John Burke

THE ILLUSTRATED

DICTIONARY
OF
MUSIC

WARNER BOOKS

A Warner Book

First published in Great Britain in 1988 by Sphere Books Ltd.
Reprinted by Warner Books 1993

Copyright (c) 1988 by BLA Publishing Limited

The moral right of the author has been asserted.

A CIP catalogue record for this book
is available from the British Library.

ISBN: 0 7515 0782 2

Printed in Spain

This book was designed and produced by BLA Publishing Limited,
East Grinstead, Sussex, England
A member of the **Ling Kee Group**

Warner Books
A Division of
Little, Brown and Company (UK) Limited
165 Great Dover Street
London SE1 4YA

Contents

Introduction

THIS IS A BOOK for concert-goers and for those listening to music at home who wish to increase their appreciation of the music they love by understanding more of its language and of the people who wrote it, rather than for the already trained musician; though it is hoped that students may also find something new and stimulating in various entries. While technicalities have been simplified where possible, and academic jargon treated with reserve, the intention is to offer enough musical explanation and evaluation to help the reader identify the individual styles of different composers and the basic theories on which they have built or against which they have rebelled.

In the case of composers, extended treatment has been given to major figures, covering as much as possible of their characteristic output in the form of symphonies, concertos, chamber music, etc. Obviously hundreds of specific titles have had to be omitted in the cases of, for example, Bach and Beethoven, since even purely nominal catalogues of their works would occupy more space than this dictionary allows. Brief additions have been made, however, to the biographical notes on other composers of undoubted significance whose full range cannot be summed up in a couple of paragraphs: in such cases, a few further representative compositions are listed under *Other Works*. Composers of lesser importance (though by no means second-rate or third-rate) are dealt with as informatively as possible in concise entries with two or three typical works named in the text.

The question of living composers, conductors, intrumentalists and singers has proved a vexed one. It would be impossible to list all contemporaries, yet it seems invidious to select some and omit others. In the end a representative choice has had to be made; and no doubt many a reader will deplore the omission of a personal favourite. This applies particularly to jazz composers and performers: where one such has established himself as being of lasting influence on the genre and on other composers (e.g. Duke Ellington), he has been included; others, more recent, will have to await the reappraisal of critics half a century from now.

Rather than scatter brief explanations of musical terms and markings throughout the alphabetical layout of the book, a number of articles have been included to cover *Interpretation Marks, Keyboard Instruments, Notation* and *The Orchestra and its Instruments*; and there are special features on *Ballet* and *Opera*.

Most musical terms have throughout the centuries been expressed in Italian, and this usage is followed here; but where certain German words are liable to be encountered at all frequently, these have been explained, as has the occasional French term. Where appropriate, the titles of works are given both in their original language and in English translation, except in cases where the original – in a Slav language, for example – is unlikely to be encountered and programmes would normally give prominence to a familiar English version.

A

ABA form A term describing a ternary form of composition: that is one in which the first section (A) is followed by a contrasting section (B), concluding with a return to (A). The minuet and trio movement of a symphony or chamber work is usually in this form, though extensive development can produce a pattern such as ABACABA, with a third quite different section in the middle.

Abbado, Claudio (1933–) Italian conductor. After studying in Milan and conducting in Vienna, he won the Koussevitsky Award at Berkshire Music Centre in 1958, and in 1963 the Mitropoulos Prize, which carried with it a five-month attachment to the New York Philharmonic Orchestra.

The conductor Claudio Abbado in pensive mood at rehearsal.

He conducted the 1965 Salzburg Festival and went on to become principal conductor at La Scala, Milan, whose repertory he broadened to include Berg and more recent composers such as Nono and Berio. His tense, invigorating style of conducting, urging every last fine little detail out of players under his baton, is effective in both opera house and concert hall, and he was welcomed as principal conductor of the Vienna Philharmonic Orchestra in 1971 and of the London Symphony Orchestra between 1979 and 1988.

A 1760 portrait by Thomas Gainsborough of the viola da gamba player and composer Carl Abel.

Abel, Carl Friedrich (1723–87) German composer and viola da gamba player who settled in London and became court musician to Queen Charlotte. He shared lodgings with J.C. Bach, and together they organized Bach-Abel subscription concerts in Soho Square, and later at Almack's Rooms in St James's, for which Abel wrote sinfonias, sonatas, and many keyboard pieces.

OTHER WORKS: Light opera *Love in a Village*.

abend German for 'evening', used in terms such as *abendlied*, an evening song, and *abendmusik*, evening performances of music of a religious nature inaugurated by Buxtehude in Lübeck during Advent. These were adopted by other German cities regularly until the early nineteenth century. *Im Abendrot*, the final autumnal piece in Richard Strauss's *Vier Letzte Lieder* (*Four Last Songs*), evokes the redness of the evening sky — the sunset.

absolute music This phrase is used to define compositions with no emotional or pictorial element, the antithesis of evocative 'programme music'.

absolute pitch Many listeners and certainly most professional performers have a sense of relative pitch in that they can relate one note they hear to its predecessor or successor, higher or lower. Much rarer is the ability (some would say an innate gift) to identify a single, isolated note correctly. A first-rate piano-tuner may possess this faculty without necessarily being able to play even the simplest melody on the instrument.

a cappella Italian phrase for music sung 'in chapel style', that is to say without instrumental accompaniment, or at most with instruments doubling the vocal lines.

accent Just as the metrical patterns of poetry derive much of their beauty from natural or calculated emphasis on certain syllables, so in music the accentuation of certain beats produces the rhythmic stress the composer requires. In a waltz the accent is normally on the first of the three beats in the bar; but an accented anticipation of the second beat can produce the syncopated lilting rhythm heard in many Viennese waltzes. When there are four beats in a bar, the accent falls generally on the first beat, often with a subsidiary, less weighty emphasis on the third; but, here again, deliberate placing of the emphasis elsewhere can produce the effect of a different, syncopated rhythm.

acciaccatura A 'grace note' deriving its name from the Italian verb 'to crush', since it is crushed in quickly before the main note to which it relates. Harpsichord and pianoforte virtuosi sometimes play the two notes simultaneously and then relieve the discord by releasing the grace note. It can also be heard as what one might call a quick breath before a full chord sounds on a regular beat in the bar.

accidental Few compositions remain in the same key from beginning to end. To add a different flavour to the melody or harmony, or to provide modulation into a different key — rather as one might provide a gate or stile and a lane in a new direction towards another main road — a note intrinsic to the original key can be sharpened or flattened one semitone by means of the appropriate sharp or flat symbol placed before the note. This alteration lasts for only the length of the bar (measure) in which it appears. If the altered note has to be restored to its original sound within that same measure, the sign of a 'natural' is inserted to cancel out previous instructions. In key signatures which from the outset stipulate a large number of sharps or flats, double sharp and flat symbols may be employed.

accompaniment The human voice or a solo pipe or fiddle were common in traditional folk music, and can still produce a moving or exhilarating effect. In addition, many later masterpieces were written for an unaccompanied instrument such as the violin, notably by Bach and Bártok. Nevertheless, even from earliest times the ear seems to have favoured the addition of some supporting rhythm, harmony or counter-melody. Primitive chants were accompanied by clapping hands,

A water-colour by L.C. de Carmontelle, 1763, of the seven-year-old Mozart accompanying his father and sister Maria Anna ('Nannerl') at a French harpsichord.

beating drums, or knocking sticks together. The recitatives and arias of early opera, and compositions for solo instruments or small groups, were underpinned by chords sketched in for a keyboard player and a bass viol or similar stringed instrument in what was known as 'figured bass'. Interpretation of these chord sequences was left to the improvisatory tastes of the players concerned, in very much the same way as parts for the pianist, guitarist and bass player in a modern dance or jazz band rhythm section allow freedom of movement within the overall harmonic pattern.

By the middle of the eighteenth century composers were beginning to prefer stricter control over this accompanying element, and wrote out the parts in full. Schubert, Schumann and Brahms created songs in which the music for the pianoforte was an integral part of the composition, weaving in and out of the sung melody with supplementary themes or adding dramatic and pictorial effects such as those of brook and mill in Schubert's *Die Schöne Müllerin* and the storm and anguish of Duparc's *La Vague et la cloche*. The increasing complexity of this relationship between voice and instrument has led to great advances in the art of the accompanist, so that an executant of the calibre of Gerald Moore has deservedly become, in the recital room and on record, an equal partner rather than merely a discreet supporter.

In opera also the composer now uses the orchestra as an essential element in conveying what he wishes to say instead of scoring no more than a pleasant background to the virtuosity of the singers. It is hard now to believe that some critics in Mozart's time complained of there being far too much going on in the orchestra during *Le nozze di Figaro* (*The Marriage of Figaro*).

accordion The invention of the accordion in the 1820s has been attributed to both Buschmann of Berlin and Damian of Vienna. Whichever of them may truly claim credit, there was no doubt about the instrument's immediate success. It was portable and could supply both melody and accompanying harmonies at considerable volume – ideal for parties, dances and community singing, though less favoured on the concert platform. The principles are simple. Bellows held between a fixed right-hand board and another board which can be pushed and pulled to and fro by the left hand (hence the nickname 'squeezebox') force air against metal reeds whose vibrations produce the desired notes. Originally the melody and harmony were played by means of studs and buttons for both hands, but in the middle of the nineteenth century the right hand was supplied with a keyboard similar to that of a piano. This,

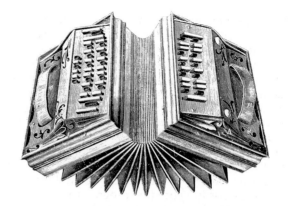

Two styles of accordion: *(above)* with button operation in both hands; *(below)* a 'piano accordion' with keyboard for the right hand.

known in full as the piano accordion, has come increasingly into favour in our own century.

acoustics Strictly speaking the term refers to all phenomena in the scientific study of hearing, but it has come to be used more frequently in connection with the sound properties of a building in relation to musical performances held there. A large hall with bare walls and floor can produce unwelcome echoes. The installation of panels and curtaining may improve matters, but too much muffling will obviously affect the required musical resonances in the opposite way. Even the most technically advanced construction of a concert hall will fail to meet the requirements of the sensitive listening ear unless allowance is made for the probable size of the audience, the positioning of soloists and/or orchestra, and the differing vibrations of various notes played by various instruments. Carefully positioned amplifiers and loudspeakers can overcome deficiencies in existing buildings: they are frequently used in churches nowadays to compensate for distortions and 'dead' areas caused by pillars and other features; but purists object to their use in the concert hall or opera house.

Adolphe Adam composed thirty-nine operas and a number of ballets, and was Professor of Composition at the Paris Conservatoire from 1849 until his death.

Adam, Adolphe (1803–56) French composer. Son of a Parisian composer and teacher, Adam was at first forbidden by his father to take up music, but at fourteen was allowed to attend the Conservatoire on the strict understanding that such talent as he might develop must never be applied to writing for the theatre. He studied the organ until his teacher, Boïeldieu, tempted him to try his hand at comic opera. His one-act *Pierre et Catherine* appeared in 1829, after which he produced a succession of popular pieces, though his attempts at grand opera were a failure. He is best remembered for the comic opera *Si j'étais roi* (*If I were King*) and the ballet *Giselle*.

Addinsell, Richard (1904–77) English composer. He originally studied law at Oxford but turned to music, studying at the Royal College of Music, London, and in Vienna and Berlin. His most fluent talent was for incidental music to revues, plays and films such as *Fire over England*, *Blithe Spirit*, and *Dangerous Moonlight*, which featured the popular *Warsaw Concerto*.

Adler, Larry (1914–) American harmonica player. He made his name as a virtuoso performer on the music halls and radio, and then extended the capabilities of the instrument to the concert platform. In 1949 he settled in England, and in 1951 Vaughan Williams wrote for him a *Romance for Harmonica, Strings and Pianoforte*. Other composers, including Milhaud, Hindemith and Malcolm Arnold, have been stimulated by him to produce works for the instrument.

Adorno, Theodor Wiesengrund (1903–69) German musicologist. A student of philosophy, Adorno also studied composition with Alban Berg, and devoted most of his philosophical enquiries to the subject of music and its relation to society. He was a fervent admirer of Schoenberg and his group and remained a close friend of Berg, walking the streets with him after the first night of the opera *Wozzeck*, influencing him in the choice of *Lulu* as the subject for his second opera, and writing a biography of him which was published in Vienna in 1968. Among his critical works translated into English are *Introduction to the Sociology of Music* and *In Search of Wagner*.

Aeolian harp According to Homer, Aeolus was the happy ruler of the islands named after him and was given by Zeus dominion over the winds. Also named after him is the harp which, probably devised in ancient times, was revived late in the sixteenth century and remained popular until the late nineteenth century. It consisted of a frame holding strings set on a window ledge or hung from the branch of a tree so that chords and resonances would be produced according to the force of the wind.

air A melody, usually of a straightforward character, with at most a simple accompaniment. An *air à boire* is the French name for a drinking song, usually in the form of a part-song; an *air de caractère* refers to dramatic themes used in ballet to highlight the appearance of strolling players, armed guards, etc; and an *air de Cour* is a courtly type of sixteenth-century French song for solo voice with lute or keyboard accompaniment. The much-played *Air on the G String* is so called because the original theme in Bach's *Suite No. 3 in D* was lowered by its nineteenth-century arranger, the German violinist August Wilhelmj, to the key of C, which enables it to be played on the violin's G string. (*See also* **aria** and **ayre**.)

Alain, Jehan (1911–40) French composer and organist. He studied at the Paris Conservatoire with Paul Dukas and Marcel Dupré, and composed mainly for the organ and for Catholic services. He served in the French army at the beginning of World War II and was killed in 1940.

Alain, Marie-Claire (1926–) French organist. She studied at the Paris Conservatoire, won the organ prize at the Geneva Competition of 1950, and has travelled widely as a recitalist. She has recorded all Bach's organ music and a number of the Widor organ symphonies.

Albanese, Licia (1913–) Italian soprano. (American citizen 1945.) She made her début in Milan at the age of twenty-one as *Madama Butterfly*, and went on to star at Covent Garden, London, and for a quarter of a century after 1940 at the New York Metropolitan Opera House. In Toscanini's recording of Verdi's *La traviata* she sang Violetta so faithfully under his guidance that she later recalled having seen tears in his eyes; and with him she also recorded Mimi in Puccini's *La Bohème*.

Albani, (Dame) Emma (1847–1930) French-Canadian soprano. Her full name was Marie Louise Cécilie Emma Lajeunesse, but having been brought up in Albany, New York, and made her first public appearance there at the age of sixteen after musical training by her father, she adopted the stage name of Albani. She studied in Paris and Milan, made her operatic début in Bellini's *La sonnambula* in Messina, and went on to appear at Covent Garden, London, and in the USA, Russia and Germany. In 1878 she married the then lessee of Covent Garden; retired in 1911 to devote herself to teaching; and at her farewell concert in the Albert Hall, London, was presented with a purse of gold. In 1925 she was created a DBE (Dame of the British Empire).

Albéniz, Isaac (1860–1909) Spanish composer and pianist. Son of a tax collector, the precocious boy played at a public recital in Barcelona at the age

Isaac Albéniz, Spanish virtuoso of the piano and composer of more than two hundred and fifty pieces for it.

of four and passed his Paris Conservatoire entrance examinations at seven, but was not allowed to study there because of his youth and unruly behaviour. He ran away from home, and for most of his adolescence travelled European and American music halls giving displays of pianistic fireworks. He composed more than 250 piano pieces in just over ten years, most of them strongly influenced by Moorish-Spanish tunes and rhythms.

Anxious both for a regular income and for success in the theatre, Albéniz accepted financial support from the English banker Francis Money-Coutts in return for converting his patron's stodgy verse dramas on Arthurian themes into operatic form. These proved worthless, as did the composer's attempt to do better with the banker's *Henry Clifford*, produced in Barcelona in 1895.

The piano compositions are his greatest achievement, reaching fruition with the twelve parts of *Iberia*, several of which were later orchestrated by Enrique Arbós.

OTHER WORKS: Operas *The Magic Opal*, *Pepita Jiménez*. Zarzuelas *Cuanto más viejo*, *Los Catalanes en Grecia*. Orchestral rhapsody *Catalonia*.

Albert, Eugen d' (1864–1932) Born in Glasgow of Anglo-French parents, Albert took his earliest music lessons from his father, a ballet master and composer of dance music. After studying in London with Sullivan and others, he won the Mendelssohn scholarship, which enabled him to spend some time in Vienna and then to become a pupil of Liszt. He became popular as a concert pianist, served for a time as Court conductor at Weimar, and composed a number of operas, of which the most successful was *Tiefland* (*The Lowland*). Married six times, he eventually took German citizenship and succeeded Joachim as director of the Berlin Hochschule für Musik.

OTHER WORKS: Symphony in F. Two piano concertos. Two string quartets. Operas including *Der Rubin* (*The Ruby*) and *Der Golem*.

Alberti bass In keyboard *continuo* parts, instead of simply sounding chords in the left hand accompaniment, the player could split the chords into their separate notes and produce a steady rhythmic pattern from them. This was especially useful with instruments such as the harpsichord and early piano, which were incapable of sustaining sounds for any length of time and so needed steady movement to bridge gaps caused by fading of the tone. The name comes from Domenico Alberti, an eighteenth-century Italian composer of operas and harpsichord sonatas who made frequent use of such 'broken' chords, though in fact they are just as common in the works of Haydn and Mozart.

Albinoni, Tommaso (1671–1750) Italian composer and violinist. He wrote about fifty operas, *concerti grossi* and other instrumental music. Today, ironically, he is best known for an *Adagio* for organ and strings to which, in fact, he contributed little: this was expanded later by Remo Giazotto, a twentieth-century Italian musicologist, from a fragment of manuscript.

alborada Derived from the Spanish *alba*, meaning 'dawn', the word refers to morning music, as with the French *aubade*. It can be a song or an instrumental piece, and in parts of Spain was frequently played on the bagpipes. A well-known adaptation of the form is *Alborada del gracioso* from Ravel's piano pieces *Miroirs*.

albumblatt German for an 'album-leaf', in musical terms this is generally a small composition for piano in intimate, personal style, such as one might adopt when writing a few lines in an autograph album.

Aldeburgh Festival In 1948 the composer Benjamin Britten and the tenor Peter Pears, living at the little fishing town of Aldeburgh in Suffolk, England, founded an annual festival built, in the first instance, around the talents of a few of their professional colleagues and friends. In spite of the cramped conditions of the town's Jubilee Hall, which Britten took into consideration when composing *Let's Make an Opera*, the festival grew in scope and soon incorporated recitals in neighbouring churches.

By 1966 it was obvious that the annual event must seek a worthier home. A lease was signed for the conversion into a concert hall of old maltings at nearby Snape. This was made possible by grants from the Arts Council, the Gulbenkian Foundation, and the Decca record company, who in due course used the hall for many major recordings. The converted building was opened by Queen Elizabeth II in June 1967; but at the beginning of the 1969 season the interior was gutted by fire. Twelve months later, restored and acoustically improved, it was reopened by the Queen. Since the deaths of Britten and Pears the administration has passed into other hands, but a high standard of performance and the encouragement of new works continue, with the addition of weekend concerts and other functions throughout the year.

Snape Maltings concert hall, centre of the annual Aldeburgh Festival, seen across the flooded saltings.

aleatory music The Latin *alea*, meaning 'dice', indicates the element of chance in works by composers who allow instrumentalists not merely to interpret the music as written but to choose what to play and what not to play, and to reshuffle the order of different sections of the work. In some cases the composer himself has relied on chance before setting down any notation whatsoever: he may feed random ideas to a computer and see how these chance fragments can be assembled. Charles Ives wrote a great deal of music offering deliberate challenges to the orchestra, which could not play the sequences as actually written but had to find ways of imposing their own discipline on fanciful or eccentric notations. One of Stockhausen's piano compositions was made up of disjointed phrases spread out for the performer to link up in any way he chose. John Cage has applied theories of indeterminacy to a large proportion of his output, and in *Music of Changes* tossed coins to establish pitch, duration and dynamics of notes.

Alfvén, Hugo (1872–1960) Swedish composer and conductor. After studying at the Stockholm Conservatory, he became a violinist in the Court orchestra, and in 1910 director of music at the University of Uppsala. His musical style was largely influenced by the French Impressionists and by his affection for local folk songs. The work of his which is still most frequently played is the first of his Swedish Rhapsodies, *Midsommarvaka* (*Midsummer Vigil*).

Alkan (1813–88) French composer and pianist. Born Charles Henri Valentin Morhange but later adopting the pseudonym of Alkan, the boy began piano studies at the Paris Conservatoire when only six, and won a major prize at the age of ten. His technical mastery as a performer is said to have been phenomenal, and his compositions for the piano, employing a chromaticism well in advance of his time, present problems for even the most talented instrumentalists of the present century. His *Grande Sonate* is a massive, ambitious work portraying in four movements the 'Four Ages of Man' — at twenty, thirty, forty and fifty. The second movement develops towards a mighty eight-part fugue and carries a subtitle demanding from the player a symbolic treatment difficult to interpret: *Quasi-Faust*.

OTHER WORKS: Two piano concertos. Piano trio. Piano studies, including one for the left hand only and one for the right hand only.

Allegri, Gregorio (1582–1652) Italian priest and composer who sang tenor in the Sistine Chapel and composed for it a nine-voice *Miserere*, jealously guarded until the fourteen-year-old Mozart wrote it out from memory after only two hearings.

Allegri Quartet A British string quartet founded in 1953 with Eli Goren as the leader. In 1968 it was refounded with Hugh Maguire leading. It has been responsible for many first performances and recordings of modern British works.

alleluia The Latin translation of the Hebrew 'Praise Jah' (Jehovah), taken into the Christian doxology in the time of the fourth-century Pope Damasus and extended from a brief response at the end of a psalm into more elaborate melodies set to appropriately celebratory music. The incorporation of a plainsong alleluia in Haydn's thirtieth symphony accounts for its title of *Alleluiasymphonie*. Alleluia is also an alternative spelling of 'Hallelujah', as in Handel's *Messiah*.

allemande The name given to a dance movement introduced into France from Germany in the late seventeenth century (*allemande* being French for 'German'), usually with four beats, or sometimes two beats, to the bar. At a moderate tempo and in simple binary (two-part) form, but with plenty of scope for ornamentation, it was widely used as the first movement of suites by, among others, Bach and Handel. Variant spellings include almain, almayne and almand.

alt An abbreviation derived from the Italian meaning 'high', usually in the form of *in alt* or *in altissimo*, referring to notes higher than the G on top of the treble clef.

alto A voice or instrument in the range between soprano and tenor, such as a male falsetto in a church choir or close-harmony quartet, and the viola in an orchestra or string quartet. The female equivalent voice is known as contralto. Several instruments have alto versions, including the clarinet, flute, oboe, saxophone and trombone.

alto clef On the musical staff, or stave, it was once common to use a special clef for the alto voice, setting middle C on its middle line and thus simplifying the notation of the voice's characteristic range around it. Today this has largely been abandoned, but the clef is still used for viola parts.

Alwyn, William (1905–85) English composer. Born in Northampton, he studied at the Royal Academy of Music in London and later became professor of composition there. He wrote a wide variety of orchestral and chamber music and an opera, *Miss Julie*, and was also a gifted poet, a translator of French poetry and a painter. Film scores include those for *Desert Victory* and *The Way Ahead*.

OTHER WORKS: Six symphonies. Concerto for harp and strings. *Fantasy Waltzes* for piano. Song cycles including *Mirages* and *A Leavetaking*.

Amadeus Quartet A string quartet made up of a group of friends — Norbert Brainin, Sigmund Nissel, Peter Schidlof and Martin Lovett — who

The Amadeus Quartet: *(left to right)* Norbert Brainin and Sigmund Nissel (violins); Peter Schidlof (viola); Martin Lovett (cello). Each was awarded an OBE (Order of the British Empire).

gave their first formal recital in London early in 1948 and won worldwide fame for their interpretations of Mozart and Schubert. Benjamin Britten's Third Quartet was written for them. Peter Schidlof died in August 1987, upon which the other members decided to dissolve the partnerhsip.

Amati family Violin makers of Cremona, Italy, flourishing between the middle of the sixteenth century and the middle of the eighteenth. Along with the Stradivari and Guarneri families they developed bowed four-stringed instruments to supersede the six-stringed, softer-toned viols which had hitherto prevailed.

Ameling, Elly (1938–) Dutch soprano. She studied at The Hague Conservatory and made her début at the age of sixteen. Her first appearance in the USA was with the New York Philharmonic Orchestra in 1964; since then she has made annual tours of the USA and Canada. A distinguished interpreter of lieder and of the songs of Fauré and Debussy, she has an equally high reputation in Bach cantatas. Among awards won for her many recordings have been the Edison Award, the Grand Prix du Disque, and the Preis der Deutschen Schallplattenkritik.

amen The word of affirmation concluding a Hebrew prayer means 'So be it', also adopted in Christian and Muslim worship. As with *alleluia*, its use in musical settings has been elaborated in some cases to provide a complete work in itself, as in Naumann's *Dresden Amen*.

amore The Italian word for 'love' occurs in several different contexts in the world of music. As a written instruction to a conductor or instrumentalist, *con amore* asks for the passage to be played

The Rotterdam-born soprano Elly Ameling.

'with love' – that is, with passion and dedication rather than tenderly, which would call for the marking *amoroso*. In connection with instruments the term denotes a lower (and implicitly more attractive) pitch than the standard one, as in *oboe d'amore* and *viola d'amore*. The sweetness of the latter was enhanced by the fitting of sympathetic strings which added resonance when the bow touched the main strings.

Anda, Geza (1921–76) Hungarian pianist. A pupil of Dohnányi and winner of the Liszt Prize, he fled Hungary during World War II and made his home in Switzerland, becoming a Swiss citizen in 1955. He was noted for his performances of Beethoven and Brahms, and especially for those of works by his fellow countryman and fellow refugee, Bartók.

Anderson, Marian (1902–) American contralto. After winning a competition to appear with the New York Philharmonic Orchestra in 1925 and making a number of concert appearances, she studied for two years in Europe and sang in London. Toscanini spoke of her rich, ample voice as the kind that 'comes once in a hundred years'. She was the first black singer to star at the Metropolitan Opera House, New York, and in 1962 was invited to sing at the inauguration of President John F. Kennedy.

Victoria de Los Angeles (*née* Victoria Gomez Cima) as Elisabeth in Wagner's opera *Tannhäuser*.

Marian Anderson was the first black singer to appear at the New York Met, taking the part of Ulrica in Verdi's *Un ballo in maschera*.

Angeles, Victoria de los (1923–) Spanish soprano. She made her début in Monteverdi's *Orfeo* while still a student at the Barcelona Conservatory, and made her first London appearance in 1949, and her New York début in 1950. At 'The Met' she achieved great success as a touching, dignified *Madama Butterfly* and, in complete contrast, a fiery *Carmen*. Her compatriot Manuel de Falla dedicated his unfinished 'cantata scenica' *L'Atlantida* to her, though it was not staged until after his death. In spite of operatic triumphs, the true qualities of her warm *bel canto* style have been best exhibited in song recitals and recordings. She can move with ease from Spanish songs to German lieder, and Gerald Moore, her accompanist for so many years, found each collaboration with her 'still more thrilling to me than the last'.

anglais or **anglaise** A French term used in the eighteenth century to describe pieces with a supposedly English flavour, such as country dances and hornpipes.

anhang A German word meaning an 'appendix' or 'supplement' – in musical usage, a coda.

Ansermet, Ernest (1883–1969) Swiss conductor. For a time professor of mathematics at the University of Lausanne, Ansermet received some music lessons from Bloch but was largely self-taught. After conducting in Montreux he became principal conductor to Diaghilev's Ballets Russes and made many international tours with the company. In 1918 he founded the Orchestre de la Suisse Romande, made many recordings with it, and remained its principal conductor until his death. He was a notable interpreter of Stravinsky's works, though in later life he and the composer disagreed on a number of subjects, including serialism. In 1946 he conducted the first performance of Benjamin Britten's *Rape of Lucretia* at Glyndebourne.

answer In a fugue, the second voice's imitation of the first theme is known as the answer. (*See* **fugue**.)

Antheil, George (1900–59) American composer. Of Polish descent, Antheil studied with Bloch in 1920 but two years later moved to Europe, continuing his studies and giving piano recitals which featured his own jazz-influenced compositions with provocative titles such as *Airplane Sonata*. He revelled in uproar, both in the orchestra and in the audience, and scored his *Ballet mécanique* for a clamorous combination of pianos, xylophones, doorbells, car horns and two airplane propellers. This was first performed in Paris and later recorded.

From 1936 onwards Antheil wrote film scores in Hollywood, becoming an associate producer in 1939 but continuing to work on symphonic and other works. His autobiography, published in 1945, was aptly entitled *Bad Boy of Music*.

OTHER WORKS: Six symphonies. Operas *Transatlantic* and *Volpone*. Piano and violin concertos. Chamber music and songs.

anthem Sacred music for solo voice or choir, usually based on Biblical texts, in an Anglican equivalent of the Roman Catholic motet. Although not a formal part of the liturgy, the anthem is designed for inclusion in a church service and has been used by many composers for specific festive occasions. The so-called full anthem calls for a choir throughout, in its purest form without accompaniment; a verse anthem is for one or more soloists with choral interludes and the accompaniment of organ and perhaps a stringed instrument.

Purcell and others developed the concept more ambitiously into virtual cantatas. Handel's twelve Chandos Anthems, written when he was in the service of the Duke of Chandos, are extended works calling for a choir, orchestra and organ. (*See also* **national anthems**.)

anticipation The playing of one note of a chord before the full chord is sounded, often 'crushed' in *acciaccatura* fashion, or as in the anticipatory note common before the first full bar of an *allemande*.

antiphony Derived from the Greek, the word means an opposition of sounds and the harmonic blend produced by such opposition. It is usually applied to double choirs or instrumental groups set well apart in church or concert hall so that the listener can appreciate the separate contributions. In religious use an antiphon is in essence a versicle sung by the second choir in response to a statement by the first. The Gabrieli family of Venetian composers made great use of the acoustic properties of St Mark's cathedral to build up resounding antiphons for choirs and bass players. Berlioz's *Grande Messe des morts* (usually referred to as his *Requiem*) was first performed in Les Invalides, Paris, with four widely separated brass bands, one at each corner of the vast choral and orchestral forces. In the twentieth century Stockhausen's *Gruppen* (*Groups*) calls for three distinct orchestras at the points of a triangle, with the audience inside the triangle.

anvil Real anvils are used for dramatic effect in the Anvil Chorus of Verdi's *Il trovatore* and in Berlioz's *Benvenuto Cellini*. In Wagner's *Ring* cycle the anvil sounds are produced by artificial percussion instruments in the orchestra.

appoggiatura From the Italian 'leaning', this defines an ornamentation in which a tone that is not a member of the forthcoming chord anticipates or leans towards it. To some extent it resembles the *acciaccatura* but is less abruptly sounded, being often a full half the value of its succeeding note, and in many instances falling directly upon the beat before taking its step up or down on to the actual chord. Singers in opera as late as Mozart's day were accustomed to add such grace notes of their own accord, a habit which lapsed until it was revived in some later twentieth-century productions.

arabesque Originally referring to florid decorations in Arabian and especially Moorish architecture, the term has come to mean similarly ornate passages in music, or entire compositions in decorative rather than abstract or even emotional mood, as with Debussy's piano *Arabesques*.

Arensky, Anton (1861–1906) Russian composer. A pupil of Rimsky-Korsakov, he became professor of harmony and counterpoint at Moscow Conservatory. Of his operas, symphonies, string quartets and other works the only substantial survivor is a tuneful piano concerto; but he is remembered by most listeners for the *Variations on a Theme of Tchaikovsky*, familiarly known simply as the *Arensky Variations*.

aria, arietta and **arioso** The Italian word for an air generally implies something more extensive than a simple short song. In the early eighteenth century the *aria da capo* was established, largely due to the influence of Alessandro Scarlatti, in ABA form, its third section being a repetition of the first, with an intervening stretch of new material, often in a different key. This was duly developed into the more elaborate form of the operatic recitative and aria, though the basic pattern remained a firm foundation for more than a century.

An *arietta* is in effect a simpler aria, usually without the middle section. An *arioso* can be a short operatic air or a more tuneful version of the usually declamatory recitative.

Armstrong, Louis (1900–71) American jazz trumpeter. Grandson of a slave, he was raised in the slums of New Orleans and loved following the band parades so popular in the town. After an over-riotous New Year's Eve, 1912, he was committed to the Coloured Waifs' Home for Boys and there learned to play the bugle and trumpet. Hearing in his head a turmoil of unorthodox harmonic progressions, he proved in his first days with jazz bands, including that of the great

The internationally acclaimed jazz trumpeter Louis Armstrong.

Joe ('King') Oliver, that he could convey these on his trumpet with dazzling technique.

He soon became a leading soloist, recorded with small groups of like-minded players, and for some years fronted a large touring band, becoming known as 'Satchmo' (Satchelmouth) because of his leathery lips and indomitable blowing. At Carnegie Hall in 1947 he returned to the smaller-scale group with his 'All Stars', playing in the relaxed creative style he had known in New Orleans. The group made so many international tours in the 1960s that he was nicknamed 'Ambassador Satch'. He was a major influence on his contemporaries and successors, including not merely players but singers such as Billie Holiday, who tried to emulate his instrumental phrasing.

In later years he suffered from an increasingly bad heart condition. When he died in July 1971 his body lay in state at the National Guard Armory, visited by 25 000 mourners.

Arne, Michael (1740–86) English composer. The illegitimate son of the composer Thomas Arne, he appeared on stage as a child singer and at an early age produced a volume of his own songs. He composed incidental music for the theatre and an opera, *Almena*, and also dabbled in alchemy. His best-loved piece is the song *The Lass with a Delicate Air*.

Arne, Thomas (1710–78) English composer. Born at the Crown and Cushion tavern in Covent Garden, son of a London coffin-maker, Arne used to practise the spinet secretly at night with its strings muffled by a handkerchief. He married the daughter of a church organist but was more interested in secular music, especially that written for the theatre, than in religious composition: he declared that the test of a good tune was whether it could be ground about the streets on a street organ.

Arne wrote incidental music for many plays and at various times was resident composer at Vauxhall Gardens, Drury Lane, and Covent Garden. The production of his masque *Alfred* in the grounds of the Prince of Wales' home at Cliveden above the river Thames included the first performance of a patriotic ode entitled *Rule, Britannia!* His instrumental works include sets of trio sonatas, overtures, harpsichord sonatas and concertos for organ or harpsichord, one of which was played by his illegitimate son Michael at a concert in 1759.

OTHER WORKS: Comic operas *The Temple of Dullness, Artaxerxes*. Oratorio *Judith*.

Arnell, Richard (1917–) English composer. A pupil of John Ireland, Arnell established many connections in the USA. In 1942 Thomas Beecham conducted the premier of his *Sinfonia quasi variazioni* at Carnegie Hall. Between 1943 and 1945 he was consultant to the BBC's North American service and in 1947 composed *Punch and the Child* for the New York City Ballet. From 1948 he was on the teaching staff of Trinity College, London, but maintained his American interests as Fulbright Exchange Professor at Bowdoin College, Maine, 1970–72 and with other visiting professorships.

OTHER WORKS: Opera *Moon Flowers*. Seven symphonies. Symphonic portrait *Lord Byron*. Song cycles and film scores.

An etching after Francesco Bartolozzi (*c.*1770) of Thomas Arne, lauded as combining 'Harmony and Sentiment' to prove that 'By Music minds an equal temper know'.

Malcolm Arnold, prolific English composer whose brilliance owes much to his own experience as a leading orchestral player.

Arnold, Malcolm (1921–) English composer. He studied with Gordon Jacob at the Royal College of Music, London, and for some years played the trumpet in the London Philharmonic Orchestra and the BBC Symphony Orchestra, which gave him an invaluable insight into orchestral techniques and possibilities. Income from film scores such as that for *The Bridge on the River Kwai* helped him to turn to full-time composing.

Arnold's work is invariably tuneful and exuberant, and often witty as well. He is quite content to operate within the diatonic system, and pays homage to no fashionable theories. One of the most prolific composers of his generation, he has written rewarding concertos for flute, clarinet, harmonica, horn, and guitar (with a movement dedicated to the memory of the French jazz guitarist Django Reinhardt); symphonies, incuding a *Toy Symphony* and a *Symphony for Brass*; and, not surprisingly in view of his own instrumental experience, a large number of other pieces for brass band and smaller wind ensembles. Among the most exhilarating of his works are the sets of *English Dances*, *Scottish Dances* and *Cornish Dances* and the concert overture depicting a boisterous urchin, *Beckus the Dandipratt*.

OTHER WORKS: Orchestral suite, *Homage to the Queen*. *A Grand Grand Overture* for three vacuum cleaners, four rifles, floor polisher and orchestra. Choral works including *A John Clare Cantata*. Piano *Variations on a Ukrainian Folk Song* and *Children's Suite*.

arpeggio From the Italian 'harp-like', indicating the spread of a chord's individual notes from bottom to top, or vice versa, instead of sounding them simultaneously. In the seventeenth and eighteenth centuries it was usual for the composer to explain his wishes by writing the full chord and adding the word *arpeggione* above it. Today the instruction is given by means of a vertical wavy line preceding the chord.

arrangement Many pieces of music written for a particular instrument have been adapted for other instruments, either by the composer himself or by some later arranger. Folk songs which caught the imagination of musicians in their own and other countries were transcribed and provided with an accompaniment. The work of earlier composers has often been filled out or adapted to modern tastes: 'realized', as some prefer to put it.

Before the days of radio and the gramophone record, when the chances of hearing a wide repertory of music were rare for most of the population, often the only way of hearing a symphony or other major orchestral work was by means of a piano transcription. Before becoming a composer in his own right the young Philip Heseltine (pseudonym Peter Warlock), despairing of ever hearing full-scale performance of Delius scores which he had read, set about arranging them for piano solo or duet.

In the field of dance music and jazz, or of theatre musical shows, the word 'arrangement' really means 'orchestration'.

Arrau, Claudio (1903–) Chilean pianist. He studied in Santiago and Berlin, and made his début with the Berlin Philharmonic Orchestra in 1920. In the same year he first appeared in London and in 1924 he performed in New York, a venture which left him nearly penniless. Back in Germany, he built up his resources again – and his reputation – and in Berlin in 1930 performed the complete solo clavier works of J.S. Bach in twelve

The Chilean pianist Claudio Arrau, noted for his marathon performances of major solo cycles: all Bach's keyboard music in a series of 1930 recitals, and all Beethoven's piano sonatas in post-war recitals.

recitals, but later expressed dissatisfaction with the sound of Bach on the piano.

Early in World War II he left Germany for the USA, became an acknowledged interpreter of Brahms with a powerful, majestic style which brought out the full chordal richness without obscuring the contrapuntal lines, and both in New York and in London gave complete performances of the Beethoven piano sonatas.

ars antiqua and **ars nova** The Latin *ars antiqua*, or 'old art', is applied in music specifically to the austere style of plainsong and organum composition favoured in France during the twelfth and thirteenth centuries. Early in the next century Philippe de Vitry wrote a treatise entitled *Ars nova* in which he described a 'new art' of dividing and measuring time, allowing for greater rhythmic and harmonic variety. From this developed the elaborate polyphony which led to the full flowering of the madrigal.

Ashkenazy, Vladimir (1937–) Russian pianist. He studied at Moscow Conservatory and was joint winner of the Tchaikovsky competition in Moscow in 1962. Defecting from Russia, he settled for a time in England, but after marrying an Icelandic wife shared his home life between Iceland and Switzerland. His performance and recordings of the Beethoven and Prokofiev piano concertos are outstanding, and he is equally gifted as a solo recitalist and as a conductor. In 1987 he became music director of the Royal Philharmonic Orchestra, London, in partnership with its principal conductor, his friend André Previn.

atonality Until comparatively recent times most music in the Western world has been written in specific keys, and even the most adventurous modulations from one key to another have preserved a recognizable tonal basis. There are occasional indications of a departure into less rigidly circumscribed tonality in Debussy's impressionist pieces, but it was not until Schoenberg and his disciples began consciously experimenting with chromatic sequences freed of any key restraints that atonality became a favoured method of composition, in revolt against what had gone before. Webern declared uncompromisingly that tonality was truly dead, and there was 'no point in continuing to deal with something dead'.

Theoretically an atonal composition should dispense with all hitherto accepted rules not just of melody but also of harmony. In place of the familiar key-oriented cadences to which the ear had become accustomed, the music progressed largely according to the composer's own intuition, in the belief that all earlier disciplines had led to staleness and lack of any possibility of further development. The immediate effects of such cerebral new music were not readily acceptable to the untutored ear, quite unaccustomed to the amassing of dissonances and the spreading of themes over all twelve notes of the chromatic scale. Even the most dedicated advocates of atonality soon began to find the lack of a fundamental discipline unrewarding: although he was in accord with its general principles, Alban Berg, for example, frequently hinted at echoes of the old tonic-dominant relationships in his work. In due course the experimenters, again under the influence of Schoenberg, turned their attention to the formalities of serialism.

aubade Morning music, from the French *l'aube*, 'the dawn'. Similar to the Spanish *alborada*.

An engraving of Daniel Auber, a dedicated but shy opera composer who was reported never to have summoned up the courage to attend any performance of his own works.

Auber, Daniel (1782–1871) French composer. Sent to London by his father to learn the business of selling paintings, he spent a large part of his time writing songs and soon opted for a musical career. His first published works, four cello concertos, were issued under the name of the virtuoso Jacques Lamare, but word soon spread of the true identity of the composer and brought him various commissions.

Frequently collaborating with the popular dramatist Eugène Scribe, Auber turned his attention to opera, causing a political storm with *Masaniello*: based on the story of a seventeenth-century Neapolitan uprising against tyranny, its production in Brussels in 1830 led to a Belgian revolt against union with the Dutch. Among his greatest successes were *Fra Diavolo* and *Manon Lescaut*.

Appointed director of the Paris Conservatoire in 1842, he served there until his death, and in 1857 also became *maître de chapelle* to Napoleon III.

OTHER WORKS: Opera *Le Cheval de bronze* (*The Bronze Horse*). Ballet *Marco Spada*. Violin concerto. Songs.

augmentation The term is used in two senses. Notes of a basic melody can be lengthened, usually by doubling their time value, to produce, for example, the solemn finale to a symphony or choral work or to enhance the subjects of a fugue. Intervals between notes of the scale are said to be augmented when they have been widened by a semitone: in the case of a common C major triad, the C-E-G of the chord would become an augmented triad as C-E-G sharp. (*See also* **diminution**.)

Auric, Georges (1899–1983) French composer. Youngest of the adventurous group known in the 1920s as *Les Six*, and much influenced by Satie, he wrote at first with a sort of flippant elegance and worked with Diaghilev on ballets such as *Les Matelots*. Disappointed by the critical reception of later more serious piano and chamber compositions, he concentrated on stage and screen music, providing film scores for Cocteau's *La Belle et la bête* and *Orphée*, and achieving a worldwide best-seller with his theme song written for *Moulin Rouge*. From 1962 to 1968 he was general administrator of the Paris Opéra and Opéra Comique.

OTHER WORKS: Symphony. Piano concerto. Opera *Sous le masque* (*Under the Mask*). Ballet *Les fâcheux* (*The Bores*). Piano pieces including *Imaginées 1-6* and *Adieu, New York*. Incidental music for film *Caesar and Cleopatra*.

auxiliary note A passing note which belongs neither to its preceding nor to its succeeding chord, creating a temporary discord between leaving one note of the chord and returning to it. Many ornamentations such as the trill and *acciaccatura* make use of auxiliary notes.

Avison, Charles (1709–70) English composer. Born in Newcastle upon Tyne, he studied with Geminiani in London but returned to become organist of his parish church, later Newcastle cathedral. In spite of a growing reputation as a composer, critic and concert organizer, he refused all invitations to settle and work in London. He introduced subscription concerts 'at the Assembly Rooms in the Groat Market and at Mr Parker's Long Room in the Bigg Market', wrote an influential *Essay on Musical Expression*, and gave lessons to local students. As well as adapting several Scarlatti sonatas for string orchestra, he published three volumes of his own harpsichord sonatas, two volumes for harpsichord and violin, and fifty *concerti grossi*, including the group now known as the 'Newcastle concertos'.

ayre Although the word is merely another spelling of 'air', it relates especially to songs of the sixteenth and seventeenth centuries in the style perfected by lutenist composers such as Thomas Campion and John Dowland, in effect the earliest form of 'art-song' in England. As a rule these were conceived for a solo voice with the accompaniment of lute and possibly a viol; but arrangements were often prepared for four voices so that they could be performed by amateur groups on a less demanding level than the more complex madrigals.

B

Babbitt, Milton (1916–) American composer. Son of a mathematician, Babbitt has shared his interests between mathematics and music, frequently combining the two disciplines. He became a member of the music faculty at Princeton University in 1938 and from there disseminated his views on serial technique not merely as applied to tone rows but also in the desirable logical relationship between pitch and rhythm. One of his concepts is that of 'time point', in which the subdivisions of beats in a measure (or bar) produce rhythmic intervals much as the varying steps between notes in a scale produce tonal intervals. The structure of a piece conceived in this style is conditioned not by note duration but by the time point at which the composer chooses to start, proceeding thereafter in a rhythmic series very much in accord with the 12-tone melodic system.

For quite some time Babbitt believed that the string quartet was the ideal medium for the performance of 'absolute' music, but later he became a leading exponent of electronic devices, working frequently with the RCA sound synthesizer at the Columbia-Princeton Electronic Music Center. Works he has created in this vein include *Composition for Synthesizer* and *Phenomena* for soprano and tape, and he has written and lectured widely on the subject.

OTHER WORKS: Jazz octet, *All Set*. Choral *Music for the Mass*. Piano *Reflections*, with tape. *Philomel* for soprano, recorded soprano, and tape.

B A C H In German usage the note B is the equivalent of our B flat, while our B is referred to as H. This provides a sequence of B flat/A/C/B natural on which a sort of musical pun can be built. Johann Sebastian Bach himself used the notes in the unfinished final contrapunctus of *The Art of Fugue*. Other composers offering homage to his name by this means include Busoni, d'Indy, Karg-Elert in the *Basso ostinato* of his organ pieces, *Semplice*, and Reger in his *Fantasy and Fugue for organ*.

Bach, Johann Sebastian (1685–1750) Son of an organist at Eisenach in northern Germany, the boy was orphaned at the age of ten and went to live in Ohrdruf with an older brother, Christoph, also an organist. There had been musicians in the Bach family for several generations, and young Johann Sebastian soon showed talent of his own. Unfortunately his brother seems to have been jealous of his precocity and tried to withhold from him copies of clavier and organ music by the great masters; but the story has it that the boy surreptitiously borrowed a volume and copied it out by moonlight – which has been advanced as a possible cause of later trouble with his eyes.

When he was fifteen he joined the choir of St Michael's in Lüneberg as a boy soprano. He also made himself useful as an accompanist on the

The only authenticated portrait of Johann Sebastian Bach, by Elias Haussmann. He is holding a copy of his 'Canon Triplex a 6 Voci'.

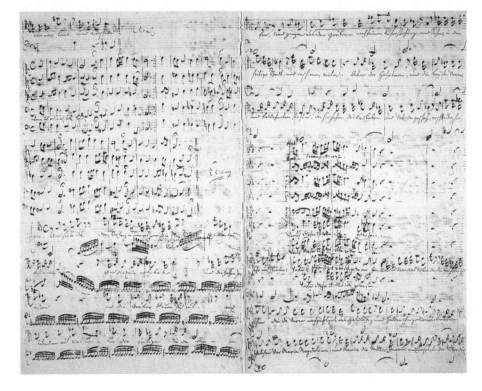

The chorale 'Wenn ich einmal soll scheiden' and part of the Evangelist's narrative from the original autograph score (1736) of the *Matthäuspassion* (*The Passion According to St Matthew*).

harpsichord and began composing, mainly for the organ. When his voice broke he continued there as an accompanist, until in 1703 he became for a short time a violinist in the Court orchestra at Weimar. During his next post as organist at Arnstadt and in several subsequent church appointments, he was required to provide cantatas regularly for Sunday services, and so began the stream of masterpieces in this form.

In October 1705 he was granted a month's leave so that he could visit Lübeck in order to hear the great Danish organist Buxtehude, whose playing and compositions for the organ and for soloists and choir were to have a fruitful influence on Bach's own style. He walked the whole 300 miles on foot and, once there, was reluctant to return to his own post. Overstaying his leave by three months, he found himself under a cloud in Arnstadt, not lightened by the distaste of his employers, choir and congregation for the complex, demanding music he was now writing. He very soon looked for another position, and was taken on at a church in Mühlhausen. Things soon proved to be no better: puritanical elements in the congregation frowned on any idea of music being an important, least of all an enjoyable, part of their church services. Bach was soon on his way again, this time back to Weimar as Court organist and chamber musician, with plenty of scope for composing and for supervising the performance of his own work. He was to stay for nine years, and during this time broadened his knowledge of the Italian masters of orchestral technique, while also creating many of his own great organ fugues and the chorale preludes of the *Orgelbüchlein* (*Little Organ Book*). Not until the post of *kapellmeister* at Cöthen was offered to him did he decide to move once more, a decision rashly made without consulting his employer, who imprisoned him for several weeks before relenting and allowing him to leave.

Prince Leopold of Cöthen was a gifted instrumentalist and was delighted to have Bach in his household, conducting the orchestra and composing orchestral pieces such as violin concertos, suites, and the *Brandenburg Concertos*. His enthusiasm was such that on a number of occasions he took Bach with him on his travels. It was during one of these absences in 1720 that another cloud darkened Bach's life, this time one of personal grief. While in Mühlhausen he had married his cousin Maria Barbara. They had been very happy together, and Prince Leopold was godfather to the most recent of their children, who sadly died in infancy. Now Maria Barbara herself died, and by the time Bach got home from his trip she had already been buried. A year and a half later he

married 20-year-old Anna Magdalena Wilcken, daughter of a musician and herself a gifted soprano. She became step-mother to his four surviving children, helped him by copying his scores, and was presented by him with the delightful little practice pieces in the *Anna Magdalena Notebook*.

In that same year Prince Leopold also married. His young wife, unlike Bach's, had no liking whatsoever for music and no time for the friendship between the prince and his resident genius. When the cantor of St Thomas's School in Leipzig died in 1722, Bach applied to fill the vacancy and, after conducting a performance of his own *St John Passion*, was appointed. Here, weathering occasional differences with the authorities, he remained for the rest of his life, teaching at the school, conducting a Leipzig musical society, and producing a steady output of superb cantatas.

In 1749 he went blind, in spite of an operation performed by John Taylor, an English surgeon who later tried to save Handel's sight also. Ten days before his death from a stroke, his eyesight suddenly returned. He was buried in the cemetery of the Johanniskirche, Leipzig, without any memorial tablet. His remains were rediscovered in 1894, but were seriously damaged during an Allied air raid in World War II.

Bach's musical beliefs were inextricably bound up with those of his Lutheran religion. He offered all his creative talents to the glory of God. And in music, as in his religious faith, he was in most ways a traditionalist. His contemporaries and those who came immediately after him considered him old-fashioned. Never an innovator for the sake of innovation, all he sought to do was to take existing forms to their ultimate: he was, as Alfred Einstein put it, the 'great river into which all things flowed'. Whatever he touched, no matter how commonplace its origin or familiar its treatment at the hands of other practitioners, he transformed.

CHORAL WORKS: For a large part of his working life Bach was committed to the regular presentation of new cantatas, musically underlining the Gospel for the day, to be sung at the services of whichever church was employing him at the time. It is estimated that he composed about 300 in all, 250 during his time in Leipzig, and many of them reaching the scale almost of a short oratorio: indeed, Bach himself referred to Cantata No.11, *Lobet Gott in Seinen Reichen* (*Praise God in His Heaven*) as an *Ascension Oratorio*. In all of them he made use of old German metrical hymn-tunes known as chorales, and in one or two cases built the entire work around variations on one such melody. The most outstanding example is the cantata *Ein' feste Burg ist unser Gott* (*A Safe Strong-hold is Our God*), based on the battle hymn adapted by Martin Luther from a plainsong melody and sung by himself and his followers as they marched into Worms. Above the *cantus firmus* (or fixed song) Bach erects a massive polyphonic structure radiant with trumpets, oboes, organ and voices, with only a few short spells of reflective solo singing before the mighty chorale fantasia takes over again, culminating in a straightforward, richly harmonized setting of the chorale for full chorus and orchestra.

Several arias from the cantatas have won popularity on their own account in transcription, such as *Jesu, joy of man's desiring* from *Herz und Mund* (*Heart and Mouth*) and *Sheep may safely graze* from the secular cantata *Was mir behagt* (*What pleases me*). There is also a body of solo cantatas for special occasions, including the joyful *Wedding Cantata* composed at Cöthen, *Weichet nur, betrübte Schatten* (*Begone, dull shadows!*).

Bach's two greatest achievements in choral music were the *St Matthew Passion* and the *Mass in B minor*. In the *Passion*, as in its predecessor the *St John Passion*, an Evangelist narrates the Biblical story in recitative, with a chorus taking the part of the crowd and soloists providing meditative arias on the Gospel texts. It is interesting to note how Bach gives unique emphasis to the words of Jesus himself by underlining them with a sustained string accompaniment. Interspersed with scenes of the story are familiar chorales in which the congregation of his time could join.

The *Mass in B minor* has caused considerable argument among scholars. Why should the staunchly Lutheran Bach write a Catholic Mass? It has been suggested that he wished to ingratiate himself with the new Roman Catholic Elector of Saxony in 1733; but in fact the *Sanctus* had been written a full nine years before that; only a *Kyrie* and *Gloria* were submitted to the Elector as separate pieces, and not until two years later did Bach integrate them into a full-scale Mass. Despite the apparent patchiness of the assembly, the overall effect is magnificent in performance.

The so-called *Christmas Oratorio*, although also telling a Biblical story – this time that of the Nativity – is in fact a sequence of six cantatas designed for performance on six separate days over Christmas and the New Year. Bach, thrifty as ever, introduced into this religious context a number of pieces from earlier secular cantatas of his own.

ORCHESTRAL WORKS: Most concertos, suites and other orchestral works were written when Bach was playing and conducting at Cöthen. Stimulated by the Italian styles with which he was now coming into contact, he transcribed several Vivaldi violin concertos as clavier concertos, fortifying the counterpoint and often writing out ornaments in full. He also wrote a string of violin and keyboard concertos of his own. Many have been lost, including the original violin version of the well-known *Concerto in D minor for Clavier and Strings*; and it seems that Bach's favourite son, Wilhelm Friedemann, sold off many of his father's MSS for what they could fetch.

Today the most frequently played of the orchestral works are probably the six *Brandenburg Concertos*, written between 1717 and 1721 and dedicated to Christian Ludwig, Margrave of Brandenburg, on his 44th birthday. There is no record of the Margrave having ever heard them or of his having even acknowledged receipt: if Bach had not retained a copy for himself, they might have been lost forever. It does seem likely that they were performed by the Cöthen orchestra, whose forces would have been just about right for the music, perhaps supplemented by visitors such as the two horn players catered for in the first of the set. They represent the ultimate development of the *concerto grosso*, with dazzling displays of contrast between soloists, *concertante* units, and the orchestral strings. One of them, the Third, for strings only with harpsichord *continuo*, has left us some questions. In two movements only, it suggests that a central movement must have been mislaid: today it is common for a keyboard player to improvise a bridge passage.

KEYBOARD WORKS: Bach's mastery of polyphony is most compellingly displayed in his organ music, where all his creative resources are poured into a sequence of monumental fugues, many prefaced by a prelude, toccata or fantasia in freer form: some of the preludes are contrapuntal masterpieces of equal weight with the culminating fugue, as in the massive *Fantasia and Fugue in G minor*. Similar inventiveness was shown in his collection of forty-eight preludes and fugues in all the major and minor keys, *Das Wohltemperierte Klavier* (*The Well-Tempered Clavier*).

Left unfinished at his death was *Die Kunst der Fuge* (*The Art of Fugue*), demonstrating the various contrapuntal possibilities in the development of a simple basic theme.

Bach's sons Records of J.S. Bach's ancestors, relatives and descendants produce over fifty names of musicians active throughout the sixteenth, seventeenth and eighteenth centuries. Of his sons, four are still remembered:

Carl Philipp Emanuel (1714–88)
After studying for a legal career in Leipzig and Frankfurt, he turned to music and became one of

A romanticized nineteenth-century view of J.S. Bach at the keyboard surrounded by members of his family, all of whom were expected to contribute to the household's musical activities. His two wives presented him with twenty children in all, of whom only nine survived to maturity.

the most successful practitioners in his whole family: attracting the attention of Frederick the Great, he worked for him for over a quarter of a century and dedicated six *Prussian Sonatas* to him. While in the royal service he wrote a treatise on 'the True Art of playing the Clavier', covering the whole technique of the keyboard and the interpretation of ornaments and paving the way for the shift from the harpsichord to the fortepiano and pianoforte. The most important influence of his time on the development of sonata form, he was forward-looking and daring in all aspects of music: turning his back on his father's polpyhony, he aimed at expressing feeling through dramatic melodic leaps and dynamic changes, all carried out with a delicacy of expression which entranced his contemporaries. Although no one composer can be said to have 'invented' the symphony and string quartet as later generations have known them, C.P.E. Bach was undoubtedly a major formative influence on Haydn and his successors, linking the baroque and classical periods.

Growing weary of the stuffy restrictions of Frederick's entourage, in 1767 he escaped to Hamburg to take over musical administration of the five churches previously under the control of his godfather Telemann, and stayed there for the rest of his life.

OTHER WORKS: Oratorio *The Resurrection and Ascension of Jesus*. Twenty symphonies. Twenty-two Passions. Clavichord and fortepiano sonatas. Keyboard variations on *Folies d'Espagne*.

Johann Christian (1735–82)

The youngest son (eighteenth child) of J.S. Bach, he studied music in Italy and there turned away from his father's Lutheran faith to become a Roman Catholic. He is known as 'the English Bach' because, after an invitation to produce two Italian-style operas in London, he settled in England and became music master to Charlotte Sophia, wife of King George III.

Among operas composed in London were *Orione*, *Carrattaco* (*Caratacus*), and *Lucio Silla*. With his compatriot C.F. Abel he presented subscription concerts in Soho and St James's, and it is believed that the first public recital given on the recently perfected pianoforte was by Johann Christian Bach at the Thatched House tavern in St James's. He befriended young Mozart on the eight-year-old's visit to London and introduced him to the new keyboard instrument. Like Mozart, he died in poverty; his popularity faded, and thanks largely to a dishonest housekeeper he ended his days heavily in debt, to be buried in Old St Pancras churchyard.

OTHER WORKS: Opera *La Clemenza di Scipione*, composed for the Haymarket, London, in 1778. Forty piano concertos. Twenty string quartets. Piano solos and trios. English songs, many performed at Vauxhall Gardens.

Johann Christoph Friedrich (1732–95)

He spent all his working life as chamber musician in the household of Count Wilhelm of Schaumburg-Lippe, and married the Court singer, Lucia Münchhausen. It was his job to provide Court music as required, and he produced a number of competent if unoriginal symphonies and concertos, string quartets, and oratorios and cantatas for religious occasions.

OTHER WORKS: Opera *Brutus* and a lyric opera, *Die Amerikanerin*.

Wilhelm Friedemann (1710–84)

His father's favourite, the boy was provided with a notebook to which keyboard pieces of graduated complexity were regularly added: many of these were to form part of *The Well-Tempered Clavier* and the *Two-* and *Three-part Inventions*. After a position as church organist in Dresden, he moved to the livelier world of Halle and worked there for over twenty years before seeking more congenial and better-paid work in Brunswick and Berlin, in which he failed.

W.F. Bach wrote about twenty cantatas, nine symphonies, and a number of organ and clavier works. Those few which are occasionally revived in our own time prove to be imaginative in concept, often audacious, with a mastery of counterpoint allied to understanding of the new forces that his brother Carl Philipp Emanuel and his contemporaries were so avidly exploiting. It is impossible not to wonder whether his waywardness, allied with a prickly sensitivity, did not derive from the high hopes his father so cripplingly invested in him. A psychologist might make much of the fact that it was J.S. Bach's most beloved son who finally got whatever few pence he could from the sale of that doting father's MSS.

Bach trumpet A misleading name for any small-bore trumpet used to produce the high-pitched 'clarino' bravura passages of the baroque period, so-called because of its use in high parts written by Bach, though he was only one among many of his contemporaries. Originally long, straight and without valves, it was supplied in the nineteenth century with two valves, pitched in A; later there was a version in D with a crook.

Bacharach, Burt (1929–) American pianist, composer and arranger. Born in Kansas City, he studied at McGill University in Montreal and then in New York and Santa Barbara. This was followed by two years of playing at Army concerts, and for a time he made a living as a night club pianist and accompanist to popular singers, among them Marlene Dietrich. As a songwriter and arranger he became fluent in the use of Latin American and 'rock' fashions. He wrote many film scores, including *What's New, Pussy Cat?* and *Alfie*, and won an Academy Award in 1970 for *Raindrops keep falling on my head* from *Butch Cassidy and the Sundance Kid*.

Backhaus, Wilhelm (1884–1969) German pianist. He studied at Leipzig and Frankfurt, and made his first concert tour when sixteen years of age. In 1905 he won the Rubinstein prize in Paris and that same year was appointed professor of piano at Manchester Royal College of Music. He continued to travel through Europe and America until well after eighty, when he made definitive recordings of nearly all the Beethoven piano sonatas.

bagatelle From the French and German word meaning 'a trifle'. In music it is applied to short, lighthearted pieces, generally for the piano, as with the Beethoven sets which include *Für Elise* (*For Elisa*), so well-worn as a practice piece.

bagpipe In French *musette*, in German *dudelsack*. A development of the primitive reed-pipe in which

A pipe major of the Scots Guards, with Windsor Castle in the background, portrayed on the cover of an 1893 issue of George Newnes' weekly, *The Million*.

the fingered 'chanter' providing the tune is supplied from a wind reservoir fed by a mouthpiece, or by bellows under the arm. An accompanying fixed drone is supplied by other pipes which can be tuned by means of adjustable joints. A characteristic form of Highland bagpipe playing is the pibroch (from the Gaelic for a pipe-tune), consisting of complex variations on a set theme. Great skill is called for in the treatment of the melody line, since it is difficult to repeat a note without introducing some intervening grace notes, known to pipers as 'warblers'.

South of the Scottish border, the Northumbrian pipes are gentler in tone and, inflated by a bellows pumped by the arm as in most European types, offer greater opportunities for staccato playing over a wider compass of notes. In 1953 the English composer Alan Bush was so much taken by the playing of the local virtuoso Jack Armstrong on the 'small pipes' that he wrote *Three Northumbrian Sketches* for the instrument. The last ducal piper in England is in the employ of the Percy family at Alnwick castle, Northumberland.

Baillie, (Dame) Isobel (1895–) Scottish soprano. She studied in Manchester and Milan, and became one of the leading singers in British oratorio performances, noted especially for her appearances in *Messiah*. Her first American appearance was in 1933. She was one of the original sixteen soloists in the *Serenade to Music* written by Vaughan Williams for Sir Henry Wood's golden jubilee as a conductor in London in 1938. After World War II she continued concert appearances and recording, and also became a teacher at the Royal College of Music, Cornell University, and the Manchester School of Music. The title of her autobiography expresses her view on musical interpretation: *Never Sing Louder than Lovely*.

Baker, (Dame) Janet (1933–) English mezzo-soprano. In 1956 she won second prize in the Kathleen Ferrier Competition, and in the same year joined the Glyndebourne chorus and made her operatic début with the Oxford University Opera Club in Smetana's *The Secret*. She was soon singing leading rôles with the Handel Opera Society, but made one of her greatest impressions as Dido in Purcell's opera *Dido and Aeneas*, a part which she was to make very much her own, singing it in many places, from Glyndebourne to Aix-en-Provence. She also excelled in Gluck's *Orfeo et Eurydice*, with which she ended her operatic career at Glyndebourne in July 1982, thereafter devoting herself to concert and recital work.

Janet Baker made many American appearances, and in *Full Circle*, the diary of her last year on

Janet Baker, English mezzo-soprano from Doncaster in Yorkshire, sang in the Leeds Philharmonic Choir and the Ambrosian Singers before going on to win fame with the Handel Opera Society and in Purcell's *Dido and Aeneas*.

the opera stage, wrote of New York as being 'for sixteen years the place which has held the most precious musical memories of my career'.

Balakirev, Mily (1837–1910) Russian composer. Originally a mathematics student, the fervently nationalistic young man was encouraged to express himself in music by Glinka. Largely self-taught, he was influential in founding the Russian Free School of Music and also became the guiding light of 'The Five' or 'Mighty Handful' of young composers with similar patriotic leanings. He was a major influence on Mussorgsky and Rimsky-Korsakov, and even Tchaikovsky was under his spell for a while.

Balakirev made collections of folk songs and wrote a symphonic poem, *Russia*, and an Oriental fantasy for piano, *Islamey*. After dismissal from the Free School as a result of quarrels with bureaucratic academics, he had a nervous breakdown and worked for a while as a minor railway official before returning to the school in 1881 and then being made director of the Imperial Chapel, when he started composing again.

OTHER WORKS: Two symphonies. Overtures *King*

Mily Balakirev took over leadership of the circle of Russian nationalist composers after the death of its father figure, Glinka, and became the 'Benevolent Despot' of the 'Mighty Handful' of younger idealists.

Lear, On Three Russian Themes, and *On Czech Themes.* Symphonic poem *Tamara.* Many songs and piano pieces.

balalaika A triangular, three-stringed instrument much used in Russia for accompanying folk singers and playing at peasant dances and celebrations. As it has no sustaining power, its chords need to be strummed like those of a banjo or ukulele.

Balfe, Michael (1808–70) Irish composer, violinist and baritone. He was taken to Italy by his patron Count Mazzara, sang in Paris, London and at La Scala, Milan, and produced his own operas in theatres all over Europe. *The Siege of Rochelle* was an instant success at Drury Lane, London, in October 1835, but an even greater one was *The Bohemian Girl* in 1843, full of the easily memorable tunes for which Balfe had such a gift.

His operas were staged in many places in many languages, and he travelled to Berlin, Vienna, St Petersburg and a number of Italian centres to supervise their production. In later years he retired to Rowney Abbey in Hertfordshire, where he combined farming with the revision of old scores and started a new opera.

OTHER WORKS: Operas *Falstaff, Geraldine, The Rose of Castile.* Ballet *La Pérouse.* Three cantatas. Many songs.

Ball, Ernest (1878–1927) American composer of popular songs. He studied at Cleveland University, but after moving to New York had to earn a living as a vaudeville pianist. He began writing songs, had a hit with *Will you love me in December as you do in May?*, and followed up with other sentimental successes such as *Mother Machree* and *When Irish Eyes are Smiling,* some of them popularized by the tenor John McCormack.

ballad The word was used originally to denote a lyrical narrative poem in short rhythmic stanzas, telling some heroic or sentimental tale, though its basically musical provenance is clear in its relation to the Latin *ballare,* to dance. In music it came to mean a song either in dance time or at any rate designed to accompany a dance, or a musical setting of verse narratives such as *Chevy Chase* and *Edward,* reaching its highest peak in transformations such as Schubert's *Erlkönig.* Many less ambitious ballads tell of everyday subjects, of personal, social and political troubles. The English historian Lord Macaulay said of seventeenth-century folk, for example: 'It was in rude rhyme that their love and hatred, their exultation and distress found utterance. A great deal of their history is to be learned from their ballads'. The same is true of the human history of the United States of America, rich in ballads sad, optimistic, wry or violent, some traditional, some rising from the minds of popular composers: *Frankie and Johnnie* and many 'hill-billy' numbers belong in the mainstream of such a musical form; and there are related versions of ballads such as *The Foggy Foggy Dew* in both England and America.

'Ballad Opera' is a stage piece made up of topical verses set to the music of folk songs and popular songs of the day, linked by spoken narrative. The form was introduced to London in 1728 by John Gay and Dr Johann Pepusch in *The Beggar's Opera,* and revived with striking effect in 1928 by Bertolt Brecht's *Der Dreigroschenoper (The Threepenny Opera).*

ballade Although the basic meaning is synonymous with 'ballad', in this spelling the word has come to refer to extended piano pieces. The romantic, frequently heroic element in troubadours' songs and the poetic ballads set by, for instance, Schubert became instrumental 'programme music' in the hands of Brahms, Chopin, Liszt and Fauré. Grieg also adopted the name of *Ballade* for his *Variations on a Norwegian Folksong.*

In 1929 John Ireland gave the name to a large-scale piano piece which, after a fragmented introduction, introduces an expressive melody over richly amassed harmonies, expressing some emotion into whose secret the composer does not admit us. The following year he wrote a second one, the *Ballade of London Nights,* but for some personal or perhaps purely technical reason was never happy with it and did not allow it to be performed in his lifetime. It was not heard until the BBC transmitted it in 1966.

Marie Taglioni, the first ballerina to dance *sur les pointes*, here shown on tiptoe
in a Paris Opera production of *La Sylphide* in 1832.

BALLET

The word, like 'ballad', stems from the Latin *ballare*, 'to dance'. Music and dance have been allied since ancient times, but the dramatic presentation of ballet as we know it today did not truly begin until the late sixteenth century. Italian dancing masters at the French Court devised stately measures for courtiers to perform, often with royal participation. The first really ambitious staged entertainment of which there is any record was *Le Ballet comique de la reine*, devised for the wedding of the Duc de Joyeux and Mlle de Vaudemont in Paris in 1581 when Catherine de' Medici, a keen encourager of the arts, was on the throne. Later Louis XIV was to continue this encouragement.

Such dance sequences did not for some time become a separate art form. They were usually incorporated with opera, but grew in importance during the reign of Lully, Louis' pampered favourite, who was himself a skilful dancer. By the early eighteenth century dance and songs were almost equal partners in an outstanding success, Rameau's *Les Indes galantes*. Later in that same century came a significant change. Ballet subjects had hitherto been confined to mythological themes, danced in formal style in heavy formal clothes. Rameau had introduced more lively movements and even incorporated descriptive music to heighten the mood, and the dancer Camargo developed a more energetic style in spite of the restrictions imposed by the costumes. Now, in their wake, Jean-Georges Noverre set about the dismissal of any lingering vocal elements and advocated a blend of mime and dance, explaining his theories in an influential publication of 1760, *Lettres sur la danse et sur les ballets*. Although many opera composers were still called upon to provide set pieces for ballet interludes in their scores – Wagner, much later, not merely allowed *Tannhäuser* to be sung in French for its Paris production but inserted a ballet in Act 2 to pander to local taste – the form had established its independence.

One of the first examples of this liberation, still performed today, was *La Fille mal gardée*, for which the music was originally drawn from popular French airs. Later a mixture of other tunes was provided by Hérold, some of his own and some taken from operas by his contemporaries. Hérold's contributions were adapted for the 1960 production in London, with one number from a nineteenth-century German version composed by Johann Hertel.

Noverre's elevation of ballet from the status of a mere divertissement to a dramatic art form brought into prominence the choreographer (from the Greek, a 'dance writer'), who had to work out the story of the ballet in dance steps and devise a way of recording the sequences by graphic symbols. Then and now there have been different approaches to the creation of a new work. Collaboration between composer and choreographer can begin with music already composed, around which the choreographer must fit the movements of the danced and mimed narrative, or with a scenario presented by choreographer to composer, sometimes sketching in only the essential outlines, or more rigorously laying down the number of measures, the rhythm, and the nature of music required.

Also the star performers were coming into their own. There had already been popular idols such as Gaetano Vestris, who praised Noverre but praised himself even more fulsomely, saying, 'There are only three great men in Europe: the King of Prussia, Monsieur de Voltaire, and myself'. When he danced in London with his son, Parliament suspended a sitting in order to attend their performance. His sister Teresa made a big hit in Vienna and became the mistress of Prince Esterhazy before going on to further triumphs in Florence and Paris. But it was the introduction of the satin slipper in place of the noisy heeled shoe worn by female dancers until early in the nineteenth century which really opened the way for improved techniques and the apotheosis of the *prima ballerina*.

In 1832 the Swedish ballerina Marie Taglioni entranced her audience by dancing *sur les pointes* – that is, on the extreme tips of her toes – in the romantic ballet-pantomime *La Sylphide*, choreographed by her father. The freedom conferred by the new slipper also made possible the pirouette and other graceful movements which had hitherto been impractical. Rivals in technical skill and poetic interpretation

Four great rivals appearing together in *Pas de Quatre* at Her Majesty's Theatre, London, in 1845: Grisi, Taglioni, Grahn and Cerrito.

soon threatened Taglioni's pre-eminence. Carlotta Grisi, who had been trained in the *corps de ballet* at La Scala, Milan, was forcefully promoted by her lover, Jules Perrot, a French dancer and choreographer who had for some time partnered Taglioni but had fallen out with her over his contract. Grisi created the title rôle of *Giselle*, specially written for her by one of her most doting admirers, the author Théophile Gautier, and went on to further adulation in a number of productions, usually accompanied by the outstanding male *danseur noble*, Lucien Petipa. The more fiery Fanny Elssler — Gautier described her as a pagan ballerina in contrast with the gentler Taglioni — popularized an accentuated, staccato style of dancing on the points, often rather noisy but winning her a faithful following of her own until she made the mistake of trying to outdo Taglioni in *La Sylphide*.

In 1850 Grisi took her performance of *Giselle* to the Maryinsky Theatre in St Petersburg and again achieved a resounding success. Ballet, originally rooted in Paris, was putting up shoots in many other countries, and in fact, when interest waned for some decades in France, the tradition was not merely preserved but strengthened and given new grafts elsewhere. Major ballet schools and companies developed, and new generations of dancers found new ways of expressing themselves and new themes to stimulate adventurous choreography. Many national, not to say nationalistic, traits emerged at one time and another, but throughout the twentieth century there has been a healthy international exchange of dancers, teachers, choreographers and composers between one school and another.

DENMARK: The Royal Danish Ballet has the longest unbroken tradition in Europe. A ballet school was functioning in the 1750s, training dancers for the Royal Theatre, but the present school was founded in 1771 by the French dancer Pierre Laurent. Four years later the Florentine Vincenzo Galeotti was lured from the King's Theatre in the Haymarket, London, to take over as dancer, choreographer and ballet master in Copenhagen. He created some fifty original works, of which *The Whims of Cupid and the Ballet Master* is still in the Danish repertory, danced to the oldest known surviving choreography.

In 1805 August Bournonville was born, son of a French father and Swedish mother. At the age of fifteen he joined the Royal Danish company and won a scholarship to study with Vestris in Paris. For a short while he danced in Copenhagen, but then returned to Paris and frequently partnered Taglioni. When he finally settled in Denmark it was as ballet director and choreographer, with only brief spells at the Vienna Court Opera and the Stockholm Opera; but he travelled from time to time and drew inspiration from Russia, the Netherlands and Italy for many of his productions. Among those still most frequently performed, in a style almost as codified and immutable as the comic operas of Gilbert and Sullivan, are *Napoli*, *Kermesse in Bruges*, *La Ventana*, *A Folk Tale*, and his own version of *La Sylphide*, which originally starred beautiful Lucille Grahn, thought by some to have bested Taglioni.

In later years a major formative influence in the company was Vera Volkova, who had studied in Russia and, after teaching at Sadler's Wells in London between 1943 and 1950, became artistic adviser to the Danish ballet. Many of her protégés went on to become ballet masters and teachers in other national companies. Harald Lander became director of the Paris Opera School and guest choreographer to many European and American companies before returning full-time to Copenhagen in 1962 and working there until his death in 1970. Erik Bruhn, one of the company's outstanding solo dancers, appeared as a guest with English, American and Swedish companies, won the Nijinsky Prize in 1963, and became associate director of the National Ballet of Canada. Peter Schaufuss, son of two stars of the Royal Danish Ballet, made guest appearances all over the world, became principal dancer of the New York City Ballet in 1974, and later directed the Royal Ballet in London. Henning Kronstam, who created the part of Romeo in Frederick Ashton's *Romeo and Juliet* (to Prokofiev's music), stayed in Copenhagen after his days as *premier danseur* and became director of the Royal Danish Ballet School.

RUSSIA: In 1738 the French ballet master Jean-Baptiste Landé was engaged to teach dancing at the Imperial Theatre School in St Petersburg, which fed local talent to the Bolshoi (Great) Theatre in the capital until that was replaced in the 1860s by the Maryinsky Theatre. From 1862 until the turn of the century the dominant figure in the Russian ballet world was Marius Petipa, who choreographed about fifty pieces for theatres in St Petersburg and Moscow, including Tchaikovsky's *Sleeping Beauty* and the libretto for the *Nutcracker*, although he was unable to complete the full choreography because of illness.

Tchaikovsky was one of the first major composers in his or, indeed, any country to turn his attention to full ballet scores. His *Swan Lake*, *Sleeping Beauty* and *Nutcracker* have never lost their freshness, and many of his other compositions have provided the basis for works by choreographers all over the world: for example, the Third Suite for Orchestra was used in Balanchine's *Theme and Variations* for the Ballet Theatre, New York, later expanded for the New York City Ballet as *Suite No. 3*; and the First and Third Symphonies provided material for the first two acts of Kenneth MacMillan's *Anastasia* for the Royal Ballet at Covent Garden, London.

Moscow was not slow to follow the example of St Petersburg. The Bolshoi Ballet company began life in 1776 and from 1780 performed at the Petrovsky Theatre until 1805, when it burned down, to be replaced twenty years later by the present Bolshoi Theatre. In 1877 *Swan Lake* had its first production here – an unsuccessful, almost disastrous first night. Not until a completely revised version was presented by the choreographer Alexander Gorsky in 1901 did the work become popular. Later versions by Soviet producers and choreographers have been based mainly on Gorsky's refashioning. Gorsky himself lived on into the post-Revolution world of Soviet Russia and helped to reorganize the company. He died in 1924, revered as a prophet of realistic, dramatic ballet and, with Mikhail Fokine, as a major reforming influence, favouring a more energetic and passionate style of male dancing in place of Petipa's formalized, old-fashioned style.

During the early Soviet years the ballet company in St Petersburg still took pride of place – though now the city had become Leningrad. It was not really until after World War II that the Bolshoi, returning to Moscow after evacuation to Kuibyshev, came to the fore and dancers such as Ulanova and Plisetskaya moved from Leningrad to what was now the capital not just of the USSR but also of the Russian ballet world. The company made its first visit to London in 1956 and to New York in 1959. They were not, however, the first Russian dancers to take the outside world by storm.

DIAGHILEV and the **BALLETS RUSSES:** Born in 1872, Serge Diaghilev became a law student in St Petersburg but from the start was more interested in the arts than in the legal profession. He founded an art magazine and for two years worked at the Maryinsky Theatre, resigning to devote himself to mounting exhibitions of Russian art in St Petersburg and Paris. In Paris he also organized concerts of Russian music and presented Mussorgsky's opera *Boris Godunov* with Chaliapin in the title rôle.

In 1909 he took the leading dancers from St Petersburg and Moscow to Paris, and presented Nijinsky, Pavlova and Karsavina to enraptured audiences, dancing to choreography by Fokine and with scenery by Benois. This and subsequent productions caused a sensation. Other choreographers emerged, their individual styles influencing companies throughout the world: Massine, Balanchine, and Lifar.

Sir John Lavery's painting of Anna Pavlova in her famous performance of *Le Mort du Cygne* (*The Dying Swan*) arranged for her by the choreographer Fokine from Saint-Saëns' music.

The Bolshoi Ballet in a 1963 production of *Les Sylphides*, originally called *Chopiniana* because the music was orchestrated from piano pieces by Chopin.

Composers who wrote for Diaghilev included Ravel, Prokofiev, Satie and Stravinsky, whose *Le Sacre du printemps* (*Rite of Spring*) caused an uproar when it was first performed in 1913, with its harsh discords, pounding, sensual rhythms, and Nijinsky's daring choreography.

After the Revolution, Diaghilev did not return to Russia but continued to run the Ballets Russes as a private company until his death, when survivors merged with the opera ballet of Monte Carlo and continued successfully as the Ballets Russes de Monte Carlo with Colonel de Basil as director.

GREAT BRITAIN: In the middle of the eighteenth century Noverre had worked for a short time with David Garrick, but it was not until well into the next century that romantic ballet began to appeal to London audiences. In 1897 Adeline Genée, creator of the rôle of Swanilda in *Coppélia*, was the idol of the London Empire Theatre. Later Diaghilev's company stimulated a surge of new interest; Pavlova settled in England; and the Polish-born Marie Rambert, who had worked with Diaghilev, founded her school in 1920 to train, over many decades,

A 1912 programme for Diaghilev's Ballets Russes shows Leon Bakst's costume design for Nijinsky in *L'Après-midi d'un faune*, with music by Debussy.

dancers and outstanding choreographers such as Frederick Ashton, Antony Tudor, and John Cranko. Irish-born Ninette de Valois set up a London Academy of Choreographic Art in 1926, closing it in 1931 in order to take over the ballet school at Sadler's Wells and develop, in conjunction with the Old Vic Theatre, what became the Vic-Wells Ballet.

Frederick Ashton joined in 1933, and it was to his choreography of *Rio Grande* that Margot Fonteyn made her first appearance in a major rôle. The music for this was written by Constant Lambert, who made a major contribution to the company as conductor.

During World War II the company toured Britain, with Fonteyn and Robert Helpmann as its stars, and premièred several important new works, including Bliss's *Miracle in the Gorbals*. In 1956 the name of Sadler's Wells gave way, by royal charter, to that of The Royal Ballet. The Ballet Rambert continued as a major experimental force, and other vigorous companies included the London Festival Ballet, the Scottish Ballet, and the Welsh Dance Theatre.

UNITED STATES OF AMERICA: European dancers made successful tours of the USA throughout the eighteenth and nineteenth centuries, but an indigenous ballet company did not see the light of day until 1909, when a school was founded as an adjunct to the Metropolitan Opera House. In 1940 the American Ballet Theatre was established, to be followed after World War II by the New York City Ballet, thanks largely to the influence of George Balanchine as artistic director, with Jerome Robbins as co-director. The two of them also contributed material generously to the Dance Theatre of Harlem, which staged its first productions in 1971.

A remarkable number of gifted individual soloists have played a large part in the development of American ballet. Isadora Duncan, born in San Francisco in 1878, cast aside all prescribed techniques and expressed herself in emotional, often melodramatic free dance forms. She ended life melodramatically, too – strangled near Nice when her scarf became entangled in the wheel of a car. Katherine Dunham's School of Dance developed the potentialities of Afro-American music and, together with her travelling troupe, was a forcing ground for black dancers. Above all, Agnes de Mille and Martha Graham opened up new vistas of contemporary dance-drama, often in partnership with leading American composers: de Mille supplied libretto and choreography for Copland's *Rodeo*; Graham commissioned his *Appalachian Spring* and Barber's *Cave of the Heart*.

Other leading ballet companies of today include those of Chicago, Philadelphia, San Francisco, Ballet West of Utah, and Merce Cunningham's group.

Martha Graham in *Legends of Judith*. Founding her own company in 1929, she became the most influential exponent of modern dance in the USA, and commissioned works from many leading composers including Copland, Hindemith, Barber, Menotti, Schuman and Dello Joio.

bamboula A West Indian tambourine, and also the name of the dance for which it provides rhythmic accompaniment.

band The word is used to describe any group of instrumentalists, either a section within a full orchestra – as in 'string band' or 'wind band' – or a self-contained orchestra such as a brass band, military band, or jazz band. Town bands were once maintained by most sizeable communities for local festivities, and often provided backing to hymns and chorales in the parish church: such an ensemble is immortalized in the 'Mellstock Quire' of the English novelist Thomas Hardy's *Under the Greenwood Tree*. Band concerts were popular throughout the eighteenth and nineteenth centuries, and there are still many European and American towns which preserve their public park and seaside bandstands.

Military bands, sometimes consisting purely of brass instruments and drums but often with woodwind added, existed to provide a brisk, steady rhythm for marching feet. Even for the general listening public, marching bands have been perennially popular. In the USA, John Philip Sousa led the Marine Corps Band for twelve years and went on to even greater public acclaim with his own touring concert band, composing invigorating music expressly for such a combination.

Civilian wind bands, especially brass and silver bands, have been most common in industrial areas of Continental Europe and northern England. Yorkshire cotton factories took intense pride in the achievements of their local musicians such as the Black Dyke Mills Band, which toured frequently in its homeland and in America; and from a mining town in the same county came the Grimethorpe Colliery Band. Great annual events during the heyday of such ensembles were the festivals at the Crystal Palace and Royal Albert Hall in London, and the championship contest at Belle Vue, Manchester.

Some serious musicians and critics tended for a while to deride the limitations and, in effect, the 'brassiness' of brass bands; but when approaches were made to them by leading conductors of such bands they rallied round with considerable effect. Elgar's *Severn Suite* was commissioned for the 1930 Crystal Palace contest; the following year John Ireland contributed his *Downland Suite*; and Edmund Rubbra converted one of his piano pieces into *Variations on 'The Shining River'*, which has since become a favourite test piece.

The dance bands which flourished in the years before, during and immediately after World War II (sometimes trying to improve their status with the designation of 'orchestra' rather than 'band') varied in personnel and makeup, but in general consisted of a saxophone section, one or more trumpets and trombones, with perhaps one wind player 'doubling' on violin, a rhythm section of piano, guitar, double bass and drums, and a singer (or 'vocalist') who might or might not be one of the instrumentalists. Jazz bands, though bearing a family relationship to dance bands, varied even more widely in number and instrumentation, from an improvising quartet to ten or twenty players capable of reading intricate orchestrations.

banjo A stringed instrument with a long neck, usually divided by frets to simplify the fingering, producing its resonance by means of vellum stretched across a metal hoop similar to a drumhead. Supposedly brought in its most primitive form from Africa to North America by black slaves, it became the favourite accompanying instrument for plantation songs and dances. At first with three strings only, it acquired a fourth, and there are models with anything from five to nine strings, offering a wider melodic range and richer supporting chords. Gut strings are played with the fingers; wire strings with a plectrum. In the early days of jazz it proved to be an ideal rhythm section instrument, especially when no piano was available to fill out the harmonies, and was in regular use until recording techniques and amplification led to its replacement by the guitar, too quiet to compete in normal circumstances but much more flexible and less strident. In the later twentieth century the banjo has come into its own again as a backing for folk singers.

Banks, Don (1923–80) Australian composer. After studying in Melbourne he became a private pupil of Mátyás Seiber in London and Luigi Dallapiccola in Florence, and later worked with Milton Babbitt, whose explorations into electronic composition stimulated his own creative response in works such as *Commentary* for piano and tape and *Intersections* with tape. Although a devotee of serialism, he could produce music which was often haunting rather than austere, as in the spare but captivating *Three Episodes* for flute and piano. He also conveys a strong rhythmic drive, which is not surprising, since another of his interests was jazz: in Australia he worked as a jazz pianist and arranger. Between 1965 and 1970 he was musical director of Goldsmiths' College, London, and then became professor of music at Canberra University.

OTHER WORKS: Concertos for violin and horn. *Assemblies* for orchestra. *Settings from Roget* for jazz singer and quartet. *Nexus* for jazz quintet and orchestra. *Psalm 70* for soprano and chamber orchestra.

Bantock, (Sir) Granville (1868–1946) English composer and conductor. He became known first as a conductor, courageously introducing new music in his concerts at the Tower, New Brighton, across the river Mersey from Liverpool. Among composers whose work he urged upon his audience was Sibelius, who dedicated his Third Symphony to Bantock. In 1904 he became conductor of the Worcestershire Philharmonic Society, a post which Elgar had once held, and later took on another of Elgar's duties, that of professor of music at Birmingham University.

Bantock was one of the most energetic and prolific composers of his time, always full of enthusiasm for some new project. He wrote two symphonies for voices alone, divided into a vast complexity of vocal parts, and a cantata based on the whole of Fitzgerald's translation of the *Rubáiyát of Omar Khayyam*; and dreamed of a sequence of twenty-four symphonic poems which should be played during one extended concert. Entranced by songs collected by Marjory Kennedy-Fraser from the Hebridean islands, he composed a *Hebridean Symphony*, a piece for soprano and chorus called *Sea Sorrow*, and with her libretto a Celtic folk-opera, *The Seal Woman*, all of them genuinely moved by the island folk-song cadences but perhaps too smoothly ironed out for the benefit of the average audience's melodic and harmonic expectations.

Tuneful and ravishingly scored as so much of his music was, little of it is heard nowadays apart from the comedy overture *The Pierrot of the Minute*, a romantic piece evoking Pierrot's dream of love and lasting happiness with a Moon Maiden – a dream which he finds, on waking, has lasted only one minute. Although Bantock uses the resources of a full orchestra in this piece, he does so with a delicacy which matches the gossamer, dreamlike texture of the story.

OTHER WORKS: Orchestral ballad, *The Sea Reivers*. Tone poem *Fifine at the Fair*. Overture *The Frogs*. Oratorio *The Pilgrim's Progress* for soloists, choir and orchestra.

bar The vertical line on a stave (or staff) marking the division of a composition according to its basic rhythm: e.g. 3/4 time, 'three in a bar', or common time, 'four in a bar'. In Britain the word has come to be applied to the space between the lines, which are now called bar-lines. In the USA the original usage has been retained, the space between the bars or bar-lines being known as a measure. The whole system was introduced at the beginning of the seventeenth century as a means of regulating by metrical division the progressions and patterns of music which had hitherto been allowed to range freely, depending for its accentuations and timing very much on the intuitive capabilities of the performers.

Barber, Samuel (1910–81) American composer. Taught singing by his aunt, a distinguished contralto in her day, at the age of fourteen he became one of the first charter students at the Curtis Institute in Philadelphia. His graduation piece was an exuberant overture to Sheridan's play *The School for Scandal*, winning immediate public acclaim when it was performed by the Philadelphia Orchestra. In 1935 he won a Pulitzer travelling scholarship, and the following year the American Academy's *Prix de Rome*. Over twenty years later he was to win the Pulitzer Prize for his opera *Vanessa*, with a libretto by his friend of long standing, Gian-Carlo Menotti.

A traditionalist in outlook, Barber's neo-romantic, elegant style flowers most rewardingly from the diatonic scale, in spite of some experiments with 12-tone methods. During service with the Army Air Corps during World War II he conceived some wartime effects from a tone generator in his Second Symphony, but deleted them in a post-war revision. It has been acutely said of him that he can offer modern music in a way which will not torture the ears of the listener, and much of this gift must surely be due to his own youthful days as a singer.

An early characteristic work was his lyrical setting of Matthew Arnold's poem *Dover Beach* for baritone and string quartet or string orchestra, in which he was the first to sing the vocal part. His string quartet of 1936 contained an adagio of such beauty that it became a popular success when conducted in orchestral form by Toscanini, and as *Adagio for Strings* has remained a favourite concert piece ever since. *Antony and Cleopatra*, his second opera, was commissioned for the opening of the new Metropolitan Opera House at Lincoln Center, New York, in 1966. Barber published a revised version in 1976.

OTHER WORKS: Symphonies 1 & 2. Orchestral *Essays* 1 & 2. Concertos for violin, cello and piano. *Knoxville: Summer of 1915* for soprano and orchestra, to words by James Agee. *Four Excursions* in jazz style for the piano.

barbershop harmony Although the term is thought of mainly in connection with the close-harmony singing of 'barbershop quartets' in the USA, its origin lies back in England of the sixteenth and seventeenth centuries, when barbers kept a selection of musical instruments on their premises so that waiting customers could while away their time. Collaborating in such casual fashion, the participants needed to stick to some fairly straightforward, well-known piece if they were to produce any sort of tolerable ensemble, and the same is true of the twentieth-century vocal inheritors of the tradition: the songs performed are usually popular ballads with predictable, easily distributed harmonies tightly following the tune, which is carried as a rule by the tenor in the foursome, with a higher tenor (or falsetto alto) singing a line above him.

Barbirolli, (Sir) John (1899–1970) English conductor. London-born of French-Italian parentage (actually christened Giovanni Battista), he studied as a cellist but made his name as an opera and orchestral conductor in Britain and the USA. From 1936 to 1943 he conducted the New York Philharmonic Symphony Orchestra, and then returned to England to begin a memorable association with the Hallé Orchestra in Manchester which lasted until his death. Between 1961 and 1967 he was also principal conductor of the Houston Symphony Orchestra. In 1939 he married the oboist and teacher Evelyn Rothwell, for whom he adapted many classical works as oboe showpieces. He was knighted in 1949.

barcarolle The word derives from the Italian *barcarola*, meaning a 'boat song', more specifically the kind sung by Venetian gondoliers in a lilting rhythm in accord with the lapping waves of the canals – which usually oblige with a lulling 6/8 time. Various composers have used the name for pieces in this style, e.g. Chopin, Fauré and Mendelssohn, probably the best known being that from Offenbach's opera *The Tales of Hoffmann*.

Barenboim, Daniel (1942–) Israeli pianist and conductor. Born in Buenos Aires, Argentina, he was given piano lessons by his mother and father

and made his first public appearance at the age of seven. After the family had moved to Israel in 1951 he was sent to Rome to study, and also had private tuition with Edwin Fischer and Nadia Boulanger. In 1956 he made his solo début in Paris, and the following year appeared in London and New York.

As well as achieving worldwide success as a pianist, especially in cycles of Beethoven piano sonatas, Barenboim made good use of his studies at Salzburg conducting classes under Igor Markevitch, and has frequently played the dual rôle of conductor-soloist in London, New York and Berlin. He has accompanied many lieder singers, played in chamber groups, and recorded definitive versions of the two Brahms clarinet sonatas with Gervase de Peyer. In 1967 he settled in England and married the brilliant cellist Jacqueline du Pré, with whom he recorded the Elgar Cello Concerto before she was sadly forced to retire because of a crippling illness.

baritone The male voice 'deep-sounding' (from the Greek) between the tenor and even deeper bass, with a range from the lower A on the bass clef to the lower F or F sharp on the treble clef. The word is also used to identify certain instruments in the same range, as in a brass band, and the baritone saxophone, of which one of the greatest exponents was the jazz musician Harry Carney, an early and long-lasting member of Duke Ellington's orchestra.

barn dance A boisterous rural dance for sets of partners, usually in brisk 2/4 or 4/4 time, held on local festive or informal occasions – not necessarily in a barn. Originating in the USA, it was sometimes called the military schottische, and has elements in common with Highland and Virginia reels, though on a much more free-and-easy basis and with fewer traditional movements. The dancer and choreographer Catherine Littlefield of Philadelphia built a ballet called *Barn Dance* around a medley of American folk songs in 1937.

baroque In architecture the word is used to describe something oddly shaped or over-ornamented, in the florid style of late Renaissance Austria and Germany. Musically it is applied to the period between the earliest true dramatic operas and the death of J.S. Bach, that is, from about 1600 to 1750. During this period the transition was made from predominantly religious vocal stylization and the similar formalities of instrumental music to a more humanistic approach. In opera the expression of emotion was not merely permitted

Daniel Barenboim, pianist and conductor, husband of the superb cellist Jacqueline du Pré from 1967 until her death in 1987.

but encouraged: the division of a melody into recitative and aria, and the refinement of *bel canto* singing, together with the reinforcement of more richly harmonized or contrapuntal instrumental parts, made possible the depiction of a wide variety of moods and affections. Oratorios ambitiously contrasted the resources of solo singers, chorus and orchestra.

In the instrumental field itself there were also great advances. As an accompaniment to singers or string and wind soloists the *basso continuo* provided rhythmic and harmonic support. At the same time larger forces were used in the developing forms of the *sinfonia, concerto grosso, concerto* and *suite*. Sonata form grew out of older vocal polyphony to become the main pattern for keyboard works and then for chamber and full orchestral composition.

At the same time the very character of music tonality was undergoing significant changes. The eight modal systems on which plainchant and other church music had been based gave way to the two rationalized major and minor scales which have served well ever since in spite of modern attacks by atonalists and quarter-tone experimenters.

During the ensuing 'classical' period it became customary to sneer at baroque composers as being crude, old-fashioned, and addicted to over-ornamentation. When one considers that the composers thus denigrated included Monteverdi, Vivaldi, Bach and Handel, one can only be thankful that later generations reconsidered the matter and came up with a revised verdict.

barré The French word meaning 'barred' describes the method by which the player of a guitar or similar instrument stops all the strings in one movement by laying a finger straight across them, thereby raising their pitch simultaneously.

barrel organ Originally used in churches which could not afford a full-scale organ, the instrument is played by winding a handle to turn a cylinder whose raised pins, like those of a musical box, engage with metal tongues to open small pipes. At the same time the cranking of the handle operates bellows to supply air to these pipes. The selection of hymn tunes available is conditioned by the pre-set pins.

The name has frequently been misapplied to the street piano or street organ, and to the hurdy-gurdy, both quite different.

Bartók, Béla (1881–1945) Hungarian composer and pianist. Born in a part of Hungary which is now Romanian, and studying in Pozsony which is now Bratislava in Czechoslovakia, Bartók was fascinated by the differences in folk tunes and rhythms between one region and another. Taught by his

Béla Bartók, the Hungarian composer whose work is suffused with the folk melodies and rhythms of his native land.

mother to play the piano, and then continuing his studies at the Royal Academy in Budapest, he became an avid collector of Hungarian, Slovak and Romanian songs, travelling with a phonograph to record the authentic sound, often collaborating with his compatriot and friend Zoltán Kodály. Later he was to extend his researches to Arab music in North Africa and to Turkey.

After trying to make a name as a solo pianist, in 1907 he became professor of piano at the Academy and tried to find time for composition. Parts of a violin concerto which he started that year were played, but the manuscript was put aside and not rediscovered until 1959. Much impressed by the music of Richard Strauss and, as his First String Quartet of 1908 shows, by that of Debussy, it took him time to find his own voice – and when he did, it was not much to public taste. The cadences of folk song, the uneven and often savage rhythms – as in the famous *Allegro barbaro* of 1911 – and the clashing dissonances which arose as he pursued a growing interest in the re-use of old modes to redefine the whole concept of key, seemed ugly to many listeners, and the painstaking symmetry of his works was far from immediately obvious. He certainly did not indulge in sweeping romantic melodies to charm the ear: his most impressive works use the briefest of motifs as the basis for inventive, beautifully structured variations. In many instances he adopted an 'arch' form, as in the Second Piano Concerto, where thematic material is shared by the first and third movements, while the central movement is itself an *adagio-presto-adagio* arch.

Racked by illness brought on by bronchitis and pneumonia in his youth, Bartók was nevertheless a ferociously vigorous pianist, and through all his music there seems to be a struggle between barely suppressed passion and a prideful intellectual discipline. He was a patriot, but never a noisy one: as well as his many returns to the idiom of folk music, his devotion to the countryside emerges in the *Out of Doors* suite for piano and the evocative 'night sounds' which so frequently insinuate their way into his compositions. On the festive occasion of the merging of Buda, Pest and Obuda in 1923 he wrote his exhilarating *Dance Suite* full of national and other almost oriental lyrical and rhythmic elements.

Twice married, Bartók dedicated his only opera, the one-act *Bluebeard's Castle*, to his first wife Márta, one of his piano pupils. Rejected by a committee seeking the most outstanding Hungarian lyrical work of 1911, it had to wait until 1918 for a successful production in Budapest. The theme makes an odd gift to a wife, dealing as it does with the sorrowful but implacable justice meted out to meddling wives by the rich, much-married Duke Bluebeard. After divorce, Bartók married another young pupil, Ditta Pásztory, and composed the *Sonata for Two Pianos and Percussion* for the two of them to perform. Its slow movement is pervaded with his characteristic 'night music'.

Among his many solo piano works, the most influential has probably been *Mikrokosmos*. This set of 153 progressive piano pieces was written for his second son Peter as a guide to the rhythms, harmonies and dissonances of modern music, as well as being a graduated series of fingering exercises. Short as they are, they encompass the whole of Bartók's creative, emotional and intellectual range, from experiments with pentatonic scales, minor seconds and divided arpeggios to the symbolism of Leonardo da Vinci's 'golden section', from *Homage to J.S. Bach* to dances in Bulgarian rhythm.

In 1940 wartime conditions drove him to emigrate to the USA. Deprived of all European royalties on his work, he was kept alive by fees for cataloguing folk song collections and by enlightened patrons such as the Koussevitsky Foundation, which commissioned the now admired *Concerto for Orchestra*, and the jazz clarinettist Benny Goodman, who commissioned the trio *Contrasts* and recorded it with Szigeti and Bartók himself. His last gift to his wife Ditta was the Third Piano Concerto, of which seventeen bars were unfinished at his death.

His greatest legacy must be the six string quartets, from the fairly conventional beginning to the knotty, challenging atonalities and unorthodox counterpoint of the later ones.

OTHER WORKS: Two violin concertos. Three piano concertos. *Music for Strings, Percussion and Celeste. Cantata Profana* for soloists, choir and orchestra. Ballets *The Wooden Prince* and *The Miraculous Mandarin*. Two violin sonatas. Forty-four violin duos.

baryton An obsolete string instrument, occasionally revived in our own time by 'early music' consorts seeking historical authenticity. It resembles the viola da gamba but was fitted, like the viola d'amore, with sympathetic strings which vibrated when the bow played on the main strings. One of its best-known exponents was Prince Nikolaus Esterházy, whose resident musician Haydn wrote nearly two hundred pieces for it.

bass Refers to the lower register human voice, the lowest note in a chord, and the lower range of musical instruments. A true bass singer able to preserve quality of tone over the vocal range of D above the bass clef to F below it is rare: most are in the baritone or, at most, bass-baritone class. In its instrumental sense the word is colloquially applied to a string double bass in a symphony orchestra, dance band, or jazz group. (*See also* **basso continuo**, **basso profondo**, **clef**, and **The Orchestra and its Instruments**.)

basso continuo Meaning 'continuous bass', often shortened to *continuo*. Also known as 'figured bass' because, instead of writing out harmonies in full, the composer simply indicated by numbers above the bass part what chords he required and left the keyboard player to choose what inversion, arpeggio or other treatment of the chord he thought most appropriate at the time. The actual bass line or continuo was played as written by a low register stringed instrument. (*See also* **accompaniment**.)

basso profondo A truly deep bass voice capable of maintaining a full, rounded quality in the lowest register. The part of the Commendatore in Mozart's *Don Giovanni* demands such a voice.

baton In early opera and other works for a large ensemble it was usual for the director to establish tempo by pounding a heavy stick on the floor, sometimes keeping this up throughout a large part of the performance. Jean-Baptiste Lully managed to kill himself by a misplaced blow from such a pole. During the classical period the orchestra was generally directed by intermittent gestures from the keyboard, or the first violinist would beat time with his bow. With the growth of larger orchestras the use of a baton, often called a stick, began with virtuoso conductors in nineteenth-century Germany. It is first recorded in England at a concert directed by Ludwig Spohr in London.

Bax, (Sir) Arnold (1883–1953) English composer. Of independent means, Bax could please himself as to the neo-romantic music he wrote and the places he visited or lived in. 'My music is the expression of emotional states,' he said: 'I have no interest whatever in sound for its own sake or in any modernist 'isms or factions.'

Captivated early by Celtic mythology, he allowed many an implication that he himself was Irish, and tried his hand at poetry under the pseudonym of Dermot O'Byrne. Among his compositions suffused with this western spell were a *Celtic Song Cycle*, the setting of a Gaelic hymn in *St Patrick's Breastplate*, and the symphonic poem *The Garden of Fand* with its invocation of the hero Cuchulain under the spell of the abandoned wife of the god of the ocean. When he died during a musical adjudication in Cork, it was fitting that he should be buried in the cemetery there.

The sources of much of his work are made clear in his charming memoirs, *Farewell, My Youth*, published in 1943.

OTHER WORKS: Seven symphonies. Tone poem *Tintagel*, inspired by Arthurian legend. *Winter Legends* for piano and orchestra. Choral music. Song cycles. Four piano sonatas.

Bayreuth Festival Anxious to have his music-dramas, especially the *Ring* cycle, performed in an ideal setting, Richard Wagner designed a *Festspielhaus* (Festival-play House) in the small Bavarian town of Bayreuth. It opened in 1876, after which there were annual festivals of Wagnerian opera, administered after his death by the composer's descendants. Singers and conductors of international standing appeared regularly; but during the years of Nazi domination the conductor Toscanini, who was at the height of his fame and was the favourite of Wagner's daughters and their sister-in-law Winifred, then manager of the festival, refused to take part. Many adventurous, often noisily controversial, productions have enlivened the post-war seasons.

beat The basic unit of musical rhythm, established by the time signature at the beginning of a composition or subsection of a composition. In

A postcard of about 1875 showing the Bayreuth Festival Theatre (or Festival-play House, to translate Wagner's *Festspielhaus* in the meaning he intended). The 'Hojotoho!' at the top is the cry of the Valkyrie from the *Ring* cycle.

Gruss vom Wagnerhort.

Hojotoho! Hojotoho!
So grüße mir Gott die Burg, die Walhall der Germanen.

Verlag: Sammet, Wagnerapostel.

Hüterin des heiligen Grals.   Erbe des Horts.   Walvater deutscher Kunst.   Schirmherr des Horts.

waltz time, for instance, the signature 3/4 indicates three beats to the bar. The word is also used for the conductor's movement conveying the time to orchestral players. A downbeat from the conductor's hand or baton comes usually at the beginning of a piece, or when a particular rhythmic accent needs to be stressed; an upbeat is the opposite motion, often used at the end of a bar or phrase to indicate a forthcoming downbeat emphasis. 'A good stance, a flexible and distinctive beat' were Sir Henry Wood's fundamental recommendations for anyone aspiring to become a conductor.

Beatles, The Four young Liverpool pop singers and instrumentalists whose performances and recordings won them vast popularity during the 1960s, and an MBE (Medal of the British Empire) for each of them. The group consisted of John Lennon, Paul McCartney and George Harrison, guitars, and Ringo Starr, drums. Among the most successful songs written for them by Lennon and McCartney were *She loves you*, *Yesterday*, and *Yellow Submarine*. After making several films and best-selling records, the group split up at the end of the decade.

Paul McCartney continued as a soloist, and appeared with a group of his own called Wings. He wrote many more songs, including *The Mull of Kintyre*, which became the first 'single' disc to pass sales of two million in the United Kingdom. In 1969 John Lennon had married Yoko Ono

The Beatles' eighth album *Sgt. Pepper's Lonely Hearts Club Band*, released in 1967, sent repercussions around the world providing the theme for the summer of love, the psychedelic culture, and heralding the beginning of a social, sexual and musical revolution.

shortly before The Beatles disbanded. After some problems arising from his possessing marijuana, he was allowed in 1976 to settle in the USA, but in December 1980 was murdered outside his New York home by a psychopathic fan.

bebop A jazz offshoot of the 1940s, sometimes simply called 'bop', which involved fast unison playing by small groups of instrumentalists, interspersed with solos or scat-singing above complex harmonic changes. Among leading exponents were the alto saxophonist Charlie Parker, known as 'Bird', and the trumpeter Dizzy Gillespie.

Bechstein, Friedrich Wilhelm Karl (1826–1900) German pianoforte maker. Born in Gotha, he worked in piano factories in Germany, France and England before establishing his own firm in Berlin. His instruments became famous for their depth of tone. In the year after his death a London recital centre was named Bechstein Hall, but in a later change took the name of the street in which it stands, to become Wigmore Hall.

A bronze head and separate hands of Sir Thomas Beecham by David Wynne, incised and dated on the support 1957.

Beecham, (Sir) Thomas (1879–1961) English conductor. Grandson of the founder of the Beecham's Pills pharmaceutical business, he was devoted to music from an early age, taught himself conducting, assembled an amateur orchestra, and used family money to subsidize concerts and opera in London from 1905 onwards. He founded the New Symphony Orchestra (which later became the Royal Albert Hall Orchestra and then was disbanded), the Beecham Symphony Orchestra, the London Philharmonic Orchestra, and in 1947 the Royal Philharmonic Orchestra.

It was Beecham's personal enthusiasm which brought opera into British public consciousness, often plunging him into dire financial straits. In 1910 he became lessee of Covent Garden, introduced works by Richard Strauss and Delius, of whom he was a tireless champion, and was the first to produce Russian ballet in England. Throughout World War I he continued, at great expense, to produce opera; and in the years immediately before World War II he was back at Covent Garden Opera House as artistic director.

A great source of witty, scathing and musically provocative remarks – many of the attributed stories being perhaps apocryphal – he travelled widely as a guest conductor in Europe and the USA. His character comes across vividly in his autobiography, *A Mingled Chime*.

Beethoven, Ludvig van (1770–1827) German composer. Of Flemish descent, he was born in Bonn where his grandfather and father had both been Court singers to the Elector. At a very early stage his father sensed the boy's talent and forced piano and violin lessons on him in the hope of creating a prodigy who would keep the family in luxury. When the widowed and frequently drunken father was dismissed from his post, Ludvig at the age of nineteen found himself responsible for the upkeep of father, two brothers, and a sister who died young. He gave lessons and played viola in the Opera orchestra until, under the patronage of Count Waldstein (to whom he was later to dedicate the *Waldstein Sonata*, or Piano Sonata Op. 53), and possibly with a recommendation from Haydn, he was given introductions to contacts in Vienna, where he spent most of the rest of his life. Other distinguished patrons were, in the fashion and necessity of the time, to receive dedications from Beethoven in subsequent years, though his wayward and often boorish temperament led him to quarrel with many of them and with many musicians, relatives and friends.

A key figure within the Romantic movement, Beethoven broke with all previous traditions of patronage and servitude. Not for him the steady employment of Haydn, the humiliations of Mozart

An 1819 portrait of Beethoven by Ferdinand Schimon.

at the hands of archbishops, or the deference of composer and player to petty princelings: he believed that a great artist should be free to create without the constraints of regular employment. He accepted a small regular income from three noblemen without ever deigning to bow to their dictates; and when an audience failed to treat him with the adoration to which he felt entitled, as when they laughed after he had knocked over a couple of candles while performing one of his own concertos at a concert, he was capable of storming off the stage and refusing to reappear.

In his own time he was more highly regarded as a pianist than as a composer, especially as an improviser in aristocratic houses and the concert hall. It was not unreasonable that during such highly acclaimed recitals he should introduce piano and chamber works of his own. The passion of his playing, his compositions, and his rough speech entranced many wealthy listeners and patrons; but at the same time the mere whiff of such patronage was enough to enrage the composer. He met many attractive and well-to-do women, and seems to have fallen in love with quite a number; but his gaucheness made it impossible for him ever to pursue these desires, and he never married. To add to his frustrations and torments was the morbid possessiveness he showed towards his nephew Karl, son of his dead brother Karl – a possessiveness so suffocating that at one stage the young man tried to commit suicide.

Even before this emotional entanglement began to weigh down on his innately thwarted and rancorous mind, Beethoven had felt the approach of the greatest tragedy a musician can experience. At the height of his performing career he began in 1801 to go deaf. The horror of this, coming as it did on top of one of his disappointments in love – on this occasion with a seventeen-year-old pupil, Countess Giulietta Guiccardi – led him, too, to contemplate suicide. Although he turned away from the temptation, he had to endure the steady worsening of the affliction. Yet at the onset of this he was only just embarking on his Second Symphony. One might regard this fact as his salvation: it was only art, he himself wrote, that saved him from putting an end to his own life. But the agonies he underwent while wrestling with that art under such a handicap are heartbreakingly summed up in a manuscript which he wrote while brooding in seclusion at the little spa of Heiligenstadt. In what has come to be known as the *Heiligenstadt Testament* he inveighed against those men 'who think or say that I am malevolent, stubborn or misanthropic' and failed to understand the 'tender feeling of goodwill' he had always longed to express to others. How could he ask people to 'Speak louder, shout, for I am deaf'; how admit 'an infirmity in the *one sense* which ought to be more perfect in me than in others'?

The disease waxed and waned, and his temper behaved very much in accordance with these fluctuations. At one time he had been an ardent revolutionary and admirer of Napoleon. Later he became Teutonically patriotic, and in 1813 composed and conducted a Battle Symphony or, to give it its full title, *Wellington's Victory or the Battle of Vittoria*. The composition, originally conceived for his friend Maelzel's mechanical panharmonicon, was a blatant piece of programme music including a number of familiar tunes, national anthems, and cannon effects. In rehearsal the conducting was a near-disaster, thanks to Beethoven's deafness, but at the actual concert the public went wild with delight.

By 1819 it had become impossible for anyone to hold a conversation with Beethoven. Everything had to be painstakingly written down on paper and answered in the same way. Yet this was the time when he embarked on one of his most searching works, struggling for years with sections of what at last became the *Missa Solemnis*, or *Mass in D*.

One illness was added to another. In 1827 he was enfeebled by pneumonia, pleurisy and dropsy. But in spite of his physical deterioration, the difficulty of communicating with him, and his own prickliness, he had become a much-revered figure in Vienna. When he died on 26 March that year, his funeral at the Währing cemetery was an occasion of national mourning. In 1888 the body was moved to the Central cemetery in Vienna.

Beethoven's liberating influence on all musical forms from the classical period was far-reaching. Never a quick worker, he wrestled with sonata form and bent it to his will, escaping from the tidy predictability of four self-contained movements by melodic and harmonic links introducing motto themes which were to foster the concept of Wagner's *leitmotiv* and Berlioz's *idée fixe*. The symphony orchestra of Haydn and Mozart was too restricted to express the whole range of his ideas: he not only enlarged it but used its individual instruments to the limit of their own capabilities, instead of confining some of them, such as the viola, cello and bass, to a routine supporting rôle. His use of the piano, too, took that instrument to its limits, with the left hand no longer confined to bland accompanying figures but battling with the right hand on equal terms as the composer faced each new work as a new challenge – yet still, trying to hammer its sounds through his deafness, he was to describe it as an 'unsatisfactory instrument'.

SYMPHONIES: Symphony No. 1 in C is very much in classical style, but thereafter Beethoven was to seek a more intense spiritual expression of ideas through music, with more startling key changes and a continual striving from a fundamental idea towards a symphonic totality: 'It rises up higher and higher', he himself explained, 'and grows before my eyes until I hear and see the image of it, moulded and complete, stand there before my mental vision'. In his search for perfection he rewrote No. 2 three times. Alterations to No. 3 were due to emotional changes caused by political fluctuations during the course of composition. Originally called 'Bonaparte' in honour of the French general for whom Beethoven at the time had a great admiration, it eventually acquired the title *Sinfonia Eroica*; but Napoleon Bonaparte ceased to be a hero in Beethoven's eyes after he proclaimed himself Emperor, and the famous *Funeral March* incorporated in it may be regarded as symbolizing the funeral of a destroyed ideal. Not long after this he started work on his only opera, *Fidelio*, with its theme of conflict between tyranny and freedom. Its rarely mentioned alternative title is *Die eheliche Liebe* (*Married Love*).

Of the remaining symphonies, No.5 in C minor is probably the most frequently played. Its unforgettable opening theme represents, according to the composer's own words, Fate knocking at the door. The same notes pound out, by chance, the Morse code rhythm for the letter V, and were used in Allied broadcasts during World War II as a 'V-for-Victory' symbol. No.6, the *Pastoral*, evoking Beethoven's own happy feelings when in the countryside, provided material for one sequence in Walt Disney's cartoon *Fantasia* and is indeed one of the most vividly pictorial of all the composer's works, evoking birdsong, peasant merry-making, running brooks, a thunderstorm and shepherds' songs.

In his last, No.9 in D minor (usually referred to simply as the *Choral Symphony)*, Beethoven built a vast edifice starting in mystery, thundering out through an overwhelming scherzo, and culminating in a setting of lines from Schiller's *Ode to Joy*, together with some stanzas of his own, for soloists, choir and orchestra.

CONCERTOS: Beethoven wrote five piano concertos. The first three were markedly under Mozart's influence, and No.3 in C minor might almost be regarded as a personal tribute from the great living composer to the great dead one. No.4 is purely Beethoven, in his most lyrical and sublime mood, communicating a vision beyond all personal ills. The final one, in complete contrast, is so majestic and powerful that it was soon dubbed the *Emperor*.

The violin concerto in D, his only venture in this field, begins unforgettably with four muffled drum beats and leads on through a radiant allegro and a dreamlike second movement to one of Beethoven's most joyful, exuberant finales.

A sketch of Beethoven by J.P. Lyser, and the composer's signature.

CHAMBER MUSIC: Beethoven's string quartets are venerated by most musicians as a veritable range of mountain peaks. Some are bathed in sunshine; some dark and shadowy; some craggy, defiant and difficult to conquer. The Rasoumovsky Quartets, dedicated to the Russian ambassador in Vienna who played violin in his own quartet, were so unorthodox that at first hearing Beethoven

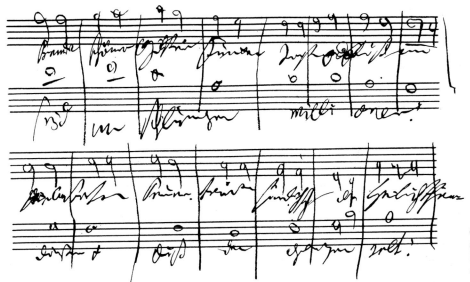

One of the composer's rough sketches for the finale of his Ninth Symphony, the *Choral Symphony*.

45

was asked, 'Do you consider these works to be music?' He replied: 'They are not for you, but for a later age'.

No. 13, Opus 130, is a favourite among many string players, and contains an exquisite *cavatina* which so moved the composer himself that he declared he could not hold back tears whenever he thought of it. Its original last movement, however, a *Grosse Fuge* (*Great Fugue*), was so long and technically gruelling that the publisher persuaded Beethoven to substitute a less demanding finale. This movement was, in fact, to be Beethoven's last completed composition.

PIANO SOLO: In addition to a great number of bagatelles and sets of variations, Beethoven wrote thirty-two piano sonatas, several of which have been given descriptive titles. Beethoven himself called No.8 in C minor a *Grande sonate pathétique*; the *Moonlight* acquired its name from a reviewer who found the first movement evocative of moonlight on Lake Lucerne; and the *Appassionata* was so called by Beethoven's publisher. The *Hammerklavier* implies nothing as violent as it may sound: it is simply the German for a pianoforte, which the composer once said he wished to appear on his MSS rather than the Italian word.

bel canto The Italian phrase meaning 'beautiful song' or 'singing' is used to describe a method of voice production and intonation giving a rounded, melodious effect rather than strident virtuosity.

bell From sets of handbells to a full-size carillon in a church belfry, the principles of bell-ringing are

The Liberty Bell, rung at the adoption by Congress of the Declaration of Independence, and now preserved in Independence Hall, Philadelphia. It gave its name to a famous march by John Philip Sousa.

Three days after Beethoven's death, surrounded by close friends, on 26 March 1827 some 20000 more admirers gathered in the streets of Vienna for the funeral, to pay tribute to their favourite adopted son.

basically the same. The cup-shaped metal body is struck by a clapper, either by moving the clapper and 'chiming' the bell, or by swinging the bell itself and so 'ringing' it. The tubular bells sometimes called for in an orchestral score are metal cylinders whose varying lengths produce different pitches, hung from a frame and struck by a hammer. (*See also* **change-ringing**.)

The word 'bell' is also used to describe the open end of a wind instrument.

Bellini, Vincenzo (1801–35) Italian composer. Born in Sicily, Bellini was at first dissuaded by his father from studying music, but his natural talent attracted the attention of a nobleman who paid for his studies in Naples. He composed eleven operas of uneven quality, the most popular being *La sonnambula* (*The Sleepwalker*) and *Norma*. In these he offered prima donnas a wealth of long, flowing legato melodies to test their vocal and dramatic virtuosity.

In 1835 *I puritani* (*The Puritans*) was a success in Paris but a flop in London, where critics found the tunes pretty enough but the orchestral writing inadequate. That same year, while working on a commission for the Paris Opéra, Bellini was stricken by an intestinal inflammation and an abscess on the liver, and died in a friend's house outside Paris.

Benda family A family of eighteenth-century Bohemian composers and instrumentalists whose activities spread throughout Europe. At one time there were four violinist brothers in the Berlin Court orchestra. František (1709–86) became *konzertmeister* to Frederick the Great and wrote several flute and violin concertos. His younger brother Jiři composed a number of symphonies and musical melodramas in the fashionable Italian style.

Bennett, Richard Rodney (1936–) English composer. He studied at the Royal Academy of Music and in Paris with Pierre Boulez. His wide range of interests includes experiments with atonality alongside more traditional forms, more than thirty film scores including *Murder on the Orient Express*, jazz recitals, and concerts and recordings with the jazz singer Marian Montgomery.

His opera *The Mines of Sulphur* was first produced at Sadler's Wells, London, in 1965, and the opera *Victory* at Covent Garden in 1970.

OTHER WORKS: Opera *A Penny for a Song*. Orchestral suites. Concertos for piano, violin, viola, oboe, guitar. Four string quartets and other chamber music.

Bennett, Robert Russell (1894–1981) American composer and arranger. He studied in his birthplace, Kansas City, with Carl Busch and later in Paris with Nadia Boulanger. He was awarded a Gug-genheim fellowship and two Victor prizes for symphonic works, but his real flair was for orchestration of stage musicals. Among more than three hundred such arrangements were the scores for *Rose Marie*, *Showboat*, *South Pacific*, *My Fair Lady* and *The Sound of Music*. He also prepared a symphonic suite from George Gershwin's opera *Porgy and Bess*.

Among his own compositions were an *Abraham Lincoln Symphony*, a Concerto Grosso for small dance band and symphony orchestra, and an opera, *Maria Malibran*, around the true story of the tragic death of the early nineteenth-century soprano. After World War II he was for some time musical director of the National Broadcasting Company (NBC).

OTHER WORKS: Six Variations on a Theme by Jerome Kern. Eight Etudes for Symphonic Orchestra. Concerto for Violin. *Overture to an Imaginary Drama*. Four Nocturnes.

Bennett, (Sir) William Sterndale (1816–75) English composer. Born in Sheffield, at seven years of age he became a chorister at King's College Chapel, Cambridge, and after studying in London and Germany, where he met Mendelssohn and Schumann, he was elected a member of the Royal Society of Musicians in London. In 1849 he founded the Bach Society. He composed a number of competent symphonies and concertos, but is best remembered as a conductor and teacher: he became professor of music at Cambridge, conductor of the Philharmonic Society, and in 1866 principal of the Royal Academy of Music.

OTHER WORKS: Cantata *The May Queen*. Overtures *The Naiads* and *The Wood Nymphs*. Piano trio and piano sextet. *Three Musical Sketches* for piano, the second of which was inspired by the millstream at Grantchester, near Cambridge.

Berberian, Cathy (1925–83) American soprano. She studied at Columbia University and in Milan, and between 1950 and 1966 was married to the Italian composer Luciano Berio, who wrote a number of works for her and whom she greatly influenced: his *Omaggio a Joyce* (*Homage to Joyce*) sprang from her recording of a reading from James Joyce's *Ulysses*. She performed many avant-garde pieces by other composers, including Sylvano Bussotti and John Cage.

berceuse A vocal or instrumental cradle song, from the French *bercer*, to rock or dandle a baby.

Berg, Alban (1885–1935) Austrian composer. Son of a German father and Viennese mother, Berg suffered all his life from bronchial asthma and fits of depression, but always maintained the air of a suave man-about-town. After a brief spell in the civil service he studied composition under Schoenberg and became an advocate first of atonality and then of the 12-tone discipline without ever allowing such restrictions to cripple his emotional, romantic nature. In 1911 he married Helen Nahowski, the beautiful blonde daughter of a civil servant – though it was rumoured in Vienna that she was really an illegitimate child of the Emperor Franz Josef. On the surface she and her husband seemed a well-matched and affectionate couple.

Another of Helen's suitors had been the poet Peter Altenberg, some of whose brief, bitter verses Berg used in his *Altenberglieder* for soprano and orchestra. When two of these were first performed in March 1913, with Schoenberg conducting, the musical language proved so new and frightening that the audience grew violent and the concert had to be abandoned.

Berg's first opera, *Wozzeck*, begun in 1914, was not performed until December 1925 in Berlin. Based on a grim play by Büchner about a victimized soldier and his doomed mistress, its apparently unpromising material was developed by the composer into a sequence of short scenes, each in a strict musical form of its own, whose cumulative effect is spellbinding in the opera house. In the same year he began work on his *Lyric Suite*. Only much later did it become clear that this erotically charged work owed its inspiration to Hanna Fuchs-Robettin, Alma Mahler's sister-in-law and Berg's mistress for the last ten years of his life. After his death his widow learned of the relationship, and this may have been behind her devious refusals to let anyone work on the supposedly unfinished last act of his second opera, *Lulu*.

He had started on *Lulu*, the savage story of a courtesan sinking to the lowest depths of prostitution until she is murdered by Jack the Ripper, in 1928. It was not until 1934 that he was able to set about full instrumentation of the short score, and even then the task was interrupted by a commission from the American violinist Louis Krasner for a violin concerto. While Berg was working on this a beloved friend, Manon Gropius, daughter of Alma Mahler by her second husband, died of polio at the age of eighteen. Now he poured his heart into the concerto, dedicating it 'to the memory of an angel' and building the conclusion around the choral *Es ist genug* (*It is enough*), well known from Bach's Cantata No.60.

Berg himself died a few months later of blood poisoning from a foot abscess. *Lulu* was staged in due course with a truncated, fragmentary third act. Even when Berg's almost complete short score was unearthed after being hidden away for years, the widowed Helen refused to sanction its release. Only after her own death

Alban Berg, one of the most influential composers of the 'Second Viennese School' together with Schoenberg and Webern.

was it finally 'realized' by Friedrich Cerha for its first full performance in 1979.

OTHER WORKS: Chamber Concerto for piano, violin and fourteen wind instruments. Piano sonata. Four clarinet and piano pieces. Seven Early Songs. Song cycle *Der Wein*.

bergamasque In Italian *bergamasca*, describing a sixteenth-century dance from the province of Bergamo. It is also used to describe a form of ground bass employed by composers of the time. Fauré's suite *Masques et bergamasques* was inspired by Verlaine poems, one of which uses the phrase; and Debussy wrote a *Suite bergamasque* for piano.

Berganza, Teresa (1935–) Spanish mezzo-soprano. She made her début in Madrid in 1955; at La Scala, Milan, in 1957; and at Covent Garden,

London, in 1960. Her particular talent is for overcoming the stringent technical and stylistic requirements of operatic composers such as Rossini and Donizetti without the effort being too obvious – a florid yet mellifluous coloratura described by the conductor John Pritchard as 'typically Spanish soft-grained vocal quality'. She made an immediate impression as Cherubino in *Le nozze di Figaro* (*The Marriage of Figaro*) at Glyndebourne, followed by the title rôle in Rossini's *La Cenerentola* (*Cinderella*), but is also capable of a passionate interpretation of *Carmen*.

bergerette A rustic song or dance (from the French *berger*, a shepherd). Mannered versions of it were popular in eighteenth-century France during the craze for dressing up prettily as shepherds and shepherdesses and pretending to live a simple pastoral life.

Bergonzi, Carlo (1924–) Italian tenor. His studies were interrupted by World War II, and for a time he was imprisoned for his anti-Nazi activities. In 1948 he made his début as a baritone, but after two years decided to train as a tenor, making a fresh début in *Andrea Chénier*. He appeared regularly at La Scala, Milan, and later at Covent Garden in London. His first US appearance was in Chicago in 1955 in *Il tabarro*, and he was to sing at the New York Met for over twenty years.

Berio, Luciano (1925–) Italian composer. Having been taught the piano and organ as a boy, he studied at the Milan Academy with Giorgio Ghedini. After marrying the singer Cathy Berberian he visited the USA and there met and studied serialism with Dallapiccola. At the same time he became interested in electronic music, and helped to found the electronic music studio in Milan.

Combining live voices and instruments, dramatic action and tape-recordings to express his poetic and philosophical ideas, he has also favoured the methods – or lack of preordained method – of aleatory music. In his *Sequenze*, a series of pieces for various solo instruments, commands are given to the piano and oboe, for example, to sound sometimes 'like themselves', and sometimes not. In *Circles* the singer can choose whether to sing the actual notes or something in the near neighbourhood. Berio also enjoys arranging, disarranging, and combining other composers' music: his *Sinfonia* of 1968 throws into the melting-pot quotations from Wagner, Mahler and Ravel along with shouted phrases from eight singers in jarring polyphony.

OTHER WORKS: *Allez Hop*, mimed tale for voice, mimes, dancers and orchestra. *Recital 1* (*for Cathy*), for soprano and seventeen instruments; and electronic music *Visage*, also for his wife Cathy

Berberian. *Variations* for piano; and *Rounds* for harpsichord.

Berkeley, (Sir) Lennox (1903–) English composer. He studied at Oxford and then for six years with Nadia Boulanger in Paris, where he met Ravel and was greatly influenced by his views on clarity and balance. This outlook and his own innate elegance of style led him in later years to favour a Stravinskian neo-classicism.

A meeting with Benjamin Britten at the 1936 ISCM Festival in Barcelona led to their collaborating on the *Mont Juic Suite* based on Catalan folk songs. Each wrote two movements, but it has never been revealed who was responsible for which. In 1940 Berkeley's Symphony No.1 (he wrote four in all) achieved a great success at a wartime Promenade concert. In the latter half of the war he worked on the BBC music staff, and in 1946 became professor of composition at the Royal Academy of Music.

In 1954 two of his operas were produced – the witty chamber opera *A Dinner Engagement* at the Aldeburgh Festival and the larger-scale *Nelson* at Sadler's Wells.

OTHER WORKS: Two piano concertos. Flute concerto. Guitar concerto. Three string quartets. Serenade for Strings. Choral *Hymn for Shakespeare's Birthday*. Piano preludes and concert studies.

Berkshire Festival In 1934 a Berkshire Symphonic Festival was held in Berkshire county, Massachusetts, and expanded in 1936 when the Tanglewood estate was offered as a permanent venue by the descendants of William Aspinwall Tappan. It was administered by the Boston Symphony Orchestra trustees, and Koussevitsky became its first director, followed by Munch, Leinsdorf, and Schuller. The 1937 concerts took place in a tent, but by the following year a more substantial 'Music Shed' had been built.

For a quarter of a century from 1940 onwards Aaron Copland taught composition at Berkshire Music Center, becoming dean of the faculty in 1946. Distinguished visiting lecturers included Olivier Messiaen.

In 1945 the annual event took the name of the Berkshire Festival, and from 1964 incorporated a major element of contemporary music. Because of its setting it is frequently referred to as the Tanglewood Festival.

Berlin, Irving (1888–) American composer. Born in Russia, he was taken as a child by his immigrant parents to east-side New York and started his career as a singing waiter under the name of Izzy Baline. With no formal tuition, he displayed an instinctive flair for composing popular songs, from the 1911 *Alexander's Ragtime Band* to *Easter Parade* and *White Christmas*. He contributed words

and music to many successful musical comedies and films, including *Annie Get Your Gun*.

Berlioz, Hector (1803–69) French composer. Defying his father's wishes that he should follow a medical career, Berlioz entered the Paris Conservatoire but was more interested in his own musical theories than in those he was taught. He fell foul of the director, Cherubini, whose pedantic style he was later to pillory in a mocking vocal fugue in *The Damnation of Faust*. Cherubini tried to stop Berlioz's first concert and intrigued against his application for the valuable *Prix de Rome*, which he won only on his fourth attempt.

Exalted by Beethoven concerts and productions of Shakespeare's plays, the romantic young man fell in love with the Irish actress Harriet Smithson, and dramatized his feelings for her in his *Symphonie fantastique*. The symphony, subtitled 'Episode in the Life of an Artist', is suffused with an *idée fixe*, a repetitive theme evoking the image of the Beloved One. At its second performance, in December 1832, Harriet met the composer and in the following year they married after he had threatened to poison himself should she refuse him. It was a stormy liaison, ending in a separation in 1840. After her death in poverty in 1854 Berlioz married his mistress, a singer of French and Spanish parentage who died of a heart attack eight years after the wedding.

For many years he had to eke out his living with music criticism, as pungent as his music which the public found so disturbing. He was commissioned by Paganini to write a viola concerto, but although later generations were to love the result, *Harold in Italy*, the great soloist felt it did not offer him enough display material. Fired with the ambition of writing a successful opera, Berlioz was distracted by another commission, this time for a Requiem Mass to be performed at government expense on the day of the annual commemoration of those who had died in the 1830 revolution. His old enemy Cherubini attempted to sabotage the whole thing, but the *Grande Messe des morts* was duly performed under different auspices as a tribute to General Damrémont, who had died in Algeria. Using huge choral and orchestral forces, including a whole battery of tuned timpani and four brass bands in strategic positions, its première in Les Invalides in Paris caused the priest to weep at the altar and later to embrace Berlioz in the sacristy; and the composer was gratified by the terror induced by the *Tuba mirum*, of such grandeur that, he wrote, 'One of the lady singers had a nervous attack.'

A cartoon of 1846 mocking Hector Berlioz's grandiloquent music and his love of thunderous special effects.

The opera to which he returned, *Benvenuto Cellini*, was a failure at the time but has since been successfully revived, and themes from it formed the much-played concert overture, *Le Carnaval romain*. In spite of his eagerness to profit from the fashionable operatic craze, Berlioz's drama remained largely in the head and was best transmuted in work for the concert hall. The phrase *opéra de concert* has been used pejoratively in connection with *La Damnation de Faust* and *Roméo et Juliette*, yet it is doubtful whether any other composer has ever conjured up such sonorously convincing musical reinterpretations of literary masterpieces.

The huge orchestral forces and 'Babylonian immensity' of some works antagonized his contemporaries and immediate successors, but since World War II his operas and religious music have been critically revalued to show that even this arch-romantic built upon an underlying classical discipline. Thanks largely to the dedication of the conductor Colin Davis, the huge opera *Les Troyens* (*The Trojans*) has been revived, as well as the scintillating comic opera *Béatrice et Bénédict* (from his adored Shakespeare's *Much Ado About Nothing*). And, contradicting every generalization made about the sprawling vastness of his conceptions, there is the delicate little oratorio *L'Enfance du Christ* (*The Childhood of Christ*), which grew gradually in his mind from a few scattered ideas into its present impeccable form.

Of his critical and autobiographical writing, the malicious essays of *Evenings in the Orchestra* and the soul-searchings and rages of the *Memoirs* are as colourful as his music.

OTHER WORKS: Overtures *Les Francs juges* and *Le Corsaire*. *Te Deum*. Song cycle *Les Nuits d'été*.

Berners, Lord (1883–1950) English composer. A diplomat and musical dilettante who studied for a while with Stravinsky, he wrote many parody pieces and composed some idiosyncratic ballet music, including *The Wedding Bouquet*, with a vocal commentary to words by Gertrude Stein, and *The Triumph of Neptune* for Diaghilev, with choreography by Balanchine and some of the scoring handled by the young William Walton. Travellers near Faringdon in Oxfordshire can glimpse the lofty tower of Faringdon Folly, for whose construction Berners paid in order to alleviate local workers' hardship during the Depression of the 1930s.

Bernstein, Leonard (1918–) American composer and conductor. After studying conducting under Fritz Reiner at the Curtis Institute, Philadelphia, and then working as assistant to Koussevitsky at the Berkshire Music Center, he was offered the post of assistant conductor to the New York

Philharmonic Symphony Orchestra and sprang to overnight fame when called on at short notice to deputize for Bruno Walter, who had fallen ill. As well as taking on other major conducting posts and appearing as guest conductor with orchestras all over the world, he became musical adviser to the Israel Philharmonic Symphony Orchestra and returned to Tanglewood as a faculty member of the Berkshire Music Center, later head of its conducting department.

In 1944 his ballet *Fancy Free*, with choreography by Jerome Robbins, told the story of three sailors on leave who become involved with girls in a Manhattan bar – and told it so successfully that it was transformed into a musical film, *On the*

The American composer and conductor Leonard Bernstein at a recording session.

Town. Bernstein and Robbins were to collaborate again, even more rewardingly, on a New York gangland transformation of *Romeo and Juliet* into *West Side Story*, to a libretto by Arthur Laurents.

His three symphonies are far from orthodox in approach. No.1 uses a soprano soloist in the final movement, with words from the *Book of Jeremiah*. No.2, subtitled *The Age of Anxiety*, is in essence a piano concerto. No.3, the *Kaddish*, incorporates a setting of the Jewish mourners' prayer for woman narrator, soprano, chorus, and boys' chorus, with orchestra. Other individualistic works include a highly theatrical *Mass* for singers, players and dancers, and the *Chichester Psalms* for counter-tenor, chorus and orchestra, written to a Hebrew text for the 1965 Chichester Festival, England.

Berwald, Franz (1796–1868) Swedish composer. Starting as a violinist in the Stockholm Opera House Orchestra, he won a scholarship to Berlin in 1928 and, after initial wounding criticism of his earliest compositions, spent some years running an orthopaedic institute there. After further disappointments with string quartets and two symphonies, he became manager of a glassworks and then a sawmill in Sweden, but continued to compose and became professor of music in the Stockholm Royal Academy of Music the year before his death. It was only later that such works as his *Symphonie singulière* became internationally recognized.

Billings, William (1746–1800) American composer. Originally a tanner by trade, he taught himself to read and write music, especially hymns and anthems, and published little contrapuntal essays which he called 'fuguing tunes'. Among his patriotic pieces was *Chester*, which was adopted as the hymn of Washington's army. The twentieth-century American composer William Schuman honoured his memory with a *William Billings Overture* and used three of his tunes as the basis for the orchestral *New England Triptych*.

binary form A song or instrumental piece in two sections, such as the dances in Bach and Handel suites and the one-movement sonatas of Scarlatti. The composer opens the first section in one key but progresses towards the key of the dominant, and then in the second part works his way back through development of the original material to reach the tonic key again. If the piece begins in a minor key, the halfway stage is often marked by a shift into the relative major.

Birtwistle, Harrison (1934–) English composer. One of an influential group of students at the Royal Manchester College of Music, he spent four years as a school music director before travelling to the USA as visiting fellow at Princeton. On his return to England he collaborated with Peter Maxwell Davies in the formation of the Pierrot Players for the performance of new chamber music. As a teacher he encouraged children to become collaborators in writing and improvising music rather than slavishly playing just what somebody else had written.

His own compositions have covered a wide experimental range, often building on apparently minuscule fragments to a complex synthesis of great blocks of repetitive, driving sound; or, in quite different vein, moving with grave, intro-spective slowness. In *Verses for Ensembles* the players are required to take varying positions about the platform, and at times to play from three staves at once: each instrumentalist chooses any one of the three lines offered at the outset and must then adhere to it until there is an indication on the score that he may switch to one of the other lines.

OTHER WORKS: Operas *Punch and Judy*, *The Mask of Orpheus*, and *Yan Tan Tethera*. Orchestral suite, *Chorales*. Brass band and chamber music. *Chronometer* for tape. Dramatic pastoral, *Down by the Greenwood Side*.

Bishop, (Sir) Henry (1786–1855) English composer and conductor. He both conducted and composed at Covent Garden, became founder member and director of the London Philharmonic Society, and was the first musician to be granted a knighthood. He wrote over a hundred stage pieces, producing many of them himself; edited collections of national songs; but is best remembered for two of his own songs, *Home, Sweet Home* and *Lo, Hear the Gentle Lark*.

Bishop-Kovacevich, Stephen (1940–) American pianist. Born in Los Angeles of Yugoslav parentage, he made his début in San Francisco in 1951 but then moved to London to study with Myra Hess. He has made an international reputation as a concert and recital pianist, and has recorded compelling versions of Beethoven and Bártok concertos. Richard Rodney Bennett's piano concerto of 1968, which he was the first to perform, is dedicated to him.

bitonality The uses of two keys at the same time, even if they are not indicated in the key signature. An effective example is the clarinet duet in Stravinsky's ballet *Petrushka*, and there are examples in the works of other modern composers such as Holst and Milhaud.

Bizet, Georges (1838-75) French composer. He was admitted to the Paris Conservatoire at the age of ten, studied under Jacques Halévy, composer of the opera *La Juive* (*The Jewess*), and some years later married his daughter. After several unsuccessful attempts at composing operas of his own, Bizet achieved little immediate acclaim for his incidental music to Daudet's play *L'Arlésienne* until it was performed in the concert hall rather than in the orchestra pit.

He had an even less favourable reception for his opera *Carmen* and, dying of a throat infection only three months after its première, did not live to see it take its place as one of the most popular operas in the repertory. Another piece, rediscovered in 1933, has found favour in the concert hall: the Symphony in C, composed when Bizet was eighteen.

A poster for a performance of Bizet's opera *Carmen* in 1901 in the arena at Bayonne, incorporating an actual bullfight.

OTHER WORKS: Operas *Les Pêcheurs de perles* (*The Pearl Fishers*) and *La Jolie fille de Perth* (*The Fair Maid of Perth*). Suite of piano duets, *Jeux d'enfants* (*Children's Games*).

Björling, Jussi (1911–60) Swedish tenor. After being taught singing by his father, he studied at the Royal Opera School in Stockholm and made his début in 1930 as Don Ottavio in Mozart's *Don Giovanni*, a part ideally suited to his lyrical yet robust voice. From 1938 until his death he appeared regularly at the New York Met.

Blacher, Boris (1903–75) German composer. Born in China, Blacher studied music there and in Russia before settling in Berlin in 1922. He experimented with jazz, 12-note music, and electronic methods, but also developed an individual treatment of variable metres, in which metrical changes from one bar to another are calculated according to a prearranged mathematical pattern. This is clearly demonstrated in his *Ornamente* for piano.

OTHER WORKS: Operas *Romeo und Julia* and *Abstract Opera No.1*. Ballet *Lysistrata*. Five string quartets. Violin, viola and cello concertos. *Two Poems* for jazz quartet.

Bliss, (Sir) Arthur (1891–1975) English composer. Son of an American father and an English mother, Bliss was born in London and studied music under Stanford and Vaughan Williams. After service with the Guards in World War I he came under the influence on Stravinsky, but later acquired a much more sober, Elgarian tone of voice. Echoes of wartime tragedy resound in his choral symphony *Morning Heroes*, dedicated to the memory of his brother 'and all other comrades killed in battle'.

Bliss made two protracted visits to the USA and dedicated his *Introduction and Allegro* to Leopold Stokowski. During World War II he became director of music at the BBC, and in 1944 his ballet *Miracle in the Gorbals* was a great success on a Sadler's Wells wartime tour. He wrote the film score, very ambitious for its time, of *Things to Come*, and arranged the music for the film version of *The Beggar's Opera*.

OTHER WORKS: *A Colour Symphony*. Opera *The Olympians*. Clarinet quintet. Viola sonato. Cello concerto.

Blitzstein, Marc (1905–64) American composer. He studied in Paris and Berlin with Nadia Boulanger and Schoenberg, and when he returned to the USA his sympathies – although he belonged to a wealthy Philadelphia family – were all with the victims of the Depression. He wrote his own libretto for his one-act 'play with music', *The Cradle will Rock*, dealing with the clash between magnate and men in the steelworks, and after World War II translated and adapted *The Threepenny Opera* from the German.

Bloch, Ernest (1880–1959) Swiss-American composer. Born and brought up in a devout Jewish household in Switzerland, Bloch was imbued with the melodies, rhythms and textures of Hebrew religious chant. He composed a number of major works in a 'Jewish cycle', including an *Israel Symphony* and the rhapsodic concert piece *Schelomo* (*Solomon*) for cello and orchestra. In 1916 he arrived in the USA to conduct for the dancer Maud Allan, and in 1924 took American citizenship, celebrating this with an 'epic rhapsody', *America*. He founded the Cleveland Institute of Music, and between 1915 and 1930 was director of the San Francisco Conservatory.

After the intensely emotional Jewish works he turned for a time to neo-classicism, but came back to his original sources of inspiration in such pieces as *Avodath Hakodesh* (*Sacred Service*), written for the New York Reform Synagogue, and the *Rhapsodie Hébraique*.

OTHER WORKS: Violin concerto. Five string quartets. Three suites for solo cello. *Concerto symhonique* for piano and orchestra. Opera *Macbeth*. *Last Poems* for flute and orchestra.

block harmony A progression of chords in which all the notes move in parallel, without change of interval and with no contrapuntal divergence.

Blow, John (1649–1708) English composer and organist. One of the first choirboys in the Chapel Royal after the Restoration of King Charles II, he later became organist of Westminster Abbey and numbered Purcell among his pupils. He wrote over a hundred anthems, including coronation anthems for James II and William and Mary, a set of 'Lessons' for the harpsichord, sacred and secular songs, and a masque-cum-opera, *Venus and Adonis*.

blue note Jazz players and composers make frequent use of slurred notes around the third and seventh degrees of the diatonic scale. When written down this produces in, for example, the key of C major an E flat usually dropping to the D, and a B flat dropping to the A. Wind or string instrumentalists usually produce a more indeterminate sound than a clear semitone. The device appears in many places in the works of George Gershwin (most notably in the descending phrases of *Rhapsody in Blue*), and several modern composers attempting the jazz idiom have employed it, usually with clumsy results.

blues The word is used loosely to describe any slow lamentatory song of Black American origin and appears in hundreds of song titles equating sadness with 'feeling blue' or 'having a fit of the blues'. In its strictest sense it refers to a 12-bar musical form around which the most gifted singers and instrumentalists have woven some of their most imaginative improvisations. Since the original blues songs were largely the product of downcast people making up the words of their tale as they went along, the first phrase was repeated while the singer tried to find a rhyme and matching rhythm for the final line. This resulted in the 12-bar pattern: two sections of four bars each, with a repeated vocal line and closely related melody in the second, rounded off by a 4-bar phrase resolving both the lyric and the music. The basic supporting chords (transformed by inventive passing harmonies in the hands of an outstanding pianist or guitarist) would read, in the key of C:

3 bars C major common chord; 1 bar C dominant 7th (C7)

2 bars F major common chord; 2 bars C major common chord

2 bars G dominant 7th (G7); 2 bars C major common chord

Blüthner, Julius Ferdinand (1824–1910) German piano manufacturer, born in Falkenhain, who founded a piano manufacturing firm in Leipzig in 1853.

bocca chiusa Italian phrase (in French, *bouche fermée*) meaning 'closed mouth' and referring to wordless humming, as called for in certain choral works.

Boccherini, Luigi (1734–1805) Italian composer. After making his name as a cellist in his native land, he went first to Spain, and then to Prussia as chamber composer to Frederick the Great. He was a prolific composer of tuneful, lightweight symphonies and chamber music of great charm and accomplishment – over two hundred string quartets and quintets, sacred and secular vocal music, and guitar arrangements of his own works. His most frequently played piece is the minuet from his string quintet in E major.

An anonymous engraving of Luigi Boccherini.

Boehm, Theobald (1793–1881) German composer and flautist. His name is preserved in the 'Boehm system' for flute, clarinet, oboe and bassoon, in which the awkward placing of finger-holes was revised and provided with levers, keys and rings to facilitate playing.

Boïeldieu, François (1775–1834) French composer. His first opera, *La Fille coupable* (*The Guilty Girl*), was produced when he was eighteen. In 1802 he married a dancer, but the marriage lasted only a year and he left for Russia, where he composed and conducted at the Imperial Opera in St Petersburg for ten years. After returning to Paris he wrote his most successful work, *La Dame blanche* (*The White Lady*), an 'amiable conversation opera' taking his melodies from a number of Scots folk songs.

Boito, Arrigo (1842–1918) Italian composer. After studying music at Milan, Boito found himself equally interested in literature, and although he composed the operas *Mefistofele*, produced at La Scala, and *Nerone* he is better remembered as librettist for his friend Verdi's *Otello* and *Falstaff* and for Ponchielli's *La Gioconda*.

Although a composer in his own right, Arrigo Boito *(left)* is better remembered for the librettos he provided for the friend with whom he is seen here, Giuseppe Verdi.

bolero A Spanish dance with a pronounced 3/4 rhythm usually with fast triplets on the second half of the first beat and sometimes on the second beat also, emphasized in its basic form by castanets. Ravel's *Bolero* of 1928 consists of one melody played over and over again, shared between different sections of the orchestra above an insistent pounding rhythm and growing in volume. It was composed for a ballet featuring Ida Rubinstein, who played the part of a gipsy dancing on a table and driving the drinkers in the tavern into a frenzy.

bombardon A brass instrument in the bass tuba or saxhorn register, taking the deeper bass parts in brass and military bands.

Bond, Carrie Jacobs (1862–1946) American writer of popular songs. One of them, *When you come to the end of a perfect day*, sold five million copies of the sheet music long before the era of pop stars and 'top of the charts' records.

bongos Small drums of Cuban origin, usually fastened together in pairs and played with thumb and fingers. They are frequently used in dance bands, especially for Caribbean and Latin-American numbers. The American composer John Cage has used them in some of his experiments with percussion groups.

Bononcini, Giovanni (1670–1747) Italian composer. The name is sometimes spelt Buononcini, which the composer himself is said to have favoured. Although born in Modena, he spent over ten years in Vienna as Court composer and from 1720 onwards worked in London, sometimes with Handel and sometimes as his rival. The public disagreements over their relative merits produced the rhyme:

> Some say that Signor Bononcini,
> Compar'd to Handel's a mere ninny;
> Others aver, to him, that Handel
> Is scarcely fit to hold a candle.
> Strange! That such high dispute should be
> 'Twixt Tweedledum and Tweedledee.

Bononcini composed twenty-two operas as well as chamber cantatas and much religious music, including the funeral anthem for the Duke of Marlborough in Westminster Abbey in 1722. After being accused of plagiarism he left England in a rage for France and Italy, and died in Vienna.

boogie-woogie A style of jazz piano playing around the chord sequence of the blues, involving a repeated figure in the left hand, often of broken octaves up and down the chord. It is said to have originated in Harlem and other 'honky tonk' settings where the instrument might have several notes missing and the pianist had to cover the gaps with fast fingering. 'Pinetop' Smith was one of the first executants to make the form popular with the public. Other figures, often with a dotted rumbling, rocking quaver and semiquaver rhythm, were employed by performers such as Jimmy Yancey and Meade Lux Lewis.

A painting by J. Rjepin in 1883 of Alexander Borodin, influenced by Balakirev into becoming one of the 'Mighty Handful' of Russian nationalistic composers.

Borodin, Alexander (1833–87) Russian composer. The illegitimate son of a Russian prince, he studied chemistry and founded a women's medical school, but turned to music and became one of 'The Five', though not so fiercely dedicated to nationalist ideals as his associates. He wrote two symphonies and two string quartets, but found his true voice in the romantic orchestral evocation of a passing caravan, *In the Steppes of Central Asia*, and the opera *Prince Igor*, unfinished at his death and completed by Glazunov and Rimsky-Korsakov. Themes from his work were used in the successful twentieth-century stage musical and film, *Kismet*.

Boskovsky, Willy (1909–) Austrian conductor and violinist. For many years leader of the Vienna Philharmonic Orchestra, he became known all over the world for his recorded and televised appearances conducting the New Year's Day concerts of music by the Strauss family.

Boughton, Rutland (1878–1960) English composer. Under the spell of Wagner and his mother's Celtic ancestry, Boughton attempted an Arthurian cycle on the lines of *The Ring*, and at the same time envisaged an annual socialistic-musical festival at Glastonbury, supposed resting-place of King Arthur and Queen Guinevere. His muddled marital and extra-marital emotional life made a disciplined artistic approach difficult. At the first festival in 1914 and some years later in London he achieved some success with his tuneful music-drama *The Immortal Hour*; but although he eventually completed his more ambitious cycle towards the end of World War II with a vision of the red star rising in the east, none of its ingredients appealed either to critics or to the public.

OTHER WORKS: Three symphonies. Four concertos. Two string quartets. Opera *Alkestis*, based on Euripides' play. Choral ballet *The Moon Maiden*. Male choral scene *Agincourt*, from Shakespeare's *Henry V*.

Boulanger, Nadia (1887–1979) French composer and teacher. Her father Ernest had won a *Prix de Rome* first-class, and expected his two daughters to follow in his footsteps. After studying with Fauré, Nadia won only a second-class award in 1908, while in 1913 her younger sister Lili became the first woman to win it first-class. Nadia decided to devote herself to furthering her sister's genius, but the partnership ended with Lili's early death in 1918.

The inspiring teacher Nadia Boulanger on the conductor's podium.

Thereafter Nadia became one of the most influential teachers of her time, most notably from 1921 at the American Conservatory in Fontainebleau, of which she was appointed director in 1948. Starting with groups of pupils and friends, she played a major part in the revival and recording of Monteverdi's long-neglected madrigals, even though some of her own piano accompaniments sounded intrusive and out of character.

Among her students at one time and another were Aaron Copland, Roy Harris and Walter Piston. According to another of them, Virgil Thomson, she felt that American music was about to 'take off' in the way that Russian music had done in the previous century. She also accepted as a pupil the jazz trumpeter Quincy Jones, whose belief that in music the head must work with the heart was in tune with her own convictions: she sternly demanded that anyone working with her must have a 'properly trained ear' in *solfeggio* (the English tonic sol-fa), without which they would never be able to combine what they heard in their heads with what they needed to write down.

In 1937 Nadia Boulanger was the first woman to conduct a Royal Philharmonic Society concert in England, and she went on to conduct the Boston, New York Philharmonic, and Hallé orchestras. Having worked closely with Stravinsky on composition classes at the Ecole Normale in 1935, she conducted the first performance of his *Dumbarton Oaks Concerto* in Washington in 1938.

Boulez, Pierre (1925–) French composer and conductor. Interested from the start in Schoenberg's 12-note theories, which he tried to integrate with the beliefs of his first teacher, Messiaen, Boulez was soon convinced that similar principles should be applied also to metre and dynamics, so producing 'total serialism'. His *Structures* for two pianos and two *Etudes* in *musique concrète* began a period during which he exerted an evangelical influence over his avant-garde contemporaries. One of his most influential works has been *Le Marteau sans maître* (*The Hammer without a Master*), in which contralto settings of poems by René Char are commented on and wildly argued over by an orchestral grouping of flute, viola, guitar and percussion, with eastern and African timbres added by the use of vibraphone and xylorimba (an instrument combining xylophone and marimba).

The indeterminancy which Boulez also favours is shown in his third piano sonata, where the performer may play the movements in any preferred order, and in *Pli selon pli* (*Fold upon fold*), which not merely allows for individual decisions on the part of the conductor but has from time to time been basically revised by the composer on the grounds that no composition can ever be really completed.

As a conductor, Boulez has espoused the works of Schoenberg and Webern and has appeared as guest conductor all over Europe and America. He was responsible for a controversial centenary interpretation of Wagner's *Ring* cycle at Bayreuth, and for the first definitive performance of Berg's complete *Lulu*. From its opening in 1977 he has been director of the *Institut de Recherche et de Co-ordination Acoustique/Musique (IRCAM)* at the Pompidou Centre, Paris, for research into com-

Pierre Boulez conducting the BBC Symphony Orchestra, of which he was chief conductor between 1971 and 1975.

puter and other electronic compositional devices.
OTHER WORKS: *Poésie pour pouvoir* for orchestra and
tape. *Répons* for voices, small orchestra and electronics. Sonatina for flute and piano. Tape *Etudes*
for one and seven sounds.

Boult, (Sir) Adrian (1889–1983) English conductor.
One of the most devoted interpreters, at home
and abroad, of English music, especially that of
his friends Elgar, Vaughan Williams and Holst.
He was musical director of the BBC for twelve
years, and conductor of the BBC Symphony
Orchestra for twenty.

bourdon From the French for a drone, the word
applies to the drone of a bagpipe or a hurdy-
gurdy, a deep-toned bell, the lower-voiced
support to a melody (as in 'burden'), and a 16-ft
pitch organ stop.

bourrée A brisk dance movement often found in
baroque and classical suites, deriving from a
vigorous old French and Spanish peasant dance
in 2/4 or 4/4 time, beginning on an upbeat.

bow and **bowing** Sound is produced from instruments of the viol family by drawing across the
strings a narrow swathe of horsehair stretched
between the ends of a slightly convex wooden
staff, the tension being adjusted by a nut at one
end. Individual players develop different techniques of bowing to produce virtuoso effects,
and some composers specify the particular effects
they require, such as bouncing the hair across
the strings, or even bouncing the wooden back
of the bow off them. Violinists and other string
players, and sometimes conductors, insert bowing
marks on to the score to indicate an upward or
downward stroke.

Boyce, William (1711–79) English composer and
organist. Son of a London cabinet-maker, he
became a chorister in St Paul's Cathedral and
later a church organist. In 1736 he was appointed
composer to the Chapel Royal, and also served
as one of the earliest directors of the Three
Choirs Festival. A prolific composer of masques,
anthems, overtures, symphonies and trio sonatas,
he was encouraged by Garrick to write entertainments for Drury Lane Theatre, one of which, *The
Chaplet*, was such a success that it was also given
in Philadelphia in 1767.

One of Boyce's greatest achievements was his
editing of a comprehensive collection of English
Cathedral Music, which he took over from
Maurice Greene, the St Paul's organist to whom
he had once been apprenticed; but by most people
he is best remembered for his patriotic song,
Heart of Oak, composed for a David Garrick
pantomime in 1759.

Boyce is buried beneath the dome of St Paul's
Cathedral.

A portrait of Johannes Brahms as a youth.

Brahms, Johannes (1833-97) German composer.
The second of three children, the boy was born
in Hamburg. His father, a horn and double bass
player working in any orchestral job available,
including some in dockside taverns and dance
halls, soon realized the boy's innate gifts, gave
him violin lessons, and found the money to send

Brahms's oval piano.

him to good local schools. Later after piano lessons from Friedrich Wilhelm Cossel and piano and theory lessons from the greatly respected Eduard Marxsen, the fifteen-year-old Brahms made a number of local concert appearances, but to earn a living had to give piano lessons and play in the same squalid dives which had provided his father with an income. His ability to transpose at sight, and to adapt music to any immediate need, prompted a publisher to commission arrangements from him for bands in the pleasure gardens, as well as a number of songs and salon pieces of his own.

In 1853 he was asked by the Hungarian violinist Eduard Reményi to become his accompanist on a tour of neighbouring towns. They made a very successful duo, more than paying their way, and on a number of occasions being asked back for repeat performances. Also, thanks to Reményi's contacts, Brahms made many new friends, among them the even more celebrated Hungarian violinist, Joseph Joachim. The first impression which Brahms made on most people was one of awkwardness and sometimes downright bad manners, but Joachim saw through the shyness, encouraged the younger man to play some of his piano compositions, and gladly gave the two of them letters of introduction to Liszt and the Schumanns. Although Liszt received them hospitably and played a Brahms Scherzo at sight, Brahms felt ill at ease, did not really approve of Liszt's own flamboyant romanticism, and was not as respectful as Reményi felt he should have been. The two partners quarrelled, and Brahms was left without a job.

Now he took two steps which were to alter his whole life. He got in touch with Joachim and was invited to join him at a lecture course at Göttingen University, where they played music together, discussed one another's playing and compositions, and on Joachim's suggestion gave a recital together to raise some money for Brahms. More important, Joachim again urged that Brahms should visit the Schumanns.

Robert and Clara Schumann took to him immediately and recognized his potential genius. Their home at Düsseldorf became the closest thing to a real home of his own which Brahms was ever to know. They admired his compositions and predicted a great future for him, and when Joachim arrived on a visit it was agreed that Schumann, a friend and pupil Albert Dietrich, and Brahms should each compose one movement of a violin sonata which the virtuoso could introduce at one of his forthcoming concerts. They achieved their aim, but only one movement is heard at all frequently today: Brahms's central

Scherzo. In it is a motto theme which Brahms was to repeat in several later works. The three contributors had agreed to use the notes FAE as a musical echo of Joachim's dour personal slogan, *Frei aber einsam* (*Free but lonely*). Brahms, more optimistic, adopted the formation FAF to represent *Frei aber froh* (*Free but happy*).

Although Schumann was in declining health and had given up writing regular music criticism ten years earlier, he now contributed a glowing tribute to the progressive magazine he had helped to found and had edited until 1844, *Neue Zeitschrift für Musik*, proclaiming young Johannes Brahms as the newly emergent composer, 'destined to give expression to the times in the highest and most ideal manner', not step by step but 'springing like Minerva fully armed from the head of Jove'. He also urged his own publishers, Breitkopf and Härtel, to take Brahms under their wing.

After Schumann's illness had led him to attempted suicide and into a mental home, and even more devotedly after his death in 1856, Brahms almost abandoned his career in order to comfort the widowed Clara. Although Clara was fourteen years older than Brahms, he acknowledged that he had fallen in love with her, and during a holiday together in the company of Brahms's older sister and two of Clara's sons there seemed a likelihood of her agreeing to marry him. Wiser than he, she drew back. They remained close friends thereafter: he always consulted her about his work, and she included many of his pieces in her recitals.

Facing the world alone, Brahms now unleashed all the tormented energy within him. His D minor piano concerto, which had been fermenting during the tragic period of Schumann's decline, burst upon a world so unprepared for what appeared to be a vast symphony with piano, rather than a piano with orchestra in accepted concerto form, that its first performance, which was conducted by Joachim, brought only incomprehension, while the second one drew noisy hissing from the audience. Brahms brought further scorn on himself by putting his signature, along with those of Joachim and two others, to a manifesto attacking the 'New German' romantic school of Liszt and Wagner. Brahms was always a classicist by conviction, suspicious of the 'so-called music of the future', and capable of using old, well-established forms to produce magnificent, individual results; but he was not yet well enough established with the public to make such pronouncements at such a time.

To add to his unpopularity, in his home town of Hamburg he had been so much taken by a young soprano, Agathe von Siebold, and had written such ardent songs for her, that she and her friends and family assumed he was about to propose marriage. At the last minute he apologized to her, writing that he could not wear fetters, though perhaps mentally admitting that he would always be fettered emotionally to Clara Schumann. Deciding a change of scene would be wise, he went to Vienna, was soon invited to become conductor of the Singakademie, and was so much taken by Viennese life that in due course he settled there.

After the death of his mother in 1865, Brahms took some music he had written for, but not used in, the First Piano Concerto, and built around it *Ein Deutsches Requiem*. He conducted the première in Bremen Cathedral himself, in the presence of Clara Schumann, who was as delighted as he was by the warm approval of those present.

Always a perfectionist, and awed by the great shadow of Beethoven, he had made only tentative attempts at tackling a symphony until at last, in 1876, his First Symphony in C minor was performed in Karlsruhe. Once the dam had been breached, works came flowing out. The following year he spent some idyllic weeks by the waters of the Wörthersee in southern Austria and produced the radiant Second Symphony in D major, which begins with a confident transposition of his pet FAF motto and, as his friend Theodor Billroth observed, 'is all rippling streams, blue sky, sunshine, and cool green shadows'. In the same key of D major, and conceived by the same lakeside, there followed the Violin Concerto, whose second movement again sings out the FAF notes and whose last movement dances with the Hungarian rhythms he had learned to love in the company of Reményi and Joachim.

The Third Symphony's key of F major naturally invites further play with FAF, this time battling with an A flat in the middle, the whole work being in a cyclic form unusual for Brahms, with subjects recurring right through the four movements and the starting theme coming gently to rest right at the end. With the Fourth Symphony, Brahms rounded off in a tribute to Bach, using the chorale from one of the cantatas as the basis of a towering passacaglia.

Towards the end of his life Brahms reserved his efforts for chamber music, piano pieces, and the collecting and setting of folk songs. His last real creative outburst was inspired by the clarinet playing of Richard Mühlfeld: just as Mozart had been impressed by the virtuosity of Anton Stadler, so was Brahms impressed by Mühlfeld, to the extent of composing a Clarinet Trio and the autumnally beautiful Clarinet Quintet, and finally two sonatas playable either by clarinet and piano or by viola and piano, but in their very essence clarinet music and unforgettable once heard in that voice.

Less than a month before he died of cancer of the liver, he heard, from his box at a Vienna Philharmonic concert, a performance of his Fourth Symphony. At the end of each movement the audience applauded as if to wish him well on his way. Prickly, uncompromising, and true to a classical tradition already under attack from louder practitioners, Brahms went to his grave one of the best-loved musicians who had ever resided in Vienna.

brass Wind instruments made not of wood (cf. **woodwind**) but of metal, usually brass but sometimes other amalgams. A common feature of all of them – including bugle, cornet, French horn, trombone, etc. – is a narrow tube which expands at the end into an amplifying bell. The player compresses his lips to squeeze a current of air through a mouthpiece into the tube: in the earliest form of such instruments, the notes were produced by variations of mouth shape and pressure (the 'embouchure'), later extended by means of valves and, in the case of the trombone, a slide. Even with the aid of such modifications, the player's performance still depends to a large extent on his ability to produce a series of harmonics (or overtones) by means of lip tightening or loosening. (*See also* **band** and **The Orchestra and its Instruments**.)

bravura A passage of music demanding a daring display of technique from singer or instrumentalist, often planted as a deliberate challenge by the composer. The word – Italian for 'courage' or, more closely, 'swagger' – is also applied to the performance itself, meriting applause derived from the same root: 'Bravo!'

break When a boy treble's voice sinks to a lower register at puberty, it is said to have broken. The term is also used for the changeover point between lower and higher registers of certain wind instruments, notably the clarinet, covered by the depressing of the 'octave key'. In jazz it refers to a brief solo improvisation at some point when the rest of the band stops for a few bars, in a melodic cadenza or most showily in the form of a 'drum-break'.

Bream, Julian (1933–) English guitarist. He made his first recital appearance at the Cheltenham Festival at the age of fourteen, his London début a year later, and his first American appearance in 1958. He has transcribed a great deal of early music for both guitar and lute, and has given frequent duet performances (including some jazz sessions) with the Australian guitarist John

Julian Bream, the English guitarist and lutenist for whom Britten, Walton and Arnold have all composed works.

bridge The wooden support on stringed instruments which lifts the strings clear of the belly or soundboard and transmits their resonances to the body of the instrument. The term is also used as a shortened version of *bridge passage* (see below).

bridge passage A short musical transition from one part of a work to another, often modulating into a different key. It appears most frequently between the first and second subjects of a piece in sonata form.

Bridge, Frank (1879–1941) English composer. A gifted viola player, Bridge appeared with several string quartets and also as an orchestral and opera conductor in London, but spent most of his creative life in his native county of Sussex. His first public impact as a composer was made with an orchestral tone poem, *The Sea*, in 1912. The tone poem *Summer*, whose première he conducted himself during World War I, represents him at his most idyllic, evoking his love of the countryside yet hinting, as always, at personal stress underneath.

After that war Bridge, a pacifist much given to inner questioning, turned his attention to the experiments of Schoenberg and his school and adapted them into an English idiom which alienated some who had enjoyed his earlier songs and chamber works but proved an inspiration to others, including his pupil Benjamin Britten.

OTHER WORKS: Five string quartets. Elegiac concerto *Oration* for cello and orchestra. *Divertimenti* for wind instruments.

Bridgetower, George (1780–1860) African-Polish violinist. A mulatto virtuoso, he made such an impression on Beethoven that the composer dedicated a *Bridgetower Sonata* to him, but then quarrelled with him and renamed the work the *Kreutzer Sonata* in honour of another violinist.

Britten, Benjamin (1913–76) (Lord Britten of Aldeburgh) English composer. Son of a Lowestoft dentist, Britten was born on St Cecilia's Day, and under the auspices of this patron saint of music began composing when he was five years old. During school holidays he studied the piano with Harold Samuel and composition with Frank Bridge, to whom in 1937 he gratefully dedicated *Variations on a Theme of Frank Bridge* for strings, based on a passage from his tutor's *Three Idylls* for string quartet. While at the Royal College of Music he heard *Wozzeck* and wanted to study with Berg in Vienna, but official disapproval brought this to nothing.

To earn a living, Britten wrote incidental music for documentary films and the theatre, and attracted the attention of the music publisher Ralph Hawkes, who offered a contract for anything he

Williams. Among the works written specifically for him is Malcolm Arnold's Concerto for Guitar and Strings.

Brian, Havergal (1876–1972) English composer. Largely self-taught, eccentric, and combining a personal romanticism with outbursts of surprisingly violent modernism, Havergal was born in Staffordshire but in 1919 settled in Sussex because in a dream he had seen a towered, turreted city which he later identified as the town of Lewes. Much of his work was mystical and idiosyncratic. In all he wrote thirty-two symphonies, but few were played or attracted critical attention until in 1961 the first performance was given of the earliest complete one, the so-called *Gothic Symphony*, which calls for an orchestra of two hundred, four brass bands, and five hundred singers plus soloists and an organ.

produced. Towards the end of the 1930s he was able to buy an abandoned windmill at Snape, a village in his home county of Suffolk.

In 1939 he went to America to give a series of recitals with his lifelong companion Peter Pears, the tenor for whom he wrote so many individual pieces and song cycles, including the *Seven Sonnets of Michelangelo*, composed while they were living on Long Island. During this same period his Violin Concerto and *Sinfonia da Requiem* were conducted at Carnegie Hall by John Barbirolli.

The two friends, who were both pacifists, were in no mood to return to Europe during the early part of World War II, until a magazine article by E.M. Forster about the Suffolk poet George Crabbe conjured up such nostalgia that in 1942 they were drawn back home. Registering as conscientious objectors, they were granted exemption from military service provided they gave concerts for the troops and the war-wounded. Not until 1944 did Britten have the opportunity of starting serious work on a project commissioned by the Koussevitsky Foundation in the USA: then, his imagination seized by Crabbe's poem *The Borough*, with its tale of a brutish yet tragic Aldeburgh fisherman, he embarked on an opera, *Peter Grimes*. It was finished in 1945 and first performed at the post-war reopening of Sadler's Wells Theatre, London, in June that year. An immediate success not only in England but all over the world, it established Britten as a major operatic composer and allowed him to embark on other compositions and projects.

Near their Suffolk coastal home Britten and Pears founded a local festival which was later to branch out over the neighbouring countryside. (*See* **Aldeburgh Festival**.) Much of Britten's music was written for performance in specific churches or other local settings, and he made great use of local schoolchildren, as in *Let's Make an Opera* and *Noye's Fludde*. His intuitive rapport with children and his ability to share with them a direct yet never over-simplified language is shown in many other works, such as the *Welcome Ode* and the vividly communicative *Young Person's Guide to the Orchestra*, written originally for an educational film, and based on a theme by one of Britten's favourite composers, Purcell.

He contributed a great deal to the revival of interest in composers of earlier times, and to impress modern ears with their essential beauty was skilful in editing, reinterpreting and 'realizing' the sometimes sparsely notated works of his admired predecessors. From folk-song adaptations to the loving recreation of such neglected stage pieces as the Dryden-Purcell *King Arthur*, he sought to convey his own delight in other people's music – an understanding and generosity which showed up equally well in his work as an accompanist and as a chamber music performer at so many Aldeburgh Festivals.

Britten's hatred of war and its results was expressed in his *War Requiem*, first performed in 1962 at the consecration of the new Coventry Cathedral, rising from the ashes of the edifice destroyed in a Nazi air raid in 1941. Within a

A painting by Kenneth Green in 1943 of Benjamin Britten *(right)* with Peter Pears, the tenor and lifelong friend for whom he wrote many outstanding songs, song cycles, and leading rôles in opera.

setting of the traditional Mass the composer incorporated nine poems by Wilfred Owen, killed in action during World War I.

It is difficult to make any generalization about the compositional style of a man who worked in so many different genres, but throughout his creative life there could always be found certain characteristics: a preference for working with singers and instrumentalists who had become friends and for whose capabilities he could write specifically (such as Rostropovich, Vishnevskaya, Fischer-Dieskau, and above all Peter Pears); an unquenchable interest in new musical forms and the reinvigoration of old ones; an innate ability to put across musical or dramatic ideas in short, direct phrases and then build upon them with equal directness yet with unique, untiring imagination; and a personal sympathy with the persecuted, the bereaved and the innocent threatened with the loss of that innocence. This last theme dominates the operas *The Turn of the Screw* and *Owen Wingrave*. In his last work, his Third String Quartet, he was still exploring and enlarging his horizons.

From 1973 onwards Britten's activities were severely curtailed by heart trouble. In 1976 he was created a life peer as Lord Britten of Aldeburgh, only a short time before he died and was buried in Aldeburgh churchyard, to be joined ten years later by Sir Peter Pears, who had been knighted in 1978. In November 1986 a gala performance attended by Queen Elizabeth II and the Prince of Wales was given to mark the opening of the Benjamin Britten Theatre, a small opera house behind the Royal College of Music in London.

OTHER WORKS: Operas *Albert Herring, Billy Budd, A Midsummer Night's Dream, Death in Venice*. Choral *Ceremony of Carols, Hymn to St Cecilia, Spring Symphony*. Cantata *St Nicholas*. Song cycles *Holy Sonnets of John Donne, A Charm of Lullabies, Winter Words*. *Serenade* for tenor, horn and strings. Ballet *The Prince of the Pagodas*. Various chamber works.

Brixi, František Xaver (1732–71) Bohemian (Czech) composer. After studying philosophy at Prague University he took on various church appointments, and when appointed organist at St Vitus' Cathedral in 1756 wrote a *Probation Mass* for the occasion. In all he produced about five hundred church compositions, including masses and oratorios, and a number of keyboard pieces: several of his lively and inventive organ concertos have been revived and recorded in recent years.

Broadwood, John (1732–1812) British pianoforte manufacturer. Born in Berwickshire, Scotland, he walked to London to learn the trade of cabinet-maker. Employed by a Swiss-born harpsichord manufacturer, Burkat Shudi (original full name Burkhard Tschudi), Broadwood married the boss's daughter and became a partner in the firm. In 1772 he took over the management just before his father-in-law's death, and in 1781 produced the first Broadwood grand piano. Later the firm became first John Broadwood and Son and then 'and Sons'. John's great-granddaughter was Lucy Broadwood (1858–1929), who collected English folk-songs and became a founder member, and for a time the Honorary Secretary, of the Folk Song Society.

Bruch, Max (1838-1920) German composer. After winning a Mozart scholarship in Frankfurt at the age of fourteen, Bruch studied in various musical establishments in his homeland and in Austria. He wrote three indifferent operas, but won great acclaim with a choral work *Frithjof*, based on a Nordic saga. Another composition in similarly heroic vein, *Schön Ellen*, appealed particularly to British audiences with its tale of a Scottish girl's part in the relief of Lucknow during the Indian Mutiny. Bruch also composed a *Scottish Fantasy* for violin and orchestra while working in England for three years as conductor of the Liverpool Philharmonic Society. A fluent if over-sentimental tunesmith, he is remembered mainly for his melodious First Violin Concerto in G minor, written for the virtuoso Joachim, and *Kol Nidrei* for cello and orchestra, which evokes the opening prayer on the evening before Yom Kippur, the Jewish Day of Atonement.

Bruckner, Anton (1824–96) Austrian composer. Born into a family of schoolteachers, young Bruckner followed the family tradition: after a spell as chorister in a monastery, he trained as a teacher and returned to the monastery to teach there and play the organ, on which he made a reputation as a brilliant improviser. Belated orchestral studies led him at last to attempt composition for himself, but at first he remained in religious mood with two masses. He continued to teach, from 1868 in the Vienna Conservatoire and from 1875 as lecturer in harmony and counterpoint at the University.

His symphonies won the approval of Wagner, to whom he dedicated the third, but Viennese audiences scorned them. The powerful critic Hanslick attacked him; Brahms derided him. The sixth symphony was not performed until after the composer's death, and the ninth was left incomplete because right up to the end of his life he was devoting much of his time to rewriting earlier works in accordance with contradictory advice from friends and critics.

Bruckner's music could never be classified in any tidy, acceptable tradition, classical or roman-

A silhouette of Richard Wagner *(left)* and Anton Bruckner, each of whom claimed to be Beethoven's true successor. Such claims may, as one sees, be taken with a pinch of snuff.

tic. To many he seemed — and still seems — a clumsy, even boorish, country boy with a limited, naïve religious faith and little creative self-confidence. Yet the overall impression left by a worthy performance of his work is of a mighty orchestral architecture, broad and expansive, with major sections formed from great blocks of ravishing sound above a spacious landscape. Often there seems little intellectual relationship between one element and another, and little development of thematic material: it is elemental, intuitive music which relies greatly on the listener's own enthralled acceptance — or analytical rejection. Yet, contradictory in this as in so many things, Bruckner startles the ear in his seventh symphony with interrelated sequences and inversions, and in the eighth with its inevitable, almost fatalistic progress towards a finale of epic grandeur.

OTHER WORKS: Choral masses, *Te Deum* and *Requiem*. String quintet. Orchestral *Overture in G minor*.

buffa, buffo Italian for a puff or a jest, from the same root as 'buffoon'. The phrase *opera buffa* is applied to comic opera, as opposed to the seriousness of *opera seria*; and the singer of comic or merely jovial parts, such as that of Leporello in Mozart's *Don Giovanni*, is described as a *basso buffo* or, less frequently, *tenore buffo*.

bugle A simple brass instrument in the treble register, consisting of a wide, looped tube, mouthpiece and small bell. By tightening or slackening his lips while blowing, the player can produce notes in a harmonic series above the lowest obtainable note but cannot vary these by valves, as in the trumpet. The few simple tunes which can be played are used mainly as military commands or in marching bugle bands.

Bull, John (1562–1628) English composer and keyboard virtuoso. In the time of Queen Elizabeth I he served as a chorister in the Chapel Royal and later as its organist. A highly regarded performer on the virginals, he composed a great deal of keyboard music and a number of anthems and secular songs. For some time his name was associated with the English national anthem, but in fact the piece he entitled *God Save the King* in no way resembles the tune to which we are accustomed.

In 1613 Bull left England, supposedly to avoid punishment for some misdemeanour. He became organist first in Brussels and then, from 1617 until his death, at Antwerp Cathedral.

bull-roarer A primitive instrument used by Australian aborigines and American Indians, consisting of a flat piece of wood whirled round the head on the end of a piece of string, sometimes called a 'thunder stick' because the noise thus produced sounds as much like thunder as like the roaring of a bull.

Bülow, Hans von (1830–94) German conductor and pianist. He studied with Liszt and married the composer's daughter Cosima. After becoming chief conductor at the Royal Opera in Munich and then director of the Conservatorium, he enthusiastically promoted the works of Wagner, and went on doing so for some time after Wagner had taken his wife away from him. In due course, however, he defected to the camp of Wagner's arch-rival, Brahms. Von Bülow became the dedicatee of Tchaikovsky's First Piano Concerto after the Russian pianist Anton Rubinstein, to whom it had originally been dedicated, declared it was clumsy, unplayable, and ought to be burnt.

Bumbry, Grace (1937–) American mezzo-soprano. She studied with Lotte Lehmann and made her début at the Paris Opéra in 1960 as Amneris in Verdi's *Aida*. In 1961 she became the first black singer to appear at Bayreuth — as Venus in *Tannhäuser* — but really made her name with her dramatic, richly temperamental interpretations of Verdi heroines, and even more stunningly as Carmen. Always flamboyantly unconventional in her personal life, with an unashamed passion for motor racing and a glamorous life-style, she resolutely sought in her career to set new standards, literally higher ones: tired of too many mezzo rôles and especially that of Carmen, she decided to train her voice up into the soprano range, and in 1970 gave an electrifying performance in Richard Strauss's *Salome* at Covent Garden.

Burney, Charles (1726–1814) English organist and musicologist. As choirboy and deputy organist at Chester Cathedral, he so impressed the visiting Dr Thomas Arne with his youthful compositions that Arne took him to London as a musical apprentice. Later Burney fell ill and had to seek a healthier country atmosphere as organist and teacher in King's Lynn, Norfolk, where he conceived the idea of his great four-volume *History of Music*, published between 1776 and 1789 after extensive travels through Europe. From 1783 until his death he was organist at Chelsea Hospital, London.

Busch, Adolf (1891–1952) and **Fritz** (1890–1951) German brothers, Adolf a violinist and Fritz a conductor. Adolf moved to England in 1933, made many concert appearances and recordings with the quartet bearing his name, and gave sonata recitals with his son-in-law, the pianist Rudolf Serkin. Fritz left Germany in the same year, after being dismissed from his conductorship in Dresden by the Nazis, but went first to Buenos Aires before being installed at Glyndebourne as its earliest conductor. He conducted at the New York Met between 1945 and 1950.

Bush, Alan (1900–) English composer and pianist. He studied with John Ireland and remains one of the finest interpreters of Ireland's piano music. His Marxist political beliefs have influenced personal activities and his choice of subjects as a composer, though without impeding the fine lines of his favoured modal idiom or his gift for melody. He has served as conductor of the London Labour Choral Union and chairman of the Workers' Music Association (which he founded in 1936), and has written many choral works for amateur choirs. Among his operas, *Wat Tyler* deals with the fourteenth-century Kentish uprising against social injustice; *Men of Blackmoor* with the tribulations of nineteenth-century Northumbrian miners, to a libretto by his wife, Nancy. After World War II his *Lidice*, a lament for Czech villagers murdered by the Nazis, was conducted by the composer on the site of the massacre.

OTHER WORKS: Three symphonies (including the *Nottingham Symphony*). String quartet. *English Suite* for strings. *Three Northumbrian Sketches* for bagpipes. Song cycle *Voices of the Prophets* (commissioned by Peter Pears).

Busoni, Ferruccio (1866–1924) Italian composer and pianist. Son of an Italian clarinettist and an Austrian pianist mother, the boy was exploited by his father as a child prodigy at the piano. He began composing at the age of eleven, travelled widely as a recitalist, and conducted and taught in Finland, Moscow and the USA before settling in Berlin. His early compositions were in romantic vein, owing a lot to Mendelssohn and Brahms, but later he was to be torn between the world of Bach and that of the Debussyian expressionists, and even of atonal and electronic experimenters. As well as his own compositions, from the neo-classical *Konzertstück* for piano and orchestra to the almost atonal Sonatina No. 2, he made a reputation as a transcriber for the piano of works by Beethoven, Liszt, Mozart and even Schoenberg.

OTHER WORKS: Operas *Turandot* and *Doktor Faust*. Piano concerto. *Fantasia contrappuntistica* on the Contrapunctus XVIII of Bach's *Art of Fugue*.

Bussotti, Sylvano (1931–) Italian composer. He studied as a violinist but became more interested in composing and won prizes at an International Society for Contemporary Music festival and a Vienna Biennale. Much influenced by Webern and serialist theories, and also by Boulez and John Cage, his music has veered between the fragile and the declamatory. Aiming at an inextricable mingling of theatre and musical resources, his *La Passion selon Sade* (*The Passion according to Sade*) combines echoes of the old *commedia dell'arte* with parody opera, an orchestra on stage, and suggestive gestures such as a soloist caressing his instrument.

OTHER WORKS: Opera *Lorenzaccio*. Five piano pieces for David Tudor. *The Rara Requiem* for voices and orchestra.

Butt, (Dame) Clara (1872–1936) English contralto. She made a couple of well-received operatic appearances early in her career, and in 1899 gave the first performance of Elgar's *Sea Pictures*, composed with her in mind; but after marrying the baritone Kennerley Rutherford concentrated on touring Britain and the British Empire in recitals of popular ballads and patriotic songs.

Butterworth, Arthur (1923–) English composer. He played trumpet in the Scottish National and Hallé orchestras, and composed and transcribed many works for brass band. He has admitted that much of his work has been inspired by the atavistic significance of places rather than by people or purely theoretical construction. Moorland vistas from the north of England have been especially influential, as in the orchestral tone poems *Path across the Moors*, *The Quiet Tarn*, and *A Dales Suite*. There is also a northern leaning in his second symphony, celebrating the centenary of Scandinavian composers Nielsen and Sibelius in 1965.

OTHER WORKS: Overtures and suites for brass ensembles. Organ concertos. Music for school plays and children's ballet.

Butterworth, George (1885-1916) English composer. He was an avid collector of folk songs, and his love of the countryside infused his own pastoral pieces such as *The Banks of Green Willow*, his settings of A.E. Housman poems, and their related orchestral rhapsody *A Shropshire Lad*, first performed at the Leeds Festival of 1913 under the baton of Artur Nikisch. Butterworth was killed on the Somme during World War I.

OTHER WORKS: Orchestral *English Idylls 1 & 2*. Arrangements of Sussex folk songs. Carols for choir.

Buxtehude, Diderik(Dietrich) (1637–1707) Danish composer and organist. Born in Elsinore, Denmark, Buxtehude followed his father as organist at St Olaf's church there. In 1668 he became organist of the Marienkirche in Lübeck, Germany, and in the prevailing custom of the time married his predecessor's daughter. When there was talk of his retirement, both Handel and Mattheson came in search of the job, but neither of them was willing to marry one of Buxtehude's own daughters.

Bach also came to visit, lured by the organist's reputation as a consummate improviser. Buxtehude's keyboard style and his organ fugues,

An allegorical painting by Johannes Voorhout in 1674 of the composer Buxtehude (with a sheet of music) and his friends from the *Amstkollegen* of St Katharine in Hamburg, with Johann Adam Reincken at the keyboard.

chorale preludes and sacred cantatas were a major influence on Bach's work.

BWV In 1950 the German musicologist Wolfgang Schmieder compiled a thematic catalogue of Bach's compositions whose numbering has become the accepted *Bach Werke-Verzeichnis* (*Index to Bach's Works*): for example, the Goldberg Variations are indentified as BWV988, the Brandenburg Concertos are BWV1046-51, and so on.

Byrd, William (1543–1623) English composer. Organist of Lincoln Cathedral at the age of twenty, Byrd was appointed a Gentleman of the Chapel Royal and moved to London, where from 1575 onwards he and Thomas Tallis were granted by Queen Elizabeth I the monopoly of music printing and publishing for twenty-one years, a sinecure which Byrd duly bequeathed to his pupil Thomas Morley. Although a Roman Catholic during times of persecution, Byrd remained in royal favour and, as well as writing music discreetly for recusants, contributed with equal skill and dedication to Anglican services. His contrapuntal genius shines most brightly in *Gradualia*, two volumes of motets, and in his Great Service, but he was just as inventive in madrigals and other secular works. Many of his keyboard pieces are included in the *Fitzwilliam Virginal Book*.

His profits were sufficient to buy him a country estate at Stondon Massey in the county of Essex after his first wife's death. Here he remarried, and here there is a memorial stone set in the church wall.

C

cabaletta A variation of the Italian *cavatina*, usually referring to the final bravura section of an operatic aria in more than one part.

Caballé, Montserrat (1933–) Spanish soprano. After working in a factory to help support her parents, she began training for the ballet in Barcelona but later turned towards opera. She made her singing début in Basle in 1956 but did not begin to establish a real reputation until 1965, when at short notice she appeared at Carnegie Hall, New York, in a concert performance of Donizetti's *Lucrezia Borgia*, astounding the audience with her warm sumptuous voice and rhythmic urgency.

Her first appearances in Britain, in that same year, were at Glyndebourne. She became a favourite at the New York Met, most notably in operas by Donizetti and Bellini. She made her Covent Garden début in 1972 as Violetta in Verdi's *La traviata*, but her English reputation depends much more on her successful concert appearances. In 1973 she announced that she was retiring to

The Spanish soprano Montserrat Caballé, who made an international impact after appearing at the New York Met in 1965 and in Mozart's *The Magic Flute* at Glyndebourne in that same year.

spend more time with her husband and daughter, but in fact went on singing though with frequent gaps and cancellations.

caccia Italian for the chase, or the hunt. Madrigals *alla caccia* dealt with hunting subjects, and the phrase was used in Italy for a canon in which the voices 'chased' each other. The *corno da caccia* is a hunting horn; the *oboe da caccia* was a low-pitched member of the oboe family, an early version of the *cor anglais*.

cadence Also called a close, because it completes a section of a composition or the entire composition. Western music over several centuries has accustomed the ear to expect a melodic and harmonic resolution which virtually announces 'We've got there at last'. In its simplest and most satisfying form, in the key of C major this would involve the 'waiting' sound of the dominant chord of G (even more effective if the seventh note of that is added to give a chord of G7), followed by the tonic chord of C. This is known as a perfect cadence or full close. Composers have often, however, followed other paths in their return to the tonic from which they started out.

In a plagal cadence in C, instead of the dominant preceding the tonic we have the chord of the subdominant, i.e., F. This is often called an Amen cadence because it is so familiar in the concluding 'Amen' of so many hymns.

An interrupted cadence is one in which the chord of the dominant, instead of settling back on to the tonic, is followed by the chord of the submediant, which in the key of C would be a chord of A minor.

An imperfect cadence, or half close, in effect reverses the perfect cadence by putting a dominant chord after the tonic chord, thus suggesting that there is more to come – and in fact it often appears as a sort of suspension or taking of breath between one movement and another in such things as *concerti grossi*, especially those of Handel.

One sound for which the ear frequently waits during a piece in a minor key is a brightening shift on to a final major chord. Known as a *tierce de Picardie* (*Picardy third*), in the key of C minor this would involve a penultimate dominant chord of G and then, instead of the awaited triad of C/E flat/G, the triad C/E natural/G.

In all cases if the final chord falls on a strong beat it is known as a masculine cadence, if on a weak beat as a feminine cadence, as in the masculine and feminine endings of poetry.

cadenza The word is essentially the same as 'cadence', but has come to be applied to a showpiece solo passage between the chords of a cadence towards the end of a concerto movement or in an operatic aria. In its earliest form it gave the player a chance to display his technical skill and imagination in improvisation, warning the orchestra with a long trill or prearranged rhythmic figure when he was ready for them to join in again. There are still soloists who prefer this, especially those performing aleatory music. From Mozart onwards, however, most composers preferred to write out their cadenzas in full, and many of them supplied cadenzas for the work of others: Beethoven provided some for Mozart piano concertos, while some of his own cadenzas were rejected in favour of contributions by Busoni and others; Brahms wrote cadenzas for Mozart and Beethoven concertos; and the soloists Joachim and Kreisler each supplied his own fully composed cadenzas for the Beethoven and Brahms violin concertos.

Cage, John (1912–) American composer. He studied with Cowell and Schoenberg, and at a very early stage became interested in 12-note techniques

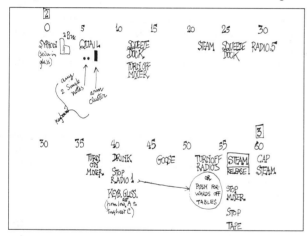

and percussion. He organized a number of purely percussion ensembles, and wrote extensively for them. The influence of eastern philosophy led him to favour chance operations, tossing coins or using tables of random numbers to determine pitch and duration, exemplified in his *Music of Changes*. Experimenting with varying sonorities, he devised a 'prepared piano' by fitting screws, rubber bands and pieces of wood and glass between the strings, and for it wrote a number of pieces, including *Bacchanale* and *Sonatas and Interludes*.

Equally interested by electronic potentialities, Cage began in 1967 to create a 4½-hour work involving seven harpsichords, fifty-two tape machines and two hundred computer-generated tapes, with a battery of amplifiers and loudspeakers, all accompanied by slide and movie projectors. It was performed two years later in the University of Illinois under the title HPSCH, the nearest thing to 'harpsichord' suitable for computer programming. In complete contrast was his notorious *4'33"*, in which the pianist is required to remain silent throughout three supposed movements and let the audience imagine whatever it chooses to hear.

OTHER WORKS: *Imaginary Landscape 1* for muted piano, cymbal, two variable speed gramophone turntables, and frequency recordings. Music for amplified toy piano. *Double Music* for percussion quartet. *0'00"* 'to be performed in any way by anyone'.

Callas, Maria (1923–1977) Greek soprano (born in USA). Every generation demands one flagrantly temperamental *prima donna* to enliven the whole experience of opera-going; but also demands that

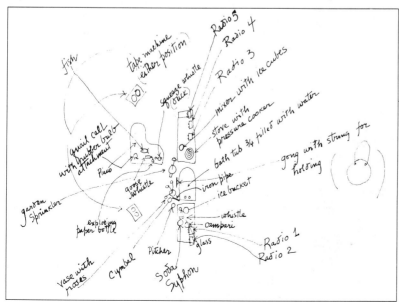

John Cage's *Water Walk* requires the solo performer to combine instructions in the score *(above)* with movements around the stage *(left)* between objects including a pressure cooker, a partly filled bathtub, a tape machine, and various whistles.

Maria Callas in the title rôle of Bellini's *Norma* in 1954. In January 1958 she caused a scandal by walking out after the first act of this same opera in spite of the presence of the Italian President and some of his distinguished guests.

the voice shall match the melodrama. Soon after World War II there came on the scene a coloratura soprano of such power that in due course she was adoringly referred to simply as Callas. Beginning her studies in Athens, she made her début there in 1940. Her first appearance in Italy was in 1947, and in the following year she caused a sensation when she was called in by the conductor Tullio Serafin as a last-minute substitute Elvira in Bellini's *I puritani*. Serafin was a major formative influence, and she later admitted that she 'drank all she could' from him.

Some critics found her voice strident; yet at her best she was one of the greatest twentieth-century exponents of *bel canto*. Opera and concert promoters found her explosive rages difficult to cope with. The interventions of her first husband and business manager Giovanni Battista Meneghini, whose name she linked with her own for a while as Meneghini-Callas, did little to smooth the way. Yet in spite of frequent harshness in voice and professional relationships she had a rare gift of hypnotizing an audience by sheer interpretative and dramatic power. The perspicuous American critic Henry Pleasants has referred to her ability to 'cast a spell that deafens the listener to executive imperfections and inadequacies'. She was unforgettable in *Norma*, and in spite of increasing shrillness gave, in her last Covent Garden appearance in 1965, a performance with Tito Gobbi in *Tosca* which is unlikely ever to be equalled.

After leaving Meneghini she entered into a much-publicized liaison with the Greek shipping millionaire Aristotle Onassis; but in the end he married Jacqueline Kennedy, and in an attempt to resume her creative career the disillusioned Callas gave master classes, appeared in a film of *Medea*, and made a patchy concert tour with the tenor Giuseppe di Stefano.

Calvé, Emma (1858–1942) French soprano. She studied in Paris, made her début in Brussels, and appeared at Covent Garden in 1892 and the following year at the New York Met, where she was immediately recognized as not just a superlative singer but an unusually gifted actress – not too surprising, since her own stage idol had been the great Italian actress Eleanora Duse. In *Carmen*, which she first sang at the Met before making it one of her major rôles elsewhere, she was almost too dramatically convincing, and horrified even admirers such as George Bernard Shaw, who, like many others, had loved her virginal quality and 'nightingale tone' as Ophelia in Ambroise Thomas's *Hamlet*, but now experienced 'much the same sensation as might be given by the reality of a brutal murder'.

Massenet conceived the title rôles of *La Navarraise* and *Sappho* for her, but at the height of her career she abandoned the opera house for the concert hall. During World War I she toured the USA raising money for the war-wounded, and died in France during World War II nearly destitute after the Nazi invasion.

Campion, Thomas (1567–1620) English composer and lutenist (name also spelt Campian). After practising medicine in London he turned to writing words and music for songs with lute accompaniment and for fashionable masques. He published several books of *Ayres*, among them the immortal *There is a Garden in her Face* and *My Sweetest Lesbia*.

canon A form of composition in which the introductory melody is taken up by a second voice (vocal or instrumental) and is imitated in strict rule (i.e. canon): the second line, although starting before the first has finished its phrase, must repeat the first line note for note, and so on with any additional voices. The principle is the same as that in a 'round', but in the hands of a skilful composer can be used for complex contrapuntal displays. In strict canon the intervals between notes remain the same, however many voices are used; canons by augmentation or diminution allow for lengthening or shortening notes in subsidiary voices; and a 'canon cancrizans' has the second voice echoing the melody backwards. When a subsidiary line is not in exact notational imitation but starts an interval away, it is identified by that interval, as in 'canon at the third', 'canon at the fith', and so on. Neo-classical and serialist composers have made considerable use of canonic form.

cantata An Italian word from *cantare*, to sing, differentiated from a sonata, an instrumental 'sounding'. The term was originally used to describe a piece for soloist accompanied by a single instrument such as a lute or with *basso continuo*. Later it was applied to a choral and orchestral work, with or without soloists, usually on a sacred subject. Buxtehude and Telemann worked fruitfully in this medium, but it was Bach who really perfected the form. He put it to secular use also, as in the *Coffee Cantata*; and Bartók was to compose a *Cantata profana* around a Romanian ballad.

canticle Basically a 'little song', usually a hymn of Scriptural origin used in Christian liturgy; but the term has been adopted for concert pieces with a religious flavour such as Benjamin Britten's five *Canticles* for various small vocal and instrumental groups.

cantilena Originally applied to the plainsong melody in early church music and then, more generally, to the main melody in any composition, the word has come to define a smooth, graceful vocal line, exemplified in the extended, flowing operatic arias of Richard Strauss.

cantor The leading singer in a synagogue, or the musical director of a Lutheran church, as Bach was at Leipzig. The same implication is to be found in the word *cantoris*, which in cathedrals denotes that part of the choir placed on the north side near the cantor, or precentor, while the rest sit on the southern *decani* side near the dean. Some musical scores for such choirs specify which parts should be taken by the *cantoris* section and which by the *decani*.

cantus firmus A fixed melody, as in plainsong or a single chorale tune, upon which a composer could build a contrapuntal structure.

canzone and **canzonet** A troubadour's solo song or light-hearted madrigal, the *canzonet* or *canzonetta* being a 'little song' of even less weight. The names have also been applied to fairly simple instrumental pieces.

cappella See **a cappella**.

capriccio A whim or caprice: that is, a brisk, light little morsel for a solo instrument (as in many piano pieces so entitled), or a fanciful orchestral piece such as Rimsky-Korsakov's *Capriccio Espagnol* (*Spanish Caprice*) and Janáček's *Capriccio* for piano only, commissioned by a player injured in World War I. The word was also used as the title of Richard Strauss's last opera, dealing with a woman torn between love for a poet and for a composer, symbolizing the clash between the rival arts involved in opera.

Carissimi, Giacomo (1605–74) Italian composer. Choirmaster in Assisi and then for almost fifty years in Rome, he pioneered cantata and oratorio forms in works such as *Job* and *Jephtha*, blending religious and operatic styles.

Carnegie Hall New York's major concert hall until the opening of the Lincoln Center in 1972. It was founded in 1891, with Tchaikovsky among the guest conductors. Originally called The Music Hall by its main benefactor, the steel magnate and philanthropist Andrew Carnegie, it was later renamed in his honour, largely because visiting foreign musicians were reluctant to appear in anything so plebeian as a 'music hall'. Carnegie himself is said to have been displeased by the change of name.

carol Although we nowadays associate carols with the Christmas religious message, they originated as boisterous dances with songs echoing old pagan pleasures in opposition to the puritanism of church observances. Many were roistering part-songs, such as the *Boar's Head Carol* printed in Wynkyn de Worde's collection of 1521. Even when an overtly Christian element was woven in, there was still a materialistic expectation of some reward for singing them outside the houses of the well-to-do, preferably including some warming food and drink. Many composers have used the form, including Gerald Finzi in one of the loveliest of his *Bagatelles* for clarinet and piano, and Benjamin Britten in his *Ceremony of Carols*. In France a carol is called *Noël*; in Germany, *Weihnachtslied*.

Carpenter, John Alden (1876–1951) American composer. From 1897 onwards he was employed in the family firm of maritime suppliers, but he also took private music lessons, including some in Rome with Elgar. A lightweight, elegantly impressionist composer, he wrote an entertaining little orchestral suite *Adventures in a Perambulator*, very much in the vein of Ravel, and then was influenced by jazz in compositions such as the ballets *Krazy Kat* and *Skyscrapers*.

OTHER WORKS: Two symphonies. Violin concerto. *Improving Songs for Anxious Children*. Symphonic poem *Sea Drift*.

Carter, Elliot (1908–) American composer. He studied with Walter Piston at Harvard and then with Nadia Boulanger in Paris, and has himself taught in a number of American Universities. His first important work was a ballet, *Pocahontas*. Stravinsky wrote approvingly of him, and for a time was a major influence on his work; but Carter moved away from neo-classical austerity into increasingly complex atonality, cross-rhythms and 'metric modulation', as in his Sonata for Cello and Piano with its interplay of lyrical cello and a piano used at times almost as a percussion instrument. His first and second string quartets went in for even more clashes of individual parts and tempi, though always with the composer's own logical framework.

OTHER WORKS: Double concerto for harpsichord, piano and two chamber orchestras. Concerto for orchestra. Ballet *Caravan*.

Caruso, Enrico (1873–1921) Italian tenor. He made his début in his home town, Naples, in 1894 and thereafter built up a reputation as the most velvet-toned of all tenors. His fame was helped by the growing popularity of the gramophone: during his career he was to make some two hundred and fifty recordings.

His vocal agility, which was never allowed to distort his tone or lyrical phrasing, so enraptured New York audiences that in all he appeared more then six hundred times at the Met. His repertoire was wide: although he never cared to sing in German, he was equally at home in Italian and French operas such as *Les Huguenots* and *William Tell*; he created the tenor rôles in several, including *Adriana Lecouvreur* and Puccini's *La fanciulla del West (The Girl of the Golden West)*.

Casals, Pablo (1876–1973) Spanish cellist. Although Casals was also a composer and conductor, he was revered mainly for his cello interpretations, especially in trio performances and recordings with the violinist Jacques Thibaud and the pianist Alfred Cortot. Between 1906 and 1912 he was

Pablo Casals, the Spanish cellist, in 1950, the year in which he founded the Prades chamber music festival.

As well as being the most admired tenor of his day, Enrico Caruso was also a gifted cartoonist, and did not hesitate to laugh at himself in this 1906 sketch made in London.

married to the outstanding Portuguese cellist Suggia, and then in 1914 married an American singer, Susan Metcalfe. Made Citizen of Honour in Madrid and Member of Honour of the Spanish Academy in 1935, he left his homeland four years later, publicly vowing never to return while it was under Franco's dictatorial system. In 1950 he founded a chamber music festival at Prades in the Pyrenees, and later a festival in Puerto Rico, where he had settled and where he died in 1973.

castanets Small cup-shaped clappers fastened by a string between thumb and fingers of Spanish dancers to produce a rhythmic accompaniment. They are made of ivory, or more usually of chestnut – the Spanish word for which is *castafia*. The pair held in the left hand, providing the basic beat, is called 'the man'; the smaller pair in the right hand, called 'the woman', adds swifter, heavily syncopated patterns.

An engraving of a pair of wooden castanets.

Castelnuovo-Tedesco, Mario (1895–1968) Italian composer. After the success of his prizewinning opera *La Mandragola*, he immersed himself in Shakespearean themes and wrote operas around *The Merchant of Venice* and *The Taming of the Shrew*, a number of concert overtures to several of the other plays, and settings of all Shakespeare's songs. His extensive, delightful output for the guitar includes a concerto, concerto for two guitars, a quintet, and a sonata. In 1939 he settled in the USA, and died in Hollywood.

OTHER WORKS: Opera *Aucassin et Nicolette*. Oratorio *Ruth*. Orchestral *Concerto italiano* and *American Rhapsody*.

castrato Since for many centuries the Church clung to St Paul's injunction that women should be silent in church, female singers were forbidden in all liturgical music. To provide the soprano lines needed to develop this music to its full potential, boy trebles were in great demand, but their careers were short because in puberty their voices broke. One solution was castration, which would enable the male singer to maintain his vocal purity in the high register. Church authorities officially proscribed castration, but in fact made regular use of *castrati*, as did operatic composers and producers when restrictions upon women were imposed on the stage also. Many boy children of large families were forced to undergo the operation in order to guarantee them a paid career: it has even been recorded that both Haydn and Rossini had narrow escapes from being mutilated in this way in childhood.

catch Very similar to a 'round', in which one singer starts an echo phrase after an earlier singer has embarked on the melody; but in this case the aim is to make an entry in such a way as to distort the overlapping words and produce absurd double meanings – often lewd ones, as was the fashion in the eighteenth century.

Cavalli, Pietro Francesco (1602–76) Italian composer. The son of a small-town church musician, Cavalli studied with Monteverdi but for many years was known primarily as a singer, first in the Doge's chapel in Venice and then in a noble household. He sprang to public notice when, after restrictions had been lifted to allow the opening of public opera houses in Venice, he swiftly wrote a string of operas full of melodious arias and elaborate set-pieces. In all he composed and produced around forty, among them *Serse*, which was performed at the wedding in Paris of Louis XIV.

Although acknowledged as an influential pioneer of dramatic opera form, Cavalli's own work fell into neglect until in 1967 *L'Ormindo* was revived at Glyndebourne in a 'realization' by Raymond Leppard, and then taken by the company to Munich. This was followed at Glyndebourne by *La Calisto*, repeated in subsequent seasons.

Towards the end of his life Cavalli, made organist at St Mark's Cathedral and then *maestro di cappella*, turned towards religious composition. He left a number of skilful motets and vespers and a Requiem Mass which was performed at his own funeral.

cavatina A simple self-contained, short melody, as in an operatic aria without a second section or the *da capo* repetition of the first. The word has also been applied to lyrical instrumental pieces such as the exquisite movement in Beethoven's String Quartet Opus 130.

cebell or **cibell** A seventeenth-century English dance appearing in harpsichord or ensemble suites by Purcell and his contemporaries, in imitation of the gavotte *Déscente de Cybelle* in Lully's opera *Atys*.

A sixteenth-century painting by Michael van Cuxie of St Cecilia, patron saint of music.

Cecilia, Saint Patron saint of music and musicians, her feast day being on 22 November. She is believed to have been martyred by Marcus Aurelius towards the end of the second century AD and her relics now lie beneath the high altar of Santa Caecilia in Rome. Her connection with music is problematical, but may be related to tales of her defiance of her persecutors by praising God in song and the playing of instruments – in her case, according to so many paintings and stained-glass windows, the organ: there is a representation of this on an outside wall of the Royal College of Organists in London. Odes for St Cecilia's Day were set by Handel and Purcell, and Britten's *Hymn to St Cecilia* reminds us that he was, most fittingly, born on her feast day.

Černohorský, Bohuslav Matěj (1684–1742) Bohemian composer. A friar and organist, he worked for a time in Padua and Assisi and had Tartini among his pupils. In 1735 he returned to Prague as organist and choirmaster of St James's church, whose choir today specializes in performances of his motets. Unfortunately a large quantity of his music was destroyed by a fire in 1754.

Chabrier, Emmanuel (1841–94) French composer. Born into a well-to-do family in the Auvergne, he took a law degree and worked in Paris for almost twenty years as a civil servant. At the same time he studied music in a somewhat dilettante fashion but became growingly interested in Spanish tunes and rhythms, displayed in his exuberant orchestral rhapsody *España* and the *Habañera* for piano.

As an opera composer Chabrier fell under the spell of Wagner, helping Lamoureux with a French production of *Tristan und Isolde*, but his own opera *Le Roi malgré lui* (*King despite himself*) stands up well in its own right. Many of his harmonic and orchestral experiments look forward to Debussy and Ravel. Towards the end of his life he sank into acute melancholia, bordering on madness.

OTHER WORKS: Operas *L'Etoile* and *Gwendoline*; opera *Briséis* left unfinished at his death. Many songs and 'picturesque pieces' for piano.

chaconne Originally a processional dance form in a stately rhythm of three beats to the bar, similar to a *passacaglia*, it was used by composers for variation writing above a *basso continuo*, though the bass part itself could be transferred to other registers. The *Crucifixus* of Bach's Mass in B minor is in essence a chaconne; and one of the most famous is that which concludes his second Partita for solo violin.

Chadwick, George Whitefield (1854–1931) After a spell in the family insurance business he studied at the New England Conservatory and then in Berlin and Leipzig. Although his operas, such as *Judith* and *The Padrone*, a number of concert overtures, and the symphonic ballad *Tam O'Shanter* have a great deal of dramatic force, they never commanded large audiences, and he is better remembered as a gifted teacher, conductor and church organist.

Chaliapin, Fyodor (1873–1938) Russian bass. With very little musical training, he sang a number of operatic rôles with a provincial travelling company and then in St Petersburg and Moscow. The resonant depths of his voice and the larger-than-life exaggerations of his dramatic interpretation startled critics when he first appeared at the New York Met in 1907 in Boito's *Mefistofele*: they found him 'stupendously picturesque' but, on the whole, uncouth. It was not until Diaghilev presented him as *Boris Godunov* in Paris in 1908 that his full stature was acknowledged. It became one of his most celebrated rôles, and marked his London début in Thomas Beecham's 1913 season.

Impulsive and domineering in both private and public life – he was capable of storming off stage in the middle of a performance after the slightest disagreement with the conductor or a fellow singer – Chaliapin did not settle happily into post-Revolutionary Russia. For a while he worked at the Maryinsky Theatre, and even after several disagreements there his reputation was so great that he was declared Premier Singer to the Soviet People. In 1922 he left the country and was anathematized as an anti-revolutionary, but continued his international career with great financial success, including seasons at the New York Met and many concert recitals. He died in Paris in 1938.

An autographed photograph of the Russian bass Fyodor Chaliapin in the title rôle of Mussorgsky's *Boris Godunov* in 1924.

chamber music In Italian *musica da camera*, in German *kammermusik*, the meaning in all languages is that of music for a room rather than a theatre or concert hall. Essentially a domestic form of entertainment, it was often written for and played by amateurs: many a composer in royal or ducal service regularly provided pieces for a small number of instrumentalists with parts adapted to their known capabilities.

In medieval times and throughout the Renaissance such intimate music was sung by madrigal groups or played by 'consorts' of similar instruments – for instance, a quartet of viols or recorders. If wind and stringed instruments were mixed, it was known as a 'broken consort'. Gradually certain formalities were adopted, the commonest pattern being that of the short trio sonata for, say, a viol, flute and continuo. When composers dropped the free-and-easy continuo in favour of fully scored parts for every instrument, the keyboard chords were replaced by more ambitious harmony and polyphony, and the string quartet developed towards the commanding heights of Haydn and Mozart.

Although additional and diversified instruments soon became acceptable, numbers were kept within reasonable bounds. The harpsichord continuo had gone, but the fashionable pianoforte was introduced into piano quartets and quintets – meaning a piano *plus* three or four other instruments, not a group of four or five pianos. There have been clarinet quintets, including the beautiful works by Mozart and Brahms, horn trios, all-wind quintets and sextets, and pieces for chamber orchestra of up to a dozen or so players, but still designed for performance in an intimate setting: e.g. Schoenberg's *Kammersymphonie* (1906), and Hugh Wood's *Chamber Concerto* (1971).

So-called *chamber opera* involves small vocal and orchestral forces, but is more appropriately sung in a small hall rather than a room; though some works in this category, such as Benjamin Britten's *The Turn of the Screw* and Richard Strauss's *Ariadne auf Naxos*, are more likely to be seen on stage then in a hall of this kind.

Chambonnières, Jacques Champion de (1602–72) French composer. Considered to be the founder of the French school of *clavecinistes*, or keyboard players, he established a style for the clavier quite separate from that of the organ, and published two influential volumes of *Pièces de clavecin*. He made great use of ornamentation, known as *agrémens*, and inspired the later work of his pupils and friends, among them the Couperin family. His father had been *claveciniste* to Louis XIII; he himself served Louis XIV in the same capacity.

Chaminade, Cécile (1857–1944) French composer. A gifted piano recitalist, she began composing at the age of eight and played many of her own works on tour in France and England. Among larger works are an opera and a 'symphonic ballet' *Callirhoë*, a lyric symphony *Les Amazones* for chorus and orchestra, and a *Konzertstück* for piano and orchestra; but her name is associated mainly with the 'salon music' style of her elegant, lighter piano pieces and songs.

change-ringing Campanology, the art of ringing church bells in rounds or changes by teams pulling on control ropes, is practised almost exclusively in Britain. Skilled members of a team can play a wide variety of sequences: a complement of seven bells, for instance, can produce a peal of more than five thousand changes, and the ultimate challenge, complete peals of what is known as Plain Bob Major, involves more than forty thousand.

chanson The French word for a song has been applied to many vocal forms, from early partsongs to the *canzonet* and even the modern French cabaret piece: performers such as Jean Sablon and Charles Trenet have frequently been described as *chansonniers*. Medieval minstrels sang of heroic deeds in versified *chansons de geste* – literally 'songs of exploits'.

Chapel Royal The 'Chapel' in this phrase refers not simply to a building but, like the German *Kapelle*, to a body of clergy and musicians, attached in this case to the reigning English monarch. Henry I employed a group of singers whose main task was to provide him with music at religious services in whichever of his royal residences he was occupying at the time. In subsequent reigns, letters patent confirmed the Chapel Royal by name. When the Court went on tour, the ensemble went too: Henry VIII took them all with him to France and the Field of the Cloth of gold. Honorary appointments were much sought after, and over the centuries much of English music was fashioned by 'Gentlemen of the Chapel', especially by its organists and choirmasters such as Tallis, Byrd and Orlando Gibbons.

A permanent base was provided by Henry VIII during the building of St James's Palace in London, where today certain Sunday choral services are open to the public. A Scottish Chapel Royal, founded in Stirling Castle but moved to Holyrood in Edinburgh, still has the duty of providing a dean and six chaplains whenever the sovereign is in residence at Balmoral Castle.

Charpentier, Gustave (1860–1956) French composer. As a boy he worked in a textile factory in northwest France, but managed to get himself into the Lille Conservatoire and won a scholarship to study under Massenet in Paris. Existing on money raised by his townspeople, and most of the time on the edge of poverty, he lived a Bohemian life and always felt a deep sympathy for the underprivileged. When he could raise funds he founded a 'Popular Conservatoire' which offered free music, dancing lessons and operatic performances to working-class girls.

One such girl became the heroine of his opera *Louise*, the tale of a poor dressmaker and Julien, her poet lover, a theme so bleakly, socially moralistic that for ten years no opera house would risk staging it. In due course it became an international success, which Charpentier tried to follow up with a sequel, *Julien*, carrying on the story after Louise's death. It achieved only twenty performances in Paris and has disappeared from the repertory.

OTHER WORKS: Song cycles *Les Fleurs du mal* (from poems by Baudelaire) and *Impressions fausses* (from Verlaine).

Chausson, Ernest (1855–99) French composer. The son of a prosperous building contractor, the young man was privately educated and remained of a solitary, introspective disposition. Captivated by Wagner's music, he undertook studies with Massenet and Franck and, in spite of his intrinsic aloofness, became one of a wide social circle of musicians and painters.

Always self-critical, Chausson wrote generally in elegiac mood. His Wagnerian leanings did not help him to achieve any success with *Le Roi*

Arthus or any of his other operas. His most characteristic voice is to be heard in his songs and in the *Poème* for violin and orchestra, given its first public performance by Ysaÿe in London a week after the composer had died in a bicycle accident.

Cheltenham Festival An annual festival of contemporary music held in the summer at Cheltenham Spa, England. When it started in 1945 it was devoted exclusively to modern British works and saw many first performances of these, but it has since expanded to take in composers of all nationalities.

Cherubini, Luigi (1760–1842) Italian composer. After studying in his native Italy he visited London to produce two operas and for a short time served as Court composer to King George III. In 1788 he settled in France and ultimately became director of the Paris Conservatoire. He made his name as producer of Italian opera seasons, to which he contributed more than thirty of his own works including *Médée*, greatly applauded in Paris, Berlin and London.

Later in life Cherubini concentrated on religious compositions, including some superb masses,

The score of the Introit to Cherubini's *Requiem in C minor* in the composer's own hand.

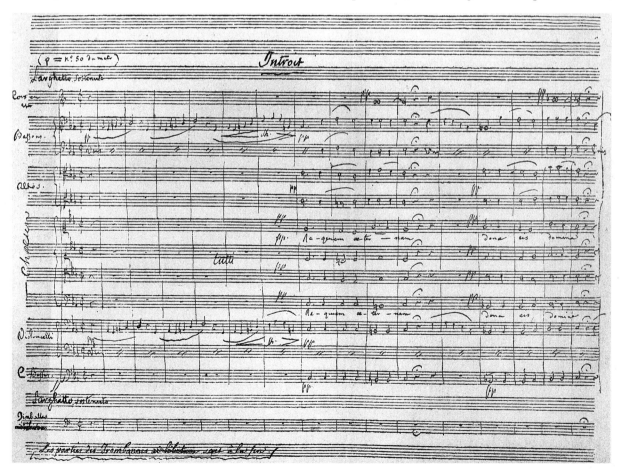

and chamber music. Vitriolic attacks were made on him by Berlioz in his *Memoirs* and in the parody of his pedantic fugal style in *The Damnation of Faust*.

chest of viols In the sixteenth and seventeenth centuries it was as common for most well-to-do households to have a set of six viols of different sizes for the family and visitors to play on as it was from the nineteenth century onwards to have a piano in the parlour. The viols were kept in a cupboard or a chest.

chest voice A low register voice or the deeper notes of such a register, so called because the resonances feel as if they come from the chest rather than the head. (*See also* **head voice**.)

choir A body of singers, usually in a church: a secular group is generally referred to as a chorus. The name is also given to that part of a cathedral where the singers are placed, often as a double choir positioned to produce the best antiphonal effects.

A *choir organ* was once a small instrument set to one side to accompany the choir in certain passages and also for rehearsal purposes. Nowadays the term is applied to a section of the main organ with a special keyboard controlling softer stops suitable for this purpose.

Peace on Earth and Goodwill to all Men: an engraving after J. Wengel, 1894, of a choir in a church organ loft.

Chopin, Frédéric (1810–49) Polish composer and pianist. The second of four children of a French father and Polish mother, his full forenames were Fryderyk Franciszek. He took piano lessons in Warsaw from the age of seven and, hearing Polish folk tunes during country holidays, began writing polonaises and mazurkas. Studying composition at Warsaw Conservatoire, in a mood of unrequited love for a fellow student he wrote two piano concertos and a number of nocturnes – a form which, in the wake of the Irish composer John Field, he perfected.

His travels took him to Paris, where he became a darling of the fashionable salons, pouring out for them a succession of waltzes and other pieces based on Polish national dances: in all he was to write fifty mazurkas and sixteen polonaises. Fanciful romantic names have been attached to several of these pieces, but Chopin himself frowned on the habit, believing that his music should speak for itself without programmatic titles. Also in his piano style he was opposed to heavy dramatic touches and shunned the pyrotechnics in which most post-Beethoven performers indulged. He often preferred to use an old style of square piano rather than the more resonant grand.

In 1837 he met the novelist George Sand, who carried him off for a love affair on Majorca, accompanied by her two children. Always frail in health, Chopin fell ill and had to return to France, with George Sand still close by his side. In her country house at Nohant he continued to write ballades and other works such as the *Fantaisie in F minor* and the *Sonata in B minor*.

Two things drove Chopin out of France to England, and then on to Scotland: the relationship with George Sand broke up, and the revolution of 1848 broke out. For a time he was the guest of a Scottish ex-pupil, Jane Stirling, whose praise of his genius so flattered him that he dedicated the two nocturnes of Opus 55 to her. Piano manufacturers in London rushed to provide him with instruments: at one time he had three grand pianos in one room. He played privately for Queen Victoria and Prince Albert, but otherwise was not much impressed with his English audiences, whom he described as having wooden ears where music was concerned.

The adoring Miss Sterling, several years his senior, grew far too possessive, and after she had lured him to a number of houses in Scotland he took fright and fled. Back in London he gave his last public recital and, weakened by worsening tuberculosis, returned to Paris, where he died. In spite of his defection, Jane Sterling paid the funeral expenses and bought up his personal effects to establish a Chopin museum in Scotland. After her own death these were sent to Warsaw, only to be destroyed by the Russians in 1863. His heart, kept in the Church of the Holy Cross in Warsaw, was hidden from the Germans during World War II but afterwards returned to its resting-place.

Apart from a handful of songs and a few cello pieces, Chopin's whole career was devoted to

An imaginative painting by Siermiradsci, 1877, of Chopin performing in Prince Anton Radziwill's Berlin salon in 1829.

performing at or composing for the piano. His poetic style embraced harmonic and dynamic inventiveness which made great use of *rubato* and the instrument's sustaining pedal to produce flowing, singing lines and unexpected sonorities. In spite of his preference for 'absolute music' over the picturesque and romantic, he was throughout his short life passionately nationalistic, as shown in the dance rhythms of so many of his pieces and in the intensity of the *Marche funèbre* in C minor and the 'Funeral March' in the Sonata No.2 in B flat minor. Themes from some of his works were linked into a ballet choreographed by Fokine in St Petersburg in 1907, originally called *Chopiniana* but now better known as *Les Sylphides*.

'Chopsticks' A simple repetitive tune in fast waltz tempo which can be played with two fingers on the piano. Its origin is unknown, but the piece is familiar in most European countries, and a volume of variations on it for three hands was published with contributions from Borodin, Cui, Lyadov, Rimsky-Korsakov and Liszt.

chorale Among Martin Luther's many ecclesiastical reforms was the introduction into church services of simple hymn tunes which the congregation could sing in unison, based either on old plain-chant themes or on folk songs with which everyone would be familiar. When composers such as Schütz, Buxtehude and ultimately Bach wrote cantatas for church performance, they not merely included or ended with a straightforward chorale of this kind, but often wove it into the texture of the rest of the work, sometimes as a *cantus firmus*, sometimes as a theme for polpyhonic variations. In the *St Matthew Passion*, Bach makes repeated use of the deeply moving chorale *O Sacred Head Sore Wounded*.

As an introduction to this piece of communal singing it was common practice, as it is today at the beginning of a hymn, for the organ to play a few chords to set the key and establish the tune. Such introductions were frequently seized on by the church organist as an opportunity to display his skill at improvisation, and composers wrote out extended variations on the well-known themes until the *chorale prelude* became a musical form in itself, with or without the subsequent voices: Bach arranged and harmonized over four hundred chorale preludes.

chord A combination of notes sounded together in harmony rather than contrapuntally. The *common chord* is a triad with intervals of a third and a fifth above the tonic in whatever the key may be: in C major this would consist of C, E, and G; in C minor of C, E flat, and G. Other notes can be added to form discords, which may be resolved or further complicated by following chords. The handling of chord sequences is as vital to composition as the creation of a melody, and can in fact throw quite different lights on the melody itself.

Chording is a term with three meanings: it refers to the spacing of the notes in a chord; to vocal intonation when singing a chord; and, in the field of popular music, to the production of chords on a stringed instrument such as a guitar or banjo.

chorus A body of singers who sing the ensemble parts in opera or oratorio. In the original Greek the word covered a combination of dance and song. Today it retains this meaning only in stage musicals with a 'chorus' or 'chorus line' of dancers.

Another usage is in a popular song, when the verse is followed by a refrain or chorus, and in the music-hall the audience may be invited to 'Join in the chorus'.

Christoff, Boris (1919–) Bulgarian bass. He began a career in the legal profession but turned to music and studied in Rome and Salzburg. He made his début in Rome in 1945, and between 1958 and 1963 sang with the Chicago Opera. After Chaliapin he became the most highly acclaimed interpreter of Mussorgsky's *Boris Godunov*.

The powerful Bulgarian bass, Boris Christoff, in the part of King Philip II in Verdi's opera *Don Carlos*.

chromatic From the Greek *chromos*, 'colour', the word refers in music to notes which do not belong to the basic key of a composition and which therefore add, as it were, fresh colouring to the piece. An ordinary *diatonic scale* consists of eight notes: in the key of C these are all, in terms of the piano, 'on the white notes'. Any 'black note' which is introduced in the development of the piece, whether in the melody or in the underlying harmonies, is defined as a chromatic note. A full *chromatic scale* consists of twelve semitone intervals, covering the whole range of black and white notes. Indication of chromatic insertions into a diatonic scale is given by the marking where appropriate of a sharp or flat on the written stave.

Chromatic harmony also uses notes alien to the prevailing key. Composition making use of such chromaticism has been known from the times of Gesualdo's complex madrigals, and was intensively practised by Bach; but it spread most widely during the nineteenth century as a means of conveying romantic, dramatic emotion as in the works of Wagner and his followers. During this period there was still, nevertheless, an underlying tonality, and a piece usually returned to its basic key. In the twentieth century, composers have frequently shaken off even that rein, and pursued the paths of atonality and serialism.

Cilèa, Francesco (1866–1950) Italian composer. He studied at Naples Conservatory and later became its director. His opera *L'arlesiana* first brought the tenor Caruso to fame in 1897. Although he wrote other operas, Cilèa was more highly regarded as a teacher than as a composer; but he did leave us one outstanding romantic work rich with lyrical arias and brilliant orchestration – *Adriana Lecouvreur*, based on the real-life story of a French actress supposedly poisoned by one of her lover's other mistresses.

Cimarosa, Domenico (1749–1801) Italian composer. A master of comic opera and a major influence on later compatriots such as Rossini, this son of a poor Neapolitan family became fashionable and well-rewarded in Naples and Rome and at the court of Catherine II in St Petersburg. In 1790, after the dismissal of Mozart's famous rival Salieri, he was appointed *kapellmeister* to the Court of Leopold II in Vienna, and there wrote *Il matrimonio segreto (The Secret Marriage)*, based on an English comedy by Colman and Garrick.

Returning to Naples after Leopold's death, Cimarosa fell into disgrace for supporting the French republican forces against his employer, King Ferdinand. After a spell in prison he set out for Russia again, but died before he could get beyond Venice.

OTHER WORKS: About sixty operas, including *Artaserse* and *L'italiana in Londra* (*The Italian Girl in London*) – cf. Rossini's *L'italiana in Algeri* (*The Italian Girl in Algiers*). Masses, cantatas and oratorios.

claque From the French verb 'to clap', the word refers to groups of supporters hired to applaud a particular performer in the theatre or opera house – or hired by rival factions to boo and hiss a production off the stage. Claques were common in Paris from the late eighteenth century onwards, and were imitated in Vienna and Milan and at the New York Met. Fighting frequently broke out: at the première of his opera *The Barber of Seville*, Rossini's gaudy clothes aroused so much derision that he was attacked and driven out of the theatre; after hecklers had tried to shout down Maria Callas at La Scala, Milan, a team of her admirers set upon them and the police had to be called; and in the 1930s things had grown so bad in Vienna under a claque organizer named Schostal that the conductor Clemens Krauss banned the *claqueurs* from the Opera House – but could enforce this only by paying off the main rival groups out of his own pocket.

Clarke, Jeremiah (1659–1707) English composer and organist. A pupil of John Blow in the Chapel Royal, he became organist at Winchester College and later of St Paul's Cathedral and the Chapel Royal. His *Trumpet Voluntary*, for many years wrongly attributed to Purcell, was based on a march associated with Queen Anne's consort, Prince George of Denmark, acquiring its popular name because it imitated the open notes of the natural trumpet stop of an organ. Clarke's life ended by his own hand: he shot himself after a disappointment in love.

clàrsach An ancient Celtic harp which accompanied bardic singing in Gaelic communities. It was reintroduced in Scotland at the beginning of the twentieth century as part of the Hebridean song revival stimulated by the researcher, Marjory Kennedy-Fraser.

classical The word is loosely used to distinguish 'serious' or 'art' music from popular songs, dance music, etc. but this is misleading. Closer to the mark, though still unsatisfactory, is its distinction of older music from modern music. In a more limited sense it has come to be applied to the period between the Baroque and Romantic eras (roughly from 1750 to the third decade of the nineteenth century), when a taste for orderly, well-proportioned music without either undue ornamentation or self-indulgent dramatic extravagance prevailed. Obviously, different styles overlapped or intermarried, but in general one may regard, for example, J.S. Bach as a baroque composer, his son C.P.E. Bach as a classical one; Mozart as classical, Beethoven as romantic.

claves Round wooden sticks, used in pairs, the one in the left hand being rhythmically beaten by the right-hand one. Of Cuban origin, they are most frequently used in dance bands as part of the percussion for rumbas and Latin-American numbers, but they also appear in some of Harrison Birtwistle's experiments with percussion groups and rhythmic patterns.

clef Literally the 'key', or symbol placed at the beginning of the stave (staff) to establish the pitch of the notes. (*See* **Notation**.)

Clementi, Muzio (1752–1832) Italian composer and pianist. Son of a silversmith in Rome, Clementi at the age of fourteen so impressed the wealthy English traveller Peter Beckford that he took the boy to his home in Dorset. Clementi left Beckford's service to become an admired teacher in London, and in 1786 was appointed 'principal composer and performer' of the Hanover Square Grand Professional Concerts. He travelled widely in Europe, and on one occasion entered a piano contest with Mozart, the verdict on which has unfortunately not been recorded.

Clementi composed symphonies, about a hundred piano sonatas, and the progressive keyboard exercises, *Gradus ad Parnassum*, which have since tormented many hundreds of aspiring players; but in due course abandoned such activities to devote himself to the manufacture of improved pianofortes. In 1832 the firm he had established became the famous Collard & Collard. He died in comfortable retirement at Evesham and was buried in Westminster Abbey, where an 1887 memorial stone replacing the original one can be found in the cloisters.

clusters Groups of adjacent notes played on the piano simply by putting the fist or elbow down on the keyboard. One of the first to explore their technical possibilities was the American composer Henry Cowell. They are found in the works of Bartók and Stockhausen; and Stockhausen has also experimented with orchestral clusters.

Coates, Eric (1886–1957) English composer. He played the viola in a number of string quartets and in the Queen's Hall Orchestra, London, but is best known for his well-crafted suites of light music and songs. Listeners to British radio are unlikely to forget the *Knightsbridge* march which introduced the 'In Town Tonight' programme, the march he composed for World War II 'Workers' Playtime', or the song *By a Sleepy Lagoon*, associated with distinguished selectors of 'Desert Island Discs'.

coda and **codetta** The Italian word for a tail, or tailpiece, identifies the brief closing section of a piece of music, usually the conclusion of a movement in sonata form. It rounds off the piece without developing any of the preceding music further.

An alternative usage is applied to the more ambitious coda found in symphonies after Haydn's day, especially those of Beethoven, where it was often built into the body of the composition and could become effectively a second development section.

A *codetta* is a 'little tail', often attached to a section of a movement rather than ending the whole movement; or in a fugue is the linking episode between sections of the exposition.

Coleridge-Taylor, Samuel (1875–1912) British composer. Son of a Sierra Leone doctor and an English mother, he sang in a Croydon church before taking up violin studies and then turning to composition under Stanford. Encouraged by Elgar, he achieved many successes with festival compositions, most notably *Hiawatha's Wedding Feast*, first performed at a Royal College of Music concert, and two choral-orchestral sequels based on Longfellow's poetry. In 1904 he was appointed conductor to the Handel Society, and that same year made the first of several visits to the USA.

OTHER WORKS: Opera *Thelma*. Oratorio *The Atonement*. Orchestral *Symphonic Variations on an African Air*. Concert march *Ethiopia Saluting the Colours*. Violin concerto. Chamber music and songs.

coloratura Flexible, florid (i.e. 'colourful') singing using decorative trills and other virtuoso elaborations, especially by operatic prima donnas – hence *coloratura soprano*.

colour The word generally appears in the phrase 'tone colour', referring to the timbre of various instruments in various combinations. A number of composers and theoreticians have attempted from time to time to relate musical textures directly to visual colour effects: Bantock's *Atalanta in Calydon* calls for the concert hall to be lit with different hues for each movement; Scriabin used a special keyboard to produce accompanying colours for his tone poem *Prometheus*; and the score of Schoenberg's expressionistic stage piece *Die Glückliche Hand* (*The Lucky Hand*) specifies coloured lighting effects.

common chord *See* **chord** and **Notation**.

common time The frequently, if loosely, used definition of 4/4 time, i.e. four beats to the bar.

compound interval An interval which exceeds an octave: e.g. a leap from C to the note D nine notes above it (in effect an octave above its own adjoining D) is the compound interval of a ninth.

compound metre (or time) This is also sometimes known as *triple time* because it defines a rhythm produced by subdividing the pulse into three parts, as in 6/8 and 9/8 time.

concert In its broadest sense the word implies people coming together in an agreement – 'in concert' – but in the musical sense it can mean either a 'consort' of singers and instrumentalists or a public performance by a large ensemble (though distinct from an operatic production in a theatre). A performance by a soloist or small group is usually called a recital.

Music-lovers in early times gathered together for private singing and playing, or went to church. The first known concerts for a paying secular audience were given in London in 1672 'over against the George Tavern in White Friars, near the back of the Temple' by one John Bannister, a violinist dismissed from the King's Musik after misappropriating money which ought to have been shared out between his fellow musicians. He was soon followed by a musically minded coal merchant, Thomas Britton, above whose store Handel, Dr Pepusch and others met and played. Other concert societies were formed, often taking the names of the inns which housed them: the Castle Concerts from the Castle Tavern in Paternoster Row, and later the Angel and Crown in Whitechapel, which specialized in performances of Purcell's music.

The first recorded concert hall designed specially for such productions was built in Oxford in 1748. The idea spread through Europe and the USA, and today there is hardly a major city in the world which does not have a venue of this kind, as well as many in unexpected small-town and rural settings.

concertante This usually indicates work in the style of a concerto, featuring a group of instrumentalists rather than a soloist. In the *concerto grosso* of the seventeenth and eighteenth centuries the 'display' group or 'little consort' was called the *concertante*, *concertino* or *concertato*, and the main orchestra the *ripieno*.

concertina The instrument's action of squeezed bellows forcing air against vibrating metal reeds has a lot in common with the accordion, but the concertina has no keyboard and is played by studs on hexagonal boards for both hands. Compact and easily portable, it was invented in 1829 by the English physicist Sir Charles Wheatstone, who in his youth had worked for an uncle as a musical instrument maker.

concertmaster In Great Britain it is more usual to speak of the *leader* of an orchestra (normally the principal first violin), but in the USA a literal translation of the German *konzertmeister* has been adopted. It is largely his responsibility, in conjunction with the conductor and sometimes virtually

Concert in the Garden, an eighteenth-century painting by Peter Jakob Horsemans of *alfresco* music-making.

as deputy conductor, to supervise conformity of bowing and intonation throughout the orchestra, and also to represent the players' interests to the conductor and concert management.

concerto and **concertino** In its earliest form the concerto was conceived as a vehicle for small groups of instrumentalists playing against a background of a full orchestra. This was known as a *concerto grosso* (*great concerto*), having much in common with an orchestral suite, and was richly exploited by composers such as Corelli and Handel. (*See also* **concertante**.)

Just as the public preferred virtuoso 'star' singers to vocal ensembles, so it began to favour the solo instrumentalist playing with, or to some extent against, the orchestra. Many composers also liked the idea of writing pieces, especially for piano and orchestra, in which they could display their own interpretative talents. In the actual writing they moved away from the suite form and in general adopted sonata form for their concertos.

As a rule the classical or romantic concerto begins with an orchestral *tutti* (meaning everybody except the soloist) stating the main theme or themes. Instead of following with the usual sonata form repeat, a second exposition is provided by the soloist, either stemming from the preceding orchestral statement or offering quite new material. After this the two elements work out concords and contrasts until the end of the first movement, with one pause for the soloist to play a *cadenza* on his or her own, perhaps as written out by the composer, perhaps invented by the soloist or some virtuoso predecessor.

In the concerto, as in so many other musical forms, a rigid pattern did not exist for long. The soloist might make an immediate entry with the orchestra, or even precede it. Two or more soloists might compete with each other, as in Mozart's *Sinfonia concertante* for violin and viola. An early fashion for three movements, dropping the minuet and trio common in symphonies and string quartets, was ignored by composers with ideas of their own which they wished to develop: Brahms, for instance, introduced a thunderous *scherzo* between the second and final movements to break up the almost conversational, chamber quality of his Piano Concerto No.2.

Twentieth-century composers have bent the form itself to their own wishes, and have also introduced a number of unusual solo instruments such as percussion (Milhaud), prepared piano (Cage), and harmonica (Hindemith, Arnold and Vaughan Williams). Some have revived the *concerto grosso* form, while others have developed the Concerto for Orchestra as a way of displaying the talents and orchestration possibilities of an entire ensemble – among them Hindemith, Bartók, Kodály and Tippett.

A *concertino* is either the solo group, also known as the *concertante* in a *concerto grosso*, or a small-scale concerto for soloist and orchestra, such as those for piano by Honegger and Piston, and Weber's for clarinet.

concert pitch Before beginning to play, all instrumentalists tune up to an agreed pitch, established in an orchestral concert by the oboist sounding the A above middle C. The exact pitch of this has varied over the centuries, but the standard now internationally recognized is that of 440 vibrations per second for the A, though some soloists – and even some conductors – like to tune higher for added brilliance.

concord The sounding of notes in a consonance which satisfies the ear as complete in itself and requiring no resolution from its opposite, a discord. A perfect example is the major triad: in the key of C major this is C, E and G.

concrete music *See* **musique concrète**.

conducting When orchestras grew in size and could no longer be directed from the keyboard or simply have the tempo established by a leading violinist, it became necessary to have what one might call a full-time overseer to establish speed, balance and dynamics and to conduct the often massive forces through the labyrinth of sound and bring them out triumphant at the other end. The conductor must be able to read and digest the composer's score for however many instruments are involved, be able to bring in soloists and sections where necessary, and ensure smooth changes of volume or tempo. He must familiarize himself in advance with any work to be performed so that he can be always on the alert for what is going on in the orchestra or chorus or on the opera stage, and at rehearsal must be able to convey to his players the nuances required, disciplining or encouraging them as necessary. It has been rightly observed that a conductor should have the score in his head, not his head in the score.

He can also be of great value to an attentive audience, not as an over-demonstrative entertainer but as a guide to which part of the orchestra he is about to draw out, what phrasing to listen to, and where the current of ideas is at any given moment. The late Sir Henry Wood once explained that if a concertgoer would follow the conductor's baton and left-hand gestures ('I always say I paint the picture with my baton') he would understand the results and be able to form his own conclusions – and in fact should *hear* more, especially in an unfamiliar composition, than if there were nobody there to direct his attention towards significant detail.

Many composers wished to conduct their own music rather than entrust it to others.

Characteristic poses and directions given by Arturo Toscanini while conducting. In his legendary rages he often broke his baton, and shouted 'No, no, *no*' so frequently at the orchestra that he was nicknamed 'Toscanono'.

Mendelssohn, Wagner, Mahler and Richard Strauss were outstanding in this field. The professional conductor as such did not really emerge until the late nineteenth century, the more flamboyant soon acquiring the admiring title of *maestro* (Italian for 'master'). Among outstanding practitioners, often associated on a long-standing basis with certain orchestras, have been Arturo Toscanini, Bruno Walter, Otto Klemperer, George Szell, Herbert von Karajan, Leonard Bernstein, Sir Georg Solti and Sir Charles Mackerras. (*See also* **baton** and **beat**.)

conservatory or **conservatoire** In Italy, especially in Naples and Venice, it was common to establish a local *conservatorio* where orphans and illegitimate children could be 'conserved', educated as useful citizens, and taught music. From this was derived the name given to leading schools of music such as the Paris *Conservatoire de Musique*, the Leipzig *Konservatorium*, and the National Conservatory of Music of America in New York. In Britain the word is rarely used: instead there are institutions such as the Royal College of Music, Royal Academy of Music, and Guildhall School of Music.

continuo *See* **basso continuo**.

contralto A lower-range female voice, the word meaning literally 'against the high'. Its normal range is from the G below middle C to the E a tenth above middle C.

Copland, Aaron (1900–) American composer. The youngest of the five children of Russian Jewish immigrants, he was born above a Brooklyn department store, and his first musical memories were of hanging over his sisters as they practised the piano. His parents were at first not keen on paying for his musical education also, but after taking some lessons from a sister – during which time, he later confessed, instead of practising he was making up tunes in his head and trying to work out what harmonies would fit them – he went at seventeen to Manhattan and studied with Goldmark. Four years later in France he became one of the first of Nadia Boulanger's pupils at the recently opened American Conservatory, Fontainebleau. She introduced him to the conductor Koussevitsky, who was just about to leave Paris and take up conductorship of the Boston Symphony Orchestra, and who at once commissioned from him a symphony for organ and orchestra. Nadia Boulanger played the solo part in 1925 for her American début under the baton of Walter Damrosch. For several succeeding years each of Copland's new works was first performed by the Boston Symphony Orchestra under Koussevitsky.

After his return from France, Copland became a leading figure in the League of Composers, taught at the New School for Social Research, and collaborated with Roger Sessions on seasons of concerts introducing many new American and European works. Later he continued such concerts with Roy Harris and with Walter Piston. His own early experimental, dissonant music caused some scandals among audiences and critics: Damrosch commented, 'If he can write like that at twenty-three, in five years he'll be ready to commit murder,' and the *Boston Post* condemned his use of jazz styles in his Piano Concerto as a 'concatenation of meaninglessly ugly sounds and distorted rhythms'.

Copland soon turned away from jazz, which he had originally felt would purge his style of too restrictingly European influences but which he found would somehow not work in harness with his other ideas. He toyed with serialism, and there are hints of Schoenberg's influence in his spiky Piano Variations (though at the same time these led to his being dubbed the 'Brooklyn Stravinsky'); but the biggest shift of direction came with his

decision to aim at pleasing a wider audience by simplifying his style and choosing themes and treatments which would be truly American and in no way derivative from other sources.

During the Depression he visited Carlos Chavez in Mexico, and in due course produced a suite full of intoxicating Latin-American dance-hall rhythms, *El salon México*. Then came music for ballets with a Wild West setting: *Billy the Kid*, which used a number of folk tunes, and, to Agnes de Mille's choreography, *Rodeo*. Music for another ballet, the Pulitzer Prize-winning *Appalachian Spring*, incorporated a number of old Quaker songs, and later became a favourite orchestral suite in the concert hall. Copland also provided a number of film scores, including those for *Of Mice and Men* and *Our Town*, and won an Academy Award with his score for *The Heiress*.

During World War II Eugene Goossens commissioned from him an orchestral *Fanfare for the Common Man*, and around the same time Copland chose a patriotic theme in *A Lincoln Portrait* for speaker and orchestra, with words chosen from Abraham Lincoln's speeches, including the noble declaration, 'As I would not be a slave, I would not be a master'.

This attitude has been Copland's own in his extensive teaching and lecturing activities. For twenty-five years he was head of the composition

The composer Aaron Copland has been not only an authoritative conductor of his own work but also a generously encouraging interpreter of contemporaries and younger American composers.

faculty at Berkshire Music Centre, Tanglewood, where many colleagues and pupils have testified that he never wanted any of them to be 'little Aarons'. Leonard Bernstein has spoken of his ability to communicate excitement while at the same time displaying unfailing 'refinement, care and commitment'. His book *What to listen for in Music*, largely transcribed by a student from easy-going lectures which Copland once gave at a New York centre for adult education, does more than any solemn treatise could to promote enjoyment and understanding through perceptive listening rather than earnest analysis.

In 1977 Copland was awarded the Congressional Medal of Honour.

OTHER WORKS: Four Symphonies. Clarinet concerto (for Benny Goodman). Opera *The Tender Land*. Orchestral *Music for a Great City*, and Orchestral Variations based on the Piano Variations. Song cycles *Twelve Poems of Emily Dickinson* and *Old American Songs*.

Corelli, Arcangelo (1653–1713) Italian composer. Born in a small town near Bologna after his father's death, the boy studied music from the age of thirteen, travelled through Europe as a virtuoso violinist, and finally settled in Rome to a comfortable life in the household of the Pope's nephew Cardinal Ottoboni. As well as directing concerts, playing, and teaching, he became internationally famous with his output of scintillating trio sonatas and *concerti grossi* (including the well-loved *Christmas Concerto*), forms which were virtually invented by him and which paved the way for works in similar vein by Vivaldi, Bach and Handel. Unlike so many great musicians, he died a rich man.

counterpoint Support for the melodic line of a simple song is most commonly provided by blocks of chords in harmony with the notes of that melody. In contrast, a great deal of early church music and later instrumental music favoured polyphony, the sounding of two or more separate melodic lines together, crossing and colliding so that notes work sometimes together and sometimes against each other – hence 'counter-point' and 'contrapuntal'. Each line should sound satisfying in itself on the horizontal plane while at the same time creating interesting clashes or concords when closing in, moving away, or intersecting vertically with another. In a way it is rather like knitting or the warp and woof of weaving: individual strands of differing but complementary colours are intertwined in combinations which may sometimes be puzzling in the early stages but which at the end reveal a complete and coherent pattern – in this case audible instead of visible.

Double counterpoint and invertible counterpoint are interchangeable terms for the process of reversing upper-and-lower contrapuntal lines. Triple, quadruple or quintuple counterpoint allows for more complex interchanges. Linear counterpoint is a modern method which concentrates on the horizontal or linear development of themes without paying too much heed to any harmonic clashes or problems which may arise. (*See also* **Bach** and **fugue**.)

Couperin, François (1668–1733) French composer and harpsichordist. There were several musicians in different generations of the Couperin family, but the genius of François was so outstanding that he was dubbed 'Couperin le Grand'. For many years Court musician and keyboard tutor to Louis XIV's children, he devised regular Sunday concerts at Versailles and contributed a wealth of trio sonatas and *ordres* (or sets) of harpsichord pieces (about two hundred and thirty in all) incorporating a wide variety of dance measures. Many have programmatic titles such as *Les Petits Moulins à vent* (*The Little Windmills*) with its rippling semiquavers, and *Les Barricades mystérieuses*

The title page of the first edition in 1689 of Corelli's Trio Sonatas, Opus 3, bearing the arms of Duke Francis II of Modena, to whom the set is dedicated.

(*The Mysterious Barriers*) with its complicated syncopation of tied notes and stumbling rhythm. 'I always have a definite idea in mind,' Couperin wrote: 'the titles correspond to those ideas.'

He was adamant that all his *agrémens*, or grace notes, should be played strictly as written and not, as in so many performances by his contemporaries, freely interpreted to suit personal tastes. Thus played, many of his distinctive turns of phrase provoke not merely a technical appreciation of their imaginative mannerisms but an indefinable sense of something which the great harpsichordist Wanda Landowska once called 'elusive anguish'.

In 1717 Couperin published a definitive book on keyboard technique, *L'Art de toucher le clavecin*.

OTHER WORKS: 'Royal Concerts' for chamber ensemble. Chamber sonatas in memory of Lully and Corelli. Forty-two organ pieces. Psalms for Holy Week, *Leçons des ténèbres*.

courante A seventeenth-century dance in 3/2 time with 'running', or gliding, steps. Its music was much used in suites by Bach, Handel and others, coming usually between the *allemande* and the *sarabande*, though other dance movements might be interpolated.

Covent Garden Opera House The Royal Opera House in London takes its name from a convent garden which once existed here. Founded in 1732 purely as a theatre for drama, it was nevertheless the setting for some of Handel's operas and for all his later oratorios from *Samson* onwards. The theatre was burnt out in 1808, replaced in 1809, gutted by fire again in 1856, and reconstructed on its present lines between 1856 and 1858. During World War II it was used as a dance hall, reopening in 1946 with a resident opera and ballet company. Among famous conductors who have served as musical directors are Beecham, Kubelik, Solti, Colin Davis, and Haitink.

Coward, (Sir) Noël (1899–1973) Described in the British *Dictionary of National Biography* as 'actor, playwright, lyricist, producer, occasional poet and Sunday painter'. Coward's air of languid ennui as singer and actor was misleading: in his field he was a hard-working, skilled craftsman, with a gift for witty lyrics and well-wrought melodies in musical shows such as *Bitter Sweet* and *Conversation Piece*.

Cowell, Henry (1897–1965) American composer. A pioneer of experimental music, Cowell in his youth had already tried to explore new ways of playing the piano, and introduced 'clusters' of clashing adjacent notes in a piece called *The Tides of Manaunaun*, composed when he was about fifteen. He made his début as a pianist in San Francisco just before his seventeenth birthday,

A silk programme for a Gala Performance by command of King Edward VII at Covent Garden Opera House in July 1903 in honour of the President of the French Republic.

and after World War I travelled in the USA and Europe playing many of his own compositions. He introduced the technique of the 'string piano', where the player brushes or hits the strings directly, and collaborated on the construction of a musical machine called a rhythmicon to sort out complex rhythms electronically.

Like his pupil John Cage, he was interested in aleatory music, and in his *Mosaic Quartet* provided the instrumentalists, as the title suggests, with fragments which they had to assemble for themselves. Under the spell of Indian, Persian and Japanese music, philosophy, and instruments, he composed two concertos for koto and orchestra, the koto being a Japanese stringed instrument rather like a psaltery. He was also busy as a teacher and promoter of American music, and wrote a book, *New Musical Resources*, to explain his beliefs about modern trends and techniques.

OTHER WORKS: Twenty-one symphonies. String quartet, *Quartet Euphometric*. Piano *Snows of Fujiyama; Aeolian Harp; The Banshee*. Choral pieces and songs.

Craft, Robert (1923–) American conductor and musicologist, associated with the music of Schoenberg and his circle. From 1948 he collaborated closely with Stravinsky on his memoirs and many recording sessions.

Cramer, Johann Baptist (1771–1858) German pianist and teacher. Born in Mannheim, the boy was taken when only a year old to London by his father Wilhelm, who became leader of the royal band. Taught music by his father and Clementi, Cramer himself became a distinguished teacher and the author of eighty-four *Studies* for piano in two volumes and other sets of exercises. The first publication of these was by the firm of Chappell, of which Cramer became a partner until, in 1824, he and two colleagues founded the publishing house of J.B. Cramer & Co.

crooning The word once referred to the gentle humming of soothing music to a baby, but in the 1930s came to be applied to soft, sentimental singing of popular dance-band tunes in a way made possible by the introduction of the microphone and electric amplification. One of its earliest, and certainly most accomplished, practitioners was Bing Crosby.

cross relation The juxtaposition of a note in its diatonic form with a passing chromatic note in another voice – a polyphonic device frequently employed by William Byrd.

crumhorn One of the most popular medieval wind instruments, usually made from boxwood with a reed-cap which kept the player's lips away from the actual reed. It had a number of finger-holes and sometimes a few keys for lower notes, with the bell end curved like a hockey-stick.

csárdás The national dance of Hungary, consisting of a slow movement called the *lassú*, usually in a minor key, followed by an increasingly fast *friss* in the major.

cyclic form A method of using a musical theme throughout a composition to give the whole structure an organic unity, as in the *leitmotiv* of Wagnerian operas and the *idée fixe* of Berlioz, or as a bond between movements of a piece such as Brahms's Symphony No. 3, César Franck's Symphony in D minor, and many of the 12-tone rows in serialist works.

Czerny, Karl (1791–1857) Austrian composer and pianist. Son of a piano teacher, Czerny at the age of fourteen set himself up also as a teacher. Liszt was one of his pupils. He gave the first performance of Beethoven's *Emperor* concerto; wrote about a thousand pieces of his own and made innumerable piano transcriptions of other composers' orchestral works, including some for eight pianos; but is best known for his sets of piano exercises and studies.

D

Dallapiccola, Luigi (1904–75) Italian composer. Born in what was then the Austrian province of Istria, which was later a part of Italy before being incorporated into Yugoslavia, Dallapiccola studied music at the Cherubini Conservatoire in Florence and for a while was professor of pianoforte there, but incurred official disfavour because of his opposition to Fascism. At first his compositions showed a considerable debt to Italian madrigalists, blended with his political beliefs in the *Canti di prigionia (Songs of Captivity)* for chorus, two pianos, two harps and percussion, a protest against Mussolini's racial laws. He was the first and most influential Italian composer to develop a keen interest in 12-note serial techniques, as in his three sets of *Liriche greche (Greek Lyrics)* for soprano and various instrumental combinations.

After World War II Dallapiccola spent some time in the United States, but continued to be a major influence in his homeland. Hatred of tyranny still affected his choice of subjects: one of his most powerful works of the immediate post-war period is the one-act opera *Il prigionero (The Prisoner)*, combining an intellectual exercise in the deployment of different tone-rows (in defiance of serialist orthodoxy) with a lyrical and strongly theatrical sense. Towards the end of his life he favoured a spare, delicately intricate style in the vein first of Berg and then of Webern.

OTHER WORKS: Operas *Job; Ulisse*. Ballet *Marsia*. Orchestral *Piccola musica notturna (A little night-music)*. *Dialoghi* for cello and orchestra.

Damrosch, Walter (1862–1950) American (German-born) conductor. He began studying composition and the piano in Breslau and then, when the family moved to the United States, continued his studies in New York. His father Leopold, a violinist and conductor, founded the New York Oratorio Society and staged a season of German opera at the Met between 1884 and 1885. Walter became assistant conductor and, on his father's death, conductor of both the New York Oratorio and the New York Symphony Societies. In 1895 he organized the Damrosch Opera Company with German singers, took it on tour in the United States, and was offered many other conducting posts. In World War I he was responsible for the bandmasters' training school for the American Expeditionary Force in France. Damrosch was the first to conduct radio orchestral concerts relayed nationwide; and in 1927 he was appointed musical adviser to NBC.

Da Ponte, Lorenzo (1749–1838) Italian librettist. Venetian by birth, of Jewish descent, his real

Lorenzo Da Ponte, who on their first meeting promised Mozart a libretto: 'But who knows whether he will be able to keep his word – or be willing either?' In due course he more than fulfilled that promise.

another work in the same vein, and Da Ponte came up with an original story of his own, *Cosi fan tutte* (*Women are all the same*), a great success at the time but later condemned for its stupidity and immorality. There were even attempts in the nineteenth century to use the music for other stories, including a French production of Shakespeare's *Love's Labour's Lost*. Fortunately such prejudices have died away, and a critic and translator such as Edward J. Dent could roundly declare it 'as perfect a libretto as any composer could desire, though no composer but Mozart could ever do it justice'.

Out of favour with a new Emperor, and in serious financial trouble, Da Ponte fled from Vienna, fell in love in Trieste, and set out with his 'companion', as he called her, to make a living in England. He took up his old profession of poet and librettist, this time for the Italian Opera in London, supplementing his income by selling books. Once again in trouble with creditors and in danger of imprisonment for debt, he fled with his family to New York, where in 1805 he set up as a grocer and tobacco dealer and gave Italian lessons. In his seventies he was offered a post as Professor of Italian at Columbia University, and a decade later he was instrumental in bringing to America an Italian opera company and in raising money which was used to build New York's first Italian opera house.

dargason A sixteenth-century English dance and folksong which has been used in the twentieth century by Gustav Holst in his *St Paul's Suite* for strings, where it appears contrapuntally with another old English tune, *Greensleeves*.

Davies, (Sir) Peter Maxwell (1934–) English composer. During the 1950s Maxwell Davies (known to friends and admiring contemporaries as 'Max') studied at the Royal Manchester College of Music in a group which included Harrison Birtwistle, John Ogdon, and Alexander ('Sandy') Goehr. Because of a similarity of interests and creative approach, it became known as the 'Manchester School'. On an Italian government scholarship Maxwell Davies studied in Rome with Goffredo Petrassi and won the 1958 Olivetti prize. Between 1959 and 1962 he taught at Cirencester Grammar School, where, it was said, he 'had children composing as other teachers had them writing essays'.

Following that spell as an inspiring teacher he went to the USA as a student at Princeton with Roger Sessions and Earl Kim, and began work on his opera based on the life of the sixteenth-century English composer John Taverner. His predilections were for a music born of a strange union of medieval modes and isorhythms, with

name was Emanuele Conegliano, but after being converted to the Roman Catholic faith by Bishop Lorenzo Da Ponte he adopted his spiritual tutor's name. After a spell in Dresden, which he had to leave hurriedly because of a scandal involving the wife of a painter and her two daughters, he managed through the influence of Salieri to be officially appointed resident poet to the Court opera in Vienna. Here he wrote libretti for many composers, most memorably for Mozart: so great was the demand for his talented lyrics that on one occasion he was writing three operatic libretti at once – *Don Giovanni* for Mozart, and works for Martin y Soler and Salieri which have not stood the test of time quite so well.

The first great collaboration between Mozart and Da Ponte was on *Le nozze di Figaro* (*The Marriage of Figaro*) which, according to Da Ponte himself, was completed in six weeks. It was he who later suggested the Don Juan (*Don Giovanni*) theme to the composer: there is some suspicion that he did so because he already had the work of a lesser librettist to hand and knew he could adapt it with very little effort. After a revival of *Figaro* in 1789 the Emperor Joseph II demanded

A scene from the première of Peter Maxwell Davies' *Blind Man's Buff* at the Roundhouse, London, in 1972. This masque for soprano, mezzo, mime and stage band was conducted on that occasion by Pierre Boulez.

his own interpretation of serialism. To achieve what they hoped would be ideal performances of contemporary music, and especially of their own, he and his colleague Harrison Birtwistle founded an ensemble which they called the Pierrot Players because its instrumentation derived from that of Schoenberg's *Pierrot lunaire*, which they greatly admired. In 1969 Maxwell Davies wrote for them his wayward, provocative *Eight Songs for a Mad King*, a theatrical piece which made the combination and its material something of a fashionable cult.

In 1970 the players were reformed as the Fires of London, with Maxwell Davies as sole director and major contributor. After years of performing his and other experimental works, the ensemble was disbanded in 1987 because Maxwell Davies found the dual burden of composing and handling administration too much, and felt that in any case the group had outlived its stimulating purpose. A final concert in January of that year included many works with which they had been associated from the start, and also the première of *Winterfold*, a setting of verses by the Orkney poet George Mackay Brown.

From the early 1970s onwards, the composer had spent a large part of his time in the Orkney Islands and had been much influenced by their landscape and traditions, especially as expressed in Mackay Brown's poetry. The atmosphere began to suffuse his compositions: he worked with local children and amateur groups, helped to set up the annual St Magnus Festival (composing a chamber opera *The Martyrdom of St Magnus* for the first event), contributed to the 'Yellow Cake Revue', which opposed the mining of uranium ore ('yellow cake') in the Orkneys, and listened to the historic resonances of the region.

His first major orchestral work drawn from that commitment was the *Stone Litany*, inspired by runic inscriptions left by Viking raiders on the prehistoric stones of the Maes Howe tomb and temple. The composer has stated that he was trying not so much to make verbal sense of the graffiti as to evoke the timeless elements of the site itself and its haunted environment. Even the vocal part is not an explanation but an eerie obbligato to the orchestral imagery. The listener may be allowed to wonder whether the composer was particularly attracted by the inscription declaring that the runes were carved by 'Max the Mighty'!

For the 1979 festival he wrote the *Solstice of Light* in fourteen movements around poems by George Mackay Brown. In essence it is a chronicle of 'incomers' to the Orkneys, including rovers who 'rowed blindly north and north', the 'hewers of mighty stone' who built Maes Howe, the farmers and fishermen, priests and pagan Vikings, and in our own time the greedy mineral hunters and exploiters. Another poem by Mackay Brown on the devastation of crofting communities let to an orchestral work originally conceived as *Black Pentecost*, which was eventually reworked as Davies's First Symphony; the Second was inspired by wave swirls in Scapa Flow.

In spite of his rich palette of orchestral and vocal tone colours, none of these compositions could be called tone poems or programme music. The original inspiration may be visual and intensely personal; but the resulting music is pure music, invigorating in its thrusting urgency, often startling in its vocal eccentricities, and perhaps most compelling when, apparently static and meditative, it shifts subtly between major and minor harmonies conditioned by its creator's abiding love of medieval modes.

OTHER WORKS: Opera *The Lighthouse*. Ballet *Salome*. Three symphonies. *Sinfonia* for chamber orchestra. Orchestral *St Thomas Wake*, a foxtrot based on a pavan by John Bull. Voices and Fires of London ensemble, *From Stone to Thorn*. Two Taverner fantasias.

Davis, (Sir) Colin (1927–) English conductor. His first appearances were with the Kalmar Chamber Orchestra and the Chelsea Opera Group, but he was not widely recognized until at short notice he took over a concert performance of *Don Giovanni* and soon became for five years musical director of Sadler's Wells Opera. After guest appearances in the United States with the Minneapolis, Boston and other orchestras, and international tours with the London Symphony Orchestra, he again went, late in 1966, to the United States for a highly successful performance of Britten's *Peter Grimes* at the New York Met. In 1968 he returned to conduct the New York Phil-

harmonic in a series of works by Berlioz. Davis probably did more than anyone else to revive Berlioz's music and refine its interpretation for modern audiences, conducting concert performances and full-scale stage productions as well as directing definitive recordings, including one of *Les Troyens* (*The Trojans*) which won seven major awards. From 1971 to 1986 he was chief conductor and musical director of the Royal Opera, Covent Garden.

Debussy, (Achille-) Claude (1862–1918) French composer. Treated somewhat offhandedly by his parents, who ran a china shop in St-Germain-en-Laye, Debussy took his first piano lessons while staying with an aunt in Cannes and then had further instruction from Verlaine's mother-in-law in Paris. At the age of ten he was admitted to the Conservatoire, where he was regarded as a pianist of great promise who, perversely, seemed to dislike the instrument but to adore music itself. In 1880 he switched to composition classes, winning a second-class *Prix de Rome* and in 1884 a first with his cantata *L'Enfant prodigue*. He did not much enjoy his spell in Rome, and was glad to return to Paris, even though it meant living

The cover of the first edition of Debussy's *La Mer*, adapted from a painting by the Japanese artist Hokusai, of whom the composer was a great admirer.

LA MER

Copyright by A. Durand & Fils, 1905

with his far from understanding parents. For a while he fell under the spell of Wagner, visiting Bayreuth and becoming involved in the growing cult; but then he reacted against 'the old poisoner'. His own style was much more influenced by the sounds of the eastern gamelan players heard at the Paris Exposition of 1889 and by his impressionist painter friends and symbolist poets: he set Verlaine poems in *Ariettes oubliées* (*Forgotten ariettas*), and the celebrated *Prélude à l'après-midi d'un faune* (*Prelude to the Afternoon of a Faun*) was inspired by Mallarmè. From an early stage he was employing harmonies and dissonances which he heard in his head but which proved difficult to translate into regular written format, and even more difficult to offer with any hope of approval to his teachers and contemporary critics. He was accused of being either careless or wantonly perverse.

His personal life caused equal controversy. For some years he lived in straitened circumstances with a mistress, Gabrielle Dupont. During this liaison he became engaged to another woman, a singer, but the engagement was broken off with unpleasant recriminations. In 1897 Gabrielle tried to commit suicide. He became involved in another affair with one of her friends, Rosalie Texier, a mannequin, and in his turn threatened to commit suicide – if Rosalie would not marry him. She succumbed; but in 1904 he left her for a banker's wife, Emma Bardac, who paid for the apartment in the Avenue du Bois de Boulogne which was to be his base thereafter. Rosalie attempted suicide, and his friends were so outraged that for a time Debussy and Emma sought refuge in England, where at the Grand Hotel in Eastbourne he completed the three orchestral sketches which make up *La Mer* (*The Sea*). In 1908 he married Emma, who more than two years previously had presented him with a daughter, for whom he wrote the *Children's Corner* suite.

Throughout all this he was exploring a new musical landscape and trying to capture it in sound as a painter might capture a scene on a canvas. He felt intuitively that musical themes should of their own essence suggest their only possible orchestral colouring, even if this involved breaking every academic rule. Rhythms, too, must arise spontaneously: they could not, he said, be contained within bars. Yet there was no hint of anarchy in this. Striving to convey his meanings, he sought simplicity and concentration of emotions and resources rather than any self-indulgent sprawl. At the same time he was venturing into a symbolic, impressionist world whose harmonic resonances he had assimilated as a pianist, built around block chords and 'layers' of sound which defied traditional theories. He revivified old modal styles, exploited the whole-tone scale, and dwelt lovingly on long sequences of interlinked dissonances instead of promptly resolving them, so that everything he wrote seemed to flow on inexorably, enchantingly, in its own translucent logic, tempting the ear rather than dictating to it. *Reflets dans l'eau* (*Reflections in the Water*) depicts not merely the convolutions of rippling water but their almost mathematical relationships. The books of *Etudes*, studies dedicated to the memory of Chopin, are as much an affirmation of his own beliefs and chromatic adventurousness as 'The 48' are of Bach's dedication to the contrapuntal forms of his time.

Such breaks with tradition accorded admirably with the elusive text of Maurice Maeterlinck's play *Pelléas et Mélisande*, in the operatic version of which the composer modelled his vocal lines on the playwright's prose rhythms rather than on four-square conventions of recitative and aria bar-lengths. It was first produced in Paris in 1902, and remained in the repertory as one of his greatest achievements. He sought different tone colours in major orchestral works such as *Images*, the ballet music for *Jeux* (*Games*), staged by Diaghilev in 1912, and the smaller scale, exquisite *Danse sacrée et danse profane* (*Dances Sacred and Profane*) for harp and strings.

In 1915 Debussy, after a period of failing health, had an operation for cancer of the rectum, and for the last three years of his life wore a colostomy appliance which was so uncomfortable that work was impossible: 'Music has quite left me,' he lamented. His final public appearance was as pianist in a performance of his own last work, the sonata for violin and piano.

OTHER WORKS: Orchestral *Nocturnes. Rapsodie* for saxophone and orchestra. Incidental music to mystery play *Le Martyre de Saint-Sébastien* (*The Martyrdom of St Sebastian*). Piano suites and pieces including *Clair de lune* (*Moonlight*) and *Préludes*, which include *La Cathédrale engloutie* (*The Submerged Cathedral*). Song cycle *Chansons de Bilitis* (*Songs of Bilitis*), settings of prose poems by Pierre Louÿs.

degree Notes of a major scale are classified, from the tonic upwards, as 1st, 2nd and 3rd degrees, and so on. In each scale there are 7 degrees before the full octave is reached, 8 becoming once more a 1st degree. As well as numerical identification they are also named as follows (using, in this example, the key of C major as a guide): tonic(C), supertonic(D), mediant(E), subdominant(F), dominant(G), submediant(A), leading note(B) ... and so to the tonic(C) an octave higher.

Delibes, Léo (1836–91) French composer and organist. While studying at the Paris Conservatoire he sang in various church choirs, and at the age of seventeen was appointed to the first of several organ posts. He also became accompanist at the Théatre Lyrique and, in 1865, second chorusmaster at the Opéra. He composed a number of bright, accomplished operettas, and in 1883 wrote the opera *Lakmé* with an exotic Indian setting and the celebrated 'Bell Song'; but his reputation rests more securely upon two earlier ballets, *Coppélia* and *Sylvia*.

Delius, Frederick (1862–1934) English composer. One of the fourteen children of a German immigrant who set up in the Bradford wool trade and served on the management committee of the Hallé concerts, Frederick was expected to join the family business. When he revolted against this idea his father, Julius, sent him to Florida to run an orange plantation. Instead of concentrating on administration, young Delius took music lessons from Thomas Ward, a Catholic church organist from Jacksonville. After further family conflict Julius relented and agreed to pay for his son's music studies in Leipzig; but Scandinavia and Paris proved greater attractions, and the composer shunned any further formal musical training.

His style was influenced by the flowing textures of Wagner and the chromatic harmonies of French composers, producing rhapsodic, richly orchestrated evocations of places and emotions – usually those of nostalgia for a lost world, drifting irreclaimably into a shimmering past. It could be self-indulgent, and falls too often into a lazy 6/8 or 9/8 gait; but at its best it conjures up a quite individual, iridescent landscape. Negro melodies

Frederick Delius during his years of blindness and paralysis, with his wife Jelka.

93

from Florida run through *Appalachia*, variations on a slave song for baritone, chorus and orchestra, and through his opera *Koanga*, again on a slavery theme. In spite of this, and although he met and married a Danish painter, Jelka Rosen, in Paris and made a home with her at Grez-sur-Loing near Fontainebleau for the rest of his life (apart from a spell in England during World War I), the sheer sound of his music more often evokes scenes of his Yorkshire childhood than any American or European atmosphere. The opera *A Village Romeo and Juliet* is based on a German story and had its first performance in Berlin; but the intermezzo, *The Walk to the Paradise Garden*, immediately conjures up a vision of pastoral England. The same could be said of the Scandinavian-inspired *Eventyr (Once upon a time)* and even of the supposedly eastern flavour of the incidental music to Flecker's *Hassan*. It is open and unmistakable in the *North Country Sketches* and his orchestral adaptation of a folk song from Lincolnshire, *Brigg Fair*.

More affirmative and less nostalgic is the setting of some rather declamatory master-race philosophy from Nietschze's *Also sprach Zarathustra (Thus spake Zarathustra)* in *A Mass of Life*, first conducted by one of Delius's most dedicated champions, Thomas Beecham.

In 1922 Delius was attacked by a paralysis brought on by syphilis, which within four years left him blind and helpless, unable to write down any of the music he wished to create. In 1928 a young Yorkshire admirer, Eric Fenby, came to live in the house and painstakingly acted as his amanuensis. Delius died and was buried in France, but a year later was reinterred in the churchyard of St Peter's at Limpsfield, Surrey, to be joined almost immediately by his widow Jelka, who had accompanied the corpse to England and died of pneumonia two days later.

OTHER WORKS: Opera *Fennimore and Gerda*. Orchestral suites and tone poems including two *Dance Rhapsodies, Summer Night on the River* and *On hearing the first cuckoo in spring*. Choral and orchestral *Sea Drift*. Violin concerto. Double concerto for violin and cello. String quartet. Three violin sonatas. Songs including *Three English Songs* and *Seven Danish Songs*.

Deller, Alfred (1912–79) English counter-tenor. After singing in a local church choir, Deller trained his voice to use the high range which had been popular in the time of Handel and Purcell, quite distinct from and purer than the falsetto or castrato tone. In the years immediately following World War II he revived much forgotten music, brought new lustre to the songs of the great lutenists such as Dowland and Campion, and led the way for other counter-tenors. He was the first to sing the part of Oberon in Britten's opera *A Midsummer Night's Dream*. His Deller Consort was formed in 1948 to give authentic performances of baroque sacred and secular music, and made many invaluable recordings.

Dello Joio, Norman (1913–) American composer and organist. The son of a New York Catholic church organist and choirmaster, he followed in his father's footsteps and became organist at St Ann's Church in New York. Much influenced by Gregorian chant, Italian opera and American popular music, he has composed a number of expansive, melodic concertos and other orchestral works such as *Air Power* and *Colonial Variations*. His dramatic sense steered him towards opera, including *The Triumph of St Joan*, and most successfully towards ballet: he wrote several works for the dancer and choreographer Martha Graham, including *Seraphic Dialogue*, also based on the St Joan theme.

descant The word was originally used in connection with early counterpoint to describe the addition of extra melodic parts to plainsong. Its most common application today is to the provision of a new melodic line above the straightforward chorus of a hymn, either written or improvised, usually by a treble or soprano voice.

Desprès, Josquin (1440–1521) Flemish composer and singer. He sang at Italian courts and later in Milan Cathedral, the Papal Chapel at Rome, and the household of Louis XII of France. Composing more than a hundred motets and a great number of masses, he achieved an unusually wide circulation for his works because they were printed in book form, a new and rare procedure. His advanced polyphonic style and the contrasts he achieved between high and low voices had a great influence on succeeding composers.

development Sometimes known as 'working out', the term has several different musical applications. In general it refers to the modifying or developing in a sonata form movement of themes stated earlier. A second section may, for instance, be built around fragments of a motif from the first section, or a version of that motif augmented, diminished, or played upside down or backwards. New material may be introduced to conflict with or disguise the original: Beethoven made considerable use of this, and with the advance and expansion of the symphony the development, working-out element could also be found in other parts of the work, including the coda. The development section is also of great importance in a fugue.

diapason The Greek word means 'all through' and so is applied in a musical sense to a full octave. The French also use it to describe a tuning-fork, and *diapason normal* defines accepted concert pitch. A more common usage is in connection with the organ: diapason stops are the foundation stops which provide the instrument's distinctive tone, either open or plugged (stopped), the stopped pipes being an octave lower than the open ones.

diatonic The diatonic scale and harmonies are those which stay within the key indicated in the key signature at the beginning of a composition, whether in the major or minor. Any notes introduced into the piece which do not belong within the diatonic melodies or harmonies are called chromatic.

Dibdin, Charles (1745–1814) English composer. Born in Southampton and christened in the Sailors' Church there, Dibdin always had a patriotic admiration for merchant seamen and the Royal Navy. When he became a successful writer of popular songs (including *The Bells of Aberdovey*) for the stage and for tavern concerts where he performed his own material, he produced many tributes to gallant mariners such as the faithful *Tom Bowling* and to 'the lass that loves a sailor'. When the fleet mutinied at Spithead and the Nore in 1797 he was sent to sing his stirring nautical airs to the mutineers, and Napoleon was reported as saying that Dibdin had done more for England's glory than any of Nelson's achievements. Official recognition, however, was long in coming, until William Pitt granted him an official pension, which Dibdin supplemented by selling rights in over three hundred of his more than a thousand songs, many of them later plagiarized or misappropriated by his own sons. A change of government resulted in the sudden abolition of his pension, but the incensed public raised a subscription and also ultimately shamed the government into restoring the pension.

differential tone Sometimes called a *resultant tone*, this refers to the extraneous sound which may be heard when two notes are played together in such a way as to produce a lower or higher tone, either as a result of the difference between their vibrations or as the sum of their vibrations. A 'difference tone' can be calculated by means of clashing harmonics to produce a sort of buzz for dramatic or provocative effect.

diminution In canonic and fugal forms, or in development sections of sonata form, notes of the original theme can be 'shrunk' by shortening their time values to produce a livelier echo of an originally stately theme or to work contrapuntally against that theme. Also, intervals between notes of the scale are said to be diminished when they have been reduced by a semitone: this occurs most commonly in the diminished triad, when in the key of C, for example, the chord of C/E/G becomes C/E/G flat, and in the useful modulation device of a diminished seventh within which all intervals are minor thirds: on a root of C, this produces C/E flat/F sharp(or G flat)/A/C. (*See also* **augmentation**.)

D'Indy, Vincent (1851–1931) French composer. The boy's mother died at his birth, and he was brought up by his paternal grandmother, an accomplished pianist. He served during the Franco-Prussian war, and upon his return sent the music of a piano quartet and other pieces to César Franck, who agreed to take him as a pupil. To supplement his income and widen his experience he also joined the Colonne Orchestra of Paris as a drummer, and in 1875 became chorus-master of their regular concerts. In 1894 he was one of the founders of the Schola Cantorum for the study of church music, teaching there and at the Conservatoire.

Major influences on d'Indy's floridly orchestrated work were Liszt and Wagner, but he also espoused his tutor Franck's 'cyclic' form. At the same time he drew upon simple folk melodies, as in his *Symphonie sur un chant montagnard français* (*Symphony on a French Mountain Song*), based on a tune from the Cévennes region, which has led to its alternative name of *Symphonie Cévenole*. His choral and orchestral work *Le Chant de la cloche* (*Song of the Bell*) is of almost Berliozian dimensions.

OTHER WORKS: Operas including *La Légende de Saint-Christophe* (*The Legend of St Christopher*). Orchestral tone poem *Jour d'été à la montagne* (*Summer Day on the Mountain*). Three string quartets. Piano *Promenades*.

discord One of the most frequently misused words in the musical language. It does not mean anything noisy or necessarily ugly, but merely an assembly of notes that create a waiting, slightly jarring effect which the ear demands should be resolved into a simple satisfying concord. The whole palette of musical coloration demands the deployment of stimulating discords to keep the mind alert and lead it towards a self-sufficient resolution.

dissonance The sounding together of notes which produce a discord, or the use of an interval between notes in a melody which disturbs the ear, as opposed to a satisfying consonance. Mozart's string quartet in C, K465, has been nicknamed the 'Dissonance Quartet' because of the intricate chromatic interweavings and clashes of its opening bars.

Dittersdorf, Karl Ditters von (1739–99) Austrian composer. The son of a Court and theatrical costumier, the gifted boy was taken on as violinist in the orchestra of a provincial prince, who included his musicians in his entourage during campaigns in the Seven Years' War. After serving with several other high-ranking patrons, including the Prince-Bishop of Breslau, Karl Ditters was able to buy himself into the nobility and add a fine flourish to his name. His compositions include forty operas and operettas, including the comic *Doktor und Apotheke*, a great success in Vienna in 1786, and he even attempted his own versions of *The Marriage of Figaro* and *The Merry Wives of Windsor*. In addition he produced over one hundred symphonies, some thirty-five concertos, and a vast quantity of chamber works and church music.

divertimento and **divertissement** As the words imply, the music so described is meant to divert and amuse. Consisting as a rule of a number of short movements in contrasting tempos, the divertimento (sometimes called a serenade or cassation) became very popular in the eighteenth century: Mozart wrote over thirty for various instrumental combinations, and Haydn about one hundred

and seventy-five. A divertissement was much the same, but often included songs and dances, especially when used as an interlude in a theatrical production.

Dixieland One of the earliest forms of jazz to capture the imagination of the general public, originating from the street marching tunes of New Orleans, largely improvised by wind instrumentalists who could play 'by ear', with the backing of drums and frequently a banjo: not until it settled indoors could it afford the luxury

King Oliver's Creole Jazz Band, a more lasting influence on jazz history than the white musicians of the Original Dixieland Jazz Band. The players were Baby Dodds (drums), Honoré Dutrey (trombone), Joe ('King') Oliver (cornet and leader), Louis Armstrong (second cornet), Bill Johnson (double bass and banjo), Johnny Dodds (clarinet), and Louis Armstrong's second wife Lil Hardin (piano).

of a piano. The rough and raucous, rhythmically stimulating syncopation made its first impact on Europe in 1919 with the London appearance of the five players of the Original Dixieland Jazz Band. In its homeland there were developments in different directions, most notably into the gangland speakeasy music of Chicago style, from which came players like Pee Wee Russell, Bud Freeman, and the flamboyant guitarist and session organizer, Eddie Condon. The swing era damped down interest in Dixieland until in the late 1930s Bob Crosby's orchestra revived it in a form which offended some purists, setting improvised solos against orchestral arrangements with a Dixieland flavour, and then using a small group closer to the original style in Bob Crosby's Bob Cats. Another talented group which contributed to the revival with a series of vigorous recordings in 1939 was Muggsy Spanier's Ragtime Band. More recent re-creations by what might be called jazz neo-Dixielanders have tended to be too earnestly contrived, lacking the spontaneity which is the essence of the genre. (*See also* **jazz**.)

dodecaphonic *See* **twelve-tone system**.

Dohnányi, Ernö (Ernst von) (1877–1960) Hungarian composer. Born in what was then Pozsony to Hungarians but Pressburg to Austrians, and is now Bratislava in Czechoslovakia, Dohnányi became an international concert pianist of some reknown but decided to give this up in favour of teaching and composition. He taught for several years in Berlin before returning to his homeland and becoming director of the Budapest Conservatoire at the end of World War I. He was also appointed conductor of the Budapest Philharmonic Orchestra; received a generous grant from the State; and in 1931 took over directorship of Hungarian broadcasting. In 1948 he again left, this time for political reasons, and became professor of pianoforte and composition at Florida State College.

Although both Bartók and Kodály were closely associated with and influenced by him, his own music showed fewer nationalist tendencies than theirs, clinging rather to a Brahmsian tradition. He wrote several operas, symphonies and chamber works, but is remembered today mainly for his inventive *Variations on a Nursery Song* for piano and orchestra.

Dolmetsch family The German word *Dolmetscher* means an interpreter, and Arnold Dolmetsch and his successors have undoubtedly presented the world with some of the most rewarding interpretations and reinterpretations of early music and the best ways in which to play it. Born in France of Swiss descent, Arnold Dolmetsch (1858–1940) studied the violin in Brussels and London before going to work in a piano factory in Boston, USA. In 1911 he began making clavichords and harpsichords in Paris, before settling at Haslemere in England in 1914 and founding the firm in which all members of his family were supposed not merely to manufacture instruments, but to learn how to play them correctly.

Their revival of the recorder, long abandoned in favour of the modern flute, has had a lasting influence on the musical activities in British schools. They also produced viols and other half-forgotten instruments in order to play music of past centuries in authentic style: Arnold's son Carl (1911–) is known to have mastered at least twenty-five different ones. In 1925 the annual Haslemere Festival of Early Music was originated, and in 1928 the Dolmetsch Foundation was established to promulgate Arnold's ideals and to help with festival organization.

dominant In any diatonic scale, major or minor, the dominant is the fifth degree above the tonic. In the key of C, for instance, this would be G. The chord of the *dominant seventh* is one of the most familiar discords in music, when the ear waits for its ritual resolution on to the tonic triad. Early modes also gave the dominant great importance, but its placing was less inevitable, depending on whether the mode was authentic or plagal. (*See also* **modes**.)

Domingo, Placido (1941–) Spanish tenor. After a tour with the composer and guitarist Federico Tórroba, Domingo's parents settled in Mexico with their two children and founded their own *zarzuela* company. (A *zarzuela* is a Spanish form of operetta-cum-drama.) The boy took private piano lessons and was entered in the National Conservatory, where he studied music among other subjects. When it was realized that he had an exceptional singing voice he was taken on in his parents' company as a baritone, but friends persuaded them to let him audition for the National Opera. He was accepted – as a tenor – and sang many minor parts before his real début in a major rôle as Alfredo in *La traviata*, in Monterrey in 1961. A few months later he had engagements in Dallas, New Orleans and Hartford, and then went with his newly-wed wife Marta for a six-month season with the Hebrew National Opera in Tel Aviv, where in fact they stayed for a full year.

Domingo's début at the Metropolitan Opera House, New York, in 1968 took place several days earlier than planned. At less than an hour's notice he had to stand in for Franco Corelli in *Adriana Lecouvreur*, and made an instant sensation. He went on to establish a worldwide reputation

(Left) Placido Domingo, the Spanish-born singer who began as a baritone but was to make his reputation as an operatic tenor.

(Below) A self-caricature by Donizetti, whose early operas made such an impact on Rome audiences that after one performance he and his leading tenor left the theatre to the accompaniment of a military band along torchlit streets.

in lyrical, heroic Italian rôles — including in 1987 a memorable appearance at Covent Garden, London, as Verdi's *Otello* — but has also sung Wagner's *Lohengrin* in Hamburg and recorded the part of Walther von Stolzing in *Die Meistersinger*. Among other recordings, quite apart from his operatic interpretations, are recitals of the *zarzuelas* with which he began his career, and a number of South American tangos.

Donizetti, Gaetano (1797–1848) Italian composer. One of the six children of a north Italian pawnshop employee, Donizetti studied music in his home town of Bergamo before going on to the Liceo Filarmonico in Bologna. For a while he served in the Austrian army, but managed to compose a number of operas in his spare time. His fluency and facility in turning out stage pieces at short notice made him in his middle twenties a favourite of producers and performers all over Italy. He had already turned out some thirty operas before his great international success,

Anna Bolena. Two years later came the comic opera *L'elisir d'amore* (*The Elixir of Love*), followed by a string of what today might well be called 'hit musicals'.

All Donizetti's writing catered for the fashion in dazzling displays of vocal pyrotechnics, exhibitionistic yet intoxicating when performed by gifted coloratura singers with the right dramatic gestures. Frequently he returned to fruitful sources from British history such as the true stories of Mary Stuart, Robert Devereux, Alfred the Great and others, along with fictional creations such as Sir Walter Scott's *The Bride of Lammermoor*, radiantly transformed into *Lucia di Lammermoor*.

At the height of his fame the composer was struck down by venereal disease which led to paralysis, insanity, and a final collapse into a protracted coma, until in 1848 he was taken home to Bergamo to die.

Dorati, Antal (1906–) Hungarian conductor (American citizen 1947). After studying in Budapest and Vienna he took on a succession of operatic conducting posts before establishing himself as a leading ballet conductor with the Ballet Russe de Monte Carlo, Original Ballet Russe, and Ballet Theatre, as well as arranging music for the ballet. After World War II he was engaged as principal conductor by a number of leading American orchestras, and between 1962 and 1966 was conductor of the BBC Symphony Orchestra. He has recorded definitive versions of all Haydn's symphonies with the Philharmonia Hungarica.

double stopping On stringed instruments, stopping (i.e. fingering) two or more strings at once to produce chords or to provide harmony on certain strings while playing the melody on another. This can in fact be more easily achieved when some of the notes are played on an open, non-fingered string. Corelli and Vivaldi made frequent use of such methods in their sonatas and concertos, and the virtuoso Paganini made great play with fast double-stopping to impress his listeners.

doubling The word has two musical connotations. Two instruments or groups of instruments playing a sequence of notes in unison are said to be doubling. The word also applies to an orchestral player switching from oboe to cor anglais, and to the dance band saxophonist who 'doubles on' clarinet.

Dowland, John (1563–1626) English composer and lutenist. Records are unclear as to whether Dowland was born in London or County Dublin in Ireland, and little is known about his early life or musical education. It is well established, however, that at the age of seventeen he went to Paris in the service of the English ambassador, Sir Henry Cobham, and was converted to Catholicism. This made it difficult for him to obtain an appointment he craved as one of Queen Elizabeth I's lutenists so he returned to the Continent, singing and playing in noble households for a spell before reverting to Protestantism.

In 1597 he published his *First Book of Songs or Ayres of foure parts with Tableture for the Lute*, shrewdly dedicating it to the influential George Carey, a leading persecutor of English Catholics. Still there seemed no opening in his homeland, so for seven years from 1598 onwards he served as lutenist to King Christian IV of Denmark, and there he wrote and published many of his most compelling songs.

The searching harmonies of Dowland's accompaniments were far in advance of their time, and the melodies themselves show a genius for expressive nuances and free rhythms which never failed him even in his moods of deep depression. He himself made many sidelong references and puns about the melancholy and tribulations of 'Doleful Dowland'. Among the most moving of his songs is *In Darkness let me Dwell*, contrasting with the sprightliness of *Fine Knacks for Ladies* — both flawlessly interpreted in our day, like many other Dowland pieces, by the counter-tenor Alfred Deller. In *Lachrimae* he published twenty-one pieces for viols and lute, consisting of dance movements with seven pavans built around his song *Flow, my Tears*.

Belatedly Dowland was appointed to the English Court as a second lutenist, and played at James I's funeral; but in weary and embittered mood he composed little more music.

D'Oyly Carte family *See* **Gilbert and Sullivan**.

drum The most ancient form of musical instrument must have been a percussion instrument of some kind, either a simple piece of wood or a piece of wood hollowed out, which would have improved its resonance. Animal hides stretched over a hollow body of wood or clay became the basis of drums as they still are today. They have been used for sacred purposes, as signalling devices, and as a means of stirring up excitement with the throbbing of war drums. Excitement has also been a major ingredient of dance band and jazz drummers' playing, not merely keeping the tempo behind the 'front line' of wind instruments but indulging in complex solo 'breaks' and long passages using all the resources of bass drum, snare drum, cymbals, and other features of the drum kit. (*See also* **The Orchestra and its Instruments**.)

duet and **duo** Instrumental or vocal pieces for two players or singers. Piano duets are usually performed by players at separate instruments, but some arrangements cater for four hands at one piano. A piece for, say, a tenor and soprano, whether accompanied by piano, guitar or full orchestra, is referred to as a duet, and many Victorian drawing-room ballads for amateur singers (frequently tenor and baritone) were written in this form. The word *duo* should, strictly speaking, be reserved for an instrumental piece. Weber composed a Grand Duo Concertant for clarinet and piano; Ravel's sonata for violin and cello is in effect a duo; and Bartók's forty-four violin duos are among the most challenging yet rewarding in the repertoire.

Dufay, Guillaume (1400–74) Flemish composer. A chorister who studied music while at Cambrai Cathedral, he became a singer in the Papal choir in Rome, and in 1431 composed a motet to celebrate the election of Eugenius IV as Pope. After a period in the service of the Duke of Burgundy, Dufay spent most of his later life back in Cambrai as the cathedral's director of music. The ambitious polyphony of his compositions was allied with a sweetness of harmonic intervals which led the way to the tonic-dominant balance of music conditioning most Western music up to our own century. His isorhythmic themes, with changing sequences of notes above a steady pulse pattern, were forerunners of 'cyclic' composition. One of his greatest masses, *L'Homme armé* (*The Armed Man*), introduces a popular song as its *cantus firmus*; and he wrote a number of delightful secular part-songs.

Dukas, Paul (1865–1935) French composer. A student at the Paris Conservatoire, he missed winning a first *Prix de Rome* by one vote, but managed a second. His own musical fastidiousness and his critical writings caused the Conservatoire authorities to regard him as a subversive influence, in spite of which he became in later life an inspector of provincial conservatories and, from 1909 until his death, professor of composition in the Paris one.

'Music more than any other art embodies our aspirations towards the infinite,' he wrote. Puritanically he refused to have any photograph of himself published, on the grounds that he owed the public nothing but his music – and of that music he destroyed a great deal shortly before he died. His characteristic style might be said to be a refinement, even in his larger works, of the romantic excesses of Wagner and even of Beethoven, much as he admired both of them. He composed a symbolic, impressionistic fantasy-opera based on Maeterlinck's play *Ariane et Barbe-bleu* (*Ariadne and Bluebeard*), and a ballet *La Péri*, from which he later made a frequently played orchestral suite. One work which he failed to destroy was his most successful composition, the orchestral scherzo *L'Apprenti sorcier* – the Sorcerer's Apprentice who featured in Walt Disney's cartoon *Fantasia*.

OTHER WORKS: Overture *Polyceute*. Symphony in C. Piano variations on a theme of Rameau. Piano *Prélude élégiaque* (*Elegiac Prelude*).

Dukelsky, Vladimir (1903–69) Russian composer (American citizen). He studied with Glière but left Russia for Constantinople after the Revolution and in 1922 settled in the USA, becoming an American citizen. Diaghilev commissioned music for a ballet, *Zephyr et Flore*, from Dukelsky, and he composed an operetta, three symphonies, and a number of songs. He is better known, however, under the pseudonym of Vernon Duke, which he used when writing popular songs such as *I Can't Get Started with You* and *April in Paris*.

dulcimer An ancient instrument in which strings are attached across a shallow wooden sound-box and struck with small hammers. Of Persian origin, it found its way to Europe in the hands of Crusaders on their homeward journeys, and established itself as a popular instrument in peasant communities: the gipsy *cimbalom* is a direct descendant.

dumka Of Ukrainian origin but more frequently heard in Czech and neighbouring lands, the music is an alternation between melancholy passages and fast, more cheerfully rhythmic ones. Dvořák's *Dumky Trio*, the piano trio Op.90, introduces such movements.

dump or **dompe** A rather heavy, doleful piece of keyboard music presumably deriving its name from the common expression 'down in the dumps', and perhaps intended as a respectful, grieving memorial to someone recently deceased: many such pieces bear the names of high-ranking people.

Duparc, Henri (1848–1933) French composer. The son of a well-to-do family, Duparc was supposed to take up a legal career but proved more interested in private musical studies with César Franck. Intensely self-critical, he destroyed many early compositions. Wagner was a major influence on his work, but although he wrote one orchestral work, *Lénore*, Duparc's real gift was for introspective, impressionist songs. One of the most remarkable is his setting of Baudelaire's *L'Invitation au voyage*; while *Phydilé* is almost too expansively orchestral in the texture of its accompaniment to be contained within the capabilities of a piano. Duparc allowed only sixteen of these songs to survive, and after 1885 succumbed to severe neurasthenia which, together with tormenting rheumatism, robbed him of virtually all desire to compose any further.

Du Pré, Jacqueline (1945–87) English cellist. She studied with leading cellists William Pleeth, Tortelier and Rostropovich, made her first public appearance at the age of seven, and after a performance in 1962 of Elgar's Cello Concerto at the Festival Hall, London, became closely associated with the work: she played it on her first New York appearance in 1965 and made two recordings of it, one with Barbirolli and one with Daniel Barenboim, whom she married in 1967. One of the most gifted players of her generation, she was tragically stricken by a crippling illness in 1972 which brought her concert career to an end, and died in 1987.

dur In German the word means a major key, as in *C dur*, C major.

durchkomponiert German for 'through-composed', referring either to a song in which successive verses are set to a progressive flow of changing music instead of having the same tune or harmonies repeated; or, similarly, to a work which has been consistently planned throughout, in one piece rather than in episodic style.

Duruflé, Maurice (1902–86) French composer and organist. A pupil of Dukas and organ pupil of Vierne, he was organist at St-Etienne-du-Mont in Paris from 1930, and professor of harmony at the Paris Conservatoire from 1943. He has composed organ works, finely fashioned motets, and a moving, melodious *Requiem*.

Dušek, František (1731–99) and **Josepha** (1754–1824) Bohemian composers and performers. Dušek was a highly regarded pianist in Prague, and composed symphonies and chamber music. Two of his lively piano concertos have been revived and recorded in recent years. His wife was a pianist and singer, for whom Mozart wrote the concert aria *Bella mia fiamma*. Mozart stayed in their villa, the Bertramka, on the outskirts of the city while feverishly completing *Don Giovanni* for its première at the Nostitz (now the Tyl) Theatre.

Dvořák, Antonín (1841–1904) Bohemian composer. As the eldest of nine children of a village butcher and innkeeper, the boy was expected to take over his father's business, but when he was sent to stay with relatives in Zlonice his schoolmaster there taught him piano, organ, viola, and musical theory, and urged that he should go to Prague for further training. After a spell in the organ school there he made a living by playing violin and viola in a café orchestra and then joined the Czech National Opera Orchestra under the baton of Smetana. His early compositions aroused little interest but, determined to allow himself more time for creative work, he left the orchestra in 1873 for a post as church organist. Submitting two symphonies in the hope of obtaining a State grant available to needy composers, he was lucky enough to have Brahms on the panel of judges. Brahms recognized his talent, and two years later persuaded his own publisher to bring out the *Moravian Duets* based, like so much of Dvořák's music, on the songs of his beloved native countryside. Soon the publisher commissioned a set of *Slavonic Dances* for piano duet and in an orchestral version.

Dvořák's first four symphonies, including the earliest, *The Bells of Zlonice*, an affectionate tribute to the small town where his musical imagination had first been fired, were for some time set to one side, and numbering began with what is now classified as his Fifth Symphony. The muddle has since been sorted out, and although those first four may not be regarded as in the same class as the subsequent superb symphonies, they are full of his lively, lilting folk melodies treated with incomparable orchestral skill and exuberance. These native songs and dances, integrated into his orchestral, chamber and piano works rather than simply 'set to music', appealed to an international audience. His *Stabat Mater*, composed during a period of mourning for the death of his eldest child, was a great success in England. Many of his most inspired works, including the Seventh Symphony, the entrancing fantasy-ballad for singers and orchestra, *The Spectre's Bride*, and the *Requiem*, were thereafter written for first performance in England, and in 1891 Cambridge gratefully bestowed an honorary degree on him.

A study of the Czech composer Dvořák in 1894, when he was Director of the National Conservatory of Music in New York.

Between 1892 and 1895 Dvořák was lured by the wealthy Mrs Jeanette Thurber to become director of the New York National Conservatory of Music which she had founded and endowed. Although she was far from meticulous in meeting her financial assurances, his work was enriched by the friendships he formed and the sounds he heard, though he stoutly denied that he had used overtly local idioms in his compositions. Programme notes frequently refer to the inspiration he had received from Negro spirituals, but although his Ninth Symphony is named *From the New World*, and in spite of the adaptation of its *largo* as a song called *Goin' Home*, Dvořák himself denied 'all that nonsense about my making use of original American national melodies'. Most of the themes in the symphony, as in the superb Cello Concerto, speak eloquently of nostalgia for his homeland. He did, however, express a real affection for the United States in his choral tribute *The American Flag*, and spoke of writing an opera on the theme of *Hiawatha*, a promise unfortunately never fulfilled.

Back in his homeland, Dvořák turned his attention to symphonic poems evocative of nature and local legend, and to operas in similar vein. Among them were the tone poem *The Noonday Witch* and the opera about a water sprite, *Rusalka* — inspired, oddly enough, not by any Czech legend but by the librettist's admiration for Hans Christian Andersen's Danish story of the Little Mermaid.

Few composers have ever managed to combine so successfully the charm, even naîvety, of the beloved folk tunes of their own region with a great symphonic scope and orchestral brilliance: the shining example is surely the utterly delightful, utterly Czech Sixth Symphony. Dvořák integrated simple melodies into classical symphonic form with such mastery — and such love — that even his senior and generous helper Brahms was awestruck, declaring how happy he would be if something occurred to him 'as a main idea which occurs to Dvořák only by the way'. His chamber works are indeed almost as compressed and intense as those of Brahms himself, but with a spontaneous lyricism which even Brahms would have found it hard to equal. Among the treasury of vocal pieces, few listeners are ever likely to forget the simple yet forever enchanting *Songs my Mother taught me*.

OTHER WORKS: Operas *The Jacobin* and *The Devil and Kate*. Overtures *Carnival*, *Othello*, and *My Home* (based on a patriotic song which later became the Czechoslovak National Anthem). Symphonic poems *The Golden Spinning Wheel* and *The Wood Dove*.

E

ear, playing by The ability to play a tune on an instrument, or a correctly harmonized piece on a piano, guitar, etc., without needing to use a written score. The phrase is applied particularly to jazz improvisers, many of the greatest of whom never learned to read music.

Ebert, Carl (1887–1980) German operatic producer. Born in Berlin, he directed the Berlin State Opera between 1931 and 1933, but left with the coming of Hitler and became first producer of the Glyndebourne Festival in England from 1934 until the outbreak of World War II, and for another six years after the war. After that he worked at the University of California, returned to Berlin for opera seasons, and between 1959 and 1962 was at the New York Met. His son Peter Ebert (1918–) has also contributed much to the operatic scene as producer at Glyndebourne, Copenhagen and Hanover, among other places, and as director and then general administrator of Scottish Opera.

Edinburgh Festival Every year since 1947 a three-week arts festival has been held in the old Scottish royal capital around the end of August and beginning of September, attracting major orchestras, opera companies and international soloists. Several modern works have had their first performances here, including Scottish Opera's production in 1977 of a truly local subject, Thea Musgrave's *Mary, Queen of Scots*.

Egk, Werner (1901–83) German composer. Largely self-taught apart from some early lessons with Carl Orff, Egk conducted for Bavarian radio and then, between 1936 and 1940, at the Berlin State Opera. He won an award from the Nazis for his music for the Berlin Olympic Games but fell into disfavour with his opera *Peer Gynt*, banned on the grounds that it mocked the Hitler régime. His dissonances, colourful orchestral textures and surging rhythms owed much to Stravinsky. Later operas, rarely performed, include *Irische Legende* based on W.B. Yeats's *The Countess Cathleen* and the comic opera *Der Revisor* from Gogol's *The Government Inspector*. A ballet, *Casanova in London*, had its première in Munich in 1969.

Einem, Gottfried von (1918–) Austrian composer. An administrator of the Salzburg Festival in the years immediately after World War II, and teacher of composition in the Vienna Academy since 1963, von Einem studied composition with Boris Blacher. His own first operas were influenced by his teacher and by Alban Berg's work. Later he adopted a more conservative tonal idiom, with considerable melodic appeal and dramatic orchestral tone colourings, as in *Dantons Tod* (*Danton's*

Death) based on Büchner's play; *Der Prozess*, from Kafka's novel *The Trial*; and *Der Besuch der alten Damen* (*The Visit of the Old Lady*) from Dürrenmatt's play, staged in Vienna in 1971 and in 1973 at Glyndebourne.

Eisler, Hanns (1898–1962) German composer. After studying with Schoenberg, his Marxist leanings led him to collaborate with the dramatist Bertolt Brecht on 'committed' propagandist songs and theatre music. Threatened by the Nazis, he left for the USA and in Hollywood wrote music for more than forty films, but was caught up in the McCarthy anti-Communist campaign and forced to move again, this time to East Germany. Although he frequently expressed criticism of Schoenberg and preached a musical gospel of social usefulness, his works continued to show his old teacher's influence in their twelve-note methods.

eisteddfod The annual bardic gathering in Wales, the word meaning a sitting of the learned. In its original form, probably dating from the seventh century, it was a triennial congress of Welsh poets and teachers who subjected candidates for admission to their circle to a number of tests. After a period of neglect the ceremonies were revived in the early nineteenth century, and today they incorporate a strong musical, especially choral, element. In 1947 an annual International Eisteddfod of singing, orchestral music and folk dancing was established in Llangollen, North Wales, attracting soloists and groups from all over the world.

electronic music The development of the gramophone record and then of tape recorders not only brought music into the homes of millions who might never have had the opportunity of frequent visits to concert halls, but in due course made it possible to reproduce vocal and instrumental sounds with a finer acoustic balance than in a public performance, to eliminate distracting background noises, and even to record sounds beyond the range of the human ear which nevertheless enhanced the tone of what the ear *could* encompass. An inevitable consequence was the employment by twentieth-century composers, already breaking away from diatonic music into atonality, serialism, aleatory music, and other explorations, of the electronic devices themselves as sound creators.

If musical notes could be converted into electrical signals, why not try converting electrical signals into coherent sounds? As early as 1906 Thaddeus Cahill of Massachusetts displayed his 'dynamophone', a vast contraption which produced notes by means of dynamos and telephone wires. It was too unwieldy to catch on at the

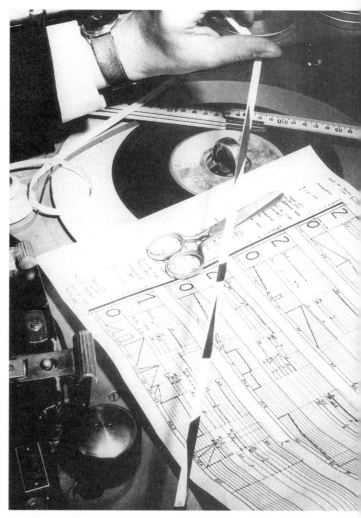

Composition with the aid of a graphic score, scissors, ruler and recording tape.

time, and there was no real way forward until the invention of the valve oscillator made possible the controllable emission of tones of any desired pitch, and gave rise to such oddities as the *ondes martinot*, capable of producing 'musical waves' and glissandos from two oscillators. Later advances led to experiments with *musique concrète*, a term invented by the French composer Pierre Schaeffer to describe his recordings of natural sounds – in 1948, the noise of railway locomotives and rolling stock – played at different speeds, back to front, sometimes blended and sometimes fragmented.

Artificially produced and arranged sounds could be used as an adjunct to live performances with conventional instruments or the human voice, as in Stockhausen's *Mantra* for two pianos and electronics, or the Norwegian composer Arne Nordheim's *Epitaffio*, where the orchestra echoes tape phrases, with the interpolation of choral passages. From the early 1950s onwards, however, in electronic music studios founded by Schaeffer in Paris and at Cologne radio by Herbert Eimert, ventures were being made into the creation of pieces entirely from electronic sources, with no use of natural or traditional instrumental and vocal resources. Stockhausen, collaborating with Eimert, was one of the pioneers of this 'pure' deployment of artificial sound.

Other influential studios for electronic music were established in Milan, the BBC Radiophonic Workshop in London, and the Columbia-Princeton Electronic Music Center in New York. Composers associated with their aims and resources have included Cage, Babbitt, Boulez and Ligeti. One of the major technical breakthroughs came with the construction by the American inventor Robert Moog of a 'synthesizer' capable of supplying any desired sound by electronic signals without the necessity for manual adjustment or the complications of mixing and splicing tape, and incorporating a 'sequencer' which could memorize and repeat protracted sequences of music. The original model could play only one note at a time, but this was soon superseded by polyphonic synthesizers. Today there is hardly a popular 'rock' group which does not rely on synthesizers for stage, television and recording performances, and even the background music to films and television commercials is regularly produced exclusively by electronic means.

Along with this have gone developments in computer technology which make it possible for a piece to be programmed in such a way, with general instructions and allowances for varying choices, that the apparatus itself might be said to be the true composer of the music. Classical notation plays no part in this: the scores are prepared in the form of graphs and technical directions which can be translated into computer language – calling in the end merely for reproduction and amplification equipment, without any need for instrumentalists or a conductor. (*See also* **Hammond, Laurens**.)

elegy In French *élégie*, in Italian *elegia*. A composition of a melancholy, commemorative nature, sometimes dedicated to a specific person recently deceased in the manner of classical elegiac poetry, but in music more frequently evoking a general rather than personal mood, as in Elgar's *Elegy for Strings* or Busoni's strangely introspective, epigrammatic Elegies for piano.

Elgar, (Sir) Edward (1857–1934) English composer. William Elgar was a piano tuner in Worcester, England, who, though Protestant, served as organist at St George's Catholic Church there. His wife was converted to Catholicism and their fourth child, Edward, born in their cottage in Broadheath in Worcestershire, was baptized and brought up as a Catholic. From an early age he took piano and violin lessons, and was addicted to sitting on the banks of the River Severn trying to write on music manuscript paper 'what the reeds were singing'. As a venerated composer in later life he was still bound up with childhood memories, echoing in *The Wand of Youth* suites, based on material he had written when twelve years of age and revived yet again in 1915 as incidental music for the fairytale play *The Starlight Express*.

After leaving school at fifteen he worked for a while in a solicitor's office but then joined his father in his Worcester music shop, trying his hand at composition and taking any casual jobs he could get as violinist in local concerts and social functions. He also conducted the orchestra in the local lunatic asylum, and gave piano lessons. In 1889 he married Caroline Alice Roberts, one of

Edward Elgar's love of music was almost matched by his interest in chemistry: after experiments in his garden shed he patented the Elgar Sulphuretted Hydrogen Apparatus.

his piano pupils, for whom he wrote the popular *Salut d'Amour*, a frequently played salon piece which he sold outright to the publishers for two guineas. She encouraged him to try his luck in London, but his work made no immediate impact and after various sorties they returned over and over again to Worcester and Malvern.

Yet slowly his message began to get across, encouraged by the faith not only of his wife but of August Jaeger, reader and editor to the music publishers Novello. Among the character sketches in Elgar's *Enigma Variations*, first performed in June 1899, the noblest is surely that of *Nimrod*, a classical interpretation of Jaeger's German name. The 'Enigma' at which Elgar hinted as 'another and larger theme' underlying the whole sequence, though never actually played, has caused much musical and philosophical speculation ever since.

His earlier ambitious compositions were choral works, for which there was a healthy demand at various festivals in northern England and the Midlands, and especially at the annual Three Choirs Festival, in whose orchestra Elgar and his father had both played regularly. For Birmingham in 1900 he wrote his setting of Cardinal Newman's *The Dream of Gerontius*, at first poorly received in his own country but arousing interest in Germany, where Richard Strauss declared Elgar to be the leading English composer of his time. He followed with oratorios, songs with orchestra, and the choral ode *The Music Makers*, but now was committing himself more and more to symphonic forms. His two symphonies developed poignant, very English thematic material dear to the composer's heart in rich, chromatic harmonies whose tone of voice, once heard, is forever after recognizable. He was no experimentalist: rather he might be regarded as one of the very last major composers to use traditional diatonic methods with complete conviction.

Elgar's local patriotism was almost matched by his sturdy national pride. London, which had once rejected him, inspired the exuberant overture *Cockaigne*. Patriotic fervour and a swaggering grandeur suffuse the rousing *Pomp and Circumstance* marches, though the otherwise devoted Jaeger strongly advised against the use of the trio section from No.1 as a setting for the words of the bombastic *Land of Hope and Glory*.

His Cello Concerto is one of the richest and most melodic works written for the instrument. In 1932 he conducted a memorable recording of his Violin Concerto with the young Yehudi Menuhin as soloist — he was indeed one of the earliest composers to realize the full potential of the gramophone record, and conducted many other of his own works. By the time of the Menuhin performance, however, he was ill and increasingly despondent, having composed little since his wife's death in 1920, of which he said: 'My active creative period began under the most tender care and it ended with that care.' Settled back in Worcester (in a house now replaced by a block of flats called Elgar Court), he revisited old haunts and dreamed old dreams. In great pain from a malignant tumour, from his sickbed he supervised by telephone landline a recording of two pieces from his secular cantata *Caractacus*, and was able to approve the playback just before he died.

OTHER WORKS: Orchestral overtures *Froissart*, *Falstaff*. Suite, *Crown of India*. Brass band (and orchestral version), *Severn Suite*. String orchestra, *Introduction and Allegro*. Oratorios *The Apostles*, *The Kingdom*. Song cycle, *Sea Pictures*.

Elizalde, Federico (1908–79) Spanish composer and pianist. He studied at Madrid Conservatory and at Stanford University, California, before settling for a while in England and studying law at Cambridge University. He composed a few jazz pieces which were played by Bert Ambrose's band, brought over some leading American jazz musicians to help him form his own band to play at the Savoy Hotel, and made several recordings under the name of Fred Elizalde. The group was disbanded on Christmas Eve 1929.

In 1930 Elizalde was appointed conductor of the Manila Symphony Orchestra. He served in the Spanish Civil War, and spent World War II in France, where among other works he completed an opera, *Paul Gauguin*, and a violin concerto. In 1948 he returned to Manila as president of the broadcasting company.

OTHER WORKS: Symphonic poem *Bataclan*. Piano concerto. String quartet. *Music for fifteen soloists*. Settings of Lorca poems.

Ellington, Duke (1899–1974) Edward Kennedy Ellington, known from his youth as 'Duke' because of his suave manner and stylish dressing, grew up in a middle-class Washington black family. He won a scholarship to art college but was too busy playing the piano and organizing dance band dates to take it up. Moving to New York he formed his own band — but in characteristic Ducal fashion called it an orchestra — and was soon making his name at the Cotton Club in Harlem. The nucleus of the orchestra remained the same over many years, with distinguished soloists whose creative playing styles the Duke moulded into his compositions. Billy Strayhorn, the pianist and arranger who joined the ensemble in 1939, explained: 'Each member of his band is to him a distinctive tone colour and set of emotions … Ellington's concern is with the individual musician, and what happens when they

The fame of Duke Ellington as a composer and bandleader tended to obscure his talent as a jazz pianist of varied styles from 'stride' piano to rhapsodic explorations.

put their musical characters together.' Among those who made major contributions to the development of the distinctive orchestral sound and to the development of his composing ambitions were the alto saxophonist Johnny Hodges, 'growl' trumpeters including 'Bubber' Miley and 'Cootie' Williams, the trombonist Joe 'Tricky Sam' Nanton, and the fluent New Orleans clarinettist Barney Bigard.

Many earlier compositions were jazz numbers and songs in fairly conventional measures, though with distinctive harmonies and dissonances. Some which had originally been written for instrumental performance acquired lyrics and became popular songs: among them, *Solitude* and *Don't Get Around Much Any More*. As the years went on, Ellington experimented with longer pieces than the usual jazz number, hitherto conditioned by the time limits of the 78-rpm gramophone record. He took four 10 in. sides for his rhapsodic *Reminiscing in Tempo*, and later tried a combination of jazz and near-symphonic flavours in the *Black, Brown and Beige Suite*. His recordings made him famous outside the USA, and he toured Europe several times, influencing composers such as Stravinsky and Constant Lambert. In the early seventies he took the orchestra behind the Iron Curtain and toured the Soviet Union.

From 1965 onwards Ellington became deeply interested in presenting sacred concerts in jazz (or perhaps one should say Ellingtonian) idiom in settings which included Grace Cathedral in San Francisco, Beverly Hills Synagogue, and Coventry Cathedral in England, and also on educational television in the USA.

embouchure The action and shaping of the lips against or around the mouthpiece of a brass or woodwind instrument to produce the sound. It is also sometimes used to refer to the mouthpiece itself.

encore The French for 'again', shouted by an enthusiastic audience wanting a performer to repeat a piece or play a further item. Also used as a noun to define small instrumental or vocal pieces which soloists or conductors keep in reserve as possible additions to the end of their programme.

Enescu, George (1881–1955) Romanian composer and violinist. (The name also appears as Georges Enesco.) He studied in Vienna and became a virtuoso violinist and influential teacher, among his most famous pupils being Arthur Grumiaux and Yehudi Menuhin. From a blend of national folksong themes and an orchestral style deriving from Brahms he fashioned his own romantic language in his two *Romanian Rhapsodies*, three symphonies, and the opera *Oedipus*.

enharmonic tones and intervals The word 'enharmonic' identifies tones which sound alike but have different names because of their place in their own basic scale. On the piano, for instance, C sharp is played on the same black key as D flat; though on stringed instruments there can be a slight distinction between the two, according to the player's fingering. Such coexistence of two differently written but similarly sounding notes facilitates modulation from one key to another around, as it were, this pivot.

ensemble From the French meaning 'together', usually referring to a group of singers or players, or both combined, smaller than a full symphony orchestra. In opera, an ensemble of singers may perform certain passages within the larger scope of the work. The word can also be used in comment on the 'togetherness' quality of a group or even a full orchestra while playing: e.g. 'good ensemble' or 'ragged ensemble'.

entr'acte French for the interval between acts of a play or opera, but in music applied to a piece designed for playing during such intervals. (*See also* **intermezzo**.)

episode Generally this refers to an incidental passage in a composition which departs from the main theme or themes, though it may be loosely based on a fragment of that thematic material. In a *rondo* it is usually quite fresh material set between two recurrent subjects; in a *fugue* it

serves as a development or commentary on a theme from the exposition, connecting with subsequent entries of the subject.

epithalamium A wedding song or hymn, the name deriving from the Greek *Epithalamion* in which the boys and girls of ancient Greece sang blessings upon the bride and groom at their marriage.

Erard, Sébastien (1752–1831) French manufacturer of harps and pianos. He built his first piano in 1777, and after opening a London branch developed a double escapement action which revolutionized the possibilities of keyboard playing. The invention of double pedals for the harp was another of his liberating inventions. His nephew Pierre took over the London business, which closed down in 1890.

étude Literally a 'study', as in a technical exercise for piano pupils, but used by composers as a useful description for short pieces complete in themselves, without development sections other than sets of graduated variations on the original theme, displaying academic and technical virtuosity. Chopin and Debussy excelled in the creation of such 'practice makes perfect' pieces, of a calibre suitable for public performance. Schumann took the idea to extremes in his dazzling *Etudes symphoniques* (*Symphonic Studies*) for piano.

euphonium A brass instrument of the tuba family, rarely heard in symphonic works but a mainstay of military and brass bands, producing a mellow sound in the tenor range.

eurhythmics A fashionable interpretation of the beliefs of Emile Jaques-Dalcroze (1865–1950), Swiss composer and teacher, whose physical exercises in *gymnastique rhythmique* were designed to relate to musical pulses. The method has proved valuable in the training of ballet dancers, and is also much favoured by those in need of losing weight by reasonably pleasurable means.

Evans, (Sir) Geraint (1922–) Welsh baritone. After his operatic début at Covent Garden in 1948 he became one of the mainstays of the annual Glyndebourne seasons and, there and abroad, established himself as one of the great *buffo* singers in parts such as Figaro, Papageno and Leporello; but he was equally impressive in the tragic title rôle of Alban Berg's *Wozzeck*. In 1960 he had sung another, quite historic title rôle – that of Verdi's *Falstaff* in a BBC and Eurovision transmission of the complete opera.

Since retirement from the operatic stage, Sir Geraint has devoted a great deal of time to teaching, including a number of televised master classes.

exposition The first part of a composition in which the basic themes of the work are first stated, especially in sonata and rondo form. In a fugue it is the opening section in which the subject is stated by each voice in turn.

expressionism A rather vague term borrowed from painting, in which it was first applied to the works of Kandinsky and the *Blaue Reiter* school around 1910. Their close associate Schoenberg adopted the word as a description of music which similarly tried to express a purely intuitive psychological reality, free from traditional academic forms and outwardly programmatic elements. It has been most commonly applied to the atonal works of Schoenberg and Webern in the period before they committed themselves to serialism.

extemporization The same as *improvisation*, meaning the ability of an instrumentalist to play music from his own imagination instead of following a composer's score. Buxtehude and Bach were noted for their extempore performances at the organ. Many cadenzas in classical concertos were improvised by the soloist. Improvised choruses against the background of a steady rhythm are an essential part of jazz playing.

Manuel de Falla with Leonid Massine, composer and choreographer of the ballet *The Three-Cornered Hat*, at the Alhambra, 1918.

F

fado A form of Portuguese popular song, usually accompanied by the guitar and often dealing in melancholy or cynical vein with personal disillusionment or expressing wry social comment.

Falla, Manuel de (1876–1946) Spanish composer. Privately educated in Cádiz, where he studied the piano and dabbled with early attempts at composing, Falla continued private lessons in Madrid and passed the Conservatoire examinations without actual formal attendance there. He composed two *zarzuelas*, a Spanish form of operetta-cum-drama, but made his first impact with an opera *La vida breve* (*The Short Life*) – not in his homeland, in spite of winning a prize for it, but in Paris, where it won the applause of Debussy, Ravel, and others of their circle.

A more resounding success was the ballet score *El sombrero de tres picos* (*The Three-cornered Hat*), staged by Diaghilev during his first London season after World War I, with designs by Picasso and choreography by Massine. The tang of Andalusian folk melodies and rhythms appealed to the public, and one of Falla's most popular works has been the *Ritual Fire Dance* from his ballet music for an Andalusian gipsy tale, *El amor brujo* (*Love, the Magician*): he himself made a transcription for solo piano.

In later years Falla turned to austerer forms, as in the harpsichord concerto he dedicated to Wanda Landowska, though his basic personal style did not alter too drastically: he always favoured lively, often witty melodies against an accompaniment which suggested a happy marriage between Debussyish chords and Spanish guitar chords. During the Spanish Civil War he fell ill, and in 1939 left Spain to settle in Argentina, from which his body was brought back in 1946 for burial in Cádiz Cathedral. Left unfinished was a large-scale 'scenic cantata' *L'Atlantida* (*Atlantis*) on which he had been working since 1928. Completed by his pupil Ernesto Halffter, it was staged in Milan and Edinburgh in 1962.

OTHER WORKS: Piano and orchestral *Nights in the Gardens of Spain*. Chamber concertos for flute, oboe, clarinet, violin and cello. Many piano pieces and transcriptions. Cycle of *Seven Spanish Popular Songs*.

false relation See **cross relation**.

falsetto The forced production of notes above a male singer's usual range, especially that of a tenor, to achieve a sound resembling that of a choirboy's unbroken voice.

fandango A Spanish dance which may have originated in South America in the early eighteenth century. It is generally in brisk triple time, speeding up and then coming to abrupt halts. The musical accompaniment is nearly always provided by guitar and castanets. A slower Basque version was the basis for a fandango in Gluck's *Don Juan* ballet, and Mozart emulates this in the last act of his opera *The Marriage of Figaro*.

fanfare A flourish of trumpets announcing the entry of some person of high rank, in official ceremonies or on the operatic stage. Other instruments are sometimes used to imitate the trumpet notes, as in Purcell's *Dido and Aeneas*. During World War II Aaron Copland wrote a patriotic orchestral *Fanfare for the Common Man*.

fantasia Sometimes referred to in sixteenth- and seventeenth-century England as a *fancy*, though it then denoted a polyphonic instrumental piece in fairly strict form rather than anything fanciful. Later it came to mean a solo or ensemble piece written according to the composer's whim, without the formalities of sonata or fugal form. Sometimes a free-ranging fantasia could provide the introduction to a more disciplined movement, as with Bach's *Chromatic Fantasia and Fugue in D minor* for the harpsichord. In different vein are large-scale works such as Schubert's *Wanderer Fantasia* for piano, so called because it is based on the melody of his song *The Wanderer*. Brahms used the name on short piano pieces, as Schumann had done in his *Fantasiestücke* (*Fantasy pieces*). It has also proved useful to describe transcriptions of and variations on the works of other composers, as in Liszt's fantasias on Beethoven pieces, and in our own century Vaughan William's majestic *Fantasia on a Theme by Thomas Tallis* and Walt Disney's full-length cartoon on musical subjects, *Fantasia*.

farandole A dance from Provence, though possibly of Greek origin. In 6/8 time, the music of fife and tabor accompanied dancers in a procession weaving through the streets. The example in Bizet's incidental music to *L'Arlésienne* has the authentic local flavour, though not in the correct tempo.

Farinelli, Carlo (1705–82) Italian *castrato* (male soprano). His real name was Guido Broschi, but it was as Farinelli that he became famous for the purity and sonority of his voice and for his skill in florid embellishments. A pupil of the opera composer Porpora, he joined his tutor's company in London when it set up an *Opera of the Nobility* in rivalry to Handel, and was acclaimed for 'the finest voice that Europe affords'.

In 1737 Farinelli visited Spain, and sang so expressively that he drew King Philip V out of a chronic melancholia, and was invited by the Queen to stay on at a high salary. He remained

A portrait by Nazari in 1734 of the castrato Farinelli. The original painting hangs in the Royal College of Music, London.

in Madrid for twenty-five years, and during the first ten of these sang the same four soothing songs each night to the King. He was kept on by Philip's successor, but then returned to Italy a rich man, buying himself a palatial home near Bologna and spending the rest of his life entertaining noblemen and other friends from all over Europe.

Fauré, Gabriel (1845–1924) French composer. As a child, Fauré's talent was so obvious that Louis Neidermeyer, founder of a Parisian school of church music, gave him a free musical education. At the age of twenty-one he became organist at Rennes, served in the army during the Franco-Prussian war, and then took on further organ posts. His most characteristic compositions, however, owe little to church influences: he became one of the subtlest and most inventive creators of elegant French song cycles and piano and chamber music. The cycle *La Bonne Chanson*, based on nine poems by Verlaine, has supple modulations of voice and piano perfectly matching the emotional cadences of the verse. There is the same grace and miniaturist delicacy in his large output of piano preludes, impromptus, barcarolles and nocturnes.

On a larger scale, Fauré's *Requiem* (in memory of his father) has grown in public esteem since World War II, built as it is upon what has been described as an affirmation of faith in the simplest musical terms, aiming at spiritual serenity rather than grandiose dramatic statements. He became director of the Paris Conservatoire in 1905; but in the last decade of his life suffered from deafness, during which his music became sparer and more withdrawn, symbolizing his own remoteness within his silent world.

OTHER WORKS: Operas *Prométhée* and *Pénélope*. Orchestral divertissement *Masques et bergamasques*. Two piano quintets. Piano duets, including the *Dolly* suite. Song cycle *L'Horizon chimérique*. *Sicilienne* for cello and piano.

Gabriel Fauré's large output of piano compositions included a number of duets, from one of which, the *Dolly* suite, was taken the theme tune of a long-running BBC children's radio programme, *Listen with Mother*.

Feldman, Morton (1926–87) American composer. In 1950 he met John Cage, and thereafter was markedly influenced by Cage's theories as well as by the techniques of contemporary New York painters. He visualized music in terms of coloured threads spreading and interweaving over extended periods of time. To express these principles he used graphs rather than convential scores in chamber works such as *Projections* and orchestral works such as *Atlantis* and *Intersection*. In *Marginal Intersection* he experimented with two oscillators and the pre-recorded sound of riveting. His Second String Quartet, completed in 1983, takes four hours to play.

OTHER WORKS: Percussion piece *The King of Denmark*. Soprano and chamber ensemble, *Journey to the End of Night*.

feminine Just as an unaccented syllable following an accented syllable at the end of a line of poetry is described as a feminine ending, so in music the phrases *feminine ending* or *feminine cadence* describe a final chord falling on a weak beat of the bar.

Fenby, Eric (1906–) English composer and organist. His compositions include a symphony and an overture *Rossini on Ilkla Moor*; but he will be most admiringly remembered as the devoted amanuensis who so arduously transcribed the music of the paralysed Delius in his later years.

fermata A pause, indicated by the sign⌒above the relevant note or chord. It allows the player to prolong a note or rest *ad lib*, detached from the specified tempo of the written music: in effect it suspends time rather than extends it. (*See also* **Interpretation Marks**.)

Ferrier, Kathleen (1912-53) English contralto. After winning a competition in 1937 she took up serious study of singing, but did not make her London début until 1943, in *Messiah*. She was greatly in demand in oratorio performances and then established herself also on the operatic stage at Glyndebourne in Britten's *The Rape of Lucretia*, followed by Gluck's *Orfeo ed Eurydice*, with which she became identified as much as Janet Baker did in later years: it was in fact as Orpheus that she made her final appearance at Covent Garden when already dying of cancer. Her radiant voice and equally glowing, affectionate personality made her one of the best-loved English singers of the century. The voice is, happily, preserved on many records, including a performance of Mahler's *Das Lied von der Erde* (*Song of the Earth*) which has yet to be equalled, let alone surpassed.

A chalk drawing by B. Dunstan of the contralto Kathleen Ferrier.

Fibich, Zdeněk (1850–1900) Czech composer and conductor. He studied in Leipzig, Paris and Mannheim, went to teach in Poland, and then in 1874 became assistant conductor at the National Theatre in Prague. He composed over 600 works including seven operas (of which *The Bride of Messina* with its dark, dramatic male voice choruses is among the most compelling), three symphonies, three hundred and fifty piano pieces and a large amount of chamber music. He was considered one of the most gifted men of his day by his associates, but is remembered now mainly for one small piece: the *Poème* from his orchestral serenade *At Twilight*.

Fiedler, Arthur (1894–1979) American conductor. He studied violin in Boston and Berlin, became violinist and then violist with the Boston Symphony Orchestra, and founded the Boston Sinfonietta. From 1930 onwards he became a household name as conductor of popular music concerts, many of them recorded and broadcast, known as the Boston 'Pops' concerts.

Field, John (1782–1837) Born in Dublin, Field had music lessons from his father and grandfather, and then from Giordani, who presented his precocious pupil with great success at the Rotunda Assembly Rooms. When the family moved to London he was apprenticed to Clementi's piano manufactory, where he improvised at the keyboards to display their capabilities. In 1802 he and Clementi travelled together through Europe, and for a time Field settled in St Petersberg. It was widely felt that Clementi exploited his employee, and after retiring cared little for him. After a dismal spell in London, Field returned to Russia, took to the bottle, and died in Moscow in near-poverty. Only long after his death was the worth of his sonatas, piano concertos and, even more, of his solo piano pieces recognized. He was the first to apply the name of *Nocturne* to such pieces, and his style of writing led to Chopin's further development of the form. Like Chopin, he was opposed to the heavy touch on the instrument favoured by so many of Beethoven's successors, and aimed both in his own playing and in the music he wrote at a lyrical, sustained quality.

fife A small soprano transverse flute with finger-holes but originally without keys. Its main use is in military or drum-and-fife bands, the modern version frequently having a number of keys.

fifth An interval covering three whole tones and one semitone – i.e. five notes between the lowest and highest. The fifth above the tonic C, for example, is G, which is known as a perfect fifth: the diminished fifth would be C to G flat; the augmented fifth, C to G sharp.

figured bass *See* **basso continuo**.

finale The last movement of an instrumental work, or the concluding ensemble of any act in an opera – but the term is not used if the conclusion is provided by a solo singer.

fingering The placing of fingertips on the strings of a bowed or plucked instrument to produce the desired notes is more generally known as *stopping*, though the neck of the instrument against which the strings are pressed is referred to as the fingerboard. In keyboard playing, different teachers and performers have favoured several different techniques in playing sequences of notes and chords; and some composers or editors mark figures above certain notes to indicate which fingers should preferably be used. So-called *English fingering* employed a cross to denote the thumb and the fingers 1-4 to represent the fingers. *Continental fingering*, now in general use, makes the thumb number 1 and the fingers 2-5.

Finzi, Gerald (1901-56) English composer. He first studied music with Ernest Farrar, and was deeply shocked when Farrar died in action only a few days after going to France in World War I. Reticent in his life and in his music, Finzi was fastidious in his setting of poems which appealed to him, especially those of Thomas Hardy, allowing the words themselves to dictate the form of each musical phrase rather than forcing them into a rigid bar or rhythm pattern. He is at his most expressive in the three sets of Hardy songs, *A Young Man's Exhortation, Earth and Air and Rain*, and *Before and after Summer*. During World War II Finzi worked for the Ministry of War Transport but continued to compose: his sprightly *Five Bagatelles* for clarinet and piano had their première at a lunchtime concert in the National Gallery, London.

In 1951 Finzi learned that he was suffering from leukemia. This did not deter him from work or from attending musical functions, but made him an easy prey when exposed to a case of chickenpox at the 1956 Gloucester Festival. At a memorial concert his most evocatively English, loving and lovely *Eclogue* for piano and strings was the most appropriate piece which could possibly have been offered in tribute.

OTHER WORKS: Concerto for clarinet and string orchestra. *Introit* for violin and orchestra. Orchestral elegy *The Fall of the Leaf*. Cantata *Dies Natalis* for soprano or tenor and strings.

fioritura From the Italian for a flowering or decoration, the word refers to ornamentations of a straightforward melody line, sometimes indicated by the composer but frequently extemporized at the keyboard or by a string soloist. It also applies to similar florid decorations of an operatic aria.

fipple A member of the flute family held vertically rather than transversely, and played through a wooden mouthpiece in which air is channelled by a plug known as a fipple, is called a fipple flute (in German *blockflöte*) – basically what we now think of as a recorder.

Fischer-Dieskau, Dietrich (1925–) German baritone. One of the most consistently mellifluous and versatile singers of his generation, Fischer-Dieskau made his Berlin début in 1948 in *La forza del destino*; first English appearance in Delius's *Mass of Life* in 1951; and first New York appearance in 1955. As well as distinguishing himself on the operatic stage, he became a profound interpreter of *lieder*, who could provide 'startling revelations' to even such an experienced accompanist as Gerald Moore. He has appeared and recorded with singers of the calibre of Elizabeth Schwarzkopf and Victoria de Los Angeles in perfect accord; and from 1975 onwards devoted part of his time to equally informed, flawlessly balanced conducting.

In spite of a packed and prosperous performing and recording schedule, the baritone Dietrich Fischer-Dieskau has remained a perfectionist, returning again and again to the re-interpretation and re-recording of such challenging works as Schubert's *Winterreise* cycle.

Fitzwilliam Virginal Book Among the manuscripts housed in the Fitzwilliam Museum in Cambridge, England, a folio volume of music which had once belonged to Dr Pepusch before finally coming into the hands of Lord Fitzwilliam was for a long time known erroneously as *Queen Elizabeth's Virginal Book*. It contains nearly 300 keyboard pieces by English composers such as John Bull, William Byrd and Thomas Tallis and by a few leading European musicians. It was set down in the seventeenth century by Francis Tregian, probably to while away a ten-year incarceration on a charge of recusancy in the Fleet prison, London, where he died. The collection, re-edited in 1899, is an invaluable guide to notation of the time, accidentals and ornamentation, and the development of bar-lines.

'Five, The' Sometimes known as *kutchka* in Russian, an abbreviation of *mogutchaya kutchka*, the 'Mighty Handful'. The reference is to five composers whose nationalist fervour led to their attempted establishment of a school of music based on folk songs and rhythms. The instigator was Balakirev, who gathered round him Borodin, Cui, Mussorgsky and Rimsky-Korsakov.

flageolet A woodwind instrument of the fipple flute family, similar to a recorder, end-blown and with two thumb-holes on the lower side to supplement four upper fingerholes.

Flagstad, Kirsten (1895–1962) Norwegian soprano. She made her début and many subsequent appearances in Oslo, much admired in Scandinavia but little noticed in the outside world until invited to Bayreuth, where she was to become one of the greatest of all Wagnerian sopranos, noted there and elsewhere for performances in *The Ring* and as Isolde. As well as many Wagnerian recordings she recorded Sibelius and Grieg songs incomparably. After retiring from operatic and concert life she directed the Norwegian State Opera from 1958 to 1960.

flam A rhythmic side-drum figure of single strokes rather than a roll.

flamenco A passionately declamatory style of singing from southern Spain, and an equally dramatic whirling dance interspersed with staccato heeltaps known as *zapateados*. In both cases the standard accompaniment is a guitar, and dancers can make great use of castanets. The name is thought to have arisen from the flamingo-hued costumes of the gipsy originators, though there is some mystery over the fact that it also means 'Flemish'.

flat The sign ♭ placed before a note on the staff to indicate that it should be lowered a semitone. (*See also* **Notation**.) Another use of the word describes singers or instrumentalists whose poor intonation leads them to produce notes marginally lower than the correct pitch: i.e. singing or playing 'flat'.

flügelhorn A valved brass wind instrument in various pitches, the most commonly used being the alto in B flat, similar to a cornet but with a wider bore and mellower tone. It is used mainly in military and brass bands, but can also be found in Stravinsky's *Threni* and Vaughan Williams's Ninth Symphony. In recent decades it has been increasingly used in jazz groups: the trumpeter Miles Davis, for example, has exploited its tonal richness to great effect.

An autographed photograph of the soprano Kirsten Flagstad, usually associated with Wagnerian rôles but also capable of smaller-scale interpretations such as that of Purcell's Dido at the Mermaid Theatre in London in 1951.

A 1912 postcard depicting a Slovak National Dance from the old 'High Hungary' region.

folk music Peasant songs and dances from any country, be they the Magyar melodies of Hungary, the street songs of medieval London, or the work and love songs of the Appalachian mountains, have often crept into the work of major composers or been deliberately appropriated by them. In danger of dying out during the twentieth century, many have been saved by devoted collectors such as Bartók in Hungary, Carl Sandburg and others in American white, black and Indian communities; and Cecil Sharp, whose travels and researches led eventually to the foundation of the English Folk Dance and Song Society. Holst in his *Somerset Rhapsody* and Vaughan Williams in *Six Studies in English Folk-Song* were inspired by rural melodies they had collected and by the old modal patterns underlying many of them. Aaron Copland arranged a set of *Old American Songs*. Even composers like Stockhausen and Berio have introduced folk material into their electronic experimentations.

Since World War II there has been a growing trend for the creation of contemporary folk music, much of it urban rather than rural. Burl Ives led the way with his treasury of songs learned from his family and during his wanderings throughout the United States. Young practitioners such as Pete Seeger and, in due course, Bob Dylan and John Denver mixed simple melodies and harmonies with the lyrics of protest against a materialistic, brutal, nuclear-threatened world. Nationalist traits were as recognizable as before in many performers and their songs: in Britain there was a revival of interest in Scots, Irish and Welsh airs, and in the use of instruments such as fiddles and concertinas, sometimes affectedly but often in character and with exuberant, authentic ensemble feeling.

Foster, Stephen (1826-64) American composer. Foster's father was a pioneer who had established himself in a prosperous business and expected his son to follow him into the firm. From early years, however, the boy was entranced by music, especially the Negro songs and spirituals he heard around his Pennsylvania home. He had no formal training, but taught himself to harmonize simple tunes and wrote a few of his own. In 1846 he went to work in his brother's office in Cincinnati, but, after selling a group of songs including the evergreen *Oh, Susanna!* to a New York publisher who made over $10,000 without giving Foster any credit, decided to go into full-time composing.

Many of his pieces were bought by Edward P. Christy of the popular Christy's Minstrels, who allowed Foster to retain publishing rights and receive a royalty; but he, too, gave no acknowledgment on the song sheets and took credit himself for pieces such as *Old Folks at Home*. Among Foster's subsequent output were such long-lived songs as *Camptown Races, My Old Kentucky Home, Beautiful Dreamer, Massa 's in the Cold Cold Ground,* and *Come Where my Love Lies Dreaming.*

Foster married in 1850. His wife found herself with a husband always in debt, inept at managing his work, and with a leaning towards the bottle. After several attempts to reform him she left. In 1864, in a seedy New York hotel with only thirty-eight cents in his pocket, Foster fell and cut himself, dying a few hours later in Bellevue Hospital.

After Stephen Foster's lonely death in poverty the draft of a final song was found in his pocket, beginning with the line *Dear friends and gentle hearts.*

fourth An interval covering two whole tones and one semitone – i.e. four notes between the lowest and highest. The fourth above the tonic C, for example, is F, which is known as a perfect fourth: the diminished fourth would be C to F flat (in effect a third, C to E); the augmented fourth, C to F sharp (also known as a *tritone*).

foxtrot A ballroom dance popular from World War I onwards. The tempo is 4/4, with heavy accents on the first and third beats. Most slow popular tunes provided dance bands with the material for a *slow foxtrot*. A faster number was usually referred to as a *quickstep*. There is an exaggeratedly jazzy foxtrot in William Walton's 'entertainment' *Façade*, and Peter Maxwell Davies has also used the form for flippant or ironic commentary.

Françaix, Jean (1912–) French composer and pianist. He studied composition with Nadia Boulanger, and was much influenced by Poulenc and Ravel. His music is elegant and mostly light-hearted, and as a pianist he has been the best interpreter of much of it. Among his large output are an opera *La Main de gloire* (*The Hand of Glory*), concertos for harp, violin, and piano; and many piano pieces and songs. He has also written film music for a number of Sacha Guitry films.

Franck, César (1822–90) Belgian composer. A gifted pianist, Franck toured Belgium at the age of eleven with his violinist brother. When the family moved to Paris he studied privately before entering the Paris Conservatoire, where he caused a sensation with his improvisations at the keyboard – a gift which brought him further acclaim as a church organist and on concert tours. After marrying in 1848 he abandoned his touring activities and settled down to teaching, at the Conservatoire and privately, and serving as organist and choirmaster in a succession of local churches.

Although he had been composing for a large part of this time, getting up early in the morning to do so before his working day began, his works attracted little public attention; but he had a devoted band of disciples whose advocacy was so strong that they became known mockingly as '*la bande à Franck*'. One of them, Vincent d'Indy, organized a concert of Franck's work in 1887 in tribute to the composer, himself too diffident ever to arrange such an event.

The compositions fall roughly into three main periods. Franck's earliest work was competent but imitative, as he sought to satisfy the then fashionable taste for comic opera. Then, doubtless because of his duties as church organist, he wrote a great deal of religious music, including the oratorios *Rédemption* and *Les Béatitudes*, the latter taking ten years to complete. Later he turned to symphonic poems with Wagnerian undertones and a tendency towards sonorities reminiscent of the organ, as if he were composing at an organ keyboard as other composers would at a piano. At the same time his contrapuntal excursions suggest the influence of his idol, Bach. The mightiest of the works from this period must be the *Variations symphoniques*, symphonic variations for piano and orchestra, soon followed by the challenging Symphony in D minor. By this time he was becoming more deeply interested in cyclic form, giving different movements of a work an extended coherence by using the same themes throughout. Hardly less massive than the orchestral works are the piano *Prélude, choral et fugue* and the *Prélude, aria et final*.

Franck's marriage was no great success, and any happiness he could achieve was due to the admiration of his group of friends and his own seclusion within his music. It was perhaps this absorption which led to the circumstances of his end: he died a short while after being knocked down by an omnibus.

OTHER WORKS: Symphonic poem *Le Chasseur maudit*. String quartet in D major. Piano quintet. Piano pieces including *Fantasia on two Polish airs*.

Frederick the Great (1712–86) King of Prussia, composer and flautist. Taught the flute by Johann Quantz, he later employed Quantz in his Court orchestra, and also C.P.E. Bach as harpsichordist. J.S. Bach visited Potsdam in 1747, to the joy of the King, who cried out to his courtiers, 'Gentlemen, old Bach has arrived', and provided his visitor with a somewhat wandering theme around which the composer fashioned the thirteen contrapuntal pieces of *The Musical Offering*.

Frescobaldi, Girolamo (1583–1643) Italian composer and organist. After a spell in Antwerp, where he produced a set of splendid madrigals, he became organist at St Peter's, Rome, in 1608, by which time his reputation was so great that thousands attended his first performance. For a time he was lured away to Florence by one of the Medicis, but duly returned to St Peter's and remained there until his death. He composed many motets and further collections of madrigals, but his most creative work was in the field of keyboard toccatas and fugues, introducing adventurous variations, syncopations and dissonances, yet always adhering to the disciplines of old contrapuntal forms at a time when florid dramatic effects were all the rage, and giving instructions to the performer which have proved invaluable to modern interpreters of such music.

frets Slightly raised strips of wood or metal set across the fingerboard of stringed instruments such as the guitar, banjo, balalaika, etc. against

The coat of arms on the title page of this edition of Frescobaldi's second set of keyboard pieces is that of Luigi Gallo, to whom the collection is dedicated.

which the player stops the strings to produce the required notes – unlike the violin family, where the player has to find his own correct placing for fingers on the strings.

Fricker, Peter Racine (1920–) English composer. He studied at the Royal College of Music in London and later with Mátyás Seiber. Although influenced by Schoenberg and Berg and fond of dissonances which at times suggest Bartók, he seems not to have been tempted down the road to serialism, and used these varying resources to establish his own vigorous contrapuntal style. He has written five symphonies, concertos for piano, violin, and viola, and a wide range of chamber music. In 1964 he became composer-in-residence at the University of California.

Friml, Rudolf (1879–1972) Czech composer. After studying piano in Prague he visited the USA in 1901 as accompanist to the violinist Jan Kubelik. He composed a piano concerto in which he was the soloist with the New York Symphony Orchestra, but his real talent was for the writing of operettas such as *Rose Marie* and *The Vagabond King*.

Froberger, Johann Jacob (1616–67) German composer and organist. A pupil of Frescobaldi and much influenced by him, Froberger became a major figure in German keyboard playing and composing of the baroque era, but not until he had survived some lean times: trying his luck in London in 1662, he was so close to destitution that he had to serve for a while as organ-blower in Westminster Abbey. Later he established himself as one of the first German players and composers to use the stylized grace notes and ornaments of the French school, and wrote toccatas, fantasias and dance suites in a free, expressive style. Towards the end of his life he was given accommodation and facilities for work in the home of the dowager duchess of Württemberg near Montbéliard in France.

fugue and **fugato, fughetta** The word is the French derivation of the Latin *fuga*, still used in that form in Italian and meaning flight or fleeing. Musically this describes the flight of a theme from one melodic line (usually called a *voice* even when carried by an instrument rather than a singer) to another. In the sixteenth century many contrapuntal pieces such as canons were labelled *fuga*, but it was not until the seventeenth century that Bach's immediate predecessors and then Bach himself really exploited the complex possibilities of these interweaving linear patterns.

The first part of a fugue is called the *exposition*. It begins with a single voice establishing the main subject, which may be no more than four notes or may run to four or even eight measures. Once this first theme has been stated, it is taken up by a second voice (known as the *answer*) beginning on a different note, usually a fifth higher or a fourth lower than the original pitch but then echoing the original intervals and note lengths exactly. This is known as a *real answer*. If the answer is not an exact parallel to the first subject, it is called a *tonal answer*. In either case, when the answer has begun, the original voice sets off on a different theme known as a *counter-subject*. If there are three, four, or more voices in the fugue, each must enter in turn with a declaration of the first subject while the preceding voices pursue inventive counter-subjects until all the stipulated voices have had their say.

With the *exposition* thus completed, its polyphonic possibilities can be further explored in a variety of ways. It is usual to introduce a number of *episodes* in this *development* section, where the music can change key or be subjected to expansions (*augmentation*) and contractions (*diminution*) of all voices or separate voices in contrapuntal conflict with one another. Episodes may be based on a mere fragment of the subject, counter-subject or answers. Such phrases reiterated at higher or lower pitch are known as *sequences*.

Invertible counterpoint changes the position of upper and lower voices. A device known as *stretto* ('squeezed') lets voices overlap so that the answer or answers enter before the subject has ended. The subject may also be *inverted* (i.e. turned upside down), or treated in *retrograde* or *cancrizans* (back to front). All such variations can of course be employed simultaneously, so that culminating sections of a truly inventive fugue may combine the basic subject played in one voice as originally stated, doubled in time values in another voice, halved in time values and played backwards in a third voice, all above a sustained pedal note on which the fourth (usually bass) voice has temporarily halted. In a *mirror fugue* the intervals appear right way up and upside down at the same time, as if one reflected the other.

There are those who regard fugal writing as a purely mathematical exercise providing no lyrical or emotional pleasure. Certainly it gives more pleasure to listeners capable of hearing several distinct lines at once rather than to those seduced purely by harmonic richness; but the overall sound of a great Bach organ fugue, or the vitality of his preludes and fugues in the *Well-tempered Clavier*, exist as beautiful sound quite apart from their academic accomplishments. Even the apparently austere essays of *Die Kunst der Fugue* (*The Art of Fugue*) can be enjoyed for their sheer sonorities.

Other fugal explorations can be found in the last movement of Mozart's Symphony No 41 in C Major (the *Jupiter*), Beethoven's *Grosse Fuge* at the end of his String Quartet Op.130, (also published separately as Op.133), the second movement of Stravinsky's *Symphony of Psalms*, and concealed or slyly manipulated in many works by Bartók, Schoenberg, and Berg.

Fugato (meaning, in Italian 'fugued') refers to passages written in the style of a fugue, usually as a passing section in another work and not fully developed into a true fugue. A *fughetta* is literally a 'little fugue', properly developed but of short duration. (*See also* Appendix III.)

fundamental The lowest or root note of a chord – e.g. C at the bottom of a chord of C major or C minor. The term is also used to identify the basic tone produced by an instrument as opposed to the harmonics deriving from that resonance. A *fundamental bass* is the correct root bass of a chord or sequence of chords, whether actually sounded or not: according to a now discredited theory of Rameau's, no composition could be aesthetically satisfying unless such root notes were present and progressed according to a certain musical logic.

furiant A traditional Bohemian (Czech) dance with frequent rhythmic changes, lively but in no sense 'furious', often used by Dvořák.

Furtwängler, Wilhelm (1886–1954) German conductor and composer. He studied composition in Munich with Josef Rheinberger and Max von Schillings, but, although he wrote three symphonies, a piano concerto and a quantity of chamber music, it was as a conductor that he made his name. From 1906 he worked in a number of provincial opera houses before being appointed conductor of the Berlin Philharmonic Orchestra in 1922, a post he was to retain for most of his life. His first London appearance was in 1924, and in New York in 1925. He became a noted Wagnerian interpreter, taking all his work with a serious, intense commitment which left little room for awareness of the outside world. Although disapproving of the Nazis' attitude to music and their persecution of Jewish musicians, he made no great public gesture as Toscanini had done; and in 1936 his appointment as conductor of the New York Philharmonic-Symphony Orchestra was cancelled. After World War II he faced charges of pro-Nazi activity, but was cleared and resumed his career as conductor.

futurism An Italian artistic movement beginning in 1909 which advocated the production of 'dynamic sensation' in the arts and a rejection of past aesthetic theories in favour of the speed and mechanical forces of modern times. Its musical parallels called for aggressive noise, some of it provided by specially made whistles and explosive devices. Although it attracted the attention of Debussy, Varèse, Honegger and Prokofiev, its limitations made it a short-lived fashion.

G

Gabrieli, Andrea (*c*.1520–86) and **Giovanni** (*c*.1557–1612) Andrea, born in Venice, sang in St Mark's Cathedral choir, and after some appointments in various German courts, during which he met and worked with Lassus, returned there as organist. He wrote a number of motets, madrigals and organ works, and collaborated with his nephew Giovanni – who was also his pupil – on a set of concertos for voices and instruments.

Giovanni, also a Venetian, followed in his uncle's footsteps, working with Lassus and serving for some years at the Bavarian Court. On his return to Venice he became deputy organist at St Mark's, and later its principal organist. He was quick to exploit the distinctive resonances of the building, writing antiphonal music for voices and brass: in several instances he specified the exact placing of choirs and instrumental groups in various galleries. Among sets of 'Sacred Symphonies' is his celebrated *Sonata pian' e forte*, one of the first pieces to be entitled *sonata* and one of the first to be written out with detailed expression marks, including stipulations as to the playing of loud and soft passages.

On his deathbed, Giovanni Gabrieli gave his ring to his most distinguished pupil, Heinrich Schütz, who kept his name and influence alive in Germany after it had been virtually forgotten in Venice.

Gade, Niels (1817–90) Danish composer and violinist. Son of a Copenhagen cabinet-maker, Gade was granted a royal stipend which enabled him to travel. He made friends with Mendelssohn and became joint conductor with him of the Leipzig Gewandhaus, until he returned to Copenhagen and was appointed Court *kapellmeister* in 1861. He composed eight symphonies, a popular ballet *The Fairy Spell*, and a number of choral works and songs. His son Jacob also became a symphonic composer, but is best known for his much-played tango *Jealousy*.

galliard A sprightly fifteenth-century dance in triple (3/4) time through which the dancers leapt and jumped in lively patterns. It was sometimes called a fivestep because the performers skipped over the fifth step, played as a quaver after a dotted crotchet on the fourth beat. This was known as 'cutting a caper'. The same melody was often used in a complementary slow *pavane*: the combination of the two became the origin of the suite.

Galli-Curci, Amelita (1882–1963) Italian soprano. She studied piano and composition in Milan, but as a singer was self-taught. At the outbreak of World War I she was in America, and as she did not care to risk the homeward voyage across the Atlantic she looked for work in the opera houses of the USA. In Chicago she was an instant success, and became one of the best-loved, warm-voiced coloratura sopranos of her day. Her records brought her a worldwide reputation, though audiences were sometimes disappointed by her tendency to sing flat at live performances. After facing some hurtful criticism, she finally retired from the operatic and concert stage in 1937 and devoted herself to teaching, spending her later years contentedly in California.

galop A brisk nineteenth-century ballroom dance in 2/4 time, featuring a hop or skip at the end of each melodic phrase. Among compositions using the form are Lumbye's exhilarating *Champagne Galop* and Koenis's *Posthorn Gallop*.

Galway, James (1939–) Irish flautist. He studied in London and Paris and privately with Jean-Pierre Rampal. He became principal flautist with the London Symphony Orchestra and the Royal Philharmonic Orchestra, and between 1969 and 1975 with the Berlin Philharmonic Orchestra. Since then he has been a leading soloist with orchestras and chamber groups, and has recorded all the major works in the flute repertoire as well as a variety of popular recitals.

gamba A common abbreviation for the *viola da gamba*, the bass member of the viol family, *gamba* being Italian for a leg and the phrase meaning in effect a leg-viol. Also the name given to an organ stop which produces a sound like that of a stringed instrument.

gamelan An Indonesian orchestra made up largely of gongs, drums and tuned metallophones. The appearance of a Javanese gamelan at the Paris Exposition of 1889 had a great effect on Debussy and Ravel. In 1931 Messiaen was equally impressed, and began using similar ensembles in his orchestral writing, followed by Boulez and Stockhausen. A visit to the Far East in 1955 inspired Benjamin Britten to introduce tuned percussion into his ballet music for *The Prince of the Pagodas*.

gamut The word is commonly used to describe a complete scale or the whole range of notes of a voice or instrument, from lowest to highest. Deriving from the Latin *gamma*, it more strictly applies to the lowest note in a medieval scale, the note G on the bottom line of our bass stave. John Cage has used the word to define the collection of sounds available within a composition and the austere discipline of their deployment, as in his String Quartet.

Gamut-Way was a term used in the seventeenth century to distinguish music written in ordinary notation from the older systems of tablature.

An 1873 cartoon shows the perils to which instrumentalists were exposed by the frenzy of *The Last Galop*.

Garden, Mary (1874–1967) Scottish soprano. Taken to the USA as a child, she was brought up in Chicago and studied in Paris, where she distinguished herself as an interpreter of French opera: at short notice she took over the title rôle in Charpentier's *Louise*, declaring 'I have never been nervous in my life and I have no patience with people who are'. She was chosen by Debussy as the first *Mélisande* in his opera *Pelléas et Mélisande*. Debussy even offered to write another opera specially for Mary Garden if she would marry him, which she refused to do, pointing out that he already had a wife. Returning to America, she sang with the Manhattan Opera and then the Chicago Opera, of which she became

Mary Garden in the rôle of Mélisande. The soprano said of her own career, 'I believed in myself, and I never permitted anything or anybody to destroy that belief'.

director for a season. Having remained a British citizen, during World War II she set up a military convalescent home with her sister in their home town, Aberdeen; and after the war continued giving lectures on music until well into her eighty-first year.

Gardiner, Henry Balfour (1877–1950) English composer. For a time music master at Winchester College, he wrote a symphony, songs and chamber music, and the attractive *Shepherd Fennel's Dance* for orchestra, named after a character in one of Thomas Hardy's *Wessex Tales*. As a generous patron of his more gifted friends, before World War I he sponsored concerts of contemporary British music and paid for the production of new works by Bax, Holst, and Percy Grainger – who spoke of his 'endless life-saving generosity to fellow composers'.

gavotte Originally a lively French peasant dance in 4/4 time beginning on the third beat, this was adapted into a more lilting, elegant form in the sixteenth and seventeenth centuries and incorporated in suites and sonatas by Rameau, Bach, Handel and others. Some gavottes have a contrasting middle section known as a *musette*, from the French name for bagpipes. In our own century the form has been revived by Prokofiev in his *Classical Symphony*, and more unexpectedly by Schoenberg in his Suite for Piano, Opus 25.

Gay, John (1685–1732) English poet, dramatist and theatrical producer. A friend of Pope, Swift and Congreve, he wrote the libretto for Handel's *Acis and Galatea* but had little success in his own right until he came up with *The Beggar's Opera*, a ballad opera for which his satirical lyrics on the corruptions of society were set to music arranged by Dr Johann Christoph Pepusch from a number of popular tunes and other composers' works. It was first produced in London in 1728 by the theatrical manager John Rich, and after successful repetitions throughout Britain was said to have made 'Gay rich and Rich gay'. A sequel, *Polly*, was banned at the time and not seen on the London stage until 1777, in New York 1925. A free adaptation of the original story was used in 1928 by the German playwright Bertolt Brecht and the composer Kurt Weill for their anti-capitalist allegory *Die Dreigroschenoper* (*The Threepenny Opera*).

gebrauchsmusik German for 'utility music', promulgated in the 1920s by Hindemith and others, including Kurt Weill and Darius Milhaud, as a creed of producing works for educational and social use, including political themes and pieces for amateur groups, rather than simply writing music for music's own sake. Hindemith himself later rejected the whole arid concept.

Geminiani, Francesco (1687–1762) Italian composer and violinist. A pupil of Corelli and Scarlatti, he played the violin in the orchestra of the Naples Opera and then based himself in London, with frequent spells in Dublin and Paris. His contemporary, Charles Avison, considered him far superior to Handel; but although Geminiani wrote large numbers of *concerti grossi* and violin and cello sonatas, his influence was much greater as a teacher: he developed a progressive method of violin tuition and wrote the first true methodical study of the subject in his *Art of Playing the Violin*, published in 1740.

Gerhard, Roberto (1896–1970) Spanish composer and pianist (Swiss parentage, British citizen). After parental opposition he began belated piano and composition studies with Granados and Pedrell in Spain and then with Schoenberg in Vienna. He felt a strong affinity with Spanish, especially Catalan, music, and taught in Barcelona until the outcome of the Spanish Civil War persuaded him to emigrate to England, where he settled in Cambridge on a research scholarship. Although he experimented with serialism under the influence of Schoenberg, notably in his First Quartet, he was never committed to strict 12-note theories and never lost his love of Spanish rhythms and melodies, which surface unmistakably in his opera *The Duenna*, based on Sheridan's play. He worked with his own electronic equipment and at the BBC Radiophonic Workshop, and in his Third Symphony ('Collages') used electronic tape in conjunction with the orchestra.
OTHER WORKS: Ballets *Ariel* and *Don Quixote*. Four symphonies (No.4 subtitled 'New York'). Harpsichord concerto. *The Akond of Swat* for voices and percussion. *The Plague* (after novel by Camus) for speaker, chorus and orchestra. Piano Impromptus. Guitar Fantasia.

German, (Sir) Edward (1862–1936) Welsh composer (born at Whitchurch in England). His full name was Edward German Jones. Educated in Chester, he formed and conducted his own band, learned the violin, and after studying at the Royal Academy of Music played in theatre orchestras until 1888, when he became conductor and musical director at the Globe Theatre, London. He wrote incidental music for Shakespearean plays, completed Sir Arthur Sullivan's unfinished operetta *The Emerald Isle*, and achieved resounding successes with his own two operettas *Merrie England* and *Tom Jones*.
OTHER WORKS: Operetta *The Princess of Kensington*. Two symphonies. *Welsh Rhapsody* for orchestra. Incidental music *Romeo and Juliet*, *Nell Gwyn*.

Gershwin, George (1898-1937) American composer. The son of Russian Jewish immigrants, Gershwin showed no particular interest in music until he heard an automatic piano playing in the street, and later began thumping out popular tunes on a piano bought not for himself but for his elder brother Ira. His first serious teacher was Charles Hambitzer, to whom Gershwin remained unwaveringly grateful. Although he studied as a concert pianist and wrote a string quartet, his real affection was for jazz and popular songs: his first job was as a Tin Pan Alley song-plugger, playing a publisher's new tunes to entertainers in search of material. By the age of twenty-one he had written a number of songs of his own, produced a full-length musical called *La La Lucille*, and achieved his first great popular success when Al Jolson sang his song *Swanee*.

In 1924, at the urging of the dance band leader Paul Whiteman, he tried his hand at something more ambitious and composed the *Rhapsody in Blue* for piano and orchestra. He followed this with a Piano Concerto, an orchestral piece *An American in Paris* which included four taxi horns in the score, and a *Cuban Overture*. At the same time he was writing a stream of musical comedies and individual songs, most of them with lyrics by his brother Ira. The show *Lady be Good* starred the dancers Fred and Adèle Astaire, and its title tune became one of the most frequently played of Gershwin's numbers. Many stage shows were transformed into Hollywood films, including *Rosalie* and *Strike up the Band*. In both his popular and serious music Gershwin used jazz idioms, especially 'blue notes'; and combined his two parallel talents in the Negro opera *Porgy and*

George and Ira Gershwin with Du Bose Heyward, whose play *Porgy* inspired the opera *Porgy and Bess*.

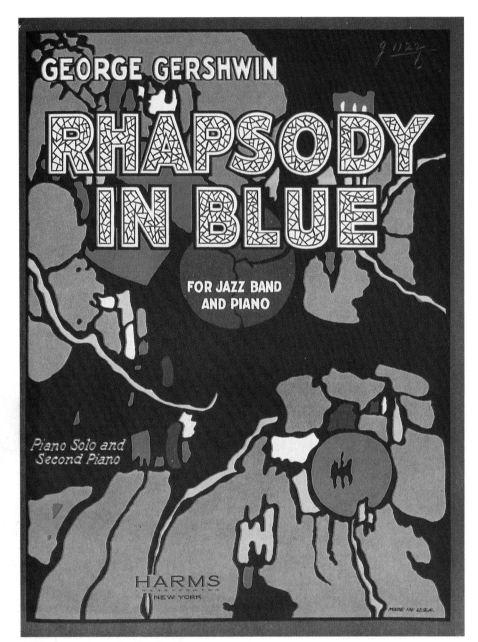

The original title page for George Gershwin's *Rhapsody in Blue*.

Bess, based on a novel by his friend Du Bose Heyward. At its première in Boston in 1935 it made no great impact, but gradually won over more and more appreciative audiences, was a great success in Russia in 1955, and was made into a film in 1959. In place of the traditional operatic aria the composer used songs in folk and jazz style, and many of them have been recorded by singers and bands as separate popular numbers, such as *Summertime* and *It Ain't Necessarily So*.

Early in 1937 he suffered a brief blackout while performing his own Piano Concerto in Los Angeles, but recovered and continued playing. Within a few months he died of a brain tumour.

OTHER WORKS: Second Rhapsody for piano and orchestra. *I Got Rhythm* Variations for piano and orchestra. Musicals *Funny Face, Of Thee I Sing*. Three Preludes for piano. Films *Shall we Dance?, A Damsel in Distress*.

Gesualdo, Don Carlo (c.1560–1613) Italian composer and lutenist. As Prince of Venosa he could deign to appear only a gifted amateur, but in fact before succeeding to the title he had taken musical studies seriously and become an accomplished performer on the lute. He composed seven books of harmonically and contrapuntally adventurous madrigals which in our own time had a strong influence on Stravinsky. He married his first cousin, who had already been married twice and seemed perpetually eager for fresh relationships: she became the mistress of the Duke of Andria, but on a night in October 1590 Gesualdo had the two of them murdered.

Gibbons, Orlando (1583–1625) English composer and organist. In 1596 he became a chorister in King's College Chapel, Cambridge, and composed some works there for special occasions. At the age of twenty-one he was appointed organist to the Chapel Royal in London, and held this post for the rest of his life, as well as becoming virginal player to the Court of James I and organist at Westminster Abbey. He conducted the music at James's funeral in 1625. At the behest of Charles I he went with the Chapel Royal to Canterbury for the reception of the king's bride Henrietta Maria from France, but died of an apoplectic fit before she arrived. His music, sacred and secular, had a sensitivity and nobility which greatly influenced his immediate successors, especially the pieces in his 1612 collection of *Madrigals and Mottets*. His madrigal *The Silver Swan* is a lasting favourite with singers; and among his keyboard pieces *The Earl of Salisbury's Pavan and Galliard* is outstanding.

Gigli, Beniamino (1890–1957) Italian tenor. At the age of seven he became a chorister in Recanati Cathedral, where his father was sacristan. He studied in Rome, and made his operatic début in 1914 in Ponchielli's opera *La Gioconda*. After extensive European travels he made his first appearance at La Scala, Milan, with Toscanini, and in 1920 began a long association with the New York Met. Among his favourite rôles were those of Rodolfo in *La Bohème* and the Duke of Mantua in *Rigoletto*.

The Italian tenor Beniamino Gigli, who in the mid-1920s could command $16000 a month for eight performances.

gigue In Italian, *giga*. An energetic dance popular in the early seventeenth century, with a bustling rhythm of triplets familiar to village fiddlers and gladly taken up by virginalists and other keyboard players and composers. It became a common lively conclusion to suites by Bach and Handel. Hearing the country music of *jigs* during a stay in England, Debussy used the rhythm for the *Gigues* movement of his suite *Images*.

Gilbert and Sullivan English librettist and composer of operettas. William Schwenk Gilbert (1836–1911) made his name as a writer of light verse and also worked as a drama critic and aspiring playwright before being introduced to Arthur Sullivan (1842–1900) as a possible collaborator. After a first failure, they were encouraged by the theatrical manager Richard D'Oyly Carte to try again, and in 1875 produced the one-act *Trial by Jury*.

A scene from an early production of *The Mikado*, one of the 'Savoy Operas' of Gilbert and Sullivan.

This was followed by a string of successes in a vein of light comedy, with Sullivan's jovial but skilfully phrased and orchestrated tunes perfectly matching Gilbert's sardonic lyrics, some of them suggesting sophisticated versions of 'patter songs'. From its opening night *HMS Pinafore* ran for seven hundred performances. When D'Oyly Carte opened a new theatre, the Savoy, solely for production of what came to be known as the Savoy Operas, it housed in profitable succession pieces such as *The Mikado, The Yeoman of the Guard*, and *The Gondoliers*.

Smoothly as their talents blended, however, the two men were not always on friendly terms. Sullivan wished to be taken more seriously as a composer and frequently objected to Gilbert's apparently flippant outlook on life. During the run of *The Gondoliers* a petty squabble over a new carpet at the Savoy led to a long rift between them. They came together again to write *Utopia Limited* and *The Grand Duke*, but soon broke up again. Both were knighted – Sullivan in 1883, Gilbert not until 1907. (*See also* **Sullivan, Sir Arthur**.)

Gillis, Don (1912–78) American composer. He was much in demand as a jazz trombonist and was influenced in his compositions by jazz and other forms of dance music. Between 1932 and 1935 he worked for Fort Worth Radio, Texas, and later as programme director for NBC in New York in collaboration with Toscanini. He composed ten symphonies, two piano concertos, and in characteristically amiable style a Symphony No.5½.

Ginastera, Alberto (1916–83) Argentinian composer. Born and educated in Buenos Aires, he achieved immediate national acclaim in 1937 with his ballet suite *Panambi*. In 1945 he began an extended stay in New York and became friendly with Aaron Copland. After his return he gradually involved himself in blending his exuberant nationalist impulses with exploration of 12-note methods, as in his Piano Sonata and Second String Quartet, and of quarter tones and aleatory rhythms. His three operas, *Don Rodrigo, Bomarzo* and *Beatrix Cenci*, are filled with violence, in vocal and instrumental treatment as in the action, and with explicit sexuality. At the same time he occupied teaching posts and founded a number of music schools, including the Centre for Advanced Music Studies in Buenos Aires, in spite of frequent clashes with the Perón régime. In 1970 he left Argentina and settled in Geneva.

OTHER WORKS: Orchestral *Variaciones concertantes* and Concertos for harp, piano, violin, and cello. Choral and orchestral *Psalm 150*. Piano *Argentine Dances; Twelve American Preludes*. Songs including *Five Popular Argentine Songs*.

Giordano, Umberto (1867–1948) Italian composer. Son of a Neapolitan chemist, he was enabled to study music by the generosity of a wealthy neighbour, and later to survive on an allowance from a music publisher while he struggled to write operas. His first success was *Mala vita* in 1892; but his only real lasting achievement was *Andrea Chénier*, a romantic opera about the French Revolution, originally rejected by La Scala, Milan, but finally put on at the urging of Mascagni. Subsequent work included the briefly popular *Madame Sans-Gêne*, which opened in New York in 1915 with the American soprano Geraldine Farrar in the title rôle.

Giulini, Carlo Maria (1914–) Italian conductor. He was musical director of Italian Radio from 1946 to 1951, then spent five years at La Scala, Milan. He has conducted at the Glyndebourne and Edinburgh Festivals and at Covent Garden in London, and was joint conductor with Solti of the Chicago Symphony Orchestra between 1969 and 1972. In 1978 he became conductor of the Los Angeles Philharmonic Orchestra.

Glass, Philip (1937–) American composer. He studied in Chicago, in New York at the Juilliard School, and in Paris with Nadia Boulanger. While in France he met and worked with the Indian composer and sitar-player Ravi Shankar, and later with Alla Rakka, acquiring a taste for 'minimal music' in which slow change and repetition of fragmentary musical figures achieve a stark simplicity as in his *Music in Fifths*. He has conceived most of his pieces for an ensemble which he founded for performance of his own music and with which he has travelled widely. The technique of chanted, slowly cumulative repetitive phrases is expanded in his operas such as *Einstein on the Beach* and *Akhnaten*.

OTHER WORKS: Opera *Satyagraha*. Ensemble *Music in Similar Motion; Music for Changing Parts; Music for Twelve Parts*.

Glazunov, Alexander (1865–1936) Russian composer. He was taught music at home, and then became a pupil of Rimsky-Korsakov. At the age of sixteen he composed a symphony which Balakirev conducted, and which so impressed Belaiev, a wealthy acquaintance, that he established a publishing house to promote the works of young Russian composers. Belaiev also organized Russian concerts at the Paris Exhibition of 1899, at which Glazunov's orchestral tone poem *Stenka Razin* was first heard. Although one of 'The Five', Glazunov was more cosmopolitan in the style of his music and less fervently nationalistic than his friends. As director of the St Petersburg Conservatory he showed himself conservative in his administration and in the style of his own large output of nine symphonies, tone poems, chamber music and songs. In 1928, unhappy with his post-Revolutionary homeland, he left the Conservatory, visited the USA, and finally settled in Paris.

OTHER WORKS: Ballets *Raymonda*, *The Seasons*. Violin concerto. Saxophone concerto. Concert overture *Carnival*. Seven quartets.

glee An unaccompanied part-song for not fewer than three male voices, simpler than the madrigal and usually harmonic rather than polyphonic. It became a popular form of entertainment in the eighteenth and nineteenth centuries with the formation of 'glee clubs' in London for after-dinner relaxation, or for conviviality in coffee houses and taverns. The lyrics were usually as unsophisticated (sometimes mildly bawdy or suggestive) as the melodies; though some composers such as Samuel Webbe, secretary of the Catch Club and librarian to the original Glee Club, exploited the form with considerable artistry.

Glière, Reinhold (1875–1956) Russian composer and conductor (of Belgian descent). He studied in Kiev, Moscow and Berlin, and in his turn became professor at Kiev and then at Moscow. He researched widely into regional folk song, and used many of its themes in his later work. His 'socialist-realist' style met with the approval of Soviet bureaucrats, and in 1939 he was appointed chairman of the Organizing Committee of USSR Composers. He composed three symphonies, patriotic marches and songs (123 songs in all), and ballets including the officially admired *The Red Poppy*.

Glinka, Mikhail (1803–57) Russian composer. One of the first overtly nationalist composers to make his mark on the outside world, he became known as 'the father of Russian opera' after the success of *A Life for the Tsar* (originally called *Ivan Susanin*

The 1906 title page of a Moscow publication of the score of Glinka's opera *Ruslan and Ludmilla*, a tale of fantasy and magic adapted from a poem by Pushkin.

and now so referred to in Soviet Russia) and the less popular but distinctive, exotic *Ruslan and Ludmilla*. Starting as a wealthy dilettante in music, pampered at home and feckless in his relations with women – he was persistently unfaithful to his wife, who ultimately went off with another man – Glinka did not turn to serious study until he visited Italy in 1830. Homesickness sowed the seeds of that first opera, and although Italian influences are obvious in the vocal lines, the orchestration has a national flavour which was to influence all his sucessors. In addition there are some inventive surprises: Glinka was well ahead of Wagner in the use of *leitmotiv*, recurrent themes which give dramatic unity to successive scenes and characters; and in *Ruslan and Ludmilla* the *leitmotiv* identifying the wicked magician is a whole-tone scale.

Easily depressed by lack of public recognition of his subsequent works, Glinka resumed his self-indulgent existence and wandered about the capitals of Europe. He died and was buried in Berlin, but later reinterred in St Petersburg.

Gluck, Christoph Willibald von (1714–87) German composer. The son of a forest ranger on the Bohemian border who disapproved of music as a career, Gluck left home at the age of eighteen to study in Prague, supporting himself by playing the organ in churches and stringed and keyboard instruments at balls and other social occasions. Surrendering, his father prevailed on his patron, Prince Lobkowitz, to take him on as chamber musician, after which he was helped to study further in Milan. When he began composing operas it was largely under Italian influence, so fashionable that he was invited to work in London, where he met Handel, who thought poorly of him. After this he spent some time as conductor to a travelling Italian opera company, writing a number of pieces which made no impression whatsoever until he fell in with a group determined on the reform of showy Italian opera and ballet which would subordinate temperamental singers and dancers to the overall concept of the work itself. One of the guiding lights of the movement was the ballet-master Noverre, whose *Lettres sur la danse et sur les ballets* declared that the only function of singers and dancers was to contribute to the basic story and to understanding of the characters.

In 1761 Gluck wrote the ballet music for *Don Juan*, and followed it the next year with the opera *Orfeo ed Eurydice*, a classical legend interpreted not through melodramatic arias but intensity of orchestral writing within which the vocal parts were an integral element rather than highlighted showpieces. He took his beliefs even

The title page of the first edition of Gluck's *Orfeo*, published in Paris in 1764.

further in his opera *Alceste*, for which he wrote a preface stating his artistic aim of restricting music 'to its true rôle of sustaining the poetry by means of expression and by following the situations of the plot without impeding the action or stifling it with a meaningless superfluity of ornaments'. It was such declarations, presaging the concept of an integrated music-drama, which later appealed so strongly to Richard Wagner. They did not, however, impede Gluck's ability to write beautifully flowing melodies when the situation really called for them, as in the heartrending lament by Orpheus, 'I have lost my Eurydice'.

Not everybody approved at the time. Many devotees still felt that an evening at the theatre called for the florid extravagances of Italian opera rather than Gluck's essentially Germanic music sung in French. A spurious contest was set up by partisans of Niccolò Piccinni, composer of more than a hundred operas, in which both composers were to write an opera in French, *Iphigénie en Tauride*, based on Euripides' treatment of the Greek legend. Gluck's version was already in rehearsal before his rival's was finished, whereupon Piccinni – who in fact admired Gluck and had wanted no part in such a squabble – retired for a time to Naples.

Partly paralysed by minor and then by more serious strokes, Gluck retired to Vienna and became friends with both Mozart and Salieri. He died after lunching with two old friends from Paris, supposedly as a result of ignoring his doctor's orders and having a large drink to round off the meal.

OTHER WORKS: Operas *La clemenza di Tito, La Rencontre imprévue*. Nine symphonies. Six trio sonatas.

Glyndebourne Festival An opera festival founded by John Christie in his house below the Sussex Downs, England, originally to display his wife, the soprano Audrey Mildmay, at her best in Mozartian rôles. The theatre opened on 28 May 1934 with a production of *Le nozze di Figaro*, and after some original scepticism on the part of critics and public was to become a fashionable venue during the annual season. In World War II the premises served as a children's home, but opera returned in 1946 with Benjamin Britten's *Rape of Lucretia*. Most of the world's leading singers have appeared at Glyndebourne and lived up to the challenge of its stringent production standards.

Gobbi, Tito (1913–84) Italian baritone. He studied law before becoming a singer, making his début in 1935 in *La sonnambula* in Rome. His first American appearance was in San Francisco in 1948, and he went on to become a favourite at

A view of the house at Glyndebourne across the gardens. Champagne and picnic baskets on the grass are an almost obligatory adjunct to attendance at an opera production.

Tito Gobbi as the jealous, forever suspicious Count Almaviva in Mozart's opera *The Marriage of Figaro*.

the New York Met as well as in London and Salzburg. He was an outstanding *Wozzeck*, and a quite unforgettable Scarpia in Maria Callas's final *Tosca* at Covent Garden. Gobbi also proved himself a profoundly knowledgeable opera producer at Covent Garden and Chicago.

Goehr, Alexander (1932–) English composer. Born in Berlin, son of the conductor Walter Goehr, he was taken to England a year later. He studied at the Royal Manchester College of Music in the early 1950s, where he was a colleague of Harrison Birtwistle and Peter Maxwell Davies. Later he worked as a BBC producer, and held appointments at the New England Conservatory and Yale. Much of his earlier music seemed calculated to provoke a deliberate clash between medieval modes and serialism; later he explored harmonic serialism. His opera *Arden müss Sterben* was first produced in Hamburg in 1967 and only later translated into English. His basic urge has always been traditionally symphonic in spite of affinities with the Schoenberg school, and in 1987 his Symphony No.3 ('Symphony with Chaconne') demonstrated his command of a language that combined poetic vision with a strong commitment to musical unity,

Goldberg, Johann Gottlieb (1727–56) German organist, harpsichordist, and composer. Although he wrote many keyboard pieces and instrumental trios, his name owes its immortality to a work requested from another source by his patron Count Keyserling, who wished for music to soothe his insomnia. Commissioned to provide this, J.S. Bach offered thirty variations on a sarabande he had already written for his wife Anna Magdalena. Played regularly by Goldberg when the Count could not sleep, these were known thereafter as the *Goldberg Variations*.

Goldmark, Károly (Carl) (1830–1915) Hungarian composer and violinist. Son of a poor Jewish cantor, he showed early promise as a violinist and entered the Vienna Conservatoire in 1847. While earning his living in theatre orchestras he narrowly escaped being arrested and executed as a rebel during the 1848 Revolution. From 1850 onwards he worked as a teacher, and also composed seven operas, including one based on Shakespeare's *Winter's Tale*, two violin concertos, a great deal of vocal and chamber music, and a symphony still frequently performed, *Rustic Wedding*. His nephew Rubin, born in New York, became a well-known teacher, numbering Copland and Gershwin among his pupils.

Goodman, Benny (1909–86) American clarinettist. After playing jazz on a Mississippi steamboat and with various recording groups, he formed his own band in 1934 and, after some early setbacks, developed a driving orchestral style with freedom for gifted soloists (notably himself) which led to his being dubbed the 'King of Swing'. He also introduced a style of what might be called jazz chamber music, first with a trio, then a quartet, and later other small combinations

The clarinettist Benny Goodman was a courageous pioneer of integrated bands, introducing black instrumentalists into his swing orchestra and his small recording groups.

of instruments. In a different form of chamber music he played the Mozart clarinet quintet with the Budapest and other string quartets, and concertos with leading symphony orchestras. He commissioned works from a number of contemporary composers, including Bartók (*Contrasts* for clarinet, violin and piano), Milhaud, Hindemith, and Copland. The Copland clarinet concerto was later used as basis for a ballet by Jerome Robbins.

Goossens family Conductors and instrumentalists of Belgian descent. Eugene Goossens (1845–1906) conducted opera in Belgium, France and Italy before settling in England and becoming for many years principal conductor to the Carl Rosa opera company. His son Eugene (1867–1958), born in France, followed him in the Carl Rosa post. A third Eugene (1893–1962), son of the second, became assistant conductor to Sir Thomas Beecham. In 1923 he went to the USA to become conductor first of the Rochester Philharmonic Orchestra and then of the Cincinnati Symphony Orchestra, later moving to Australia for some years. He was knighted in 1955.

Leon Goossens (1896–1988), brother of Sir Eugene, became one of Britain's leading oboists, and had works written for him by Elgar, Vaughan Williams, Gordon Jacob, and his own brother. Their sisters Marie (1894–) and Sidonie (1899–) have both held positions as harpists with major English orchestras.

gopak A lively Russian folk dance for men, in fast 2/4 time.

Gottschalk, Louis Moreau (1829–69) American pianist and composer. Born in New Orleans, he went to Paris in 1842 to study with Hallé and Berlioz. Chopin spoke highly of his first recital at the age of fifteen, and he became popular on his return to the United States as a touring virtuoso performing his own showy or sentimental pieces such as *Le Banjo: Caprice américain* with piano imitations of banjo-strumming in cake-walk rhythm, *Chanson négre*, and *The Dying Poet*. He also composed two symphonies and two operas in similar naïve style, which failed to live up to the brief success of his piano solos.

Gould, Morton (1913–) American composer. He studied at the New York Institute of Musical Art and has worked as conductor and arranger for Radio City Music Hall, NBC and CBC. His own compositions have been influenced by jazz and popular music: of his four symphonies, No.4 is subtitled *Latin American*, and his *American Symphonette No.1* is subtitled *Swing*. He has written a concerto for tap dancer and orchestra, ballet music including *Fall River Legend*, and a great deal of incidental music for films and television.

A caricature by L. Petit of the composer Charles Gounod.

Gounod, Charles (1818–93) French Composer. His father was a highly respected painter who had won a second Prix de Rome. Charles Gounod, given his first piano lessons by his mother, who was the daughter of a professor of piano at the Paris Conservatoire, entered the Conservatoire himself in 1836 and the following year won a second Prix de Rome, and then in 1839 the Grand Prix de Rome. While in Rome he fell under the spell of polyphonic singing in the Sistine Chapel, began composing masses and other religious music, and on returning to Paris became a church organist and choirmaster. He even contemplated taking holy orders, from which he was distracted by the charms of a young woman to whom he became engaged. The engagement was called off, but the girl's mother, Pauline Viardot, mistress of the novelist Turgenev, was prevailed on to sing the title rôle in Gounod's first attempt at opera, *Sapho*, in 1851.

Further operas aroused little interest until in 1859 *Faust* was greeted rapturously by the public in Paris and went on to become an international favourite with its tuneful arias, vigorous 'Soldiers' Chorus', and lush orchestration. Gounod's romantic temperament, shown in this and a subsequent opera *Romeo and Juliet*, led him, in spite of his innate religious austerity, into a tangled relationship with an eccentric English singer, Augusta Weldon, during five years in England after the outbreak of the Franco-Prussian war. While in England he conducted at the Crystal Palace and was first conductor of what eventually became the Royal Choral Society. The quality of English choirs so impressed him that on his return to France, failing to appeal to the public with further operas, he concentrated again on religious works, composing two large-scale oratorios for performance at festivals in Norwich and Birmingham and several more masses.

OTHER WORKS: Operas *Le Médecin malgré lui*, *Polyceute*. Two symphonies. *Ave Maria*, counterpoint melody to the first prelude of Bach's '48'.

grace notes *See* **ornaments**.

gradual A book of plainchant used in the Roman Catholic mass; also a term used for the antiphon sung between the Epistle and the Gospel at the Eucharist.

Grainger, Percy (1882–1961) Australian composer and pianist (American citizen 1919). After studying in Melbourne, Frankfurt and Berlin he spent some years in England, collecting and adapting many folksongs, such as *Brigg Fair*, and trying to invent a system of notation which would preserve the intonations of rural singers. In the Petrie collection of ancient Irish music he found a tune which in different arrangements he popularized as *The Londonderry Air*. Many of his own compositions adopt a folksong idiom and parody a half-disguised original, as in *Country Gardens* with its echoes of *The Vicar of Bray*.

Feeling a great affinity with Scandinavia, especially after establishing a friendship with Grieg and becoming a masterly interpreter of his Piano Concerto in A minor, Grainger attempted in his speech, writing and musical terminology to excise all Latin formations in favour of pseudo-Nordic inventions of his own. He also pleaded for liberation of music from old traditions into a 'Free Music' which should go beyond Cyril Scott, Duke Ellington, Stravinsky and Schoenberg and be played by non-human, mechanical means, for which he himself experimented with scores written in differently coloured inks. Among his other eccentricities, not fully understood by his friends at the time and only learned by his wife after their marriage, was a passion for flagellation, though he felt little shame about this, and in 1936 expressed his philosophy thus: 'Destroy nothing, forget nothing. Remember all, say all. Trust life, trust mankind.'

OTHER WORKS: Orchestral *Shepherd's Hey*, *Spoon River*, *Handel in the Strand*. Choral *Shallow Brown*, *Marching Song of Democracy*. Piano *Molly on the Shore* and other song arrangements. Wind quintet *Walking Tune*.

Granados, Enrique (1867–1916) Spanish composer. In Barcelona he won a piano competition at the age of sixteen, and while studying supported himself by playing in cafés. By the turn of the century he had established his reputation as a recitalist, and in 1901 founded his own piano school, the Academia Granados. He wrote a number of Spanish dances and popular song adaptations for the piano, as well as some unsuccessful operas, and blended his own poetic concept of Spanish history with Scarlatti influences in *Goyescas* for piano. An opera based on *Goyescas* was scheduled for production in Paris, but the outbreak of World War I prevented this. Instead, Granados and his wife attended the premiére at the New York Met in 1916. On their way home their ship was torpedoed by a German submarine, and the composer died trying to rescue his wife.

graphic scores A method of indicating the composer's wishes to the player by pictorial means without the use of conventional notation, derided by some critics as 'doodles and scribbles' scratched at random by those who lack the skill or patience to express themselves clearly. Advocates of graphic notation, however, claim that it can stimulate the interpreter's imagination, allowing him to make choices of his own and thereby take a creative part in the work. The first such score is thought to have been that for Morton Feldman's *Projections* in 1950–51. Cage and Stockhausen have frequently used similar devices.

Grétry, André (1741–1813) Belgian composer. A chorister in Liège, he began composing masses and motets at an early age and won a grant to study in Italy. Settling in Paris, he tried his hand at operas and, after an early failure, captured the public fancy and ultimately wrote about fifty, of which *Richard Coeur-de-Lion* is his most dramatically ambitious, though *Lucile* and *Zémire et Azor* demonstrate more clearly the fresh, lighter melodic style which made him popular. The *Air de ballet* from the latter is still frequently played in concert programmes and was one of Sir Thomas Beecham's favourite 'Lollipops'.

Grieg, Edvard (1843–1907) Norwegian composer. His mother taught him the piano and also instilled in him a lasting love of Norwegian folk songs. After studying at Leipzig and composing pieces very much in the Romantic vein of Schumann and Mendelssohn, he spent some time in Copenhagen, where in 1869 he was to give the first performance of his Piano Concerto in A minor. After marrying his cousin Nina Hagerup, a singer who had been brought up in Denmark, he settled in Norway and set about introducing characteristic Norwegian folk cadences and influences into his work, though he insisted that all the actual melodies were his own work with the exception of one, *Solveig's Song*, part of the incidental music to his compatriot Ibsen's play *Peer Gynt*.

Although Grieg (whose un-Nordic name was derived from a Scottish great-grandfather named Greig) produced a number of orchestral works and some chamber music, he was essentially a shy, undeclamatory miniaturist, heard at his most characteristic in the piano pieces and more than 120 songs. Even the orchestral music was in many cases an arrangement of earlier piano compositions such as the *Norwegian Dances* and *Holberg Suite*. Of the solo songs, a majority of them written for his wife, the most lasting has been his setting of Hans Andersen's poem *Jeg elsker dig* (*I love thee*), usually heard in its German translation as *Ich liebe dich*.

An 1892 painting by Theodor Werensjoeld of Edvard Grieg, who, in spite of a diffident nature and continuing poor health after a childhood attack of pleurisy, made regular concert tours to promote the music of Norwegian composers.

From 1874 onwards Grieg received a State pension to enable him to compose without financial worries. When he died, greatly revered in his own country, he was accorded a State funeral.

OTHER WORKS: Orchestral *Elegiac Melodies*, incidental music for Sigurd Jorsalfar. Three violin sonatas. String quartet.

Grofé, Ferde (1892–1972) American composer and arranger. He played the viola in the Los Angeles Symphony Orchestra and also worked with theatre orchestras. The band-leader Paul Whiteman engaged him as a 'symphonic jazz' arranger, and in 1924 he orchestrated Gershwin's *Rhapsody in Blue*. His own most frequently played composition is the *Grand Canyon Suite*.

ground bass *See* basso continuo.

Grove (Sir) George (1820–1900) English lexicographer. Linguist, Biblican scholar, and civil engineer who worked on the tubular railway bridge crossing the Menai Straits in Wales and served for twenty years as secretary to the Crystal Palace, he is best remembered for his authoritative *Grove's Dictionary of Music and Musicians*, referred to in musical circles simply as *Grove*. Produced between 1879 and 1889, it was later expanded by other scholars, the most recent edition being published in 1980 as *The New Grove* under the editorship of the English musicologist Stanley Sadie.

Guarneri family Italian violin makers. The firm was founded by Andrea (c.1626–98), a pupil of Amati at the same time as the celebrated Stradivari. His sons built up a high tradition of stringed instrument manufacture, but the most gifted was his nephew Giuseppe Antonio (1687–1745), known as 'del Gesù' because of his use of the letters IHS on his labels, who constructed strong instruments with a powerful, sonorous tone.

guitar A stringed instrument with a long neck joined to a flat soundboard, carrying six strings tuned from E below the bass staff through A, D, G, B to the E above middle C (though music for it is written an octave higher than sounded). With its ability to produce rich chordal sequences when plucked with fingers or plectrum, it has been used for accompanying song and dance in most countries of the world, but the Spanish version has proved the most popular and has become a solo instrument in its own right. Concertos written for it include those by Castelnuovo-Tedesco and Malcolm Arnold; and the *Preludes* of Villa-Lobos explore the whole range of its possibilities. Electrical amplification has made it a favourite with pop and rock groups during the later decades of the twentieth century.

Gurney, Ivor (1890–1937) English poet and composer. After studying the organ and composition, he joined the army in World War I, writing poetry until badly gassed and shellshocked. After the war he studied under Vaughan Williams and wrote some 250 songs, many of them of great beauty, others exhibiting the instability which in 1922 led to his being committed to a mental hospital. In spite of this he produced two exquisite song cycles based on poems by A.E. Housman, and a number of other pieces, before sinking finally into incurable insanity. After World War II the composer Gerald Finzi worked hard to achieve public recognition of the quality of Gurney's writing, and himself made a beautiful setting of the poem *Only the wanderer*.

H

habañera A Spanish dance named after Havana in Cuba, where it probably came from Africa, danced in slow 2/4 time with an effective rhythm of four quavers, the first one dotted and producing an effect similar to that of a tango, or with a triplet on the first beat. Familiar examples are the song *La Paloma*, the habañera in Bizet's opera *Carmen*, and one which Ravel adapted from a piece for two pianos into his orchestral *Rapsodie espagnole*.

Hahn, Reynaldo (1874–1947) French composer and conductor. Born in Venezuela, he entered the Paris Conservatoire at the age of eleven, and studied composition with Massenet. He wrote a number of operas and operettas, including *Ciboulette* and a version of Shakespeare's *Merchant of Venice*, together with a great deal of incidental music for the theatre, but is best remembered for his song cycles and especially for one song, *Si mes vers avaient des ailes* (*If my songs had wings*). A dedicated Mozart conductor, he was director of the Paris Opéra from 1945 to 1946.

Hallé (Sir) Charles (1819–95) Anglo-German conductor and pianist. Born Carl Halle, he adopted the accent to ensure that the English among whom he spent most of his life would realize that the last letter of his surname was not mute. In 1836 he went to Paris to continue piano studies, but left for England during the 1848 Revolution and settled in Manchester, where he took charge of an amateur orchestra and converted it into what became the Hallé Orchestra. He made a feature of conducting even the larger Romantic piano concertos from the keyboard, and introduced much new music to his audiences, including English premières of several major works by Berlioz. Subsequent conductors of the orchestra included Richer, Beecham, Sargent, and most notably Barbirolli, succeeded after his death by James Loughran.

Hammond, (Dame) Joan (1912–) New Zealand soprano. She studied in Sydney, Vienna and London, making her London début in 1938 in *Messiah*. Her operatic rôles included *Aida* and numerous parts with the Carl Rosa company during World War II.

Hammond, Laurens (1896–1973) American inventor. Born in Evanston, Illinois, he studied mechanical engineering at Cornell University but by mistake sat for an advanced electrical engineering exam, and passed. Shortly after World War I he worked on the manufacture of marine engines, then turned his attention to a number of inventions: a non-ticking clock, early three-dimensional movie technique, an electric clock, and then the electric organ with which his name is always associated. By fitting a secondhand piano keyboard with switches to control a mass of electric circuitry, Hammond and his team found electro-magnetic ways of using wave patterns not merely to produce and amplify different organ notes but also to alter the timbre. Shortly after the resultant invention had been patented, it was demonstrated to the public in New York on 15 April 1935, and on that first day was played on by George Gershwin, who at once placed an order.

After a gap during World War II when his company concentrated on military products, Hammond proceeded to create new models of electric spinets and chord organs. He retired in 1960, but the company continued developing techniques in automatic chording and digital rhythm units.

handbells Small bells of different pitches which can be held in the hand by handles or leather straps, and swung to produce miniature peals, often as a practice for full-scale change-ringing.

Handel, George Frideric (1685–1759) German composer. (English citizen 1726.) Born in Halle, his name was originally Georg Friedrich Händel. His father, a barber-surgeon, disapproved of any idea of a musical career, but when his noble patron heard the boy and urged that he should be encouraged to study music and extend his instinctive talent on the organ, it was difficult to refuse. Nevertheless Handel was unable to pursue a full-time musical career until after his father's death, and even then the lingering influence was so strong that for a time he combined the study of law at Halle University with duties as organist at Halle Cathedral. In 1703 he resolved to leave both, and set out for Hamburg, where he obtained employment as a violinist and later as a harpsichordist at the opera house. Almost immediately he made friends with a fellow instrumentalist and composer four years older than himself, Johann Mattheson, who later wrote somewhat

patronizingly of the young man that he was composing 'long, long arias and absolutely endless cantatas, but he had not yet got the knack of the right taste'. He admitted, however, that Handel had been able to reveal to him 'certain special tricks of counterpoint'.

Hearing of the imminent retirement of the great Lübeck organist, Buxtehude, the two friends went together to see if one could win the post. When they found that whoever was appointed would be expected to marry Buxtehude's daughter, twelve years older than Mattheson, they at once headed back to Hamburg. Life at the opera house was frequently stormy, and tempers ran so high that on one occasion the two of them quarrelled and fought a duel. But shortly afterwards Mattheson sang principal tenor in Handel's first opera, *Almira*, produced in January 1705 to great acclaim. Handel rushed out another work, *Nerone*, and again his friend sang in it; but it ran for only three days. On top of this disappointment, Handel was finding working conditions and the vicious jealousies of the opera house too harrowing. He needed to pursue his career elsewhere. In 1706 he set off for Italy to learn all he could in what was then the heartland of fashionable opera and concert life.

Supporting himself by giving virtuoso performances at the organ and harpsichord, Handel at one stage had to fight another duel: this time a keyboard contest arranged by Cardinal Ottobini in Rome between the visiting German and Domenico Scarlatti, in which they seemed fairly evenly matched, apart from Handel's superiority on the organ, which Scarlatti generously acknowledged. He wrote a number of operas in the Italian style, including *Rodrigo* and *Agrippina*, several cantatas, a great deal of religious music on Latin texts, including the *Dixit Dominus* — though he remained a staunch Lutheran — and built up such a reputation that after three years he was invited to return to Germany as *kapellmeister* to the Court of Hanover.

He was scarcely settled into his new post when he received an invitation to compose an opera for production in London. Seeking temporary leave of absence, he composed *Rinaldo* in two weeks, and was overwhelmed by its immediate success and by the English admiration for 'Signior Hendel, the composer of Italian musick'. After a brief spell back in Hanover he sought permission to visit London again; and this time stayed on. Queen Anne was so impressed by the *Birthday Ode* he composed for her and the great *Te Deum* celebrating the Peace of Utrecht that she granted him an annual pension. When she died, Handel found himself faced with the alarming

A portrait by Thomas Hudson of Handel in 1756. Handel, like Bach, suffered from blindness in later years and both suffered unsuccessful surgery at the hands of the same English surgeon.

in the Haymarket. For this he composed a succession of operas, among them *Giulio Cesare*, *Rodelinda*, and *Alessandro*. He became a British subject in 1726. In the following year George I died, and for George II's coronation Handel wrote an anthem, *Zadok the Priest*, which has been used for every British coronation since.

In 1728 the success of John Gay's English ballad opera, *The Beggar's Opera*, suddenly drew the public away from the Italian fashion. Handel's company went bankrupt, and a new company did little better. Even in his own field he was threatened by a rival composer and producer, Bononcini, and in 1737, as a result of overwork, suffered a stroke. After his recovery, though still struggling to maintain his operatic output, he began to turn his attention more and more to a completely different form of music, embarking on oratorios and turning them out as regularly as he had once turned out operas. In style they were not so very different, consisting of dramatic recitatives, arias, and resounding choruses, but this time on Biblical themes such as *Esther*, *Saul* and *Israel in Egypt*. The most magnificent of his religious works was *Messiah*, its text selected from the Scriptures and its music composed in three weeks, though much of it consists of adaptations from other works by Handel. Like many composers of his day, he felt no compunction in re-using or re-shaping material, whether his own or other people's: of his six 1738 organ concertos, for instance, one was almost certainly written originally for the harp, and another for lute and harp. A vocal melody could happily be transformed into a violin solo, a solemn sacred chorale into an operatic set-piece. Yet somehow the overall impression left by *Messiah* is one of noble unity. It was first performed in Dublin in 1742 and admiringly received, though in London its reception was lukewarm and only gradually did it become the favourite it has remained to this day.

Although Handel's sight deteriorated and he was blind for the last seven years of his life, he continued to give recitals and direct productions of his work, including annual charity performances of *Messiah* for the benefit of the Foundling Hospital, of which he became a governor. His final appearance was as conductor of *Messiah* from the organ at Covent Garden, after which he was taken ill, dying a week later. He was buried in Westminster Abbey, where Joseph Haydn later attended a Handel festival and burst into tears, crying, 'He is master of us all!'

In spite of his German birth and early background, Handel shows few German influences in his music. He was essentially an Italianate composer modified by English requirements. His

realization that her successor was none other than the Elector of Hanover whom he had deserted. There is a popular legend that he won back the esteem of the new King George I by writing a suite of *Water Music* to be sprung as a surprise during a royal picnic on the river Thames; but in fact they had already been reconciled, and the main consequence of the *Water Music* was an increase in Handel's pension.

For three years Handel served as musical director to the Duke of Chandos at his home in Edgware, and there wrote the twelve *Chandos Anthems* and some keyboard suites, one of which includes the variations known as *The Harmonious Blacksmith*. When he left, it was to form his own Italian opera company known as the Royal Academy of Music, based on the King's Theatre

The structure for the Royal Fireworks display in Green Park, London, in 1749, for which Handel wrote a suite of music which must surely have been rendered inaudible by 'the Girandola, or letting off 6000 rockets at once'.

operas seem rather static, often more suitable for the concert hall than the theatrical stage, but their drama is in the singing and the orchestral scene-painting. Solo lines are invariably expressive, often breathtaking in their soaring beauty; in the chorus and orchestra his contrapuntal genius seems to be used effortlessly to achieve whatever he desires. The same command is shown in his keyboard orchestral works, with their unfailing mastery of structure, using the suite form, fugues, and all the possibilities of the *concerto grosso* with its solo groups pitted sparklingly against the full orchestra. Asked for a set piece on some special occasion, his inspiration never failed him: the *Dettingen Te Deum* was performed in the Chapel Royal to celebrate a British defeat of the French in 1743; *Music for the Royal Fireworks* accompanied a firework display marking the Peace of Aix-la-Chapelle in 1749 (when a large set-piece caught fire and very nearly engulfed the Royal Library); and he produced a funeral anthem for Queen Caroline and wedding anthems for Princess Anne and the Prince of Wales.

Memorials to Handel are not hard to find in London. There is a statue by Roubiliac in Westminster Abbey, and in the Thomas Coram Foundation (successor to the Foundling Hospital) a bust by the same sculptor, the composer's organ keyboard, and an original score of *Messiah*. In St Lawrence's churchyard, Little Stanmore, there is even a tombstone claiming to be that of the 'Harmonious Blacksmith'.

Handy, William Christopher (1873–1958) American composer. Often referred to as the 'father of the blues', W.C. Handy graduated from the Agricultural and Mechanical College in Huntsville, Alabama, but became interested in music and toured as a cornet soloist and bandmaster with a group of 'Coloured Minstrels' before settling as a bandmaster in Memphis. During his travels he had listened to the songs of black labourers and country guitar players, and in 1909 he began writing down many of their twelve-bar blues into more formally structured compositions such as *Memphis Blues* and, in 1914, the unforgettable *St Louis Blues* with its unexpected interlude in tango rhythm, played and sung by every jazz singer, instrumentalist or orchestra of any standing. Handy also arranged many Negro spirituals and published a number of collections of spirituals and blues.

Hanslick, Eduard (1825–1904) Austrian music critic. Of Czech descent, he studied music and law in Prague and Vienna, and became one of the most influential lecturers and critics of his day, especially as music critic of the *Neue Freie Presse* in Vienna for more than thirty years. Although he had hailed Wagner's *Tannhäuser* with enthusiasm, his real taste was for 'pure music' rather than the so-called 'music of the future' with its dramatic and other extraneous elements. During the bitter quarrels between partisans of Wagner and Brahms, Hanslick sided with Brahms and thereby brought down Wagnerian torrents of abuse on his head.

harmonica Two quite different instruments carry this name. The glass harmonica was originally a set of drinking glasses whose notes were produced by pouring in varying quantities of water and then rubbing a wet finger round the rims. Benjamin Franklin later developed a form which he called *armonica*: in this the tuning depended on the varying sizes of the glasses, which were fixed to a spindle and moved through a trough of water so that they were kept permanently damp. Mozart and Beethoven both wrote pieces for the glass harmonica.

The more common use of the word today refers to the mouth-organ, whose metal reeds work on the same principle as the accordion, but with wind provided for the vibration of those reeds by the player blowing into the edge of the instrument or drawing breath through it, at the same time moving it to and fro against his lips to produce the required notes. (*See also* **Adler, Larry**.)

harmonics Also known as *partial tones*, these are the secondary sounds or overtones resonating (often barely audibly) at fixed intervals above the sound of a fundamental tone. It is possible to produce a harmonic in the series without actually sounding the fundamental: on stringed instruments by lightly stopping a string so that only a fraction of its length vibrates; on the harp by placing the palm of one hand lightly on the middle of the string while plucking it; and in wind instruments by overblowing.

harmonium A small organ developed by various European manufacturers early in the nineteenth century. Sounds are produced by reeds vibrating in currents of air forced through by foot-operated bellows. The instrument became popular in small churches which were unable to afford a larger organ, and portable versions are frequently used by organizations such as the Salvation Army. The so-called *American organ*, a French invention which soon caught on in the USA, operates by the suction of exhaustion bellows instead of forcing the wind through. Few major composers have written for the harmonium, though Percy Grainger employed it on a few occasions, and it appears in Dvořák's *Bagatelles*.

harmony From the Latin *harmonia*, itself a derivative of the Greek for 'fitting together', the word is used in music to denote a combination of notes sounded simultaneously to produce a vertical chord, as opposed to the horizontal movement of counterpoint. It does not necessarily mean an immediately agreeable sound, though it is frequently misused in this way: the opposite of discord is not harmony but concord – and discord plays a large part in the harmonic progress of a composition.

Early music was sung in unison until the introduction of *organum*, in which the melody was echoed by another voice at the interval of a fourth or a fifth. By the fourteenth century composers were experimenting with the use of thirds and sixths also, and finding that certain combinations and sequences made a particular appeal to the ear and, as it were, coaxed the listener along. Harmony could well be defined as a system of organizing concords and discords so that, both in theory and in the listener's head, they follow logically from what has gone before and lead on logically to what follows.

Each degree of a major or minor diatonic scale has its own triad (three-note chord), built up by the added intervals of a major or minor third and a fifth above the root note. The tonic triad is sometimes called the *common chord*. When the chord is written with its root actually at the base, it is said to be in root position. Triads can, however, be spread out in different ways. In what is known as the first inversion, the lowest note is moved up an octave to appear above the other two notes. In the second inversion the root of the chord is in fact the dominant of the key, and in strict harmony this formation cannot be used on its own because the ear is dissatisfied by the gap of a fourth between the bass and its next higher note (the tonic), and it will have to move on to a more acceptable resolution. *Tertiary harmony*, a system based on the third rather than the fourth of fifth, proved agreeable to the western European ear at an early stage. Supposing that the fourth had predominated, and old modes had continued to be used, would our minds, now so used to the chord of root, third and fifth, have adapted themselves to expectation of the kind of sounds which Bartók was later to bring to unreceptive ears that in due course became receptive?

Not all notes of successive chords need to be sounded each time. One or two passing notes can keep a melody moving along through different stages with only a hint of the full chord sequences;

and can slyly deceive the listener by implying continuance in one key, only to modulate by an unexpected full chord into another key. The element of surprise and of subtle shifts through imaginative deployment of harmony is at the heart of all composition. Throughout the Baroque and Classical periods the prevailing pattern was one of starting from a tonic chord on a trip through the dominant and back to the tonic, with any number of variations, explorations, and temporary key changes to enliven the journey. The Romantic movement broke away from such a simple formula, venturing out across colourful landscapes of chromatic harmony; but still, at the end of a composition, tended to surrender to the old imperative of a perfect cadence. In the twentieth century the older disciplines have been further shattered by atonality and the twelve-note system. But in music, as in all the arts, the codification of rules is inevitably a challenge to the instinctive law-breaker. Even such strictly banned progressions as *consecutive fifths* or *consecutive octaves*, shunned because it was felt their perfect consonances stood out too strongly for the balance of the other elements in part writing, were defiantly used by Beethoven and other composers of his time, and have appeared with calculated effect in much modern writing, including that of Roy Harris.

Diatonic harmony keeps to the key established at the beginning of the piece. *Chromatic harmony* introduces extraneous notes. *Open harmony* refers to writing in which the notes of the chords are widely spread. In *close harmony* the notes are packed together in their closest triad form. This phrase is also used in connection with a style of singing, as in barbershop quartets or popular vocal groups such as the Mills Brothers, when the voices keep close together, usually within the range of an octave. (*See also* **chord** and **cadence**.)

Harris, Roy (1898–1979) American composer. He studied first at the University of California, Berkeley, and then privately before going to Paris in 1926 to study with Nadia Boulanger. Between 1932 and 1940 he taught at the Juilliard School, and organized a number of music festivals and summer schools for young instrumentalists. The first of his sixteen symphonies was conducted by Koussevitsky in Boston in 1934. After this he soon established himself as one of the most distinctively American symphonists, using folksong and hymn tunes as a basis for his flowing melodies, rugged rhythm, and grandly structured orchestration. Several of the symphonies have titles denoting national pride, such as No. 6 (*Gettysburg Address*) and No. 10 (*Abraham Lincoln*).

OTHER WORKS: Symphonic overture *When Johnny Comes Marching Home*. String quartet *Impressions of a Rainy Day*. Concerto for accordion. Concerto for amplified piano. Choral *Songs for Occupations*, *Symphony for Voices*, *Canticle to the Sun*.

Hartman, Karl Amadeus (1905–63) German composer. He studied in Munich and then, early in World War II, with Herman Scherchen and Anton von Webern. He destroyed all his early compositions and lived in discreet retirement during the Nazi years, emerging in 1945 to found the Musica Viva concerts in Munich, performing works banned by the Nazis. His own eight symphonies are markedly polyphonic, and show the influence of Berg, Bartók and Hindemith.

Harty, (Sir) Hamilton (1879–1941) Irish composer and conductor. He played as a church organist in Belfast and Dublin from the age of twelve before settling in London in 1900 and establishing a reputation as a pianist and conductor. After conducting opera at Covent Garden and concerts with the London Symphony Orchestra he became permanent conductor of the Hallé Orchestra from 1920 until 1933. His farewell concert with the orchestra included his own *Irish Symphony*, with which he had won a prize in Dublin in 1902 for a work based on traditional Irish melodies.

OTHER WORKS: Symphonic poem *With the Wild Geese*. Choral and orchestral *Mystic Trumpeter*. Modern orchestrations of Handel's *Water Music* and *Music for the Royal Fireworks*.

Haydn, Franz Joseph (1732–1809) Austrian composer. Often referred to as father of the symphony and the string quartet, Haydn's musical beginnings were far from auspicious. The second son of a poor wheelwright, he became a chorister at St Stephen's Cathedral in Vienna but was summarily dismissed when his voice broke, and had to scrape a living by playing in street bands. For a while he worked as manservant and accompanist to the Italian composer and singing teacher Niccola Porpora in return for music lessons, and began to compose a number of divertimenti, cassations, and string quartets. After serving in two posts as music director to the lesser nobility, he felt secure enough to marry. His wife, Maria Anna, proved to be a shrew, and he was glad to avoid her company by accepting an appointment in the country palaces of the wealthy Esterházy princes, first at Eisenstadt and then at Esterház. He was to play an important rôle in the music-loving household for some thirty years, conducting the orchestra, writing and producing operas, playing in chamber concerts, and providing quartets, symphonies and religious music as required. With a full-time body of instrumentalists at his disposal, and the chance of playing with and writing for visiting virtuosi, he had everything a composer needed, and gratefully acknowledged the fact:

> As a conductor of an orchestra I could make experiments, observe what produced an effect and what weakened it … I was cut off from the world, there was no one to confuse me, and so I was forced to become an original.

His originality asserted itself most markedly in his development of sonata form in chamber music and the symphony. Moving on from the semi-operatic nature of the baroque trio sonata with its 'singing' lines of one or two soloists above a continuo, he passed through the early phase of quartet writing in which only the top part had any real significance, demanding from the other instruments only a rhythmic and harmonic under-pinning, to compositions in which each of the four parts had its own contribution to make. His *Sun* quartets of 1772 reintroduced fugal develop-ments of a kind that had been discarded for some years after the death of Bach, but employed them as an integral part of symphonic develop-ment rather than as academic contrapuntal exer-cises in their own right. Ten years later his *Russian* quartets (dedicated to Grand Duke Paul of Russia) had made great strides into a new world of chromatic harmony, thematic development, and use of each individual instrument as a worthy partner in the whole. No longer following the rigid formula of main subject, second subject, and academic development therefrom, Haydn allowed each movement to declare its own identity from the very first bar and pursue its own destiny. It was these pieces of Op.33 in 'an entirely new and special manner' which so enthralled and influenced Mozart.

A portrait of Haydn painted during his first visit to London, 1791-92, by the English artist Thomas Hardy.

Sonata form in the symphony had already been urged from its original formalities by composers such as Stamitz and C.P.E. Bach, but it was Haydn who definitively freed it of its rigidity and introduced rondos, variations on folksong, byroads into remote keys, and an emotional content which was to lead ultimately to the grandeurs of Mozart and Beethoven. Some of the dramatic and pictorial elements led to the adoption of titles and nicknames for a number of these works: rural life at Esterházy was encapsulated in the symphonies *Le Matin*, *Le Midi* and *Le Soir* (*Morning*, *Noon* and *Evening*); the last galumphing movement of No.82 combines a bagpipe tune and growling noises to suggest a dancing *Bear*; the *Surprise* (No.94) has a sudden loud chord and drumbeat in the slow movement, supposedly designed to awaken a drowsy audience; and the *Farewell* (or *Abschiedsymphonie*) is so called because the departure of the orchestral players one by one in the final *adagio* was meant to remind their patron that he had overstayed his welcome and was demanding too much of their working time.

Haydn also wrote a number of splendid masses in vivacious, virtually operatic vein, including the *Paukenmasse* (*Mass in Time of War*) when Vienna was under threat from Napoleon, and the *Nelson Mass* celebrating Nelson's victory at Aboukir Bay. When condemned early in his career for writing cheerful music in religious works, he pleaded, 'Since God has given me a cheerful heart, He will forgive me for serving Him cheerfully'.

The style of some of these later religious compositions owed a great deal to his experiences in England. When his patron Prince Nicolaus died in 1790, Haydn accepted an invitation by the impresario Salomon to visit London, where his concerts were an immediate success. He composed six *London* symphonies, was made an honorary Doctor of Music by Oxford University, and after a brief spell back in Vienna returned to London with six more symphonies. Contact with Handel's religious works led him to compose an oratorio *The Creation*, following it with *The Seasons*, based on verses by the Scottish poet James Thomson. Also, his emotional response to the singing of *God Save the King* while he was in England determined him to provide Austria with a fitting national anthem − based on a Croatian folk melody from his childhood but dignified as the *Emperor's Hymn* and used in his string quartet Op.76 No.3, the *Emperor* Quartet.

During his long lifetime Haydn wrote so much in so many different fields that later critics tended to dismiss him as an accomplished but uninspired hack. Few real musicians have ever thought so. Within his vast output there is hardly a phrase which is not challenging and original. Mozart, who admired him as a composer and as a man, and was equally admired in return, summed it up: 'There is no one who can do it all … and all equally well: except Joseph Haydn'.

Haydn, Michael (1737–1806) Austrian composer. Younger brother of Joseph Haydn, he was also a chorister at St Stephen's Cathedral in Vienna, and became deputy organist. From 1762 until his death he was musical director to the Archbishop of Salzburg, and married the Court singer Maria Magdalena Lipp, who sang principal soprano in some early Mozart operas. Michael is reputed to have been a long-term drunkard, but managed during his tenure of office to write thirty symphonies, concertos for various solo instruments and orchestra, and some dignified masses in more austere style than his brother's.

head voice A high vocal register in which the sound produces a resonance seemingly inside the singer's head rather than in the chest, as in a *chest voice*.

Heifetz, Jascha (1901–87) Russian violinist (American citizen 1925). Taught the violin by his father, he gave his first public performance at the age of five, and at eight began studies in St Petersburg Conservatoire. He played in Berlin, Vienna and Leipzig, and in New York after his family had emigrated there in 1917. Heifetz became known as one of the world's outstanding virtuosi on his instrument, and in 1939 commissioned William Walton's violin concerto.

heldentenor German for 'heroic tenor', as opposed to a lyric tenor, demanding a strong dramatic voice capable of coping with the exacting solo parts written for Wagnerian heroes in particular.

hemiola A rhythmic figure in which contrasting accentuations of notes in triple time are set one against the other in simultaneously sung or played parts, so that six beats in two bars are divided in one voice as $3 + 3$, while the other voice employs a cross-accent of $2 + 2 + 2$ or $1\frac{1}{2} + 1\frac{1}{2} + 1\frac{1}{2} + 1\frac{1}{2}$. Handel and Brahms were both fond of such devices, and there is a famous example in the waltz from Tchaikowsky's *Sleeping Beauty*.

Henze, Hans Werner (1926–) German composer. His musical education was interrupted when he was conscripted into the army in World War II and taken prisoner by the British. After the war he studied at the Heidelberg Institute for Church Music and in Paris with an advocate of twelve-note music, René Leibowitz. His earliest compositions were in neoclassical style, including his first symphony and a chamber concerto, but then he turned for a while to serialism. Disliking the post-war materialism of Germany, he went to live in Italy, which inspired his music with a warm lyricism and sensuality, both in orchestral work and in a succession of operas, among them *Der Prinz von Hamburg* and *Elegy for Young Lovers*. This opera was written to an English libretto by W.H. Auden and Chester Kallman, though first performed in a German translation; its English première was at Glyndebourne, where it was deemed to be effective in theatrical terms but less so in its music and poetry. Later Henze became a committed Marxist and wrote works with a social content, including the song cycle *El Cimarrón* about a runaway Cuban slave, and a 'military oratorio' *The Raft of the Medusa*, which caused such a clash between students and police in Hamburg in 1968 that its première had to be cancelled and postponed until 1971 in Vienna.

OTHER WORKS: Operas *Boulevard Solitude*, *The Bassarids*, *The English Cat*. Six symphonies. Five string quartets. *Voices* for two singers, small orchestra, and tape.

Herbert, Victor (1859–1924) Irish composer and conductor (American citizen 1902). Born in Dublin, Ireland, he studied the cello and became an orchestral player in Germany, where his mother had taken him after his father's death and her remarriage. In 1885 he composed and played a cello concerto. Shortly after his own marriage to an opera singer, he and his wife were hired by the New York Met, and subsequently he became a regimental bandmaster and then conductor of the Pittsburgh Symphony Orchestra. Although he struggled for recognition as a serious composer, his fame derived mainly from light-hearted operettas, among them *Naughty Marietta* and *Sweethearts*, with songs such as *Ah, Sweet Mystery of Life*.

heroic tenor *See* **heldentenor.**

Hess, (Dame) Myra (1890–1965) English pianist. She became one of England's leading interpreters of Beethoven and Schubert. Her piano transcription, *Jesu, joy of man's desiring* from Bach's cantata No.147, established itself as a firm favourite with recitalists and record collectors. During World War II she founded a morale-boosting series of lunchtime concerts in the National Gallery, London.

hidden fifths and **hidden octaves** Consecutive fifths or octaves which may escape immediate notice because of concealment by a passing note, but which nevertheless remain 'bad grammar' in musical terms. (*See also* **fifth** and **harmony**.)

Hindemith, Paul (1895–1963) German composer (American citizen 1945). One of the most prolific composers of the century, Hindemith favoured different techniques at different phrases of his career. An expressionist in youth, he became a neoclassicist and for a while an advocate of socially committed *gebrauchsmusik* ('utitlity music'), which he later repudiated. Overall his tendency was towards an exploration of musical tensions and the construction of highly chromatic edifices on the simplest fragments, without ever abandoning a firm tonal centre.

After military service in World War I he played violin and then viola in a string quartet, became concertmaster in the Frankfurt Opera orchestra, composed three short operas whose sexual themes made them a *succès de scandale*, and in 1927 became professor of composition at the Berlin *Hochschule für Musik*. At the time of Hitler's seizure of power, Hindemith was working on an opera *Mathis der Maler* (*Matthias the Painter*), an affirmation of artistic values which did not appeal to the Nazis: they banned its proposed first performance in 1935. Hindemith set out on travels which took him to Turkey, England (where overnight he composed the mourning *Trauermusik* on the death of King George V), Switzerland, and in due course the United States. In 1940 he became visiting professor of musical theory at Yale University. In 1953 he settled finally in Switzerland, conducting and writing.

In 1957 Hindemith completed a work which had long occupied his mind, an opera *Die Harmonie der Welt* (*The Harmony of the World*), based on the life and philosophical concepts of the astronomer Kepler. It was produced in Munich, but without any great success. Having started out as something of an *enfant terrible*, Hindemith spent his last few years in declining health and declining esteem, considered by younger composers as a conservative in spite of his searching mind and his continued encouragement of other musicians.

OTHER WORKS: Opera *The Long Christmas Dinner*. Requiem *When Lilacs Last in the Dooryard Bloom'd* for soloists, chorus and orchestra (on a Walt Whitman text). Choreographical suite *Nobilissima Visione* (*Most noble vision*) based on the life of St Francis of Assisi. *Kammermusik* (*Chamber music*) for various small groups.

Hoddinott, Alun (1929–) Welsh composer. He studied at University College, Cardiff, became a lecturer there, and in 1967 was appointed professor of music. His compositions include five symphonies, a number of instrumental concertos, and chamber music, all in a deeply romantic vein, sometimes employing serial techniques but on the whole remaining firmly tonal. Of his operas, *The Beach at Falesá*, based on a story by Robert Louis Stevenson, has been produced at Cardiff, and *Murder the Magician* had its première on television in 1976.

Hoffmann, E.T.A. (1776–1822) German music critic, composer, and conductor. Although he scraped

A cartoon by Paul Hindemith of a string quartet – possibly his own Amar Quartet – playing a fugue upon the chorale theme *Von Himmel Hoch*.

a living as an opera conductor and composer before dying of alcoholism, he is best-known for his fantastic tales, which provided the basis for Offenbach's opera *The Tales of Hoffmann*.

Hollywood Bowl An open-air amphitheatre near Los Angeles where the problem of performing music out of doors has been solved by the construction of a large acoustic shell. As well as individual productions, there is an annual season of concerts given by the Los Angeles Philharmonic Orchestra between July and September.

Holmboe, Vagn (1909–) Danish composer. He studied in Copenhagen and Berlin, and was himself a teacher at the Royal Danish Conservatory between 1950 and 1965. The major Danish composer since Carl Nielsen, he has written eleven symphonies, ten string quartets and a number of concertos. A fluent and rhythmically vigorous composer, he was influenced in his early quartets by Bartók, to whose memory the first is dedicated. Other elements of which Bartók would surely have approved have been assimilated as a result of Holmboe's researches into Danish and Romanian folk music.

Holst, Gustav (1874–1934) English composer. Of Swedish descent, he was born in Cheltenham

(where his birthplace has now become a Holst museum) into a musical family, and went to study composition at the Royal College of Music in London. Here he established a lifelong friendship with a fellow pupil, Ralph Vaughan Williams. Both of them were fired at about the same time with an interest in neglected English folk music, and Holst's orchestral *Somerset Rhapsody* of 1906 makes lyrical use of local folk melodies. For some years he supported himself as trombonist on seaside piers and with the Carl Rosa opera company, until he decided to go in for teaching. From 1905 until his death he was director of music at St Paul's Girls' School in London, and here he wrote his evocation of Hammersmith people, traffic and the riverside scene in his *Hammersmith* Prelude and Scherzo.

It was also here that he worked on *The Planets* orchestral suite based on astrological symbols and his interpretation of Eastern mysticism. Girls from the school copied out parts so that his friends Balfour Gardiner and Adrian Boult could arrange a performance for him to hear before leaving for Istanbul at the end of World War I as organizer of musical education for troops awaiting demobilization. Similar influences led to his settings of Hindu hymns in the *Rig-Veda*; but his favourite among his own works was the very English tone poem *Egdon Heath*, based on the stark picture of swarthy, haggard land in Thomas Hardy's novel *The Return of the Native*. His daughter Imogen wrote in later years of his recurrent taste for 'grey isolation'.

Mars, the first episode of *The Planets* to be composed, had actually been begun while he was living in the Essex village of Thaxted, where he founded a festival of music and dance and where he returned frequently to stay and work. His carol setting *The Dancing Day* was written here, and sung in May 1934 at his funeral in Chichester Cathedral, Sussex.

OTHER WORKS: Opera *The Perfect Fool*. String orchestral *St Paul's Suite, Brook Green Suite*. Choral Symphony. Choral Fantasia.

Holst, Imogen (1907–84) English conductor and writer. Educated at St Paul's Girls' School, where her father Gustav taught music, she edited and conducted several of his works and wrote a biography of him. For some years she was assistant to Benjamin Britten and was a Festival director at

Gustav Holst and Ralph Vaughan Williams, friends with a shared interest in English folk themes, resting on a walking tour in Northumberland, c.1913.

Aldeburgh, where, like Britten himself, she died.

homophony From the Greek for 'sounding the same', the word is applied in music mainly to unison singing or playing of a single melody, as in hymns, perhaps with chordal accompaniment but distinct from polyphony in that there are no contrasting themes or rhythms.

Honegger, Arthur (1892–1955) Swiss composer. After studying in Zürich and Paris he became a member of the French *avant-garde* group *Les Six*, but was too innately serious to indulge wholeheartedly in their vagaries. He first made his own earnest, somewhat rhetorical voice heard in a 'dramatic psalm' *Le Roi David* (*King David*). His energetic style and liking for direct, diatonic counterpoint in contrast to the atonal and other experiments of his contemporaries made him a sought-after provider of descriptive music for films (more than thirty in thirty years) and radio. His symphonic portrayal of a steam locomotive gathering speed, *Pacific 231*, made use of every possible musical device to summon up the feeling of power and speed, and even the scream of the brakes. (2-3-1 refers to the American nomenclature for axle arrangement – a leading bogie of two axles, three pairs of driving wheels and a single trailing axle. In British usage, based on wheels, the title would have had to be changed to *Pacific 462*! In utterly different vein, Honegger's emotional intensity is displayed to its full in the dramatic oratorio *Jeanne d'Arc au bûcher* (*Joan of Arc at the stake*), to a text by the Catholic poet Paul Claudel.

OTHER WORKS: Biblical opera *Judith*. Five symphonies. Symphonic movement *Rugby*, portraying a football pitch. Three string quartets. Film music for *Mayerling* and *Pygmalion*.

hornpipe A lively solo dance of British origin, originally in 3/2 time and used in concertos and suites by Handel and Purcell, but later in brisk 2/4. It is generally associated with sailors dancing to the accompaniment of a reed pipe with a horn bell to amplify the sound.

Horowitz, Vladimir (1904–) Russian pianist (American citizen 1944). After studying in Kiev and touring Europe as a virtuoso recitalist, he made his New York début in 1928 and settled there, marrying Toscanini's daughter Wanda. He is quoted as saying that the longest walk in the world is the walk from the Carnegie Hall wings to the piano stool. Serious illness during the late 1930s interrupted his career, but after World War II he returned to London and, after an agonizing time trying more than sixteen pianos provided for him by Steinway, gave a bravura recital boldly introducing unfamiliar Scriabin to his audience among the expected Chopin pieces. From 1953 he concentrated on recording before reappearing on the concert stage in New York in 1965.

Hotter, Hans (1909–) German bass-baritone. After working as an organist and choirmaster he made his operatic début in 1939, becoming an incomparable Wotan in Wagner's *Ring* cycle and appearing frequently at Bayreuth. In spite of the great power of his voice he has also been a sympathetic interpreter of Brahms *lieder*, and took part in an outstanding recording of Brahms's *Liebesliederwalzer*.

Howells, Herbert (1892–1983) English composer. He studied at the Royal College of Music, London, and in 1920 joined the staff there. In 1936 he followed Gustav Holst as music director at St Paul's Girls' School. His music has much in common with that of Elgar and Vaughan Williams in its pastoral moods, such as those so gently evoked in his early piano quartet and the string quartet *In Gloucestershire*. From the late 1930s onwards he concentrated on Anglican church music. After the death of his only son from spinal meningitis he poured his grief into a *Hymnus Paradisi* for voices and orchestra, but hid it away for twelve years until Vaughan Williams persuaded him to let it be performed at the Three Choirs Festival in Gloucester in 1950.

Humfrey, Pelham (1647–74) English composer. He was a Chorister and later Gentleman of the Chapel Royal. In 1664 King Charles II sent him to France to study the methods of Lully, though his expenses were so lavish that it was rumoured he was really engaged in espionage. In 1672 he was appointed Master of the Children of the Chapel Royal, where Purcell was among his pupils. His own compositions included sacred and secular songs and choral works, though the diarist Pepys wrote of him: 'an absolute monsieur ... disparages everything ... understands nothing, nor can he play on any instrument, and so cannot compose'.

Hummel, Johann Nepomuk (1778–1837) Austrian composer and pianist. He studied piano with Mozart and made his début in Vienna in 1787 at a Mozart concert. He succeeded Haydn as *kapellmeister* to Prince Esterházy, served in similar posts at Stuttgart and Weimar, toured widely as a virtuoso recitalist, and conducted the German Opera in London in 1833. His copious output includes operas, oratorios, chamber music and concertos for mandolin and bassoon. The A minor piano concerto and trumpet concerto have won a new lease of life in the latter half of the twentieth century.

humoresque A piece, usually for solo instrument, in a 'humour' or temperamental mood, not necessarily amusing. Schumann and Dvořák wrote lively sets for the piano. (German *humoreske*.)

Humperdinck, Engelbert (1854–1921) German composer. Upon winning the Mendelssohn Prize in 1879 he travelled to Italy, met Wagner, and fell under his spell. For the next two years he worked as assistant on the production of *Parsifal* at Bayreuth, then found it necessary to take teaching appointments in Spain and Germany in order to make a living. Asked by his sister to provide accompanying music for a children's play she had written around the fairy-tale *Hansel and Gretel*, he became so immersed in the project that it ended up as a full-length opera, much influenced by Wagnerian idiom. Its production in 1893 was an immediate success, and the following year it caught on with London audiences. It was the first opera to be broadcast complete in both Europe and the USA. Attempts to repeat the triumph failed, and by 1900 Humperdinck had settled back into the academic world as director of the Berlin Meisterschule of Composition.

hurdy-gurdy The word is often misused to denote a barrel organ or street piano. The instrument, dating from medieval times, was in effect a cross between a lute and a guitar, whose treble strings or *chanterelles* carried the melody while other strings acted as drones. Sound was produced by cranking a handle to rub a resined wheel across the strings. The resonant lengths of the melody strings were controlled by wooden keys attached to movable frets which stopped the strings very much in the manner of a violinist's or guitarist's fingers.

hymn A religious song of prayer or praise sung in temple, church or chapel. Fragments have survived of early Greek hymns to Apollo; the earliest known Christian hymns, two unidentifiable texts accompanied by notation in Greek lettering, were found at Oxyrhynchos in Egypt on fragments of third-century papyrus. Christian hymns began as settings of Biblical psalms, usually sung in plainchant. Later, special words were written, often set to simple themes derived from folksong which would be familiar to the congregation. Martin Luther set challenging new words to many well-known German melodies, and composed further melodies of his own, often developing into chorales expanded to wonderful effect by Buxtehude, Schütz and Bach.

The first book to be printed in the English colonies in America was the *Bay Psalm Book*, which included the much-loved doxology known in Britain as the *Old Hundredth*, in America as the *Old Hundred*. Versions of this have been arranged by several composers, including Vaughan Williams, who made ceremonial use of it for Queen Elizabeth II's coronation. It was sung at his funeral in Westminster Abbey.

Isaac Watts and the Methodist brothers, John

and Charles Wesley, spread their beliefs through the medium of simply expressed verses and simple folklike melodies. Around the time of the American Civil War, 'revival' hymns became popular, most notably *Mine Eyes have Seen the Glory of the Coming of the Lord*. In an attempt to assemble a definitive edition of English hymns and tunes, *Hymns Ancient and Modern* was published in England in 1861, and frequently updated.

|

Ibert, Jacques (1890–1962) French composer. He studied at the Paris Conservatoire, won the Prix de Rome in 1919, and while in Italy travelled extensively around the Mediterranean. The atmosphere influenced his brightly impressionistic *Escales (Ports of call)*. After working in France for some years he returned to Rome in 1937 as director of the French Academy there. Among other works he contributed one of the movements to the ballet *L'Eventail de Jeanne (Jeanne's Fan)*, commissioned from ten composers by Jeanne Dubost for her Paris ballet school; collaborated with Honegger on an opera, *L'Aiglon*; composed a concertino for alto saxophone; and adapted his witty orchestral *Divertissement* from music written for the play *The Italian Straw Hat*.

idée fixe A term applied by Berlioz to a motto theme which recurs in different guises throughout his *Symphonie fantastique*, each time conjuring up in the imagination of a morbid, drugged young musician a tormenting memory of his beloved – 'an obsessive idea that he keeps hearing wherever he goes'. It foreshadowed the *leitmotiv* of Wagner, but also has much in common with the repeated themes in Tchaikowsky's fourth and fifth symphonies and Liszt's 'transformation' studies.

imitation A device in which a figure stated at the beginning of a piece is repeated, either in the same form or displaced to an interval above or below, perhaps augmented, diminished, or in other ways refashioned. Where each subsequent voice or instrumental line keeps strictly to the same melody, though possibly interrupting before the first has finished the phrase, this forms a *canon*. In a *round*, the second voice has to wait until the first has finished.

impressionism The term originated in late nineteenth-century art criticism, and was soon applied to music such as Debussy's, whose pictorial elements, allied with shifting, unorthodox harmony, produced much the same intangible, elusive effect. In contrast, the phrase 'subjective impressionism' has been applied to the atonality and advanced chromaticism of Schoenberg and Webern.

impromptu A short piece of music whose style suggests the inspiration of the moment, to be played without formality, rather as if improvising. Many Schumann, Schubert and Chopin piano pieces are so titled.

improvisation *See* **extemporization**.

incidental music Overtures, entr'actes and 'atmospheric' background music written to accompany a play or film or provide processional flourishes and linking passages, as distinct from the integrated music and libretto of an opera. Two of the best-known examples are Mendelssohn's incidental music to Shakespeare's *A Midsummer Night's Dream* and Grieg's to Ibsen's *Peer Gynt*.

indeterminacy *See* **aleatory music**.

in nomine The plainchant phrase of *In nomine Domini* in the mass became in sixteenth-century England the basis of contrapuntal variations for keyboard, lute or consorts of viols and gave its name to the form, used rewardingly by composers such as its originator John Taverner, the Chapel Royal organist William Blitheman and his pupil John Bull.

instrumentation The scoring of music for individual instruments in relationship to one another, preferably with knowledge of the timbre and technical possibilities of each instrument. (*See* also **orchestration**.)

interlude A musical passage introduced between other musical features, as in organ chorale preludes between parts of a cantata, or sections of a play or revue. Handel was accustomed to playing the organ between acts of his operas. The *Four Sea Interludes* by Benjamin Britten, frequently performed in the concert hall, originated as descriptive passages between dramatic scenes in his opera *Peter Grimes*. In the theatre, *intermezzo* and *entr'acte* have much the same meaning.

intermezzo As mentioned above, this refers to a piece of music played between dramatic or operatic acts in the theatre. In the early days of Italian opera it was customary for quite separate instrumental, ballet or madrigal groups in costume to interrupt the proceedings with what in variety theatre parlance have come to be known as 'novelty items'. When used to more serious effect by operatic composers, the intermezzo could become an essential bridge between one act and another, perhaps to indicate the passage of time or simply to soothe the ear while the scene-shifters did their work. The title has been bestowed on several such pieces now frequently played in their own right, as in the *Cavalleria Rusticana* intermezzo, or *The Walk to the Paradise Garden* from Delius's opera *A Village Romeo and Juliet*. Brahms used it to describe some of his shorter piano pieces.

INTERPRETATION MARKS

Music written for solo or ensemble instruments carries instructions from the composer (and sometimes from a conductor or the actual player) to indicate tempo, style and dynamics. The words used are, by tradition, generally Italian, but in the following list a number of the more frequent German and French expressions are also included; common abbreviations are shown in brackets. In addition to verbal instructions there are symbols for accentuation, phrasing and other niceties of performance, illustrated within this section.

ACCELERANDO: (*accel*) Gradually increase speed.

ADAGIO: Slow and easy. *Adagietto* indicates a slightly slower speed; *adagio assai*, very slow.

AD LIBITUM: (*ad lib*) At will — 'as you please'. This can be applied to tempo, rhythm and interpretation, and to improvised passages as in the cadenza of a concerto or a chorus in a jazz number.

A DUE CORDE: To be played on two strings.

AFFETTO or **AFFETTUOSO:** Affectionately, expressively. Also occasionally *affettuosamente*.

AFFRETTANDO: Urging on — applied either to the speed of the passage or to its dramatic intensity.

AGITATO: Agitated, restless. The French term is *agité*.

À LA CORDE: Keep the bow on the string smoothly from note to note.

À LA MESURE: Keep in strict time.

AL or **ALLA:** 'At the' or 'in the style of'. Appears frequently in the following formations:
  al fine Play to the end (often given as an instruction after repeat of a subsection within a piece).
  al loco Return to original pitch (e.g. after a passage marked *8va*, an octave higher or lower).
  al niente Fade away to nothing.
  al segno To the sign (*see* **dal segno**).
  alla breve 'In short style' — that is, in a piece written with four beats to the bar but at a tempo which may make performance difficult, the player should treat it as being effectively in 2/2 time.
  alla marcia In march style.
  alla turca In the Turkish style (as in Mozart's *Rondo alla turca*).

ALLARGANDO: Broadening and slowing gradually.

ALLEGRO: Bright and lively, i.e. fast. *Allegro moderato* means moderately brisk; *allegro con brio*, fast and with spirit. *Allegretto* is slower and less vigorous than *allegro*, but still lively.

ALLMÄHLICH: Gradually.

A MEZZO VOCE: Singing or playing in subdued style — 'at half the voice'.

ANDANTE: Moving along at a moderate pace. *Andantino* also indicates this 'strolling' mood, but with a slightly quicker step.

ANIMANDO or **ANIMATO:** Animated, with spirit. (French *animé*.)

ANWACHSEN: Gradually louder.

APPASSIONATO or **APPASSIONATA:** With passion.

ARCO: The bow of a stringed instrument. (German *bogen*.) The instructions *coll' arco* or *arcato* indicate that the player should resume use of the bow after plucking a PIZZICATO passage.

ASSAI: Very.

A TEMPO: Return to the original speed.

ATTACCA: (In French, *suivez*.) Go straight on — e.g. from one movement of a sonata or concerto to the next — without pause.

AUSDRUCKSVOLL: With expression.

À VOLONTÉ: French for 'at will' or AD LIBITUM.

BALLABILE: In dancing style.

BEWEGT: Speeded up or emotionally moving. *Bewegter*, quicker.

BIS: In French, 'twice', meaning that a passage should be repeated. In the opera house or concert hall it is the same as 'Encore!'

CALANDO: (*cal*) Slowing and softening gradually.

CANTABILE: (*cant*) To be played smoothly and lyrically, in the style of a song.

COL, COLL' or **COLLA:** 'With the' — as in *coll' arco*, with the bow; *col legno*, with the wood (meaning to strike the strings of a violin, for instance, with the back of the bow); and *colla parte*, meaning that the accompanist to a singer or instrumentalist should follow the soloist rather than adhere strictly to the written instructions regarding rhythm and tempo.

COMODO: Leisurely, at a moderate speed.

CON: 'With' — as in the following formations:
  con amore With love, in the sense of playing with enthusiasm and dedication.
  con brio With spirit and animation.
  con dolore With melancholy.
  con fuoco With fire.
  con moto With movement.
  con sordino With mute (as on the bridge of a violin or in the bell of a brass instrument).

CRESCENDO: (*cresc*) Gradually increasing in volume.

DA CAPO: (*D.C.*) Repeat from the beginning: literally 'from the head'. *D.C. al segno* indicates that the music should be played from the beginning to a point marked by a sign; *D.C. al fine* that it should be played right from the beginning to the end.

DAL SEGNO: (*D.S.*) Repeat from the sign, i.e. do not go right back to the beginning as in preceding *D.C.* entry, but return and resume only at the marked point.

DECRESCENDO: (*decresc*) The opposite of CRESCENDO: fading gently from loudness to softness. More frequently used nowadays is the word DIMINUENDO.

DÉTACHÉ: French for 'detached', meaning to play in a STACCATO style.

DIMINUENDO: (*dim*) Gradually decreasing in volume.

DIVISI: (*div*) Divided. The instruction is given on the score where a section of instruments which would normally play in unison (such as the first violins) are now given two or more separate lines to play, which must be divided among them and not attempted in chord form by, for instance, double stopping.

DOLCE: Sweetly. *Dolcissimo*, very sweetly. The German is *leise*; French, *doucement*.

DOLENTE: Doleful.

DOLOROSO: Sorrowful (similar to DOLENTE). Also *dolorosamente*.

DOPPIO: Double. In *doppio movimento* this calls for adopting a new tempo twice as fast as the preceding one. The German is *doppelt*.

EMPFINDUNG: German for 'feeling'; *empfindungsvoll*, feelingly.

ENERGICO: Forceful. German, *energisch*.

ESPRESSIVO: Expressively.

ESTINGUENDO: Dying away. Similarly, *estinto*, meaning 'extinct' – i.e. to be played as softly and levelly as possible.

FINE: End. Not strictly necessary at the end of a musical score, but used at a bar-line where the actual conclusion is reached by repetition of an earlier section. (*See also* DA CAPO.)

FORTE: (*f*) Loud. *Fortissimo* (*ff*) means very loud: some composers demanding the greatest possible volume have been known to write *fff* and even *ffff*.

FORTEPIANO: (*fp*) Calls for a swift change from loud to soft.

FORZANDO: (*fz*) Forceful: meaning that the note so marked should be strongly emphasized. A more common form is SFORZANDO (*sfz*).

GIOCOSO: Playful.

GIOIOSO: Joyful.

GIUSTO: Exact. Generally appears in the phrase *tempo giusto*, instructing the player or conductor to adopt a reasonable pace and adhere strictly to it throughout.

GLISSANDO: (*gliss*) Sliding. Usually seen as an instruction to a pianist or harpist to slide a thumb or finger swiftly down the keyboard or across the strings. It can also be achieved by the trombone and by members of the violin family. The word is a jocular derivation from the French *glisser*. In Italian the more formal term is *strisciando*.

GRANDIOSO: Majestically.

GRAVE: Slow, solemn.

GRAZIOSO: Gracefully.

INCALCANDO: 'Heating up' — that is, increasing speed and volume.

ISTESSO: The same. Usually found in *l'istesso tempo*, signifying that even though the score may be showing a change of rhythm in the time signature, the player(s) should maintain the same beat value.

L, L.H. or **l.h.:** On a piano part, indicates that a passage should be played by the left hand, even though it may be in a high register and may cross over the right hand.

LACRIMOSO: Tearfully.

LAMENTOSO: Mournfully.

LANGSAM: Slow. *Langsamer*, slower.

LARGO: The word really means 'broad' rather than 'slow', but has come to define a spacious slow movement. Similarly, *largamente* asks for a stately style of performance. *Larghetto* means a 'little largo', to be played with dignity but not quite so slowly.

LEGATO: (*leg*) Tied. The application here is to a style of joining notes smoothly together in a sustained phrase — the opposite of STACCATO.

LEGGERO and **LEGGIERO:** Light and swift. Sometimes written adverbially as *leggieramente*.

LEISE: German for soft or gentle.

LENTO: Slow, but not quite as slow as LARGO. French *lent*, German *langsam*.

LESTO: Quick. *Lestissimo*, very quick.

LIBERAMENTE: Freely — i.e. allowing free interpretation of rhythm, RUBATO, and other aspects of a piece. (French *librement*.)

LOCO: Literally 'place', usually found in an instruction to a player to return to the music's original register after the conclusion of a passage marked *8va* — an octave higher or lower than the written part. Frequently shown as *al loco*.

LONTANO: Faint and distant. French, *lointain*.

LUNGA and **LUNGO:** Prolonged. *Lunga pausa* indicates a long rest, to be sustained entirely at the performer's wish, without regard to whatever formal length of rest appears in the score.

LUSINGANDO and **LUSINGHIERO:** Coaxing: asking for the piece or passage to be played in a charming, endearing manner.

LUTTO, LUTTOSO or **LUTTUOSO:** Mournful.

MAESTOSO: Majestic, stately.

MARCATO: (*marc*) Marked: i.e. the notes should be accentuated and the piece as a whole played decisively. When one part in an ensemble is so marked, the intention is that it should stand out from the rest of the music. Sometimes written *marcando*. In French, *marqué*.

MARTELLATO: Hammered. Indicates that a string player should hit the strings hard with his bow to accentuate the notes. French, *martelé*.

MARZIALE: In martial style.

MENO: Less. In *meno mosso*, less lively, it calls for the speed to be slowed down slightly.

MESTO: Gloomy, woeful.

MEZZA or **MEZZO:** Half. The markings *mezzo-forte* (*mf*) and *mezzo-piano* (*mp*) ask for a volume between loud and soft; *mezza voce* is a 'half voice', produced softly as if under the breath.

MISTERIOSO: Mysteriously.

MODERATO: At a moderate pace. French, *modéré*.

MOLTO: Much, or very, as in *allegro molto* — very fast.

MORENDO: Dying away, either in volume (often indicated by a decrescendo mark) or in speed, especially towards the end of a piece.

MOSSO: Moved, lively. *Più mosso* means quicker, *meno mosso* slower

MOTO: Movement. *Con moto* asks for a piece to move along at a good pace.

NACH: German for 'after' or 'in the manner of' (French *à la*, Italian *alla*). So *nachdenklich*, to be played in thoughtful manner; *nach gefallen*, the equivalent of AD LIB; *nachlassend*, slowing gradually; *nachslag*, a grace-note; and *nach und nach*, bit by bit.

NOBILMENTE: In a noble (all too frequently pompous) style.

OSSIA: Or else. Denoting an alternative sequence of notes to those provided by the composer, which may not be within the player's technical capabilities. These substitute passages are usually written in smaller notation in parallel with the original.

OTTAVA: (*ott*) Usually written as *8va*, signifying that the performer should play the passage so marked an octave higher (if the symbol appears above the notes) or an octave lower (if it appears below). This obviates the need for an accumulation of extra ledger lines above or below the staff.

PARLANDO: An injunction to an instrumentalist to play in a communicative 'speaking voice'; or to a singer to produce vocal lines in a conversational style.

PED: A marking on piano music to indicate that the sustaining pedal (commonly but wrongly called the 'loud pedal') should be engaged.

PERDENDO or **PERDENDOSI:** Gradually weakening ('losing') in volume, though not necessarily slowing down.

PESANTE: Weighty – i.e. to be played firmly and heavily throughout.

PIACEVOLE: Agreeable, in pleasant style.

PIANGENDO or **PIANGEVOLE:** Mournful; plaintive.

PIANO: (*p*) Quiet. The passage so marked should be played softly. Even softer is *pianissimo (pp)*, and the extreme in this direction is marked *ppp*.

PIÙ: More, as in *più allegro*, faster, or *più lento*, slower. *Un poco più* indicates just a little more.

PIÙ FORTE: (*pf*) Means play a little louder.

PIZZICATO: (*pizz*) Pinched. The string player should not bow the strings but pluck them with a finger. In some alternating passages the bow is used in the right hand while a finger of the left hand plucks intervening notes. *Pizzicato* playing of the double bass is normal usage in dance and swing bands.

PLACIDO: Tranquil.

POCO: A little, as in *poco lento*, rather slow. *Poco a poco* means, like the German *nach und nach*, bit by bit, or little by little.

PRÈS DE LA TABLE: An instruction to a harpist to finger near the sounding board.

PRESSANTE or **PRESSANDO:** Pressing on; increasing in speed. Similar to ACCELERANDO. French, *pressant*.

PRESTO: Very fast – faster than ALLEGRO – and lively. *Prestissimo* indicates that the piece should be played as fast as possible.

PRIMA and **PRIMO:** First. It identifies the top part in a piano duet, and is used in several other markings: *come prima*, to repeat a passage in exactly the same style as before; *tempo primo (t.p.)*, return to the original tempo; and *prima volta (p.v.)*, marking the transaction to a repeat of the 'first time' section of a piece, while *seconda volta (s.v.)* leads on after the repeat to a different section.

QUASI: As if; simulating. The word suggests that a piece should be played in a way which hints at something slightly at variance, or even downright contradictory – seemingly but not really, as it were. *Quasi allegro*, for instance, might indicate something which can be made to sound fast because of complex notation even though the basic tempo may be no more than ANDANTE.

R, R.H. or **r.h.:** On a piano part, indicates that a passage should be played by the right hand, even though it may be in a low register and may cross over the left hand.

RALLENTANDO: (*rall*) Gradual slowing down.

RASCH: German for fast.

RAVVIVANDO: Reviving; generally used to urge a speeding-up after the slowing-down of, for example, a *rallentando*.

RELIGIOSO: In solemn devotional style.

RINFORZANDO: (*rf, rinf,* or *rfz*) Reinforcing. Applied to an abrupt emphasis or CRESCENDO over a short phrase or, as with SFORZANDO, on an individual note or chord.

RISOLUTO: Determined; resolute.

RITARDANDO: (*ritard* or *rit*) Retarding, holding back. The implication of slowing down is virtually the same as RALLENTANDO. The direction RITENUTO, also shortened to *rit*, has the same implications, though some critics and players interpret it as defining a more immediate slowing down than in the case of the other two terms.

RITENUTO: *See* RITARDANDO.

RUBATO: Literally 'robbed'. *Tempo rubato* allows the performer freedom to linger upon one note or phrase and 'steal' from another (usually against a steady pulse in the orchestra or, in the case of a pianist, against a regular left-hand rhythm) in order to produce an expressive effect. Some players introduce it to suit their own tastes; but if a composer himself wishes a piece to be treated with this freedom he may write on the score *rubato, molto rubato* (a lot of *rubato*), or perhaps *rubato ma non troppo* (*rubato* but not too much).

SALTANDO or **SALTATO:** Leaping. An instruction to a string player to bounce the middle of the bow on and off the strings. Interchangeable SPICCATO. French, *sautillé*.

SANFT: German for gentle, easy.

SCHERZANDO: Skittish; humorous. On a score it asks for the piece or passage to be performed lightly and playfully. A whole movement may be treated this way, as with one marked, for example, *allegretto scherzando*.

SCHNELL: German for fast. *Schneller*, faster.

SCIOLTO: Untied. Meaning to play in a relaxed, easygoing style.

SCORRENDO or **SCORREVOLE:** Scurrying. Means the same as GLISSANDO.

SEGNO: Sign. *See* AL SEGNO and DAL SEGNO.

SEGUE: Follow on without a pause. Similar to the command ATTACCA. Sometimes used at the bottom

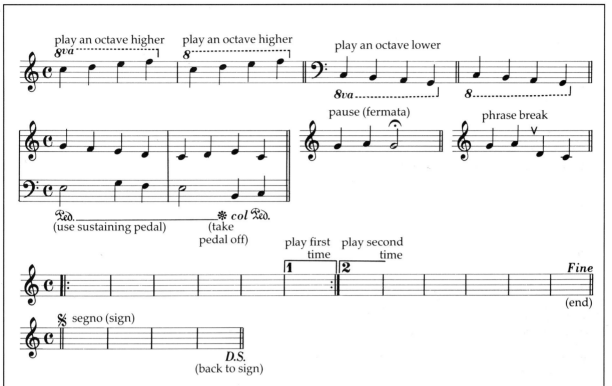

of a page to indicate that, even though a phrase may appear to be complete, there is more to come and one should be ready to turn over.

SEHR: German equivalent of MOLTO, or very.

SEMPLICE: Simple. Used by a composer when he wishes to warn players against over-indulgence in romantic interpretation or excessive RUBATO in a piece which ought to be performed without affectation.

SEMPRE: Always. Joined, for example, to the previous entry to give *sempre semplice*, it would emphasize the composer's wish that the piece or passage so marked should be played straightforwardly throughout; *sempre staccato* means that all succeeding notes should, until otherwise directed, be played STACCATO — which saves writing a dot above each note in the sequence.

SENZA: Without. Used in many contexts, as in *senza rallentando*, warning the player not to slow down, and *senza sordino*, without mute, usually at the end of a string or brass passage earlier marked *con sordino*: on a piano part *senza sordini* indicates that the sustaining pedal should be used, thereby removing the dampers from the strings.

SFORZANDO or **SFORZATO**: (*sf* or *sfz*) Reinforced. A note or chord so marked should be strongly accentuated.

SIMILE: (*sim*) Like. It indicates that a subsequent passage should be performed in exactly the style already established in a similar preceding passage. This saves repetition on the score of every expression mark, bowing, GLISSANDO and ornamentation instruction, etc.

SLENTANDO: Slowing down gradually. The same as the command RALLENTANDO.

SMORZANDO: (*smorz*) Smothered. The sound should gradually fade away — not necessarily linked to a slackening of speed, unless so marked.

SOAVE: Sweet; gentle.

SOPRA: Over; on. *Sopra una corda* on violin music means that the phrase so marked should be played on one string.

SOSPIRANDO: Sighing. Indicates that the music should be played in a melancholy style.

SOSTENUTO: (*sost* or *sosten*) Sustained. A warning to the performer, vocal or instrumental, to hold on to a note for its full length, or maintain a melodic phrase on a broad, flowing line. (*See also* TENUTO.)

SOTTO: Under. The most common use is in *sotto voce*, meaning that a singer or instrumentalist should perform the melody 'beneath the voice' — i.e. in an undertone.

SPIANATO: Planed; level. Music to be performed in an even, smoothed-out fashion.

SPICCATO: Separated. In this context meaning to bounce a violin bow on the strings. Equivalent of the leaping SALTANDO.

Stringed instrument markings:

downbow upbow   tie   slur   tremolo   trill

STACCATO: (*stacc*) Detached. The opposite of LEGATO, this calls for crisp, clearly separated playing of the notes in a phrase, usually marked on the music by a dot above each note to be so played (but *see also* SEMPRE STACCATO). In effect the note is shortened by the introduction of a brief pause between it and its neighbour, the length of the gap being determined by the composer's use of different dot markings — though some modern composers prefer to write out the exact length of note required. String players tackle STACCATO passages by stopping the bow abruptly before continuing to the next note; by bouncing the bow in SALTANDO fashion; or by PIZZICATO plucking of the strings. Wind players combine short expulsions of breath with tonguing. A pianist will strike a key and lift his finger as quickly as possible.

STESSO: *See* ISTESSO.

STRINGENDO: (*string*) Tightening. An injunction to the performer to increase the tempo and intensity, usually when approaching the exciting climax of a work.

SUBITO: (*sub*) Suddenly. Instructs the player to go on immediately, without a pause. *See particularly* VOLTI SUBITO.

SUL: On; or close to. *Sul G* indicates playing on the G string of a violin. *Sul ponticello* instructs a string player to bow close to the bridge of the instrument and so produce a nasal, rather scraping sound. *Sul tasto* has the opposite effect: playing with the bow over the fingerboard produces a warm, mellow sound.

TACET: Silent. The player concerned has nothing to do until instructed otherwise. If in fact he has nothing further to contribute throughout all that remains of the piece, his part will often be marked *tacet al fine*.

TANTO: As much; so much. Usually employed in a warning sense as *non tanto* — not too much. Similar to TROPPO.

TARDO and **TARDAMENTE:** Slow; slowing. *Tardando* implies delaying, i.e. playing the music in a lingering fashion.

TENENDO: Sustained. To be played without hurrying.

TENERO and **TENERAMENTE:** Tender; tenderly. German, ZART, ZÄRTLICH.

TENUTO: (*ten*) Held. The note, chord or phrase marked should be given its full value and even held a fraction longer, but not to the extent of holding *back*, as with RITENUTO.

TRANQUILLO: Calm; peaceful.

TREMOLANDO: (*trem*) Trembling. The word once referred to an exaggerated *vibrato*, but is now used to indicate a *tremolo*, or shaking, produced on stringed instruments by rapid to-and-fro bowing or by fast fingering between two notes, rather like a speeded-up trill.

TRILL: (*tr*) Shake. An ornamentation provided by rapid alternation between the main note and a tone or semitone above it, according to key or the composer's specific markings. The instruction is almost invariably accompanied by a wavy line, extended over the music to define the length of trill required.

TROPPO: Too much. Usually found, like TANTO, in the negative, as in *allegro ma non troppo* — fast but not too much so.

UNA CORDA: One string. An instruction on piano music to use the damping ('soft') pedal, which shifts the hammers so that instead of playing all three of the strings to each note they strike only one.

VIVACE: Animated; with vivacity. It refers to the enthusiastic style of playing as much as the speed, but in essence means fast and lively.

VIVO: Lively. Much the same as VIVACE, but less frequently used.

VOLANTE or **VOLATE:** Flying. Indicates a swiftly running passage, usually for a stringed instrument in which the bow 'flies' over a near-STACCATO sequence of notes.

VOLTI SUBITO: (*v.s.*) Turn over quickly — a command at the bottom of a page of music which, in moments of stress, can tempt the player to demand, 'How many hands does he think I've got?'

ZART and **ZÄRTLICH:** German for tender, tenderly.

ZURÜCKHALTEN: German for holding back — equivalent of RITARDANDO.

interval The distance, or difference in pitch, between two notes, whether played simultaneously or in succession. The intervals are identified by numbers according to the size of the gap between them: e.g. in the major scale starting on C, the note F would be a fourth, G a fifth. The fourth, fifth and octave are regarded as *perfect intervals*; the others in the scale are called *major second*, *major third*, *major sixth* and *major seventh*. Any such interval reduced by a semitone becomes a *minor third*, *minor sixth*, etc. Enlarged by a semitone, it is an *augmented interval*. *Compound intervals* are those wider than an octave, e.g. from C to the D a *major ninth* above. The way in which a composer uses intervals in his melody, harmony or counterpoint is often as distinctive as a thumbprint.

intonation The way of singing or playing music in tune and producing overall phrasing which pleases the ear. The word can also be applied to the *intoning* of an introductory phrase on one note by a plainchant singer to establish the correct pitch.

introduction The beginning of a piece of music, often a slow section leading into the first movement of a sonata-form symphony or concerto, or a separate section as in Ravel's *Introduction and Allegro* for harp, flute, clarinet and string quartet.

introit From the Latin for 'entrance', the word applies in a Roman Catholic mass to an antiphon or part of a plainchant psalm intoned by the priest, or to a psalm sung by the choir as the priest approaches the altar to celebrate the Eucharist.

invention A short contrapuntal composition stating one theme and then developing it in two or three parts, with frequent use of imitation. The best-known examples are J.S. Bach's Two-part Inventions and what he called 'Symphonies', now referred to as his Three-part Inventions.

inversion The turning upside down of a chord from its root position, or of a melodic theme so that its intervals go down instead of up, and vice versa. (*See also* **fugue** and **harmony**.)

Ippolitov-Ivanov, Mikhail (1859–1935) Russian composer and conductor. After studying in the choir school of the Isaaky Cathedral, he became a composition pupil of Rimsky-Korsakov at the St Petersburg Conservatory. In 1883 he became head of Tiflis Conservatory, where he composed his *Caucasian Sketches* for orchestra. After the Russian Revolution he became director of the Moscow Conservatory and conductor of the Moscow Opera. He composed six operas and a number of pieces favourable to the régime, such as the choral and orchestral *Hymn to Labour* and the march *Song of Stalin*.

Ireland, John (1879–1962) English composer. His parents died when he was fourteen, leaving him a small income which he supplemented by work as a church organist and as accompanist at smoking concerts while studying the piano and composition at the Royal College of Music. For many years he held organ posts in Chelsea, and in 1923 became professor of composition at the RCM. Many of his own compositions, including the piano pieces *Chelsea Reach* and *Ragamuffin*, portray his pleasure in the London scene, though he was also drawn into the countryside and particularly to prehistoric sites which awoke mystical, haunting resonances in him.

Ireland favoured a restrained, often austere French style in his music, yet at the same time he was entranced by romantic visions of ancient mounds and their ghosts. His symphonic rhapsody *Mai-Dun* evokes the battle-torn history of

A portrait by Guy Lindsay Roddon of John Ireland in 1960, two years before the composer's death. His gravestone at Shipley in Sussex bears the inscription, 'One of God's noblest works lies here.'

Maiden Castle in ancient Wessex; while staying in Jersey he worked on *The Forgotten Rite*, a tone poem inspired by the neolithic dolmens of the Channel Islands; and his vision of a group of dancing children below Chanctonbury Ring in Sussex led to his *Legend* for piano and orchestra.

The horrors of World War II depressed Ireland deeply, as shown in the pain and nostalgia of the *Concertino Pastorale*. In 1953 he settled in a Sussex windmill, where his sight deteriorated and he grew unwilling to travel even as far as London. In 1962 he was buried in the nearby churchyard of Shipley, and the grave was marked by a sarsen stone in sight of his beloved Chanctonbury Ring.

OTHER WORKS: Orchestral *A London Overture*. *Downland Suite* for brass or strings. Cantata *These Things Shall Be*. Carol *The Holy Boy* (also arranged for piano and other instruments). Song *Sea Fever*. Piano suite *Sarnia*, inspired by Guernsey scenes.

isorhythm From the Greek 'equal', here stipulating the same rhythmic pattern (or *talea*) to be maintained against a melodic pattern (or *colour*), although the notes sung or played above the repeated pattern may differ, so that restatements of the rhythm may occur against different pitches. In the fourteenth-century motet, isorhythms were restricted to the tenor part, but later the principle was applied to other voices also in order to achieve greater coherence.

Ives, Charles (1874–1954) American composer. The son of a Connecticut bandmaster, and himself a church organist at the age of thirteen, Ives studied composition at Yale University but decided there was little money in music and became an insurance agent. Nevertheless he spent all his spare time composing, in an experimental vein whose originality was only fully appreciated many years later, since he made few attempts to have his work actually performed at the time. In seclusion he created his own language of atonality, polytonality, polyrhythms and piled-up dissonances, assembled out of incongruous materials such as hymn tunes, vaudeville numbers and the clashes of different brass bands in a parade playing in different keys and different rhythms. When at last his music began to be heard, difficulties in performance were not eased by the disorderly state of his manuscripts or the eccentric demands he made. In *Central Park in the Dark* he wanted the orchestra to be subdivided, part on stage and part off. In *The Unanswered Question* the conductor is left to cue in various parts when it suits him. Ives's ultimate ambition was to write a *Universe Symphony* for performance by vast orchestras and choirs set upon mountain tops and in the valleys below.

A 1950 lithograph of Charles Ives. Business commitments meant that Ives could compose only at weekends, yet he produced a vast amount of symphonic, chamber and vocal music and was forever revising and rethinking his work.

In 1919 he published his second piano sonata, the huge *Concord Sonata*, at his own expense, and followed this with the publication of 114 songs. Gradually other American composers began to appreciate his creative uniqueness and his 'truth to experience' in the use of native American themes, and most of them today freely acknowledge his seminal influence upon their own work. In 1947 a performance of his third symphony had such an impact that he was awarded a Pulitzer Prize. But by the time he had been thus 'discovered', he had virtually ceased composing: afflicted by heart trouble and diabetes, he retired both from music and, in 1930, from the insurance business, though he lived on for almost another quarter of a century.

OTHER WORKS: Orchestral *Three Places in New England*; *Firemen's Parade on Main Street*. Choral *General William Booth Enters Into Heaven*. Two string quartets. Four violin sonatas. *Three Quarter-Tone Pieces* for two pianos. Collections of sacred and secular songs.

J

jam session A spell of improvisation around well-known tunes or chord sequences by a group of jazz instrumentalists. (*See also* **jazz**.)

Janáček, Leoš (1854–1928) Czech composer. Born in the Moravian village of Hukvaldy, he studied music in a monastery school in Brno and then went on to a teachers' training college and to Prague Organ School, but always retained an intense feeling for the folk music and dialect of his childhood surroundings. Audiences and academic critics unfamiliar with the everyday rhythms and characteristic repetitions of that provincial speech found it difficult at first to come to terms with the musical interpretations he attempted in his songs and operas.

Janáček's earliest attempts at opera, after some years of teaching, collecting folk music and writing for local choral groups in Moravia, were made under the influence of Dvořák, but he broke out into a quite different world with *Její Pastorkyna* (*Her Stepdaughter*), better known under its later title *Jenůfa*, first performed in Prague in 1916. This tragedy of a village girl, her two lovers, her illegitimate child and her 'church-woman' stepmother presents the darker side of the bucolic life so jovially portrayed in Smetana's opera *The Bartered Bride*. The composer was completing the work just as his daughter Olga died, and his agony at the loss is echoed in the music of the second and third acts, and in his piano pieces *Down an Overgrown Path*, one of which echoes with the sound of an owl hooting a repeated prophecy of death.

The real, vibrant life of the countryside continued to provide Janáček with themes and the 'melodic curves' of demotic speech, set against strangely spaced chords and often harsh, challenging orchestration. His song cycle *The Diary of a Man who Disappeared* was provoked by a story in a Brno newspaper about a farmer's son who vanished from his home in pursuit of a gipsy girl who had borne his child. The exquisite opera *The Cunning Little Vixen* derived from, of all things, a newspaper cartoon strip: its cast of singing animals could make it, in lesser hands, as naïve as a Christmas pantomime, but it has proved to be one of his best-loved, most moving masterpieces.

The Czech composer Leoš Janáček, portrayed in a charcoal sketch by his compatriot K. Svolinsky. Janáček summed up his lifelong aim in music: 'I want to cry myself into the core of yearning; all this in full intensity.'

During his country's brief spell of independence between World Wars I and II, the composer dedicated a *Military Sinfonietta* to the Czechoslovak armed forces, originating from a brass fanfare written for a Prague gymnastic festival and now referred to simply as *Sinfonietta*. Towards the end of that first war he and his wife had met and spent holidays with an antique dealer David Stössl and his wife Kamila. From then on Janáček was infatuated by this woman thirty-eight years younger than himself, pouring his heart and all his genius into operas such as *Katya Kabanova* with its tale of illicit love, *The Makropoulos Affair* about a ravishingly beautiful, ageless woman, and his second string quartet with its significant

Miles Davis, influential modern exponent of intellectual 'cool jazz' deriving from the experiments of Charlie Parker and Dizzy Gillespie but reaching into new, remoter worlds and harmonic progressions.

title, *Intimate Letters*. At the age of seventy he wrote his rapturous wind sextet *Mladi* (*Youth*).

OTHER WORKS: Opera *From the House of the Dead*. Orchestral *Lach* Dances; rhapsody *Taras Bulba*. Choral and orchestral *Glagolitic Mass*. Two volumes of *Moravian Dances* for piano.

jazz The word seems to have been coined as a derogatory term for what was considered in polite society a raucous and even an immorally suggestive development of ragtime, but was swiftly adopted into normal usage as a useful description of all rhythmic popular music with a strong beat and syncopated phrases above it. Its birth is generally credited to the Negro marching bands and blues singers of New Orleans, with a tradition stemming from Africa; though the leader of the pioneering Original Dixieland Jazz Band, which first brought the sound to Europe, claimed that it owed much more to white musicians using European melodies and harmonies.

The music is characterized by a misplacing of accents between basic time signature and the solo or ensemble melodic lines. In many pieces the emphasis falls on weak beats of the bar. Steps in the dance rage of the 1920s, the *Charleston*, were governed by the division of four beats in a bar into 1½ + 2½. Parts of Meade Lux Lewis's piano piece *Honky Tonk Train Blues* set a steady figure of dotted quaver and semiquaver in the left hand against 12/8 time in the right. Such waywardness jarred on many but appealed to others: Milhaud, Hindemith, Stravinsky and Poulenc all tried to adapt these eccentric cross rhythms to their own ends, and Krenek's fashionable opera *Jonny spielt auf* (*Johnny strikes up*) had a black jazz player as its hero.

Few of these earnest experiments contributed much to the true development of jazz, which rests much more on the extemporization of gifted soloists and an unteachable instinct for relaxing against what might seem to unbelievers a frenetic, pounding rhythm and amplified wind instruments, than on carefully calculated scoring of orchestral parts. Even allowing for the high quality of compositions by, for instance, Duke Ellington, the real jazz enthusiast remembers players above all: trumpeters like King Oliver, Louis Armstrong, Buck Clayton and Miles Davis; saxophonists like Johnny Hodges, Charlie Parker and Lester Young; pianists like Earl Hines, Teddy Wilson, 'Fats' Waller and Thelonious Monk.

Ragtime, forerunner of jazz, was in essence a piano style with a strong rhythm, but usually composed by such executants as Scott Joplin rather than improvised. *Dixieland* (and later the so-called 'trad jazz' which aimed to revivify such earlier 'pure' styles) was played by small groups of players such as trumpet, trombone and clarinet (to which was added in due course a saxophone) with the backing of a rhythm section which in its simplest form consisted of drums, banjo and brass or string bass, with a piano if the group was playing indoors. As jazz grew more popular, attempts were made to provide a 'respectable' version with the *symphonic jazz* arranged for large orchestras such as that of Paul Whiteman. Less formally, real devotees found release and refreshment in the driving *Chicago style* featuring players such as Bix Beiderbecke, Jack Teagarden and, through several distillations, Benny Goodman.

Goodman and rivals such as the Dorsey Brothers and Artie Shaw opened up the *swing* era of big band sound, still relying on imaginative soloists but providing a background of ensemble orchestration, either in the form of block chords and insistent 'riffs' to urge the clarinet, trumpet or saxophone star along, or as increasingly complex works for contrasting sections of the full orchestra. Count Basie emerged with a Kansas City style of fast blues playing. Glen Miller's tightly disciplined band provided the definitive, now sentimentally evocative sound of World War II radio programmes. After the war there were some who tried to cling to the older forms either in New Orleans revivalism or a compromise music dubbed *mainstream*, while others sought a marriage of jazz forms with other modern music and called it *progressive jazz*. Whatever its directions in the future, it has established itself as the most influential music of the twentieth century, American in origin and accent but now an international language with a vast vocabulary.

Jew's harp A misnomer for what should be called a *jaw's harp*, a small metal frame carrying a thin metal strip. The player's teeth grip the frame while one or two fingers pluck the strip to produce a twanging sound which can be varied by altering the shape of the open mouth. There are varieties of this instrument throughout Europe and Asia.

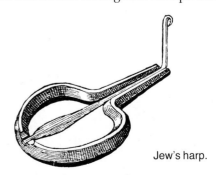

Jew's harp.

jig A lively dance popular for centuries throughout the British Isles, similar in its triple time to the *gigue* but usually more bucolic and often with a boisterous semi-comic element. It has survived in Ireland and in some of the outer islands of Scotland as a popular feature with country fiddlers and folk dance groups.

Joachim, Joseph (1831–1907) Hungarian violinist. He made his first concert appearance at the age of seven, and during his years of study in Leipzig played at concerts there and also visited London. Further visits to England led to an honorary Mus.D. from Cambridge University in 1887. In that same year he received a magnificent gift from Brahms. The two had been close friends but had quarrelled when, after Joachim's divorce, the composer sided with his wife. Regretting the rift, Brahms wrote a double concerto for violin and cello and sent it to Joachim as a peace-offering. Joachim himself composed three violin concertos and a number of overtures and songs.

The violin virtuoso Joseph Joachim on a summer holiday with his family in Gründelwald.

Jochum, Eugen (1902–87) German conductor. He conducted many leading German orchestras, and even during World War II was able to continue as principal conductor of Hamburg Opera, keep Jewish musicians in his orchestra, and perform banned composers such as Hindemith and Stravinsky. He was the only German conductor the Concertgebouw Orchestra of Amsterdam would accept during the Nazi occupation. In 1949 he founded the Bavarian Radio Symphony Orchestra and expanded his recording repertory. He was a sympathetic exponent of Bruckner, and an early enthusiast for the works of Carl Orff. Late in life he became a much revered visiting conductor of the London Philharmonic Orchestra, and in 1975 was appointed Conductor Laureate of the London Symphony Orchestra.

Joplin, Scott (1868–1917) Black American composer and pianist. His parents, brothers and sisters were talented amateur musicians, and young Scott's attempts at piano playing led to his father buying him a secondhand instrument. He was given free lessons in piano and harmony by a German teacher in their hometown in Texas. At fourteen he started a career playing in the saloons and brothels of St Louis and Chicago, developing his own style of percussive, rhythmic piano playing and composing a number of what he called *rags*, among them *Maple Leaf Rag* and *The Entertainer* (enjoying a popular revival since its use in the film *The Sting*). He emphasized that these pieces should be played brightly but not too fast. Anxious to establish himself as a serious, original composer, in 1911 he wrote a 'ragtime opera' *Treemonisha*. It was a failure at the time, but was staged again and recorded in the 1970s. Much of the rekindled interest in Joplin's work has been due to the dedication of the American musicologist and pianist Joshua Rifkin.

Shortly before Scott Joplin's death he asked for *Maple Leaf Rag* to be played at his funeral, but when the time came his widow could not bear to have this done.

K

Kabalevsky, Dmitri (1904–87) Russian composer. He studied piano in Moscow towards the end of World War I and then made a living for some years as a teacher and cinema pianist before returning to his studies, this time in composition. In 1929 the first of his three piano concertos won acclaim in his homeland. Elsewhere his 'Socialist realism' made little impact, and outside the Soviet Union he is little heard apart from performances of his orchestral suite *The Comedians*. During

World War II he wrote patriotic pieces, including an opera *V Ogne* (*Into the Fire*) about the Red Army's defence of Moscow; but even that did not save him from official censure in 1943 for 'bourgeois formalism'.

OTHER WORKS: Operas *Colas Breugnon, The Taras Family*. Three symphonies. Choral and orchestral *Leninists*. Songs including *Seven Merry Songs* based on English nursery rhymes.

Kálmán, Emmerich (1882–1953) Hungarian composer. He lived in Vienna and Paris before World War II, and then in the USA until 1946, when he returned to Paris. He wrote a string of popular operettas including *Die Csardastfürstin* (*The Gipsy Princess*) and *Gräfin Mariza* (*Countess Maritza*).

kapellmeister The German name for the conductor or director of a *chapel*, originally in the sense of a body of musicians in the employ of a king or nobleman, largely for religious functions, but later coming to mean any kind of orchestra. The term *kapellmeistermusik* is sneeringly applied to works written to formula with no creative flair.

Karajan, Herbert von (1908–) Austrian conductor. A commanding presence on the rostrum, and flamboyant in his life style, Karajan began his musical studies with the piano, but turned to conducting and was with the Berlin State Opera throughout World War II. From 1954 onwards he was conductor of the Berlin Philharmonic Orchestra. His scope has been enormous, preserved for posterity in his dazzling recordings of Beethoven, Holst's *The Planets*, Verdi and Mozart operas. His performance of Richard Strauss's *Thus Spake Zarathustra* was heard by audiences who might otherwise never have encountered it, when it provided background music for Stanley Kubrick's film *2001*.

Karg-Elert, Siegfrid (1877–1933) German composer and organist. He studied at Leipzig Conservatory, and in 1919 succeeded to Reger's professorial post there. It was Reger who advised him to adapt to organ use a large number of pieces he had written for the harmonium. Adaptation was one of his particular skills: he arranged Elgar's symphonies as piano solos. In spite of a vast output of piano pieces and songs, he is particularly associated with works for the organ, including preludes, postludes, fifty-four variation studies, sixty-six chorale improvisations and the mighty *Fantasia and Fugue* in D major.

Kennedy-Fraser, Marjory (1857–1930) Scottish folksong collector. She taught singing, and, after coming across a volume of Breton songs 'with apt accompaniments and singable French translations', was much taken by the idea of making similar translations and adaptations of original verse and music from the Hebridean islands west of Scotland. Since she herself did not speak Gaelic, many of her revisions became too politely tidy, harmonized according to current drawing-room taste; but without her and her colleague Frances Tolmie it is doubtful whether many now familiar Celtic airs such as *Land of Heart's Desire* would have survived.

Kern, Jerome (1885–1945) American composer. After piano lessons from his mother in New York he studied piano and theory at the New York College of Music. From the start his interest lay with popular music, and he became pianist for a music publisher and then a rehearsal pianist on Broadway shows. After collaborating on a number of musicals with Guy Bolton and P.G. Wodehouse, he made a hit with the show *Sally*, and went on to write other successful scores, including *Show Boat* (which introduced the song *Ol' Man River*) and *Roberta*, later made into films. He contributed to many other films with such numbers as *I Won't Dance* and *The Way You Look Tonight*, a large proportion of them with melodic phrases and harmonic sequences unusual for the average popular song. Few major jazz or dance band singers or instrumentalists have not at some time produced their own renderings of his songs *Smoke Gets in Your Eyes* and *The Last Time I Saw Paris*.

key and **key signature** For over a thousand years, up to the beginning of the seventeenth century, music was normally based on modal systems, but composers then began to adjust these into scales starting on a *tonic* note which established the aural 'feel' of the piece and gave its name to the predominating *key*. In C major the scale begins on the tonic or keynote C. A *Symphony in C major* may modulate through other keys and may have movements in contrasting keys, but on the whole the ear expects a return to the original tonal region by the end of the work.

Scales with a similar sequence of intervals can start on any other note, but to preserve that pattern it is necessary to introduce sharps and flats. Rather than mark these every time the notes occur, the labour-saving device of a *key signature* was invented. At the beginning of each stave the relevant sharps or flats are written in: the key of G major, for instance, has one sharp; that of B major, five sharps; and that of F, one flat. This instruction prevails throughout unless temporarily cancelled by accidentals, or unless the piece modulates for any considerable period into a different key, when the key signature is changed on the stave. (*See also* **Notation**.)

The word *key* is also applied to levers operated by an instrumentalist's fingers to produce the required notes: on a keyboard by pressing or striking them, on woodwind instruments by controlling the covering or opening of airholes.

KEYBOARD INSTRUMENTS

Designation by composers of the keyboard instrument required for a certain piece could prove very confusing. In the seventeenth and eighteenth centuries the word *klavier* was used indiscriminately in Germany for any such instrument, including the harpsichord, which could also be referred to by French or Italian variations of *clavicembalo, cembalo* and *clavecin*. All of them may be regarded as, in essence, clusters of harp strings stretched out within a box where they can be struck or plucked; but there are certain constructional and tonal categories into which they can usefully be divided.

CLAVICHORD: one of the oldest keyboard instruments, this was developed from the *monochord*, a single-stringed device thought to have been used by Pythagoras for demonstrating the mathematical relationships of musical intervals. It has a simple mechanism of a small brass blade or *tangent* fixed at the rear end of each key. When the key is fingered the blade strikes the string and stays against it until the key is released. Repeated pressure on the key produces a gentle vibrato known as a *bebung*, adding to the charm of what Schubert described as the 'instrument of solitude, of melancholy, of inexpressible sweetness'.

HARPSICHORD: This is rather a portmanteau word, including the *virginal* and *spinet*. The strings are not struck, but plucked by quills or leather tongues mounted on an upright piece of wood called a *jack*, which rises when the key is depressed. In a full-size harpsichord each set of jacks is mounted on a rail which can be moved sideways by pedals or manual controls for the simultaneous or separate playing of different octaves. There is also a lute stop producing a *pizzicato* effect. In a two-manual harpsichord both keyboards can be linked by means of a coupler.

The *virginal*, often referred to in the plural as *virginals*, was a small rectangular instrument which could easily be carried around and was very popular in the late fifteenth century and throughout the sixteenth: it was said to be Queen Elizabeth I's favourite instrument. The *spinet* was only slightly larger, triangular or trapezoidal in shape, and commoner in Italy. There is a theory that its name (*spinetta* in Italian) comes from the diminutive of *spina*, describing the thorn-like tongues which pluck the strings.

PIANOFORTE: Early in the eighteenth century Bartolommeo Cristofori produced in Florence his *gravicembalo col piano e forte*, in which the notes were produced by the action of hammers on the strings. He made twenty of these in all; one of them is preserved in the Metropolitan Museum of Art, New York. The most important feature of the instrument was the way in which gradations of force in the fingering could produce contrasts, as the name implied, between 'soft and loud'. In Germany the idea was taken up by the organ builder Gottfried Silbermann and demonstrated to Bach, who was not impressed; nor was Voltaire, who declared the *forte-piano* 'an ironmonger's invention compared with the harpsichord'.

The earliest instruments were for some time referred to as *fortepianos*, and this name is frequently used today to distinguish the type known to Mozart and Beethoven, before the development of more powerful models whose metal frames could stand up to the repeated hammering against the strings: Broadwood and Steinway produced their first completely iron-framed pianos in 1851 and 1855 respectively.

Cristofori's major pioneering device had been an escapement action for releasing the hammers swiftly after they had struck the strings. This was later improved to prevent the hammer bouncing back and hitting the string again. Early in the nineteenth century the French manufacturer Sébastien Erard invented a double escapement which, by checking

Queen Elizabeth I's virginals.

A two-manual harpsichord of 1685 from eastern France, now in the Württemberg Museum, Stuttgart.

the hammer before it fell all the way back, made faster playing possible. To produce an agreeable tone, hammers were provided with padding: over the years there was first a leather covering, then cloth over leather, leather over felt, and at last in 1826 the introduction of all-felt hammers.

Most keyboard instruments had traditionally been made with horizontal strings, as with the 'square piano' and still with the grand piano. Upright pianofortes were introduced by John Hawkins of Philadelphia around 1800. For the relatively unskilled, an impression of virtuosity could be conveyed by means of a *player piano* in which treadling pedals operated a bellows to force air through perforations in a paper roll and so play the desired notes. Piano rolls of this kind were in some cases made from actual performances by well-known executants or even the composers themselves, including Debussy, Greig and Scott Joplin. The vogue for such home entertainment died with the advent of radio and the record-player. (*See also* **organ**.)

The key action of a modern grand piano. The mechanism includes (1) a damper applied to the string; (2) a hammer which hits the string to produce a note; (3) a check to prevent the hammer rebounding; (4) levers which lift the hammer while the key is also lifting the damper from the string; (5) the hammer pivot; (6) the pivot of the key itself.

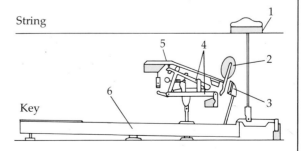

Khachaturian, Aram (1903–78) Armenian composer. He studied at the Moscow Conservatory under Myaskovsky, and was taken up by Prokofiev, who arranged a performance of his Trio for clarinet, violin and piano in Paris in 1932. He made his name with larger orchestral works filled with invigorating, uncomplicated tunes and lush scoring. The ballet *Gayaneh* features his much-played *Sabre Dance*. In 1948 he was among those composers denounced by the authorities, and turned to teaching and providing film music; but in 1956 he came back into favour with his ballet *Spartacus*, from which came the theme for a long-running British television series, *The Onedin Line*.

OTHER WORKS: Three symphonies. Piano concerto. Violin concerto. Choral and orchestral *Poem about Stalin*. Films *Battle of Stalingrad* and *Othello*. Incidental music *Macbeth* and *King Lear*.

Kipnis, Alexander (1891–1978) Russian bass (American citizen 1934). He studied in Warsaw and Berlin, making his début in Hamburg in 1915 and going on to appear in opera in Berlin, London, and Chicago, and throughout World War II in seasons at the New York Met. He appeared at all the major festivals, including Bayreuth, Salzburg and Glyndebourne, was an impressive Hagen and King Mark in Wagner's operas, and taught at the Juilliard School in New York until well into his eighties.

Kleiber, Erich and **Carlos** Erich Kleiber (1890–1956) was born in Austria but made his reputation as a conductor in Germany. He became musical director of the Berlin State Opera in 1923 and remained until a quarrel with the Nazis in 1934. He and his family went to Italy and then to Argentina, where in 1938 he became an Argentine citizen. After the war he hoped to rebuild Berlin's operatic traditions, but quarrels between East and West in the city made his position untenable. His conducting of Mozart's *Le nozze di Figaro* and Strauss's *Der Rosenkavalier* are among the most magnificent achievements of the recording industry.

His son Carlos Kleiber (1930–) born in Berlin, became an Austrian citizen in 1980. After studying chemistry he, too, turned to music as an opera conductor, including spells in Vienna and Bayreuth. Based in Munich in the 1980s, he is known to restrict himself to works about which he feels, after the most intensive study and preparation, that he has something special to say, such as Verdi's *Otello* and Berg's *Wozzeck* (which his father had been the first to conduct in Berlin and in London). Orchestral players have described him as being 'electrifying to play for'.

Klemperer, Otto (1885–1973) German conductor. He studied in Frankfurt and Berlin and, in the 1930s, with Schoenberg in Los Angeles. In 1907 Mahler, despite his own troubles in Vienna at the time, befriended Klemperer and helped him to secure the appointment of conductor to the German Opera in Prague. The young man helped Mahler with rehearsals of his massive eighth symphony, the *Symphony of a Thousand*.

After holding posts in various German towns, Klemperer became conductor of the Los Angeles Philharmonic between 1933 and 1939, when he became partially paralysed and had to give up work throughout World War II. Although illness continued to restrict his appearances, he conducted compelling performances of the Beethoven symphonies, premières of works by Schoenberg and Hindemith, and operas including *Fidelio* and *Lohengrin*. From 1955 to 1972 he was associated with the Philharmonia of London, who appointed him their conductor-for-life.

In his later years Klemperer spent much of his time in composition, producing a number of songs, symphonies and quartets.

Kobbé, Gustav (1857–1918) American musicologist and critic. He wrote a biography of Wagner, and embarked on a thoroughgoing collection of opera synopses and analyses in *The Complete Opera Book*. This was almost complete when he was killed while out sailing by a collision with a seaplane. The book was published in 1922 and has been regularly updated since then, in recent years by the Earl of Harewood.

Köchel, Ludvig von (1800–77) Austrian botanist and amateur musician. The 'K' which prefaces the chronological numbering of Mozart's work testifies to Köchel's industry in compiling a comprehensive thematic catalogue of the composer's works, a system used ever since. The Symphony No.40 in G minor, for example, is listed as K550; its immediate follower, No.41 (the *Jupiter*) in C, as K551.

Kodály, Zoltán (1882–1967) Hungarian composer. Brought up in a household of keen musical amateurs, Kodály learned the violin and cello before entering Budapest University. A keen student of Hungarian folksong, he wrote his university thesis on this subject, and after graduation spent time travelling in the company of Bartók and collaborating with him on scholarly publication of their researches. In later years the Hungarian Academy of Sciences put him in sole charge of collation and publication of all available folksong material.

Kodály's own compositions were influenced first by Brahms and then by Debussy, but were always filtered through his national consciousness. Maintaining himself for the larger part of his life by teaching, he composed a tone poem *Summer Evening* and a number of chamber works just

A drawing by Istvan Szegedi-Szüts of Zoltan Kodály in 1949, the year after production of his third opera, *Czinka Panna*.

before and during World War I. In 1923 he was commissioned, along with Bartók and Dohnányi, to supply a celebratory work for the fifteenth anniversary of the unification of Buda and Pest. He produced his choral and orchestral *Psalmus Hungaricus*, which was such an international success that he followed it with other richly scored religious works such as the *Budavári Te Deum* and, after World War II, a *Missa Brevis*. His opera *Háry János* is filled as ever with folk elements, and they are found again in the sets of *Dances of Marosszék* and *Dances of Galánta*.

OTHER WORKS: Orchestral *Variations on a Hungarian Folk Song, 'The Peacock'*; and *Concerto for Orchestra*. *Pange lingua* for chorus and organ. Two string quartets. Sonata for solo cello.

Koechlin, Charles (1867–1950) French composer. He did not tackle music studies seriously until the age of twenty-two, and although taught by Massenet and Fauré he tried to reject all influences other than his own instincts. In spite of persistent ill-health he wrote a large number of substantial orchestral works, often launching into his own concepts of atonality and imaginative polyphony, and bestowing on them titles such as *Seven Stars Symphony* (inspired by the characters of film stars) and *Symphony of Hymns*. He flirted with Marxist ideas but, always an intransigent individualist, refused to join the Communist party.

Korngold, Erich (1897–1957) Austrian composer (American citizen 1943). He was a child prodigy both as composer and as pianist: Schnabel played a piano sonata the boy had written at the age of thirteen. He wrote a number of operas, among which *Die tote Stadt* (*The Dead City*) achieved considerable success, and a number of orchestral works and concertos. When he settled in the USA in 1935, however, his gift for luscious orchestration and captivating melody – sometimes of a rather saccharine nature – was turned to the production of scores for films such as *Captain Blood*, *The Adventures of Robin Hood* and *The Private Lives of Elizabeth and Essex*. Of his more serious works, only the violin concerto has been revived with any success.

161

Koussevitsky, Serge (1874–1951) Russian conductor (American citizen 1941). He began his career as a double bass player, and became professor of the instrument at Moscow Conservatory. In 1908 he made his conducting début with the Berlin Philharmonic Orchestra, and then founded his own orchestra and a music publishing house whose profits were distributed to Russian composers. After the Russian Revolution he worked in Paris and later in the USA, where he conducted the Boston Symphony Orchestra from 1924 to 1949. During those years he introduced many new works and commissioned a number: the orchestra's fiftieth anniversary in 1930 was celebrated by his commissioning Stravinsky's *Symphony of Psalms*, and the help he gave Bartók during the composer's melancholy exile resulted in the *Concerto for Orchestra*.

In 1947 the Natalie Koussevitsky Foundation was established as a memorial to his first wife, and after his own death his second wife Olga continued the work of commissioning new pieces from composers on both sides of the Atlantic.

Kreisler, Fritz (1875–1962) Austrian violinist and composer (American citizen 1943). Friedrich, always known as Fritz, learned to read music when he was three. His father, a doctor who would himself have preferred a career in music, gave the boy violin lessons and arranged further lessons from the leader of the Ring Theatre Orchestra. Admitted to the Vienna Conservatory at the age of seven, the first time a student under ten had been accepted, Kreisler won a gold medal when he was ten, went on to Paris, and two years later won a first prize for his violin playing.

In 1888 he set out on an American tour with the Polish pianist Moriz Rosenthal, making his début in Boston. There were some doubts about the staying power of such a child prodigy, and during his late adolescence he did in fact neglect his studies and lead a wild Bohemian life in Vienna. His salvation, as he himself later admitted, was marriage to an American divorcée of German descent, who lovingly but firmly organized his life and career for him.

From then on he toured Europe and America regularly, developing a tone and bowing technique which were the envy of his rivals and an eloquence which cast new light on the standard works in the repertoire. He made his first recordings in 1903, and became the most highly paid recording artist of his day. During World War I he served with the Austrian army and was wounded – fortunately only in the leg. His first postwar appearance in New York and a subsequent concert in London were greeted rapturously by his audiences. Among his many compositions the best known is the *Caprice Viennois*.

Křenek, Ernst (1900–) Austrian composer (American citizen 1945). He studied in Vienna and Berlin, worked in German opera houses, and after a period of involvement in atonal idioms fell briefly under jazz influences and wrote his phenomenally successful opera *Jonny spielt auf* (*Johnny strikes up*), which was translated into many languages and brought in enough money for him to devote himself purely to composition. In about 1930 he turned his attention to twelve-note techniques, as in his opera *Karl V*, and in 1940 published *Studies in Counterpoint*, one of the most lucid explanations of the method. While teaching at the School of Fine Arts in Hamline University, Minnesota, he composed a moving *Symphonic Elegy* for strings in memory of Anton von Webern, shot in error by an American G.I. at the end of World War II.

OTHER WORKS: Operas *Dark Waters* and *Der goldene Bock* (*The Golden Ram*). Ballet *Jest of Cards*. Five symphonies. Orchestral variations on *I Wonder as I Wander*. Electronic *Quintina* for soprano, chamber ensemble and tape.

Kubelik, Jan (1880–1940) Czech composer and violinist (Hungarian citizen 1903). He studied and made his solo début in Prague, travelled as a virtuoso performer, and composed six violin concertos and an *American Symphony*.

Kubelik, Rafael (1914–) Czech conductor and composer. Son of Jan Kubelik, he accompanied his father in recitals but went on to make his name as conductor of the Czech Philharmonic Orchestra, leaving in 1948 for appointments with the Chicago Symphony Orchestra and then as musical director of Covent Garden, London, from 1955 to 1958. During this time he was responsible for the first stage performances in English of Janáček's opera *Jenůfa* and a shortened version of Berlioz's *The Trojans*. In 1973–4 he was musical director of the New York Met. Among his own compositions are two symphonies and four operas.

Kuhlau, Friedrich (1786–1832) German composer and flautist. The son of a military bandsman, Kuhlau gave keyboard lessons while still a young man in Hamburg, but fled when there was a threat of being drafted into Napoleon's army. He won an appointment as first flautist in the King of Denmark's band, and ultimately became Court composer and director of music. He wrote many pieces for the flute, a number of operas, and incidental music to plays, the most lasting being the music for Heiberg's drama *Elverhøj* (*The Fairy Hillock*), a perennial favourite in Denmark, which includes what became the standard orchestration of the Danish Royal Anthem.

Kuhnau, Johann (1660–1722) Bohemian composer. Bach's predecessor as cantor and organist at Leipzig, he wrote a number of practice pieces to which he gave the name *Klavierübung* (*Keyboard exercise*), a designation picked up by Bach to cover a number of his partitas and other pieces, including the *Goldberg Variations*.

Kurtág, György (1926–) Hungarian composer. He studied in Budapest and Paris, and after work with Milhaud and Messiaen began to favour the sparse textures of Webern and Bartók: some of his lapidary, miniaturist works have been described as making even Webern sound long-winded. Although he has written a wide range of piano and chamber music, he works at his fullest stretch in a combination of voice and other instruments, including the characteristic Hungarian cimbalom, or with the voice alone, as in his *Attila Joszef Fragments*. Since 1968 he has taught at the Budapest Academy, one of his pupils being his composer son, also György Kurtág.

L

Lalo, Edouard (1823–92) French composer. Of Spanish descent, Lalo studied the violin and cello in Lille and Paris, and also took private lessons in composition. As his early compositions made little impact, he supported himself as a chamber instrumentalist until he married a singer who urged him to write for the stage. His first opera came a dismal third in a competition sponsored by the government. It was not until 1874 that he achieved recognition in a different field with a violin concerto performed by the Spanish virtuoso Sarasate, for whom he then wrote the even more widely acclaimed *Symphonie espagnole*. His opera *Le Roi d'Ys* (*The King of Ys*), based on a Breton legend of a mythical land beneath the sea, was written in a semi-Wagnerian style which worried the management of the Paris Opéra so much that they postponed production for several years – only to find that the public adored it. One of Lalo's few other compositions still heard at all frequently is the *Norwegian Rhapsody* for violin and orchestra.

Lambert, Constant (1905–51) English composer and conductor. He studied with Vaughan Williams and soon, in the company of William Walton and the Sitwell family entourage, came to be regarded as an *enfant terrible* of contemporary English music. Walton's sardonic suite to Edith Sitwell's poems, *Façade*, was dedicated to him. He was the first English composer to have ballet music commissioned by Diaghilev, resulting in his *Romeo and Juliet*, though he is better remem-

bered for the ballets *Horoscope* and *Tiresias*, both with choreography by Frederick Ashton. Lambert was music director of Sadler's Wells Ballet from its foundation in 1931, toured with it during World War II, and after giving up full-time conducting became its musical adviser from 1948 onwards. Among his orchestral works the most exhilarating is the colourful *Rio Grande* for piano, chorus and orchestra. His prejudices and insights are admirably expounded in his book *Music, Ho!*.

Lamoureux, Charles (1834–99) French conductor and violinist. After studying at the Paris Conservatoire he played in a theatre orchestra and then at the Opéra, where he later became conductor. In 1880 he helped to found a chamber music society for the introduction of new works, and in 1881 founded his *Nouveaux Concerts* or *Concerts Lamoureux*, which also concentrated on the introduction of unfamiliar works to the public, especially those of Wagner. The Lamoureux Orchestra has continued the tradition and made many recordings under a number of distinguished conductors, including Pablo Casals, Bernard Haitink and Igor Markevitch.

ländler An old rural dance originating in Ländl, a region of Austria. It is in 3/4 time, like a slow waltz, with leaping phrases covering wide intervals in the music, to which couples gyrate in a large circle, sometimes separating and circling each other. Many of the so-called minuets in Haydn's symphonies are in effect ländler, and Mahler frequently used the rhythm. Among the most attractive examples are those composed by the Schubert.

Landon, H.C. Robbins (1926–) American musicologist. After studying in Boston he settled in 1948 in Vienna and became an expert on the life and music of Haydn, editing a collected edition of his music, a study of the symphonies, and his collected correspondence and London notebooks. He has also served on the Committee for International Mozart Research and edited a collected edition of Mozart's music. With Donald Mitchell he was joint editor of *The Mozart Companion* (1956).

Landowska, Wanda (1879–1959) Polish harpsichordist and music researcher. A child prodigy, she became a virtuoso piano recitalist, but through her contact with music of the seventeenth and eighteenth centuries was lured into reviving older styles and older instruments. In 1900 she eloped to Paris with the journalist and ethnologist Henry Lew, who became her husband and her mainstay during her tours of Europe and the USA, when she gave harpsichord recitals which brought the instrument back into fashion. Between 1919 and 1938 she taught and continued performing in France, but after the looting of her school by the

·Wanda Landowska at a harpsichord built for her. (Note the
pianoforte black-white key pattern rather than the older style
of keyboard in which the accidentals were white.) Of the
instrument's subtleties she quoted an admirer of Mattheson
on that player's ability 'to charm the mind, to bewitch our
ears, to make a harpsichord speak under the hands.'

Lanner, Josef (1801–43) Austrian composer and
violinist. The son of a glovemaker, he taught
himself music, and by the age of twelve was
playing the violin in a light orchestra in Viennese
taverns and dance halls. Five years later he left
to form his own quartet, in which Johann Strauss
the elder played the viola. The group enlarged
and finally became two separate orchestras, with
Lanner conducting one, Strauss the other. With
his output of more than a hundred waltzes and
two hundred other dance pieces, including a
number of ländler, Lanner was for a long time
regarded in Vienna as the musical equal of the
Strauss family, but the rivalry remained a friendly one.

La Scala, Milan The *Teatro alla Scala* has been the
most famous Italian opera house since its opening
in 1778 on the site of the church of Santa Maria
alla Scala. Composers who wrote specifically for
it included Salieri, Rossini, Verdi and Puccini;
among conductors who have established great
reputations there are Toscanini and Abbado;
among singers, Callas and Tebaldi. Almost destroyed by bombing in World War II, the theatre
was rebuilt in its former style by May 1946.

Nazis in World War II she left to make her home
in the USA. De Falla and Poulenc wrote
harpsichord concertos for her.

A painting by Angelo Inganni
in 1852 of La Scala opera
house, Milan, whose first
performances included many
by Rossini, Bellini, and
Puccini.

Lassus, Roland de (1532–94) Flemish composer (known in Italy as Orlando di Lassus). It is said that as a chorister he had such a beautiful voice that numerous attempts were made by rival churches to kidnap him. He travelled in Italy as a boy and young man, and for a while was choirmaster to St John Lateran in Rome. On moving to Antwerp in 1555 he published his first book of madrigals and motets. The following year he entered the service of the Duke of Bavaria, and spent most of the rest of his life in Munich. Among more than two thousand compositions his secular songs are charmingly tuneful, often in dancing rhythms, while in his religious music he wove long, soaring lines in a seemingly effortless polyphony earning him a place on a level with Palestrina.

Lawes, Henry and **William** Henry Lawes (1596–1662), English singer and composer, became a Gentleman of the Chapel Royal in the time of King Charles I. He was commissioned to write the music for Milton's masque *Comus*, produced at Ludlow Castle in 1634, and sang a part in it himself. After the Commonwealth interregnum he was reinstated as Court musician, and for Charles II's coronation wrote an anthem *Zadok the Priest* – which has not stood the test of time as well as Handel's version.

William Lawes (1602–45), Henry's brother, also served with the Chapel Royal and wrote music for masques, a number of anthems and psalms and accomplished, if rather obvious, pieces for consorts of viols. He was killed while serving with the Royalist army at the siege of Chester.

lay (or **lai**) A medieval French poem and song form in twelve stanzas of differing metres, sung to different tunes. The word has come to be more loosely applied to any short verse meant to be recited or sung.

leading note The seventh note of an ascending scale, which 'leads' the ear to expect a further semitone step up to the summit of the octave, especially when the note is on top of a chord of the dominant seventh. In a rising scale of C major or minor, B would be the leading note, though in a descending C minor scale the B is flattened.

ledger (or **leger**) **lines** Short lines written above or below the stave to accommodate notes too high or low to be accommodated within the five lines of the stave.

Legge, Walter (1906–79) English impresario. He was for many years recording manager of HMV and Columbia (later EMI) and signed up many leading artists under contract. In 1945 he founded the Philharmonia Orchestra, mainly with a view to making records for his company, and managed it until 1964, when it became a self-governing body, notably associated with conductors such as Klemperer, Maazel, Muti and, from 1984, Sinopoli. In 1953 Legge married the soprano Elisabeth Schwarzkopf.

Lehár, Franz (Ferencz) (1870–1948) Hungarian composer. Son of the youngest bandmaster in the Austrian army, Franz acquired a love of music

Costume designs for a December 1939 production of Lehár's *The Merry Widow* at the Berlin State Opera.

while travelling with his parents, and at the age of twelve won a scholarship to study the violin at Prague Musical Academy. Advised by Dvořák to give up playing and concentrate on composition, he nevertheless decided to follow in his father's footsteps and become, in his turn, the youngest bandmaster in the army. Once he had tried his hand at a stage piece, however, he recognized his own true métier. His first opera, *Kukuschka*, was produced in Leipzig, Budapest and Vienna. In 1905 came *Die Lustige Witwe* (*The Merry Widow*), a dazzling, lilting work as fresh today as when Lehár wrote it.

He followed with a string of operettas, from *The Count of Luxembourg* to *Frasquita*, the first of many designed especially for the tenor Richard Tauber. During World War II the composer stayed on in Austria, almost losing his Jewish wife when the Gestapo attempted to carry her away. They were prevented only by Lehár's direct appeal to the local Nazi administrator.

Lehmann, Lilli (1848–1929) German soprano. As a child she studied the piano and became accompanist to her mother, a soprano who also gave her singing lessons. In 1865 Lilli made her début in Prague; between 1870 and 1885 she sang with the Berlin Opera, and in the first Bayreuth *Ring* was cast as a Rhinemaiden, under the direction of Wagner himself. She was the first to sing Isolde and Brünnhilde in New York, but found herself in trouble when she returned: she had been allowed to leave Berlin only on special dispensation from the Kaiser, had overstayed her leave, and now was banned for two years from singing in opera.

In 1891 she took up teaching: the American soprano Geraldine Farrar was among her outstanding pupils. Late in her career she became virtual dictator of Mozart productions at Salzburg.

Lehmann, Liza (1862–1918) English composer and soprano. After a career as a concert singer she began composing works such as the song cycle *In a Persian Garden*.

Lehmann, Lotte (1888–1976) German soprano (American citizen 1945). After studying in Berlin she made her operatic début in Hamburg as one of the three boys in *Die Zauberflöte*. From 1916 until 1938 she was a leading star of the Vienna Opera, becoming the most rapturously acclaimed Marschallin in Richard Strauss's *Der Rosenkavalier* and creating many other Strauss rôles. Her first American appearance was in Chicago as Sieglinde in Wagner's *Die Walküre*. In 1938 she settled in Santa Barbara and began teaching there: one of her most outstanding pupils was Grace Bumbry. Her farewell recital was given in New York in 1951.

leitmotiv Frequently misspelt as leitmotif, this describes a musical theme which reappears at different stages throughout an opera or other work as a 'leading motive' to direct the listener's attention to a character or important idea. Certain chords or discordant phrases in stage and film music, for instance, unmistakably announce the arrival of the villain. The most extensive use of the device is found in Wagner's operas, especially in the *Ring* cycle, where the relationships and impending fate of the characters are musically interwoven in repeated or transmuted thematic combinations. (*See also* **idée fixe**.)

Leoncavallo, Ruggiero (1858–1919) Italian composer. After studying piano and composition in Naples, he attempted an opera based on the life of the English poet Chatterton and planned a trilogy on Renaissance subjects, but was soon so discouraged that he had to turn to giving music lessons and accompanying singers in various cafés. An idea for another opera was provided by his father, a magistrate, who had presided over the trial of an actor in a touring company accused of murdering his wife. From this Leoncavallo fashioned the libretto and music for a two-act opera *Pagliacci*, hoping to enter it in a competition which unfortunately proved to be for one-act operas only. The winner was, ironically, Mascagni's *Cavalleria Rusticana*, with which the ultimately popular *Pagliacci* was forever after to be twinned in a double bill. Leoncavallo seemed fated not to achieve first place anywhere: his opera *La Bohème* might well have been a success in 1897 if Puccini's version of the same story had not appeared only a few months earlier.

libretto Literally, in Italian, a 'little book', in musical parlance the text of an opera or outline of a ballet plot. The writer is referred to as a librettist. Outstanding exponents have included da Ponte (for Mozart) and von Hofmannsthal (for Richard Strauss). In the modern stage or film musical, happy collaborations have included those of Richard Rodgers and Lorenz Hart and of Jerome Kern and Oscar Hammerstein II; while Alan Jay Lerner, writer of three Academy Award winning films (*An American in Paris*, *Gigi*, and *My Fair Lady*), became, in 1985, the first lyricist to receive the Kennedy Center Honor for a lifetime's contribution to the performing arts.

lieder *Lied* is simply the German word for a song, but the plural form *lieder* applies particularly to 'art songs' of the German Romantic movement from the late eighteenth to the early twentieth century. These are not merely folksongs or even attractive melodies with piano or other accompaniment, but compositions which endeavour to unite the singer's words and tune with an instrumental part (usually piano) of virtually equal importance. Schubert wrote more than six hundred lieder, some of them love songs, some dramatic ballads, and some linked in song cycles with integral pictorial and emotional effects provided by the piano. Schumann worked most happily in this form, followed by Brahms; and Hugo Wolf, one of the most sophisticated explorers of the medium, always gave equal weight to the interpreters by listing his songs as being 'for voice and piano'.

ligature From the Latin *ligare*, to bind, the word refers to the twine which once bound the reed of a clarinet to the mouthpiece of the instrument, now superseded by a metal clamp. It is also used in musical notation to indicate a slur of two or more notes sung or played over one syllable or in one phrase.

Ligeti, György (1923–) Hungarian composer. After studying at the Budapest Academy he became a teacher there and composed rather in the style of Kodály, though moving gradually towards an interest in Schoenberg and Webern in spite of the difficulty of hearing such proscribed music in the political climate of the time. After the Russian invasion of 1956 he moved to Vienna and then Cologne, where he worked in the electronic music studio and produced a number of intricately textured, strikingly witty pieces such as *Artikulation* and *Glissandi* for tape. After these experiments he returned to composing for live performers in post-Webern vein (which he himself has called *micropolyphony*) exemplified in the orchestral *San Francisco Polyphony*, first performed in that city in 1975 under Seiji Ozawa.

Lind, Jenny (1820–87) Swedish soprano. An illegitimate child who never got on with her mother, she was brought up by various relatives and foster parents. At the age of nine her voice attracted the attention of a ballerina from the Royal Opera in Stockholm, and she studied and performed in Stockholm and Paris before setting out on taxing tours of Europe which made her reputation as 'the Swedish Nightingale'. All who heard her were enthralled by the sweetness of her tone and dazzling coloratura, together with an appealing shyness quite unlike the tantrums and high dramas favoured by so many temperamental singers. Wagner was taken by her 'curious pensive individuality'.

In 1847 she made her first appearance in London in Meyerbeer's *Robert le Diable* before an audience which included Queen Victoria and Prince Albert. The Queen was so overwhelmed that she threw her own bouquet to the singer, and thereafter Jenny Lind was taken up in high society. On a triumphal tour of England she visited Norwich and there met Dr Stanley, Bishop

A portrait by E. Magnus of Jenny Lind, the 'Swedish nightingale', for whose London operatic performances in 1847 the orchestra stalls cost five or six guineas each, and boxes twenty.

of Norwich, whose influence on her was so powerful that she promised him to give up the stage and devote herself to the singing of sacred works only.

Although this dismayed many of her admirers, her reputation was still strong enough for the showman Phineas T. Barnum to book her for a nationwide tour of the USA. In Boston she married Otto Goldschmitt, a German-Jewish pianist and composer, a pupil of Mendelssohn and Chopin, who had been engaged to conduct for the singer during her American tour. When they returned to Europe they lived for a while in Dresden before moving to London, where Goldschmitt became vice-principal of the Royal Academy of Music. With his wife's help he also founded the Bach Choir.

Jenny Lind's last home was a secluded house high on the Malvern Hills, facing the ramparts of an Iron Age hill fort which, ten years after her death, was to inspire the composition of Elgar's *Caractacus*. Her husband outlived her by twenty years.

Lipatti, Dinu (1917–50) Romanian pianist and composer. He studied in Bucharest and later in Paris with Cortot, Dukas and Nadia Boulanger. He composed a concertino for piano and chamber orchestra, a piano sonata for the left hand, and a set of *Romanian Dances* for orchestra, but is most enduringly remembered for his superb concert and recording performances of Bach, Mozart and, above all, Chopin. He died from leukemia while working at the Geneva Conservatory.

Liszt, Franz (1811–86) Hungarian composer and pianist. His father, a court official and cello player in the service of Prince Nicholas Esterházy, detected early on the musical promise of young Ferenc (Franz) and gave him piano lessons. An audience of local magnates was so impressed that they offered to pay for the boy's further tuition. In Vienna he studied composition with Salieri and piano with Czerny, who regarded him as his most brilliant and industrious pupil and was incensed when Liszt's father took him away to Paris. Here and in England he was acclaimed as a child prodigy; but thoughout his adolescent years he practised so assiduously and gave so many recitals that he began to tire of the whole procedure and contemplated giving up his profession and becoming a priest. Instead, after his father's death, he turned to composition.

In 1834 the young man met Countess Marie d'Agoult, with whom he started an affair. The following year he persuaded her to leave her husband and child and elope with him to Switzerland. She had three children by Liszt, one of whom, Cosima, was to marry Hans von Bülow and then abandon him in favour of Richard Wagner.

During their travels, Liszt increased his reputation as a recitalist and established himself beyond all argument by defeating the swaggering virtuoso Sigismund Thalberg in a historic piano 'duel' – what jazz players of today would call a 'cutting session'. When the love affair with Marie faded, he made another reputation: that of a philanderer, involved with Marie Duplessis, inspiration for Dumas' *La Dame aux camélias*, with Lola Montez, with Marie Pleyel, wife of the great piano manufacturer, and with the Polish-born Princess Carolyne von Sayn-Wittgenstein. With his flowing locks, handsome features and passionate temperament, Liszt was the arch-Romantic of his time.

It seems incredible that, in addition to his gruelling recital schedule and so many scheduled or unscheduled love affairs, Liszt should have found time to follow his bent as a composer. Nevertheless, while with Marie d'Agoult he produced the three books of *Années de Pèlerinage*

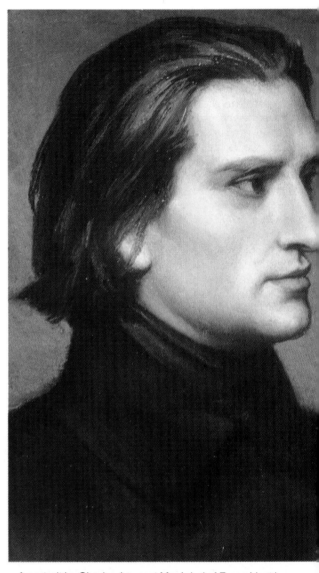

A portrait by Charles-Laurent Maréchal of Franz Liszt in Paris some months after the birth of his son Daniel in Rome, and shortly before he left the boy's mother in order to travel and raise money for a Beethoven monument in Bonn.

(*Years of Pilgrimage*), piano pieces evoking the moods and scenes of their wanderings, and his transcriptions of *Transcendental Studies after Paganini*, including the much-played *La Campanella*. Settled for a time in Weimar with his latest love, the Princess Carolyne, he was appointed conductor to the Court Opera in 1848, staged works by Wagner and Berlioz, and poured out twelve symphonic poems (including the *Faust* and *Dante* symphonies), his first piano concerto, and any number of piano pieces.

Love and work turned sour again. In 1859 Liszt left Weimar and went to Rome, where at one time there had seemed to be a possibility that the Pope might consent to Princess Carolyne's divorce from her husband. When this fell through, the relationship, too, fell apart. Again Liszt contemplated a monastic life. His compositions became almost entirely religious; he immersed himself in meditation; and in 1865 took minor orders in the Roman Catholic Church. Although he was frequently called the Abbé Liszt after this, he never actually became a priest. His love affairs were resumed, most spectacularly with a woman who had assaulted and abandoned her husband the day after their wedding. Olga Janina remained true to form: at one stage in her brief spell with Liszt she threatened him with a loaded revolver.

Still an incomparable master of keyboard technique, Liszt frequently returned to Weimar to give lessons to adoring disciples, and sometimes allowed himself to be persuaded to give benefit concerts. It could be said that he was truly a man born at the right time: his own compositions for the piano and his advanced, melodramatic style

of playing were made possible only by recent developments in the manufacture of the instrument, which he exploited to the full. The musical language of the compositions themselves, with Liszt's belief in 'transforming' one basic motif throughout an entire work, anticipated Wagner's prevailing *leitmotiv* and even some of Schoenberg's ideas.

Late in life he was a revered guest in England and France during special performances of his work. In summer 1886 he was also made welcome at the Bayreuth Festival, where his daughter Cosima was now in charge; and it was in Bayreuth that he died on July 31st.

OTHER WORKS: Symphonic poems including *Hungaria* and *Mazeppa*. Orchestral *Hungarian Rhapsodies* – also in solo piano versions. Choral *Hungarian Coronation Mass* and *Missa choralis*. Piano nocturnes *Liebesträume* (*Love's dreams*).

Liszt at his desk in Weimar: a photograph taken in 1885, about five years before his death.

Litolff, Henry Charles (1818–91) Anglo-Alsatian composer and pianist. His father came from Alsace, his mother was English, and he was born in London. He made his first public appearance as a pianist at the age of fourteen, married at seventeen in the face of parental disapproval, and went off to France. In 1851 he married again, choosing the widow of a music publisher and taking over the business, where he pioneered the sale of cheap editions. Later he settled in Paris and married yet again, this time the Comtesse de la Rochefoucauld. He composed a number of only mildly interesting operas and operettas, an overture *Robespierre*, and five *Concerto-symphoniques* for piano and orchestra, from the fourth of which comes the only piece of his that is still played frequently, usually referred to simply as 'Litolff's *Scherzo*'.

Loewe, Karl (1796–1869) German composer. The youngest of a schoolmaster's twelve children, he sang so well in his Halle school choir that Jérôme Bonaparte, then King of Westphalia, granted him an annuity to further his musical studies. By the time his benefactor had been forced to flee, Loewe could make a living as an organist and teacher. He composed several operas, symphonies and concertos, but made his reputation with songs such as *Edward* and *Der Erlkönig* (published before Schubert's famous version). A gifted linguist, he took narrative ballad subjects from many countries, notably Scotland and England, and set them to agreeably sentimental or dramatic music.

Longo, Alessandro (1864–1945) Italian pianist and editor. He became professor of piano at Naples Conservatory and founder, in Bologna, of a Scarlatti Circle. He edited the complete works of Domenico Scarlatti and prefixed the numbering with the letter L. A later alternative cataloguing by the American harpsichordist Ralph Kirkpatrick uses a K identification, not to be confused with the Köchel numbers of Mozart's compositions.

Lortzing, Albert (1801–51) German composer and librettist. He spent much of his youth as an actor on tour with his parents, but at the same time taught himself the piano and cello. After marrying an actress he turned to composing for the stage, and struck a rich vein with his fourth opera, *Zar und Zimmermann* (*Tsar and Carpenter*), with his own libretto based on a French play about Peter the Great. Although his subsequent operas *Der Wildschutz* (*The Poacher*) and *Undine* were also successful in their own time, his large family and incompetence in financial matters made it necessary for him to take a poorly-paid conducting job in a Berlin vaudeville theatre, hastening his death the morning after the première of his own last work, *Die Opernprobe* (*The Opera Rehearsal*).

Lully, Jean-Baptiste (1632–87) Italian-French composer. The son of a poor miller in Florence, the boy (then Giovanni Battista Lulli) taught himself the violin, showed an instinctive flair for dancing, and joined a troupe of strolling players. At the age of fourteen he entered a noble household in France, where his musical talent was soon noticed during a visit by the young King Louis XIV, later to become known as the 'Sun King'. Louis took Lully into his own service, where he somehow expanded his knowledge of composition and instrumental playing (the details remain a mystery) so brilliantly that he became leader of a newly-formed string orchestra, 'the little violins of the King', wrote music for Court ballets, and danced in some of them with Louis as partner. In May 1661 he was appointed overall Superintendent of Music, in December acquired French nationality, and the following year married the only daughter of the hitherto predominant Court composer and lutenist, Michel Lambert.

Lully moved on from the rather lightweight masques and comedy ballets which had for so long been fashionable in France, and began adapting Italian operatic forms to French tastes, doing away with 'dry' recitative and substituting accompanied recitative, tackling serious dramatic subjects as well as light-hearted ones, and unifying singing, dancing and playing into a spectacular whole. While working to create a new art-form, he was not unmindful of personal profit: to prevent any rivalry, he won from Louis a monopoly for the production of opera in Paris, and then poured out a succession of pieces such as *Alceste*, *Persée*, *Amadis*, and his acknowledged masterpiece *Armide*.

In 1687 Lully wrote and conducted a *Te Deum* to celebrate the King's recovery from an illness. Beating time with a long stick, he stabbed himself in the foot and died of a gangrenous infection.

Lumbye, Hans Christian (1810–74) Danish composer and conductor. He became known as 'the Strauss of the North' while conducting the Tivoli pleasure gardens orchestra in Copenhagen during its earliest years and writing waltzes, galops, polkas and marches. A statue was erected to his memory in the gardens. The outer balcony rail of the Tivoli concert hall, rebuilt after the Nazis had destroyed it during the World War II occupation, is decorated with the opening bars of Lumbye's most popular piece, the *Champagne Galop*.

lur A Bronze Age horn with a long, curving neck, usually found in pairs in Danish archaeological

Jean-Baptiste Lully rose from humble beginnings to become Composer of Instrumental Music to Louis XIV and Superintendent of Music to the Royal Chamber.

JEAN-BAPTISTE LVLLY SECRETAIRE DV ROY ET SVR-INTENDANT DE SA MVSIQVE

ET ASPICIT ENOTRI

NIL MORTALE CANIT

Quon ne nous parle plus d'Orphée,
Par toy fameux LVLLY sa gloire est etousée,
Si de la Lyre et de la voix
La fable vente en luy les rares ouurages,
Qu'a til fait qui ne cede a tes diuins ouurages
Qui charment le plus grand des Roys.

excavations. The deep, resonant tones are restricted to a simple harmonic series, though skilled brass players can extract more by use of embouchure and breath control.

lute A long-necked, fretted stringed instrument of ancient Eastern origin, originally plucked by a plectrum but later, in Europe, by the fingers. Unlike members of the guitar family it had a rounded back. The earliest known models had four strings, extended during the fifteenth century to six pairs (two to each note) tuned in rising fourths but with the interval of a third between strings 3 and 4. Schools of lutenists (or lutanists) grew up to compose and play more and more complex works, writing them out not in musical notation but in tableture (or tablature) indicating finger positions, very much like the chord symbol grids for the ukulele and banjo printed on popular song sheets. John Dowland was probably the greatest exponent of the instrument's possibilities, but major composers continued to write for it up

to the time of Bach and Handel. For a couple of centuries it fell out of fashion, until its delicate beauties were rediscovered thanks largely to the efforts of mid-twentieth century players such as Desmond Dupré and Julian Bream.

Lutoslawski, Witold (1913–) Polish composer and pianist. After studying piano at the Warsaw Conservatory he began composing in neo-classical style, but the exigencies of World War II forced him to eke out a living playing in Warsaw cafés. After the war, political restraints allowed for little other than pieces based on folksongs and national themes, though he tackled these with a skill and subtlety owing much to Bartók. The *Concerto for Orchestra* dates from this period. Gradually he eased his way towards experiments with twelve-tone music, which did not appeal to him for long, and with aleatory techniques influenced by the works of John Cage. The dividing line between wariness and outspokenness came with the *Funeral Music* of 1958 in memory of Bartók, followed by the indeterminacies of *Venetian Games* for chamber orchestra and, in more

Caravaggio's evocative 1594 painting of a lutenist.

recent years, a return to more traditional patterns.

OTHER WORKS: Three symphonies. Violin concerto. *Silesian Triptych* for soprano and orchestra. *Dance Preludes* for clarinet and piano.

Lutyens, Elisabeth (1906–83) English composer. Daughter of the architect Sir Edwin Lutyens, she studied at the Royal College of Music and became an assiduous worker in concert promotion and the introduction of new music to Britain, in conjunction with her husband Edward Clark, who brought Schoenberg and others to London while he was working at the BBC. Under the influence of Schoenberg and Webern, Elisabeth Lutyens was one of the first English composers to use twelve-tone techniques. She wrote a number of operas, including *The Goldfish Bowl*, a wide range of orchestral and chamber works, and about two hundred film and radio scores.

Lyadov, Anatoly (1855–1914) Russian composer. He studied with Rimsky-Korsakov at St Petersburg Conservatory and later became professor of composition there. He composed a number of orchestral tone poems, including *The Enchanted Lake* and *Baba Yaga*, contributed to *Paraphrases* (on *Chopsticks*), and carried out researches into Russian folklore, but was kept from any great achievement by a congenital idleness: so much so that when commissioned by Diaghilev to write a score for a ballet *The Firebird* he took so long to get round to it that the task was handed over to Stravinsky.

lyre An ancient instrument related to the harp, with a wooden or tortoiseshell body holding two arms between which strings were stretched and plucked by the fingers or a plectrum. Probably originating in Sumeria, it became the favourite instrument of classical Greece, where its creation was ascribed to Apollo, and Orpheus was its legendary virtuoso. There were then two types: the large *kythara* or *cithara* (from which comes the modern word 'guitar'), and the smaller *lyra*. Both could be played using two methods at once, with the fingers of the left hand plucking some strings while the right hand used a quill as plectrum on others.

The word *lyra* is also used to describe a lyre-shaped percussion instrument carried in military bands, on which tuned steel bars are played by hammers, known in Germany as a *stahlspiel* and in effect a portable *glockenspiel*.

lyric Strictly speaking, a piece sung to the accompaniment of a lyre; but the word has come to mean any verses set to music, especially the 'lyrics' of stage and film musical shows, and the term *lyric drama* has been used by some composers as an alternative to *opera*. Short pieces of instrumental music with a poetic quality also adopt this description, as in *Lyric Suites* by Grieg and Berg.

M

Maazel, Lorin (1930–) American conductor. He conducted both at the New York World Fair and the Hollywood Bowl in 1939, and went on to appointments with most leading American orchestras before making a name for himself in the operatic field at Bayreuth, Berlin, and La Scala, Milan. In London he conducted at Covent Garden, and in 1982 became the first American to hold the position of director of the Vienna Opera.

Lorin Maazel, who as a nine-year-old conducted in New York and at the Hollywood Bowl before going on to become conductor of many of the world's greatest orchestras.

McCabe, John (1939–) English composer and pianist. He studied at the Royal Manchester College of Music and then in Munich. As a pianist he has been a leading interpreter of Haydn, at the same time working in the cause of contemporary English music both as performer and as critic. He has written two operas, one on the story of *Mother Courage*, the other on C.S. Lewis's *The Lion, The Witch, and The Wardrobe*, as well as music for the ballet *Mary, Queen of Scots*, produced in Glasgow in 1975. His orchestral piece *The Chagall Windows* was inspired by Chagall's stained glass in the Hebrew University synagogue, Jerusalem, depicting the twelve tribes of Israel. He has written a great deal for the piano and for various chamber music combinations.

McCormack, (Count) John (1884–1945) Irish tenor (American citizen 1917). Without any formal musical education, he won a gold medal in the 1902 National Irish Festival, and began to study opera. He made his operatic début in Savona, Italy, in 1906 and went on to appear at Covent Garden, London, and in the main US opera houses. He won special acclaim as an ideal partner to Melba in productions of *La Bohème*. After 1923 he gave up the theatre and became a popular concert and recording star with sweetly-sung, impeccably phrased versions of sentimental pseudo-Irish songs such as *Mother Machree*. McCormack also appeared in a well-received film, *Song of my Heart*. In 1928 he was made a papal count. His farewell concert was given in Dublin in October 1938.

MacDowell, Edward (1860–1908) American composer and pianist. After learning the piano as a child he went to Paris and Frankfurt for further studies, became teacher of piano at Darmstadt Conservatory in 1881, and in the following year visited Liszt, who helped to promote the performance and publication of his *First Modern Suite* for piano. The first American composer to be acknowledged in Europe, MacDowell decided in 1888 to return to America, where he made many concert appearances before taking charge of the newly formed department of music at Columbia University. His compositions include a number of symphonic poems, among them *Hamlet and Ophelia*, inspired by a performance by Henry Irving and Ellen Terry which he had seen in London; but, himself an accomplished draughtsman, he was most at home with pictorial, allusive piano suites and pieces. Of his *Woodland Sketches*, the best remembered is the lyrical *To a Wild Rose*.

Possibly as the result of a street accident, MacDowell lapsed into insanity for the last few years of his life.

OTHER WORKS: Symphonic poem *Lancelot and Elaine*. Two piano concertos. *Norse* and *Keltic* piano sonatas. Many songs.

Machaut, Guillaume de (*c.*1300–77) French composer. As secretary to John of Luxembourg, King of Bohemia, and later in the service of other regal and noble masters, Machaut travelled throughout Europe and acquired a wide knowledge of musical sources from folksong to courtly ballads. In 1337 he was made a canon of Rheims Cathedral, and remained there for the rest of his life. In 1364 he celebrated the coronation of Charles V with his so-called *Mass of Nôtre Dame*, the first full setting of the mass for four voices with instruments emphasizing the vocal lines where appropriate, the whole work being a veritable cornucopia of devices such as syncopation, isorhythm, and syllabic setting of vocal phrases.

A protagonist of the *ars nova*, Machaut proved an adventurous pioneer in polyphonic setting of rondeaux and virelais for mixed voices and instruments. His motets often produce remarkable effects with two voices singing popular love songs against a sacred text in the third voice. In addition, Machaut was a gifted poet who greatly influenced Chaucer. He combined his interests in his *Voir Dit* (*Tale of Truth*), a collection of verse, letters, and song settings in praise of a lady.

Mackerras, (Sir) Charles (1925–) Australian conductor. He studied in Sydney, and was principal oboist in the Sydney Symphony Orchestra between 1943 and 1946. After later studies as a conductor (notably with Vaclav Tálich in Prague) he turned increasingly towards opera, first in Hamburg and then in England, and in 1951 conducted the first English performance of a Janáček opera, *Katya Kabanova*, at Sadler's Wells. In that same year he arranged Sullivan pieces for the Sadler's Wells Ballet in *Pineapple Poll*. Following this he has been responsible for editing and directing many other Janáček productions and recordings.

Maconchy, (Dame) Elizabeth (1907–) English composer (of Irish parentage). She studied with Vaughan Williams in London and with Karel Jirak in Prague, where her *Concertino* for piano and orchestra was first performed in 1930. She has written operas, including *The King of the Golden River*, and a variety of orchestral pieces and concertos, but is more closely identified with her large output of chamber music in a tense, concentrated Bartók vein.

madrigal A composition for a number of voices (usually five, though fewer or more can be employed) in which each has its own individual part, like an instrument in a string quartet, woven into a polyphonic structure. It was a form of domestic entertainment which lasted from the fourteenth century until the mid-seventeenth. The words were almost invariably short stanzas of secular verse and demands on the singers were not too great, though madrigals became more complex in the hands of composers such as Palestrina, Monteverdi and Gesualdo. Around 1650 the style gave way to that of the cantata.

maestro In Italian, 'master'. It has been used to dignify great executants in any instrumental field, but is most commonly applied to conductors. In the seventeenth and eighteenth centuries, the player who guided an orchestra from the keyboard and filled in the continuo part was described as the *maestro al cembalo*; and a *maestro di capella* was the equivalent of the German *kapellmeister*. Italian orchestral players who disapprove of a conductor have a wide choice of derivatives:

maestrino for a little teacher, *maestruccio* for a pathetic little one.

maggiore *See* **major**.

maggot A medieval English word for a whimsy, often used by composers for a fanciful instrumental piece in light-hearted mood and rhythm. In 1974 Peter Maxwell Davies revived the concept in his theatre piece *Miss Donnithorne's Maggot* for a frivolous combination of metronomes, football rattle and glass harmonica effects with mezzo-soprano and chamber orchestra.

magnificat The first word of the Latin version of *My soul doth magnify the Lord*, the canticle of the Virgin Mary, based on St Luke's account of her meeting with Elizabeth in the house of Zacharias. It is sung in Roman Catholic Vespers and Anglican Evensong. Originally sung in plainchant, it was in due course expanded by many composers into large-scale church or concert works, including settings by Dunstable, Buxtehude, Bach, and Vaughan Williams.

Mahler, Gustav (1860–1911) Austrian composer and conductor. Born into a Jewish family on the Bohemian-Moravian border, he was the eldest survivor of twelve children, five of whom died in infancy. His mother, whom he adored, was lame and suffered from heart disease; his own limping gait may have begun in imitation of hers and become an irreversible habit. His father owned a small distillery and paid for Gustav to have piano lessons, go to Prague for more advanced studies, and then enter the Vienna Conservatoire. In the hope of winning the annual Beethoven Prize offered by the Conservatoire, Mahler submitted a dramatic cantata, *Das Klagende Lied* (*Song of Sorrow*); and ascribed its rejection to the malice of a reactionary establishment.

Unable as yet to make a living as a composer, he accepted a conducting post and after a number of minor appointments became deputy at the Royal Prussian Court Theatre in Cassel. An uncompromising perfectionist, he soon became unpopular with the orchestra for insisting on long rehearsals of works which they thought they knew off by heart, but popular with audiences who felt a fresh vitality in the music and production. Invited by admirers to conduct a three-day festival, he achieved too great a triumph for the liking of his superiors, and realized he would have to seek employment elsewhere. He applied for a twelve-month engagement at Leipzig; and, while waiting to take this up, spent some months as second conductor in Prague. There he fell under the spell of Wagner, one of whose most devoted interpreters was the senior conductor, Anton Seidel. In spite of Wagner's virulent anti-Semitism, Mahler remained an ad-mirer, but because of Cosima Wagner's even more fanatical hatred of Jews he was never, even at the height of his career, invited to Bayreuth.

In Leipzig, as assistant to the great but domineering Artur Nikisch, he made time to work on a 'symphonic poem' which became his First Symphony. Also during this period he was asked by Weber's family to complete the unfinished opera *Die Drei Pintos* (*The Three Pintos*), and did so with great success.

After an equally controversial spell at Hamburg, whose opera company he took to London in 1892 on his only visit to England, and a spell in Budapest, Mahler converted in 1897 from Judaism to Roman Catholicism and at last reached the heights by becoming director first of the Vienna Court Opera and then of the Vienna Philharmonic. His reign there was a stormy one, but for a large part of the time he enjoyed the loyalty and friendship of his second conductor, Bruno Walter. There was also a strong bond between himself and Richard Strauss, whose operas he insisted on presenting in the teeth of scandalized opposition, and who reciprocated by urging on the German musical establishment performances of Mahler's own works.

He tried to divide his life methodically between conducting in Vienna during the season and working on his own music during summer in the countryside. A great nature lover, he was happiest among hills and meadows, and worked most creatively in little rural cottages which he referred to as his 'Composing Houses'. When Bruno Walter visited him during the writing of the Third Symphony and seemed impressed by the towering crags above, Mahler dismissed the need even to look at these splendours: 'I've composed them already'.

Some critics expressed contempt for his introduction of naïve little folk tunes into the most intense passages of his work, not to mention cowbells (in the Sixth and Seventh Symphonies), 'farmyard chatter' (in the Fourth), and other bucolic sounds. But these were among his own happy memories, to be set against the anguish and struggle of life, though at other times such ordinary little tunes had the opposite effect: during a consultation with Freud, while trying to save his marriage, he recalled how a frightening quarrel between his parents would forever be associated in his mind with a barrel-organ playing in the street, grinding out a hackneyed Viennese popular song.

So much of Mahler's own emotional personality went into his music that it is difficult to discuss his methods of composition objectively. He himself regarded each of his symphonies as a com-

Silhouettes by Böhler of Gustav Mahler, who shaved off his beard so that his facial expressions would more clearly express his intentions to the orchestra when conducting.

plete world, an all-embracing resolution of innumerable themes, emotions and philosophy. The Second Symphony makes great play with images of death, quoting from the *Dies Irae* and suggesting in the composer's own programme note that the entire audience should imagine itself standing beside the coffin of a dead hero; introduces a lyrical, rural element only to stress the loss of youth and innocence; turns to mockery; then offers up a prayer to the Virgin Mary, and ends in such a thunderous invocation of the terrors and grandeurs of Judgment Day that it has come to be known as the *Resurrection Symphony*. In this, as in the Third, Fourth and Eighth Symphonies, human voices are used to enhance some of the composer's passionate, lyrical, or religious 'programmes'. The Eighth is known as the *Symphony of a Thousand* because of the vast forces needed to perform this amalgamation of hymn and drama, where the Pentecostal *Veni, Creator Spiritus* is set against the final scene of Goethe's *Faust*.

Many joys and miseries were associated with his wife Alma. Hitherto shy of women and gloomy about his own suitability as a husband, at the age of forty-one he had declared to this beautiful twenty-one-year-old that she was going to marry him, and when he got his way made it clear that she must consider herself a handmaiden to genius — while Alma saw herself rather in the rôle of his inspirational Muse, to whose advice he ought always to listen. There was constant conflict, yet he undoubtedly adored her, and was stricken when he learned that she had fallen in love with the architect Walter Gropius (whom she later married). Marital stresses, continual forebodings such as those which produced the *Kindertotenlieder* (*Songs of the Death of Children*), presaging the death of his elder daughter, and the strain of conducting in his ruthlessly idealistic way, aggravated a chronic heart condition. In 1907 he was invited to conduct in New York, first at the Metropolitan – where he opened in January 1908 with a production of *Tristan und Isolde* – and then at the Philharmonic. Taken ill early in 1911, he returned to Europe to die.

Left unperformed at his death were the Ninth Symphony and a song cycle which in orchestral forces and overall proportions is essentially a symphony: *Das Lied von der Erde* (*The Song of the Earth*), in which Mahler used Chinese lyrics as the basis for another of his meditations on death and the impermanence of beauty, ending with the drawn-out poignancy of *Der Abschied* (*Farewell*). It was thought for some years that two movements were all that had been completed of a Tenth Symphony, but in 1960 the musicologist Deryck Cooke found a complete short score and from it prepared a full performing version.

OTHER WORKS: Song cycle *Lieder eines fahrenden Gesellen* (*Songs of a Wayfarer*). Song settings of folk poetry, *Des Knaben Wunderhorn* (*Youth's Golden Horn*). Piano quartet and quintet. Violin sonata.

major Italian *maggiore*, German *dur*. Used to describe a diatonic scale from, for example, C to the C an octave above in a succession of full tones except for a semitone between the third and fourth degrees and between the seventh and eighth degrees; or an interval within a chord such as the *major common chord* which includes the major third of C to E, while the minor chord would have an interval of C to E flat. (*See also* **chord** and **scale**.)

malagueña An Andalusian song originating from Malaga, beginning and ending in the key of the dominant, or an instrumental piece in similar style.

Malcolm George (1917–) English harpsichordist and conductor. For some years master of the music at the Roman Catholic cathedral of Westminster, London, he is also a pianist, organist, composer, arranger, and one of the most gifted harpsichord recitalists in Britain. Among his transcriptions and witty pastiches have been harpsichord arrangements of the *Flight of the Bumble Bee* and a semi-jazz, semi-fugal version of the *Sailor's Hornpipe* called *Bach before the Mast*.

Malibran, Maria (1808–36) Spanish mezzo-soprano. Under her maiden name of Maria Garcia she made her opera début in London at the age of seventeen as Rosina in *The Barber of Seville*, and the following year went to New York with her father's touring Italian opera company. He seems to have been her main teacher, credited with developing her vehement, dramatic voice by 'hardy and tremendous exercise' and brutally 'beating trills into his daughter'. In New York she married an elderly Frenchman, Eugène Malibran, but left him when he went bankrupt, and later married a Belgian violinist, Charles de Bériot. Her frenzied career, which took in a performance of *La sonnambula* that 'quite besotted' its composer, Bellini, and a great success in *Norma* and *Fidelio*, reached its climax when, shortly after falling off a horse while pregnant, she insisted on giving a taxing encore in competition with a rival performer in Manchester, resulting in her collapse and speedy death.

A lithograph of the soprano Maria Malibran, whose competitive rather than musically perfectionist outlook led the painter Delacroix to complain that 'she was completely lacking in the sense of the ideal.'

Malipiero, Gian Francesco (1882–1973) Italian composer. He studied in Vienna, Venice and Bologna, and while in Venice immersed himself in the then half-forgotten works of Italian composers such as Monteverdi and Tartini, many of which he transcribed and arranged, publishing a full edition of Monteverdi's works and editing many volumes of Vivaldi. He became a composition professor and in critical mood destroyed many of his own earlier works before discovering his real voice in a music stimulated by Stravinsky but conditioned by his own lasting love for early Italian music: influences which led him to revolt against the operatic conventions of contemporary Italy and produce his trilogies *L'orfeide* and *Il mistero di Venezia*. He experimented with atonality but shied away from serialism, and in later years achieved a fine synthesis of all his different yet complementary interests.

OTHER WORKS: Operas *Guilio Cesare, Don Giovanni*. Ballet *Stradivario*. Eleven symphonies. Eight string quartets. Choral and orchestral *Missa pro mortuis*. Songs and piano pieces.

mandolin or **mandoline** A Neapolitan stringed instrument of the lute family, but with a more pear-shaped back and metal instead of gut strings, set in pairs and played with a plectrum whose fast thrumming can produce a tinkling tremolo effect. It has been used most effectively in the serenade in Mozart's *Don Giovanni* and in Mahler's *Das Lied von der Erde*.

Mandolin.

Mannheim School In the eighteenth-century electoral court at Mannheim in Baden-Württemberg the orchestra was noted for its instrumentalists, many of them from Bohemia and many of them composers in their own right, including Stamitz and Richter. They were famous throughout Europe for their disciplined dynamics, especially their dramatic, perfectly controlled crescendos, sometimes called the 'Mannheim Rush' or, in later histories, the 'Mannheim Steamroller' – a wild anachronism, since such a machine had not then been invented. Similar effects were attempted in the drumming urgency of bass parts in the German *trommelbass* and the so-called 'Rossini crescendo' in Italy.

Manns, (Sir) August (1825–1907) German conductor. (British citizen 1894.) He was engaged as sub-conductor of the military band providing light music at the Crystal Palace after its move from the Great Exhibition site in Hyde Park, London. When the orchestra was enlarged he became its full conductor, and organized the Saturday concerts which were to feature much new English music as well as old favourites. Later he instituted an annual Handel Festival. He became a naturalized Englishman and was awarded a knighthood.

manual A keyboard played by the hands, especially organ keyboards as distinct from the pedals. Large harpsichords frequently have two manuals.

maracas The word is generally used in the plural, since maracas tend to be played in pairs. They consist of dried gourds containing beads or pellets, and in Latin-American dance band numbers are shaken to produce a rattling effect. Appearances in other compositions are rare, though Varèse has made some use of them in his percussion ensembles.

march A piece of music with a strong beat, usually in 4/4, 2/4 or 6/8 time, originally intended to keep marching soldiers in step but also employed for processions, funeral ceremonies and on the operatic stage. March movements appear in music for virginals, some of them with dramatic titles. Beethoven introduced a Funeral March into his *Eroica* symphony, and Chopin into his piano sonata in B flat minor. The wedding marches from Wagner's *Lohengrin* and the incidental music in Mendelssohn's *Midsummer Night's Dream* are heard in the majority of church weddings in our own time. Elgar wrote a famous set of *Pomp and Circumstance* marches, to the first of which have been set the words of *Land of Hope and Glory*; and in America the bandmaster Sousa wrote such rousing examples that he became known as 'the March King'.

marimba A Mexican percussion instrument of the xylophone family, but with a deeper tone produced by metal resonators under the wooden keys. It is large enough for a number of players to use mallets on it together, and in Central

America there are entire marimba bands. It is heard in Boulez's *Pli selon pli* and Stockhausen's *Gruppen*, and Milhaud wrote a concerto for marimba and vibraphone.

Markevitch, Igor (1912–83) Russian composer and conductor. He was brought up in Switzerland and Paris, studying with Nadia Boulanger. Diaghilev was impressed by his work and commissioned the piano concerto of 1929. Markevitch wrote several ballet scores, including *Icare*, and a cantata based on Milton's *Paradise Lost*. He spent World War II in Italy, and afterwards concentrated on conducting, appearing as guest conductor with leading European and American orchestras and becoming director of the Monte Carlo Opera in 1968.

Marriner, (Sir) Neville (1924–) English conductor and violinist. He studied at the Royal College of Music, and in 1950 became professor of the violin there. In 1956 he founded the Academy of St Martin-in-the-Fields chamber orchestra, named after the London church in which its concerts were originally given, and directed it until 1978. From 1968 he was also conductor of the Los Angeles Chamber Orchestra.

Marschner, Heinrich August (1793–1861) German composer. He began playing the piano and composing as a boy, but without formal training until, when he was supposedly studying law in Leipzig, he turned full-time to music. Weber produced his opera *Henrich IV und d'Aubigné* at Dresden, where Marschner became his deputy conductor. He held other such posts until becoming *kapellmeister* at the Court in Hanover, and continued composing romantic operas, of which *Hans Heiling* made the greatest public impression.

Martin, Frank (1890–1974) Swiss composer. The son of a Calvinist minister, he studied in Geneva and Rome, became a teacher at the Geneva Conservatory, and only slowly developed his own delicate, expressive style of composition. For a time he was much influenced by French music, which he heard at Ansermet's concerts, but began his own exploration of note series without ever committing himself too rigidly to twelve-tone systems. One of his best-known and most frequently played works is the luminous *Petite symphonie concertante* for harp, harpsichord, piano and strings. Martin experimented with other unusual instrumental combinations such as trombone and saxophone, and wrote ballades for solo alto saxophone. In 1946 he settled in Amsterdam with his Dutch wife, although after 1950 he had to commute between there and Cologne to work as professor of composition in Cologne Conservatory.
OTHER WORKS: Opera *Dur Sturm*. Secular oratorio *Le vin herbé* (on Tristan legend). Two piano concertos. Two string quartets.

Martinů, Bohuslav (1890–1959) Czech composer. (American citizen 1952.) He was born and spent his early years in an apartment high up in a church tower (of which his father was keeper), and frankly attributed the academic, neo-classical cast of his music to the remoteness he always felt looking down on other people from this eyrie. He went to Prague to study the violin with Suk, but was dismissed for laziness. For over ten years he worked on and off as a violinist in the Czech Philharmonic Orchestra, then in 1923 went to Paris to study with Roussel and stayed there until 1940.

Largely self-taught, he became one of the most prolific composers of the century, pouring out symphonies, concertos, chamber music for various combinations, and choral works. His first international success was *La Bagarre* (*The Tumult*), an orchestral celebration of Lindbergh's flight across the Atlantic. French influences are clear in much of his writing, especially in the dream-world opera *Julietta*, together with jazz echoes here and there, but always with the underlying melodiousness and melancholy of Czech folk music which haunted him throughout years of exile. He rarely strayed from the paths of diatonic harmony, but was capable of using it to the full limits of dissonance and imaginative progressions.

After the fall of France in World War II, he and his French wife left for the USA, where he spent most of the rest of his life apart from a few periods in Europe. In 1943 he wrote an orchestral *Memorial to Lidice* in tribute to the villagers massacred by Nazis during their occupation of Czechoslovakia. In 1955 his expansive sixth symphony, subtitled *Fantaisies symphoniques*, was first performed by the Boston Symphony Orchestra under Charles Munch, of whom Martinů said 'I like Munch's spontaneous approach to music – the music takes shape in a free way, flowing …'
OTHER WORKS: Opera *The Greek Passion*. Ballet *La Revue de Cuisine* (*Kitchen Revue*). Orchestral *Jazz Suite*, *Frescoes of Piero della Francesca*. Six symphonies. Seven string quartets. Choral *Field Mass*.

Martin y Soler, Vicente (1754–1806) Spanish composer (known in Italy as Vincenzo Martini). He started his musical career as an organist, but then began composing operas, several of them to libretti by Lorenzo Da Ponte. One of them, *Una cosa rara*, is quoted in Mozart's *Don Giovanni*. In 1788 he became Court conductor to Catherine II in St Petersburg, left for a spell in London to work with Da Ponte on a joint production of two operas, and then returned to Russia as a teacher.

Mascagni, Pietro (1863–1945) Italian composer. His father, a baker, forbade him to take up music; but the boy took lessons in secret until he was found out, when a sympathetic uncle took him into his household. Later the father and son were reconciled after the much applauded performance of a cantata, *In Filanda*. A wealthy patron paid for Mascagni to study in Milan, but he found theory so dull that he fled and went off as conductor to a touring opera company. When he married, he was forced to give up this sort of life and settle down as director of a municipal school of music in Cerignola and as a piano teacher.

In 1889 Mascagni entered a music publisher's competition for a one-act opera, and won first prize with *Cavalleria Rusticana*. When produced in Rome it was an immediate success – a success repeated all over the world. Later operatic attempts made little impact and, although comfortably provided for by the royalties on this opera and by his work as a touring conductor and for a time conductor at La Scala, Milan, the composer often regretted that he was 'crowned before becoming king'.

During Mussolini's dictatorship Mascagni played along with the régime and wrote banal patriotic pieces. Later he was to pay for this by having to surrender all his property and honours, and finished his life in near-poverty in a small hotel in Rome.

masque In seventeenth-century England the most popular form of aristrocratic entertainment was a combination of dance, drama and song with instrumental accompaniment, performed with great pageantry and based on allegorical or classical themes. In many ways it resembled the French opera-ballet, from which modern opera and ballet both stem. Milton's *Comus*, with music by Henry Lawes, is one of the most celebrated examples. Arne's masque *Alfred*, performed in the Prince of Wales's amphitheatre at Cliveden above the River Thames, included the first performance of the song *Rule, Britannia*!

Mass In Latin *Missa*, in French and German *Messe*. The main ritual of the Roman Catholic church, also used in some Anglican and Episcopalian churches, can be either a spoken Low Mass or a High Mass in which music is used. Five sections known as the Ordinary, which remain unchanged throughout the year, consist of the *Kyrie*, *Gloria*, *Credo*, *Sanctus and Benedictus*, and *Agnus Dei*. Settings of these have been made by composers from the days of plainchant, through the polyphony of Machaut and Palestrina, up to the towering achievements of Bach in his *Mass in B minor* for soloists, chorus, organ and orchestra, and Beethoven's *Missa solemnis*. Some Popes objected to the use of orchestral music in church, suspecting that its purpose was self-indulgently dramatic rather than devotional, and banned its use, so that concert performances became more frequent than integration with religious services.

Another five parts of the Mass vary according to seasons and feast days. Known as the Proper, they consist of the *Introit, Gradual, Alleluia or Tract, Offertory*, and *Communion*. Settings of these sections have usually been restricted to plainchant.

Haydn wrote some brilliant celebratory Masses, including one in honour of Lord Nelson, and an especially beautiful one called after Theresa, wife of the Emperor Francis II of Austria. In our own time, Stravinsky and Vaughan Williams have used the form. Delius adapted it to his pantheistic tastes in *A Mass of Life*, based on Nietzsche's *Also Sprach Zarathustra*.

Massenet, Jules (1842–1912) French composer. During a period of financial stringency Massenet's mother took on piano pupils, and gave her son lessons. At the age of eleven he was accepted by the Paris Conservatoire, helping to keep himself by playing in the percussion sections of local theatres. He won the *Grand Prix de Rome* and spent three years in Rome, where he gave piano lessons to a girl whom he married and took back with him to Paris. After winning some acclaim for oratorios and operas, he achieved a great success in 1884 with the opera *Manon*. Among later works were *Werther* and *Don Quichotte*, in which Chaliapin sang the title rôle. He was a conservative musician with limited creative resources but an undeniable melodic gift and with the ideal temperament for teaching: he became professor of composition at the Paris Conservatoire and remained popular there in spite of the opposition of younger men with post-Wagnerian leanings.

Master of the King's (Queen's) Music The post was created by King Charles I of England for the leader of his royal orchestra. Since the end of the nineteenth century it has been a purely honorary appointment bestowed on a leading composer of the day, who will usually provide a few celebratory pieces for coronations, royal weddings and other special occasions. Holders of the post since 1626 have been:

Nicholas Lanier 1626
Louis Grabu 1666
Nicholas Staggins 1674
John Eccles 1700
Maurice Green 1735
William Boyce 1755
John Stanley 1779
William Parsons 1786
William Shield 1817
Christian Kramer 1829
Franz Kramer 1834
George Frederick Anderson 1848
William Cusins 1870

Walter Parratt 1893
Edward Elgar 1924
Walford Davies 1934
Arnold Bax 1941
Arthur Bliss 1953
Malcolm Williamson 1975

Mattheson, Johann (1681–1764) German composer and harpsichordist. Born in Hamburg, he was for some years secretary to the English Legation there, and later *chargé d'affaires*. As a young man he had sung female rôles in opera, and he wrote several of his own as well as oratorios, cantatas, harpsichord suites, a dozen or so sparkling flute sonatas, and several important books, including *Der vollkommene Capellmeister* (*The Perfect Conductor*). He was a close friend of Handel, and on one occasion went with him to Lübeck to explore the possibility of succeeding Buxtehude there.

mazurka A Polish national dance from the old region of Masovia, in 3/4 time with a heavily accented second beat. The melody finishes also on the second beat of the final measure. In spite of its marked rhythm it is a stately dance rather than a fast one. Chopin used the form and developed it in many of his piano pieces.

measure *See* **bar**.

mediant The third degree of an ascending major or minor scale, so called because it comes halfway between the tonic and the dominant.

Medtner, Nicolas (1880–1951) Russian composer and pianist. He studied at the Moscow Conservatory and later became professor there. After the Revolution he taught for a while in a Moscow school, but during a tour abroad as a virtuoso pianist he decided not to return. He spent some time in Paris, made his American début in 1924 with the Philadelphia Orchestra, and settled in England in 1936, sharing his time between London and a place in the country. He composed a large number of solo piano pieces, including sets of *Fairy Tales* and *Forgotten Melodies*, and settings of German and Russian texts for voice and piano, many of which he recorded himself with singers such as Oda Slobodskaya and Elisabeth Schwarzkopf. He wrote a book condemning modern techniques and remained staunchly in favour of tonality.

OTHER WORKS: Three piano concertos. Twelve piano sonatas. Three sonatas and three nocturnes for violin and piano. *Hymn in Praise of Toil*.

Mehta, Zubin (1936–) Indian conductor, violinist and pianist. Son of the founder of the Bombay Symphony Orchestra, Mehta studied in Vienna and in 1958 won the first prize in an international conductors' competition at Liverpool. He made his American début in 1961, and became music director of orchestras including those of Montreal,

Los Angeles and New York. In 1968 he became musical adviser to the Israel Philharmonic Orchestra.

meistersinger German guilds between the fourteenth and sixteenth centuries cultivated regular poetry and music recitals at which strict rules were enforced regarding apprenticeship and, through a series of competitions, elevation to higher grades and ultimately to the accolade of 'mastersinger'. The form of the songs was equally rigid: it must always consist of a first section, the *stollen*, which was repeated and then followed by the *abgesang*. Wagner's opera *Die Meistersinger von Nürnberg* (*The Mastersingers of Nuremberg*) gives a vivid picture of the rituals and conflicts of such a guild, basing one of the characters on the real-life Hans Sachs, who is reputed to have composed thousands of verses and melodies.

Melba, (Dame) Nellie (1861–1931) Australian soprano. Born Helen Mitchell in Richmond, a suburb of Melbourne, she later adopted the stage name of

An autographed photograph of Dame Nellie Melba, the self-willed Australian soprano whose 'beautiful, effortless tone' was matched by her strident declaration during any contretemps whatsoever, '*I* am Melba.'

Melba in tribute to the city, and resoundingly claimed, 'I put Australia on the map'. She sang in churches and at local concerts as a child, but could not study seriously until after her marriage to a sheep farmer went awry, and she was in desperate need of money. Travelling to Europe with her father, she was taken on as a pupil of Mathilde Marchesi in Paris. Her purity of tone and brilliance in coloratura rôles led her to Covent Garden in London, La Scala in Milan, and a long succession of seasons at the New York Met. At the height of her career she became the epitome of the temperamental *prima donna*, dictating to managements the supporting cast she required, and rearranging lighting even during a performance to present herself in the most flattering conditions. Melba toast and the ice-cream dish *Pêche Melba* are named after her.

An autographed photograph of the Danish tenor Lauritz Melchior when appearing in the title rôle of Wagner's *Siegfried* during the 1930/31 Berlin State Opera season.

Melchior, Lauritz (1890–1973) Danish tenor (American citizen 1947). He studied in Copenhagen and made his début there as a baritone in *Pagliacci*, turning to tenor parts in 1918 in a production of *Tannhäuser*. He soon became the outstanding Wagnerian *heldentenor* at Bayreuth, as well as at the New York Met between 1926 and 1950, singing the rôle of Tristan more than two hundred times.

melisma A group of notes sung to a single syllable, most frequently employed in plainsong.

mellophone A brass instrument with three valves, similar in tone to the French horn but less rich, used mainly in marching bands.

melodeon A portable reed instrument like a concertina (the names often being interchangeable); or a version with foot pedals, an early form of the so-called 'American organ'. (*See also* **harmonium**.)

melody A succession of notes which by means of varying pitch and rhythm produce a pleasant effect on the ear. The word is often used as a substitute for 'air' or 'tune', but a melody is not necessarily complete in itself and may in fact be only a fragment of the whole. Like a tune, however, it is essentially horizontal music as opposed to the vertical construction of harmony; though most listeners hear an implied harmony beneath even the most spare, unaccompanied melody.

Mendelssohn, Felix (1809–47) German composer and pianist. His father Abraham, a Jewish banker in Hamburg, made an addition to his surname to become Mendelssohn-Bartholdy on his conversion to Christianity. Felix never lacked for money or for stimulating acquaintance with artists in every field, and he was not only encouraged in his musical interests by his father but made to get up at five o'clock every morning to study and

A painting of the twelve-year-old Felix Mendelssohn.

The entrance to Fingal's Cave on the isle of Staffa, inspiration for Mendelssohn's tone-poem overture, *The Hebrides*.

compose. As well as learning the piano and making a concert début at the age of nine, he began learning the violin also. He was ten when one of his compositions, a psalm setting, was sung in Berlin; fourteen when he completed a comic opera; and seventeen when he wrote the overture to his fresh, lyrical incidental music for *A Midsummer Night's Dream*.

As well as composing and proving himself a virtuoso pianist, Mendelssohn worked as a conductor and was largely responsible for reviving the music of the neglected Johann Sebastian Bach: in March 1829 he gave the first performance since Bach's death of the *St Matthew Passion*. Another 'first' was his introduction of Beethoven's *Emperor* Concerto to English audiences in 1829.

Interest in the works of Bach was largely responsible for his own attempts at large-scale choral works which proved especially popular in England. His visits to London and other parts of Britain won him admirers everywhere. He dedicated his first symphony to the Philharmonic Society, and soon became an honorary member. He conducted the first performance of his oratorio *Elijah* in Birmingham, and in several different towns during his tenth and final visit to the country. Travels in Scotland resulted in the *Hebrides* overture, better known as *Fingal's Cave*, and in the idea for a *Scottish Symphony* which became his Symphony No.3 in A minor and was dedicated, with her permission, to Queen Victoria. His tuneful, sometimes almost too facile music, his elegant style of playing, and his charm of manner made him a great favourite with the queen and her consort, Prince Albert. When news of his death in Leipzig reached her, Victoria recorded in her diary their distress at the loss of 'the greatest musical genius since Mozart, & the most amiable man'.

Of Mendelssohn's other works, among the most lasting favourites have been his *Italian Symphony* (No.4), the violin concerto in E minor, and the *Songs without Words* for piano. In all of them he combined a classical background with nineteenth-century Romanticism, always faultlessly accomplished, even though he never really attained the heights of unquestionable genius to which Queen Victoria sentimentally wished to elevate him.

OTHER WORKS: Orchestral overtures *Ruy Blas*, *Calm Sea and Prosperous Voyage*. Two piano concertos. Symphony-cantata *Lobgesang (Hymn of Praise)*. Six string quartets. String octet in E flat. Many piano capriccios, preludes and studies. Six sonatas for organ.

Menotti, Gian Carlo (1911–) Italian composer. He studied in Milan and then at the Curtis Institute in Philadelphia, where he became a friend of Samuel Barber, for whose opera *Vanessa* he was later to write the libretto. As a youth he had written two operas, and he continued in this field, most successfully with *The Medium* and the deeply felt attack on cruel bureaucracy, *The Consul*. Most of his working life has been spent in the USA, and he has undoubtedly been influenced by the Broadway theatre in his approach to opera. In 1951 his *Amahl and the Night Visitors* was the first opera to be written directly for television. In 1974 he began restoring a house in the Lammermuir Hills, Scotland, with the intention of opening a small concert hall there.

Menuhin, Hephzibah (1920–81) American pianist. Sister of Yehudi Menuhin, she made her début in 1928 in San Francisco, and thereafter appeared not only as a soloist but in recitals with her brother. In 1938 she made her home in Australia, but continued touring, and died in London.

Two knights: the violinist Sir Yehudi Menuhin *(right)* and the composer Sir Lennox Berkeley.

Menuhin, Yehudi (1916–) American violinist. His parents, Russian-born Jews, had each emigrated first to Palestine and then to the USA, where they met and married, naming their oldest son Yehudi – 'the Jew' – because his mother insisted on demonstrating her pride in the face of anti-Semitic prejudice. A child prodigy, he made his first public appearance in San Francisco at the age of eight, going on to study with Enescu in Paris. In 1929 he played three violin concertos (by Bach, Beethoven and Brahms) in one concert with the Berlin Philharmonic Orchestra, and that same year visited England for the first time for concerts and recordings. In 1932 he recorded Elgar's violin concerto with the composer conducting; and in 1942 Bartók dedicated a solo violin sonata to him. After World War II he continued concert appearances, but in 1959 he settled in England and for ten years was musical director of the Bath Festival. When he gave up this post he was made a Freeman of the City.

A gifted teacher, enthusiastic in communicating with young musicians, he founded the Menuhin School of Music in 1963, and in 1965 became an honorary KBE (Knight of the British Empire).

Messager, André (1853–1929) French composer and conductor. A pupil of Saint-Saëns, he was for many years a church organist before becoming an opera conductor. Debussy dedicated *Pelléas et Mélisande* to him. Between 1901 and 1905 he was artistic director of Covent Garden, and then director of the Paris Opéra. He composed a number of light operas of his own, including the agreeable *Véronique* and *Monsieur Beaucaire*, and music for a ballet, *Les deux pigeons* (*The Two Pigeons*), which was revived in London in 1961 with new choreography by Frederick Ashton.

Messiaen, Olivier (1908–) French composer. His father was a professor of literature, his mother a poet, and the boy was brought up in a devoutly Roman Catholic atmosphere. After studies at the Paris Conservatoire he became organist at the Sainte Trinité church and remained there for more than twenty years, during which he developed his own style of composition in organ music and symphonic realization of what he saw as static concepts rather than continuous development. His studies in Hindu music and birdsong reinforced his tendencies towards highly decorated rather than dynamic music, all in the service of Catholic theology, which he wrote must be the best, 'for it comprises all subjects, and the abundance of technical means allows the heart to expand freely'. In spite of this, his generous acknowledgment of other exploratory methods made him in post-war years a valued and influential teacher of younger composers such as Boulez and Stockhausen.

During World War II Messiaen was captured and sent to a prisoner-of-war camp, in which he composed, and managed to have performed, his *Quatuor pour la fin du temps* (*Quartet for the end of time*), for violin, clarinet, cello and piano. Released in 1942, he became professor of harmony at the Paris Conservatoire. Between 1946 and 1948 he worked on a vast symphony commissioned by Koussevitsky, called *Turangalîla* after a Sanskrit word implying movement and rhythm in the interplay of divine action and reaction throughout the cosmos, all woven in and around the love motive of the Tristan legend – a rewarding combination for Messiaen in his commitment to what have been called his artificial musical universes. This ten-movement work employs not merely a large orchestra but a number of pitched and unpitched percussion instruments, as well as the electronic *ondes Martenot*.

Messiaen has continued to be concerned with rhythm units and the relationships of sound to colour in music, all of them typified in the songs, plumage and movements of birds, which repeatedly find their way into his organ music, religious

Oliver Messiaen at an Oxford Festival with the score of his massive *Turangalîla* Symphony.

choral pieces, and orchestral works such as *Oiseaux exotiques* (*Exotic birds*).

OTHER WORKS: Orchestral *Chronochromie*. Choral and orchestral *La Transfiguration de Notre Seigneur Jésus-Christ*. Organ *Livre d'orgue* (*Organ book*). Piano preludes and rhythmic studies.

Metastasio, Pietro (1698–1782) Italian poet and librettist. Original name Trapassi. Of humble origins in Rome, he was taken up by a distinguished singer and in 1730 became Court poet in Vienna, where his main function was to provide librettos for the operas which were then all the rage, mainly on classical themes. Among composers who used his words were Gluck, Handel, Alessandro Scarlatti, and Mozart (the opera *La clemenza di Tito* and several of the concert arias). Some of his texts are thought to have been used as many as sixty or seventy times, and were reused or reworked even after Gluck's fresh approach to opera had led to the shedding of many fashionable conventions.

metre In music, as in poetry, the word is used in connection with the pattern of successive rhythmic pulses produced by notes of similar or varying

On 16 September 1966 the new Metropolitan Opera House opened in Lincoln Center, New York, with Thomas Schippers conducting the première of Barber's *Antony and Cleopatra*.

length within a measure. To avoid too loose an application of the term, it is generally accepted today that in a time signature such as 6/8 the basic eight beats are the metre, while the six notes actually played are the rhythm.

metronome A mechanical device for establishing the correct tempo of a piece according to the composer's wishes. It was invented by a Dutchman named Winkel but around 1814 was taken over and developed by a German, Johann Mälzel. The basic principle is that of a pendulum driven by a spring and wheel which tick off a steady beat, adjustable by means of a movable weight. If a composer writes M.M. ♩ = 80 (or simply ♩ = 80, discarding the 'Mälzel Metronome' attribution), he is asking for a timing of 80 crotchets to the minute rather than using a less specific indication such as *andante* and leaving interpretation of this to the player's own feeling for relative speeds. Mälzel's friend Beethoven used the tick-tock effect as an amiable tribute in the slow movement of his eighth symphony. In 1962 György Ligeti composed a 'Symphonic poem' for a hundred metronomes.

Metropolitan Opera House, New York 'The Met', as it has been affectionately known for generations, opened in 1883 with a performance of Gounod's *Faust*. Its first conductor died before the end of his first season, but his son Walter Damrosch later took over, presenting all productions in German. Famous directors and conductors, both guest and resident, have included Mahler, Toscanini, Serafin and Szell. Between 1950 and 1972 the controversial Rudolf Bing was manager, modernizing the whole approach to operatic staging. In 1966 a new Met was incorporated in the Lincoln Center for the Performing Arts, opening with Samuel Barber's *Antony and Cleopatra*. In 1975 James Levine, principal conductor since 1971, was appointed musical director.

Meyerbeer, Giacomo (1791–1864) German composer. His real name was Jakob Liebmann Beer. 'Meyer' was added to his surname at the request of an uncle who left him a legacy, and after studies in

Italy he dropped the Jakob in favour of its 'Italian equivalent. His musical interests were also transformed. Having previously tried his hand at religious choral work and operas in German, he fell under the spell of Rossini and produced six well-received Italian operas. One of them, *Il crociato in Egitto* (*The Crusader in Egypt*), was an immediate success in Venice, Munich and Paris. Already a wealthy man, the composer won further riches by insisting on expensive, first-class production standards and by spending lavishly on self-publicity.

An engraving from a photograph of Meyerbeer. Under the spell of Italian opera he earned Weber's disapproval as one who had 'become an imitator in order to win the favour of the crowd'.

In Paris Meyerbeer met the playwright and librettist Eugène Scribe, and soon turned his attention to French opera. Collaboration with Scribe produced another money-spinner, *Robert le Diable* (*Robert, the Devil*)), (presented with spectacular effects and a ballet of ghostly nuns, and adding to the reputations of both men. They followed up with *Les Huguenots, Le Prophète*, and one not produced until shortly after Meyerbeer's death, *L'Africaine*, on which he had worked with mounting mistrust of his own failing powers. Others did not share his doubts. In 1842 the King of Prussia had appointed him General Music Director in Berlin, where he helped the young Wagner – to be repaid later by an attack on him in Wagner's essay about 'Judaism in Music'. In 1862 he represented German music at the International Exhibition in London.

mezza and **mezzo** Italian for 'half' (feminine and masculine). The phrase *mezza-voce* instructs the singer to produce a 'half voice', under the breath. A *mezzo-soprano* is a singer whose voice falls into the range between soprano and contralto.

microtones Intervals smaller than those between the semitones of a chromatic scale can be achieved by singers or string players, and have provoked interesting experiments in composition since the end of the nineteenth century. Bartók and Charles Ives introduced quarter tones into some of their works, Ives using pairs of pianos tuned a quarter of a tone apart. In the 1920s in Prague there were attempts to use sixth-tone methods as well. Electronic resources have made even finer gradations possible; but most listeners still find it difficult to accept such deviations from expected intervals and progressions.

Milhaud, Darius (1892–1974) French composer. When he entered the Paris Conservatoire he envisaged a career as a violinist, but almost immediately plunged into composition, producing a string quartet, a violin sonata, and even an attempt at an opera. In spite of an arthritic condition which led to frequent confinement to a wheelchair, he became one of the most prolific and energetic composers of the century, producing about four hundred and fifty known works, including cantatas, operas, eighteen string quartets, ballet music, and a variety of pieces for varying instrumental combinations. In Paris he became a member of the anti-establishment group *Les Six*. He was also an enthusiastic teacher, working from 1940 until 1947 at Mills College (now part of the University of California), and continuing there part-time until 1971.

Although Milhaud has been associated primarily with a distinctive use of bitonality, Latin-American rhythms and jazz – as in the cabaret atmosphere

Bad health meant that from the late 1920s Darius Milhaud could conduct only sitting down and move about only in a wheelchair.

of the ballet *Le Boeuf sur le toit*, with its Cocteau libretto – he was equally capable of turning his talents to a recreation of old French themes and atmospheres. His wind quintet *La Cheminée du Roi René*, first performed at Mills College in 1941, evokes scenes and episodes from a famous Troubadour Court at Aix-en-Provence, near a country spot known as 'King René's Fireplace', in a witty, modally allusive vein, with a hint of madrigal influences.

OTHER WORKS: Operas *Bolivar, David*. Ballet *La Création du monde*. Six chamber symphonies. Five piano concertos. Three violin concertos. Suite *Scaramouche* for two pianos.

minnelied and **minnesinger** German for a love song and singer(s) of love. The *minnesinger* were mem-bers of minstrel groups, equivalent of the French troubadours, of aristocratic origin in contrast to their merchant-class successors, the *meistersinger*. Wagner depicts one of their vocal rituals in *Tannhäuser*, the full title of which is *Tannhäuser and the Singing Contest at the Wartburg*, the hero being himself a *minnesinger*.

minor Italian *minore*, German *moll*. In a scale or chord, a lesser interval than the major interval, involving the introduction of a semitone at certain places. The minor scale is similar to the discarded Aeolian mode (A to A on the white keys of a piano) but with alterations to the sixth and seventh degrees in certain formations. In the key of A minor, for instance, with a key signature the same as C major (i.e. without sharps or flats), the natural minor scale ascends and descends without accidentals. In the melodic minor, however, both the sixth and seventh are sharpened on the way up but natural on the way down; and in the harmonic minor, just the seventh is sharpened on the way up and is again natural on the way down. (*See also* **major** and **Notation**.)

Minor chords include the minor triad (with a minor third and a perfect fifth above the root) and the minor seventh (equalling a minor triad with a minor seventh above the root). (*See also* **chord** and **Notation**.)

minstrel The word was taken into English from the French *ménestrel*, a public or guild singer (similar to the German *meistersinger*), but came to mean almost any wandering performer. Some of these were welcomed along their way; others, regarded as vagabonds, were liable to be burned through the ears with a hot iron. In the last quarter of the nineteenth century the 'Minstrel Show' of songs and vaudeville acts, usually presented by white men with blackened faces, became popular in the USA and spread to Europe, making great use of rhythmic numbers which were among the formative influences of ragtime and jazz. They also inspired *Minstrels* in Debussy's *Préludes* and the *Golliwogg's Cakewalk* in his *Children's Corner* suite.

minuet A graceful Court dance in 3/4 time of French origin, popular from the seventeenth century onwards. Composers introduced it into suites and then into the symphony, where it usually consisted of one section repeated; a different section called the trio because for a time it was written in three-part harmony or played by three players only; and a final section repeating the first. After Beethoven's time it tended to be replaced in orchestral works by the faster *scherzo*.

Mitropoulos, Dimitri (1896–1960) Greek conductor (American citizen 1946). He studied in Athens and Berlin, becoming répétiteur at the Berlin State Opera and later conductor of the Paris Symphony Orchestra. In 1936 he made his American début with the Boston Symphony Orchestra, and later conducted the Minneapolis Orchestra for twelve years and the New York Symphony Orchestra for eight. An international competition for young conductors is named after him.

modes Until the present major and minor scales were generally accepted, from the late sixteenth century onwards, as being more useful in the development of harmony, the patterns of musical composition were usually conditioned by the mode (or scale) chosen. The seven in medieval use were of Greek origin, evolved from scientific principles and taken over by the early Christian church, on which Greek influence was strong.

To pick them out today, the easiest method is to play on the white notes of the piano, starting on a specific keynote and introducing no accidentals, even for the leading note – unlike the minor scale now commonly used. A modal piece normally begins on the keynote and should invariably return to it. The dominant is the tone around which most of the main theme is sung, especially in plainchant.

There are two forms of each mode, the *Authentic* and the *Plagal* or *Hypo*. Starting notes for the Authentic modes are:

D — Dorian   E — Phrygian   F — Lydian
G — Mixolydian   A — Aeolian
B — Locrian   C — Ionian

In the Authentic modes, the melody must lie within the octave above the keynote. In Plagal modes, it lies within the octave formed by the note a fourth below the keynote and the one a fifth above the keynote. In other words, the HypoDorian mode (*hypo* being Greek for 'below') encompasses A below the Dorian keynote D to the A above that D; and so on in a parallel mathematical relationship through all the other Authentic formations.

modulation A composer wishing to refresh the ear of his audience will frequently change from the key in which he started into another key by means of certain intermediary harmonies. This transition can be achieved either by means of a pivot chord between one key and a related major or minor key, or by weaving an enticing or deliberately baffling path through a protracted sequence of chord changes and melodic clashes. Dramatic effects can be produced by a sudden unheralded shift to an apparently remote key; but there should always be at the very least an implicit logical progression to satisfy not merely the musical grammarians but the attentive listener. Composers such as Wagner and Liszt produced continuously shifting effects by employing *chromatic modulation*, altering chords by means of inner chromatic changes. *Enharmonic modulations* are achieved by using as a pivot two notes which differ in name and in their relevance to their own basic key, but which actually sound the same – e.g. C sharp and D flat.

Moeran, E.J. (Ernest John) (1894–1950) English composer (Irish descent). He studied at the Royal College of Music and, after service in World War I, with John Ireland. A keen collector of folksong, especially in Norfolk, where he lived for some years and explored with his friend Peter Warlock, he also used the near-modal sounds of folk music in small orchestral pieces such as *Lonely Waters*, with its genuine Norfolk song played on the oboe, and piano vignettes such as *Stalham River*.

OTHER WORKS: Symphony in G Minor. Rhapsody *Whythorne's Shadow* for small orchestra. Song cycle *Ludlow Town* (from A.E. Housman poems). String quartet. Oboe quartet.

moll German for *minor*, e.g. *A moll* = A minor.

monody Derived from the Greek for a 'single song', the word has become virtually synonymous with *monophony*, implying a single melody without harmonic enrichment or polyphonic development, though generally allowing for at least a ground bass accompaniment.

monotone The singing of a number of syllables without change of pitch, as in prayers and psalms. The word does not imply monotony in the sense of being dull and boring.

Monteux, Pierre (1875–1964) French conductor (American citizen 1942). He studied the violin and played in the Paris Opéra-Comique orchestra before becoming conductor of Diaghilev's Ballets Russes, with whom he gave the first performances of *Petrushka* and the *Rite of Spring*, among other challenging works. He was conductor at the New York Met at the end of World War I, and after appointments in Boston, Paris and San Francisco returned to it in 1953. He rounded off his career, distinguished above all by his handling of Russian and French music, as principal conductor of the London Symphony Orchestra.

Monteverdi, Claudio (1567–1643) Italian composer. His father was a barber-surgeon and apothecary working near Cremona Cathedral, where the boy sang in the choir and studied music with the *maestro di capella*. He became a talented organist and viol player, composed a number of well-received madrigals and canzonettas, and in his twenties obtained a post with the ducal family of the Gonzagas in Mantua. The Duke held Monteverdi in high esteem and took him on trips to spas in Flanders and on military expeditions against the Turks in Hungary. During this period he composed his opera *La favola d'Orfeo* (*The Legend of Orpheus*), notable for its pioneering use of a large orchestra. Even more memorably, during despondent years after the death of his wife in 1607 he produced the exquisite set of *Vespro della Beata Vergine* (*Vespers of the Holy Virgin*, sometimes called the *Vespers of 1610*).

A year after his patron's death in 1612, Monteverdi was appointed *maestro di cappella* at St Mark's in Venice, where he later took holy orders. He composed a great corpus of sacred works, but retained his interest in opera, and when restrictions on operatic performances in Venice were lifted in 1637 he promoted a revival of one of his earlier works, *Arianna*, and contributed two new masterpieces, *Il ritorno d'Ulisse in patria* (*Ulysses' return to his homeland*) and *L'incoronazione di Poppea*

Claudio Monteverdi (painting by Bernardo Strozzi), who answered criticism of his unconventional madrigals by asserting that he built 'on the foundations of truth'.

(*The Coronation of Poppea*), a work full of sensual melody and dramatic fire quite astounding for a man then aged seventy-five. Neglected for centuries, in spite of scholarly work by Malipiero, Monteverdi's operatic genius was only fully recognized again with performances at Glyndebourne of *Poppea* in 1962 (280 years after its première in Venice) and *Ulysses* in 1972, bringing out the full splendour of his melodic and harmonic adventurousness.

Moody and **Sankey** American 'gospel hymn' writers. Dwight Moody (1837–99) had been director of the YMCA in Chicago for four years when he met Ira Sankey (1840–1908), an evangelistic singer and hymn-writer. The two went on tour and led revivalist meetings across the USA and in England. The words and much of the music of their hymns were the work of Sankey, including *The ninety and nine* and *Faith is the victory*. Their *Sacred Songs and Solos*, published in 1873, sold over fifty million copies.

Moog, Robert (1934–) American inventor. In the early 1960s he pioneered an electronic *synthesizer* which enabled composers or performers to produce required sounds and sound patterns by voltage control. (*See also* **electronic music**.)

Moore, Gerald (1899–1987) English pianist. Born in Watford, he spent much of his boyhood in Canada and studied piano in Toronto. On returning to England he decided to concentrate on a career as accompanist rather than attempt the solo concert platform, and became the acknowledged master in this field. In recitals and recordings he established himself as an equal partner with singers of the calibre of Fischer-Dieskau and Schwarzkopf, intuitively blending his tone and phrasing with theirs. His books *The Unashamed Accompanist* and *Am I Too Loud?* manage to be both entertaining and deeply informative.

Moore, Grace (1898–1947) American soprano. After singing in night clubs and revues she began to study music seriously in Paris, and after a New York début at the Met in 1928 sang there regularly up to 1946. She appeared in popular films, including *One Night of Love*, a great success in its day with a much-played theme song. In 1947 she was killed at Copenhagen in an air crash.

Moore, Thomas (1779–1852) Irish poet, satirist and musician. The son of a Dublin grocer, he studied law in London, obtained a sinecure which left him in debt, and wrote a number of biographies. His most lasting work was on collections of *Irish Melodies*, usually with lyrics by himself and sometimes the music as well. Among the best known are *The Minstrel Boy* and *The Last Rose of Summer*. Flotow used this latter in his opera *Martha*, and several other minor composers availed themselves of Moore's words and music.

morceau French for a 'morsel', or 'small piece', hence a small musical piece for orchestra or solo instrument, especially the piano.

mordent *See* **ornaments**.

Morley, Thomas (*c.*1557–1602) English composer. A protégé of Byrd's in the Chapel Royal, Morley inherited from him the monopoly of printing and publishing music granted by Queen Elizabeth I. One of the most gifted composers of madrigals and canzonets, he influenced his contemporaries and successors with his skill and the introduction of a native cheerfulness into the hitherto Italian-dominated forms of part-singing. His *Madrigalls to Four Voyces*, published in 1594, was the first truly English collection of its kind; and in 1599 his *First Booke of Consort Lessons* was both the first printed volume of ensemble music in England and the first treatise to specify the exact instrumentation required. Shortly before his death Morley edited an anthology of madrigals, *The Triumph of Oriana*, issued in honour of the ageing Queen Elizabeth.

morris dance An English folk dance performed by men to the accompaniment of pipe and tabor, in various kinds of fancy dress with jingles attached to the dancers' legs. Originally a Whitsuntide pageant, it gave way to performance by local village groups at any festive time they chose, and there are still troupes which dance regularly outside inns for charity or simply for the entertainment value.

Mossolov, Alexander (1900–73) Russian composer. He studied Central Asian folk music and used such themes in his *Kirghiz Rhapsody* and *Uzbek Suite*, but made his name as a protagonist of 'constructivist music' in pieces such as the ballet *The Factory*, later revised as a symphonic poem *Music of Machines*. This attempt at 'Socialist realism' did not appeal to the authorities and for a while he was out of favour, but came to the fore again during World War II with battle songs and other works for massed choirs and orchestra.

Moszkowski, Moritz (1854–1925) Polish-German composer and pianist. He studied in Dresden and Berlin, making his début as a pianist in Berlin at the age of nineteen and later becoming a professor there. He composed opera, orchestral works and a number of songs, but is best remembered for his salon pieces for piano, especially the *Spanish Dances* for piano duet.

motet A short choral composition deriving from the thirteenth-century *conductus*, which had a vocal part rather like a *cantus firmus* (though not a plainsong melody) around which other voices wove other themes. Although popular tunes were introduced, the motet remained for several centuries basically a composition for religious use, without accompaniment. Its secular parallel was the madrigal. Machaut, Victoria and Tallis were among the greatest exponents of the motet; Palestrina wrote about a hundred and eighty in all, and Bach wrote six considerably extended examples.

motif and **motiv** French *motif*, German *motiv*, and English *motive* all apply to a brief melodic or rhythmic theme of recognizable significance in a composition, even if it consists of only a few notes, as at the beginning of Mozart's Symphony No.40, Beethoven's No.5, and Brahms's No.3. (*See also* **idée fixe** and **leitmotiv**.)

motion The term describes the movements up or down of a melodic theme, usually clarified by a further definition of their nature:

Conjunct motion A single part moving on through a succession of notes one step at a time.

Disjunct motion A single part moving through intervals larger than one step.

Similar motion Two or more parts moving together in the same direction.

Contrary motion Two or more parts moving together in different directions.

Oblique motion One part staying on one note while another moves up or down.

mouth organ *See* **harmonica.**

mouthpiece The part of a brass or woodwind instrument into or against which the player blows to produce the required sound. (*See also* **embouchure.**)

movement Strictly speaking, a separate, self-contained section of a symphony, concerto, or chamber or instrumental sonata, these sections being usually in different tempos and often in different keys. The term has, however, come to be loosely applied also to separate pieces in a suite.

Mozart, Leopold (1719–87) German violinist and composer. He became Court composer and deputy *kapellmeister* to the Prince-Archbishop of Salzburg, published a treatise on violin playing, and composed a number of symphonies and divertimenti, among them a *Toy Symphony*, with musical toys added to the small orchestra. Of his six children, only two survived, a daughter Maria Anna (nicknamed Nannerl), and the youngest, a son Wolfgang Amadeus. Leopold soon realized that Wolfgang had all the makings of a child prodigy, both as pianist and composer, and he set about introducing him to as many as possible of the aristocratic households of Europe.

Mozart, Wolfgang Amadeus (1756–91) Austrian composer and pianist. His father began teaching him the piano at the age of four, and within two years he had become so accomplished that he was taken on a series of European tours as a 'wonder child'. In Munich he impressed the Elector of Bavaria; in Vienna he charmed the Empress Maria Theresa; and on a London visit at the age of eight he played several times for King George III, met and admired J.C. Bach, and spent his spare time writing his first three symphonies. His first comic opera in the Italian style, *La finta semplice* (*The Make-believe Simpleton*), was composed in Vienna when he was twelve, but local jealousies frustrated its production.

In 1771 Mozart took up duties in Salzburg which his father had so long obsequiously desired for him, playing for the Court and composing violin concertos, the *Haffner Serenade* and other divertimenti, and religious pieces as required; but he was frequently tempted away by commissions elsewhere and by money earned from personal appearances as a piano virtuoso. Unfortunately a new Prince-Archbishop in Salzburg proved less amenable than his predecessor. Colloredo treated his musicians as lower-ranking servants, and expected them to be on call whenever required. Mozart endured many snubs in silence

To all Lovers of Sciences.

THE greatest Prodigy that Europe, or that even Human Nature has to boast of, is, without Contradiction, the little German Boy WOLFGANG MOZART; a Boy, Eight Years old, who has, and indeed very justly, raised the Admiration not only of the greatest Men, but also of the greatest Musicians in Europe. It is hard to say, whether his Execution upon the Harpsichord and his playing and singing at Sight, or his own Caprice, Fancy, and Compositions for all Instruments, are most astonishing. The Father of this Miracle, being obliged by Desire of several Ladies and Gentlemen to postpone, for a very short. Time, his Departure from England, will give an Opportunity to hear this little Composer and his Sister, whose musical Knowledge wants not Apology. Performs every Day in the Week, from Twelve to Three o'Clock in the Great Room, at the Swan and Hoop, Cornhil. Admittance 2s. 6d. each Person.

The two Children will play also together with four Hands upon the same Harpsichord, and put upon it a Handkerchief, without seeing the Keys.

When touring Europe as a child prodigy, Mozart was often billed in terms which might well have been applied to a performing monkey.

(though reporting them resentfully in his correspondence), but tried to find employment elsewhere. In 1777 he visited Paris and Munich, where the Elector of Bavaria regretted he had no vacancies. In Mannheim he met and fell in love with Aloysia Weber, but was prevented from marrying by his father's intervention. A commission for an opera took him to Munich, where *Idomeneo* was an outstanding success. Immediately after its first performance he was summoned to Colloredo's residence in Vienna, to be received so deplorably that he lost his temper and resigned. His employer maintained that he had in fact been dismissed, and had him literally kicked off the premises. From now on Mozart had to try his luck as a free-lance.

Vienna was the obvious place on which to base a musical career. Mozart took lodgings with his friends the Webers, who had moved here from Mannheim. Having failed to win their daughter Aloysia, he married her sister Constanze, took piano pupils to eke out a living, and composed a string of piano concertos in which he appeared as soloist. Having won official approval for his opera in the German language *Die Entführung aus dem Serail* (*The Abduction from the Seraglio*), he hoped for further public successes, but attained none until the appearance of *Le nozze di Figaro* (*The Marriage of Figaro*) in 1786. He now, without knowing this, had only five years to live; yet in spite of frustrations, tribulations and utter lack of comprehension of his innate

A painting by Thaddeus Heibling of Mozart at the age of ten.

genius he plunged into one of the most fruitful periods known in the whole history of music.

It was, unhappily, not financially fruitful. Always in need of money to maintain his wife and family, Mozart was reduced to sending begging letters to a fellow member of a Masonic order which he had joined. In 1788, while composing his three most radiant symphonies, he had to grovel to Puchberg, his 'Dearest Brother' Freemason, admitting that he still owed eight ducats yet daring 'to implore you to help me out with a hundred *gulden* until next week, when my concerts in the Casino are to begin'. He had obtained a poorly paid post as Court Composer to the Austrian Emperor, but did not have the will to improve it when offered better remuneration by the Prussian Emperor. When his erstwhile librettist Lorenzo Da Ponte invited him to further collaboration in London, a place of happy memories, this was declined also. Sinking into despair, he was alarmed by the appearance of a mysterious envoy commissioning a Requiem Mass for an unknown nobleman. Interrupted several times in its writing, Mozart became superstitiously convinced that he was preparing it for his own death. On the night he knew he was about to die he gave instructions for its completion to his pupil Franz Süssmayr. After an ill-attended funeral he was buried in an unmarked and by now unidentifiable grave in the churchyard of St Mark's, Vienna. Great dramatic profit has been made from a theory that he was poisoned by his rival composer Salieri (even before a twentieth-century play and film, Rimsky-Korsakov had written an opera on the subject), but there is not a scrap of evidence to support such a theory.

Of all great composers, Mozart is the most difficult to assess as a person, and the most difficult to comprehend in every aspect of his all-embracing genius. It could be said that he invented nothing: all his works owe their backgrounds and basic language to his immediate predecessors and to contemporaries such as Haydn and the younger Bachs. His operas could not have existed without the prior work of the Italians, just as J.S. Bach's organ works and cantatas could hardly have sprung to life but for the seminal influences of Buxtehude and Schütz. Yet, like Bach in his own contrapuntal world, Mozart in his world simply did everything better than anybody else: he assimilated everything, transformed and refined it, and finally offered his audience perfection. Such accomplishment reduced his successors not so much to emulation or competition as to despair.

OPERAS: All Mozart's letters reveal a keen interest in people rather than places or scenery, which enabled him to create real characters in his operas instead of artificial puppets who were simply required to sing well. The music draws out their true nature, comments wittily or lovingly upon them, and echoes the tensions, joys and despairs of real life. In *Le nozze di Figaro* (*The Marriage of Figaro*) the quick-witted Figaro is set in vivid personal and musical contrast against the arrogant Count and his beautiful but sad Countess. The very choice of subject was daring: Beaumarchais' play had been banned because of its political content, but the librettist Lorenzo Da Ponte cunningly got round the prohibition without sacrificing the irony and implicit social criticism. In *Don Giovanni*, rapturously received in Mozart's favourite city, Prague, the story moves inexorably towards a climax in which the swaggering lecher and the women seeking revenge are brought step by step to a confrontation led up to not merely in dramatic but in inspired musical development.

Da Ponte provided the composer with further opportunities for subtle characterization in *Così fan tutte* (*Women are all the same*) where the distinctions between the two women are enhanced by the musical depiction of Dorabella's instinctive coquetry and Fiordiligi's deeper, more disturbing passion. In the exquisite quintet in Act I these are interwoven with strands of rapture, anguish, self-deception, and ironical comment. *Die Zauberflöte* (*The Magic Flute*) seems on the face of it a rather contrived Masonic pantomime, but its symbolism is interpreted by some of Mozart's most radiant melodies.

CONCERTOS: Mozart wrote concertos for a wide range of instruments, including four superb ones for French horn, one for clarinet which has been described by a leading German musicologist as 'of unearthly beauty', and others for bassoon, oboe, and violin; but it is perhaps the twenty-three surviving piano concertos with which we most closely associate him. Throughout his life he was a performer as well as a composer, and even while giving lessons to make a living he wrote for the instrument so that he could give public recitals. Many are heard today on a large piano with full orchestra, but they were written for a much lighter instrument, and Mozart scored the orchestral parts so that they could be played by any combination available, from a string quartet to a chamber orchestra with or without wind players. Among the most impressive are the intense, dramatic No.20 in D minor (K466) and the lilting No.23 in A (K488).

SYMPHONIES: The earlier symphonies were in smooth, conventional style, though full of fine passages and subtle touches. Even in his maturity some, like No.31 (the *Paris*), were virtually written to order in somewhat perfunctory fashion, and No.35 (the *Haffner*) was hurriedly cobbled together from the *Haffner Serenade* in answer to a request from his father. In contrast, the composer could burst out into the loving, lively tribute offered to a beloved place in No.38 (the *Prague*). Most amazing of all were the last three symphonies, written in seven weeks during the summer of

1788, at a time when he was in financial trouble and growing despondency yet could display his genius at its full range, culminating at the pinnacle of No.41, named the *Jupiter* not by Mozart himself but, it is thought, by the impresario Salomon.

CHAMBER MUSIC: If Mozart brought the string quartet to its ultimate perfect blend of grace and passion with technical invention, it has to be admitted that he owed a great deal to Haydn – and Mozart himself was the first to admit it. Haydn had declared to Leopold Mozart that his son was 'the greatest composer I have ever heard', and became a loving friend and adviser. In gratitude Mozart dedicated to him six string quartets, known forever after as the *Haydn Quartets*, in which the older man played first violin during visits to Mozart's home: they include the lively *Hunt* quartet and the so-called *Dissonance*, with its remarkably wayward introduction. Among other chamber works the loveliest must surely be the quintet for clarinet and strings, inspired by the playing of the Viennese clarinettist Anton Stadler, for whom Mozart also wrote a concerto and trio.

Munch, Charles (1891–1968) French conductor and violinist. He became professor of the violin first at Strasbourg and then at Leipzig, where he was also leader of the Gewandhaus Orchestra. His conducting début was made in Paris in 1932, followed by appearances in London and then in Boston. Between 1949 and 1962 he was conductor of the Boston Symphony Orchestra, with which he toured Europe, Australia and the Far East. Between 1951 and 1962 he also directed the Berkshire Music Center.

Münchinger, Karl (1915–) German conductor. Born in Stuttgart, in 1945 he founded the Stuttgart Chamber Orchestra, with which he has toured widely and made many recordings, including fine interpretations of Bach.

Munrow, David (1942–76) English instrumentalist and early music expert. In 1967 he founded the Early Music Consort, with which he played recorder and other authentic old instruments. An enthusiastic communicator, he toured with the ensemble, lectured, made many broadcasts and recordings, and arranged scores for films and television.

musette A small French bagpipe. The word is also applied to a part of an instrumental piece which mimics the drone of a bagpipe in its bass part, usually in a suite as a brief diversion within a gavotte. Bach's third *English Suite* has such a movement, and Prokofiev used the effect in the gavotte of his *Classical Symphony*.

musical box When the lid of this decorated toy instrument is lifted, a cylinder operated by clock-

A musical box using a disc rather than a cylinder, but operating on a similar principle of metal tongues twanging a slowly revolving pattern of graduated metal teeth.

work turns and produces a tune by means of pins twanging graduated metal teeth, rather like those of a comb.

musica reservata A sixteenth-century term of doubtful origin, generally referring to the expressive but austerely unornamented (i.e. reserved) style of composition and performance favoured by polyphonists such as Josquin Després.

music drama *See* **Opera.**

musicology A twentieth-century neologism adopted as a useful term for the scholarly study of musical history and aesthetics, as opposed to purely practical study of composition or performance.

musique concrète The name 'concrete music' was bestowed by Pierre Schaeffer in 1948 on his experiments in Paris, with the blending of natural sounds recorded and then speeded up, reversed, or otherwise electronically manipulated, together with instruments and voices. Originally the term was used exclusively for 'concrete' sources as opposed to synthetic sounds produced entirely by electronic means, but in time the distinction became blurred.

Mussorgsky, Modest (1839–81) Russian composer. He was destined for an army career, but while at military academy learned a great deal about early church music from one of his tutors. During service with the famous Preobrajensky Regiment he played piano in his spare time at parties and in cafés, drank heavily, and in due course decided to leave the army and devote himself to music. Family money enabled him to study with Balakirev, and he was drawn into the group of The Five, or 'Mighty Handful'. He was too impatient

A painting by Ilya Repin which all too vividly portrays Mussorgsky's decline into drunkenness and *delirium tremens*.

to study theory in any depth, but his instinctive creativity impressed his friends, fuelling their determination to establish a national music freed from German and Italian influences.

When his family lost a large part of its income as a result of Tsar Alexander I's freeing of the serfs, Mussorgsky had to take on a dismal clerical job in government service, but still tried to compose in spite of bouts of alcoholism. In 1869 he completed his opera *Boris Godunov*, based on Pushkin's dramatic views of Russian life and history, but it was turned down by the Imperial Opera, whose directors were bewildered by its mixture of folk music, dissonant harmonies, unorthodox orchestration, and a natural rather than stereotyped vocal line which followed the patterns of everyday speech.

To supplement his income he worked as piano accompanist to a singer and teacher. Friends raised money to buy him time to complete two further operas, *Khovanschina* and *Sorochintsy Fair*, but the struggle wore him down and he turned again to drink. Committed to a military hospital, he survived only a few weeks in a state of near-insanity. After his death, his friend Rimsky-Korsakov decided to smooth over the apparent

roughnesses of *Boris Godunov*, producing a version which audiences gladly accepted. It is only in the latter part of the twentieth century that the full quality of Mussorgsky's original writing has been appreciated.

OTHER WORKS: Orchestral *Night on the Bare Mountain*. Piano *Pictures at an Exhibition* (also orchestral version by Ravel). Many solo songs including *The Song of the Flea*.

mute A device attached to an instrument to dampen its tone or alter the quality of that tone. On stringed instruments it is clipped on to the bridge. In the case of brass instruments, the horn player can muffle his tone simply by pushing his fist into the bell; trumpeters and trombonists insert a cone-shaped mute made of metal, rubber, plastic or wood; and jazz players especially employ a variety of devices to produce growling, piercing or 'wah-wah' effects.

Myaskovsky, Nikolay (1881-1950) Russian composer. He studied with Lyadov and Rimsky-Korsakov at the St Petersburg Conservatory, and became a friend of Prokofiev. He fought in World War I and with the Red Army, and in 1921 was appointed to the staff of Moscow Conservatory. He was a conscientious, conventional composer, producing twenty-seven symphonies (one of them for a military band) and thirteen quartets, yet like others was temporarily out of favour after the 1948 official denunciation of 'formalism'.

Mysliveček, Josef (1737–81) Bohemian composer. The son of a miller, he studied music in Prague with one of the Benda family before travelling and studying further in Italy. His twenty skilful, fashionable operas earned him the nickname of *Il divino Boemo* (*The divine Bohemian*) and had a great influence on the style of Mozart, whom Mysliveček befriended in 1770.

N

Nabokov, Nicolas (1903–78) Russian composer (American citizen 1939). A cousin of the novelist Vladimir Nabokov, he studied in St Petersburg, Yalta, Stuttgart and Berlin before settling for some years in Paris, where Diaghilev commissioned his ballet-oratorio *Ode*. He left for the USA in 1933 and was employed in several teaching posts, returning to Paris only in 1952 to organize a festival of twentieth-century music. Between 1951 and 1966 he was secretary-general of the Congress for Cultural Freedom. Among his compositions were an opera, *Love's Labour's Lost*, to a libretto by W.H. Auden and Chester Kallman; a number of ballets, including *Union Pacific*; and three 'lyric symphonies'.

nachtmusik and **nachtstück** German for 'night music' and a 'night piece'. The former is the same as a serenade, one of the most celebrated being Mozart's *Eine Kleine Nachtmusik* (*A Little Night Music*). *Nachtstück* is the equivalent of a *nocturne* or a piece evoking night feelings, as in much of Bartók's work.

national anthems Every country has its own patriotic song or hymn for ceremonial occasions. Among those of leading Western nations are:

AUSTRIA: *Land der Berge, Land am Strome*. Before 1919 it was *Gott erhalt unsern Kaiser*, on a tune composed by Haydn and used in his 'Emperor' quartet.

BELGIUM: *La Brabançonne*, composed in 1830 to mark Belgian independence from Holland.

DENMARK: *Kong Kristian stod ved højen mast*. There has been a tendency in recent years to use this as a royal anthem, and for the national song to be *Der er et yndigt land*.

FRANCE: *La Marseillaise*, composed in 1792 by Rouget de l'Isle, deriving its name from Marseilles volunteers who sang it as they entered Paris and stormed the Tuileries.

GREAT BRITAIN: *God Save the Queen*. The melody has been used frequently by other countries to different words. Although attributed to John Bull, the real source is obscure.

HOLLAND: *Wilhelmus von Nassouwe*. Verses in praise of William of Orange-Nassau were written by Philip van Marnix in the late sixteenth century at the time of the Netherlands' struggle against Spain, with music by an unknown composer added and published in 1626.

ITALY: *Fratelli d'Italia*. Various patriotic songs were associated with different Italian principalities before their union in 1861, after which, apart from an interruption by Mussolini's Fascist anthem *La giovinezza*, these verses by G. Mameli and music by M. Novara, composed in 1847, have been used.

UNITED STATES OF AMERICA: *The Star-spangled Banner*. Words by F. Scott Key written after watching the bombardment of Fort McHenry by the British in 1814. Music by J. Stafford Smith. Officially adopted as the national anthem by a Senate Bill in 1931.

WEST GERMANY: Before 1945, *Deutschland über Alles* was the anthem for all Germany, from the same source as Haydn's melody for the Austrian anthem. The Federal Republic now uses *Einigkeit und Recht und Frei*, also from Haydn.

natural A note neither flattened nor sharpened. To lower or raise its pitch, a flat or sharp is introduced on the stave immediately before it. To cancel out such alterations, the sign for restoring the natural pitch is ♮. A natural key is one without sharps or flats in the key signature. *Natural harmonics* are those produced from open strings and not by means of stopped strings.

neo-classicism A term applied to the style of twentieth-century composers rebelling against nineteenth-century romanticism and favouring the approach of classical and baroque predecessors such as Haydn and Bach. Among leading exponents were Prokofiev with his *Classical Symphony* and Stravinsky in *Pulcinella* and other works.

neo-romanticism This is a very suspect term, sometimes used in the form 'new romanticism' to sum up the tendency of some composers in the 1970s to turn away from serialism, electronic music and other contemporary forms and hark back to the larger symphonic styles of the nineteenth century.

Nicolai, Otto (1810–49) German composer and conductor. He studied in Berlin and Rome, and after a spell as singing master in Vienna returned to

The flamboyant eighteenth-century soprano Brigitta Banti began as a Parisian street singer and, according to Da Ponte, 'brought to opera ... all the habits, manners and customs of an impudent Corsican'. Here she is shown singing *God Save the King* – of which, to the annoyance even of her admirers, she never managed to learn all the words.

Rome to write several operas in the Italian style. In 1847 he became director of the Berlin Opera, and there composed his most successful work, *Die Lustigen Weiber von Windsor* (*The Merry Wives of Windsor*), staged two months before his death.

Nielsen, Carl (1865–1931) Danish composer. Born in the village of Nørre Lyndelse some eight miles south of Hans Christian Andersen's birthplace, the boy was the seventh of the local house-painter's twelve children. He worked as a goose-herd and cowherd, but soon showed an aptitude for music and accompanied his father as second fiddle at village dances and festivals. At the same time he was practising the cornet, and was encouraged by his father to attend auditions for a regimental band in Odense. Although only fourteen at the time, he came well ahead of older contestants and won a place in the band. Once settled in the town, he began experimenting in the field of composition. In May 1883 he left his home island of Fyn, just as Hans Andersen had done before him, to seek fame and fortune in Copenhagen.

Having shown the manuscript of his first string quartet to Niels Gade, head of the Conservatory there, he was accepted as a violin and piano student, though he never felt really at home with the piano and was increasingly involved in composition. The violin, however, stood him in good stead: needing to make a living when his studies ended, he won a position in the Chapel Royal, the opera and ballet orchestra of the Royal Theatre, where he was to work for the next sixteen years. In 1905, after unfortunate experiences as a deputy conductor and other chores which interfered with his real interests – 'I have sometimes wept because I must leave my compositions when being really inspired in order to attend rehearsals at the theatre' – he resigned and concentrated on completing his opera *Maskarade* (*Masquerade*). Nielsen himself conducted the first performance at the Royal Theatre in November 1906, a performance which drew an enthusiastic letter from Edvard Grieg: 'I'm in no doubt that it is the work of a new master, who says "Here I am!"' In 1908 Nielsen was invited back to the theatre as conductor. This again interfered with his composing, but he soldiered on until quarrels with the theatre authorities led to his resignation in May 1914.

During studies abroad in 1889–90 he had met and married the young Danish sculptress Anne Marie Brodersen. During their honeymoon in Italy they were deeply impressed by Titian's painting in Padua of a man slaying his beloved in a fit of jealousy. The idea haunted the composer, who took five years to produce the choral *Hymnus Amoris*, in which different generations laud the joys of love or lament its agonies.

From 1915 onwards Nielsen conducted for the Music Society in Copenhagen, and in the following year joined the board of the Royal Danish Conservatory, of which he became chairman in 1931, less than a year before his death. He was invited to become a member of the Swedish Academy and of the *Akademie der Künst* in Berlin. In spite of the esteem in which he was now held by his contemporaries in northern Europe, he never lost his deep, intuitive love for the simple country life of his home island of Fyn, and during the national celebrations for his sixtieth birthday in 1925 he published the delightful auto-biographical sketch *Myn fynske barndom* (translated into English by Reginald Spink as *My Childhood*). Although there are rarely any traces of a folk-song element in his major works, he collected many such songs and wrote more of his own in the same vein.

The first of his compositions to be heard in public was the *Little Suite for Strings*, performed in Copenhagen's Tivoli pleasure gardens. In 1894 came the first performance of his Symphony No.1 in G minor – which, to the surprise of the audience, began and ended with a chord of C major. The second symphony was given a title, *The Four Temperaments*, inspired by a set of naïve paintings which Nielsen had seen in a country inn. Each movement represents one of the temperaments illustrated: choleric, phlegmatic, melancholic, and sanguine. Without indulging too obviously in 'programme music', Nielsen frequently attempted to interpret characteristics of nature and individual human beings in musical terms. His wind quintet was built around the personalities of the original performers, and two of them were to receive similar treatment in the spiky, turbulent clarinet concerto dedicated to the choleric Aage Oxenvad, and the flute concerto in which the solo part for the fastidious Gilbert Jespersen is mocked by grotesque interruptions from a bass trombone.

It is in the later symphonies that Nielsen shows his greatest creative intensity. The third, entitled *Sinfonia espansiva*, is a joyful work opening with an exuberant flourish and driving on through a sequence of shifting tonalities. The idea of progressive tonality, in which a work evolves by means of shifting relationships until it establishes its ultimate 'right' key, was one which caught the imagination of both Mahler and Nielsen. In Nielsen's tumultuous fourth symphony, *The Inextinguishable*, the violence of World War I which so horrified the composer (even though Denmark was not actually involved in the fighting) is

To the end of his days the Danish composer Carl Nielsen loved the 'matchless song' in the dialect of his home island, Fyn, which could be recalled 'every day if only we will listen' and which he himself recalled again and again in his music.

echoed in the roar of the music, the titanic battle between two timpani, and the struggle to free one recurrent theme from the toils of conflicting keys. In the end the ear of the listener is satisfied by the triumphant E major.

The fifth symphony has no title. After a mysterious, misty opening not unlike some passages from works of Nielsen's friend Sibelius, the first of the two movements struggles through a complexity of keys, stated or hinted at, with an insistent intervention from the note D, until a long, magnificent melody emerges. Here Nielsen's characteristic quirkiness seems to become almost self-destructive: having produced this soaring tune, he sets about demolishing it by instructing the side-drummer to improvise 'as if at all costs to stop the progress of the orchestra'. To assert his undying optimism after the chaos of the first movement, the composer lets fly in the second with a sinewy, unstoppable fugue. The work ends in confident mood: a confidence not echoed in the sixth and last symphony, a harsh and embittered piece echoing Nielsen's physical weariness at the time.

At one stage he had to shelve work on the fifth in order to fulfil a long-delayed commitment for the Danish Choral Society. The result was one of his most engaging, tuneful works: *Fynsk Foraar* (*Springtime on Fyn*), a 'lyric humoresque' for soloists, choir and orchestra, returning happily to the scenes of his childhood.

After his death his widow created two statues of him, one of which now stands near his birthplace, the other in Copenhagen.

OTHER WORKS: Six string quartets. Two violin sonatas. Piano pieces. Opera *Saul and David*. Danish song collections. Organ *Commotio*.

Nikisch, Artur (1855–1922) Hungarian conductor and violinist. He began his musical career as a child prodigy on the piano, but it was as a violinist that he played in the orchestra at the ceremony of laying Bayreuth's foundation stone. Later he was to conduct in opera houses and concert halls all over Europe, and he took the London Symphony Orchestra on its first tour of the USA in 1912. A generous advocate of contemporary English composers, he conducted a compelling performance of Elgar's first symphony.

Nilsson, Birgit (1918–) Swedish soprano. She made her operatic début in Stockholm in 1948 and went on to appear in the world's major opera houses, becoming the acknowledged successor of Kirsten Flagstad in Wagnerian rôles such as Brünnhilde and Isolde, as well as achieving enormous success on stage and on record as Richard Strauss's *Salome*.

ninth An interval of one step more than an octave,

Birgit Nilsson as Brünnhilde in Wagner's *Ring* cycle, a part she sang on the complete recording made between 1958 and 1965 under the baton of Georg Solti.

e.g. from C to the D nine notes above. It is also the name of a discord achieved by adding the seventh and ninth notes to the three basic notes of a common chord.

nocturne From the French, meaning a piece of music related to the night (Italian *notturno*, German *nachtstück*). The word was applied by John Field and most memorably by Chopin to their small romantic keyboard pieces. Debussy expanded the concept into an orchestral suite; and Benjamin Britten composed a song cycle under this title for tenor and small orchestra.

nonet A composition for nine voices or instruments. One of the most popular examples is by Spohr, the Nonet in F for five wind instruments and string quartet.

Nono, Luigi (1924–) Italian composer. At first he favoured Webern's serialism, allied with his own concepts of duration control, and shared many of the ambitions of Boulez and Stockhausen. Later his growing Communist commitment led him to choose didactic and declamatory subjects with a political flavour, such as his opera *Intolleranza* (*Intolerance*) and the choral and orchestral *Epitaffio per Garcia Lorca* (*Epitaph for Garcia Lorca*). He has been a leading experimenter with the blending of voices, instruments (especially percussion), and pre-recorded tape.

Norman, Jessye (1945–) American soprano. She made her operatic début in Berlin in 1969, and first appeared at La Scala, Milan, the following year. Her American début was in the Hollywood Bowl in 1972, after which her flowing, legato style of *bel canto* singing brought her into great demand all over the world. Her operatic successes have never obscured the more intimate beauty of her interpretations of *lieder* or such cycles as Berlioz's *Les Nuits d'été* and, in quite different vein, Berg's *Der Wein*.

Nørgård, Per (1932–) Danish composer. He studied in Copenhagen with Vagn Holmboe and in Paris with Nadia Boulanger, returning to Denmark as a teacher and setting up a compositional school of free-ranging ideas at Århus. His own compositions seemed influenced by Sibelius at first, but then he began working in fragmented style with rhythmic syncopations which give a dancing urge to much of his music, most effectively in the ballets *The Young Man Shall Marry* (with a scenario by Ionesco) and *Gipsy Tango*. He has also experimented with an extension of twelve-note series into what he calls an 'infinite row', with rhythmic patterns shown in graphic score.

OTHER WORKS: Operas *The Labyrinth*, *The Divine Tivoli*. Four symphonies. Cello concerto. Orchestral *Constellations* for twelve solo strings or string groups. Oratorio *Babel*.

NOTATION

Fourteenth-century Italian notation on a four-line staff.

For centuries music, like folk tales and sagas, was passed down in all parts of the world by word of mouth (or by teaching one's successors traditional tunes and rhythms on primitive instruments). Greeks and Romans attempted a method of writing down notes in alphabetical form, but more for the sake of mathematical and philosophical discussion than to help singers or players. Around the late sixth or early seventh century a system of plainsong notation was developed called *neumes*, at first merely a set of accents along a single horizontal line above the words to cover the note lengths and phrases to which each syllable should be sung. Later a clearer indication of pitch was attempted by markings showing where it should rise and fall, but these did not specify by how much, and were still little more than reminders of tunes which the singers were expected to know already. Not until the addition of extra horizontal lines was it possible to define pitches and lengths of notes and their relationships one to another. By the eleventh century the four-line staff was in use for plainsong and for the newly developing polyphony; by the thirteenth the five-line staff was proving its worth for writing down any conceivable kind of music.

To establish a firm tonal centre for any piece, a *clef* is set at the beginning of the staff, followed by other symbols to specify basic key and metre.

TREBLE (or **G**) **CLEF**: The symbol has a curling tail which loops around the second line of the staff to establish the note G there, a fifth above middle C. Middle C itself is too low to be shown on this staff, so a *ledger line* has to be added below the bottom (E) line.

BASS (or **F**) **CLEF**: The curve of the symbol begins on a large blob set on the fourth line of the staff, with dots above and below that line, to establish the note F, a fifth below middle C. Middle C itself is too high to be shown on this staff, so a *ledger line* has to be added above the top (A) line.

ALTO and **TENOR** (or **C**) **CLEF**: This rather convoluted symbol can be centred on any line of the staff to define middle C, which varies between the tenor, alto, mezzo and soprano ranges. It is rarely used nowadays except for viola parts in the alto clef, and sometimes for the higher registers of the cello, bassoon or tenor trombone.

KEY SIGNATURE: To establish the basic key in which a piece is to be played, it is necessary to show, immediately after the clef signs, the number of sharps or flats which will prevail throughout that piece unless cancelled out by accidentals or by a signalled change to another key altogether. Some keys, though theoretically viable, are not used: C flat major, A sharp major, D sharp major, G sharp major, D flat minor, or G flat minor. On a keyboard instrument these have equivalent keys with fewer sharps and flats (plus double sharps and double flats) to contend with: A sharp major, for example, with its daunting clutter of sharps and double sharps, is for all practical purposes B flat major (with only two flats). Each key signature shows two possible keys, one major and one minor. In performance the seventh note of the ascending melodic or harmonic minor scale has to be sharpened to provide a leading note, but this is done

by an accidental, not incorporated in the key signature: e.g. although there are two flats in the key signature of B flat major and G minor, the G minor key takes F sharp as its leading note and in the harmony of the dominant seventh chord. (*See also* **key, major**, and **minor**.)

TIME SIGNATURE: After establishing the key it is equally necessary to specify the rhythm of the piece, i.e. how many beats there should be in the bar, and the value of those beats. This is usually done by means of one numeral on top of another: the top figure defines the number of beats, the bottom one the type of beat. In common or 4/4 time, the figure 4 upon 4 indicates that there are four quarter-notes (crotchets) in each measure (or bar). Waltz time, 3/4, gives us three beats of quarter-notes. It should be emphasized that these figures do not refer to the number of notes actually played in a measure: in a florid passage there may be a flurry of thirty-two tones, perhaps interrupted by a few rests, but these should always add up to the numerical relationship established in the time signature.

The time signature also implies the strong and weak beats in a measure. In 2/4 time, the first beat is strong, the second weak; in 4/4 time, the first and third are strong, the second and fourth weak. 'Common time', or 4/4, is often shown simply by the letter C on the staff; with a vertical stroke through it, this becomes 2/2 time, also known as *cut time* or *alla breve*.

NOTE VALUE: American and British usages differ in the description of note values, but the basic time relationships are the same. Rests between notes are also calculated as integral parts of the measure. Starting with one note which occupies a full measure in common (4/4) time, the divisions are as follows:

United States of America	Great Britain
whole note	semibreve
half note	minim
quarter note	crotchet
eighth note	quaver
sixteenth note	semiquaver
thirty-second note	demi-semiquaver
sixty-fourth note	semi-demi-semiquaver

Double whole note or breve is rarely used outside church music.

Eighth notes and shorter notes can be grouped together by *beams*.

Clefs

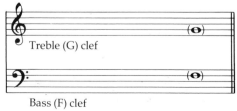

Treble (G) clef

Bass (F) clef

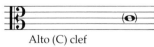

Alto (C) clef

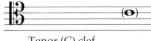

Tenor (C) clef

Key signatures

C major or A minor | C# major or A# minor | Db major or Bb minor

D major or B minor | Eb major or C minor | E major or C# minor | F major or D minor

F# major or D# minor | Gb major or Eb minor | G major or E minor

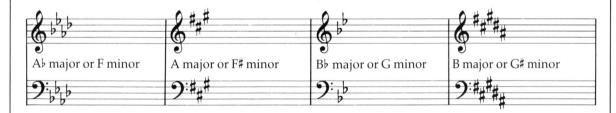

Ab major or F minor | A major or F# minor | Bb major or G minor | B major or G# minor

Time signatures

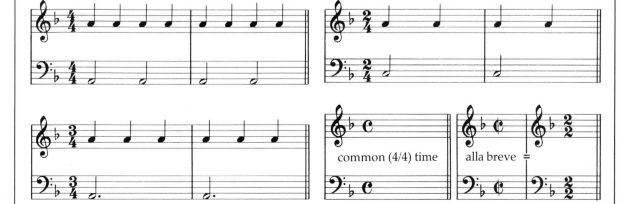

common (4/4) time | alla breve

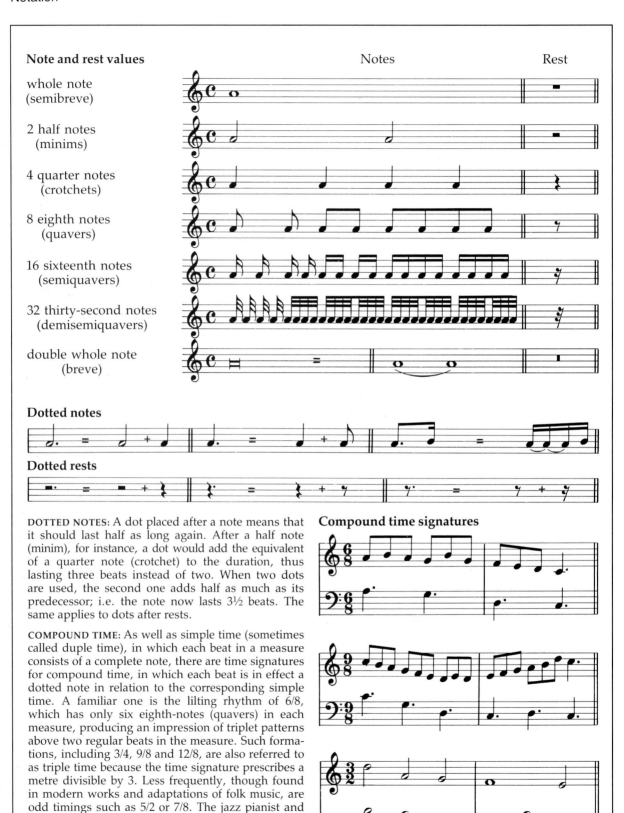

Note and rest values — Notes — Rest

whole note (semibreve)

2 half notes (minims)

4 quarter notes (crotchets)

8 eighth notes (quavers)

16 sixteenth notes (semiquavers)

32 thirty-second notes (demisemiquavers)

double whole note (breve)

Dotted notes

Dotted rests

DOTTED NOTES: A dot placed after a note means that it should last half as long again. After a half note (minim), for instance, a dot would add the equivalent of a quarter note (crotchet) to the duration, thus lasting three beats instead of two. When two dots are used, the second one adds half as much as its predecessor; i.e. the note now lasts 3½ beats. The same applies to dots after rests.

COMPOUND TIME: As well as simple time (sometimes called duple time), in which each beat in a measure consists of a complete note, there are time signatures for compound time, in which each beat is in effect a dotted note in relation to the corresponding simple time. A familiar one is the lilting rhythm of 6/8, which has only six eighth-notes (quavers) in each measure, producing an impression of triplet patterns above two regular beats in the measure. Such formations, including 3/4, 9/8 and 12/8, are also referred to as triple time because the time signature prescribes a metre divisible by 3. Less frequently, though found in modern works and adaptations of folk music, are odd timings such as 5/2 or 7/8. The jazz pianist and composer Dave Brubeck wrote an interestingly eccentric number entitled *Take Five* in 5/4 time.

Compound time signatures

note The name given to a single symbol on a musical score, indicating the pitch and duration of what is to be sung or played, and to the single sound actually heard. (In the USA this is usually called a *tone*.) The word can also be applied to a piano or organ key. (*See also* **Notation**.)

note-row *See* **tone-row**.

Novello, Ivor (1893–1951) Welsh composer and playwright. Son of the soprano Clara Novello Davies, the young man dropped his surname and ultimately became a 'matinée idol' as playwright and actor-manager. His first success was a World War I song, *Keep the Home Fires Burning*. After the war he wrote and appeared in a number of plays before embarking on a run of popular musical comedies in London, including *Glamorous Night* and *King's Rhapsody*.

O

obbligato The term is often mistakenly used as meaning some extraneous vocal or instrumental flourish added more or less at will. In fact it means the opposite: any passage so marked is *obligatory*, usually drawing attention to a soloistic passage of great significance in the composer's mind, as in 'violin obbligato' or 'oboe obbligato' parts accompanying some of the arias in Bach cantatas.

octave The eight notes of a diatonic scale starting from the tonic. The eighth note or octave always produces exactly twice the number of vibrations per second of its tonic, creating an impression of unison. Names given to the ascending steps, using the scale of C major as an example, are:

    C = tonic
    D = supertonic
    E = mediant
    F = subdominant
    G = dominant
    A = submediant
    B = leading note
    C = octave

An *octave coupler* is a device whereby a note played on an organ or harpsichord can be doubled one or more octaves higher or lower.

octet A composition for eight singers or instrumentalists, or the group of performers itself. Most pieces so written are in the form of suites in a number of separate movements, as in Mendelssohn's Octet for strings, and Stravinsky's for wind instruments.

ode The original Greek meaning was 'a song', implying verse which could be set to music in either lyrical or choral style. Later poets applied the word to purely spoken verse, but composers have used it in a blend of poetry and music on special occasions, as with Handel's and Purcell's *Odes for St Cecilia's Day*. The German poet Schiller's *Ode to Joy* (originally entitled *Ode to Freedom*) was used by Beethoven for the choral finale of his ninth symphony.

Offenbach, Jacques (1819–80) Franco-German composer. Seventh child of a Cologne synagogue cantor who had taken the name Offenbach from his family home town of Offenbach-am-Main, the boy learned the violin and cello at an early age, and was accepted into the Paris Conservatoire when he was fourteen. He became a fashionable salon cellist, touring France and Germany and making a great impression on Queen Victoria and Prince Albert in London. With the profits he settled in Paris, became a Roman Catholic, and married a Spanish lady. After writing incidental music for the theatre he had a couple of unremarkable comic operas staged, but made little progress

The title page of *Offenbachiana*, a pot-pourri of the most popular melodies from Jacques Offenbach's operettas.

with composition until in 1849 he became conductor at the Théâtre Français and could insinuate some of his own pieces into the programmes.

From 1853 onwards he set about composing operettas, and during the next quarter of a century turned out almost a hundred of them. To ensure the production standards he required, he leased his own theatre. In 1858 he had his first real success with the saucy, satirical *Orphée aux Enfers* (*Orpheus in the Underworld*), with its swirling can-can, followed by *La Belle Hélène* and the colourful picture of Parisian life, *La Vie parisienne*.

Anxious to establish himself with a serious opera, Offenbach embarked on *Les Contes d'Hoffmann* (*Tales of Hoffmann*) and worked earnestly at it over several years; but it remained unfinished at his death, and had to be revised and completed by the composer and teacher Ernest Guiraud. Despite its many fine moments, it will never compete in popularity with the infectious, vivacious music of the operettas.

Oistrakh, David (1908–74) and **Igor** (1931–) Russian violinists. David, the father, studied in Odessa and made his Moscow début in 1933. He became one of the greatest virtuoso violinists of his time, playing in Paris, London, and the USA and at many international events with a steely, almost frightening certainty in everything he performed. Shostakovich's two violin concertos were both dedicated to him, and he was the first to play them.

Igor Oistrakh studied under his father at Moscow Conservatory and made his début in 1948. He won the Wieniawsky competition in Poland in 1952, and went on to establish a reputation on the strength of his own merits, quite distinct from his father's, though the two of them frequently appeared together and recorded the Bach double violin concerto and Mozart's sinfonia concertante for violin and viola, with David playing the viola.

ondes Martenot In 1922 Maurice Martenot (1898–1980), a French pianist and string player, patented an electronic instrument to produce 'musical waves' (*ondes*) by generating sound modulations from oscillators controlled either by a keyboard or by a 'ruban' (ribbon), capable of glissandos and variations in volume and timbre. Messiaen used a six-piece ensemble of *ondes Martenot* in his *Fête des belles eaux*, and solo parts in other works including the huge *Turangalîla* symphony. Honegger, Varèse and Boulez have also employed it, though it has since been superseded by more complex electronic devices.

one-step A fast dance of American origin in 2/4 time, associated with minstrel shows and early jazz, as in the *Original Dixieland One-Step* per-

David Oistrakh and his son Igor, both born in Odessa. The father died in Amsterdam in 1974, leaving Igor to carry on their great virtuoso tradition.

formed by the Original Dixieland Jazz Band and subsequent 'trad' (traditional) groups.

open The adjective has several instrumental applications, as in *open string*, a violin or other string sounding its entire length and not stopped by fingering; a wind instrument not muffled by insertion of hand or a mute; and the *open diapason* of an organ, as opposed to a *stopped* ('*plugged*') *diapason*.

Open form, also known as *mobile form*, is a phrase describing compositions whose individual sections may be displayed and played in any order, as in several aleatory works by Boulez and Stockhausen.

OPERA

The word on its own is simply the plural of the Italian *opus*, meaning 'a work': the full phrase should be *opera in musica*, and there have been some composers (most vociferously Wagner) who have preferred the term *music drama*, from the older *dramma per musica*, or its German equivalent *singspiel* (*sung play*). The form as we know it today derived in fact from a blend of classical drama with singing and, predominantly for a while, dancing. In fifteenth-century Florence it had been common for sacred dramas to be interspersed with solo songs and madrigals, and gradually the same treatment was given to pagan classical themes. By the end of the sixteenth century a group of well-to-do Florentine dilettantes replaced spoken lines with direct setting of texts to monodic vocal music, resulting in what are thought to have been the first true operas, Jacopo Peri's *Dafne* and *Euridice*. The sung contribution remained for a long time in recitative, narrating and acting out the story, until enrichment came with the development of the *aria*, in which soloists intensified the mood of a scene with self-contained symmetrical melodies. Choruses were added to represent crowd scenes or to comment on the action in the manner of a Greek dramatic chorus.

In 1607 Claudio Monteverdi's *Orfeo* enhanced the vocal style with elements taken from the madrigal and church music, adding florid ornamentation to bring out the emotional content of the words, though at this transitional stage he still relied more on rectitative than on solo set-pieces. With *L'incoronazione di Poppea* (*The Coronation of Poppea*) he moved masterfully on to create a much more comprehensive form of music drama in which all the elements were perfectly combined: a highly dramatic libretto, scenes for contrasted characters in conflict, and ravishing songs. Venice was enchanted; and Venice was throughout the seventeenth century the real home of opera, which had ceased to be a purely aristocratic diversion and become the favourite fare of general audiences with the opening of the first public opera house there in 1637. Within a few decades the city possessed seventeen such theatres, most of them equipped with lavish scenery and mechanical devices for transformation scenes and special effects.

Cavalli, Stradella and others built up an Italian tradition which was to prevail for centuries. Alessandro Scarlatti wrote about a hundred and twenty-five operas for Venice, Rome, Florence and Naples, which soon began to rival Venice in importance. It was an Italian, too, who laid the foundations of French opera: becoming Superintendent of Music to King Louis XIV, Giovanni Battista Lulli also became Jean-Baptiste Lully and, combining two traditions of masque and ballet, staged grand spectacles of music, drama, dancing and pageantry. It delighted his patron but was all rather grandiose, and the establishment of a less pompous, distinctively French style had to await the advent of Rameau with the rich melodies and harmonies of *Hippolyte* and *Castor et Pollux*.

The first fully-fledged opera in England emerged, ironically, as a result of Puritan severity. Staging of plays was forbidden under Cromwell's rule, but there was no proscription of music. Sir William Davenant, who had written masques for King Charles I, slyly arranged for his play *The Siege of Rhodes* to be set to music by a number of composers including Henry Lawes and Matthew Locke, and in 1656 staged it without mishap. It was followed by others, but English opera did not really show signs of healthy growth until Henry Purcell wrote *Dido and Aeneas* in 1689 – and even that was originally conceived for private performance in a school for young ladies in Chelsea. His *King Arthur*, to a text by Dryden, though described as a 'dramatic opera' was closer to being a masque with music; but has been effectively 'realized' in our own time by Benjamin Britten at Aldeburgh.

EIGHTEENTH CENTURY: Italian operatic influences prevailed in Germany as elsewhere, despite a gifted native school of composers in Hamburg. It was there that George Frideric Handel composed three operas, among them *Almira* with a text in which German and Italian mingle. He took his talents to England and became the idol of the London theatre until Italian rivals arrived to challenge his supremacy. His music was superb, but the texts he used left a lot to be desired, and since he was not fluent in the Italian language he did not write as gracefully for it as did his competitors. After his death most of his operas were virtually forgotten and he was thought of mainly as a composer of oratorios – into which he had in fact introduced much of his dramatic musical gift – but in spite of their rather plodding formality many of the operas have been revived since World War II and revalued at any rate for their music and vocal lines, if not for the librettos.

One of the major reformers in Germany and Austria was Gluck, who, although still committed to opera in the Italian language, cut down on dances introduced merely for the sake of variety and on arias designed only to exhibit a performer's virtuosity. Everything had to contribute musically and dramatically to a unified production, including the orchestra, whose instruments he deployed with as much care as he did the singers. At the same time Haydn was composing operas – at least twenty are known – but these were mainly for private performance in his patron's residence, and although they are full of lovely music they did not advance the form with such assurance and originality as did the works of his young friend Mozart.

Of Mozart's four major operas, *Le nozze di Figaro* (*The Marriage of Figaro*) and *Così fan tutte* (*Women are all the same*) are in the form known as *opera buffa*, meaning comic; *Don Giovanni* has sardonic touches

The sumptuous interior of the Moscow Opera House in the glittering nineteenth-century days of the Tsars.

an advanced use of the orchestra, and an enthralling symphonic treatment of vocal ensembles, especially in his finales.

NINETEENTH CENTURY: Weber's *Der Freischütz (The Freeshooter)* and *Oberon* owed a great deal to Mozart's influence, but were clearly moving into the era of German Romanticism, much involved with Teutonic folk tales and fantasies. Beethoven's only operatic attempt was *Fidelio*, strictly speaking a *singspiel*, though in graver mood than one usually associates with the term. Berlioz's operas were often more suited to concert than theatrical performance; but it is surprising that the light-hearted, tuneful *Béatrice et Bénédict* has not been seen more often on stage. In France, comic and light opera seemed more to the public taste, and Offenbach's exuberant pieces have survived on equal terms with the works of his contemporaries Gounod and Bizet.

too, but is shot through with a tragic intensity which makes it hard to fit the work into any tidy category; while *Die Zauberflöte (The Magic Flute)* is, with its spoken dialogue, an ambitious example of *singspiel*. Mozart made only two attempts at *opera seria* (serious or tragic opera): one early in his career, *Idomeneo*, and one in the last year of his life, *La clemenza di Tito (The Clemency of Titus)*. But whatever the classification, he imbued all of them with a wit in characterization,

Although German opera was finding its feet, the nineteenth century still belonged mainly to the Italians. They showed equal skill in both grand opera and comic opera. Rossini, Donizetti and Bellini were followed by Verdi, who chose unashamedly theatrical themes and graced them with music to match, from *Rigoletto* to the final masterpieces of *Otello* and

A set design for Act 1, Scene 1 of Mozart's *The Magic Flute* in an 1816 Berlin production.

(Right) Stars of the London production of *Aida* in 1879 were Signor Campani as Radames, Mlle Kellog as Aida, and Mme Trebelli as Amneris, shown here in a painting of the last act by G. Durand.

(Below) On the fiftieth anniversary of the opening of Glyndebourne Opera House the celebratory production was of Mozart's *The Marriage of Figaro*, which with *Così fan Tutte* had featured in that first season in 1934.

Falstaff. The civic opera houses in which these were performed were often battlegrounds for clashing loyalties, adoration for some composers and singers being matched by derision for others. In Germany things were taken more solemnly, and the Festival Theatre at Bayreuth became a hallowed shrine to its founder, Richard Wagner, rather than a place for a lively night out.

Wagner had set off fairly conventionally in the steps of Weber and Meyerbeer, but was soon aiming for a fusion of all elements beyond anything his predecessors could have conceived, with musical concepts and stage action blended and transformed by his catalytic passions into a totality of music-drama. The demands he made on singers and the new paths he traced harmonically and orchestrally were to have an inescapable effect on music and performance in the next century.

TWENTIETH CENTURY: In spite of the work of atonalist and serialist composers, opera has never taken kindly to such divagations from diatonic melody and harmony. Even the impressionism of Debussy in *Pelléas et Mélisande*, disturbing as it was to critics at the time with its shifts between conventional harmony and elusive chromaticism, had a recognizable logic to it, shaped by the demands of the story and the heartfelt lyricism of the vocal lines. Puccini, with an established reputation late in the nineteenth century, went on in the twentieth to write *Tosca*, *Madama Butterfly*, and *Turandot*, in which he absorbed some theories of Schoenberg and Stravinsky for his own use, blended with Debussy influences.

(Below) A 1900 music cover of *Tosca*, published by the celebrated Italian (and later American) firm of Ricordi, champions of the music of Verdi, Puccini, and others.

The Catfish Row residents dancing in a 1952 Berlin production of Gershwin's *Porgy and Bess*.

In Germany, Richard Strauss was Wagner's closest successor, but had leanings towards less heavily symbolic themes and a romanticism of his own in works such as *Der Rosenkavalier* (*The Chevalier of the Rose*). Of the younger generation, Schoenberg tried to adapt his method of *sprechgesang* (*speech-song*) to a full-scale opera, *Moses und Aron*, but the result was an uneasy mixture of real feeling and earnest theory which failed to cohere. Far more accomplished were the two operas of his disciple Alban Berg, *Wozzeck* and *Lulu*, which tackled similar problems but overcame them with complete conviction.

Other compelling works of the century have been Stravinsky's *The Rake's Progress*, Britten's *Peter Grimes*, Poulenc's *Les Dialogues des Carmélites*, and a number of invigorating experiments in differing styles in the USA, including Samuel Barber's *Vanessa*, Gershwin's *Porgy and Bess*, and Bernstein's *West Side Story*.

NATIONALISM IN OPERA: During the hegemony of different imperial powers in eastern and central Europe, the only way for subject peoples to express their national identity was by keeping up traditions of folksong and dance and, in the case of composers, using such material in orchestral or instrumental pieces, and above all in opera. Although the Russians were not then under any alien rule, many creative artists in the nineteenth century felt that literature and music had been enslaved by French and German influences. Glinka's *A Life for the Tsar* was one of the first attempts to break free, followed by the works of Mussorgsky and Borodin. In the Austro-Hungarian dominions, Czechs reasserted their individuality in operas by Smetana such as *Dalibor* and *The Bartered Bride*, and later in the speech and music rhythms of Janáček. Bartók, a fervent Hungarian folksong collector, attempted only one opera, *Bluebeard's Castle*, which in spite of consisting of only one act is a powerful summation of all his musical beliefs and powers. (For more about **Opera** see Appendix II.)

operetta Literally, in Italian, a 'little opera'; in French, *operette*. The word has come to be associated with tuneful stage pieces, usually mingling spoken dialogue with song, built around a sentimental story with a happy ending and not too many demands made on the musical knowledge of the audience. At its best the form has produced such Viennese gems as Strauss's *Die Fledermaus* (*The Bat*) and the works of Lehár. In England, Gilbert and Sullivan collaborated on a distinctive series of operettas; in the USA, immigrant European composers such as Rudolf Friml, Sigmund Romberg and Victor Herbert developed their own genre in *Rose Marie, The Desert Song, Naughty Marietta*, and many other successes. Operetta is rarely devised as such nowadays, having given way to what is simply called a 'musical'.

opus Latin for 'work', most frequently used in connection with the cataloguing of a composer's works and shortened to *Op*. In such lists it may be assumed that Op.25 would have been written earlier than Op.35, but such reasoning does not always apply: a lot depends on whether the composer himself or some later scholar has done the cataloguing, and whether recent discoveries have had to be incorporated or simply tacked on the end. Further confusion can be added by the eighteenth-century habit of grouping several similar pieces together for convenience of publication: e.g. twelve of Handel's *concerti grossi*, all packaged into Op.6.

oratorio In the middle of the sixteenth century Biblical stories were presented in dramatic form in the Oratory of St Philip Neri in Rome; music was increasingly added as time went on. The distinction between these and operatic forms was that the *oratorio* was presented without costume or scenery. Although such colourful appurtenances were proscribed, the music itself became more colourful in the hands of composers such as Carissimi and Schütz, using vocal and orchestral elaboration to effect a marriage between sacred music and the vigour of early Italian opera.

It was in Germany that the oratorio reached its greatest heights and was then most rewardingly exported to England by Handel, whose *Messiah* perhaps represents the peak of its development. Haydn produced *The Creation* and a secular oratorio, *The Seasons*, but he himself acknowledged, after bursting into tears at a Handel festival in Westminster Abbey, that Handel 'is master of us all!' Using Negro spirituals in place of the more familiar Passion chorales, Michael Tippett described *A Child of our Time*, his work for soloists, choir and orchestra based on Nazi persecution of the Jews, as an oratorio.

William Hogarth's depiction of a choral rehearsal for the oratorio *Judith* by the eighteenth-century Flemish composer William Defesch, who settled in England in 1733, dying in London in 1761.

THE ORCHESTRA AND ITS INSTRUMENTS

The original Greek word defined a 'dancing place' between the stage of a theatre and its audience. With the development of seventeenth-century opera houses it was adopted as a useful description of the musicians between the singers and the audience in what came to be known (often with rueful connotations) as the orchestra pit. For several centuries now it has been applied to the instrumental ensemble itself, whether in an opera house, concert hall or recording studio.

The modern symphony orchestra has developed from instrumental groups which accompanied royal or ducal entertainments or were assembled by gifted amateurs who were, in every sense of the word, in harmony with one another. By Haydn's time the orchestral resources were expanding, but he still wrote for comparatively small forces and, in spite of modern performances of his work with outsize orchestras, sounds better in the hands of not more than thirty players. Romanticism brought the larger orchestra, together with sonorities made possible by technical improvements in the instruments themselves.

Until the nineteenth century it was rare for a permanent orchestra to exist outside a Court or wealthy private household. Musicians were assembled for some special occasion, often expected to play their parts at sight, and then paid off and disbanded. Not until 1813 were favourable conditions established by the Philharmonic Society of London (becoming the Royal Philharmonic Society a century later) for the establishment of a full-time professional orchestra. Today most large cities have their own symphony orchestras, some paying their way, most of them subsidized. There are also smaller bodies such as chamber orchestras and string orchestras: if an ensemble consists entirely of one class of instrument, especially wind instruments, it is generally called a band. (*See also* Appendix I.)

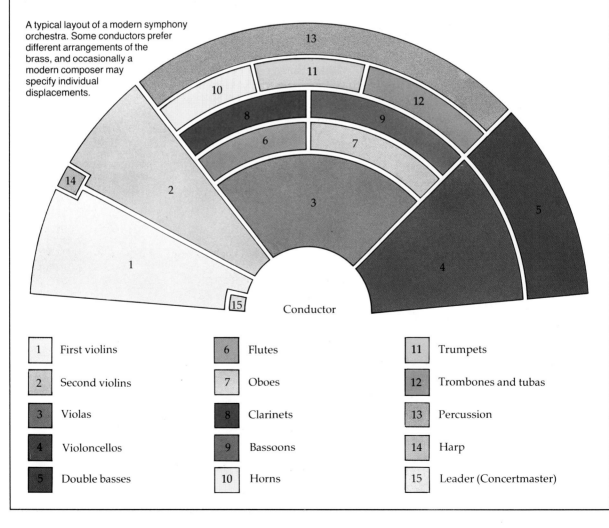

A typical layout of a modern symphony orchestra. Some conductors prefer different arrangements of the brass, and occasionally a modern composer may specify individual displacements.

Conductor

1	First violins	6	Flutes	11	Trumpets
2	Second violins	7	Oboes	12	Trombones and tubas
3	Violas	8	Clarinets	13	Percussion
4	Violoncellos	9	Bassoons	14	Harp
5	Double basses	10	Horns	15	Leader (Concertmaster)

Each different section of an orchestra has its leader, sometimes known as the principal or 'first desk'. The first violinist is the overall leader, known in the USA as the concertmaster. Conductors have differing tastes regarding the layout of the various sections of the orchestra, and some compositions demand unorthodox placings of the instruments, decided either by specific instructions from the composer (as in Boulez's *Figures-Doubles-Prismes* and works by Carter and Stockhausen) or by the conductor's own interpretation of the work's meaning; but on the whole it is usual to have first violins to the conductor's left, bass strings to his right, violas immediately in front of him, and wind sections set back between the strings and the percussion right at the rear.

Unusual instruments have at one time and another been introduced by composers seeking special effects, but the following are those in normal use in a contemporary symphony orchestra. The practical range of each is indicated (though some performers can by various technical means such as skilful fingering and lip pressure on certain wind instruments produce notes above the usual limit), together with transposition intervals where relevant. Music for some wind instruments is written not at the actual pitch of the composition but at one which produces the same sound without involving the player in awkward fingerings: parts for an A clarinet, for instance, are written a minor third higher than they are meant to sound, so that instead of playing in the key of A with three sharps, the clarinettist is actually fingering in the straightforward key of C; and if the key is E major, with four sharps, the clarinettist will be reading his part in G, with only one sharp.

BASSET HORN: An early form of clarinet, transposing in F, with a range a minor third lower than the subsequent A or B flat instrument. It was used by Mozart in his *Requiem* and other works, including his clarinet concerto, which had to be re-scored for later instruments. In modern times it is rarely used, but can be heard in two wind sonatinas and a number of operas by Richard Strauss, and in some of Stockhausen's work. The Italian translation, *Corno di bassetto*, was used by George Bernard Shaw as a pseudonym during his spell as a music critic.

BASSOON: A large woodwind instrument of the oboe family, with a double reed, shown on musical scores in its Italian form as *fagotto*, a name bestowed because of its resemblance, when dismantled for transport, to a bundle of faggots. It is pitched in C. Operating in a very low register, it is often used to produce chortling comic effects as in Mendelssohn's music for *A Midsummer Night's Dream*, but can add especial richness to an ensemble. The *vox humana* (human voice) quality in parts of its register led Prokofiev to use it for the grandfather's voice in *Peter and the Wolf*. In Dukas' *The Sorcerer's Apprentice* it represents the playful, uncontrollable broom. Mozart composed a bassoon concerto; Vivaldi composed over thirty. The standard instrument is a little over nine feet long, but there is a larger double bassoon (or contra-bassoon), pitched an octave lower, which has to be supported on a spike like that of a cello or double bass.

CLARINET: A woodwind instrument with a single reed. It was developed at the end of the seventeenth century from a simple reed-pipe known as a *chalu-*

The Theatre Museum in Nuremberg has a collection of engravings by Christoph Weigel in 1720 of contemporary musical instruments.

(Far left) This one is labelled *Faggott* (bassoon).

(Left) An eighteenth-century clarinet.

meau – a name still applied to the clarinet's lower register and to a bagpipe chanter. Early models produced a shrill, trumpet-like sound which led to their being named clarionets, a spelling now obsolete.

The so-called octave key which increases the clarinet's range does not in fact raise the pitch by an octave, as with the overblowing of a flute, but by a twelfth, which involves different fingering in the registers below and above the break. The introduction of the Boehm system of rings and levers simplified this considerably, but to cope with awkward key signatures it is usual for an orchestral clarinettist to carry a pair of instruments: the most common in B flat transposing a tone, the A version transposing a minor third. There is a C version, little used nowadays, and a high E flat one used almost entirely in military bands.

In spite of its uneven harmonics and a rather dead patch in the 'throat' register between G and B flat in the treble clef, the warmth of the instrument's tone endeared it to Mozart and Brahms, who produced some of their most lyrical work for it. Among modern composers who have written strikingly for it have been Poulenc, Finzi, Nielsen and Stravinsky (*Ebony Concerto*); and as well as writing a concerto for Benny Goodman, Copland has used the less familiar E flat clarinet to piercing effect in *El Salón México*.

COR ANGLAIS: A member of the oboe double-reed family, but pitched a fifth lower and in effect an alto oboe, the 'English horn' has been said to take its name from a hunting horn, but its dark reedy tone belies that. Another suggestion is that it derives from *cor anglé*, since the reed tube is bent back at the top and was once more acutely angled. It is tuned in F, so that it transposes a fifth down from the written

A modern Boehm system clarinet.

music. Its haunting timbre has led to its use in such evocative pieces as the slow movement of Dvořák's *New World* Symphony and Sibelius's symphonic legend, *The Swan of Tuonela*.

DOUBLE BASS: The lowest-pitched of bowed string instruments, developed from the bass viol towards the middle of the sixteenth century. Originally it had only three strings, but a fourth was later introduced. Unlike its fellow members of the violin family, it tunes those strings in fourths instead of fifths, as otherwise the wide intervals would make fluent playing almost impossible. Music for it is written an octave higher than the actual sounds, to avoid adding a veritable ladder of ledger lines below the bass staff.

Employed for a long time merely as a supporting instrument, the double bass's possibilities as a solo performer were exploited by Beethoven's friend Dragonetti. Schubert added it resonantly to the cellos in the opening of his *Unfinished Symphony*; the whale in Haydn's *Creation* and the galumphing elephant in Saint-Saens' *Carnival of the Animals* are portrayed by it; and one of its most brilliant exponents, the conductor Koussevitsky, wrote a double bass concerto. The twentieth-century dance band and swing orchestra have made great use of the double bass, usually plucked or slapped, in the rhythm section.

FLUTE: A member of the woodwind section of an orchestra, although many modern instruments are made of metal. In its basic form it has existed from earliest times as the fundamental 'blown' instrument, and is referred to in both classical texts and folklore. The term has been used to cover the recorder and similar pipes blown vertically; but the orchestral flute is played transversely (the only woodwind instrument to be so), the sound resulting from breath being blown across an open blow-hole or embouchure. Boehm's ring-key system of fingering, introduced in the first half of the nineteenth century, gave added flexibility.

Mozart disliked the instrument, yet wrote some delightful concertos and chamber music for flautists. Bach made scintillating use of it in the *Suite in B minor* and in two of the *Brandenburg Concertos*. Its sensual qualities were exploited by Debussy in *Prélude à l'après-midi d'un faune* and *Syrinx*. Modern compositions are too numerous to list, but outstanding among them are concertos by Nielsen and Arnold and a sonata by Poulenc.

FRENCH HORN: A brass wind instrument with its tubing wound into a coil, with a mouthpiece at one end and a wide amplifying bell at the other. In its primitive form as a hunting horn it could produce only the natural harmonics, governed by the player's lip pressure and breath control, and only in the key in which it was pitched. The introduction of crooks which could be fitted into the tube made it possible to change key, and other variations of note and timbre could be achieved by manipulating one hand

Travers-flaute (flute). Christoph Weigel's engraving of an eighteenth-century flute.

within the bell. Still it was difficult to achieve smooth chromatic transitions until the invention of piston and rotary valves early in the nineteenth century.

These more modern horns, called French because most of the significant developments took place in France, were generally pitched in F, so that music is written a fifth above the actual sound; but a more advanced model, the double horn introduced at the end of the last century, makes it possible to tune either in F or B flat. Music written for the instrument is unusual in that it rarely includes a key signature: the key is apparently C major throughout, with all sharps and flats marked as they occur.

In spite of the technical limitations of his day, Mozart wrote four superb concertos for the horn.

Waldhorn, a hunting horn from which the modern French horn developed.

control of string length to offer the flat, natural and sharp of each tone. A modern instrument, tuned to the key of C flat major (effectively B major), has forty-seven strings and seven pedals. Near the end of the nineteenth century the manufacturer Pleyel produced a chromatic harp with one string for each semitone, thereby doing away with the need for pedals, but its complexities outweighed its advantages.

The harp is most frequently (indeed, too predictably) employed to provide rippling *glissandi* or a guitar-like *arpeggio* intimating or accompanying some heavenly choir. As a solo instrument it has been neglected, though Mozart wrote delightful duet passages for it in his Concerto for flute, harp and orchestra. Debussy made use of all its capabilities in his *Danse sacrée et danse profane*, as did Ravel in the *Introduction and Allegro* for flute, clarinet, harp and strings. More recently Berio and Boulez have featured it, and there are a concerto by Milhaud and a sonata by Hindemith.

Harffenist (harpist) by Christoph Weigel.

Brahms wrote a trio and employed the plummy sonority of the instrument in his symphonies and the Second Piano Concerto. Mahler and Strauss were also fond of its orchestral effect, and in our own time there have been quartets by Hindemith and Tippett and Britten's Serenade for tenor, horn and strings.

HARP: A stringed instrument of ancient origin, appearing on reliefs from Assyria and Egypt, and much written about in Greek mythology and the Old Testament. Varying forms were common in Scandinavia and all Celtic lands. Its present name derives from the Anglo-Saxon *hearpe* (in German, *harfe*). Basically it consists of a frame holding a number of strings stretched in a graduated sequence, plucked by the player's fingertips. The earliest strings were made of gut or twisted horsehair, but brass and other metals came into use in later centuries.

In its fundamental form the harp could produce only one note from each string. Early in the eighteenth century a Bavarian instrument maker introduced a single-action pedal, but it was Sébastien Erard's double-action pedal of 1810 which made possible the

OBOE: A woodwind instrument producing its sound, like that of the bassoon and cor anglais, by the vibration of two cane reeds against each other when blown. The name derives from the French *hautbois*, meaning high (or loud) wood because it was once much used in large (and, one feels, surely discordant) numbers out of doors: the English version, a regular adjunct of the town waits, was for a long time known as a hautboy. The instrument as we now know it was refined in the middle of the seventeenth century by a Parisian bagpiper, Jean Hotteterre, was used to great effect by Lully, and soon became an integral part of most reasonably sized orchestras. Because its pitch cannot be altered by any mechanical adjustment, the oboe is the instrument to whose A all the other orchestral players must tune.

Bach made poetic use of it in his *Christmas Oratorio* and cantatas such as *Wachet Auf*. Handel wrote concertos and sonatas for it. Mozart's oboe quartet is almost as lyrical a work as his clarinet quintet. It crows like a cock in Haydn's *The Seasons*, and imitates a duck in Prokofiev's *Peter and the Wolf*. The twentieth-century virtuoso oboist Heinz Holliger has written for it himself and inspired compositions by Berio, Henze, Stockhausen and others.

The *oboe d'amore*, created in Germany in about 1720, pitched a minor third lower, was favoured by Bach for its soulful tone but went out of fashion, to be revived only occasionally, as in Ravel's *Boléro* and Holst's *Somerset Rhapsody*. The *oboe da caccia*, or 'hunting oboe', was used out of doors but then developed for orchestral use as the *cor anglais*.

Oboe.

PERCUSSION: Long before mankind discovered ways of producing different notes by blowing through reeds or tubes of different kinds and pitches, hands and sticks must have beaten on wood and gourds. From these beginnings have developed a number of percussive instruments in two classes – tuned (such as the timpani and xylophone) and untuned (such as the gong and side drum), which cannot alter their pitch. Some composers have experimented with a variety of unusual additions from different lands, but in general the percussion section of an orchestra consists of the following:

bass drum In a military band it is usually (and uncomfortably) supported against the player's chest and beaten with padded mallets from either side. In a jazz band the drummer operates a foot pedal to maintain the rhythm. In a full symphony orchestra the bass drum is usually suspended in a frame, with one head angled towards the player and frequently another head stretched across the other end to provide extra resonance. The deep sonority of the drum is well exemplified in Berlioz's orchestration of the *Rákóczy March* in his *Damnation of Faust*.

celesta Invented in the 1880s by a harmonium manufacturer, the celesta has a keyboard like that of a miniature piano, operating hammers which strike metal plates to produce a gentle tinkling sound which admirably suited Tchaikovsky for his *Dance of the Sugar-Plum Fairy* in the *Nutcracker* ballet. It is used to compelling effect by Bartók in his *Music for Strings, Percussion and Celesta*.

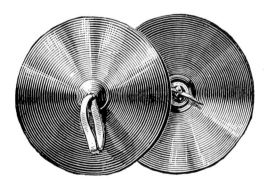

Cymbals.

cymbals Made from an amalgam of copper and tin, these wide plates of Chinese and Turkish origin usually come in pairs, held in the player's two hands by leather tags and clashed together, any unwanted reverberation being then checked by damping the cymbals against the player's chest. The larger models have no definite pitch, but smaller versions called *crotales*, of ancient Greek origin and sometimes referred to as *antique cymbals*, can be tuned to a definite pitch and have been used by Debussy and Ravel. Other varieties, more frequent in dance bands

than in symphonic scores, include 'sizzle' cymbals – with jingles or sizzles loosely attached – and 'high hat' cymbals, operated by the drummer's foot while played upon by sticks or wire brushes.

glockenspiel The German word means 'bell play', describing the bell-like sound of the instrument's graduated metal bars set in a harp-like frame, usually struck by small beaters but sometimes played from a piano-like keyboard. Papageno's magic bells in Mozart's *Die Zauberflöte* (*The Magic Flute*) are usually represented on the glockenspiel. It also appears in the *Chinese Dance* from Tchaikovsky's *Nutcracker* ballet.

gong The most widely used orchestral model is the bronze *tam-tam*, originating in China – a large disc with a shallow rim suspended from a frame and struck with a padded mallet. It is much used for Eastern or pseudo-Eastern effects, as in Puccini's *Turandot* and innumerable Hollywood film scores. It features also, in a more unusual context, in Stockhausen's *Kontakte* and works by Boulez and Messiaen.

A bandsman's side drum.

side drum The name comes from military band usage, where the drum is carried to one side of the player. It is also called a snare drum because of a set of snares (gut or wire strands) stretched across the lower head to add a bright rattle to the sound produced on the top (or batter head) by drumsticks. The tension of these snares can be adjusted to muffle the sound when required. Different effects can be produced, and frequently are in dance and jazz bands, by rolls, paradiddles, 'rim-shots' and the use of wire brushes. Two famous orchestral uses are in the repetitive rhythm, building up in a long crescendo, of Ravel's *Boléro*, and in Carl Nielsen's Fifth Symphony, where the composer instructs the side-drummer to improvise 'as if at all costs to stop the progress of the orchestra'.

Timpani, or kettledrum.

close to the top by mallets. They are heard most frequently as carillons and similar effects in programme music such as Tchaikovsky's *1812 Overture* and Janáček's symphonic rhapsody *Taras Bulba*.

xylophone The Greek word for wood, *xylo*, is incorporated in the name of an instrument which is in fact of ancient Asiatic origin and may reasonably be considered one of the earliest assemblies of tuned elements. Sticks of differing lengths laid on the ground and struck with another piece of wood produced early, primitive tunes. Today the bars of the instrument are laid out more formally like a piano keyboard, but the principle of bars hammered by beaters is still the same. Instruments in the same family include the larger marimba, and a combination known as a xylorimba. The vibraphone works in the same way but with metal bars instead of wooden ones. Saint-Saëns used the xylophone to depict skeletal cavortings in his *Danse macabre*, and there is a xylophone solo in Bartók's *Music for Strings, Percussion and Celesta*. The xylorimba is featured in Boulez's *Le marteau sans maître* and works by Stravinsky and others.

PICCOLO: The name derives from the Italian word for 'little', as in *flauto piccolo* – a little flute. It is pitched so high that its music has to be written an octave below the actual sound produced. Composers have used it, on the whole, for producing shrieking storm effects, jokey passages, and other atmospheric passages. A piccolo tune which most people can whistle (though in a lower register) is that in Sousa's *Stars and Stripes* march.

SAXOPHONE: Much maligned for its impure tone and by the snobbish for its associations with jazz and dance music, the instrument is also in reality a mainstay of military and other marching bands, producing considerable volume without too great an effort on the part of the player. With fingering similar to that of the clarinet (on which many jazz players 'double'), and with a single reed also allied to a clarinet reed, it was named after its inventor, Adolphe Sax. As a clarinet player himself, he was dissatisfied with the awkward overblowing of the instrument at the twelfth (*see* CLARINET above), and set about producing a more satisfying octave break and consistent fingering. At the same time he changed from a woodwind construction to one of brass.

There are eight different sizes and pitches of saxophone, each with a range of two and a half octaves and all of them transposing (except the 'C melody'). The three in commonest use are the alto (pitched in E flat), the tenor (in B flat), and the baritone (in E flat); but some jazz players, including Sidney Bechet and Johnny Hodges, have made brilliant use of the B flat soprano.

Although saxophones have never formed a regular section of a symphony orchestra, they have been used by some composers to introduce distinctive

timpani Also known, particularly in military band circles, as kettledrums, owing to their cauldron shape. The drum consists of an open metal hemisphere across which is stretched a vellum or synthetic skin, struck by a range of soft or hard beaters. The drumhead can be tuned within narrow limits by adjusting screws around the retaining hoop, and variations in sound are achieved by striking different areas of the head. There are also timpani whose tension is varied by a foot pedal, allowing for pitch changes while actually playing, and also for *glissandi*. Four steady beats on the instrument lead in to the first movement of Beethoven's Violin Concerto. Berlioz decreed sixteen of them for his overwhelming *Requiem*. In Carl Nielsen's Fourth Symphony there is what sounds like a battle to the death between two timpanists.

triangle A length of metal shaped, as its name makes clear, into a triangle. Struck by a metal rod, it produces a sharp, penetrating, ringing sound. A sustained jangling tremolo can be obtained by rattling the rod swiftly to and fro within the triangle. It is heard in *Anitra's Dance* from Grieg's *Peer Gynt* suite, and adds to the exuberance of the Scherzo in Brahms's Fourth Symphony.

tubular bells A graduated series of tubular metal chimes, hung in two rows from a frame and struck

Tenor saxophone.

tone colours. Richard Strauss included four in his *Symphonia Domestica*; Vaughan Williams scores for a saxophone in his ballet *Job* and in the Sixth and Ninth Symphonies; and Eric Coates wrote a *Saxo-Rhapsody* for saxophone and orchestra. In more recent decades Harrison Birtwistle has used a soprano instrument in *The Triumph of Time*, and there is a baritone in Stockhausen's *Gruppen*.

TROMBONE: This is the only wind instrument capable of true chromatic playing and *glissandi*, consisting as it does of a U-shaped tube extended by means of a telescopic slide. It derives from the medieval *sackbut* and, like it, is usually scored for in groups rather than as a single instrument. The nineteenth century invention of a trombone with valves rather than a slide proved unsatisfactory, though Juan Tizol achieved some success with it in Duke Ellington's orchestra.

The tenor trombone is the normal symphonic instrument, supplemented by a bass trombone with a larger bore. Others are rarely used, though Wagner and Mahler scored for the unwieldy contrabass, and treble and alto trombones are to be found in some baroque music. All of them are non-transposing.

Mozart made terrifying use of the instrument in the statue scene of his opera *Don Giovanni*, and Brahms produced a great dramatic effect in his Fourth Symphony by holding the trombones back until the *passacaglia* of the last movement. The Yugoslav trombonist and composer Globokar has written several avant-garde studies for the instrument, and Hindemith composed a sonata for it. Most fluent use of it has been made in jazz by Jack Teagarden and Tommy Dorsey.

Trombone.

TRUMPET: The word has been applied throughout the centuries to a variety of wind instruments capable of producing thrilling martial sounds, usually through a metal tube. Trumpets were known in ancient Egypt and Greece; some supposedly brought down the walls of Jericho; and one of their successors will sound the Last Trump on Judgment Day.

Early forms such as the hunting horn, bugle and curved trumpets with loops and crooks were vastly improved with the introduction in the nineteenth century of piston valves and valve slides, making it possible to adjust the effective length of the tubing while playing. The modern trumpet is usually a transposing instrument pitched in B flat, with the ability to retune to A; but there is a slightly higher, non-transposing version in C. A member of the same family is the cornet, smaller and with a narrow conical bore. Both trumpet and cornet are used in military, brass and jazz bands.

Throughout the classical period little use was made of the trumpet by composers except to provide routine ensemble harmonies. Haydn composed a sprightly concerto, but it was not until Wagner's time that the possibilities of the technically improved instrument were recognized. Ravel's orchestration of Mussorgsky's *Pictures at an Exhibition* assigns a solo trumpet and accompanying brass to the linking *Promenade* theme. A chromatic trumpet solo opens Elliot Carter's *Symphony for Three Orchestras*. There is a concerto for trumpet, bassoon and strings by Hindemith; and Malcolm Arnold, himself an orchestral trumpeter, has featured it in many ensemble pieces.

TUBA: The name is applied to several large brass instruments providing bass parts in brass ensembles such as military or wind bands, including the euphonium, but in the symphony orchestra it generally means the bass tuba in F. Notes on the deepest model, the double bass tuba, are so low that the human ear can hardly distinguish between them; but Wagner called for its use sometimes, and he also had special oval-shaped tubas constructed for the *Ring* cycle.

With its great mass and convoluted coils, the tuba may look unwieldy, but it is a considerable improvement on its long, hardly manageable predecessors, the serpent and the ophicleide. The introduction of valves early in the nineteenth century gave it enough

Christoph Weigel's eighteenth-century engraving *Trompette* (trumpet).

flexibility to be a useful supporter of the brass section in an orchestra. Although provided with solo passages in works by Rimsky-Korsakov, Mahler and Holst, it was rarely regarded as a particularly rewarding soloist until Vaughan Williams composed a concerto for it.

A model used in marching bands, with its bell carried above the player's head by tubing encircling the player's body, took the name *sousaphone* after John Philip Sousa, for whom it was designed.

VIOLA: A stringed instrument slightly larger than the violin and with a deeper, alto or tenor tone (and called the *alto* by the French), the viola has gone through many transformations since its early form in the viol family. The present model is, strictly speaking, a *viola da braccio* ('arm viola', as opposed to the *viola da gamba* or 'leg viola'), and in Germany it is actually known as a *bratsche*. Arguments about the acoustics and ideal dimensions of the instrument have even now not been satisfactorily settled, and there were times when composers felt its tonal inadequacies to be so insuperable that they wrote only dull inner parts for it, often little more than a doubling of bass and cello parts, leaving the more dexterous violins to do most of the real work.

The viola's four strings are tuned to C/G/D/A. Music for it is generally written in the otherwise little-used alto clef. Mozart recognized its potential richness of sound, used two violas in his string quintets, and actually offered a rare starring rôle in the *Sinfonia Concertante* for violin, viola and orchestra. Berlioz was commissioned by Paganini to write a viola concerto for him, and came up with *Harold in Italy* – which Paganini never performed. Walton and Copland have written viola concertos. Bartók left one, dedicated to the violist William Primrose, unfinished when he died, to be completed from surviving sketches. (*See also* **amore** for **viola d'amore**.)

VIOLIN: The leading instrument in all major orchestras, string chamber ensembles and string quartets, the violin (affectionately referred to even by serious musicians as a 'fiddle') has over the years been a favourite in one form and another with wandering musicians, players at local festivities, gipsy bands and virtuoso soloists. The instrument as we know it today was perfected in the seventeenth century by the Amati, Stradivari and Guarneri families of Cremona, Italy. Around the same time the convex bow used hitherto was superseded by the concave style and made longer and lighter.

The violin's four strings are tuned in *accordatura* (normal tuning) to G/D/A/E/. A method known as *scordatura* (mistuning) allows for raising or lowering the pitch to produce brighter effects or perform difficult passages with greater ease. Traditionally made of catgut (actually taken from the intestines of sheep and never from cats), strings may nowadays be of wire. The action of the bow produces, as with

Violin, viola, and violoncello.

all stringed instruments, vibrations which are carried by the bridge down into the wooden body. The resulting sounds are then emitted through the *f*-shaped sound-holes.

The violin repertoire is too vast even to be summarized in any meaningful way. Among the great concertos written for it are those by Bach, Mozart, Beethoven, Brahms, Mendelssohn, Bartók and Berg. Works for unaccompanied violin include those by Bach, Bartók and Honegger.

VIOLONCELLO: Generally referred to in its shortened form as 'cello', the instrument derives from the *viola da gamba* but is supported not by the legs, as the name implies, but on a spike resting on the floor – which on a concert platform can give it extra resonance. The *bouts* creating the waist of the cello are not, as might appear, kneeholes but, as with similar stringed instruments, contributory to the acoustic design.

The volume of sound which the cello produces did not in the seventeenth and eighteenth centuries endear it to sensitive musicians, but adaptations to its originally heavy strings toned things down considerably, and its voice was soon accepted as ideal in the lower registers of a string section and as a mainstay of the string quartet. Strings are tuned C/G/D/A an octave lower than those of the viola.

Solo passages within orchestral works are often provided for the cello in lyrical or passionately emotional mood. The second movement of Brahms's Second Piano Concerto begins with a ravishing slow melody on the cello, and Mahler uses it to the full in *Das Lied von der Erde* (*Song of the Earth*). Dvořák and Elgar wrote noble concertos; and Shostakovich and Britten both dedicated works to the contemporary cellist Rostropovich.

Instrumental compasses (the range of actual notes, not transposed)

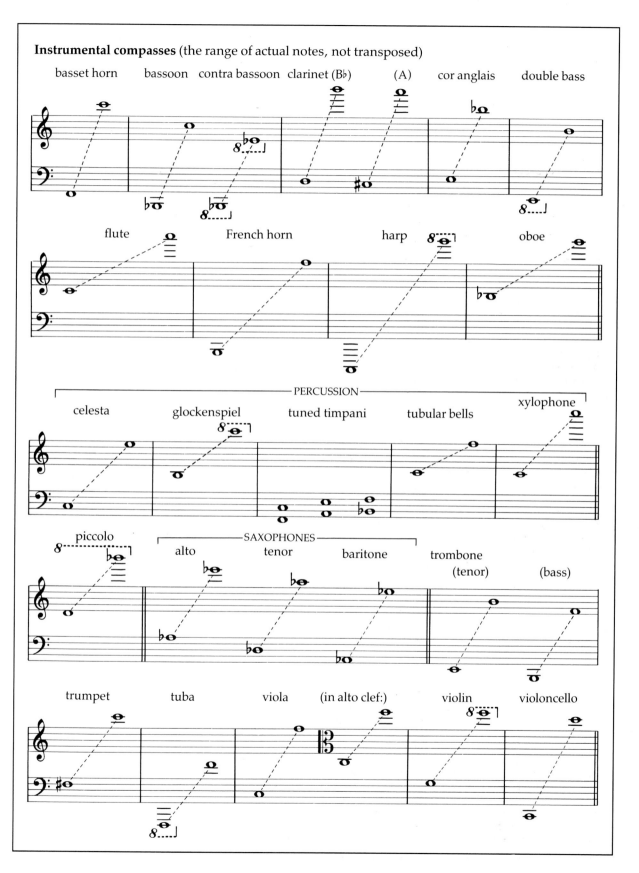

orchestration The art of writing out, or *scoring*, the various parts of a work in such a way as to make the most of instrumental resources in solo or section passages and in balance one with another, and to produce a variety of tone colours. A skilled orchestrator can adjust his demands to the resources available, or expand those resources: Haydn and Mozart understood the capabilities and limitations of their contemporary instrumentalists and could write flawlessly for them; Berlioz and Wagner demanded larger orchestras to allow them greater expression.

The word is also applied to the adaptation of a solo or chamber piece for full orchestral use, as with Ravel's orchestration of Mussorgsky's piano suite *Pictures at an Exhibition*, or Schoenberg's of the Brahms piano quartet in G minor. (*See also* **arrangement**.)

Orff, Carl (1895–1982) German composer. Resistant to formal training, he began composing at an early age, taking ideas which appealed to him from the old masters, and improvising at the piano. For a while he came under the influence of Richard Strauss and Schoenberg, but again turned back to older forms, preferring medieval music and primitive, repetitive rhythms. In 1924 he and Dorothee Günther founded a school to teach gymnastic dancing and to encourage children to sing and play on simple percussion instruments, for which Orff in due course wrote five volumes of *Das Schulwerk, Musik für Kinder*.

In 1937 he produced the work for which he is best known, *Carmina Burana* (*Songs of Beuron*), setting rumbustious medieval poems to pounding rhythms and great blocks of sound with little harmonic subtlety but with great driving force. He announced that he was discarding all his previous work, and that with this composition his 'collected works' were really to begin. Most of his later output was similarly percussive and theatrical.

OTHER WORKS: Opera *Die Kluge* (*The Clever Girl*). Theatre *Catulli Carmina* (*Songs of Catullus*). Arrangements of Monteverdi's *Lamenti* and *Orfeo*.

organ Described as the 'king of instruments' because of its great resources as a solo instrument and the majesty of its sound, the organ is known to have existed for more than two thousand years. It works on the principle of the pan-pipes, with wind provided not by human breath but by a bellows operated by various means over the ages. In Alexandria in the third century BC water pressure was used; later the force was provided

A German positive organ – i.e., one which could be stood on the floor or a table, as opposed to a portative organ which could be carried around – of about 1600.

by hand pumping; in most places today the work is done by electricity.

In spite of many technical advances, the basic principles of the organ have remained the same. Air is channelled through selected pipes to provide notes and chords required. What are called flue pipes are similar to giant recorders; reed pipes, each with a single beating reed, provide a contrasting, more penetrating tone. There are usually two keyboards, or *manuals*, and sometimes more, each controlling a particular section of the instrument – in effect separate organs within the main one. The addition of foot pedals to control the bass pipes expanded the range, and a growing number of stops made it possible to achieve different tone colours. *Crescendo* and *diminuendo* can be regulated by swell pedals.

The repertoire of organ works is enormous. Although he worked with the smaller baroque organ, Bach's fugues and chorale preludes have been unequalled by pieces written for larger models; many have been recorded on authentic instruments by Helmut Walcha. Franck and Widor produced virtual 'symphonies' to exploit the resources at their disposal. In the twentieth century the organ has lost its appeal for most composers, though Messiaen has developed a quite individual approach with his use of clashing timbres and acoustic resonances.

Since 1934 a number of purely electronic organs have been developed, providing compactness and greater flexibility; but it is doubtful whether any of them will ever replace the sound of the great pipe organ in the affections of players and listeners.

organum To break away from the monody of plainchant, ninth-century singers began adding parallel fourths or fifths to the main melody. This early attempt at harmonization led to further decorations and a more complex and satisfying polyphony and harmony, and ultimately to the abandonment of the rather stark *organum*.

Ormandy, Eugene (1899–) Hungarian conductor (American citizen 1927). He studied the violin in Budapest and toured Europe as a child prodigy until the outbreak of World War I. In 1920 he left for the USA and worked as leader and then conductor of a cinema orchestra before becoming conductor of the Minneapolis Symphony Orchestra in 1931 and of the Philadelphia Orchestra in 1936.

ornaments In Italian these are referred to as *fioriture*, in French *agréments*, in German *verzierungen* or *manieren*. Such embellishments were used by players of keyboard instruments which, until the invention of the pianoforte, had no sustaining power and therefore needed embellishments to keep the note alive on its way to the next phrase, and even more lavishly by singers wishing to enthral their audience with vocal flourishes. Operatic *divas* were accustomed to improvise florid passages around the simplest melodic sequences, sometimes displaying such self-indulgence that horrified composers decided to write any such ornamentation into the score as they wished it to sound rather than leave it to the passing fancies of temperamental performers. It has always proved difficult to codify such elaborations, but a number of indications have been accepted as standard practice, as follows:

Appoggiatura A 'grace note' not belonging to the main melody, inserted before and 'leaning' on a note integral to the theme, usually taking half the value of its successor. There are other similar anticipatory ornaments, some skipped over before the actual beat, some shortening it by incorporation into the established rhythm.

Mordent A sign above the note instructs the player or singer to include briskly before the emphasized note itself either a grace note immediately above it (in German a *pralltriller*) or below it. When the additional 'crushed' note is to be only a semitone different, with an accidental not in the prescribed key, this inflection is shown by the inclusion of a sharp or flat above or below the mordent sign. Since terminology in this field has been confused from the start, it is advisable to refer to the two main formations as *upper mordent* and *lower mordent*.

Trill (or *Shake*) The written note and the note immediately above it are played swiftly one after the other, for as long as indicated by the trill sign. Variations specified by the composer or introduced by individual performers can start on

the note above, as with a turn (*see below*), or move up to it from below; but basically the ear should be satisfied by an unequivocal return to the main thematic note.

Turn Four notes are played around the main written one, starting on the note above and describing a curve through the note itself, the note below, and then a resolution on to the main note. If indicated between two degrees in the established key, it acts as an ornamental link by cutting the value of its starting note to make time for a lead-up to the next one. An *inverted turn* begins on the note below the main one, and loops over it in a sequence of note below, written note, note above, and finally the written note.

ostinato From the Italian for 'obstinate', the word describes persistent repetition of a figure in a composition, as in *basso ostinato*, a repeated sequence of notes in the ground bass. It can equally be applied to a similar rhythmic figure.

overtone In a harmonic series, all partials at fixed intervals above the fundamental are known as overtones. (*See also* **harmonics**.)

overture From the French for an 'opening', the word can be applied to the opening movement of a suite or the introductory music to an oratorio or opera. In early stage or orchestral presentations it was sometimes called the *symphony*, but only in the sense of 'sounding together'. Many operatic overtures were self-contained and could be detached for use in the concert hall. Beethoven wrote three for his opera *Fidelio* before being satisfied: these are performed separately as *Leonora* Nos. 1, 2 and 3. In the nineteenth century the word was used for orchestral compositions designed from the start as concert pieces, e.g. Mendelssohn's *Hebrides* and Elgar's *Cockaigne*.

Ozawa, Seiji (1935–) Japanese conductor. He studied in Tokyo, and in Berlin with Herbert von Karajan. In 1960 he won a Koussevitsky scholarship, and from 1961 to 1962 was assistant conductor of the New York Philharmonic with Leonard Bernstein. Since then he has conducted several American and British orchestras, and opera in Salzburg and Vienna. In 1974 he became conductor of the Boston Symphony Orchestra.

P

Pachelbel, Johann (1653–1706) German composer and organist. Much admired by Bach and other contemporaries, he held a number of organ posts in North German cities and wrote prolifically for the keyboard. Among nearly eighty chorale preludes are settings of many tunes also used by Bach. When Pachelbel's wife and son died of the plague in 1683, he commemorated them in seven sets of chorale variations for the clavichord. In the 1970s his name reappeared in conjunction with the suddenly popular *Pachelbel's Canon* — a misleadingly definite title, since it was only one among scores, possibly hundreds, of canons which he wrote.

Pachmann, Vladimir de (1848–1933) Russian pianist. An eccentric, flamboyant performer, he treated the public as inferiors rather than as a paying audience. Even as a young man he had been unpredictable. After a début in Odessa in 1869 he disappeared for eight years in order to study, and after a few brief public performances went off again for a while. He made his American début in 1891, and became an international favourite as a Chopin interpreter, in spite of his habit of talking to himself as he played and shouting abuse of other pianists at the audience.

Six sets of keyboard variations by Pachelbel, the only work printed during his ten final years in Nuremberg.

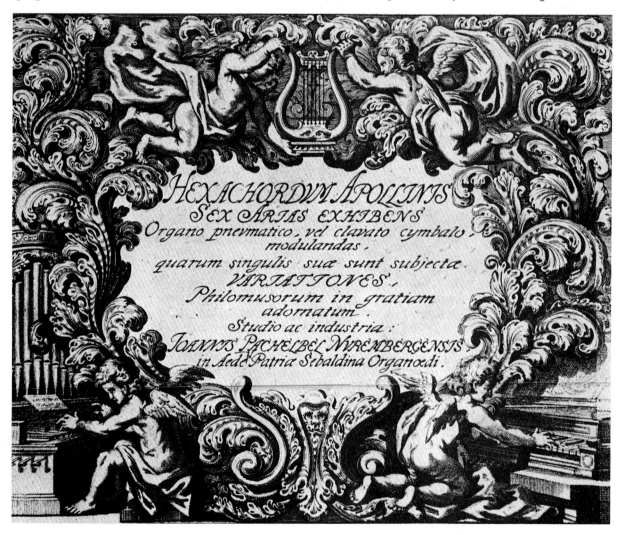

A romantic portrayal by Sir Edward Burne-Jones of the piano virtuoso Paderewski.

Paderewski, Ignace Jan (1860–1941) Polish pianist and composer. Unusually for someone who was to make a name as a virtuoso pianist, Paderewski did not concentrate on the instrument at an early stage, preferring to compose rather than play, and did not make his Paris début until 1888. Thereafter his rise in the esteem of the public and fellow performers was rapid. He was, said Saint-Saëns, 'a genius who also happens to play the piano'.

His personal background was as complicated and often as tragic as that of his country. His mother died within a few months of his birth; his maternal grandfather had died in a Siberian prison camp; and his father spent a year in a Russian prison for his nationalistic Polish views. Ignace married when he was twenty, and his wife died in childbirth within the year, leaving behind a palsied son. Later the boy was looked after by a married woman, Helena Gorska, whom Paderewski married in 1899 after her divorce.

He had his own specially furnished railway carriage, and insisted on having his own piano transported with him. He was skilful at keeping an audience waiting in anticipation of his suitably dramatic entry. He preferred London to Berlin and made no bones about it. Russians he hated. In 1891 the Steinway piano company sponsored an American tour beginning at the recently opened Carnegie Hall, where so many demands were made on him that he had to spend five hours in the middle of one night practising in the piano company's warehouse.

Paderewski became one of the wealthiest of all star performers. He bought an estate in Galicia, a farm in Switzerland, and a ranch in California, though he was not as successful with them as with his playing. In 1908 his fervent patriotism led to his commissioning from a young Polish sculptor a monument in Kraków to the Poles who had defeated the Germans at Grünwald in 1410. During World War I he gave hundreds of speeches in the cause of Polish liberation, and in 1919 became Prime Minister and Foreign Minister of his reborn country; but by 1922, disillusioned by political squabbling, he was back on the concert circuit again.

Many recordings preserve the evidence of his poetic interpretative powers. After the death of his wife in 1934, however, much of the fire went out of him, and the invasion of his country at the beginning of World War II was a bitter blow. He travelled in the USA to raise money for Polish relief and was appointed President of the Polish government-in-exile. In 1941 President Roosevelt decreed there should be a Paderewski Week on the fiftieth anniversary of his first tour of the country. In June of that year Paderewski died, and was buried with full military honours in Arlington National Cemetery.

Paganini, Niccolò (1782–1840) Italian violinist and composer. One of the most brilliant violin virtuosi of his day, and composer of especially difficult pyrotechnic solos which only he could play, Paganini was reputed by envious rivals to be in league with the devil. Although he sought to discredit slanderous imputations, including one that he had served a prison sentence for murder and had developed his fiendish technique in his cell, the dark reputation dogged him even after his death: the Archbishop of Nice forbade the ringing of funeral bells and would not consent to his burial without permission from the Pope. When this was not forthcoming, the embalmed body was carried by friends from one place to another until at last a private burial without religious rites was sanctioned. Only towards the end of the nineteenth century was a full religious service carried out, and his illegitimate son was allowed to set a tombstone over the grave.

In 1833 Paganini commissioned from Berlioz a viola concerto which became *Harold in Italy*, but never played it himself. Among his own surviving compositions are six violin concertos and twenty-four *Caprices* for solo violin. Of these, a *Caprice* in A minor has provided the theme for variations

A melodramatic staging at a Viennese theatre of 'Nicolo Zaganini, the Great Virtuoso', based on the scandalous life of Niccolò Paganini.

by several composers, including Brahms, Rachmaninov and Lutoslawski; and there is even a version recorded by Benny Goodman's swing orchestra.

OTHER WORKS: Violin and orchestra *Le streghe* (*The Witches' Dance*); Variations on *God Save the King*; *Moto perpetuo*. Twelve sonatas for violin and guitar. Six guitar quartets.

Paisiello, Giovanni (1740–1816) Italian composer. Educated by Jesuits with a view to taking up a legal career, he became interested first in church music and then in comic opera, of which he wrote over a hundred fluent examples. Though virtually forgotten now, his fame in his own time

An engraving by Vincent Aloja, after a painting by Elisabeth Vigée-Lebrun, of Giovanni Paisiello (referred to as Jean while in Napoleon's employ). He worked in Russia, Vienna, Naples and Paris in the service of anyone who would pay well enough for his musical fluency and adaptability.

was so great that he was appointed Court conductor and master of Italian opera to Catherine the Great in St Petersburg, where he produced *La serva padrone* (*The Maid as Mistress*) and a successful *Il barbiere di Siviglia* some considerable time before Rossini took up the theme. It has been suggested that to some extent this success influenced Mozart and Da Ponte, in their choice of Beaumarchais' sequel, *Le Mariage de Figaro*, as the basis for their first glorious collaboration. In addition he turned out a string of symphonies, cantatas, masses, and chamber music. In 1784 he entered the service of Ferdinand IV in Naples, but was happy to curry favour elsewhere by attaching himself to Napoleon and writing the music for the imperial coronation. This did not endear him to the Bourbons after Napoleon's fall, and he died in near poverty.

Palestrina, Giovanni Perluigi da (1525–94) Italian composer. His original name was simply Giovanni Perluigi, but later he added the name of his birthplace, Palestrina, a small town near Rome. He became a choirboy in Rome, studied music there, and then for a time returned to his home town as organist and choirmaster, until his bishop became Pope Julius III and took him back to Rome as choirmaster of the Cappella Giulia, training singers for the Sistine chapel. After Julius's death, Pope Marcellus II tried to enforce a recommendation by the Council of Trent that complicated polyphony which vexed the ears of simple congregations should be shunned in favour of the older plainchant. Legend has it that Palestrina's six-part *Missa Papae Marcelli* was composed expressly to show how the new regulations could be combined with ambitious writing for voices. Even if the story were true, the work did not fulfil its purpose: Marcellus was succeeded by Pope Paul IV, who dismissed Palestrina because he disapproved either of polyphonic music or of the fact that the musician was married and had two children, and therefore was unfitted to take part in the Sistine choir services.

Palestrina filled a number of posts in Roman churches before returning to the Cappella Giulia and working there for the rest of his life. When his wife and children succumbed to the plague he took steps towards becoming a priest, and had actually been ordained when the arrival in his life of a rich widow persuaded him to remarry. She installed him in the family fur business, and from then on he combined commerce with composition, doing well enough in both to be able to pay for the publication of collections of his own music.

In spite of his many differences with church authorities, Palestrina wrote almost exclusively for religious occasions, apart from a few madrigals and keyboard pieces of no great significance. He favoured the *a cappella* style, the pure flow of voices without instrumental accompaniment, and was unmatched in his ability to use these vocal lines contrapuntally in such a way as to create virtually an orchestra of singers. He wrote over a hundred masses and about two hundred motets, incorporating a wealth of soaring melodies deployed in canons, six-part webs, and chordal sequences which were later to be rediscovered and marvelled at by both Romantic and neoclassical composers. The antiphonal motet *Stabat Mater* for twelve voices stands high above the numerous other settings of that devotional text.

Rich and highly esteemed, Palestrina decided in 1593 to return to his birthplace and combine comfortable retirement with the job of local organist and choirmaster. Early in the New Year he fell ill and died before he could make the journey. On his coffin was set the inscription *Princeps Musicae* – 'Prince of Music'.

OTHER WORKS: Hymns for four voices. Psalms for twelve voices. *Lamentations* for four voices. Settings for four voices from the *Song of Solomon*. Sacred and secular madrigals. Thirty-five *Magnificats*.

panharmonicon A mechanical orchestra invented by Mälzel, for which his friend Beethoven wrote his garish *Battle Symphony*.

pan-pipes Also known as the *syrinx*, this was the classical forerunner of the flute and of organ pipes. Reed, cane or pottery pipes of graduated

Pan, the Greek god of pastures, flocks and shepherds, usually represented as having the legs, horns and ears of a goat, to whom the original pan-pipes are traditionally ascribed.

lengths were bound side by side, producing different notes when the player blew across them. Their use in symphonic music is limited, though Mozart imitated the sounds in Papageno's 'Magic Flute' in the opera of that name; and folk music and film themes have been played by their twentieth-century Romanian exponent, Gheorge Zamfir.

Panufnik, Andrzej (1914–) Polish composer (British citizen 1961). His father was an engineer and a part-time violin maker who had also married a violinist, but did not wish his son to pursue a musical career. Nevertheless the boy managed to study in Warsaw and Vienna, became an admired composer and conductor in his country – though much of his work was lost during the Warsaw uprising – and after World War II took over conductorship first of the Kraków and then of the Warsaw Symphony Orchestras. He attempted to write music in conformity with official pronouncements, but finally defected to London. After this, performance of his works was banned in Poland. For a time he conducted the City of Birmingham Symphony Orchestra, but gave this up to devote himself to full-time composing.

Polish themes continued to obsess him, contrasting provocatively with influences felt strongly while living in Twickenham, the home of the poet Alexander Pope. He made an intense, moving setting of Pope's *Universal Prayer* as a cantata for soloists, choir, three harps and organ. Stokowski gave the first performance of this in the Cathedral of St John the Divine in New York, but it aroused disapproval from both Catholic and Protestant communities, and Panufnik himself had American visa applications turned down on the grotesque grounds that, in spite of having fled the tyranny of his own country, he must nevertheless somehow be a Communist. In England he has composed in his own favoured style of severe, compact note groups a *Sinfonia Votiva* pleading with the Black Madonna for Poland's freedom; and his bassoon concerto is dedicated to the memory of the priest Father Jerzy Popieluszko, murdered by Polish police.

OTHER WORKS: Ballet *Miss Julie*. Nine symphonies. *Sinfonia concertante* for flute, harp and strings. Cantata *Thames Pageant*.

parallel chords When the individual degrees of a chord move through the same intervals simultaneously without altering their inner structure, this is said to be *parallel motion*. Since strict academic theory frowns on consecutive fifths or octaves, the only way that chords may be written in such sequences is in an inversion. For example, a triad of C major moving to a triad of D minor could not be played as C/E/G followed by D/F/A, but it is permissible for it to be E/G/C followed by F/A/D. Like all rules, this one is made to be broken by composers who have a particular effect in mind.

Parry, (Sir) Hubert (1848–1918) English composer. The son of a well-to-do Gloucestershire squire, Parry was educated at Eton and Oxford and for a few years pursued a business career before turning full-time to music. His first piano concerto was performed in 1880, and he achieved wide popularity with his choral settings of *Blest Pair of Sirens* and Blake's *Jerusalem*. From 1894 until his death he was director of the Royal College of Music. In 1896 he inherited the family estate, where his bailiff later reminisced about Parry's habit of taking out a tuning fork whenever he heard a cuckoo and making a note of the date, pitch and interval.

OTHER WORKS: Five symphonies. Oratorio *Judith*. Cantata *Ode on St Cecilia's Day*. Anthem *I Was Glad* for coronation of Edward VII. *Te Deum* for coronation of George V. Over 140 solo and part songs.

part The word is used to describe either one voice in music sung or played in a composition for a number of performers (e.g. soprano part, viola part, etc.), or an actual single line of such music (e.g. a fugue in four parts). (*See also* **score**.)

partials *See* **harmonics**.

partimento From the Italian for 'division', the word refers to exercises in the seventeenth and eighteenth centuries involving the playing of elaborate melodies (usually improvised) above a figured bass.

partita This was originally used as the Italian name for a *suite*, though its basic meaning is 'departure', in this sense a 'variation'. It was applied by Bach to some of his keyboard and solo violin works, though he described similar cello works as *suites*.

partitur German for a score. In French, *partition*.

part song A vocal piece for mixed voices, without the polyphonic complexities of a madrigal and relying more on a leading melody line with accompanying harmonies.

pas A dance step, especially in ballet, as in *pas seul*, a solo dance, and *pas de deux*, choreographed for two dancers (usually male and female).

paso doble Sometimes written as a single word, *pasodoble*, this is Spanish for a 'double step', a fast 2/4 dance originating in this century. It has been the basis of a number of popular dance band numbers, and was used in the parodic tango-pasodoble treatment of *I do like to be beside the seaside* in William Walton's *Façade* suite.

passacaglia In French, *passecaille*. It started out in the early seventeenth century as a Spanish dance and 'street song' (the basic meaning of the word) accompanied on the guitar. The slow 3/4 tempo was maintained when it was transformed into an instrumental piece with a repeated ground bass theme above which the composer wove intricate variations, similar to the style of a *chaconne*. Handel and Bach used the form frequently, and Brahms produced two superb examples in the *St Anthony Chorale* variations and the last movement of his fourth symphony.

passepied Meaning 'foot passing', this applied in the first place to a light courtly dance in frisky 3/8 or 6/8 time from Brittany which became popular in sixteenth-century Paris. It was used in suites by Bach, Handel and Rameau, and in a number of French operas.

passing notes (or **tones**) Many melodies make their way through sequences of tones which do not belong to the integral harmonies of the piece but intervene either as diatonic steps or in chromatic scale form. Some are skipped over quickly as an ornament, but many are played or sung straightforwardly between the principal tones. In Renaissance contrapuntal motets, deliberate use was made of passing note dissonances moving up or down between one consonance and another. Unlike several ornaments and *auxiliary notes*, a passing note should always continue moving in the direction in which it began.

Passion music Beginning with Latin recitation of the Passion of Christ in churches during Holy Week, the addition of plainsong and then polyphonic interpolations led to the development by masters such as Victoria and Lassus of a more elaborate musical narrative. The Lutherans of Reformation Germany adopted vernacular translations and introduced chorales whose message could be understood by the laity. Schütz and then Bach elaborated on the form and raised it to its ultimate heights. Few twentieth-century composers other than Penderecki have ventured to follow such exemplars.

pasticcio The Italian word (literally a 'pastry' or 'pie') means a 'hotchpotch', in the sense of a stage entertainment not composed specifically but patched together from pieces written by any number of people, or an opera or instrumental piece with contributions from various composers, as with ballad operas and the trio whose three movements were composed by Dietrich, Brahms and Schumann.

pastiche Although the French word meaning 'imitation' is sometimes used in the same sense as *pasticcio*, it should strictly be applied only to a piece written in deliberate parody of another style or period, as in Prokofiev's *Classical Symphony* or Alec Templeton's *Bach Goes to Town*.

pastoral(e) A vocal or instrumental piece suggesting a countryside atmosphere (*pastor* being Latin for a shepherd), referring in particular to some seventeenth-century French operas treating rustic themes in an artificial manner. The same mood is conjured up in the depiction of shepherds at the beginning of the second part of Bach's *Christmas Oratorio*, the *Pastoral Symphony* in Handel's *Messiah*, Beethoven's bucolic *Pastoral Symphony*, and Vaughan Williams's *Pastoral Symphony*.

Patti, Adelina (1843–1919) Italian soprano. Her father, an impresario, took his wife and child to New York in 1846, where Adelina became a singing prodigy. Here she made her concert début in 1850 and her operatic début in 1859 in *Lucia di Lammermoor*. She met with great enthusiasm in London, was the first to sing Verdi's *Aida* there, and after tours of America and Europe became the highest-paid singer of her time. Famously self-willed and demanding, she was described by the critic Hanslick as 'half timid and half wild, what the French call *sauvage*', but was praised by Bernard Shaw for her 'beauty and delicacy of surface, and her exquisite touch and diction'. In 1905, after much persuasion, she allowed gramophone records to be made of her singing in a castle she had bought in Wales, to which she retired permanently a couple of years later, apart from one charity performance for the Red Cross at the beginning of World War I.

pause *See* **fermata**.

pavan(e) A stately dance sometimes shown as *padovano*, meaning 'from Padua' in northern Italy, originating in the early sixteenth century and taken up in fashionable circles, where its mannered steps and ceremonial bowing appealed to those reluctant to hop and skip about too vigorously. Its steady 2/2 or 4/4 pace and grave, rather hymnlike melody were usually followed by a faster *galliard*, a conjunction from which the *suite* later developed. Byrd and Dowland wrote some popular pavans, but after their time the form fell into disuse until it was revived in France by Fauré, and by Ravel in his *Pavane pour une infante défunte* (*Pavan for a dead Princess*).

Pavarotti, Luciano (1935–) Italian tenor. He won an international competition at Reggio Emilia in 1961 and made his operatic début there that same year in *La Bohème*. In 1964 he made his sole appearance at Glyndebourne in Mozart's *Idomeneo*, a performance fortunately captured on record. After successes at Covent Garden he toured Australia with Joan Sutherland and appeared at

A portrait by James Sant, *c.*1885, of Adelina Patti, the preservation of whose Welsh castle and its possible use for opera seasons became the subject of controversy in the 1980s.

Luciano Pavarotti with Joan Sutherland in Donizetti's *The Daughter of the Regiment* at Covent Garden, London.

La Scala, Milan, and at the New York Met in 1968. During the 1980s he devoted an increasing amount of time to concert appearances.

Pears, (Sir) Peter (1910–86) English tenor. He studied as an organist and was musical director in a school before taking up a singing career. For years he was the close companion of Benjamin Britten, sang in the USA with him, and back in Britain became the first and most compelling interpreter of the title rôle in *Peter Grimes*. Many of Britten's works were written specifically for him, including the *Seven Sonnets of Michelangelo* and the part of Aschenbach in *Death in Venice*, with which he made his New York Met début in 1974. Together they founded the Aldeburgh Festival.

pedal A lever operated by the feet on the organ and other keyboard instruments to control stops or octave couplers, and to damp or sustain notes on the piano; also for use with the modern orchestral harp and with pedal timpani. Because of the effect created by sustaining a low note on an organ pedal, the term *pedal point* has come to be used for any deep note held while the harmony or polyphony above it alters (as at the end of many Bach fugues), and for the lowest tone of a harmonic series, especially the fundamental note of a brass instrument. When a sustained note is used in a register other than the bass, it is called an *inverted pedal*.

Penderecki, Krzysztof (1933–) Polish composer. He studied at Kraków Conservatory and later became a teacher and then director there. His own compositions attracted international attention with their avante-garde use of natural sounds such as sawing wood, allied with a variety of percussive effects and adventurous use of shrill, explosive choral and instrumental possibilities. Deeply religious, he sought to express his beliefs and aspirations first through serialism, then through these unorthodox scorings, without ever losing the emotional and moral commitment which eventually led to his major choral works.

In 1960 he wrote an orchestral *Threnody for the Victims of Hiroshima*. Commissioned by West German Radio, his *St Luke Passion* startled yet entranced its first audience in Münster Cathedral in 1966. Later he became less extreme in his orchestral methods, and worked for some years on a more accessible, painfully intense composition prompted by events in his homeland. The *Polish Requiem*, performed complete in London in 1987, was created over a long, emotionally exhausting period from a number of elements. It began in 1980 with a setting of *Lacrimosa* commissioned by the Solidarity trade union in memory of Gdansk shipyard workers killed ten years before. The following year Penderecki added an unaccompanied *Agnus Dei* prompted by the death of Cardinal Wyszynski; then the *Recordare* for the canonization of Maximilian Kolbe, and a terrifying *Dies Irae* on the fortieth anniversary of the Warsaw ghetto uprising. A number of other sections from other works have been integrated with the main parts of the *Requiem*, all in far from mute protest at the imposition of martial law on the composer's country: 'In Poland,' he told an American interviewer, 'liturgical music is not only an expression of religion: it's a way for composers to show which side they are on.'

OTHER WORKS: Opera *The Devils of Loudun*. Vocal and orchestral *Dimensions of Time and Silence*. *Strophes* for soprano, narrator and ten instruments. Orchestral *Pittsburgh Overture*. Two symphonies. Two violin concertos. *Psalmus* for tape.

penillion A form of traditional Welsh singing in which words and melody, frequently improvised, are sung as a sort of descant against a harp accompaniment usually based on a well-known tune.

pentatonic scale A scale of five notes, known in folk music from the Far East to Scotland and in American folksong. Some Gregorian chant is mainly pentatonic, and the distinctive sound was revived by more recent composers such as Puccini, Debussy and Ravel. Although it can be used by removing the minor seconds from any modern scale, it is most easily comprehended by playing the five black notes on a piano keyboard.

Pepusch, Johann Christoph (1667–1752) German composer and violinist. At the age of fourteen he was appointed to the Prussian Court, but later emigrated first to Holland and then to England, where he spent the rest of his life. He played in theatre orchestras, served for some years as organist and composer to the Duke of Chandos, and wrote a wide range of competent if ephemeral incidental music and individual items for *pasticcio* operas and masques. His most considerable achievement was the arrangement of popular tunes and the composition of the overture for John Gay's *The Beggar's Opera* in 1728 and for its less successful sequel, *Polly*.

percussion See **The Orchestra and its Instruments**.

perfect See *under* **cadence** and **interval**; for **perfect pitch** *see* **absolute pitch**.

Pergolesi, Giovanni Battista (1710–36) Italian composer. In 1731 he composed his first comic opera, and two years later another one of which all that is remembered is the intermezzo *La serva padrona* (*The Maid as Mistress*). After disappointments with other stage works he determined to devote himself to religious works, having been appointed organist at the Neapolitan royal chapel, but succumbed to tuberculosis. Several of his pieces were adapted by Stravinsky for use in the ballet *Pulcinella*.

Perlman, Itzhak (1945–) Israeli violinist. He studied in Tel Aviv and New York, and at the age of ten gave a recital on American radio. He has appeared with leading international orchestras, recorded all the great concertos and some finely balanced solo recitals, and made a particular name in chamber groups. Because of the effects of polio he has to remain seated while playing.

perpetuum mobile The Latin phrase often appears in the Italian version, *moto perpetuo*. Meaning 'perpetual motion', it is applied to a piece moving along in swift, repetitive figurations, usually for virtuoso soloist, though Johann Strauss wrote a popular *Perpetuum mobile* for full orchestra. Poulenc composed a sparkling set of *Mouvements perpetuels* for piano.

Peters, Carl (1779–1827) German music publisher. He took over an existing business and was the first to publish complete editions of Bach and Haydn. After his death his name became associated with the 'Peters editions' of inexpensive scores, while the firm's list of musicians grew to include Brahms, Wagner, and others. A subsidiary opened in London just before World War II, and another in New York in 1948, publishing the works of major American composers.

Pfitzner, Hans (1869–1949) German composer and conductor. Although little played outside Germany, Pfitzner's music has long been regarded there and in Austria as comparable with that of Richard Strauss. His grandfather and father were professional musicians, and the boy studied in Frankfurt, became a piano teacher and conductor, and composed a number of operas. Of these, his greatest achievement was *Palestrina*, which he described as 'a musical legend'. This was written during World War I around the story behind Palestrina's supposed defence of polyphony in his *Missa Papae Marcellae*. It is a profoundly felt didactic work in austere, reticent style, conservative yet thoroughly individual, as are his fine *lieder*, of which he wrote more than ninety.

After the war Pfitzner became professor of composition in Berlin and then in Munich. His loyalty to nineteenth-century Romantic traditions and his outspoken denunciations of Schoenberg and his school, and even of Richard Strauss, won him for a while the approval of the Nazis, which may have been a factor in the decline in his reputation after World War II – though he himself disapproved of the Hitler régime. Shortly after the end of that war he was found destitute in Munich, but was adopted as a pensioner by the Vienna Philharmonic Orchestra, and at his death was buried under their auspices in the Vienna Zentralfriedhof.

OTHER WORKS: Opera *Das Herz* (*The Heart*). Cantata *Von Deutscher Seele* (*From the German Soul*). Three symphonies. Violin concerto. Two cello concertos. Three string quartets. Piano quintet.

philharmonic The word means 'music-loving', whether applied to a person or to an organization. Its frequent use for Philharmonic Orchestras and Philharmonic Halls derives from the foundation, early in the nineteenth century, of Philharmonic Societies for the enjoyment and propagation of good music.

phrase and **phrasing** A phrase in music has similar features to a phrase in speech and writing. It consists of a small number of notes which make a clear thematic statement, either self-contained in a short space or capable of leading on to another short phrase. Juxtaposition or variation of phrases can enrich a composition with an interplay of regularity and irregularity, question and answer, and skilfully calculated conflict.

Phrasing is the technique of playing a written work according to the composer's instructions, allied to the performer's own technical and interpretative capabilities in fingering, dynamics and expression.

pianoforte *See* **Keyboard Instruments**.

Piatigorsky, Gregor (1903–76) Russian cellist (American citizen 1942). He studied in Moscow and became principal cellist in the opera orchestra there before joining the Berlin Philharmonic Orchestra. He made an international reputation with chamber groups and as a soloist, first appearing in the USA in 1929. William Walton's cello concerto was dedicated to him.

pibroch *See* **bagpipe**.

Pijper, Willem 1894–1947) Dutch composer. He studied in Utrecht and became a music critic there before taking up teaching posts for twelve years in Amsterdam and then seventeen years in Rotterdam. He devised a method of developing whole movements and even complete works out of cells of three or four notes. Among his works are three symphonies, six 'Symphonic Epigrams' for orchestra, and an opera, *Halewijn*.

piston A valve in brass instruments, with holes bored through it to control entry of air into the tubing of cornet, trumpet, horn, etc. It was intro-duced early in the nineteenth century to enable chromatic passages to be played instead of merely the natural harmonics.

Piston, Walter (1894–1976) American composer. He studied at Harvard and then in Paris with Nadia Boulanger and Paul Dukas, returning to Harvard to join the music faculty, where he became assistant professor in 1932 and professor in 1938. Among his pupils were Elliot Carter and Leonard Bernstein. He has written textbooks on harmony, counterpoint, and orchestration. Among his own compositions, largely in an easygoing neo-classical vein, are eight symphonies, five string quartets, and *Three New England Sketches* for orchestra.

pitch The height or depth of a sound, i.e. its pitch, is determined by the frequency with which the string, reed or metal tubing of an instrument, or the tone of a human voice, vibrates: the faster the vibration, the higher the pitch. The A above middle C has been established as the basis for instrumental tuning. After many variations this was set at 'concert pitch' of 440 vibrations a second. Choirs are often given the note by a *pitch pipe*, but a more accurate method is provided by a *tuning fork*. (*See also* **absolute pitch**.)

Pizzetti, Ildebrando (1880–1968) Italian composer. Son of a piano teacher, he studied in Parma and taught there before becoming director of the Cherubini Institute in Florence and later of Milan Conservatory, and, between 1936 and 1958, professor of composition at the Academy of St Cecilia in Rome as Respighi's successor. His main interests were shared between Renaissance music and the theories of his contemporaries such as Malipiero and Casella; but he forged his own style from a return to religious forms, contrasted with dramatic incidental music for plays by the flamboyant poet Gabriele d'Annunzio. In 1957 he wrote an opera *L'Assassinio nella cattedrale* based on T.S. Eliot's verse play *Murder in the Cathedral*.

OTHER WORKS: Operas *Fedra*, *Ifigenia*. Orchestral *Preludio a un altro giorno* (*Prelude to Another Day*). *Requiem* and *De profundis* for unaccompanied voices. Songs and chamber music.

plainchant (or **plainsong**) Medieval church music consisted of a single line of vocally intoned unison themes, derived from Jewish and Greek sources, without harmonization or instrumental accompaniment. It had no set rhythm other than that of the words sung, and interpretations varied from one ecclesiastical establishment to another until in the sixth century Pope Gregory codified the variants into a standard usage known as Gregorian chant. These were based on *modes* which eventually proved inadequate to cope with the growth of elaborate polyphony and harmony.

Playford, John (1623–86) English music collector and publisher. Born in the county of Norfolk, he went to London in his mid-twenties and two years later published *The English Dancing Master*, a collection of rural airs for the violin. Many came from his own part of the country, others are identifiably Scottish, quite probably carried to London when King James VI's royal household moved from Edinburgh upon his becoming King James I of England. A number of pieces from the collection have been arranged in this century by Herbert Howells.

plectrum A small pick made of quill, tortoiseshell or metal, held between thumb and finger to pluck the strings of instruments such as the lyre, lute, or guitar. In instruments of the harpsichord family it is mounted on a jack operated by the keyboard action.

Pleyel, Ignaz (1757–1831) Austrian composer and piano manufacturer. Haydn's favourite pupil, he was invited years later to set up in opposition to his old master in London performances, but the two men remained on terms too mutually affectionate to be ruined by contrived rivalry. Pleyel composed twenty-nine symphonies and forty-five string quartets which played almost as formative a part in the development of those media as Haydn's work had done; but he was perhaps even more influential as a craftsman after the foundation of his piano factory in Paris in 1807. The firm still survives, and it was to them that Wanda Landowska turned early this century when she sought a reconstructed harpsichord 'approaching as closely those of the middle eighteenth century when they had reached the height of their glory': with the help of their chief engineer she was able to introduce her Pleyel model at a Bach festival in Breslau in 1912.

pluralism The use of differing styles, and even different keys and rhythms, within one piece, sometimes at one and the same time, rather like a musical collage.

polka A Bohemian round dance in 2/4 time which became fashionable in European ballrooms in the first half of the nineteenth century. It was used invigoratingly in Smetana's opera *The Bartered Bride*. During World War II a popular song from its homeland, invaded by the Nazis in 1939, was *The Beer Barrel Polka*.

polonaise The French name (in Italian, *polacca*) for a stately Polish dance in 3/4 time with a processional, marching character to it. Each section ends on a feminine cadence. The form has been known since the sixteenth century and appears in the music of Mozart and Schubert, but is generally associated with the patriotic, emotional treatment bestowed on it by Chopin.

polyphony From the Greek for 'many sounds', the word refers to music of more than one part, in the sense of separate interweaving strands (as in a Bach fugue or a Palestrina motet) rather than one melody with harmonic accompaniment. It might almost be taken to define sets of simultaneous individual monophonies, and several modern composers have theorized along such lines, as in Boulez's *Polpyphonie X*. (*See also* **counterpoint**.)

polyrhythm The word is virtually synonymous with *polymetre*, meaning a number of different rhythms operating simultaneously. These appear frequently in modern compositions, including Stockhausen's *Gruppen*, but one of the most remarkable examples must still be that of the three cross-rhythms played by three separate orchestras in the Act I finale of Mozart's *Don Giovanni*.

polytonality If two keys are used simultaneously, this is known as *bitonality*. More than two key signatures take us into the realm of polytonality, little used before the twentieth century, and then with rather awkward results, since the ear finds it difficult to disentangle such collisions, even in the skilful hands of Stravinsky and Milhaud.

Ponchielli, Amilcare (1834–86) Italian composer. He grew up in near-poverty as the son of a small shopkeeper in Cremona, but managed to gain entry to the Milan Conservatoire at the age of nine. He found an organ post in his home town, and in 1856 won local acclaim for his first opera, *I promessi sposi* (*The Betrothed*). Later, working as a bandmaster, he wrote other operas and ballets to produce a reasonable income, but his name is linked with only one lasting success, *La Gioconda* (*The Joyful Girl*), first staged at La Scala, Milan, in 1876. For the final years of his life he lived in comfort on its proceeds and as professor of composition at the Milan Conservatoire.

Pons, Lily (1898–1976) French soprano (American citizen 1940). She studied in Paris and made her operatic début in Mulhouse before being invited to the New York Met, where she appeared first as *Lucia di Lammermoor* in 1931, singing coloratura rôles regularly until 1959, and appearing in several films.

pop music So-called Popular Concerts of light classical and operetta music were a feature of London life from the middle of the nineteenth century onwards, echoed in the USA from 1930 with the Boston 'Pops' concerts. In the second half of the twentieth century the word 'pop' has come to be associated with the electronically assisted performances of 'groups' and solo vocalists such as The Beatles, The Rolling Stones and Shirley Bassey. Devotees make angry distinctions between pop, rock and roll, punk, and other passing phases.

portamento The Italian word for 'carrying' implies a smooth, *legato* vocal or instrumental glide from one note to another in a phrase, in effect briefly sounding all the microtones in between. If exaggerated it is liable to be denounced by critics as *scooping*. Two other Italian words, *portando* and *portato*, and the French *port de voix* have the same meaning.

Porter, Cole (1893–1964) American composer and lyricist. The heir of a rich timber merchant, Porter began writing songs when he was ten, and his mother paid to have one of them, *The Bobolink Waltz*, published. He went on to become one of the twentieth century's most popular writers of sophisticated songs with witty or bitter-sweet lyrics, and contributed to many Broadway shows and films. During a world cruise he was inspired by native music to write one of his most memorable hits, *Begin the Beguine*. In 1937 he fell from a horse and broke his legs in so many places that he was in constant pain for the rest of his life; but shortly after the accident he was at work on other shows, one of them including the song *My Heart Belongs to Daddy*. He turned Shakespeare's *The Taming of the Shrew* into the successful musical *Kiss Me Kate*, which ran for over a thousand performances on Broadway. In 1958 his right leg had to be amputated, after which he found it impossible to continue composing.

position The word has three musical connotations. On a stringed instrument, the fingers of the player's left hand choose certain positions to produce the required notes: on a violin, 'first position' is the one closest to the tuning pegs, the others moving successively further away; on a trombone, 'first position' is when the slide is least extended. The layout of a chord is also defined in this way: when the tonic of a triad is at the bottom, the chord is said to be in 'root position' as distinct from one of its possible inversions.

posthorn An early brass instrument more like a bugle than a horn, without valves and so capable

A charcoal drawing by Soss Melik in 1953 of Cole Porter with his piano score of *Kiss Me, Kate*.

The French composer Poulenc *(right)* with Lennox Berkeley at the centenary celebrations of the foundation of J. & W. Chester Ltd, the London music publishers specializing in Russian and contemporary foreign composers.

of producing only natural harmonics. The name derives from its use by mail coach guards to announce their approach. Mozart used two in his *German Dances*, and a brass band showpiece is the *Posthorn Gallop* composed by a nineteenth-century cornet-player.

postlude A small addition at the end of a work or performance, as with church organ music played while the congregation is leaving. It is the opposite of a *prelude*.

pot-pourri The French 'rotton pot', usually applied to a mixture of dried flower petals and spices, refers in a musical context to a medley of tunes from popular musical shows or other sources, loosely strung together without any further melodic, harmonic or contrapuntal development.

Poulenc, Francis (1899–1963) French composer and pianist. His mother taught him to play the piano at an early age, and he later studied composition with Koechlin. Influenced for a while by Stravinsky, he was drawn into the company of other forward-looking young composers in the group known as *Les Six*. He soon developed a distinctive 'tone of voice' and throughout all his working life displayed a suave, semi-classical elegance, from his witty transmutations of Paris street and music-hall songs into settings such as *Cocardes* (*Cockades*) to the devout limpidity of his later religious works.

In 1923 he used jazz and other jokey elements in a ballet, *Les Biches* (*The Hinds*), commissioned by Diaghilev. His three operas are in three different moods: the comedy *Les Mamelles de Tirésias* (*The Breasts of Tiresias*), the religious drama *Les Dialogues des Carmélites* (*The Dialogues of the Carmelites*), and the one-act tragic monodrama based on Cocteau's *La Voix humaine* (*The Human Voice*).

Marked changes in his mood, if not in his always tuneful style, are apparent from 1935 onwards, when he both returned to his Catholic faith and began a long association with the baritone Pierre Bernac. For Bernac he wrote most of his exquisite songs, and accompanied him at recitals and on record. In the song cycle *Tel jour, telle nuit* (*Such a day, such a night*) Poulenc, as in other works, produced not merely a sequence of flawless pieces but made a balanced whole from them: 'In my estimation a song in a cycle must have a special colour and architecture,' he explained. 'That is why I have opened and closed *Tel jour, telle nuit* with two songs in similar keys and *tempi*.'

OTHER WORKS: Orchestral *Sinfonietta*. *Concert champêtre* for harpsichord or piano and orchestra. Oboe sonata. Clarinet sonata. Piano *Three mouvements perpetuels*. Choral motets and songs.

Praetorius A Latin version of their name adopted in the sixteenth and seventeenth centuries by a number of German musicians originally called Schulz, Schultz or Schultze, though only two were of the same family. One of the most distinguished was Michael Praetorius (1571–1621), organist and later music director to the Duke of Brunswick. He wrote a comprehensive treatise on music and instruments entitled *Syntagma musicum*, and composed several volumes of Latin and German sacred and secular songs.

prelude A piece preceding some other musical form such as a fugue, an act of an opera (e.g. *Lohengrin*), or the movements of a suite. The name has also been given to piano pieces by Chopin and Debussy. Liszt's symphonic poem *Les Préludes* is so called because, he wrote, life itself is only a series of preludes to the after-life.

prepared piano The composer John Cage was the first to seek ways of producing eccentric tone colours from a piano by 'preparing' it with bolts, screws, and pieces of cardboard inserted between the strings. His *Second Construction* and the piano concerto of 1951 were both conceived for such an instrument.

Previn, André (1929–) German pianist and conductor (American citizen 1943). Educated in Berlin and Paris, he became an influential jazz pianist and composer/arranger of many film scores in Hollywood. Between 1968 and 1979 he was conductor of the London Symphony Orchestra and, settling in England, became a keen protagonist of English music and a fluent communicator in a series of television programmes. In 1978 he and playwright Tom Stoppard collaborated on a piece for actors and orchestra, *Every Good Boy Deserves Favour* (a familiar mnemonic for the lines of the treble stave, E-G-B-D-F), revived in 1987. During the late 1980s Previn began dividing his time between conductorship of the Los Angeles Philharmonic and Royal Philharmonic Orchestras, still anxious to introduce new music and revalue the old: 'There's a great well of little-known scores out there waiting to be tapped.'

prima, primo Feminine and masculine of the Italian 'first'. The *prima donna* was originally the 'first lady' in an opera, but the word has acquired a more general application in referring to any famous woman singer. The male equivalent is *primo uomo*. To define the leading lady in the original sense the word 'absolute' is added to make the phrase *prima donna assoluta*; in the case of a ballet dancer this becomes *prima ballerina assoluta*.

On the music for piano duets the word *primo* refers to the upper part. On all scores *come prima* means 'as at first'; *prima volta* is a direction for a 'first time' repeat of a passage before leading on via a *seconda volta* to a fresh subject, or a final bar.

Prix de Rome From 1803 until 1968 the Institut de France awarded annual prizes to composition students at the Paris Conservatoire, the *Grand Prix de Rome* paying for a four-year spell of study in Rome, the second prize being a gold medal. Well-known winners included Berlioz, Bizet and Debussy. An American *Prix de Rome* was established in 1905. Since 1968 the French system has altered, and the opportunity to study in Rome is based on teachers' recommendations.

programme music Instrumental or orchestral music written to illustrate or suggest a pictorial, literary or dramatic mood or story rather than as music pure and simple. Romanticism in the nineteenth century led to the composing of many such evocative pieces, including Tchaikovsky's *1812 Overture*, Smetana's *Má Vlast* suite, and Liszt's *Mazeppa*. The tone poems of Sibelius and pieces by many composers designated 'symphonic poems' all have what might be called a programme.

progression The logical movement of one note to another or one chord to another.

progressive tonality Both Mahler and Carl Nielsen were fond of starting a work in one key and evolving it through shifting harmonic relationships until the ultimate 'right' key was established at the end of the work. Nielsen's *Inextinguishable* symphony is an outstanding example.

Prokofiev, Sergey (1891–1953) Russian composer and pianist. His father was a well-to-do businessman and his mother a gifted amateur pianist who taught him to play and encouraged him to compose. At thirteen he entered the St Petersburg Conservatory and studied with Rimsky-Korsakov and Lyadov. His first two piano concertos provoked simultaneous admiration and shock, intro-

A sketch by Natslie Gontschardwa of Serge Prokofiev, about 1915, before the Russian Revolution unsettled both his life and his work.

ducing as they did strange dissonances, wild melodic leaps, and ferocious rhythms. In 1914 he was asked by Diaghilev for a ballet score, but World War I interrupted their possible collaboration, and all that remains of the music is the *Scythian Suite*, even more aggressive than the previous works. Yet in 1917 Prokofiev chose to turn back, briefly, to an earlier world and compose his scintillating pastiche of Haydn, the *Classical Symphony*.

In May 1918 Prokofiev made a tour of the USA, meeting with great enthusiasm for his piano virtuosity but equally great antagonism to the eccentricities of his own compositions. The Chicago Opera commissioned an opera, *The Love for Three Oranges*, which was poorly received. The composer returned to Europe and settled in Paris, renewed his acquaintance with Diaghilev, and wrote three ballets for him. For a while he was happy to assimilate French influences and convert them to his own wry, adventurous style; but in spite of the existence of a Bolshevist régime in Russia he began to long for his homeland, and finally returned there in 1933.

Although no 'social realist', Prokofiev found himself able to work in many approved genres without sacrificing his individuality. He wrote a number of brilliant film scores, including that for *Alexander Nevsky*, orchestral and piano works as astringent yet lyrical as ever, and the ballet music for *Romeo and Juliet*. But in 1948, like so many of his colleagues, he was condemned for 'formalism' and had to write a grovelling letter confessing to sinful deviations. In 1951, back in favour, he was awarded the Stalin Prize, but wrote little more in the last two years of his life.

OTHER WORKS: Opera *War and Peace*. Seven symphonies. Five piano concertos. Two violin concertos. Ten piano sonatas.

promenade concerts Theoretically listeners should be able to stroll about at promenade concerts while the music is being played, but the phrase has come to mean a concert where part of the audience, having paid for the cheapest tickets, can stand or lounge. Various promoters organized seasons of such concerts in London from 1838 onwards, but the name is nowadays associated with the 'Proms' which began under Henry Wood at the Queen's Hall in 1895. The BBC sponsored them from 1927 onwards. With the destruction of the Queen's Hall by bombs during World War II, the venue shifted to the Royal Albert Hall. 'The Last Night of the Proms', during the conclusion of which the audience stamp in tempo and join in choruses, has become a traditional jollification not merely in the Hall but on television.

The handwritten score of a sixteenth-century setting by Roland de Lassus (Orlando di Lasso) of the psalm *Miserere mei*.

psalm and **psalmody** Psalms are sung in Roman Catholic and Anglican church services, the words generally taken from the Book of Psalms in the Old Testament; in the former the music is in plainsong form, in the latter it consists of chants. Verse adaptations of the original texts are known as *metrical psalms*. Many composers have used the form for choral and concert works. *Psalmody* is the action of singing psalms or the arranging of the words and music for such singing.

psaltery A medieval instrument like a dulcimer, with strings stretched across a triangular board and played with fingers or plectrum.

Puccini, Giacomo (1858–1924) Italian composer. He and his brother, a singing teacher, belonged to the fifth generation of a family of church musicians. The fifth of seven children, Giacomo was expected to continue the tradition but became entranced instead with opera. He studied in Lucca and Milan, where his talents came to the attention of the publisher Ricordi, who commissioned an opera, *Edgar*. This was a failure; but the next work, *Manon Lescaut*, was an immense success and won for Puccini an international reputation.

(Right) The cover of Ricordi's edition, 1896, of Puccini's opera *La Bohème*.

His gift for melting, melodious vocal writing contrasting with fiery dramatic outbursts to bring out the true human nature of his characters, his intuitive stage sense, and his brilliant handling of orchestration made him the true successor to Verdi, though speaking in a thoroughly modern idiom. The three operas following his first success became, and have remained, standard works in the repertory of almost every opera house in the world: *La Bohème*, *Tosca*, and *Madama Butterfly*; yet on first hearing the critics and audience were disturbed by the naturalistic conversational style of *La Bohème* and the impressionism of the orchestral scoring. It also caused distress to the composer Leoncavallo, for quite another reason. He had been working on the same subject, but his finished work was staged after Puccini's, and in spite of the presence in the cast of the remarkable young Enrico Caruso it soon faded from public notice.

Puccini's final opera, the exotic, erotic, sadistic fable of the eastern princess *Turandot*, remained unfinished at his death. The last two scenes were completed by Franco Alfano from sketches the composer had left. Conducting the première at La Scala, Milan, Toscanini laid down his baton at the point where, he announced, 'Giacomo Puccini broke off his work. Death was stronger than art.' The next evening the opera was performed with Alfano's ending.

Purcell, Henry (1659–95) English composer. He became a boy chorister in the Chapel Royal and, in 1677, composer to the string orchestra. Two years later he was appointed organist at Westminster Abbey. As well as composing for religious

A chalk drawing by John Closterman of Henry Purcell in 1695.

and formal occasions such as the birthdays and funeral of Queen Mary, and the glowing *Ode on St Cecilia's Day*, he poured out chamber music, harpsichord suites, and incidental music for the theatre. In 1689 he wrote an 'entertainment' for a young gentlewomen's boarding school in Chelsea, with libretto by Nahum Tate, which as *Dido and Aeneas* became the first tentative opera in England. Other stage presentations were masques rather than true opera, but were filled with colourful melodies woven around popular themes: *King Arthur*, *The Fairy Queen*, and *The Tempest*.

Purcell composed music for two coronations, those of James II and William III. He had an unmatchable gift for blending words and music in perfect accord, from ditties for a glee club to the most magnificent of anthems. His songs *Nymphs and Shepherds* and *Music for a While* were only two among a great treasury of sometimes simple, sometimes elaborately ornamented pieces. In his works for string ensembles he loved to build the most complex variations upon a ground bass in chaconne form, but was equally adept at producing lilting dance tunes and rousing marches, including the 'New Irish Tune', *Lilliburlero*. At his death he was buried in Westminster Abbey to the sound of the funeral music he himself had written for Queen Mary.

OTHER WORKS: Choral *Come ye sons of art*, *Magnificat*, *Te Deum*. Instrumental *Fantasias*, Twelve three-part sonatas, Ten four-part sonatos. Keyboard *Musick's Handmaid*. Organ voluntaries.

Q

quadrille A square dance popular in France early in the nineteenth century, involving five successive sections calling for different figures and different music, usually taken from popular tunes of the day, the rhythm switching between 2/4 and 6/8.

Quantz, Johann Joachim (1697–1773) German composer and flautist. From an early age he was a versatile instrumentalist, playing the double bass at the age of eight, becoming oboist in the orchestra of the King of Poland, and then studying the flute. In 1728 he became teacher of the flute to Crown Prince Frederick of Prussia, later King Frederick II, and in due course became his Court musician at Berlin. Quantz made technical improvements to the flute and wrote more than three hundred concertos and two hundred smaller pieces for the instrument.

quartet A piece for four singers or instrumentalists, or for a group of four performing such a piece. The string quartet, scored for two violins, viola and cello, has been the form of chamber music most favoured by composers since the middle of the eighteenth century. It generally consisted of four separate movements, similar to those of a symphony; and in fact many quartets were written in such a way that they could be played not merely on their own but with supplementary strings and the addition of whatever woodwind and brass instruments were available.

Haydn was the major creative influence in quartet writing. His early works gave prominence to the first violin, which carried all the main melodies above an accompaniment by the other three instruments. Later the lower parts were given more to do, and in the works of Mozart, Beethoven and their successors were treated as equal partners.

Quartets have been written for other combinations of instruments, or for one other instrument together with strings. A so-called piano quartet is a piece for piano and, usually, one violin, viola and cello. Similarly Mozart wrote an oboe quartet and four flute quartets. Other mixtures have been explored by, e.g., Webern with his quartet for piano, violin, clarinet and saxophone, and Messiaen with his *Quatuor pour la fin du temps* (*Quartet for the End of Time*), for clarinet, violin, cello and piano.

Among regular ensembles taking the name have been the Amadeus Quartet, the Budapest Quartet, the Juilliard Quartet, and jazz 'chamber groups' such as the Benny Goodman Quartet.

quickstep A popular dance tempo before, during and for some years after World War II, being basically a faster version of the foxtrot.

Quilter, Roger (1877–1953) English composer. He studied in Frankfurt and became associated with the setting of verse by Shakespeare, Herrick, Tennyson and others, writing in all about a hundred charming, melodious songs. He composed a radio opera *The Blue Boar* and incidental music for the children's fairy-tale play *Where the Rainbow Ends*. His only orchestral work played at all frequently is the *Children's Overture*.

quintet As with the *quartet*, this defines a number of singers or instrumentalists. The string quintet usually consists of the four instruments of the quartet plus another viola, but some composers have preferred the addition of a second cello. Many works have been written for a wind instrument together with string quartet, such as the Mozart and Brahms clarinet quintets; and among composers producing quintets purely for mixed wind instruments have been Elgar, Carl Nielsen, Milhaud and Hindemith.

quodlibet From the Latin 'as it pleases', the term refers to a composition including a number of familiar tunes interwoven polyphonically, most famously at the end of Bach's *Goldberg Variations*, where two popular songs of his day interlock in playful inversions and imitations.

R

Rachmaninov, Sergey (1873–1943) Russian composer and pianist (American citizen 1943). His land-owning family was beginning to fall on hard times during the boy's childhood, and by the time he was nine the estate was sold off and his parents separated. Living with his mother,

Sergey Rachmaninov (properly but less commonly spelt as Rakhmaninov), whose second piano concerto became so popular that players refer to it casually as 'Rack Two'.

brothers and sisters, he managed to gain entry to St Petersburg Conservatory on a scholarship in 1883, and two years later went to Moscow Conservatory to study piano and composition. In 1891 he completed his first piano concerto (later revised), and the following year produced one of his most celebrated piano pieces, the *Prelude in C sharp minor*, as well as winning the Great Gold Medal for an opera, *Aleko*, well received by the Moscow public.

Rachmaninov was prone to fits of depression, and after a disastrous performance of his first symphony conducted by Glazunov he abandoned composing for many months. Persuaded to take on a conducting post and then to travel to London as a piano recitalist, he was encouraged by the praises heaped on him; but it was not until after a spell of treatment by a Moscow psychologist that he returned to composing, produced his unforgettable second piano concerto, and married — with lasting happiness — Natalie Satin. In 1909 he took another concerto, his third, with him on a concert tour of the USA, and returned triumphant to Russia to become Vice-President of the Imperial Music Society and to conduct the Moscow Philharmonic Concerts until the outbreak of World War I.

When the Revolution broke out in 1917, Rachmaninov took his family on a Scandinavian tour and then, in November 1918, began a new career in the USA and on European tours, concentrating on recitals and conducting, and in due course recording many of his own works. These remained mostly in vivid romantic vein, some suffused with that melancholy which he could never quite shake off. His most powerful means of communication was the piano, to which he brought a glittering technique as a player and, as a composer, a deep understanding of its sonorities. In spite of increasing pain in the back from cancer, he continued to play during World War II, a large part of the time for war relief, but finally collapsed after a recital in Knoxville, Tennessee, in February 1943, and died in March of that year. OTHER WORKS: Opera *Francesca da Rimini*. Three symphonies. Symphonic poem *Isle of the Dead*. Piano and orchestra *Rhapsody on a Theme of Paganini*. Piano nocturnes and preludes. Songs including *To the Children*.

rāga A series of notes used in India since the fifth century, built around a system of scales in which only certain notes are used in the ascending scale, and certain others only when descending. These form the basis for melodic improvisation on instruments such as the *sitar*, according to the mood of the player or the season: many rāgas are associated with Hindu festivals and other

ceremonial occasions. The melodic lines are usually accompanied by the playing of heavily syncopated rhythms on hand drums.

Among the subjects of rāga playing and singing are seasonal Indian themes connected with Krishna and his tempting flute, more potent than that of the Pied Piper.

ragtime An early form of heavily syncopated jazz, confined for a long time to café and 'honky tonk' piano playing. Irving Berlin wrote one of his earliest successes around the idea in *Alexander's Ragtime Band*, and Stravinsky tried too earnestly to emulate the spontaneous sound in his *Ragtime* for eleven instruments. (*See* **jazz** and **Joplin, Scott**.)

Rainier, Priaulx (1903–) South African composer and violinist. After a spell in the South African College of Music she studied at the Royal Academy of Music in London and stayed on in England as a violinist and teacher, becoming between 1942 and 1959 professor of composition at the RAM. As a composer she sought a blend between African music and the influences of Stravinsky and Bartók: her *Barbaric Dance Suite* for piano owes much to these conflicting interests. She wrote with eerie, poetic conviction in the *Cycle of Declamation*, her settings of John Donne for unaccompanied solo voice.

Rameau, Jean-Philippe (1683–1764) French composer. He was the seventh of eleven children of a church organist in Dijon, and although destined for a legal career showed himself such an adept keyboard player and violinist that his father let him go off to Italy to find his own musical career. For a time he played first violin in a troupe of travelling musicians, but returned to France to become an organist in a number of churches, at none of which he seems to have stayed for very long. In 1706 he published his first volume of harpsichord pieces, and throughout his life continued to compose for the instrument in a *galant*, mannered yet always coolly intellectual style, often imitating natural phenomena or evoking pictures of birds and animals, as in *Les Tourbillons* (*Eddies*) and *La Poule* (*The Hen*). His suites were finely balanced to provide contrasts between movements: he might begin with a stately, almost processional *allemande*, and then make his way through a slow dance and a number of *danses hautes* in a frisky, leaping style which some of his contemporaries condemned as being too energetic – an accusation repeated in connection with his stage works.

In 1722 Rameau published his *Traité de l'harmonie* (*Treatise on Harmony*), explaining his views on the importance of harmonic progressions from which all melody arose. This and further theoretical works established new rules for music as it moved away from polyphony to the harmonic methods which were to condition most subsequent composition.

At the age of fifty he began to concentrate on the theatre, developing a colourful, dramatic style of French opera to rival the Italians and to break away from Lully's long-lasting influence. He won

A painting by Chardin of Rameau, here apparently playing a violin *pizzicato*, as he must often have done in youthful days when working with a troupe of wandering minstrels.

many admirers and almost as many critics with his combination of descriptive music, flowing melodic lines, lively ballets, exotic backgrounds, and daring stage and orchestral effects. Among his greatest successes were the opera-ballet *Les Indes galants*, and what he called simply *tragédies*, including *Castor et Pollux* and *Dardanus*.

Rampal, Jean-Pierre (1922–) French flautist. One of the most influential teachers of the instrument in this century, Rampal founded the French Wind Quintet and the Paris Baroque Ensemble, travelled widely as a recitalist, and has recorded many dazzling flute concertos of the Bohemian baroque era.

Rattle, Simon (1955–) English conductor. Starting as a percussion player, he later founded the Liverpool Sinfonia, conducted a number of orchestras, and with a performance of *The Rake's Progress* became the youngest conductor in the history of the Glyndebourne Festival. In 1980 he was appointed principal conductor and musical adviser to the City of Birmingham Symphony Orchestra, which soon became one of the most exciting and adventurous orchestras in Britain.

Married to the American soprano Elise Ross, he has frequently put family life in London before the opportunities of taking up tempting offers in Berlin, New York and Los Angeles.

Ravel, Maurice (1875–1937) French composer and pianist. Unlike many musicians who had to fight against parental disapproval, the young Maurice was encouraged by his father, provided with the best teachers, and sent as a harmony and piano student to the Paris Conservatoire. In 1889 he, like Debussy, was fascinated by the Javanese *gamelan* performances at the Paris World Exhibition, but his mind was always open to other influences: the music of Wagner, Satie, and Russian composers; the *Ballets Russes*; and, most markedly, Basque and Spanish melodies and rhythms perhaps inculcated in him by his Basque mother.

Ravel won no laurels at the Conservatoire, against whose academic establishment he rebelled, causing quite a public scandal in so doing. His compositions did not please the authorities; his attempts at winning the *Prix de Rome* were a failure. Yet he was establishing a reputation among his contemporaries. In one of his earliest works, the *Habañera* for two pianos, his distinctive tone of voice was already recognizable. A pastiche of the neo-classical style he favoured at one time, *Pavane pour une infante défunte* (*Pavan for a dead Infanta*), first for piano and later orchestrated by the composer, was an immediate popular success. By the early twentieth century he was composing in a fluent stream. The *Introduction and Allegro* for harp, flute, clarinet and string quartet dates from this creative period.

Further inspiration came with the arrival of Diaghilev in Paris and a commission for the ballet (or 'choreographic symphony', as Ravel described it) *Daphnis et Chloé*. He also made friends with the young Stravinsky, and in 1913 collaborated with him on a revised performing version of Mussorgsky's unfinished opera *Khovanshchina*.

During World War I, though declared unfit for military service, he managed to get taken on as a motor transport driver. In 1916 he was stricken by dysentery and sent home to Paris, only shortly before his adored mother died. Personal sadness and, from 1932 onwards, the onset of aphasia which blurred his memory and speech, darkened much of his work, but he found solace in the return to a childhood world in the opera (or 'lyrical fantasy') *L'Enfant et les sortilèges* (*The Child and the Spells*). In 1928 he made an exhausting American tour which nevertheless pleased him with its demonstration of the popularity of his music, and in that same year wrote what must

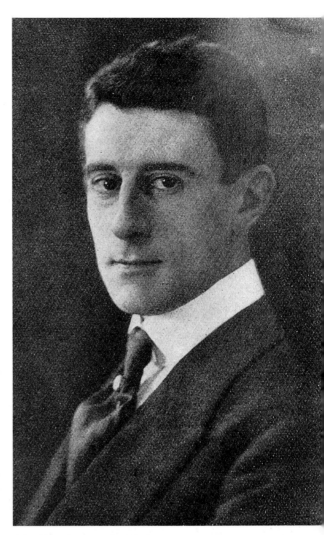

The French composer Maurice Ravel, who never married, preferring long, lonely walks at night interspersed with sessions of drinking, smoking and chatting in cafés with groups of friends.

be the most popular of all his works – the *Boléro*, composed for the ballerina Ida Rubinstein and first produced at the Paris Opéra in November 1928. Bitter memories of the war were resuscitated when he was commissioned to write a piano concerto for the left hand by Paul Wittgenstein, an Austrian pianist who had refused to abandon his career in spite of having lost his right arm on the battlefield.

Although Ravel's influence is often regarded as being much in the same vein as Debussy's impressionism, he aimed in fact at a much more self-contained, coolly technical assemblage and polishing of his ideas. Each fresh composition was a challenge which had to be solved in a different way, but solved with an inner consistency. Ravel put it austerely: 'One must spend time in eliminating all that could be regarded as superfluous in order to realize as completely as possible the definitive clarity so much desired.' He used Spanish rhythms, blues phrasing, eastern harmonies and other elements which interested him – but was not satisfied until they were integrated into his overall conception, which might have been in his mind for many months or even years. He said himself that he always needed a long period of gestation. It was difficult to communicate his own musical objectivity to others: although he assured his pupils (among whom, for a short period, was Vaughan Williams) that they should never be ashamed of imitating other composers, each of his own works was so complete in itself as to be virtually a dead end.

OTHER WORKS: Opera *L'heure espagnole* (*The Spanish Hour*). Orchestral *Rapsodie espagnole* (*Spanish Rhapsody*), *La Valse* (*The Waltz*), *Ma mère l'oye* (*Mother Goose*) – also versions for two pianos. Song cycle for voice and orchestra, *Shéhérezade*. Piano pieces *Jeux d'eau* (*Fountains*), *Gaspard de la nuit* (*Rogue of the night*), *Miroirs* (*Mirrors*).

Rawsthorne, Alan (1905–71) English composer. After a spell as a dental student, he turned to the study of piano and composition at the Royal Manchester College of Music. His own writing for the piano was lucid and immediately engaging, and in this and in symphonic and chamber music he excelled in sets of variations. The *Symphonic Studies* for orchestra are full of dance rhythms and reach a splendid climax with a skilful fugue. Fellow composers always spoke affectionately of his economy, subtlety and refinement. During World War II he served with the Royal Artillery and then with the Army Film Unit, which he found creatively fruitful. In 1954, long before the advent of a popular musical on the theme, he set a number of verses from T.S. Eliot's *Old Possum's Book of Practical Cats* for narrator and orchestra in a logical sequence, melodically and rhythmically, full of sly jokes and lyrical pleasures.

OTHER WORKS: Ballet *Madame Chrysanthème* (choreography by Frederick Ashton). Three symphonies. Two piano concertos. Three string quartets. Piano duet *The Creel*.

realize The word defines the scholarly process of filling out earlier, often only partially scored music so that it can be satisfactorily played in modern conditions. Benjamin Britten was particularly sensitive in his 'realizations' of Purcell's music.

rebec An ancient three-stringed instrument of Arab origin, shaped like a mandoline but played with a bow. After its introduction to Europe extra strings were added and different sizes were made, becoming the immediate predecessors of the viol family.

recapitulation The section in sonata form, after the exposition and development, in which the first subject returns to its original tonic key, and the second subject appears in the tonic of the dominant key.

recital The word is generally used to distinguish a performance by a soloist or small group, vocal or instrumental, from that of a large-scale orchestral or choral concert.

recitative In opera and oratorio, much of the dramatic action is carried by half-sung, declamatory exchanges between characters, or explained by a solo reciter. Even when there is some melodic content, the rise and fall of the voice and its rhythms are close to ordinary speech. There are two types of recitative: *secco* ('dry', i.e. unaccompanied or with only occasional harpsichord chords) and *accompagnato* (or *stromentato*), i.e. 'accompanied', usually by protracted string chords. Recitative in early opera generally led to a set-piece aria or chorus; but composers from Mozart onwards found ways of blending the two, so that the recitative could become more lyrical in itself and effect smooth transitions, perhaps with some dramatic flourishes in the accompaniment to underline the meaning of the scene.

recorder A woodwind instrument, ancestor of the flute but held vertically and not transversely. The sound is produced by blowing down the mouthpiece against a wooden block called a *fipple*: in German the instrument is known as a *blockflöte*. After some years of neglect, different sizes of recorders have been revived for use in schools and amateur ensembles or for authentic performances of early music. The virtuoso Michal Petri has arranged many pieces for the instrument, and in 1987 Malcolm Arnold wrote a fantasy for solo recorder specially for her.

An early alto recorder.

reed Sounds from certain woodwind instruments are produced by the vibration of cane or metal tongues, either against an air slot (when they are known as *beating reeds*) or within the slot (when they are known as *free reeds*). The clarinet and saxophone each has a single reed; the oboe and bassoon have double reeds which vibrate against each other. Free reeds are used in mouth-organs and in members of the accordion family. The *reed stops* on an organ control pipes with metal tongues to imitate woodwind sounds, also known as *lingual stops*.

reel A dance of Celtic or Scandinavian origin, in quick 2/4, 4/4 or 6/8 time divided into regular eight-bar phrases, for two or more couples. It is still popular at Irish and Scottish festivities. The American version, the *Virginia Reel*, is probably the legacy of English settlers.

refrain The burden or, in popular music, the 'chorus' of a song which is repeated after each individual verse.

regal A small portable organ of fifteenth-century origin whose beating reeds vibrated in the air that was pumped through by bellows, controlled by buttons like those on the later concertina. When hung round the neck, its bellows were operated by the player's left hand; when set on a table, it was possible to operate the bellows by foot. A *Bible regal* was one which folded up like a book and could be carried under the arm. The word is also applied to certain reed stops on a full-size organ, including the *vox humana*.

Reger, Max (1873–1916) German composer and organist. A precocious child, he became a church organist at the age of thirteen and went on to establish himself as a virtuoso recitalist and an influential composition teacher. His own works were all in conservative vein and utterly divorced from programme music: although he wrote a so-called *Romantic Suite*, two *Romances* for violin and orchestra, and over two hundred sacred and secular songs, his real commitment was to the polyphonic tradition of the past in monumental fugues and sets of variations from which he constructed free-ranging fantasias. Firm favourites among organists include the *Fantasia and Fugue on B.A.C.H.*, two organ sonatas, and a large number of chorale preludes.

OTHER WORKS: Piano concerto. Violin concerto. Orchestral *Variations and Fugue on a Theme by Beethoven*. Six string quartets. Three clarinet sonatas. Four piano sonatinas. Two organ suites.

reggae Music of Jamaican origin, mixing revival hymns with popular melodies and Rastafarian cult music to support lyrics of social comment and local or personal news, accompanied by involved drum rhythms which influenced certain jazz ensembles in the 1950s.

register and **registration** Distinctive parts of a singer's vocal ranges are referred to as the head register, chest register, etc. In the case of instruments there are varying tonal qualities between the highest and lowest notes: the mellow lower range of the clarinet, for example, is known as the *chalumeau* register. On the organ, sets of pipes controlled by particular stops are known as registers, and *registration* is the art of selecting the most appropriate ones for the piece being performed.

Reich, Steve (1936–) American composer. He studied with Milhaud and Berio, and after 1964 concentrated on experiments with tape music and with the study of gradual time changes, introducing the word *phasing* to describe the effects produced by two tape recorders getting gradually out of phase with each other. A large amount of his work has been devoted to percussion groups, as with his *Drumming* for bongos, marimbas, glockenspiels and voices, and *Music for Mallet Instruments*.

OTHER WORKS: *My Name Is* for tape recorders, performers and audience. *Phase Patterns* for electric organs.

Reicha, Antonin (1770–1836) Bohemian composer (French citizen). His uncle was musical director of the electoral court in Bonn, where young Reicha played the flute and made friends with Beethoven. He wrote a number of now forgotten operas, twenty string quartets, six quintets, and twenty-four wind quintets. In 1818 he became professor of composition at the Paris Conservatoire, numbering Liszt and Gounod among his pupils.

Reizenstein, Franz (1911–68) German composer and pianist. He studied with Hindemith in Berlin and then with Vaughan Williams in London, where he decided to settle. He taught at the Royal Academy of Music and the Royal Manchester College of Music, played in a number of chamber ensembles, and composed two radio operas, concertos for piano, violin and cello, and a great deal of chamber music.

relative Major and minor keys with the same key signature are said to be relative: e.g. a key signature of two flats establishes either B flat major or its *relative minor*, G minor; and the absence of flats or sharps indicates A minor or its *relative major*, C major.

Relative pitch refers to an individual's ability to relate one musical sound to another, though lacking *absolute pitch*, the gift of correctly identifying a single note sung or played on its own.

répétiteur A rehearsal coach in an opera house who takes singers through their parts before the conductor takes charge, and sometimes acts as prompter for those who have difficulty reading or memorizing music and words. The word is French but is used in most countries.

répétition The French word for a 'rehearsal'; the *répétition générale* is the final dress rehearsal.

reprise French for 'repeat', generally used to describe the taking up again of the first theme or whole section of a movement (especially in sonata form) after a development or different section has been completed. It can also be applied to a short section repeated at the end of variations from the original theme, and as such is frequently used in stage musicals when a chorus number is returned to.

requiem At the beginning of the Roman Catholic Mass for the Dead the words *Requiem aeternam* pray for eternal rest. Once sung entirely in plainchant, the requiem has been used more elaborately by Mozart, Berlioz and Verdi, and rhapsodically by Fauré. Benjamin Britten's *War Requiem* was virtually an oratorio, combining the Latin mass with interspersed songs based on World War I poems by Wilfred Owen.

resolution The harmonic process by which a discord resolves itself satisfactorily into a concord.

resonance All music consists of vibrations, some produced by the strings and sounding-board of, for instance, a violin, or by the interaction of a woodwind instrument and its reed; some by the acoustic qualities of a hall or studio; and some by the sympathetic resonances transmitted to reproductive apparatus through microphones or electronic equipment.

Respighi, Ottorino (1879–1936) Italian composer. He studied in Bologna and with Rimsky-Korsakov in St Petersburg after becoming first viola in the opera house there. On returning to Italy he made a living as conductor, violinist, pianist and teacher. Production of two operas led to his being offered the professorship of composition at the Conservatorio Santa Cecilia in Rome, of which he later became director.

More successful than his operas were the symphonic poems *Fontane di Roma* (*Fountains of Rome*) and *Pini di Roma* (*Pines of Rome*), with a lushness of orchestration in provocative contrast to the austere medieval influences in his *Concerto gregoriano* for violin, and the adaptation of classical lute and harpsichord pieces into the suite *The Birds*. He also adapted some of Rossini's music for a ballet, *La Boutique fantasque* (*The Fantastic Toyshop*).

rest In many vocal and instrumental parts there is a need for breathing spaces before or during certain passages; but quite apart from such practical considerations, silences between notes are an important ingredient in the composition itself. The protracted anticipatory pauses in much of Webern's work, for example, are as essential to the structure as are the pitch relations. Each length of note has an equivalent rest, of equal time value when adding up the beats in a measure. (*See also* **Notation**.)

rhapsody Originally defining an ancient Greek recitation or chanting of epic poetry, the word has been taken over to cover a wide range of music in no fixed form, often akin to a *tone poem* or *symphonic poem*, using pictorial effects or developing variations around a folk melody or other source. Liszt wrote a number of nationalistic *Hungarian Rhapsodies*, Vaughan Williams used local themes in his *Norfolk Rhapsody*, and Gershwin found the term useful in the title of his symphonic jazz fantasia, *Rhapsody in Blue*.

Rheinberger, Josef (1839–1901) German composer, conductor and organist. He studied at Munich Conservatory and from 1859 was piano professor there, with only one short break, until his death, as well as serving as a church organist and choir conductor, and for a time coaching the Court opera. He wrote a large number of operas, religious pieces and symphonic overtures, but his reputation rests on his great output of technically demanding organ music, including twenty sonatas and a large number of fughettas and other smaller pieces.

rhythm The word has come to be so loosely used in connection with jazz and modern dance music, especially in a number of song titles suggesting indiscriminate liveliness, that a formal definition is liable to be considered stuffy and academic. Nevertheless, it may be simply stated that rhythm refers to the systematic grouping of musical notes within a pattern which establishes their relationships with one another in time. Such groupings of pulses should urge the music forward at a speed which will convey the composer's wishes regarding the pace of melodic and harmonic changes. Although a preordained metre and rhythm simplify the writing of music in mathematically logical sections helpful to the performer, a true sense of the pulse can be conveyed best by a sensitive interpreter in 'free' rather than 'strict' rhythm; and the basic rhythm itself may be effectively altered by the introduction of irregular accents, and by changes of time signature. Comparatively well-disciplined metrical measures prevailed until the twentieth century, when composers dedicated to tonal dissolution have also favoured such rapid changes of time signature and such a variety of cross-rhythms that the metre has often become unstable and, to all but the most expert listener, virtually unidentifiable. (*See also* **Notation**.)

ricercare The Italian word meaning 'to research' is applied to a contrapuntal form of composition popular with composers in the sixteenth and early seventeenth centuries. It was the instrumental equivalent of a motet or madrigal, using strict fugal and canonic devices to 'search out' the possibilities of a single theme without the introduction of additional episodes. Froberger wrote a number of organ works with this title, but the best known is one from Bach's *The Musical Offering*, woven around a theme supplied to him by Frederick the Great. In modern times Norman Dello Joio has written three ricercares for piano and orchestra.

Richter, Hans (1843–1916) Austro-Hungarian conductor. He studied in Vienna and for four years worked as a horn player in a Viennese theatre. In 1866 he began working with Wagner, learned the trumpet especially to play in the private première of the *Siegfried Idyll* for Wagner's wife, and was chosen to conduct the first complete performance of the *Ring* cycle at Bayreuth. From 1877 onwards he spent a great deal of time in England, conducted the Hallé Orchestra between 1899 and 1911, and became a champion of English composers: he conducted premières of several Elgar works, and also introduced audiences in Manchester and London to the music of Bartók and Sibelius.

Richter, Sviatoslav (1914–) Russian pianist. A youthful prodigy in his homeland, he reached England and the USA in the early 1960s, distinguishing himself in interpretations of Prokofiev and, in quite different vein, recordings of Beethoven, Brahms and Schubert. He has appeared frequently at Aldeburgh Festivals with his fellow countryman, the cellist Rostropovich.

Ricordi family In 1808 Giovanni Ricordi, one of a family of Spanish origin who had settled in Italy, founded a music publishing firm in Milan which continued in the hands of his son and grandson. They published the operas of Bellini, Rossini and others, and went on to great successes with the works of Verdi and Puccini. An American branch was established in 1897.

rigaudon Known in English as a *rigadoon*, this was a lightly tripping dance originating in the Aix-en-Provence region of France, ritually performed at Corpus Christi and after the corn-threshing. In lively 2/4 or 4/4 time, beginning usually on the fourth beat of a measure with two eighth-notes (quavers), its nimble skipping movements were not unlike those of the sailors' hornpipe. Seventeenth-century composers featured it in keyboard or ensemble suites. It reappears only rarely in later times, but has been used by Prokofiev and Ravel.

Rimsky-Korsakov, Nicolay (1844–1908) Russian composer. Brought up in a musical household, he was discovered at an early stage to have perfect pitch, but there was no thought of his taking up music as a career. While training as a naval officer, however, he met Balakirev and was drawn into the activities of 'The Five' young nationalist composers. Though without formal training, and later describing himself as 'an officer-dilettante who occasionally enjoyed playing or listening to music', he composed a symphony

A sketch by Ilya Repin of Rimsky-Korsakov in 1888.

and the opera *The Maid of Pskov*, and (to his own surprise) became a professor at the St Petersburg Conservatory in 1871. He used the position to learn theory and instrumentation for himself, and from 1873 held for just over ten years an appointment as inspector of naval bands. For some time he and Mussorgsky shared lodgings and musical ideals, though Rimsky-Korsakov managed to avoid his friend's fatal drinking habits.

In his own music he revived old Russian folk themes, and combined modal and Oriental scales along with peasant dance rhythms and exotic orchestration to produce such colourful works as the symphonic poem *Sadko* and his *Russian Easter Festival Overture*. The opera *Tsar Saltan* included a piece which was to become a perennial favourite – *The Flight of the Bumblebee*. Generous in the cause of his friends, though perhaps over-zealous in altering their creative idiosyncrasies, he revised and reorchestrated works such as Borodin's *Prince Igor* and Mussorgsky's *Boris Godunov*. His own last opera, *The Golden Cockerel*, banned in his lifetime because of its undisguised satire on Tsarism and bureaucracy, was in its turn reconstituted as a ballet-with-voices in Diaghilev's *Le Coq d'or*.

OTHER WORKS: Opera *Tale of the Invisible City of Kitezh*. Three symphonies. Orchestral *Capriccio espagnol* (*Spanish Caprice*); symphonic suite *Sheherezade*. String quartet.

ripieno The name (Italian for 'supplementary') is given to passages in choral works to distinguish a small self-contained body of singers from the main choir (as in the boys' group at the beginning of Bach's *St Matthew Passion*), or – confusingly the other way round – to the main orchestra in a *concerto grosso* as opposed to the smaller *concertante* group of soloists.

ritornello A 'little return': in the case of songs (especially madrigals), the repeat of a refrain between differing verses; in an anthem or aria, the reappearance of an instrumental passage between the vocal sections; and in orchestral terms, the return of the full orchestra (*tutti*) after a solo, or the regular return of a theme in a rondo.

Robeson, Paul (1898–1976) American bass. After studying law he became an actor, but after singing *Ol' Man River* in the musical *Show Boat* and giving recitals of Negro spirituals he became in demand as a singer, appearing in several films and making a number of recordings. Popular in Britain, he fell out of favour in the USA during the 1950s because of supposed Communist sympathies.

rock Beginning in the USA in the 1950s as *rock'n'-roll*, the heavily rhythmic and electronically amplified music performed by 'groups' of vocalists and instrumentalists (usually electric guitars, drums, and electronic keyboards) was based in the main on the twelve-bar blues, with a hint of boogie-woogie in the bass. Later it was expanded to include songs of social protest in *folk rock* and increasingly fierce styles such as the anarchic *punk rock*.

Elvis Presley, 'The King' of rock, whose tomb at his Graceland home is visited annually by thousands of fans who still find it hard to believe that he is dead.

rococo Like the word *baroque*, this was originally an architectural term, in this case derived from the French *rocaille* – rock-work, as in a garden rockery. It implies ornate additions to music, delicate rather than extravagant, popular in the eighteenth century and displayed in the *galant* style of Couperin and in several works by Haydn and Mozart. The distinction between baroque and rococo might be defined as that between ornamentation which makes an integral expressive contribution to the whole structure, and ornamentation which has been added for the sheer flowery sake of it, pleasing the ear but contributing nothing to the essential underlying pattern.

Rodgers, Richard (1902–79) American composer. He studied at Columbia University and the Juilliard School. Interested from an early age in popular songs and musical shows, he met the lyricwriter Lorenz Hart and, with him, turned out a number of successful Broadway musicals including *On Your Toes* and *Babes in Arms*, and songs such as *Manhattan* and *Blue Room*. When Hart died in 1943, Rodgers went on to collaborate just as rewardingly with Oscar Hammerstein II: their *Oklahoma* and *South Pacific* both won Pulitzer Prizes, and *The King and I* and *The Sound of Music* were lasting successes both on stage and as films.

Rodrigo, Joaquin (1902–) Spanish composer. Blind since the age of three, he studied in Paris with Dukas. Most of his works are entitled *Concierto* of one kind or another, the most popular being the *Concierto de Aranjuez* for guitar and orchestra, first performed in Madrid in 1939. There are other concertos for two guitars, four guitars, harp, piano, violin, cello, and flute, and a *Fantasia para un gentilhombre* (*Fantasia for a Courtier*) for guitar and orchestra. Based on seventeenth-century courtly dances, this fantasia was written for Segovia, and was first performed in San Francisco in 1958 when Enrique Jordá was conductor of the San Francisco Symphony Orchestra. Rodrigo has said that his favourite guitar would be a 'fantastic multi-form instrument with the wings of a harp, the tail of a piano, and a soul of its own'. In 1946 he became professor of musical history at Madrid University.

romance In Italian, *romanza*; in German, *romanze*. The word, derived from medieval verse tales and songs of chivalry, became a useful term without specific musical meaning which could be bestowed by a composer on any small instrumental or orchestral piece of rhapsodic, tender or meditative nature. The slow movement of Mozart's D minor piano concerto (K466) and a movement in *Eine kleine Nachtmusik* are marked *romanze*. Schumann bestowed the title on quite a number of works for piano, women's and mixed choruses, pieces for oboe and piano, and the slow movement of his fourth symphony. Vaughan Williams's *The Lark Ascending* is described as a *Romance for violin and orchestra*.

romanticism Nineteenth-century writers and composers rebelled against the formal disciplines of classicism in prose, poetry and music, and sought for intense dramatic and pictorial expression rather than academic perfection. Although there have been romantic, rebellious elements in all periods, the *Age of Romanticism* is generally applied to the times of Schubert, Schumann, Chopin, Liszt and Berlioz, composers intent on communicating in their own emotional language. Many of them turned to romantic literature for inspiration: the novels of Sir Walter Scott and the works of Goethe provided fruitful sources, and in Germany especially there was a turning back towards mystical and supernatural themes, the culmination being Wagner's transformation of Nordic myth into the *Ring* cycle.

Romberg, Sigmund (1887–1951) Hungarian composer (American citizen). He studied in Vienna but left for the USA and settled in New York in 1913, making his name as a fluent composer of operettas. The two most successful were *The Student Prince* and *The Desert Song*, but he also showed skill as an adapter with the use of Schubert melodies in *Blossom Time*.

rondo Although this is frequently used as the last movement of a sonata or symphony, it stood for many years as a musical form on its own. Like the medieval French *rondeau*, a poem that came full circle with a last line repeating its first, the rondo relies on a theme which is interrupted by what are called episodes but which always returns to the original refrain, recognizable even if temporarily in a different key. The so-called *sonata-rondo* employed by Mozart and Beethoven fell into three distinct sections echoing the exposition-development-recapitulation layout of a sonata. Examples of a rondo can be found in the last movement of Mozart's piano sonato in D (K311), Richard Strauss's tone poem *Till Eulenspiegel*, and the closing scenes of Acts I and II of Berg's opera *Wozzeck*.

root The lowest note of a chord when that chord is in its fundamental position. In a triad of C-E-G, C is the root; and the formation is known as *root position*.

Rorem, Ned (1923–) American composer. After study in the USA, including a spell with Aaron Copland, he went to live in Morocco in 1949 and from 1951 in Paris, where he became friends with Milhaud, Auric and others and was much influenced by Poulenc's songs. In 1958 he returned to New York, and later became professor at Buffalo and Utah. He has published lively, amusing diaries of his life in Paris and New York, and also *Critical Affairs, a Composer's Journal.* Among his compositions are operas, including *Miss Julie*, three symphonies and three piano concertos, a number of song cycles and about three hundred songs for voice and piano.

Rosa, Karl (Carl) (1842–89) German conductor, violinist and impresario. He studied in Leipzig and Paris, became leader of a Hamburg orchestra, and made his British and American débuts in 1866. The following year in New York he met and married Euphrosyne Parepa, a soprano with whom he formed an opera company which they took to England. She died in 1874, but he decided to continue and established the Carl Rosa Opera Company, one of the earliest regular touring companies based in England.

Rossini, Gioacchino (1792–1868) Italian composer. His father was the town trumpeter of Pesaro and also a highly regarded singer. Although the boy was apprenticed to a blacksmith, he had managed by an early age to become a competent player of the piano, viola, and horn, as well as singing in church choirs. When his parents moved to Bologna he entered the Academy there, won a prize for counterpoint, and composed various prentice pieces including five string quartets. His bent, however, was soon shown to be for opera.

After being commissioned to write a one-act comic opera for production in Venice, he found favour with several similar pieces written to order and rushed each one out in a matter of weeks. Next he attempted a serious work, *Tancredi*, which was well received by audiences but not nearly so well as another comic opera, *L'italiana in Algeria* (*The Italian Girl in Algiers*), with its

Rossini's opera *The Barber of Seville* was composed after Mozart's *The Marriage of Figaro* but shows the same characters in earlier situations. In the first act there are many sparkling exchanges between the irrepressible Figaro and the delightfully crafty Rosina – who was to become in the sequel a more dignified, sorrowful Countess.

brisk, skittish tunes and sparkling orchestration – all the work of a twenty-one-year-old. Young Rossini was soon to take over as musical director at both opera houses in Naples, where he made his mark by providing accompanied rather than dry recitative, and in addition insisted on writing out all the ornaments for singers to follow instead of allowing them their own self-glorifying embellishments. He also began to develop what came to be known as the 'Rossini crescendo', especially in his overtures, repeating orchestral phrases with ever-increasing intensity and volume to get the audience in excited, receptive mood.

In 1816 he moved to Rome and in the same year presented there an opera composed in just under a fortnight, though making use of a lot of his earlier pieces. *Il barbiere di Siviglia* (*The Barber of Seville*) had at first a lukewarm reception from Roman audiences accustomed to a work of Paisiello's which had long been in the repertory, but in the end it was to be accepted as Rossini's finest work, a light-hearted companion piece to *The Marriage of Figaro* by Rossini's great idol, Mozart. His most characteristic arias were nearly all exacting coloratura pieces, and most of them were originally sung by the soprano Isabella Colbran, who became his mistress after being for some time the mistress of a Neapolitan impresario. He married her in 1822. Despite this his opera *Zelmira* was staged in Vienna by that same discarded lover. After Vienna, Rossini went to London, led a blithely social existence, and was reported to have sung duets with King George IV.

In 1824 he settled in Paris and became the idol of the city. To keep him in France, the government granted a substantial pension and a number of resounding musical appointments. While there he wrote a jocular little comic opera, *Le Comte Ory* (*Count Ory*), which was brilliantly revived at Sadler's Wells in London during the 1960s, and, in 1829, *Guillaume Tell* (*William Tell*), a daring change to a heroic subject after so many comic masterpieces. It was to be the last of his thirty-eight operas, although he still had just over that same number of years to live. No plausible reason has ever been offered for his subsequent silence, broken only by a couple a religious works and some small pieces which he himself disparaged as 'sins of old age'. After the 1830 Revolution he had to fight a legal battle over his pension rights, returned to Italy to become director of the Bologna Academy, left his wife for a demi-mondaine Olympe Pélissier, whom he married after Isabella's death, and returned with her to Paris in 1855. Buried there in 1868, his body was removed nineteen years later to the Santa Croce church in Florence.

OTHER WORKS: Operas *La Cenerentola* (*Cinderella*), *La gazza ladra* (*The Thieving Magpie*). Choral *Stabat Mater*. Songs, *Soirées musicales* (including *La danza*). Six string sonatas for two violins, cello and double bass. Six wind quartets.

Rostropovich, Mstislav (1927–) Russian cellist and conductor. He studied in Moscow, made his début as a cello virtuoso in 1942, and in 1960 became professor of the instrument at both Moscow and Leningrad Conservatories. He married the soprano Galina Vishnevskaya, and frequently acted as her piano accompanist in recitals at home and abroad. His support of the dissident writer Solzhenitsyn lost him the approval of the Russian authorities, and for a while he was not allowed to appear in the West. In 1974 he and his wife left the USSR and did not return, being officially deprived of their citizenship in 1978. They were friends of Benjamin Britten and appeared many times at the Aldeburgh Festival, of which Rostropovich became artistic director in 1977. In the same year he took over conductorship of the National Symphony Orchestra in Washington, USA. Prokofiev, Shostakovich and Britten all wrote works specially for him.

The Russian-born cellist Rostropovitch, who from 1974 onwards worked in the West and made a second brilliant career as a conductor.

roulade The French name for an extended vocal decorative passage, usually a fast succession of notes, and especially such a sequence sung on one syllable of the lyric.

round A dance in which the participants move in a circle, or a canonic part song whose equal sections are complete in themselves and not merely phrases. One voice starts with the first section, and as it begins the next section a second voice enters with the first section. A favourite round is *Three Blind Mice*. One of the earliest known examples is *Sumer is icumen in*, known also as the Reading Rota because, like a wheel (*rota*), its tune goes round and round.

roundelay Fourteenth-century rustic song, taking its name from the French *rondelet* which, like the *round* (*see* preceding entry), had a first section to which the singers returned repeatedly.

Roussel, Albert (1869–1937) French composer. He set out on a career as a naval officer, but in 1894 resigned his commission and began to study music in Paris, from 1898 to 1909 with Vincent d'Indy at the Schola Cantorum. His progress was such that he himself became a teacher of counterpoint there, with Satie and Varèse among his pupils. Marrying, he took his wife on a tour of India and south-east Asia, which had made a lasting impression on him during his naval service, and whose exotic influences were to show in his opera *Padmâvâti*. He served with the Red Cross during World War I, after which, broken in health, he settled into a quiet, withdrawn life in Brittany and then Normandy, composing in a neo-classical style spiced incongruously but effectively with eastern flavours, strongly rhythmic and harmonically astringent. There is a marked

difference between the impressionistic music for his pre-war ballet-pantomime *Le Festin de l'araignée* (*The Spider's Banquet*) and that for the 1930 ballet *Bacchus et Ariane* (*Bacchus and Ariadne*), suites from both of which are frequently played in concert performances. His finely wrought chamber music is particularly worthy of attention.

OTHER WORKS: Opera *La Naissance de la lyre* (*The Birth of the Lyre*). Four symphonies. Vocal and orchestral *Psalm 80. Divertissement* for piano and five wind instruments.

Royal Albert Hall A large building in South Kensington, London, erected in memory of Albert, Prince Consort, in 1871. With seating for ten thousand people, it has been the venue of prize-fights, pop concerts, conventions and wartime reunions, but is largely associated with orchestral concerts, especially the annual season of Henry Wood Promenade Concerts. Its notorious echo caused a critic to observe that this was the only place where a modern English composer could hear his work played twice; but special acoustic devices have been introduced to control this.

The Royal Albert Hall was named in honour of Queen Victoria's consort Prince Albert. His father, the Duke of Saxe-Coburg, had written comic operas, and Albert himself composed church music and songs, and was a patron of many English musical activities.

Royal Festival Hall A concert hall built on the south bank of the Thames in London, opening in 1951, the year of the Festival of Britain. The complex, incorporating a large auditorium with seats for over three thousand people and two smaller sections, the Queen Elizabeth Hall and the Purcell Room, is the main setting for orchestral concerts in London, though challenged by the more recently built Barbican closer to the heart of the City.

Rozhdestvensky, Gennady (1931–) Russian conductor. The son of a conductor, he studied in Moscow and in 1951 became assistant conductor at the Bolshoi Theatre. Later he was principal conductor there and at USSR Radio and Television. In 1973 he took the Leningrad Philharmonic Orchestra on a tour of the USA; and from 1978 he was chief conductor of the BBC Symphony Orchestra.

Rubbra, Edmund (1901–) English composer. He left school at fourteen for a job on the railway in Northampton, but hearing the music of Cyril Scott, who offered him tuition, he used his half-price employee's ticket to travel once a fortnight to London. Steeped in the joys of Tudor polyphony and modal harmony, he began composing with no heed for the atonalists and other contemporary experimenters. His *Improvisations on Virginal Pieces by Giles Farnaby* manage to combine an Elizabethan flavour with the folk music touches of Holst and Vaughan Williams. During World War II he was ordered to form a piano trio and give concerts to serving men and women in Britain and, later, in Germany. Between 1947 and 1968 he was a distinguished lecturer at Oxford.

OTHER WORKS: Ten symphonies. Piano, violin, and viola concertos. Madrigals and motets for unaccompanied choir. Four string quartets.

Rubinstein, Anton (1829–94) Russian pianist and composer. Making his début in Moscow while still only nine years old, Rubinstein made an immediate impression, and after intensive study in Paris was taken by his teacher on a European tour. In London he was received by Queen Victoria. On later tours he featured several of his own compositions, but was more famous for the phenomenally long and taxing programmes during which he would go through a vast range of pieces from Couperin, Bach, Mozart, and Beethoven to Liszt and Chopin – and then repeat the whole concert next day for the benefit of local music students.

In 1858 he settled in St Petersburg, and in 1862 founded the Conservatory there. Its basically international flavour unfortunately aroused the wrath of the young nationalist composers known

The pianist Arthur Rubinstein against a truly classical background, the Parthenon in Athens, photographed by Cecil Beaton in 1962.

as 'The Five', and after many wrangles Rubinstein resigned in disgust.

Although he wrote twenty operas and six symphonies, he is remembered as a composer mainly for his piano piece, *Melody in F*.

Rubinstein, Arthur (1887–1982) Polish pianist (American citizen 1946). A child prodigy, he so impressed Joachim that the great violinist and two friends paid for his musical training. He travelled continually, becoming the greatest twentieth-century interpreter of Chopin, and also introducing the works of de Falla to wide audiences. In 1939 he settled in Hollywood but after World War II continued his extensive recital tours. In his ninetieth year he was made an honorary KBE (Knight of the British Empire).

Ruckers firm In 1579 Hans Ruckers founded a firm of harpsichord and virginals manufacturers in Antwerp, which was taken over in due course by his two sons and then a grandson. They designed harpsichords capable of varying tone and registers, with single and double manual models. About a hundred have survived to this day. Wanda Landowska kept a 1642 model in her collection at St-Leu-La-Forêt, later looted by the Nazis.

rumba A Cuban dance, probably of African origin, played in heavily syncopated 2/4 time. It became very popular in American and British ballrooms before World War II, and was the basis of a number of stage and film dance routines. In 1938 Arthur Benjamin wrote a piano duet called *Jamaican Rumba*, later arranged for small orchestra and other combinations.

S

Sacher, Paul (1906–) Swiss conductor. At the age of twenty he founded the Basle Chamber Orchestra and, after marriage to a rich woman, devoted himself to widening its repertoire by commissioning new works from leading contemporary composers such as Stravinsky and Honegger, at the same time encouraging study of authentic performance of early music with the founding of a research institute, the Schola Cantorum Basiliensis. Among more than two hundred pieces written for him were Bartók's *Divertimento*, Martinů's *Double Concerto* for strings and piano, and Richard Strauss's *Metamorphosen*. After sixty years he decided in 1987 to wind up the orchestra, but announced his intention of continuing to collect valuable twentieth-century scores for the library of his Paul Sacher Foundation: he already had all Boulez's and Frank Martin's manuscripts, most of Stravinsky's, and a large amount of Bartók.

sackbut An early form of trombone, known from the late fifteenth century. Unlike other brass instruments, its basic construction has hardly altered over the years.

Sadie, Stanley (1930–) English editor and critic. He wrote criticism for *The Times* of London for many years, edited *The Musical Times*, and from 1970 until publication in 1980 worked on the editing of a monumental, completely revised edition of Grove's *Dictionary of Music and Musicians*, now familiarly referred to as the *New Grove*.

Sadler's Wells In 1683 Richard Sadler discovered an old well in the garden of his London house and set out to exploit the current fashion for medicinal spas. In later years a theatre was built and a number of entertainments flourished and faded. Between 1818 and 1828 the famous clown Grimaldi appeared here regularly. By the twentieth century it had fallen on hard times, but as the result of a public appeal a new theatre for drama, opera and ballet was opened in 1931 under the management of Lilian Baylis. During World War II the opera and ballet companies went on tour, but the theatre was reopened in June 1945 with the first performance of Britten's *Peter Grimes*, followed by first productions of works by contemporaries such as Malcolm Williamson and Gordon Crosse. Most works were sung in English translation, including operas by Janáček and a complete *Ring* cycle. Visiting companies included the Hamburg Opera in Hans Werner Henze's *Der Prinz von Homburg* (*The Prince of Hamburg*) and Berg's *Lulu*. In due course the Sadler's Wells Ballet transferred to Covent Garden as the Royal Ballet, and the Sadler's Wells Opera became the English National Opera with its base in the London Coliseum. The premises have since been used mainly for visiting dance companies and musical shows.

Saint-Saëns, Camille (1835–1921) French composer. A talented child, at the age of ten he appeared in public as a pianist with a Belgian violinist in a Beethoven sonata. At thirteen he entered the Paris Conservatoire to study organ and composition. In 1857 he won the coveted post of organist at the Madeleine, by which time he had written two symphonies and other pieces. He began to concentrate on opera, but the third, *Samson et Dalilah*, was his only undeniable success in this field, in spite of its disconcerting alliance of oratorio with grand opera.

A caricature of Camille Saint-Saëns as combined harp and harpist.

Saint-Saëns had become a leading figure in French musical circles when the Franco-Prussian war broke out. He gave a few charity piano recitals, then fled to London for a few weeks' respite and gave organ recitals at the Albert Hall and the Crystal Palace. His virtuosity on both instruments was to bring him international renown, and the elegant, conservative style of his compositions and graceful harmonies suited many undemanding audiences. The first three of his five piano concertos became immediate favourites, as did the *Introduction and rondo capriccioso* for violin and orchestra.

Co-founder of the *Société Nationale de Musique*, for the propagation of French music, Saint-Saëns contributed some of his best-known symphonic poems to its cause, including *Le Rouet d'Omphale* (*Omphale's Spinning Wheel*) and the vivid evocation of dancing skeletons, *Danse macabre* (*Dance of Death*). A much revered figure towards the end of his long life, he travelled widely, conducting and playing his own works, and in 1913 was accorded a Jubilee Festival of his music in London. His fifth piano concerto has echoes of some of the exotic music he heard in Egypt and neighbouring countries. The work by which he is perhaps best remembered is one whose performance he forbade in his own lifetime: the 'grand zoological fantasy' *Le Carnaval des animaux* (*Carnival of the Animals*).

OTHER WORKS: Opera *Henry VIII*. Five symphonies, including 'The Organ' Symphony (No.3). Three violin concertos. *Havanaise* for violin and piano. Bagatelles, six études, and fugues for piano. Organ preludes and fugues.

Salieri, Antonio (1750–1825) Italian composer. He studied in Venice and became conductor of the Vienna Court Opera in 1770, having nine of his own operas produced there in four years. In all he was to compose more than forty, including *Armida* and *Falstaff* in Italian, and, at Gluck's instigation, a few in French. His reputation as the possible poisoner of Mozart, against whom he admittedly intrigued, almost certainly does him an injustice.

Salomon, Johann Peter (1745–1815) German violinist, conductor and impresario. He studied in Bonn and played in orchestras there and at

Rheinsberg before settling in London in 1781 as conductor, soloist, and chamber musician. His seasons of subscription concerts in the Hanover Square Rooms featured Haydn in 1790-2 and 1794-5, and the twelve symphonies Haydn wrote for these (Nos. 93-104) are generally referred to as 'the Salomon symphonies' or 'the London symphonies'.

salon music A term sometimes used dismissively for light pieces of music which can be played in a private salon or in the palm court or restaurant of a hotel. In fact many agreeable little morsels have been produced in this vein by composers such as Chaminade, MacDowell, and Elgar (notably his *Chanson de Nuit, Chanson de Matin,* and *Salut d'Amour*).

saltarello An energetic dance of mixed Italian and Spanish parentage which calls for rhythmic leaps (*salti*). In the sixteenth century it was frequently used as an alternative to the similar *galliard* in the after-dance to a *pavane.* Later it grew even livelier, and the dancers, as in the *tarantella,* increased their pace towards the end.

Salzburg Festival It is ironic that the major annual Mozart festival should be held in the town where he had been so wretched in his servitude under the Prince-Archbishop, and which appreciated him so little while he was alive. Nevertheless it was here that the Mozarteum music college was founded in 1870, and here that the first festival was held in 1877. Regular festivals did not begin, however, until 1920, under the aegis of Richard Strauss, Hugo von Hofmannsthal, and the producer Max Reinhardt. An opera house was opened in 1927. In 1938 the Nazis took charge and turned the annual events into festivals of German culture. After World War II the programmes increasingly included contemporary works from Orff, Henze, Nono and others. Among conductors who have appeared at Saltzburg have been Toscanini, Strauss, and Karajan, who served for many years as artistic director.

samisen A Japanese long-necked lute, played with a plectrum which produces a gentle, plaintive tone from three waxed silk strings.

Sammartini, Giuseppe (1693–1751) and **Giovanni-Battista** (1698–1775) Italian composers. The name is sometimes given as San Martini. Giuseppe, the older brother, was a skilled oboist who settled in England in the 1720s and played at the opera before becoming chamber music director to Frederick, Prince of Wales. He wrote many *concerti grossi,* trio sonatas, and a setting of Congreve's masque *The Judgment of Paris.*

His younger brother Giovanni-Battista was an organist and choirmaster to several churches in Milan, where he spent his entire life. He had a formative influence on the development of sonata form, and is believed to have composed more than two thousand works, including operas, masses, motets, symphonies and quartets. Gluck was one of his pupils.

Sándor, György (1912–) Hungarian pianist (American citizen 1943). He studied in Budapest with Kodály and Bartók and became the leading interpreter of Bartók, giving the first performance of the third piano concerto and recording all the piano music. Other recordings include all the solo piano music of Kodály and Prokofiev.

Santley, (Sir) Charles (1834–1922) English baritone. He learnt music as a choirboy and made a number of amateur appearances as a soloist before taking up serious studies in Milan and London. He was soon much sought after for oratorio performances, creating an overwhelming impression in Mendelssohn's *Elijah,* and sang with several opera companies. In 1871 he toured the USA, and while there joined Carl Rosa's opera company for a time and was with it again in London in 1875. In 1890 he toured Australia. His farewell appearance was made at Covent Garden in 1911, but he emerged from retirement in World War I to sing at a concert for Belgian relief.

saraband(e) An elegant courtly dance which is thought to have originated in Spain in the sixteenth century, though its roots may have been in the Near East. In slow 3/2 time, it became a favourite at the early seventeenth-century French Court before being introduced as an almost obligatory part of the dance suite used by Bach, Handel and Couperin. The saraband also provided the basis for instrumental variations and operatic arias. For many years it fell from favour, but has been revived in works by Satie, Debussy and Honegger.

sarangi A North Indian fiddle, an early precursor of the viol family, with a deep wooden soundbox covered by skin, and three strings with ten sympathetic strings underneath.

sardana A Spanish round dance from Catalonia, accompanied by pipe and tabor.

Sargent, (Sir) Malcolm (1895–1967) English conductor. He began his career as a church organist but turned to conducting and for a time taught the subject at the Royal College of Music. From 1929 to 1940 he was musical director of the Courtauld-Sargent Concerts in London, and made a speciality of conducting choral concerts all over the country. From 1950 to 1957 he was conductor of

(Left) Three great men at the Salzburg Festival before the Nazis took charge of it: the conductors Bruno Walter *(left)* and Arturo Toscanini *(far right),* with the author Thomas Mann *(centre),* winner of the Nobel Prize for Literature.

the BBC Symphony Orchestra, and from then until his death was chief conductor of the Henry Wood Promenade Concerts. His dandyish, impeccable dress and his brisk confidence when tackling any kind of music earned him the nicknames 'Slick Malcolm' and 'Flash Harry'; but even his detractors admitted his unfailing competence in handling large orchestral and choral forces and his reliability in a crisis.

sarrusophone An attempt to combine woodwind and brass instruments, it takes its name from its inventor, Sarrus, a nineteenth-century bandmaster in the French army. Although a brass instrument, its mouthpiece has a double reed, and it was intended that a whole range of sizes should be made so that marching bands could have a substitute for oboes and bassoons. Only the bass version has been used by a few composers, including Saint-Saëns and Massenet, and Delius in *Song of the High Hills* and *Eventyr*, though in performance a double bassoon is often substituted.

S A T B The letters stand for soprano, alto, tenor and bass. Starting from the top, this is the usual grouping of a vocal quartet or the written order of their parts on the staff.

Satie, Erik (1866–1925) French composer and pianist. Son of a French father and Scottish mother, the young Eric (who later changed the spelling to Erik) was sent to live with his grandparents upon his mother's death, but returned to Paris when his father remarried and arranged for his admission to the Conservatoire. All reports upon him proclaimed that he was lazy, unreliable, unpunctual – yet gifted. Too idle to go through the full range of academic studies, he made up for this with ironic exhibitionism, both in his dress and his music; but his personality and talent were enough to win the approval of both Debussy and Ravel.

In 1888 he wrote three piano pieces, *Gymnopédies*, two of which were later orchestrated by Debussy and interested the public in Satie's wit and originality. His search for a personal style produced some remarkable harmonic innovations, often in conjunction with cabaret-style melodies. He provided absurd, fanciful titles for several of his pieces: e.g. *Trois morceaux en forme de poire* (*Three pieces in the shape of a pear*) and *Choses vues á droite et á gauche* (*sans lunettes*) (*Things seen to right and left* (*without glasses*)). Among his larger works were an operetta, a marionette opera, and a number of ballets, of which the most notable was *Parade*, with a libretto by Cocteau, décor by Picasso, choreography by Massine, and a score which incorporated a typewriter, a siren, and other effects together with a tang of ragtime.

OTHER WORKS: Choral *Messe des pauvres*, with

A photograph of the enigmatic Erik Satie taken about 1896. One short-lived group of equally whimsical composers and artists admiringly adopted the name *Ecole d'Arcueil* (School of Arcueil) from the suburb of Paris in which Satie lived.

organ or piano. Symphonic drama *Socrate* for four sopranos and chamber orchestra. Café-concert songs. Piano solo pieces.

Savoy Operas See **Gilbert and Sullivan**.

Sax, Adolphe (1814–94) Belgian instrument maker. He invented the saxhorn, a brass wind instrument resembling the bugle but with valves. The alto model is usually called a *flügelhorn*, the B flat bass a *euphonium*, and the contrabass a *bombardon*. They are used more in brass bands than anywhere else. Sax also invented the saxophone, and this too was produced in several sizes. Unlike the cup mouthpiece of the saxhorn family, it had a reed similar to that of a clarinet, and the fingering is similar to that in one register of the clarinet. In dance and jazz bands a saxophone section takes the place of what in a symphony orchestra would be a string section. (*See also* **The Orchestra and its Instruments**.)

scale The term is taken from the Latin and Italian words for a ladder. In German, *tonleiter*; in French, *gamme*. A scale is in effect a ladder of ascending or descending successive notes. A straightforward diatonic major scale begins on its tonic note and ascends or descends an octave, i.e. eight notes. The sequence consists of whole-tone gaps except for a semitone between the third and fourth degrees and between the seventh and eighth degrees. In the key of C this results in a climb of C-D-E-F-G-A-B-C.

Minor scales introduce a semitone between the second and third degrees and between the sixth and seventh, but with slight variations according to whether they are ascending or descending, and whether they are melodic or harmonic minor scales.

Scales using a complete succession of semitones are known not as diatonic but as chromatic scales. In an ascending melodic chromatic scale, the accidentals are written as sharps; when descending, as flats. This obviates the need for introducing naturals to cancel out preceding accidentals, which appear in the acending harmonic chromatic scale. (*See also* **pentatonic, twelve-tone**, and **whole-tone scales**.)

Scale of C major

Scale of C minor

(natural)

(melodic)

(harmonic)

Melodic chromatic scale

(ascending)

(descending)

Harmonic chromatic scale

(ascending)

(descending)

Scarlatti, Alessandro (1660–1725) Italian composer. He was born in Sicily. Little is known of his early life, though he is thought to have studied with Carissimi in Rome. He married a Roman girl when he was eighteen, and there is a record of 'Scarlattino, a Sicilian' having composed a Lenten oratorio there in 1679. That same year he wrote the first of more than a hundred operas, so impressing Queen Christina of Sweden, who was in the audience, that she engaged him for four years as conductor to her private theatre. After that he divided most of his working life between Rome and Naples, becoming the major influence in what has been called the Neapolitan Opera School. Opera houses were the main centres of entertainment in Naples, and audiences were ready for a new, more tuneful and flowing style than the rather rigid Venetian works to which they had been accustomed.

Scarlatti introduced the *da capo* aria, and prefaced his operas not with the French-style overture but with a bright three-part *sinfonia* (also known as the 'Italian overture') from which the classical symphony was to develop. His constructive methods were to have a great influence on Bach and Handel. All his works save one were *opera seria*, the greatest being perhaps *Mitridate Eupatore*, produced in Venice in 1707. The exception was a frivolous little *opera buffa* called *Il trionfo dell'onore* (*The Triumph of Honour*).

As well as succeeding in the theatre, Scarlatti served as *maestro di cappella* to Cardinal Ottobini in Rome and for two periods at the royal chapel in Naples. He composed twenty oratorios and more than six hundred solo cantatas, a large number of *concerti grossi*, and works for keyboard including a dazzling set of variations on the popular Portugese dance *La follia* (*The Folly*). His influence was so lasting that Dr Charles Burney could write later: 'I find part of his property among the stolen goods of all the best composers of the first forty or fifty years of the present century.'

Scarlatti, Domenico (1685–1757) Italian composer. The sixth son among Alessandro Scarlatti's ten children, he became at the age of sixteen organist and composer to the royal chapel in Naples during one of his father's spells there as *maestro di cappella*. In 1708 he met Handel in Venice. They became mutually appreciative friends and travelled together to Rome, where Cardinal Ottobini arranged a keyboard duel between them: the verdict was that Scarlatti was marginally the better harpsichordist, but Handel, as Scarlatti himself declared, was far superior on the organ.

After a number of church and other appointments, he became music director to the Portugese

Domenico Scarlatti's prowess at the keyboard was such that Dr Burney reported a fellow musician being so stricken that 'if he had been in sight of any instrument with which to have done the deed, he would have cut off his own fingers.'

Court in Lisbon, and when the Princess Maria Barbara married the heir to the Spanish throne he moved with her to Madrid, where he spent the rest of his life teaching, composing and, it has been recorded, gambling so recklessly that he frequently had to appeal to his royal patron to cover his debts. It was during this time that, as well as writing the obligatory masses and cantatas for religious and formal occasions, he produced his great collection of harpsichord sonatas, some of them as exercises for the princess (later queen), all of them innovatory in style and combining Spanish and Portugese melodic influences with brilliant technical devices. They were nearly all in binary form, yet this seemed to inspire the composer rather than limit him. He used invigorating, dancing rhythms and, with rarely more than two or three contrapuntal voices, exploited the whole range of the keyboard. He was one of the first to display, with great *bravura*, the technique of crossing hands in virtuoso passages. More than five hundred and fifty of his sonatas have survived, catalogued first by Longo (L) numbers, later by Kirkpatrick (K) numbers. It was Kirkpatrick, the American harpsichordist, who established that most of the pieces had originally been conceived in pairs, making them in effect two-movement sonatas, both sections in the same key.

scat-singing In jazz, the improvised singing of nonsense syllables to the notes of a popular tune. Legend has it that it was started by Louis Armstrong when he temporarily forgot the words of a piece he was recording, and made up rhythmic noises to fit.

Scharwenka, Franz Xaver (1850–1924) German-Polish composer, pianist and teacher. He studied in Berlin, made his solo début there, and in 1881 founded his own conservatory, later merging it with that of Karl Klindworth. Between 1891 and 1898 he lived mainly in New York, where he established a branch of his school. As well as editing the piano works of Robert Schumann, he composed extensively for the piano himself, with four concertos, two trios, and a large number of solo pieces including some Polish dances.

Scheidt, Samuel (1587–1654) German composer and organist. After appointments as a church organist, he became organist and *kapellmeister* to the Margrave of Brandenburg. He wrote a number of 'sacred concertos' for voices and instruments, transcriptions of about a hundred hymns and psalms, and in his three volumes of *Tablatura nova* not only assembled a variety of organ pieces but established the principle of staff notation for the instrument in place of the restricting tablature which had hitherto prevailed.

scherzo The Italian word for a joke. It was originally applied to light, skittish compositions, usually for voices, as in Monteverdi's *Scherzi musicali (Musical Jokes)*. As time went on it was incorporated into instrumental music such as a sonata or string quartet, and then into symphonies by Haydn, Beethoven, Mendelssohn and others, usually as a livelier, often boisterously jolly replacement in 3/4 time for the minuet-and-trio movement. Berlioz's *Romeo and Juliet* contains the popular, scintillating *Queen Mab* scherzo.

Scherzando is a direction on a score asking the performer to play in a bright, humorous style; *scherzevole* and *scherzoso* mean the same, but are less frequently used.

A *scherzetto* or *scherzino* is a small scherzo, applied only to small instrumental pieces and not to symphonic movements.

Schikaneder, Emanuel Johann (1751–1812) German singer, impresario and librettist. After some years as an itinerant fiddler and then as actor and singer in a troupe of strolling players, he settled in Vienna in 1784 and became a theatrical manager. He produced spectacular patriotic pieces and comic operas, and wrote librettos for several of them. In 1791 he asked Mozart to provide the music for one of the magic fairy-tale extravaganzas which he had found most popular: the result was *Die Zauberflöte (The Magic Flute)*, in which

Schikaneder was the first Papageno, doubtless overplaying it for all he was worth.

Schirmer firm A firm of music publishers founded in New York in 1861. Gustav Schirmer became sole owner in 1865, and later his sons were taken on as partners. They have published the works of leading American composers such as Barber, Menotti and Bernstein, and in 1915 they founded *The Musical Quarterly*. A nephew established a separate company in Boston in 1921, publishing Copland, Piston and Rorem as well as younger avant-garde composers.

Schmidt-Isserstedt, Hans (1900–73) German conductor. His conducting career began in Wuppertal, and after other posts he was appointed to the Hamburg State Opera in 1935, then to the Deutsches Opernhaus in Berlin between 1942 and 1945. After World War II he founded the *Nordwestdeutsche Rundfunk (Northwest German Radio)* Symphony Orchestra in Hamburg, helped it to build up a high reputation in spite of post-war difficulties, and stayed with it for a quarter of a century. In 1951 it was the first foreign orchestra to play in the restored Free Trade Hall in Manchester.

Schmieder, Wolfgang (1901–73) German musicologist. He compiled the definitive catalogue of the works of J.S. Bach and established the BWV standard numbering, first published in 1950.

Schnabel, Artur (1882–1951) Austrian pianist and composer. He studied in Vienna and made his début as a pianist at the age of eight. Over the years he established himself as a leading interpreter of Beethoven and Schubert, and has left many superb recordings. He edited Beethoven piano sonatas and, in collaboration with Carl Flesch, the Mozart and Brahms violin sonatas. During World War II he lived in the USA, but settled in Switzerland in 1945. Although he showed little interest in playing twentieth-century music, his own compositions, which include three symphonies and five quartets, are largely in the twelve-tone method.

Schnitke, Alfred (1934–) Russian composer. In spite of official condemnation of anything which flouts the USSR policy of 'social realism' in the arts, Schnitke has experimented with serialism, electronics, and aleatory methods. 'I am not outside the Russian school,' he has said, 'but I have had to find the right way of creating a dialogue with it.' Moving on from serialism, his *Quasi una Sonata* of 1968 led to freer fantasia writing and a growing addiction to musical paradox. The 'polystylistic' synthesis of his apocalyptic, half serious, half frivolous first symphony, dedicated to Rozhdestvensky, has led to its being called a 'tower of Babel'. His *Yellow Sound* is an attempt to evoke a Kandinsky painting by means of mime, soprano and chorus, and instrumental ensemble. In 1985 Schnitke had a severe stroke and was thought to be dead; he slowly recovered, but has since worked with more deliberation and a great deal of effort.

Schoenberg, Arnold (1874–1951) Austrian composer (American citizen 1941). He learned to play the violin and viola as a child, but had little idea of making a living from music until, bored by the job he had been forced to take in a bank to support his widowed mother and sister, he left and sought employment in a more congenial métier. He orchestrated operettas for various composers, conducted in satirical cabaret, and at the same time acquired what theoretical and practical knowledge he could from his own experiences and from his friend Zemlinsky, who gave him his only formal lessons in counterpoint. His earliest compositions were in a fulsome romantic tradition: the string sextet *Verklärte Nacht* (*Transfigured Night*) was programme music depicting a lover's forgiveness of his mistress's infidelity (later used for Antony Tudor's ballet *Pillar of Fire*); and the huge choral and orchestral *Gurrelieder* (*Songs of Gurre*) was a Wagnerian outpouring around verses of the Danish poet J.P. Jacobsen. While working on such projects he married Zemlinsky's sister and was helped by his brother-in-law to

Arnold Schoenberg about 1930, the year when he began work on his opera *Moses and Aaron*, to his own libretto.

take on pupils, among them the young Alban Berg and Anton von Webern. In 1908 his wife ran off with an artist from whom both of them had been taking painting lessons, but was persuaded to return to Schoenberg, whereupon the painter committed suicide.

It was around this time that Schoenberg moved away from nineteenth-century colourful romanticism into a more stringent discipline. His first quartet and a chamber symphony had already hinted at his dissatisfaction with accepted tonality. The song cycle *Das Buch der hängenden Gärten* (*The Book of the Hanging Gardens*) plunged right into atonality, and he followed it up with similar iconoclastic works of which one of the most influential was the *Pierrot lunaire* (*Moonstruck Pierrot*) cycle of '3 times 7' vocal pieces in *sprechstimme* (*speaking-voice*), with an instrumental ensemble of piano, piccolo, flute, clarinet, bass clarinet, violin, viola and cello. Both works aroused violent hostility from audiences and critics offended by the startling dissonances and disturbed by the alien intensity of the half-declamatory, eerie half-wailing delivery

Called up for military service in World War I, Schoenberg was released in late 1916, called up again, and finally discharged as being physically unfit. In early 1918 he settled in Vienna and began evolving his theories of 'twelve tones related only to one another', then moved to Berlin to take composition classes in the Prussian Academy of Arts. Here he wrote the first two acts of his unfinished opera *Moses und Aron*. With the advent of the Nazis his 'decadent' theories and racial origins brought vicious condemnation. In 1898 he had abandoned his Jewish faith for Lutheranism, but after leaving Germany in 1933 he returned to his family religion and just before World War II made a moving setting of the Jewish prayer *Kol Nidrei* for rabbinical speaker, chorus and orchestra.

After emigrating to the USA Schoenberg (who had hitherto spelt his name Schönberg) taught at the University of California. Though continuing to preach the virtues of dodecaphony, he often reverted to conventional tonality in compositions such as his *Second Chamber Symphony* and the *Theme and Variations* for wind band. In spite of this, his influence on his disciples remained strongest in the advocacy of serial techniques which conditioned so much subsequent music. He expressed his convictions in books such as the *Harmonielehre* (*Treatise on Harmony*) and *Structual Functions of Harmony*. 'Time,' he declared, 'will bring understanding to my works.'

OTHER WORKS: Stage monodrama *Erwartung* (*Expectation*). Oratorio *Die Jakobsleiter* (*Jacob's*

Ladder). A Survivor from Warsaw for narrator, chorus and orchestra. Four string quartets.

Scholes, Percy (1877–1958) English music critic and lexicographer. He wrote on music for several English journals, including *Radio Times*, and was author of a number of books. His major achievement was compiling and editing *The Oxford Companion to Music* and the later *Concise Oxford Dictionary of Music*, brought up to date after his death by John Owen Ward and further amended in great detail by Michael Kennedy in 1980.

schottische A round dance in 2/4 time, not unlike a slower version of the polka and in fact known, at its introduction into Britain in the middle of the nineteenth century, as the 'German polka'. To confuse matters, however, the Germans called it a *schottische* because of a supposed origin in the *écossaise*, a dance which has no known connection with Scotland and to which the *schottische* bears only a slight resemblance.

Schubert, Franz (1797–1828) Austrian composer. One of the only three of a schoolmaster's eleven children to survive infancy, he had his first music lessons from his father and elder brother. In 1808 he became a boy chorister in the imperial chapel and played the violin in the school orchestra, of which he soon became assistant conductor. His first symphony was written when he was sixteen, shortly after he had begun studying theory with Salieri. After his voice broke he had to take up employment as an assistant schoolteacher under his father. Still he longed to devote himself to

(Above) A coloured lithograph after a drawing by Wilhelm August Rieder of Schubert in 1825.

(Left) Schubert at the piano accompanies friends during one of the convivial evenings they called *Schubertiads*. Because of his small stature and dumpiness these friends dubbed the composer *Schwammerl*, an Austrian dialect word for 'little mushroom'.

music, and in his spare time continued composing. After reading Goethe's *Faust*, he took verses from it and in one day in 1914 wrote the song *Gretchen am Spinnrade* (*Gretchen at the Spinning-Wheel*).

Soon tiring of teaching, he moved into lodgings with friends frequently as poor as himself, and shared musical and literary evenings with them and other acquaintances, calling the gatherings 'Schubertiads'. A leading operatic baritone of the day, Johann Michael Vogl, heard some of his songs and introduced them into his public concerts, often with Schubert as piano accompanist. Among those written at this time were the immortal *An die Musik* (*To Music*) and *Die Forelle* (*The Trout*), the melody of which the composer was to use in his *'Trout' Quintet* a few years later while holidaying in the countryside far from Vienna.

In the Summer of 1818 he was offered the post of music tutor to Count Esterházy's two daughters, and moved to their castle in Hungary; but missed his friends and the Viennese way of life, and returned before the year was out. He now established a routine of composing every morning, spending the afternoon in coffee houses, and playing in Schubertiads with his circle of friends in the evening. Hoping to make a name and money in the operatic and concert world, he wrote a number of operettas and six symphonies, but failed to make a popular breakthrough: the only one of his symphonies which he heard in his own lifetime was the fifth, which he had devised for a small amateur ensemble that used to meet occasionally at his father's house. In 1822 he set to work on a symphony in B minor, his eighth, and filled two movements with melodies of an unearthly beauty, expressively orchestrated and perfectly balanced; but after attempting some bars of a *scherzo* as the third movement, found himself unable to continue and set it aside. This *Unfinished Symphony* was not rediscovered until forty years later.

Schubert's inability to complete that composition may have been due to the onset of the syphilis which was eventually to wear him down. In 1823 he went into hospital, and while there began to write the winningly sentimental song cycle *Die schöne Mullerin* (*The Fair Maid of the Mill*). Out of hospital, he spent a recuperative period on the Esterházy estate, and then toured the lakes and mountains of Upper Austria in the company of Vogl, singing, playing, and composing. It is thought that it was on his return that he began work on another symphony, though this has confusingly been identified by some as his seventh, by others as his ninth. It does, however,

seem probable that this was the '*Great*' C major, which he did not complete until a few months before his death. He had hoped to hear it performed, but it was rejected on the grounds of being bombastic and hard to understand. It was left to Robert Schumann to rediscover it ten years later, praising the 'heavenly length' of its movements, and arranging for Mendelssohn to conduct it in Leipzig.

In May 1827 Schubert was a torchbearer at Beethoven's funeral. His own death was not far away. In sombre mood he completed a song cycle, *Die Winterreise* (*Winter Journey*); and three piano trios and a cluster of piano impromptus show no signs of failing powers. But in spite of the beauty of his piano writing, the terrifying virtuosity of the *Wanderer Fantasie*, and the scope of his fifteen string quartets and other chamber music, it is as a *lieder* composer that he will always be remembered. He wrote over six hundred songs, creating entrancing melodies and then shaping each of them into a musically perfect, utterly individual whole. Some are strophic and sound like unspoilt folksongs; some evolve in a narrative of mounting dramatic force. Without ever essaying 'programme music', Schubert could make a rippling brook as immediately real and as important in his scheme as the lamentations of a deserted lover or, in *Der Tod und das Mädchen* (*Death and the Maiden*), the entreaties of a girl that the 'wild skeleton' should pass her by. As his mighty successor Brahms reverently said: 'There is not a song of Schubert's from which one cannot learn something.'

Schuman, William (1910–) American composer. He led a high school dance band before studying seriously with Roy Harris and embarking on the composition of large, vigorous symphonic works, several with unforced jazz rhythms and vivid orchestration. After conducting Schuman's second symphony, Koussevitsky commissioned his *American Festival Overture* in 1939. He became president of the Juilliard School of Music and, from 1961 to 1969, president of Lincoln Center for the Performing Arts in New York.

Schumann, Clara (1819–96) German pianist and composer. Clara Wieck's father was a highly regarded Leipzig piano teacher, and his daughter proved to be one of his most gifted pupils. She made her début at the age of nine, and from twelve onwards made regular recital tours of Europe. Another of Wieck's pupils was Robert Schumann, whose wish to marry Clara was thwarted several times by her angry father: he opened their letters and carried on such a campaign of slanderous attacks that in the end Schumann had to take the matter to court, finally marrying Clara in 1840. She became the leading interpreter of his piano music and continued so after his death, in spite of having to cope with eight children. In 1878 she became head of the piano faculty at Frankfurt Conservatorium. Although her own compositions have been overshadowed by those of her husband, she showed considerable talent in her piano concerto and trio and in a number of solo pieces.

Schumann, Robert (1810–56) German composer. His father was a bookseller, and for a time Schumann's ambition was to be a writer. It was soon obvious from his piano playing, however, that his real gift was for music, though he had to wait some years before taking up serious studies. After his father's death and his sister's suicide, which left a lasting impression on him, he began studying law; but a meeting with the piano teacher Friedrich Wieck, who was impressed by his musical abilities, led to his persuading his mother and guardian to let him lodge and study with Wieck. Trying to make up for lost time, he invented a device to strengthen his fingers and enable them to function separately, but succeeded only in permanently crippling his right hand. A career as a virtuoso was now out of the question. He concentrated on the study of composition with Heinrich Dorn, conductor of the Leipzig Opera, and attempted to write a symphony much sooner than he was ready for it. He found it more natural to write for the piano, and his wide reading in early youth supplied him with many a subject for romantic songs.

In spite of her father's opposition, Schumann married Clara Wieck in 1840. In the period immediately before and after the marriage he poured his emotional yearnings into the song cycles *Liederkreis* (which is simply German for *Song-cycle*), *Dichterliebe* (*Poet's Love*), and *Frauenliebe und Leben* (*Woman's Love and Life*). Piano and voice were quite inseparable, with no hint of the instrument being the subservient partner: indeed, Schumann spoke of a 'piano piece and voice' in connection with some of them, because 'the voice cannot achieve everything and relate everything'. He also sought in his blend of words and melody 'to follow a poem into its smallest detail with the finest musical material'. In all he wrote about a hundred and forty songs, and in none of them is the piano part ever conventional or less than captivating.

While he had been still a composition student, Clara had asked him for a brilliant piece which she could play at her recitals. It was not until six months after their marriage that he got down to it, producing a *Phantasie for Piano and Orchestra* which she played at a Leipzig concert where his first symphony was also performed. No publisher showed any interest in this one-movement piece, and three years later Schumann decided to add two more movements. This, as the *Concerto for Piano and Orchestra in A minor*, became one of his most frequently played works, even though it was greeted with less than rapture at the time: the critic of the London *Times* called it 'laboured and ambitious', and referred patronizingly to Mme Schumann's 'praiseworthy efforts to make her husband's rhapsody pass for music'. Perhaps he, like others, was perplexed by Schumann's integration, here as in his songs, of piano and orchestra instead of the usual pattern of soloist and orchestra in competition with each other.

In the second year of their marriage, Schumann was also inspired to write the first draft of a symphony in four days. This, performed and published as his first (the *Spring*) symphony, opens with what has been described as a jubilant cracking of the winter's ice, and moves on warmly, as an English conductor put it, in 'a golden-brown glow'.

In 1834 he and friends had founded a periodical, the *Neue Zeitschrift für Musik*, of which he later became sole editor. It was intended to establish standards for the criticism of German music past and present, condemning the second-rate and encouraging new ventures and reappraisals of old masters. Schumann was one of the first to laud Chopin's talents in Germany, and the first to foresee Brahms's great achievements. Brahms became one of the Schumanns' closest friends, and an invaluable comfort to Clara after her husband's death. Schumann gave up editorship of the periodical in 1844, the year in which they moved to Dresden from Leipzig, where he had helped Mendelssohn found the Conservatory but had also exhausted himself trying to teach while at the same time composing a large choral work. Clara hoped that Dresden would prove more restful, and for a while it seemed to be ideal for the composer.

He wrote two more symphonies, of which the third, the *Rhenish*, has worn best, though lacking the perfection of his songs or the fresh, endearing lyricism of his chamber music. He began to study Bach, to whom the textures of his late songs owe much. In 1850 his only opera, *Genoveva*, was produced in Leipzig. In the same year the Schumanns moved again, this time to Düsseldorf, where he became conductor of the orchestra. By now he was being afflicted by bouts of depression and strange noises inside his head. For three years he tried to cope with his duties as a conductor, but fared so badly that in the end he had to resign. After this he went rapidly downhill,

270

Robert and Clara Schumann, who in spite of her father's opposition married on the day before her twenty-first birthday.

and in 1854 threw himself into the Rhine. He was rescued and committed to an asylum near Bonn, where he spent the last two and a half years of his life.

Schütz, Heinrich (1585–1672) German composer and organist. He was a chorister in the chapel of the Landgrave of Kassel before taking up the study of law, which he soon abandoned when his patron paid for him to study music under Giovanni Gabrieli in Venice. He returned to Kassel as organist, and then became *kapellmeister* in Dresden and later in Copenhagen. He wrote an opera, *Dafne*, whose score was unfortunately destroyed in a fire. His secular works are of far less importance than his sacred songs, motets and passions. He achieved a happy marriage of Italian madrigal and motet styles with German polyphony, and with Buxtehude may be regarded as one of the two major influences on Bach. *The Seven Words from Christ on the Cross* are simple, restrained, yet dramatic in their narration. Towards the end of his life Schütz wrote the even more dramatic and beautiful oratorio, *The Christmas Story*.

Schwarzkopf, Elisabeth (1915–) German soprano. She studied in Berlin and made her opera début there in *Parsifal*, though Wagner was a composer with whom she was rarely associated afterwards. The great Wagnerian soprano Kirsten Flagstad said that Schwarzkopf's voice was the loveliest sound she had ever heard coming from a human throat; the accompanist Gerald Moore wrote that he had never met a singer with her capacity for work. She is heard at her best in rôles such as the Marschallin in Strauss's *Der Rosenkavalier* and Elvira in *Don Giovanni*, and in *lieder* recitals and recordings, particularly the songs of Hugo Wolf. She was the first to sing Anne Trulove in Stravinsky's *The Rake's Progress*. In 1953 she married Walter Legge, the recording impresario.

Schweitzer, Albert (1875–1965) French organist and musicologist. He studied the organ with Widor, but also studied medicine in order to take up work as a medical missionary. Combining his two interests, he gave Bach recitals, published a two-volume treatise on the composer's work and books on French and German organs, and used the profits from lectures, recitals and writings to fund his missionary work at Lambaréné in French Equatorial Africa. In 1952 he was awarded the Nobel Peace Prize.

Schwertsik, Kurt (1935–) Austrian composer and horn-player. He studied at the Vienna Academy of Music and was fascinated by the works of Hindemith and Stravinsky, little heard in his country during World War II, and by Debussy. For a while he emulated Stockhausen and Cage, but turned towards a more tuneful, sardonic style of music owing much to Viennese cabaret and modern pop music. He favours tonality and a direct approach which will 'take the audience and transform it', a style of accessible music which 'has been lost so utterly – partly because of Schoenberg'. As well as playing the horn in the Vienna Symphony Orchestra, in 1958 he founded with Friedrich Cerha a new music ensemble called *die reihe*, a title which can be translated in many ways: turn, series, progression, suite.

scordatura The deliberate mistuning of a stringed instrument to achieve greater brilliance of sound or a special effect, as in the violin tuned up a tone to make the figure of death more terrifying in both Saint-Saëns's *Danse Macabre* and Mahler's fourth symphony.

score and **scoring** In his *Essay on Musical Expression*, the eighteenth-century Newcastle composer and critic Charles Avison put it perfectly: 'Music is said to be in *score* when all the *parts* are distinctly wrote and set under each other, so as the eye, at one view, may take in all the various contrivances of the composer.' A full score laid out in this way enables the conductor to control all the instrumental strands; individual players have sheets containing only the music for their particular instruments (hence the phrase *score and parts*).

Short score, known in German as *particell*, is a working sketch in which the composer's general intentions regarding orchestration and harmonization are compressed into a manuscript which will later be elaborated into the full score.

Scoring is the process of orchestrating a work. (*See also* Appendix IV.)

Scotch snap Also known as a *Scots catch*, this is a rhythmic figure which reverses the usual order of dotted quaver (eighth note) followed by semiquaver: instead, the shorter note comes first on a strong beat, and the longer note is then maintained for the full duration of the beat. A feature of the Scottish dance, the strathspey, this 'snap' appears also in music of other countries, including that of Purcell and especially of Bartók and other East European composers whose languages accentuate the first syllable of a word. The effect is produced in English with words like 'never', 'bitter', etc..

Scotto, Renata (1934–) Italian soprano. Daughter of a policeman in Savona, she began singing from the window of her home in the hope of persuading passers-by to toss coins to her, then studied in Milan and made her opera début there in 1953, becoming a regular member of the company at La Scala for many years. She married the first violinist at La Scala, who then became her manager and coach. Like many *divas*, she was plump to start with, but later fined down without any detriment to her fluent, pulsating interpretations of the great Verdi and Puccini rôles: she has sung *Madama Butterfly* more than six hundred times, and chose it for the opening production when she became the first woman to direct herself in opera at the New York Met in 1986. In that same year she published her autobiography *Scotto — more than a diva*, containing a number of tart reminiscences of historic clashes between her admirers and those of Maria Callas.

Scriabin (or **Skryabin**), **Alexander** (1872–1915) Russian composer. His mother was an accomplished pianist and, although she died shortly after his birth, must have passed on some of her talents to enable him to become a child prodigy. While serving in the Moscow Cadet School he studied music, then entered the Moscow Conservatory and attracted the attention of the music

Alexander Scriabin (variously spelt as Skryabin, Skrjabin, etc.), who under theosophical influences came to believe that he was destined to interpret ecstatic mysteries in musical terms and prepare himself and his listeners for an ultimate transfiguration.

publisher Belaiev, who sponsored a European concert tour for him. In 1898 he became professor of piano in the Conservatory, but resigned to devote himself to composition. Between 1906 and 1907 he toured the USA and attracted the attention of Koussevitsky, with whom he toured the Volga region. Theosophical preoccupations led to his belief that music, like everything else, should contribute to an ideal state of 'ecstatic mystery', with himself as a possible new Messiah.

The 'poem of fire', *Prometheus*, a performance of which he attended in England, conducted by Henry Wood, was intended to be supported by a continuous interplay of lights from a 'colour keyboard'. It was labelled a symphony but, like another supposed symphony, the *Poem of Ecstasy*, was really a lush, erotic tone poem with the same mystical strangeness and impressionistic chromaticism as his sonatas and other eccentric, wildly athletic piano works. He planned an all-embracing musical and dramatic *Mysterium* for two thousand performers which would gather up the human race into one ultimate moment of collective ecstasy heralding a new world order; but got no further than a few tentative scribbles before dying from septicaemia brought on by a lip tumour.

Searle, Humphrey (1915–82) English composer. He studied with Vaughan Williams and John Ireland in London and with Webern in Vienna, and adopted the twelve-tone system for much of his work. He worked for some years in the BBC music department, and became professor of composition in the Royal College of Music from 1965 onwards. His opera *Hamlet* was produced in Hamburg in 1968, and in London the following year. He composed five symphonies, two piano concertos, three works for speaker and orchestra, including *The Shadow of Cain* (to words by Edith Sitwell), and a piano sonata which achieves the remarkable feat of combining twelve-tone methods with the language of Liszt, about whom Searle wrote an analytical book.

secco *See* **recitative**.

second A melodic or harmonic interval of one step (two semitones) up or down from a given tone, e.g. from C up to D or from C down to B flat. A *minor second* is a semitone up or down; an augmented second, three semitones. The word is also used for a lower part such as that of a *second violin*, and *secondo* identifies the part of the second player in a piano duet, the upper part being marked *primo*.

Segovia, Andrés (1893–1987) Spanish guitarist. He studied and made his début in Granada, abandoning early violin studies in order to teach himself the guitar. Although popular as an

The Spanish guitarist Segovia playing, appropriately enough, a Spanish guitar. 'From my youthful years', he declared, 'I dreamed of raising the guitar from the sad artistic level in which it lay.'

accompaniment for folk and dance music, the instrument had not for several centuries been highly regarded in serious recitals, and little had been written for it. Segovia worked, as his great admirer Julian Bream was to write in an obituary notice, 'to draw forth from the strings of the guitar depths of sonorities which had lain hidden hitherto'. In 1925 he began a long sequence of masterly recordings, appeared all over the world, made transcriptions of works by Bach and others, and had major works written for him by composers including Castelnuovo-Tedesco and de Falla. In 1981 King Juan Carlos of Spain created him Marquis of Salobrena.

seguidilla A sixteenth-century Andalusian dance in triple time, probably of Moorish origin. It resembles a brisker bolero, accompanied by guitar and castanets, interspersed with the singing of vocal couplets.

Seiber, Mátyás (1905–60) Hungarian composer (British citizen). He studied in Budapest with Kodály and then went to Frankfurt, where he played in an orchestra and was a pioneering teacher of jazz. In 1935 he left Germany for England. From 1942 until 1957 he taught at Morley

The Hungarian-born composer Mátyás Seiber (right) reunited with his old mentor Zoltán Kodály.

College, became a co-founder of the Society for Promotion of New Music, founded and conducted the Dorian Singers, and wrote a great deal of film music, including that for Orwell's *Animal Farm*. Eclectic in style, he sometimes introduced the jazz elements of which he was so fond, at others echoed Bartók and Schoenberg. He composed a cantata around James Joyce's *Ulysses*, and set some fragments from *The Portrait of an Artist as a Young Man*. He was killed in a car crash in the Krueger National Park during a lecture tour of South Africa.

OTHER WORKS: Clarinet concertino. Three string quartets. Two *Jazzolettes* for jazz sextet. *Missa brevis*. Violin sonata.

semitone The whole step between two notes, as between C and D, is called a tone; a half-sized step, as between C and C sharp, is a semitone.

septet A piece for seven singers or players; or a group of seven such singers or players. Several different instrumental combinations are possible: Beethoven's *Septet in E* uses clarinet, bassoon, horn, violin, viola and double bass; Ravel's *Introduction and Allegro*, though not described as such, is in fact a septet for flute, clarinet, harp and string quartet. Other composers using this medium include Hummel, Spohr, and Schoenberg.

sequence The repetition of a melodic phrase at a higher or lower pitch but without any key change. If the repetition is purely melodic, it is called a *melodic sequence*; if it involves a progression of chords, it is a *harmonic sequence*; and if slight variations are needed because the phrase involves semitones when moved up or down, this is a *tonal sequence*. When a change of key occurs but the melodic or harmonic pattern remains the same, the correct term for the sequence is a *rosalia*.

Sequences were skilfully used by Mozart (as with the repetitions at the beginning of the Symphony No.40 in G minor), and Romantic composers in the nineteenth century loved to build up dramatic tension by means of sequences urging the music on to a climax.

The word is also applied to a medieval chant which was introduced into the Mass after the Gradual and the Alleluia – i.e. a sequential addition. The practice of interpolating such hymns was widespread until 1560, when the Council of Trent abolished all save four: the *Victimae paschali laudes* at Easter; *Veni sancte spiritus* at Whitsun; *Lauda Sion* for Corpus Christi; and the *Dies Irae* for a Requiem Mass. In 1727 a further sequence was allowed, the *Stabat Mater*.

Serafin, Tullio (1878–1968) Italian conductor. He studied in Milan and became a violinist in the orchestra at La Scala. In 1900 he made his début as a conductor at Ferrara. In 1909 he was conducting at La Scala, later became a regular guest at Covent Garden, and from 1924 to 1934 conducted at the New York Met, where he presented the first American performance of *Turandot*. He worked devotedly in the revival of *bel canto*, and was a major formative influence on Maria Callas, who said later: 'He taught me exactly the depth of music.'

serenade Evening music, especially that sung or played in the open air. Originally it was the song of a troubadour wooing a girl beneath her window (and is used as such, mockingly, in Mozart's *Don Giovanni*). Later it was expanded into a form of agreeable, entertaining music for instrumental groups, and became hardly distinguishable from a *cassation* or *divertimento*. Mozart wrote a number of serenades, including the *Haffner*, for a Salzburg wedding, and the name has been attached to works by Richard Strauss, Stravinsky, and Copland.

serialism In 1921 Arnold Schoenberg assured one of his pupils that he had 'discovered something which will assure the supremacy of German music for the next hundred years'. The discovery was serialism. Schoenberg had been increasingly dissatisfied with the incoherence of atonality, which he felt threatened the great German musical tradition with a lapse into anarchy. Where there was no melodic or harmonic law, there could be no discipline and no shape. Without wishing to return to the worn-out systems of diatonic and chromatic music whose limitations had caused the atonal rebellion in the first place, Schoenberg and his circle of disciples sought a way of creating order out of the prevailing chaos.

The new principle was one of arranging all twelve notes of the chromatic scale in a fixed order or *series* which would condition the progress of the music throughout the rest of the composition. The chosen sequence, or *tone row* (usually called *note row* in Britain), is in itself the main theme of the piece and, like the theme of an earlier symphonic or chamber work, can be inverted, contracted, developed, and exploited throughout various devices and registers; the last note can become the first in a retrograde treatment, or the sequence can be played both backwards and upside down; but it is axiomatic that no one note can be used again until all the other eleven have appeared.

In spite of the rigidity of his theories, Schoenberg himself often broke his own rules, and his most gifted pupil, Alban Berg, put those theories to more flexible use. Anton von Webern was one of the few to adhere puritanically to strict serialism.

Total serialism was a strictly logical application of the basic idea of melodic and harmonic twelve-tone composition to other musical parameters such as rhythm and dynamics, fixing time values, volume, etc., in strictly calculated order.

Serkin, Rudolf (1903–) Austrian (Bohemian) pianist (American citizen 1939). He studied piano and composition in Vienna, and made his début there at the age of twelve. He married the daughter of the violinist Adolf Busch, and made many recital appearances with Busch, including his American début in 1933. Settling in the USA, he taught at the Curtis Institute and in 1968 became its director.

Sérly, Tibór (1900–78) Hungarian composer and string player. He studied in Budapest with Bartók and Kodály, and after Bartók's death completed the score of the third piano concerto and, from the composer's sketches, the viola concerto. Settling in the USA, Sérly played the viola in the Cincinnati Symphony Orchestra and the NBC Symphony Orchestra, and taught in New York. Among his compositions were two symphonies, a viola concerto, and a number of chamber works.

serpent A wind instrument originating in the late sixteenth century, coiled in a long S-shape, which gave it its name. It had a brass mouthpiece, but the body was frequently made of wood, wrapped round with leather. The bass member of the obsolete *cornett* family, it was used in military bands, and provided deep-toned support for church choirs in the days when each church had its small local band rather than an organ.

Serpent.

Sessions, Roger (1896–1985) American composer. He studied at Harvard and Yale, taught at Smith College, Northampton, and worked with Bloch at the Cleveland Institute of Music. After a spell in Italy and Germany, during which his first symphony was performed in Boston, he returned to teach at Boston and other American univer-

sities. His association with Bloch influenced his earlier works, but he became interested in Schoenberg, and his 1953 violin sonata is an essay in twelve-tone composition. Though benefiting from his scholarly knowledge of contemporary trends, he was always an individual artist who could use that knowledge as a creative spark and not merely as a source of ready-made material. His views are clarified in two books *The Musical Experience* and *Questions about Music*.

OTHER WORKS: Opera *Montezuma*. Eight symphonies. Violin concerto. Piano concerto. Two string quartets. Three piano sonatas.

seventh An interval of seven steps between one note and another. In the diatonic scale of C major, the gap between the tonic C and the B above it is a major seventh; up to B flat is a minor seventh; and up to A a diminished seventh (the same, really, as a major sixth, but here regarded as part of the C/E flat/G flat/A diminished seventh chord, useful for modulation because of its indefinite tonality).

sextet A piece for six singers or players; or a group of six such singers or players. Vocal sextets appear in some dramatic operatic scenes, including Mozart's *Don Giovanni* and Donizetti's *Lucia di Lammermoor*. Many combinations have been used for instrumental sextets. When written for strings, there are usually two violins, two violas, and two cellos, as in Brahms's two sonorous works and Schoenberg's *Verklärte Nacht*. Poulenc wrote a *Sextuor* for piano and wind instruments; Janáček's *Mládí* (*Youth*) is a charming suite in four movements for a sextet of flute, oboe, clarinet, bass clarinet, horn and bassoon; and Henry Cowell wrote *Tall Tales* for a brass sextet.

Shankar, Ravi (1920–) Indian composer and sitar-player. He worked with his brother's troupe of dancers and musicians, became director of music to Indian Radio, and founded a school of music in Bombay. His tours of Europe and the USA awoke interest in the playing of the sitar and Indian music as a whole. He has written a concerto for sitar and orchestra, as well as a number of film scores.

shanty, sea Sometimes spelt *chanty*. The hard work on a sailing ship was to some extent alleviated by singing songs whose rhythm matched that of the task in hand. There were two main types: capstan shanties, urging steady effort by men carrying out a job such as heaving on capstan bars; and halyard shanties, where occasional words were accented to encourage the men to 'sway' together, as when hoisting topmasts and yards. Some tunes and words remained popular long after the

Ravi Shankar playing the sitar, around 1950.

coming of steamships, including the very early *Haul the Bowline, Shenandoah,* and *Blow the Man Down,* and *What shall we do with the drunken sailor?.*

sharp The sign ♯ before a note indicates that it should be raised a semitone. The number of sharps in a key signature conditions all notes throughout the following composition. (*See* **Notation.**)

Another application of the word is to singing or playing which goes out of tune upwards – i.e. on the sharp side.

Sharp, Cecil (1859–1924) English folk song and dance collector. He studied as a lawyer, but was also a keen musician, and between 1889 and 1892 was organist of Adelaide Cathedral in Australia. Returning to London, he became principal of the Hampstead Conservatory and began collecting folk music from all over Britain. In 1911 he founded the English Folk-Dance Society, which after his death became the English Folk Dance and Song Society and made its home in Cecil Sharp House in London. During the latter half of World War I he visited the USA to collect songs from the Appalachian mountains which bore traces of English origin, preserved by descendants of early emigrants,

shawm A woodwind instrument with a double-reed mouthpiece, made in many sizes, forerunners of the oboe and bassoon. All models had a wide bell, and the larger ones were much used for outdoor ceremonials because of the volume they could produce. In modern times reconstructions have been made for authentic performances of early music, and similar instruments are still used in some folk music.

shofar An ancient Hebrew wind instrument made of a ram's horn, capable of producing only natural harmonics, still used in synagogue rituals.

Shostakovich, Dmitry (1906–75) Russian composer. He was born in St Petersburg, but by the time he began to study music at the Conservatory this had become Petrograd; and when, during World War II, he worked as a firefighter in the city and lauded its gallant defence in his seventh symphony, it had long been Leningrad. At one stage he had not been sure whether to concentrate on the piano or composition, but composition won, and his energetic, inventive first symphony, performed when he was not yet twenty, appealed not only to Russian audiences but to those in Germany and in the USA, where both Stokowski and Toscanini conducted it.

After harassment by the Soviet authorities, Shostakovitch subtitled his Fifth Symphony *A Soviet Artist's Practical Creative Reply to Just Criticism.*

Shostakovich was a genuine supporter of the Soviet system, and wanted his music to be part of that system. The effect of hearing music from outside Russia, however, especially that of his defecting countrymen Stravinsky and Prokofiev, led him into what was later denounced as 'abstract experimentation'. Instead of loyally churning out patriotic melodies and writing folksy operas or ballets, he wrote the grotesquely humorous opera *The Nose,* based on a story by Gogol, and then went on disastrously with another opera, *The Lady Macbeth of the Mtsensk District.* This tale of a multiple murderess, treated with great gusto, unashamed dissonances and melodic eccentricities, was well received in Moscow and elsewhere; but two years after its first performance in 1934 was suddenly denounced in a great tirade in the newspaper *Pravda* for its 'petty bourgeois sensationalism', coarseness, and 'confusion in place of music'. The opera was withdrawn, to reappear in revised form thirty years later as *Katerina Izmaylova.* The original version had to wait longer, arousing some controversy when produced at the London Coliseum in May 1987.

In the meantime the composer had been forced to go through the motions of repentance. His fifth symphony, ending in a brassy triumphal march, was offered as a 'Soviet artist's reply to just criticism'. He warily put his much more adventurous fourth symphony to one side for the time being. Back in favour, he was awarded a Stalin prize during World War II, and for his own satisfaction wrote a number of chamber works, innocuous on the surface but beautifully fashioned and full of original ideas. Trouble came again in 1948 when he was among the group of musicians condemned for 'formalism' and for inability to communicate comprehensibly with the Soviet people. In 1949 he produced a patriotic oratorio *The Song of the Forests* and a cantata *The Sun Shines over our Motherland.*

From then on until Stalin's death he struck a wary balance between the obligatory nationalist compositions and the demands of his own musical conscience. His tenth symphony, sombre yet heartening in its grandeur, conceals its personal secrets: a theme around the cipher DSCH, based on the composer's initials, plays an important part in its development. The mighty eleventh symphony won a Lenin Prize. Times were easier, and in the thirteenth symphony, with its setting of Yevtushenko's verses about the Nazi massacre of Jews at Babi-Yar, Shostakovich was able to get away with what most people recognized as a symbolic attack on Stalin's atrocities. He travelled freely, spoke out on behalf of international peace movements, and in spite of heart trouble continued to compose, producing among other works his four last string quartets, a worthy coda to all the chamber music into which he had poured more of his own aspirations than he dared risk in larger, more public declarations. After his death his contemporary Khachaturian spoke of him as 'the conscience of Soviet music'.

Sibelius, Jean (1865–1957) Finnish composer. The son of a doctor who died of cholera when the boy was still an infant, he was brought up by his mother and grandmother. Showing musical interests at an early age, he had hopes of becoming a great violinist, but at university in Helsinki started out, as so many composers seem to have done, by studying law. He then turned to the study of composition in Helsinki, Berlin and Vienna. When he returned to his homeland in 1891 he began work on his first large-scale orchestral and choral symphonic poem, *Kullervo*, based on legends in the *Kalevala*, a Finnish verse epic to which he was to return on many occasions. In that same year he married Aino Järnefeldt, who in due course presented him with five daughters.

National legend and the landscapes of his country suffused everything he wrote. From small cells of musical material he built sweeping tone poems which conjured up visions of forest, storm, and ancient mythological figures. In 1899 he contributed to an historical pageant a short orchestral piece, *Finlandia*, which became almost a national anthem in defiance of Russian hegemony. That was also the year in which he wrote the first of his seven symphonies. (Rumours

In his studio the sculptor Väinö Aaltonen compares his marble bust of Jean Sibelius with the composer himself.

have existed for some years of the existence of an eighth symphony, but although there is some evidence that he arranged for the copying of some parts of the score, it is also thought that in self-critical mood he destroyed the whole thing.)

Granted a state pension at the age of thirty-two by his grateful country, Sibelius continued to work on symphonies and tone poems which at first hearing could sound chill and forbidding, but which gradually made their mark in other countries, most impressively in England. His approach to music changed little over the years. He lived as a recluse, known to drink heavily, and slowly produced intensely emotional works which might have been hewn from his native landscape rather than from his musical experience: nature, he declared, was the book that most inspired him. His fifth symphony perhaps conveys most directly the essence of his creative methods: starting on four notes which prove to be the kernel of the whole first movement, it moves on through a reflective second movement to a nobler, swelling, forever climbing finale. Yet to set disturbingly against it there are the eerie puzzles of its predecessor, the fourth symphony, so abstract and tonally wayward that one wonders what mythical land Sibelius had ventured into this time.

The last composition of any real significance was the tone poem *Tapiola*, a masterpiece in which the orchestration is transmuted into an utterly absorbing, terrifying reality: the evocation of the howling, all-powerful forest god Tapio. After this Sibelius wrote almost nothing for the quarter of a century before his death. His unique voice nevertheless left the world a legacy which will need frequent reappraisal: even now his songs have not received their full due, and although concert programmes repeatedly feature the melancholy tone poem *The Swan of Tuonela*, there are many other gems which can glow if given the right setting. The string quartet *Voces intimae* (*Friendly Voices*) undeniably matches the title he bestowed on it.

siciliano In French, *sicilienne*. A slow, lilting dance in 6/8 time, supposedly of Sicilian origin, popular in the eighteenth century and often forming part of a suite. A more recent example is the graceful *sicilienne* in Fauré's incidental music to Maeterlinck's play *Pelléas et Mélisande*.

sight reading Some singers and instrumentalists have the ability to convert written music into the correct sounds at first sight. This depends to some extent on the equal ability to look ahead and, as it were, see what is coming round the corner of the next bar. The German equivalent is a fine linguistic cocktail: *prima vista spielen*.

signature tune Broadcasts of dance bands between the two world wars were usually prefaced by an identifying tune – a 'signature' in advance, though the number was usually repeated for a fade-out at the end.

similar motion *See* **motion**.

Simpson, Robert (1921–) English composer. He studied with Herbert Howells, and from 1951 to 1980 worked on the music staff of the BBC. His work has been influenced by Bruckner and Carl Nielsen, about whom he has written books which won him the Bruckner Medal and the Nielsen Medal. Although the large-scale nineteenth-century symphony has fallen out of fashion in this century, Simpson continues to work convincingly in that medium, but prefers the string quartet above all: by 1987 he had written eleven. In 1983 he produced a set of orchestral *Variations on a Theme of Carl Nielsen*, written with Nielsen's own pencil, presented to him by the composer's daughter.

OTHER WORKS: Piano concerto. Violin concerto. Symphonic study *Energy* for brass band. Clarinet quintet. *Variations and fugue* for recorder and string quartet.

Sinding, Christian (1856–1941) Norwegian composer. He spent most of his life in Oslo apart from a few terms teaching at the Eastman School, New York. From 1915 onwards he received a pension from the Norwegian government. He composed four symphonies, chamber music, and over two hundred songs, but is best known for his romantic piano piece, *Rustle of Spring*.

sinfonia *See* **symphony**.

singspiel German for a 'song-play', used early in the eighteenth century to describe opera in general, but later applied specifically to ballad opera styles in which the dialogue was spoken and not declaimed in recitative. Mozart's *Die Entführung aus dem Serail* and *Die Zauberflöte* are both advanced examples of *singspiel* and so, strictly speaking, in spite of its serious nature, is Beethoven's *Fidelio*. Berthold Brecht and Kurt Weill revived the form in *The Threepenny Opera*.

sitar A lute-like Indian instrument with a long, slender neck and a gourd bowl. Below seven main strings are up to twelve sympathetic strings, tuned to the notes of whichever *rāga* is being performed. The neck carries movable frets, and the strings are played by a plectrum or by fingernails. (*See also* **Shankar, Ravi**.)

Six, Les 'The Six', a name given to a group of young French composers who, influenced by the avant-garde ideas of Jean Cocteau and Erik Satie, came together in Paris in 1917 to pool ideas and further the cause of modern music. The six consisted of Georges Auric, Louis Durey, Arthur

Honegger, Darius Milhaud, Francis Poulenc and Germaine Tailleferre. In fact they each had a quite distinctive, individual style, and soon pursued separate paths.

sixth An interval of six steps between one note and another. In the diatonic scale of C major, the gap between the tonic C and the A above it is a major sixth; up to A flat is a minor sixth; and up to A sharp an augmented sixth (in effect, on a keyboard, the same as a minor seventh). The frequent 'chord of the sixth' consists of a C major triad, C/E/G, with an A added above the G. The so-called *Neapolitan sixth* (origin unknown) is the first inversion of a chromatic chord built on the flattened supertonic of a scale: in the key of C, this becomes F/A flat/D flat.

Skalkottas, Nikos (1904–49) Greek composer. He studied the violin at Athens Conservatory and then composition in Berlin under Schoenberg and Weill. Returning to Athens in 1933, he became an orchestral violinist, collected Greek folk music, and composed large-scale orchestral and chamber works which attracted little attention until after his death, when a committee was formed to publish and promote them. His sets of *Greek Dances* are vigorous nationalistic interpretations of folk music; but his other music was largely in twelve-note form, sometimes attempting a complex multi-serialism, or utterly atonal.

sketch The word can be used for a composer's first draft of a work (Beethoven kept very detailed sketchbooks of progress on various pieces), or for an actual piece of music, short and usually programmatic, e.g. Sterndale Bennett's *Three Musical Sketches*. The French equivalent, *esquisse*, is frequently used, as in the English composer Nigel Osborne's *Esquisses* of 1987, which he described as 'a short lyrical piece for strings which confronts a series of contrasting musical images'.

Costume designs by Wenig for a 1928 production of Smetana's opera *The Bartered Bride*.

Slezak, Leo (1873–1946) Austro-Hungarian (Moravian) tenor. He studied in Paris and made his operatic début in Brno as *Lohengrin*. From 1901 until 1926 he sang at the Vienna Opera under Mahler, and with Mahler gave the American première of Tchaikovsky's *The Queen of Spades*. After retiring from the operatic stage he appeared as a comedian in several films; and his son Walter followed him in this field with many Hollywood rôles.

slide The notes of a trombone are produced not by fingering but by the action of a tube, known as a slide, which is moved in and out while the instrument is being played. The word can also be applied to the movement of the finger along a string without lifting it.

slur In musical notation, a curved line above two or more notes which are to be played or sung smoothly.

Smetana, Bedřich (1824–84) Bohemian (Czech) composer. His father was a brewer and an accomplished amateur violinist who encouraged the boy's musical leanings. After studying in Prague and imbibing fervent nationalist ideals there, he helped man the barricades during an abortive rebellion in 1848 against Austrian rule. That same year, having tried and failed to command attention as a piano virtuoso, he opened his own music school, and the following year married. Only one of their four daughters survived, his wife became tubercular, and Smetana himself grew more and more depressed about future prospects in his homeland.

In 1856 he was offered the musical directorship of the Gothenburg Philharmonic Society in Sweden, made a name as a piano recitalist, and began composing symphonic poems such as *Wallenstein's Camp* and *Haakon Jarl*. In 1859 his wife died; a year later he remarried; and in 1861 they returned to Prague. His nationalist aspirations rekindled, Smetana entered a competition for the best historical and comic operas on Czech themes. His entry was *The Brandenburgers in Bohemia*. Because of the intrigues of a hostile cabal, it won only a grudging 'conditional' prize; and he was also passed over for the appointment of opera director at the new Czech Provisional Theatre. When the opera was at last staged there, five years later, its patriotic story made it an immediate success, and now at last Smetana was appointed conductor of the Provisional Theatre.

He had a second opera ready, having been working on it despite the delays in staging the first one. This was in quite different mood: from a stirring heroic theme he had turned to one of rural love and laughter. *The Bartered Bride*, with its sparkling melodies, exuberant dance rhythms

and glittering orchestration, was the first truly Czech opera – but one whose musical language has been understood all over the world. From now on Smetana shared his time between serious historic operas such as *Dalibor*, with its tale of a legendary Czech hero not unlike that of *Fidelio*, and tuneful comedies such as *The Two Widows*. Then, at the height of his career, he was forced to relinquish his theatre post and the income that went with it.

In 1874, plagued by pains in the ears for some time, he went deaf. Although he could hear nothing of his own or anybody else's music from outside, however, he was tormented by shrieks and whistling inside his head. Doggedly he continued work on more operas, and completed the superb cycle of symphonic poems, *Má Vlast* (*My Country*), conjuring up six aspects of his beloved homeland and its stormy history. In 1881 the opening of the new National Theatre was marked by the first production of another patriotic work, his opera *Libuše*, which Smetana attended although he could not hear a note.

Retiring with his surviving daughter Zofie and her husband to the country, he poured his heart and memories into the string quartet in E minor, *From my Life*, and wrote his final opera, *The Devil's Wall*, a comedy set in a great castle beside the river Vltava: a comedy which turns sardonic and sour, mocking romantic notions of chivalry while still producing the most ecstatic music, suffused with a passion as vigorous as it had ever been. Its first few performances were poorly received. 'They want nothing else from me!' lamented the composer, by now alternating between shrieking bouts and paralysed silences. In April 1884 he had to be taken to Prague lunatic asylum, where he died three weeks later. The autopsy showed the cause as syphilis.

Smith, John Stafford (1750–1836) English composer and organist. He was first a Chorister and then a Gentleman of the Chapel Royal, and wrote many canons and other church music. His song *Anacreon in Heaven* was to form the musical basis of *The Star-Spangled Banner*.

Smyth, (Dame) Ethel (1858–1944) English composer. She studied in Leipzig and Berlin, and her first three operas were first performed in Germany. An active suffragette, she composed *March of the Women* for the cause, and spent some time in gaol for her beliefs. Her operas *The Wreckers* and *The Boatswain's Mate* are finely dramatic and move along at a great pace, but she became embittered by the belief that as a woman she was being neglected by critics and audiences, and towards the end of her life suffered from near-deafness.

Söderström, Elisabeth (1927–) Swedish soprano. She studied in Stockholm and became a member of the Royal Opera there, later consolidating her reputation at Salzburg, Glyndebourne, and the New York Met. It has been said of her that few prima donnas since World War II have been so responsive to different challenges, from Monteverdi to twentieth-century operas, or so willing to work with small companies on interesting projects. She has been especially moving in her performances and recordings – in Czech – of the great female rôles in Janáček's operas.

solfeggio (and **tonic sol-fa**) A system of teaching sight-reading and training the ear to recognize tone sequences in any key by means of names instead of notes written on a staff. This is a common practice in France and Italy; the term *solfège* is generally used in France to cover elementary musical training in general. The early nineteenth-century English adaptation of *tonic sol-fa* was taken up in schools in spite of obvious drawbacks. Starting from the tonic of any key, the ascending sequence, named doh-ray-me-fah-soh-lah-te-doh, enables the singer to discern intervals well enough; but the introduction of accidentals requires vowel changes, and note lengths are shown by a complex system of dots, double dots, commas and horizontal lines.

solo A composition or part of a composition sung or played by one performer, with or without accompaniment. (The plural, for a group of performers, is *soli*.) The *solo organ* is one manual of an organ which controls melodic *solo stops*, e.g. the flute or clarinet stops.

Solti, (Sir) Georg (1912–) Hungarian conductor (British citizen 1972). He studied with Bartók, Kodály and Dohnányi, worked at the Budapest Opera, and became its conductor in 1934. In 1939 he moved to Switzerland, making a living as a pianist, but after World War II returned to conducting in Munich and Frankfurt. He made his American début in San Francisco in 1953 and later appeared at the New York Met. Between 1961 and 1971 he was a transfiguring influence as musical director of Covent Garden, London. With the Vienna Philharmonic Orchestra and a cast of the world's leading Wagnerian singers, he conducted the first complete stereo recording of the *Ring* cycle: the fascinating story of the achievement is detailed in *Ring Resounding*, a book by the project's recording administrator, John Culshaw.

Somervell, (Sir) Arthur (1863–1937) English composer. He studied in Cambridge and Berlin, taught at the Royal College of Music, and from 1901 onwards served for many years as a schools music inspector. He wrote a number of skilled if undemanding orchestral and choral works, but was much more lyrically persuasive in the song cycles *Maud* and *A Shropshire Lad*.

sonata and **sonata form** The most straightforward interpretation of the word *sonata* is 'something sounded', as opposed to *cantata*, 'something sung'. It came to be applied to one-movement instrumental pieces in contrapuntal style similar to that of vocal motets and madrigals. As other movements in contrasting tempos were added, the *trio sonata* became a favourite of the baroque era, using two solo voices (often violins, or perhaps a flute and violin or other instrument) above a *continuo*, rather in the manner of two operatic singers interweaving their dialogue above a harmonized accompaniment. For church use, such a piece was called a *sonata da chiesa*; for secular use, in the form of a dance suite, it was a *sonata da camera*.

During the classical period there were many solo keyboard sonatas, and at the same time *sonata form* was applied to movements in chamber music, symphonies, and concertos. Basically it has three sections:

Exposition A first subject (or theme) is stated. A bridge passage leads to a second subject, in a different but related key (usually the dominant). Occasionally there may be further new subjects, and contrasts of key and transitional sections enliven the chosen themes. The exposition is almost invariably repeated, and may be rounded off by a brief decorative *codetta*.

Development This takes fragments of the preceding subjects and plays about with them melodically, harmonically and contrapuntally, twisting the stated themes into new shapes and building up to a climax through modulations which leave the listener poised for a return to the original mood and key.

Recapitulation The first subject returns in its original tonic key, and this is even more firmly re-established by the fact that the bridge passage this time does not modulate to a relative key but stays in the tonic. The whole movement is concluded by an extended coda.

A *sonatina* is a 'little sonata', lighter but not necessarily trivial: Beethoven and Clementi wrote admirable ones, and there are some demanding technical problems in those by Ravel and Milhaud. (*See also* **rondo**.)

song A short composition for the human voice, solo or accompanied; though Mendelssohn wrote a set of piano pieces with 'singing' melodies which he designated *Songs without Words*. The term can cover many varieties of expression, from the simplest folk song to the highly developed works of major composers, when they are usually known in English rather clumsily as 'art songs', in French as *chansons*, and in German as *lieder*. In a *song cycle* the composer links separate pieces either by using verses from the same poet or by choosing a unifying theme such as love, death, or some legendary subject. Fauré's *La Bonne chanson* is based on love poems by Verlaine; Copland set *Twelve Poems of Emily Dickinson*; and it is difficult to count the number of English composers who have produced their own versions of lines from Housman's *A Shropshire Lad*.

sopranino A 'little soprano', e.g. instruments of higher register than soprano, such as the sopra-nino recorder and the rarely used sopranino saxophone in E flat.

soprano The highest register of the female voice (or a *castrato*, or a boy's unbroken voice – though this is generally referred to as a *treble*). Normal range is between middle C and the C two octaves above it, though composers have written up to top F above that. The term is also applied to some instruments, e.g. the soprano saxophone.

Sousa, John Philip (1854–1932) American composer and bandmaster. He joined the United States Marine Band when he was thirteen, left it five years later to play the violin in theatre orchestras,

A German collection of Sousa's world-renowned marches.

and then returned as leader of the Marine Band. In 1892 he formed his own ensemble, Sousa's Band, with which he toured all over the USA and most of Europe. Not content with playing standard works and introducing the public to arrangements of composers such as Wagner and Dvořák, he wrote about a hundred rousing marches, including *The Stars and Stripes* and *The Washington Post*, and became justifiably known as 'The March King'. He also composed eleven operettas, extracts from which he featured in his band programmes.

sousaphone A brass instrument of the tuba family, developed for use in John Philip Sousa's band. Part of its tubing winds round the player's body. In the earliest model the wide bell pointed upwards, but later was altered to face outwards, capable of being turned to project the maximum volume in the required direction. Until the introduction of the string double bass it was a common feature of jazz bands, providing a steady, audible backing in New Orleans street parades.

Speaks, Oley (1874–1948) American composer and baritone. He wrote and performed over two hundred songs, providing showpieces for many later baritones, among them *When the Boys Come Home* and *The Road to Mandalay*.

species The five strict types of counterpoint allowed by academic rules, as laid down in Fux's early eighteenth-century *Gradus ad Parnassum* (*Steps to Parnassus*), which defines the permitted treatment of one note in relation to others. These pedantic regulations, which can be broken by any truly creative composer, are useful as disciplines for the beginner, taking the following forms:

First species Second or other subsidiary voice moves at the same pace as the notes of the original subject (or *cantus firmus*).

Second species Second or other subsidiary voice moves against the original subject at twice the pace.

Third species Second or other subsidiary voice moves at four or six times the pace of the original.

Fourth species Second or other subsidiary voice moves at the same pace as in the second species, but is syncopated by ties between the second note in the bar and the first note of the next bar.

Fifth species Second or other subsidiary voice uses any or all of the devices from the other species and can also introduce shorter notes, *stretti*, etc.

speech-song *See* **sprechgesang**.

spiritual A religious revival hymn, often with folksong elements, of southern Blacks in the USA. Many were based on the pentatonic scale, sung to a rhythmic accompaniment of hand-clapping. The melodies are usually simple, suitable for use in church services, as were the Lutheran chorales of Bach's time, but with different nuances and an instinctive use of slurred or flattened notes which had a great influence on jazz. Major interpreters for the benefit of white American and European audiences have been Paul Robeson, Marian Anderson and Mahalia Jackson. Michael Tippett, while wondering what contemporary substitute he could use for Christian hymns or chorales in his oratorio *A Child of our Time*, heard someone on the radio singing the spiritual *Steal Away*, and at once knew that its mood, transcending all individual doctrines, was what he needed.

Spitta, Julius August Philipp (1841–94) German musicologist. He taught in Leipzig and Berlin, and became permanent secretary to the Berlin Academy of Arts. He edited the works of Schütz and Buxtehude, as well as some of Frederick the Great's, and wrote a two-volume treatise on the life and works of Bach, clashing in many respects with the views of Albert Schweitzer in two later volumes on the same subject.

Spohr, Ludwig (1784–1859) German composer and violinist. In public life he came to use the name

An engraving by M. Esslinger of the composer Ludwig Spohr, whose operas *Faust*, *Undine*, and *Jessonda* made him as popular in his time as any of his contemporaries: on visiting England he was acclaimed almost as warmly as Mendelssohn.

Louis rather than Ludwig. At fourteen he became violinist in the orchestra of the Duke of Brunswick, who was so impressed by his playing that he arranged for him to take further lessons and travel with Franz Eck, an admired virtuoso of the time. Later Spohr was to make many international concert tours of his own, becoming particularly admired in England, where he is thought to have been the first to conduct an orchestra with a baton instead of relying on the occasional gesture from a violin bow or from a keyboard. As a conductor, he was an early champion of Wagner's music. As a composer, he provoked protests in Norwich, England, from local dignitaries who disapproved of professional singers (including opera singers) performing his oratorio *Calvary* in the cathedral; but he was nevertheless commissioned to write another oratorio, *The Fall of Babylon*, for the city's next triennial festival. Among his chamber works, the Octet in E major and the Nonet in F major have remained perennial favourites.

OTHER WORKS: Eleven operas including *Faust*. Nine symphonies. Fifteen violin concertos. Two clarinet concertos. Thirty-four string quartets.

sprechgesang and **sprechstimme** *Sprechgesang* is German for 'spoken song', or 'speech-song'. Humperdinck employed it in the first version of his opera *Königskinder* (*The King's Children*), whose dialogue was inflected in speaking style but with parallel music played strictly in tune by instruments of the orchestra. Schoenberg demanded that in his *Pierrot lunaire* the voice should first pitch the note exactly 'but then immediately leave it on a fall or·rise'. For this he preferred the description *sprechstimme*, implying a 'speaking voice' rather than 'speech-song'. Berg used similar methods in *Wozzeck*, and Boulez adapted them for 'spoken intonation at the pitch indicated'.

Stadler, Anton (1753–1812) Austrian clarinettist. A member of the Court orchestra in Vienna, he so impressed Mozart with his clarinet playing that the composer wrote three of his most exquisite works, the clarinet concerto, quintet, and trio.

staff (or **stave**) The horizontal system of five parallel lines on which music is written. (Plainchant used four lines.) Such music is called *staff notation* to distinguish it from the symbols of *tonic sol-fa*. (*See also* **Notation**.)

Stainer, (Sir) John (1840–1901) English composer, organist and teacher. He became a choirboy at St Paul's Cathedral, London, at the age of seven, and after studying at Oxford served as St Paul's organist from 1872 until 1888. He succeeded Arthur Sullivan as principal of the National Training School for Music, and from 1889 was professor of music at Oxford University. Among

a great deal of church music he wrote a cantata much performed in his own day and frequently revived since, *The Crucifixion*.

Stamitz family Bohemian composers and instrumentalists. Jan Václav Stamic (1717–57) was engaged by the Elector of Mannheim as violinist and musical director of his orchestra, and Germanized his Czech name to Johann Wenzel Stamitz. He composed some fifty symphonies and a number of violin concertos, but was most highly esteemed for the standards which he imposed on the orchestra, impressing contemporary audiences and musicians, including Haydn and Mozart. His brother Anton joined him there, but later became a priest. Johann fathered two sons in Mannheim: the older was Karel (later Karl) (1745–1801), who played second violin in the orchestra for some time before going off to Paris with his brother Jan (later Johann Anton) (1754–1809) and becoming an even more prolific symphonist than their father.

Stanford, (Sir) Charles Villiers (1852–1924) Irish composer and teacher. He studied at Cambridge and served as organist to Trinity College from 1873 to 1892, with intervals for further study in Leipzig and Berlin. As conductor of the Cambridge University Music Society he introduced new works to audiences there, including some first performances of works by Brahms, and was invited by Tennyson to compose incidental music for his *Queen Mary*. Among his pupils when he became professor of composition at the Royal College of Music, where he also conducted the orchestra and opera classes, were Vaughan Williams, John Ireland and Gustav Holst. Some of them found his traditionalism and his adoration of Brahms stifling and referred ruefully to the 'limiting effects of his pedantry'; but he was not to be coaxed into any new thought, and his own attractive compositions are thoroughly orthodox in their handling of frequently Irish themes, as in his *Irish Symphony* and six *Irish Rhapsodies* for orchestra. He published five collections of Irish folksong.

Stanley, John (1713–86) English composer and organist. Blind from the age of two, he studied with Maurice Greene, St Paul's Cathedral organist, from the age of seven and himself became organist in various London churches, including that of the Temple. In 1760 he went into partnership with John Christopher Smith, and later with Thomas Linley, to carry on Handel's oratorio concerts. He composed an oratorio of his own, *Jephtha*, a number of cantatas and organ voluntaries, and six concertos for strings. In 1779 he succeeded William Boyce as Master of the King's Music.

steel band A familiar ensemble in the Caribbean, consisting of oil drums 'tuned' to different pitches by cutting them to different lengths and indenting or sectionalizing the tops, which act as drumheads. The sound can be as haunting as that of a marimba band.

Steinway firm A firm of piano manufacturers founded in New York in 1853 by Heinrich Engelhardt Steinweg, who had emigrated from Germany with his five sons, two of whom joined him in the business. Two years later they displayed at the New York World Fair an iron-framed instrument of greatly improved sonority. In the 1860s the family name was amended to Steinway. The third son joined the firm and developed the modern concert grand, and in 1875 the fourth opened a London branch. Their pianos are still among the finest in the world.

Stenhammar, Vilhelm (1871–1927) Swedish composer and conductor. He studied music privately in Stockholm and Berlin, and led a career divided between composing, playing the piano, and conducting, notably the orchestra of the Royal Theatre in Stockholm and, for fifteen years from 1903 onwards, the Gothenburg Symphony Orchestra. He was a friend of Nielsen and Sibelius, and his intensely romantic style had something in common with theirs, though rather more earnestly

A Steinway grand piano.

Isaac Stern rehearsing with the London Philharmonic Orchestra for a Royal Festival Hall concert in November 1961. In 1985, still at the peak of his powers, he commissioned and retained exclusive performing rights in a concerto, *The Tree of Dreams*, from Henri Dutilleux.

Germanic than Scandinavian. He wrote two operas, two symphonies, two appealing *Sentimental Romances* for violin and orchestra, and six string quartets.

Stern, Isaac (1920–) American violinist. Born in Russia, he was taken to San Francisco as a child, and made his début there in 1934 with the San Francisco Symphony Orchestra. Nine years later he made his first appearance in New York. A player who mixes technical virtuosity, unfailing accuracy and infectious enthusiasm for his work, he has played in distinguished company as a chamber musician, and performed and recorded most of the major concertos for the instrument.

stimmung German for the tuning of an instrument. It is also used for a mood or disposition, as in Richard Strauss's piano pieces, *Stimmungsbilder* (*Impressionist Pictures*). Stockhausen's *Stimmung* (*Tuning*) is a work for six singers using no actual words but combining Asian vocal nuances with electronic amplification, allowing for choices from the harmonic series.

stochastic From the Greek word *stochos*, a target or goal, this is a term taken by the composer Xenakis from the mathematical theories of probability to denote random musical elements in whose progress the degree of choice gradually narrows until there is an inevitable goal in sight. The word has come to be used to describe compositions in which overall contours are well

defined but details within are left to chance as the composer finds his way, sometimes according to his own mood and sometimes by use of a computer.

Stockhausen, Karlheinz (1928–) German composer. The son of a village schoolmaster, he studied in Cologne after World War II, at the same time playing the piano in bars and as accompanist to a conjuring act. At a Darmstadt summer school in 1951 he met Nono, Boulez and Messiaen, and was taken with the concept of organizing music 'rationally' in total serialism. One result was his *Kreuzspiel* (*Crossplay*) for piano, oboe, bass clarinet and three percussionists, involving a crossplay of twelve-tone sets of pitch classes (a term invented by Babbitt for sets of all pitches of the same name in any register – e.g. top C, middle C, etc.) and durations. He also became interested in *musique concrète* and electronic music, took on co-directorship of the West German Radio electronic studio, and was one of the first to use purely synthesized sound.

One of the most influential composers and teachers of the second half of the twentieth century, Stockhausen evolved and disseminated theories of dimensions of sound which would encompass pitch, duration, timbre and every other conceivable element in a unification of all the world's musical cultures and methods. He pre-planned his form schemes and then introduced into them a variety of musical processes, sounds from exotic backgrounds, electronic devices, and austere ritual formulas. He coined the phrase *moment form* to suggest that his audience should concentrate on each moment or short section rather than grope for relationships between such moments. This matched his belief that different sections could also be shuffled around at will. His *Momente* for soprano, four choral groups, eight brass, two electric organs and three percussionists set a number of texts in different sections which each evoked an individual aspect of colour, pitch and duration.

Taken to extremes, some of his theories could culminate in a grouping such as *Aus den sieben Tagen* (*From these Seven Days*), fifteen pieces for instrumental ensemble with a score consisting only of short texts around which the performers have to invent their own music. In spite of the mathematical disciplines which he has frequently favoured, Stockhausen has at the same time allowed more and more for these elements of chance, and in later years has shown a growing

Karlheinz Stockhausen, who has performed a great deal of his electronic music with his own ensemble, aiming for a synthesis of every musical element in the whole world.

conviction that music exists above all for inducing a telepathic communication between composer, player and listener, without the restrictions of ancient rules. He has also conceived many works for his own travelling ensemble and for entire evenings of almost Wagnerian commitment. At the Osaka Exposition in 1970 he managed to have an entire building dedicated to the presentation of his music.

OTHER WORKS: *Gruppen* (*Groups*) for three orchestras. *Inori* (Japanese for *Adorations*) for mimes and orchestra. *Gesang der Jünglinge* (*Song of the Young Boys*) for boy's voice and electronic tape. Eleven *Klavierstücke* (*Piano Pieces*). Projected cycle of seven operas, or 'ceremonies', *Licht* (*Light*).

Stokowski, Leopold (1882–1977) English-born conductor (American citizen 1915). Son of a Polish father and an Irish mother, he became a London church organist and then between 1905 and 1908 organist to St Bartholomew's in New York. After a spell conducting in London, he returned to the USA and made a name as conductor of the Philadelphia Orchestra, introducing many new works to audiences there. He conducted several other leading American orchestras, and after settling in England in 1972 was frequently guest conductor of the London Symphony Orchestra. He made a much-used orchestral arrangement of Bach's organ *Toccata and Fugue in D minor*, appeared in a popular film with Deanna Durbin, and conducted the music for Walt Disney's full-length cartoon *Fantasia*.

Stolz, Robert (1880–1975) Austrian composer and conductor. He studied in Vienna, made some appearances as a child prodigy pianist playing Mozart, and conducted the first performance of Lehár's *The Merry Widow*. He composed some sixty operettas of his own, including *Two Hearts in Waltz-time*, and more than a hundred film scores, many of them in Hollywood between 1938 and 1950.

stop and **stopping** On an organ or harpsichord, the handle used for altering the pipe or string tone is called a stop. *Stopping* refers also to the alteration of tone quality governed in a horn by pushing the fist into the bell, and to the fingering of strings (thereby shortening them) on a stringed instrument; *double stopping* being the fingering of two or more strings at once.

Stradella, Alessandro (1645–82) Italian composer. A well-born dilettante, he taught singing in Venice and Rome, and eloped with the young betrothed of a Venetian senator. He wrote a number of operas in the then fashionable style, some secular and sacred cantatas, and was murdered in Genoa. A meledramatic picture of this killing is presented in Flotow's opera *Stradella*.

The coats of arms and labels of the great Cremona violin makers – Amati, Stradivari, and Guarneri.

Stradivari family The Latinized version has become familiar as Stradivarius. The family established a tradition of violin and cello making in Cremona after Antonio Stradivari (1644–1737) had been apprenticed to Amati and then started his own workshop. He made more powerful, resonant instruments than his tutor, and experimented with different woods and varnishes to achieve the perfection he sought. It is recorded that he made well over a thousand instruments – the last of them in the final, ninety-third, year of his life – of which six hundred still survive. A number of his eleven children followed in his footsteps.

strathspey A Scottish folk dance of late eighteenth-century origin, in quadruple time with dotted rhythms and the frequent figure of a *Scotch snap*, similar to the reel but slower.

Straus, Oscar (1870–1954) Austrian composer (French citizen 1939). He studied in Vienna and Berlin, and conducted theatre orchestras in a number of German towns. Among successful operettas which he composed were *Der tapfere Soldat* (*The Chocolate Soldier*), based on George

Bernard Shaw's play *Arms and the Man*, and *Ein Waltzertraum* (*A Waltz Dream*). After 1927 he spent most of his life between New York and Paris, and had a late success with the captivating waltz for the film *La Ronde*.

Strauss family Austrian composers and conductors. Johann Strauss I (or 'the elder') (1804–49) was the son of an innkeeper near the banks of the Danube in Vienna. His mother died when he was seven. Shortly after remarrying, his father was found drowned in the river, and Johann was brought up by his stepmother and her next husband. Although at the age of thirteen he was apprenticed to a bookbinder, he was much more interested in the music made by strolling players, and ran away in the hope of joining them. Brought home, he was allowed to take music lessons, and was soon playing the viola in a popular Viennese dance orchestra along with Josef Lanner. When Lanner left to form his own successful orchestra, Strauss joined him, became leader of a second group, began composing waltzes, and then in 1826 emulated his friend by leaving to form his own fourteen-piece orchestra.

As well as playing for dancing in a large suburban hall, they presented regular interludes of concert pieces, and Strauss was appointed *kapellmeister* of the First Bürger-regiment and director of the Imperial Court fêtes and balls. He took the orchestra on tours of Europe, and played in England during the celebrations for Queen Victoria's coronation. Of his two hundred and fifty works, about one hundred and fifty were waltzes, but he was equally celebrated for the introduction of the quadrille to Viennese society, and for rousing works such as the *Radetzky March*. In 1849 he made a final visit to England, and shortly after his return home contracted scarlet fever and died.

Johann Strauss II (or 'the younger') (1825–99) was not encouraged by his father to take up music but studied in secret, and in 1844 began leading a rival orchestra in waltzes composed by Johann the elder and by himself. He became the more admired of the two, and after his father's death amalgamated the two orchestras to make himself indisputably 'the Waltz King'. Like his predecessor, he toured Europe, and in due course took over administration of the Imperial Court balls. For ten years after 1855 he presented summer concerts in St Petersburg. Even more prolific than the elder Johann, he composed about four hundred lilting waltzes, among them the unforgettable *Tales from the Vienna Woods* and what is probably the best-known piece in all Viennese music, *The Blue Danube*. His friend Brahms once sketched the opening bars of this on a fan owned

A 1901 title page of Johann Strauss II's music entitled *Jugend (Youth)*.

by Strauss's wife, and added the words: 'Unfortunately not by Johannes Brahms.' In addition to the waltzes, polkas and quadrilles, Strauss, fired by what he had seen of French operetta, set himself to write Viennese equivalents. The most glittering results were *Die Fledermaus* (*The Bat*) and *Der Zigeunerbaron* (*The Gipsy Baron*).

Having married a well-to-do popular soprano, he decided to give up conducting to devote himself to composition; though in fact he shared his time between this and philandering with other women. The orchestra was taken over by his younger brother Josef Strauss (1827–70), who had also been discouraged by their father from taking up a musical career, but had also disobeyed. He composed almost three hundred waltzes, but lacked the real verve of his father and brother. Nervous by temperament, he underwent great humiliation from Russian officers while conducting an ill-disciplined orchestra in Warsaw, collapsed, and returned to Vienna to die.

Strauss, Richard (1864–1949) German composer and conductor. The son of a Munich horn-player, he had early lessons on the piano and violin, and showed a precocious talent for composition. At the age of twenty-one he impressed the conductor Hans von Bülow and was taken on as assistant conductor of the Meiningen Court Orchestra, succeeding Bülow within a month. It

was the beginning of a career shared between conducting and composing. He had already written two symphonies, a number of songs, and two works for wind ensemble. Now, breaking away from traditional styles, he began to explore new harmonic territory and to contemplate music as a means of colourful expression rather than as a self-sufficient art form in itself. His first symphonic poem, *Aus Italien* (*From Italy*), was a summing-up of the effects an Italian journey had had on him. It was to be followed over the years by other dramatic orchestral works such as *Don Juan*, *Tod und Verklärung* (*Death and Transfiguration*), *Till Eulenspiegel*, and *Ein Heldenleben* (*A Hero's Life*), in which the 'hero' is shamelessly Strauss himself. One tone poem in which mood and music are most happily blended is *Don Quixote*, in the form of theme and variations, with the grave but sometimes awkward cello embodying the character of Quixote, and exquisite touches such as the oboe evocation of the beautiful Dulcinea.

The lushness, sometimes extravagance, of the orchestration enraptured some listeners but provoked anger from others. A critic in the 1920s looked back on Strauss's complexities and personal assertiveness as heralding only 'The false dawn of modern music'. There was further controversy with his operas. *Salome*, based on an erotic play by Oscar Wilde and evolved through appropriately sensual, fierce music, was condemned for blasphemy and obscenity. The charge of obscenity was also levelled at *Elektra*, with a libretto by the poet Hugo von Hofmannsthal. Strauss continued to work with Hofmannsthal, and they have left a treasure-house of correspondence to show all the ups and downs of collaboration between composer and librettist.

In 1911 came the resounding success of the gentler, but still provocatively, ironically scored *Der Rosenkavalier* (*The Knight of the Rose*), with Viennese waltz rhythms in the orchestra and voices displaying Strauss's gift for soaring, apparently endless *cantilena*, which was to be nostalgically conjured up again, much later, in his *Four Last Songs*. In equally engaging yet stringent, almost neo-classical style was *Ariadne auf Naxos* (*Ariadne on Naxos*), which he tackled in a couple of experimental ways before getting the final version right: it began as a musical epilogue to a German-language performance of Molière's play *Le Bourgeois Gentilhomme*, for which Strauss had

A strange linguistic amalgam: Richard Strauss's controversial opera *Salome* was based on a play by the Anglo-Irish Oscar Wilde, written in French, translated into German by Hedwig Lachmann.

provided incidental music, and then he decided to provide an explanatory prologue which introduced the composer himself as a character, and did away with the purely spoken dialogue of the play.

From 1919 to 1924 he was joint director of the Vienna Opera, resigning after many a stormy controversy. When Hitler came to power, Strauss, regarded as a truly Germanic successor to Wagner, was created President of the State Music Council without having even been asked. He carried out his duties for a while until repeated interference – including a ban on his using the Jewish writer Stefan Zweig as librettist – led him to resign. On the whole he was then left warily alone, apart from occasional harassment because of having a Jewish daughter-in-law. In spite of this he was put on trial after World War II for collaboration with the Nazis, a charge of which he was duly cleared.

Strauss's very personal, frequently bombastic style and labyrinthine 'note spinning' have led to some decline in critical and public favour in the second half of the twentieth century. There have also been sneers at the mawkishness in autobiographical works influenced by his wife Pauline, as in the *Symphonia domestica* (*Domestic Symphony*). But it would be a mistake to neglect some of his more refined, sometimes crystalline works such as the oboe concerto, the *Metamorphosen* for twenty-three solo strings, and the songs, many of the finest of which he wrote for his wife; while the operas *Capriccio*, *Arabella* and *Intermezzo* will surely stand the test of time.

Stravinsky, Igor (1882–1971) Russian composer (French citizen 1934, American citizen 1945). The third of four sons of the principal bass singer at the Maryinsky Theatre in St Petersburg, he read law at university but, after private discussions with Rimsky-Korsakov, studied music with him. In 1906 he married his cousin Catherine, who presented him with two sons and two daughters. Composing very much in the style of his mentor, he had two orchestral works performed at a concert and attracted the attention of Serge Diaghilev, who at the time was assembling material for a season of Russian opera and ballet in Paris. Diaghilev commissioned from him the music for a ballet *The Firebird*, based on a Russian fairy-tale and danced to provocatively irregular Russian rhythms. It was an immediate success in Paris in 1910. Three years later another work was to cause one of the rowdiest scandals and demonstrations ever seen in a theatre, when the barbaric beat and brutal dissonances of *The Rite of Spring* assailed Western ears unused to the shifting metres and non-diatonic harmony of pagan cultures far beyond so-called civilized boundaries. Younger musicians and audiences welcomed this new, terrifying voice. Traditionalists howled abuse at it.

Stravinsky surprised both factions with a subsequent work for Diaghilev. Having come across the joys of eighteenth-century melody and polyphony, in the ballet *Pulcinella* he adapted some Pergolesi themes as a forerunner of what came to be regarded as his neo-classical period. Barbaric Russian influences were gradually sloughed off as he toyed appreciatively with sarabande, gavotte and minuet, and worked with smaller instrumental ensembles rather than with the vast resources of a full orchestra. Yet he never lost his instinctive feeling for strong, urgent rhythm: steeped in the atmosphere of Diaghilev's ballet world, he made pastiches of Viennese waltzes, drove even his most abstract works along in remorseless, ever-thrusting metres, and incorporated jazz elements when they suited him. Even after discarding jazz as a fruitful technique in itself, he added its flavour to several pieces. As late as 1945 he was to write the *Ebony Concerto* for the swing clarinettist Woody Herman and his band.

In Switzerland when the Russian Revolution broke out, Stravinsky and his family decided not to return to their homeland. With all his property confiscated, he had to make a living, and set out on international tours as conductor and pianist – preferably performing his own work, and shrewd enough to copyright for his sole use a number of such compositions. Although the theatre piece *The Soldier's Tale* ('to be read, played and danced') used popular Russian folk tales as a basis, his neo-classical bent became more and more marked: it was as if, exiled from his native country, he could no longer use Russian themes with any conviction. The *Dumbarton Oaks* concerto, named after the Washington home of Mr and Mrs Robert Woods Bliss, was conceived as an utterly modern, utterly Stravinskyan parallel to Bach's *Brandenburg Concertos*.

Just before World War II his wife, mother and elder daughter died, and Stravinsky himself spent some months in a sanatorium. He left the USA, where he was joined by Vera de Bosset, with whom he had been in love for many years and whom he married in Bedford, Massachusetts. In 1940 he composed his *Symphony in C*, a small but quite perfect work of Mozartian timbre with happy suggestions of Tchaikovsky here and there; and to round off the war there was his *Symphony in*

Igor Stravinsky resting in a meadow, sketched in 1913 by Alexandre Benois, the art director and librettist who was a formative influence on the Diaghilev ballet company.

Three Movements, a synthesis of the many elements which had affected him over the years. Another influence was now to come into his life. Working on a neo-classical opera, *The Rake's Progress*, with libretto by W.H. Auden and Chester Kallman, he met a young American conductor and musicologist, Robert Craft, who had been a passionate advocate of the music of Schoenberg and his circle. As a regular visitor to the Stravinsky household, Craft interested the composer in recordings of the group so effectively that Stravinsky began to experiment with serialism and was soon devoting himself almost exclusively to such forms: *In Memoriam Dylan Thomas* used only a five-tone row, but by 1958 the large-scale *Threni* for soloists, choir and orchestra was committed to full serialism, a practice continuing through the *Movements* for piano and orchestra and the *Epitaphium* for flute, clarinet and harp.

In 1962 Stravinsky's reputation was such that the Russians, wishing to claim his genius as part of their heritage, invited him to Moscow and Leningrad, where he was fulsomely received by Khruschev and others. Accounts of his life and work have been lovingly preserved by Robert Craft in books of reminiscences and discussions and in collections of papers and letters. Stravinsky's final pieces were spare, austere, one might almost say bony, and were mainly religious, as in the final major composition, the *Requiem Canticles* of 1966. He died in New York but was buried, according to his own request, near Diaghilev on the island of San Michele, Venice.

stretto Meaning a tightening or squeezing, as when fugal subjects are made to anticipate and overlap, so increasing the tension and, sometimes, the tempo.

strings The cords of gut or wire on instruments of the viol and guitar families and in keyboard instruments, which are bowed, plucked or hammered. The word is also used to denote an entire orchestral section of violins, violas, cellos and double-basses. A *string quartet* consists of two violins, viola and cello; a *string orchestra* of any number and division of stringed instruments only. (*See also* **The Orchestra and its Instruments**.)

strophic The simplest form of folk song or popular chorus using the same tune for each stanza, deriving its description from the Greek *strophe*, a similar form of metric repetition in ancient choral and lyric poetry. A *strophic bass* is an instrumental bass figure which is played without alteration below a series of vocal or instrumental parts which may vary from one section to another.

stück German for 'a piece', as in *fantasiestück*, a short fantasy piece; *nachtstück*, a night-piece, or nocturne; *konzertstück*, a concert piece; etc.

subdominant The fourth degree in a major or minor scale: in the key of C, for example, this is F.

subject A musical theme of prime significance in a composition: in sonata form, the melodies stated in the exposition are known as the first and second subjects; in a fugue, the subject is the prevailing theme stated at the outset and brought in again by successive voices.

submediant The sixth degree in a major or minor scale: in the key of C major, for example, this is A (A flat in C minor). Its name derives from its position a third below the tonic, matching the mediant a third above the tonic.

suite From the sixteenth to the eighteenth centuries the suite of separate dance pieces was a favourite compositional pattern, especially for the keyboard. The basic movements consisted of allemande, courante, sarabande and gigue, usually in the same key and usually in binary form. Other dances which could be added included the gavotte, minuet and bourrée. Bach and Purcell were fond of prefixing the whole set with a prelude. After the ascendancy of the symphony, the word was more generally applied to collections of lighter pieces, as in Elgar's *Wand of Youth* suites; cycles of pieces with a linking idea, as in Ravel's *Mother Goose* suite; or arrangements of individual items from a composer's operas, ballets or other works, e.g. Stravinsky's *Petrushka* and Copland's *Billy the Kid*.

Suk, Josef (1874–1935) Czech composer and violinist. He studied in Prague with Dvořák, whose daughter he later married, and was a founder member of the Bohemian String Quartet, in which he played second violin. From 1922 until his death he was professor of composition in the Prague Conservatory. His early compositions in earnest Romantic style showed signs of his father-in-law's influence. In 1906 he wrote a dark, brooding symphony, *Asrael*, named after the Angel of Death, as a memorial to Dvořák and to his own wife, who had died the year after her father: in it there is a quotation from Dvořák's *Requiem*. Later he fashioned a more complex style bordering at times on atonality.

OTHER WORKS: Symphonic poem *Praga* (*Prague*). Orchestral *Meditation on an old Bohemian Chorale*. Two string quartets. Four pieces for violin and piano. Songs for male and female choirs.

Sullivan, (Sir) Arthur (1842–1900) English composer. The son of an Irish bandmaster and professor at the Royal Military School of Music, he became a chorister of the Chapel Royal, and at the age of thirteen wrote an anthem which was accepted for publication. Winning the newly established Mendelssohn Scholarship, he went to Leipzig to study, had his incidental music for Shakespeare's

The Tempest performed there, and on his return to England had a great success with it at a Crystal Palace concert. To make a living he took on various organ appointments, but continued to compose in both sacred and secular vein, and was highly praised for his cantata *Kenilworth* at the Birmingham Festival in 1864. In that same year his operetta *The Sapphire Necklace* was produced.

Operetta was to prove Sullivan's forte. In collaboration with the playwright W.S. Gilbert he wrote from 1871 onwards a string of popular successes, including *The Pirates of Penzance* and *The Mikado*. (*See also* **Gilbert and Sullivan**.) He himself was never happy at being regarded as a lightweight composer, no matter how brilliant and well paid. He attempted more serious opera in *Ivanhoe*, and composed an *Irish Symphony* and further oratorios; but it was the so-called Savoy Operas, hymn tunes such as *Onward, Christian Soldiers*, and the song *The Lost Chord* which made the greatest appeal to the public.

supertonic The second degree in a major or minor scale: in the key of C, for example, this is D.

Suppé, Franz von (1819–95) Austrian composer (of Belgian descent). He studied in Padua and Vienna, and became conductor at the Josephstadt and other Viennese theatres. He made a great reputation and rich profits from writing incidental music for plays at these establishments, and went on to write his own operettas, including *Pique Dame* (*Queen of Spades*). Two pieces survive today only in their overtures: his operetta *Leichte Kavallerie* (*Light Cavalry*), and his incidental music to the play *Dichter und Bauer* (*Poet and Peasant*).

suspension In counterpoint or harmony, a device which delays the arrival of a note really belonging to the interval or chord, thereby creating a dissonance until the held-over tone resolves on to the awaited one. Many so-called grace notes or ornaments are in effect suspensions.

Susskind, Walter (1913–80) Czech conductor and pianist (British citizen 1945). He studied in Prague with Suk and Szell, making his conducting début at the German Opera there. He left for England in 1938 and became pianist with the Czech Trio and then conductor of the Carl Rosa Opera Company. After working in Australia and Canada he was appointed conductor of the St Louis Symphony Orchestra between 1968 and 1975.

Süssmayr, Franz Xaver (1766–1803) Austrian composer. He studied with Salieri and Mozart and wrote a number of now-forgotten operas, but is remembered for having completed Mozart's *Requiem*.

Sutherland, (Dame) Joan (1926–) Australian soprano. She studied in Sydney, made her début there in

In spite of childhood ailments such as sinus trouble and bad circulation, Joan Sutherland became one of the most powerful yet flexible sopranos, of whose calculated rather than intuitively dramatic style Callas was to say it had 'set my work back a hundred years.'

Purcell's *Dido and Aeneas*, and sang in a number of music clubs accompanied by a young pianist, Richard Bonynge, who left for London when she did, and whom she married. In 1952 she joined the Covent Garden Opera company, where she sang various rôles before her full *bel canto* and coloratura potential was realized, largely thanks to the advocacy of Bonynge. She was soon associated with dazzling performances of *Lucia di Lammermoor* and *Norma*, though her husband's insistence from 1962 onwards on conducting and generally organizing every detail caused some strife: there were resentful murmurings about the 'Sutherland-Bonynge package deal'. Nevertheless he coached her and inspired her in some of her greatest triumphs, and she was rapturously received on her return to Australia in 1965 with her own operatic touring company. Conflicting supporters of Sutherland and Callas still contest the right of the other to be known, as both have been in Italy, as 'la Stupenda'.

Sweelinck, Jan (1562–1621) Dutch composer and organist. He spent most of his working life in Amsterdam, apart from occasional forays across the Netherlands to advise on organ construction and repair. After his father's death in 1577 he took over the post of organist at the Oude Kerk and remained there for the rest of his life. He taught singing, composition, and organ playing, and wrote a vast number of keyboard fantasias, toccatas, and dance movements and a wide range of vocal music, including secular songs and sacred psalms, most of them imaginatively bridging the changeover from modal to new major/minor tonalities.

swing See **jazz**.

sympathetic strings Some stringed instruments, including the viola d'amore and the Indian sitar, are fitted with supplementary sets of strings which vibrate in accord with those actually bowed or plucked.

symphony Taken from the Greek meaning simply 'sounding together', the symphony has been described as a sonata for orchestra. In the seventeenth and eighteenth centuries the word *sinfonia* was applied most frequently to an instrumental piece introducing or providing an interlude in an opera or oratorio. When elaborated into three movements it paved the way for the self-sufficient composition we have been familiar with since the days of Haydn and Mozart. It became customary for such symphonies to have four movements, the first in sonata form and usually at a fast tempo – though a slower, solemn introduction to this *allegro* was a device much favoured by composers wishing to establish and then relieve a taut, dramatic mood. The second movement, often also in sonata form, was slow and song-like; the third most commonly a minuet and trio; and the fourth a sparkling finale, often a rondo, though Mozart took it to unprecedented contrapuntal heights in the last movement of No.41 (the *Jupiter*), and Brahms launched into an awe-inspiring passacaglia to conclude his No.4. Twentieth-century composers have shunned the conservative connotations of the word and applied it to works as disparate as Stravinsky's *Symphony of Psalms* and Messiaen's ten-movement *Turangalîla*.

The word *sinfonietta* really means no more than a 'small symphony' but, like *sinfonia*, has been applied in this century to chamber orchestras

such as the Bournemouth Sinfonietta, the Sinfonia di Siena, the Northern Sinfonia, and others.

syncopation The medical condition of *syncope* involves an abnormality of heart beats; and in music the meaning is much the same, referring to the accentuation of a weak beat in a bar instead of placing the emphasis, as is usual, on a strong beat. All stimulating dance music involves some kind of syncopation, which by its very eccentricity emphasizes the underlying normal beat. Folksongs, especially those collected by Bartók and others in Eastern and Central Europe, have continual changes of metre and staggered accents; and jazz has always made great use of syncopation, most effectively in improvised solos against the background of a steady rhythm section.

synthesizer An electronic device invented by Robert Moog to produce by means of voltage control a range of artificial sounds or to blend and modify fragments of natural and artificial sounds without the operator having painstakingly to edit lengths of recording tape. The introduction of transistors made possible the production of portable synthesizers which could be used in live performances. Their possibilities have been explored by Babbitt, Cage, Stockhausen and other contemporaries.

Szell, Georg (1897–1970) Hungarian conductor and pianist (American citizen 1946). He studied with Reger, made his first appearance as a solo pianist at the age of ten, and conducted the Berlin Philharmonic Orchestra in a composition of his own at the age of seventeen. He made his American début with the St Louis Symphony Orchestra in 1930, and in 1939 decided to settle in the USA. From 1946 until his death he conducted the Cleveland Orchestra, establishing the highest standards and becoming a legend in his own lifetime as a perfectionist with an incredible musical memory and an interpretative range which took in Wagner, the moderns, and Brahms, whose symphonies he tackled with a steely vigour that did away with all traces of the exaggerated romanticism favoured by so many conductors.

Szigeti, Josef (1892–1973) Hungarian violinist (American citizen 1951). He made his début at the age of thirteen and set out on international tours. One of the most gifted violinists of the century, he played most of the major works in the repertory, recorded a great many, and distinguished himself especially in the concertos of Bartók and Bloch.

Szymanowski, Karol (1882–1937) Polish composer. His family owned an estate in the Ukraine and he was brought up in comfortable circumstances, but suffered from a lameness which made it painful for him to travel far or lead a very active life. Devoting himself to music, he studied the piano at home and then in a nearby town, and at the age of sixteen published a number of piano preludes. After study at Warsaw Conservatory he moved to Berlin, where he wrote his first symphony and found himself attracted to the music of Richard Strauss. He was still, however, to a large extent influenced by his compatriot Chopin, and he and three nationalist friends founded an organization which they called 'Young Poland in Music'. On his eventual return to Poland he wrote several pieces inspired by national folklore, found new interests in the work of Stravinsky and Debussy, and in 1916 wrote a visionary symphony, *A Song in the Night*, for orchestra and male chorus, the text being a Czech translation of thirteenth-century Persian pantheistic verses.

During World War I his family home was destroyed, and in spite of illness he had to travel and give recitals in Europe and America. In 1926 he became director of Warsaw Conservatory, but spent as much time as possible in the mountains, a background which inspired his ballet about wild mountain folk, *Harnasie*. His masterpiece is perhaps the *Stabat Mater*, in which he exemplified his resolve to avoid 'archaic academicism'. His sumptuous yet always clear style is also well displayed in his second violin concerto, a one-movement work deploying wide resources of mood and tempo, and unusually introducing a significant part for piano set against the solo violin.

OTHER WORKS: Opera *King Roger*. Ballet *Mandragora*. *Symphonie Concertante* for piano and orchestra. *Litany of the Virgin Mary* for soprano, women's chorus, and orchestra. Two string quartets.

T

tabla An Indian hand-drum, played in a pair of which one is conical, the other cylindrical. The drummer provides rhythms and cross-rhythms in support of stringed instruments such as the sitar and tanpura.

tablature An old system for writing music with figures and other signs instead of notes. Symbols marking the positions of the player's fingers were widely used for organ and lute tablature. Their only survivors today are the little grids on popular song sheets showing the fingering of ukulele or guitar.

tabor A small medieval drum held by a strap around the player's neck, struck by the hand or a drumstick while marching or accompanying folk dances, nearly always in conjunction with a fife or other simple wind pipe.

tafelmusik German for 'table music', meaning music to be performed at mealtimes or on convivial occasions. Telemann produced sets of pieces for various instrumental combinations under this overall title.

Tailleferre, Germaine (1892–1983) French composer and pianist. She studied in Paris as a pupil of Ravel, was drawn into Satie's circle, and so became the only woman member of the modernist group known as *Les Six*. She was eclectic in her styles, though the influences of Fauré and Ravel were never far away. Works included a piano concerto, concertino for harp and orchestra, string quartets, and ballet music.

Takemitsu, Tōru (1930–) Japanese composer. He was largely self-taught, and was greatly influenced by Western music, identifiably including Debussy, Messiaen and jazz, though always applying a Japanese economy of line and colouring to the textures of his music. The shortness of some of his carefully wrought pieces has led the conductor

The Japanese composer Takemitsu, most of whose music is written for orchestral combinations familiar to Western ears, but all with a quietly insistent, individual tone of voice.

Simon Rattle to refer to them as 'bite-sized music'. Takemitsu has tried consistently to transmit visual aspects into an aural rationale, and this interest in the visual imagination has, not surprisingly, resulted in his scoring some engrossing film music. On one occasion the director Kurosawa asked him to 'write beyond Mahler': the result was the music for 'RAN'. On the whole, Takemitsu aspires not to provide something additional to a film, but rather to force the viewer to stop, think, and 'hear something anew which will make him *see* anew'.

He has experimented with tape and other electronic methods, and in *November Steps* used Japanese instruments. His ideas cannot be fitted into forms such as the symphony or concerto: the music 'comes as it comes'. His *Rocking Mirror Daybreak* of 1983 at first suggests the remote fragmentations of Webern, but the singer's lilting lines could be none other than Takemitsu's own communication, certainly no slavishly derivative voice. Frequently using the traditional Japanese pentatonic scale, he consciously regards much of his work as a stroll through a Japanese garden.

OTHER WORKS: *Relief statique* for tape. Orchestral *Music for Tree. Gitimalay (Bouquet of Songs)* for marimba and orchestra. *Crossing* for women's voices, guitar, harp, piano, vibraphone and two orchestras. *Far away* and *Undisturbed Rest* for piano.

Tallis, Thomas (*c*.1505–85) English composer and organist. Details of his early life are obscure, but he is known to have held an appointment at Waltham Abbey, probably as organist and choirmaster, for some years before its dissolution in 1540. He became a Gentleman of the Chapel Royal and was in favour with both Queen Mary and Queen Elizabeth, who granted Byrd and himself the sole right for printing music and music paper in England. In Mary's time he wrote pieces for Catholic worship; in Elizabeth's, for the services of the English Church. The *Cantiones Sacrae (Sacred Songs)* on which he collaborated with Byrd contain a superb motet, *Salvator mundi*, and some massive polyphonic works including one for eight five-part choirs. His great output of devotional compositions and the magnificence of their scale earned him the title of 'Father of English Cathedral Music'. One of the melodies which he contributed to Archbishop Parker's Psalter of 1567 was used by Vaughan Williams in his *Fantasia on a Theme of Thomas Tallis*.

tambour French for a drum. A two-headed version known as the *tambourin* was common in medieval times, and also gave its name to a Provençal dance whose drone-bass accompaniment imitated a drum.

tambourine A shallow drum with a single head stretched over a wooden frame into which metal 'jingles' are inserted. Thought to be of Arab origin, it is much used as an accompaniment to rhythmic Salvation Army hymns and to a number of folk dances. It is played by striking the skin with fingers or knuckles, or banging it against knee or elbow, and shaking it so that the jingles rattle.

Tambourine.

tangent The metal tongue which touches a clavichord string when a key has been depressed.

Tanglewood *See* **Berkshire Festival**.

tango An Argentine dance originating from an African rhythm brought over by slaves, in 2/4 time with a dotted rhythm and frequent accentuation of the final beats in a phrase. It became a popular ballroom dance in Europe for several decades after World War I. Composers who have used the form include Albéniz, with his haunting *Tango in D*, and Walton in the *Façade* suite.

tanpura The word also appears as *tambura* or *tanbura*. One of the commonest Indian instruments, it has a long lute-like neck and a gourd bowl, with four metal strings which are plucked to produce a continuous drone.

tanz, tänze German for 'dance' and 'dances'. Liszt wrote variations on the grim plainsong theme of *Dies irae* in his *Totentanz (Dance of Death)* for piano and orchestra.

tarantella A fast Italian dance in 2/4 or 6/8 which may take its name from Taranto or, according to popular legend, from the poisonous spider native to that region, the effects of whose bite could be cured only by this whirling dance. Rossini composed a memorable tarantella, and a light tarantella pastiche can be found in the last movement of Mendelssohn's Symphony No.4, the 'Italian'.

Tartini, Giuseppe (1692–1770) Italian composer and violinist. At the University of Padua he studied law, acquired great skill in fencing, became increasingly interested in music, and eloped with the niece of a Cardinal. Threatened with arrest, he hid in a monastery at Assisi, where he made new discoveries in acoustic phenomena, invented an improved violin bow, and composed his famous (or infamous) *Devil's Trill* sonata, which he said had come to him in a dream of a pact with the devil. After being allowed to return to Padua he became famous as a virtuoso, spent two years leading Count Kinsky's band in Prague, and returned yet again to Padua to found a school of violin playing which became known as the 'School of Nations', while Tartini himself was dubbed 'Master of Nations'.

His elegant compositions were in the direct tradition of Corelli. Although he attempted some church music, he was at his most fluent in his forty-two violin sonatas, eighteen violin concertos, and a number of sparkling concertos for wind instruments.

Tate, Phyllis (1911–87) English composer. She had little formal training until a friend heard her playing on the banjo some foxtrots which she had composed. She then went to the Royal Academy of Music, and while still a student wrote an operetta, *The Policeman's Serenade*. Later she composed in a simple, accessible manner which made her particularly successful in choral and other works for children. Out of character was her choice of the story of Jack the Ripper for her opera *The Lodger*. She was married to Alan Frank, English clarinettist and for many years head of the Oxford University Press music department.

tattoo Military music for bugles and drums, used either to recall soldiers to barracks or tents at night, or as accompaniment to exercises and displays, usually by torchlight, as in the Aldershot Tattoo. In the annual Edinburgh Tattoo, the bugles are superseded by bagpipes.

Tauber, Richard (1892–1948) Austrian tenor (British citizen 1940). He made his opera début in 1913 as Tamino in *The Magic Flute* in Chemnitz, and from then until 1925 sang with the Dresden Opera, and from 1926 to 1938 with the Vienna Opera. Although highly regarded as a *lieder* and operatic singer, and giving his final appearance in *Don Giovanni* at Covent Garden with friends from Vienna only a few months before his death, he established a much greater reputation in operetta: he sang the leading tenor rôles in all Lehár's works after *Frasquita*, and will always be especially associated with *The Land of Smiles*. He and the composer remained close friends until the Nazi annexation of Austria, when Tauber fled to England.

Tavener, John (1944–) English composer. He studied with Lennox Berkeley at the Royal Academy of Music and had an early success in 1968 with his cantata *The Whale*, based on the story of Jonah. Of a questing religious nature, he used a

children's choir along with a mixed choir and orchestra to create in his *Celtic Requiem* a 'theatre piece for children' in which they play games of love and death to a poem by Henry Vaughan, a hymn tune, and a medieval Irish poem, accompanied by devices such as a gong, bagpipes, and electric guitar. His music became sparer and more luminous after he entered the Russian Orthodox Church. In his oratorio *Ultimos Ritos* (*Last Rites*) he introduced five priests as speakers, together with solo singers, choir, and orchestra.

OTHER WORKS: Opera *Thérèse. Grandma's Footsteps* for five musical boxes and chamber ensemble. Choral *Canticle of the Mother of God. Greek Interludes* for flute and piano.

Taverner, John (1495–1545) English composer. Born in Lincolnshire, he held for some years a benefice in Tattershall collegiate church until appointed by Cardinal Wolsey choirmaster and organist at Cardinal College (now Christ Church), Oxford. In 1528 he was imprisoned for heresy, but two years later was released and sent back to Lincolnshire to help Thomas Cromwell in his persecutions of supposed idolaters. He seems at this time to have abandoned music altogether, but not before writing eight majestic masses and establishing the *in nomine* style of polyphonic variation writing. His crowning achievement was the mass *The Western Wynde*, taking its name from a shred of folksong around which he fashioned thirty-six free variations into a grand design speaking eloquently of the English countryside. Peter Maxwell Davies's opera *Taverner* is based on the story of his life.

Taylor, Deems (1885–1966) American composer and critic. He was for some years music critic of the *New York World*, became musical adviser to CBS in 1936, and as well as giving many talks on the radio was responsible for the narration behind Walt Disney's cartoon *Fantasia*. Two of his operas, *The King's Henchman* and *Peter Ibbetson*, were staged at the New York Met, and he wrote a number of light, accomplished orchestral works.

Tchaikovsky, Pyotr (Peter) Ilyich (1840–93) Russian composer. A reserved and sometimes neurotic child, he showed an early fondness for the piano, but after his wayward father impulsively left his job in government service and the family moved about for some years, he was forced into legal studies and at nineteen became a clerk in the Ministry of Justice in St Petersburg. Lonely and embittered after the death of his beloved mother, he responded to no outer stimulus until, in 1863, he resigned his safe position in order to study full-time at the St Petersburg Conservatory, newly

A painting by N.D. Kurnezow of Tchaikovsky.

303

founded by Anton Rubinstein. Although his student work made little mark, he was invited by Rubinstein's brother Nicholas to teach harmony at the equally new Moscow Conservatory, a post which he occupied for twelve years. In spite of repeated nervous disorders he completed a *Winter Symphony* and, in 1866, became friendly with Balakirev and others of 'The Five'. It was Balakirev who encouraged him to write the well-known fantasy overture, *Romeo and Juliet*.

In 1874 Tchaikovsky produced the B flat minor piano concerto which has been so frequently pillaged – for use as a popular song, and as a showpiece in films. He had hoped to impress Nicholas Rubinstein with this, but Rubinstein declared it to be unplayable, poorly proportioned, and vulgar. Its first performance was given in Boston the following year by Hans von Bülow. Performances of his first and second symphonies attracted more favourable comment, though symphonic sonata form was really alien to his nature. In a letter he said frankly of his work:

> All my life I have been much troubled by my inability to grasp and manipulate form in music ... What I write has always a mountain of padding: an experienced eye can detect the thread in my seams and I can do nothing about it.

Throughout his symphonies, constructed from darting little themes tossed colourfully, often teasingly to and fro between sections of the orchestra, or expanded into long, sweeping lines, there seem always to be captivating melodies, harmonies and rhythms waiting to be transformed into ballet music. Yet the ballet scores we now regard as classics – *Swan Lake*, *The Sleeping Beauty* and *The Nutcracker* – were all poorly received in their earliest performances.

In July 1877 Tchaikovsky, not capable of facing up to the realization that his tastes were homosexual, made the mistake of marrying a pretty but unstable music student. Within a matter of days he found her physically repugnant, ran off to stay with his sister, and shortly afterwards tried to commit suicide by throwing himself into the river in Moscow. Rescued and taken for a rest cure in Switzerland, he was helped to recuperate by the generosity of a widow with musical leanings. Nadezhda von Meck, a wealthy widow with eleven children, settled an annual allowance on him so that he could give up teaching and concentrate on composition. The only proviso was that, although they could write to each other, they must not meet.

With renewed confidence he completed an opera, *Eugene Onegin*, based on the poet Pushkin's verse drama of a cold-hearted young rake who kills his sentimental friend and learns too late the value of real love. At the same time he was working on a fourth symphony, which he dedicated to Mme von Meck. The travels which her money made possible resulted in the sparkling *Capriccio italien*. In that same year, 1880, he also wrote the delightful *Serenade for Strings* which he said he had felt deeply from start to finish. There came a time when the comfort of financial security and the pleasures of holidays on his benefactress's country estate threatened to dry up his creative energies; but from the late 1880s onwards he again plunged into work, producing two more symphonies and his opera *The Queen of Spades*. In 1890 he was deeply hurt when Mme von Meck, troubled by illness, abruptly withdrew her patronage and friendship. By now, however, he was famous in his own right. He toured the USA; was present when Mahler conducted *Eugene Onegin* in Hamburg; and in 1893 visited England to receive an honorary doctorate from Cambridge University.

In November of that same year he contracted cholera in St Petersburg and died in agony, leaving a legacy of music uneven in quality but always passionately lyrical and individual in tone.

Tcherepnin, Alexander (1899–1977) Russian composer and pianist (American citizen 1958). His father Nikolay had conducted for Diaghilev. In 1921 the family settled in Paris, where Alexander made a name as a pianist. He wrote a ballet *Ajantas Frescoes* for Pavlova and experimented with the harmonic complexities of a nine-note scale. In the 1930s he toured the Far East as a teacher, and was greatly influenced by Oriental music. Between 1949 and 1969 he was professor of piano and composition at De Paul University, Chicago. Among his works are four symphonies, a harmonica concerto, and a cantata, *The Story of Ivan the Fool*, which employs electronic devices. His sons Serge (1941–) and Ivan (1943–) have both become composers.

tedesco, tedesca Italian for 'German'. The expression occurs frequently in the form *alla tedesca*, meaning that a piece should be played 'in the German style', usually in slow waltz or ländler time.

Te Kanawa, (Dame) Kiri (1944–) New Zealand soprano, of Maori ancestry. Her first singing teacher was a nun. After winning prizes in Australia she moved to England, joined the London Opera Centre, then studied with Vera Rosza, and made her Covent Garden début in 1971 as a ravishing Countess in Mozart's *The Marriage of Figaro*. Since then she has been in demand in the world's major opera houses, has proved an entertaining guest in television shows and interviews, appeared in the film *Don Giovanni*, and was invited to sing at the wedding of the Prince of Wales and Lady Diana Spencer in 1981.

Telemann, Georg Philipp (1681–1767) German composer. The son of a clergyman, he taught himself music by studying old scores, and continued to do so while also studying science and languages at Leipzig University. He wrote a number of operas for Leipzig theatres, became a church organist, and in 1721 was offered the cantorship of the Thomaskirche in preference to Bach. A

Kiri Te Kanawa, who made her opera début as the Countess in Mozart's *The Marriage of Figaro* in 1971, and in 1981 sang Handel's *Let the Bright Seraphim* at the wedding in St Paul's Cathedral of the Prince and Princess of Wales.

An engraving by G. Lichtensteger of Telemann, whose sets of *Tafelmusik* (Table Music) contain many diverting pieces for a variety of instruments, to be played at mealtimes.

higher offer tempted him away to Hamburg, where he remained music director of five churches for the forty-six years up to his death.

In his day the fertile Telemann was regarded more highly than Bach or Handel. His vast output included six hundred overtures, a wide range of concertos and instrumental suites, and church music for every occasion. Handel himself observed that Telemann could write a motet as easily as most people could write a letter. Although he never achieved the heights of his two great contemporaries, his music was – and remains – consistently well-wrought and diverting.

Telmányi, Emil (1892–) Hungarian violinist and conductor. He made his début in Berlin in 1911 with the first Continental performance of Elgar's violin concerto. In 1918 he married one of Carl Nielsen's daughters, and in 1919 settled in Denmark.

temperament On stringed instruments and a slide instrument such as the trombone, notes such as A sharp and B flat are marginally different in what is known as 'just intonation', depending on the key of the piece. Keyboard and other fixed-pitch instruments cannot make such a distinction, so some system of adjusting the tuning of intervals in the 'natural scale' is necessary to strike a balance agreeable to the ear. In 'meantone' tempering, used in the seventeenth and eighteenth centuries, some keys were in tune, others very much out of tune, and modulation from one to another could produce excruciating results. This was replaced by 'equal temperament' tuning, making equal intervals of all twelve semitones in a scale. Bach's set of 48 Preludes and Fugues is known as *The Well-Tempered Clavier* because he had set out deliberately to demonstrate the advantages of this revised system.

tempo The pace at which a piece of music is played: i.e. not the rhythm established in the time signature but the speed asked for by the composer in markings such as *lento* or *allegro*. Some composers who wish to be quite specific give metronome markings to define the number of beats of certain note values within one minute.

tenor The word derives from the Italian for 'holding on', because in early polyphony a plainsong theme would be maintained by the high male voice. It has also been applied to instruments within a similar range, such as the tenor horn and tenor saxophone, and to the C or tenor clef on the written staff. A *counter-tenor* is an even higher male voice, purer than a male alto, and not to be confused with the falsetto or castrato voice.

ternary form A composition in three sections is said to be ternary, with the first and last movements the same or nearly the same, contrasting with a second movement based sometimes on the original material but more usually on a fresh theme. The minuet and trio section of a traditional symphony is in ternary form, as is a *da capo* aria. The pattern is often referred to as A-B-A. In different vein, the average popular song is really in ternary form, though the first eight bars are usually repeated to make it A-A-B-A.

terzetto An alternative name for *trio*, meaning three voices or instruments.

tessitura Italian for 'texture'. In music it defines the compass within which a particular voice or instrument can perform most comfortably and effectively, though this range may be capable of extension in a higher or lower direction according to the demands of the composer, provided he understands the technical exigencies.

Tetrazzini, Luisa (1871–1940) Italian soprano. She studied in Florence and made her début there at the age of nineteen in Meyerbeer's opera *L'Africaine*. Her powerful coloratura voice had made her reputation in Argentina before she won a rapturous reception from New York audiences – if not from the critics – in *La traviata*. It was said that her *cantabile* was uneven, her *tremolo* as bad as that of a howling infant, and her whole voice badly schooled and badly balanced. Her over-dramatic interpretations are guyed in the novel by E.M. Forster, *Where Angels Fear to Tread*. Nevertheless she flamboyantly established herself in London, New York and Chicago, and then after World War I devoted herself to profitable concert tours before losing her money to confidence tricksters and a charlatan of a third husband. When she died in Milan, she had to be buried at the expense of the Italian state.

Teyte, (Dame) Maggie (1888–1976) English soprano. She studied in London and Paris, and made her début at Monte Carlo in 1907 in one of Offenbach's lesser operettas. Of more significance was her appearance in Debussy's *Pelléas et Mélisande* after studying her rôle as Mélisande with the composer (and giving her last interpretation of it in New York just after World War II). She made a speciality of French songs, and between World Wars I and II appeared in a number of light operas such as *Monsieur Beaucaire*. Her final operatic appearance was with Kirsten Flagstad in Purcell's *Dido and Aeneas* in London in 1951.

theme The principal melody (or subject) of any extended composition, developed and decorated throughout the piece. Many works, or movements within works, consist of a set of *theme and variations*, in which the original statement is treated in a number of contrapuntal, harmonic and rhythmic diversifications. A *theme song* is a tune within a musical stage show which reappears as a sort of motto, or restates the basic idea of the story; and is also synonymous with the *signature tune* of dance bands and broadcast shows.

Theodorakis, Mikis (1925–) Greek composer. He studied in Athens and Paris, and has written a number of oratorios and ballet scores, but is better known to the public as the composer of a film score for *Zorba the Greek*.

The composer Mikis Theodorakis in June 1970, arriving in London after being released from a Greek political prison.

theorbo An obsolete bass instrument of the lute family with a double neck, one with strings over a fingerboard, the other with bass strings which could be altered only by retuning. It was often used as a continuo instrument in Renaissance times.

theremin An electronic melody instrument invented in 1920 by the Russian physicist Lev Theremin. It produced one note at a time within a range of five octaves by movements of the player's hand at some distance from a vertical rod-and-loop aerial. Martinů wrote a quartet incorporating a theremin, but the device made much less impact than the more easily controllable *ondes Martenot*.

third An interval of three steps between one note and another. In the diatonic scale of C major, the gap between the tonic C and the E above it is a major third; up to E flat is a minor third. A diminished third, in this context written as C sharp/E flat, is for all practical, equal temperament purposes a major second. In harmony, the *third inversion* is one in which the fourth note of a four-note chord is set at the bottom: e.g. in a chord of C major seventh (C/E/G/B flat), the B flat would become the bass note.

Thomas, Ambroise (1811–96) French composer. He studied piano and violin at an early age, and at the age of twenty-one won the Grand Prix de Rome while at the Paris Conservatoire. His early interests lay with chamber music, but he discovered a dramatic gift within himself, composed a few ballet scores, and then concentrated on opera. His greatest success was *Mignon* in 1866. The later *Hamlet* made no great impact, but led to his appointment as director of the Conservatoire in succession to Auber, after which he wrote little on his own account.

Thomas, Michael Tilson (1944–) American conductor and pianist. He studied in California and then at Bayreuth and Berkshire. He made his London début with the London Symphony Orchestra in 1970, and became music director of the Buffalo Philharmonic Orchestra in 1971. In London in July 1987 he arranged and conducted televised programmes of the whole range of George Gershwin's work to commemorate the fiftieth anniversary of the composer's death, and in 1988 was appointed music director of the London Symphony Orchestra.

Thomson, Virgil (1896–) American composer and critic. He played the organ during his schooldays, but musical tuition was interrupted by World War I, during which he served in the US Military Aviation Corps. After the war he went to Harvard, then studied in Paris with Nadia Boulanger. For a while he wrote music criticism for *Vanity Fair* before returning to Paris, living there between

1925 and 1932 and becoming involved with *Les Six*: several of his compositions echo the wry, limpid style of Satie. He wrote two operas to librettos by Gertrude Stein, *Four Saints in Three Acts* and *The Mother of us All*. For fourteen years after his return to New York in 1940 he was the outspoken music critic of the *New York Herald-Tribune*. At the same time he composed musical 'portraits' of his friends in different instrumental settings, and continued to write incidental music, film scores, and other work in a clear-cut if not particularly distinctive style.

OTHER WORKS: Three symphonies. Cello concerto. Three string quartets. Orchestral suite *Portraits*. *Seven Portraits* for violin. *Four Portraits* for violin and piano. Film score *The Plow that Broke the Plains*.

Three Choirs Festival An annual musical festival held in rotation in the English cathedral cities of Hereford, Worcester and Gloucester, with the participation of their assembled choirs. The first such festival is thought to have been given around 1716 to raise money for widows and orphans of local clergy, and the proceeds still go to charity. It became a regular event after 1724, presenting oratorios and other sacred choral works, and over the years introducing many new orchestral works. Elgar, in spite of being a Catholic, frequently played the violin at Worcester and in 1890 was asked by the committee to compose a work for that year's function: the result was his overture *Froissart*. Delius conducted the first performance of his *First Dance Rhapsody* at Hereford in 1909, though unfortunately the result was widely condemned as a 'shambles'. Vaughan Williams provided a great deal of material for successive festivals, including his *Fantasia on a Theme of Thomas Tallis*, performed at Gloucester in 1910.

threnody A dirge, or song of lamentation. Stravinsky's *Threni* (*Threnodies*), his first purely twelve-tone composition, was a setting of words from the *Lamentations of Jeremiah* in the Old Testament.

through-composed See **durchkomponiert**.

Tibbett, Lawrence (1896–1968) American baritone. After an early career as an actor he turned to operetta and then to opera, making his début at the New York Met in 1923 as a monk in *Boris Godunov*. He was to sing at the Met until 1950, creating many rôles and distinguishing himself in interpretations of Verdi operas. He was also a great success in Gershwin's *Porgy and Bess*, and appeared in several films.

tie A curved line, sometimes called a *bind*, joining two notes of the same pitch to indicate that they should be held as one unbroken note and not sounded twice. This should not be confused with a *slur*, which links notes of differing pitches.

tierce French for an interval of a major or minor third. Also the fourth harmonic, which is a major third above the fundamental note two octaves higher; or an organ stop which sounds that harmonic as well as the fundamental tone. The *tierce de Picardie* is a cadence in which the major third is introduced in the last chord of a composition in a minor key: e.g. in C minor the E flat will be replaced by E natural.

timbre A French word for a chiming bell. It has come to be used in the sense of tone colour in music, distinguishing the qualities of different voice and instrumental sounds. (In German, *klangfarbe*.)

timbrel The original, and still correct, English word for a *tambourine*.

time and **time signature** The Italian word *tempo* is literally translated as *time*, but in the writing of music there is a distinction between the two: *tempo* refers to the speed at which a composition should go; *time* refers to the basic rhythmic patterns and the figures used to show these on a score. The *time signature* on a staff specifies the units of notes or rests making up a measure, e.g. in 3/4 time there are three quarter-notes (crotchets). (*See also* **Notation**.)

Tiomkin, Dimitri (1899–1979) Russian composer and pianist (American citizen 1937). He studied in St Petersburg, toured Europe as a virtuoso pianist, and made his first appearance in New York in 1926. Settling in the USA, he was much in demand as a composer of film scores, among them *High Noon*.

Tippett, (Sir) Michael (1905–) English composer. Although born in London of Cornish stock, Tippett spent his early years in a Suffolk village to which his parents moved shortly after his birth. He showed an early interest in music and took piano lessons locally. When he was twelve his mother took him to a piano recital in London, and at seventeen he attended his first symphony concert and was enraptured. He had difficulty winning his parents' permission to take up music full-time, but finally persuaded them to let him study composition at the Royal College of Music. On leaving, he did part-time teaching in Surrey, and helped to produce small-scale operas at the Barn Theatre, Oxted.

The development of his musical style went hand in hand with political convictions. He conducted for a number of workers' organizations, including Morley College for Working Men and Women, of which in 1940 he became musical director – a post once held by Gustav Holst. During World War II his stance as a conscientious objector earned him a three-month prison sentence. In March 1944 an oratorio on which he had been working for two years was performed in London with Peter Pears as tenor soloist. This was *A Child of our Time*, in which he used the true story of a Jewish boy who had killed a Nazi diplomat to convey his own tragic vision of the clash between good and the dark forces of evil. To make it immediately comprehensible and relevant to the contemporary world, he wrote his own simple text, some of it almost in folk idiom, and instead of sacred chorales introduced five spirituals. The effect was deeply moving, though disturbing to many at the time. More than forty years later, showing how far the by now revered composer had come, the work was chosen to open the 1987 season of Promenade Concerts.

Always enjoying work with young people, Tippett began in 1965 an association with the Leicestershire Schools Symphony Orchestra, for whom he wrote his invigorating *Shires Suite*, starting out with a fine treatment of the canon *Sumer is icumen in*. In spite of his affectionate evocation of this and other regions of the English countryside, he confesses to feeling himself essentially a Celt at heart. His opera *The Midsummer Marriage*, though telling a modern tale of two couples undergoing very modern psychological problems, digs deep back into myth and ritual, and the very names of Mark, Jenifer and King Fisher have obvious Arthurian and Celtic connotations. Another opera, *King Priam*, was commissioned by the Koussevitsky Foundation. A third, *The Knot Garden*, delved again into metaphor and myth to unravel the loves and hates of another group of modern English characters.

Tippett's sprung rhythms and his love of polyphony, which seemed at times to defy any stable measure and to accumulate great congestions of notes, baffled listeners for many years. Gradually, however, the sheer radiance of his idiom shone through all surface difficulties. The *Fantasia on a Theme of Corelli* contains a pastoral andante which surely harks back to the atmosphere of his Suffolk childhood. The string quartets have a knotted intensity which opens out rewardingly after several hearings. In later years Tippett has displayed a serene confidence in his interweaving of Monteverdi madrigal styles, blues idioms and a rich palette of orchestral colouring, with his personal idealism always there as a cohesive force.

OTHER WORKS: Opera *The Ice Break*. Four symphonies. Concerto for Double String Orchestra. Choral and orchestral *The Vision of St Augustine*. Song cycle *Boyhood's End*. Three piano sonatas.

toccata From the Italian *toccare*, to touch. Originally it meant merely a piece to be played, not sung, but came to be applied to keyboard pieces dis-

Of Cornish descent, Michael Tippett has declared that when travelling by train across England he can, even with his eyes shut, tell the exact moment when his compartment crosses the border of Cornwall.

playing the performer's dexterity and precision of touch. Bach and other composers frequently used a free-ranging toccata as the prelude to a more rigorous contrapuntal movement such as a fugue.

Tomasini, Luigi (1741–1808) Italian composer and violinist. He was a member of the Esterházy orchestra under Haydn, and eventually its leader. Many of the violin parts in Haydn's quartets were written to match Tomasini's capabilities. He himself composed a number of quartets and concertos, and twenty-four *divertimenti* for the baryton.

Tomkins, Thomas (1572–1656) Welsh composer and organist. One of a large family of musicians, Tomkins studied with Byrd and was appointed organist at Worcester Cathedral. In 1621 he became an organist of the Chapel Royal, and in 1625 wrote music for the coronation of King Charles I. His compositions include a hundred anthems, pieces for the virginals, and several sets of madrigals for groups of three to six voices.

Tommasini, Vincenzo (1880–1950) Italian composer. He studied in Rome and Berlin, and wrote a number of operas, among them *Medea*. He is best remembered for his setting of pieces by Domenico Scarlatti for a 1917 Diaghilev ballet *The Good-Humoured Ladies*, with choreography by Massine.

tonality The establishment in the listener's ear of a definite single key underlying an entire composition or section of a composition. If two such keys are employed within the same parameters, this is *bitonality; polytonality* is the use of several interacting keys; *atonality* is the abnegation of any set key discipline.

tone This word has several distinct meanings, and a number of loose usages. It defines a single note without supplementary harmonies; an interval of a major second; the quality of a sung or played note, as in 'beautiful tone' or 'harsh tone'; and in the USA is used instead of the word 'note', whence *tone-rows* and *twelve-tone music*.

tone cluster A group of adjacent notes played simultaneously, creating a chord made up of tightly packed major or minor seconds. The American composer Henry Cowell pioneered a method of producing such clusters by pushing the hand or forearm down on a section of piano keyboard. Stockhausen and Ligeti have experimented with orchestral clusters.

tone poem Some composers prefer to call such work a *symphonic poem*: Liszt applied this description to his thirteen dramatic, pictorial orchestral works. Richard Strauss, on the other hand, used the word *tondichtung* (*tone poem*) for compositions such as *Macbeth* and *Don Juan*. One of the most powerful works in the genre is Sibelius's *Tapiola*. Whichever term is chosen, the basic concept is of a superior form of programme music, endeavouring to convey literary or natural images by means of music.

tone row Also known as a note row (in Britain) or a set (derived by Babbitt from mathematical set theory), this refers to the order in which a composer employing the full twelve pitches of a chromatic scale arranges a sequence to form the basis of later, frequently serial, developments. No note should be repeated before the basic set is completed, though the rhythm may be altered. (*See also* **serialism**.)

tonguing The art of using the tongue in the playing of wind instruments. To emphasize a straightforward note a trumpeter, for instance, may use single-tonguing; to increase the pace or produce special effects, he will use double-tonguing and triple-tonguing; while flautists and occasionally other players use flutter-tonguing to produce a fast trilling effect.

tonic The keynote, or first degree of a major or minor scale, giving its name to the key of the piece; also the root note of a tonic triad chord. (For **tonic sol-fa**, *see* **solfeggio**.)

Torelli, Giuseppe (1658–1709) Italian composer and violinist. In 1686 he became leader of the Bologna cathedral orchestra. In 1687 he went to Germany as leader of the Margrave of Brandenburg-Anspach's band, but a few years later returned to Bologna. He composed twelve concerti grossi and a great deal of other ensemble music, and is believed to have been the first to compose a concerto for solo instrument and orchestra.

Tortelier, Paul (1914–) French cellist. He was principal cellist in a number of orchestras, including those of Monte Carlo and Boston, before embarking on a solo career and playing the major concertos and other works written for his instrument. He has been an inspired teacher, and his television 'master classes' will long be remembered.

Toscanini, Arturo (1867–1957) Italian conductor. Thanks to the perspicacity of one of his schoolteachers, who praised his musical powers to the boy's parents, Toscanini was sent at the age of nine to study the cello and composition at Parma Conservatory where, he was to say in later years, his best tutor had been the library. He spent all his spare time reading and analysing scores, building up the phenomenal memory for detail which was to carry him through many a difficult situation. In 1886 he was taken on as a cellist and assistant chorus master to an opera company touring South America. During an uproar in Rio de Janeiro when the conductor refused to appear and the deputy conductor was hissed off the podium, Toscanini took over and conducted an entire performance of *Aida* from memory.

Back in Italy he speedily made his name as an operatic conductor, and at Turin in 1895 conducted the first Italian performance of Wagner's *Götterdämmerung*. He went on to become one of the most revered Wagnerian conductors at Bayreuth until, in 1933, Hitler's racial laws against Jews in Germany led to his announcement that he would no longer appear there. Hitler tried personally to lure him back, but Toscanini was adamant, whereupon Hitler publicly denounced him. Already the conductor had quarrelled with Mussolini because of a failure to play the Fascist anthem, the *Giovinezza*, and had been beaten up in Bologna. Now there was to be yet another clash, leading to his lament, 'I have lost three countries': after triumphs at the Salzburg Festival, he saw the Nazis taking over Austria as well, and once more had to turn his back on places he had loved. Fortunately he never turned his back on music. From now on he spent more and more

Toscanini conducting a recording session of Debussy's *La Mer* in March 1947.

time in the USA, conducting legendary concerts for the Philharmonic Symphony Society of New York and later for seventeen years with the NBC Symphony Orchestra, specially formed for him. He made many guest appearances in London before and after World War II, and conducted at Covent Garden during George VI's coronation celebrations in 1937.

Some orchestral players found him tyrannical and unpredictable. Yet even from players he had quarrelled with he continued to produce the most inspired performances, pulling individual parts together into a shimmering tonal web which no other maestro has ever matched. His ability to perform an entire long work within precisely the allocated time was the envy of fellow conductors, who were said to attend his rehearsals and performances with stop watches to find out how he achieved it. They failed. There were some composers with whom he was temperamentally not in sympathy, though he rarely pronounced on the subject. His interpretations and recordings of Beethoven, and the encouragement he offered modern composers such as Samuel Barber, provided a positive legacy which cancels out any other failings.

Tosti, (Sir) (Francesco) Paolo (1846–1916) Italian composer (British citizen). He studied the violin and composition in Naples, and composed a number of light songs which he performed himself. These led to his being appointed singing teacher to the future Queen of Italy. In 1875 he visited England and found a public receptive to his tuneful ballads, persuading him to use English texts in place of his native Italian. He became singing teacher to the royal family and was a favourite of Queen Victoria; but it was not until the reign of her son, Edward VII, that Tosti was knighted in 1908. Although too readily dismissed nowadays as 'sentimental Victorian drawing-room ballads', his melodies were warm and flowing, and the lyrics no worse than a hundred others. His *Good-bye* is still a recital standby and 'party piece' for many distinguished singers.

touch There are no scientific grounds for believing that any nuance of tonal quality can be achieved by variation in the impact of fingers on a piano or other keyboard (apart from the clavichord), since the key action behaves in precisely the same way however the key is depressed. Nevertheless the subtle skills of some players enable them to combine swiftness of fingering with minute inequalities of pressure and of time (using rubato, syncopation, staccato attack or legato expansiveness, etc.) to produce distinctive interpretations and be praised for their 'touch'.

In earlier music, up to the seventeenth century, the word was used in the meaning of *sounding* a keyboard instrument, and remains as such in the term *toccata*.

Tovey, (Sir) Donald (1875–1940) English composer, pianist, teacher and writer. He accompanied the great violinist Joachim at a concert at Windsor, gave piano recitals of his own in London, Berlin and Vienna, and composed a number of chamber works, a symphony, and an opera, *The Bride of Dionysus*. From 1914 until his death he was Reid professor of music at Edinburgh University, and in that city established the Reid orchestral concerts. His programme notes for these formed the basis of several books of criticism. Among his other writings are a detailed analysis of Bach's *Art of Fugue*, for whose final unfinished contrapunctus he wrote a skilful conjectural ending.

transcription The arrangement of a composition for one instrument or ensemble to suit another instrument or different grouping: not merely a straightforward re-orchestration, but usually allowing for changes which one supposes the composer himself might have made had he written for such an instrument or instruments in the first place. Schoenberg's orchestral versions of Bach chorale preludes and of the Brahms piano quintet in G minor are in effect transcriptions, as are a number of reinterpretations by Webern.

transition A subordinate passage providing a link between two important sections of a composition, often involving a modulation from one key to another.

transposition The shifting of a passage or entire composition into another key without any alteration of melodic or chord intervals so that the result sounds exactly the same within itself apart from being at a different basic pitch. Transposing instruments are those which are notated at another pitch from that of the actual sound in order to make for simpler fingering: e.g. the A clarinet when playing music written in the key of C (without accidentals in the key signature) produces the sound of music in A major, which if it had been a non-transposing instrument would have involved three sharps throughout. (*See also* **The Orchestra and its Instruments**.)

trauermusik German for mourning music. The title was bestowed by Hindemith on a piece which he wrote overnight in London for viola and strings on hearing of King George V's death: this memorial composition, its fourth movement based on a Bach chorale, was first performed on BBC radio the following day. A *trauermarsch* is a funeral march.

trautonium An electronic instrument exhibited by its inventor, Friedrich Trautwein, in Berlin in 1930. Its principle was not unlike those of the *thérémin* and the manual version of the *ondes Martenot*, controlled by hand movements close to an aerial; but although it had an interesting range of tone colours and superior methods of establishing exact pitches, it attracted the interest of few composers other than Hindemith, who wrote a concert piece for trautonium and strings.

travesti The Italian word means a 'dressing-up' or 'disguised' part; in English theatre a 'trousers rôle', in German *hosenrolle*: in brief, a transvestite performance. In light comedy and in *opera buffa*, male characters were frequently performed by women dressed as men, leading at times to double complications in the plot when the girl-dressed-as-boy had for some contrived reason to play the part of boy-dressing-as-girl. Two of the most wittily handled of such characters are Cherubino in Mozart's *Le nozze di Figaro* and Richard Strauss's Octavian in *Der Rosenkavalier*.

treble The highest normal range in vocal compositions, usually applied to a choirboy's unbroken voice. It can also refer to a similar instrumental part, and to high-pitched musical instruments such as a treble recorder. The treble clef is the upper staff used for keyboard music and for string and wind instruments in that register.

trepak A lively Russian dance of Cossack origin in 2/4 time.

triad The common three-note chord of root, third and fifth – in C major, for instance, C/E/G. An *augmented triad* contains an augmented fifth, in this case G sharp; a *diminished triad* a flattened or diminished fifth, in this case G flat.

trio Any piece written for three voices or three instruments, or the singers or players of such pieces. A chamber music trio may consist of any instrumental combination: Haydn, Mozart and Beethoven wrote many trios for piano, violin and cello; one Brahms trio has horn, violin and piano; Poulenc wrote a sonata for horn, trumpet and trombone. The *trio sonata* of the baroque period was designed for two instruments and continuo. Bach's *trio sonatas* for organ required one performer only, though employing three distinct elements – left hand, right hand, and feet. The trio in the *minuet and trio* sections of a symphony or chamber work was so-called because it was originally written in three-part harmony, as if for three individual instruments.

triplet A group of three notes, or notes and rests, fitted into the same time length as one, two, or another even number of the prescribed beats in the time signature. The triplets are shown by a figure 3 above a bracket linking the notes.

tritone The interval of an augmented fourth, i.e. three whole tones which in fact divide an octave precisely in half: in a scale of C major, the interval reaches from tonic C to F sharp, with an equal interval from the F sharp up to the higher C of the octave. It is a difficult leap to sing in tune, and until the early seventeenth century was actually prohibited because of its sinister sound: there was a saying, derived from tonic sol-fa nomenclature, that 'Mi against fa is the devil in music'. The modern ear has become accustomed to it in dominant seventh and diminished seventh chords, and in compositions using the whole-tone scale, where the interval between any tone and a tone four steps away is inevitably a tritone.

troubadour A poet-musician from the 'Age of Chivalry' between the eleventh and thirteenth centuries. Such minstrels wrote and sang their own songs, sometimes accompanied and sometimes unaccompanied. Most of them were courtly love lyrics, but there were also epic songs known as *chansons de geste*. The word has often been applied to wandering minstrels, but most of them were gentlemen accustomed to singing in private mansions. Their noble counterparts in northern France were called *trouvères*. One of the most celebrated was Blondel, who located the imprisoned King Richard the Lion-heart by roaming the countryside singing a song known only to the two of them. The Italian term for a troubadour became the title of Verdi's opera *Il trovatore*.

tune and **tuning** The word 'tune' is virtually synonymous with 'melody', especially as the top line of a harmonized piece – 'the tune'. *In tune* means that vocal or instrumental intonation is correct;

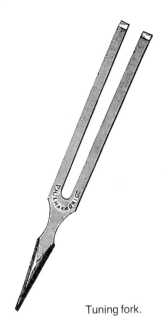

Tuning fork.

out of tune, that voice or instrument is inexact, veering sharp or flat. Adjustment of instruments before a performance is known as *tuning*. Correct pitch can be established by the vibration of a *tuning fork*, a two-pronged metal device invented in 1711 by a trumpeter, John Shore, which gives out a pure A above middle C without harmonic upper partials.

Tureck, Rosalyn (1914–) American pianist and conductor. She made her début in Chicago in 1923, in New York in 1935. From 1957 onwards she made extensive tours of Europe giving recitals of Bach on a modern piano and, in 1959, forming the Tureck Bach players in London. In 1958 she was the first woman to conduct the New York Philharmonic Orchestra. In 1971 she became a professor at the Juilliard School.

Turina, Joaquin (1882–1949) Spanish composer and conductor. He studied in Seville and Madrid, and then with d'Indy in Paris. He became a leading ballet conductor in Spain, and from 1931 professor of composition at Madrid Conservatory. His own compositions are strongly nationalistic, including an opera *Margot*, an orchestral *Sinfonia Sevillana*, *Andalusian Dances* for piano, and a number of pieces for guitar.

Turner, (Dame) Eva (1892–) English soprano. She joined the Carl Rosa Opera company in 1916 and remained with them for eight years. While there she was heard by Toscanini's assistant, auditioned for the maestro, and was engaged to sing two Wagner rôles at La Scala. Until the outbreak of World War II she lived mainly in Italy, appearing at the major opera houses. With her thrillingly expansive voice she has been unquestionably the most powerful interpreter of the ruthless princess in Puccini's *Turandot*. On the coronation night of King George VI in 1937 she led the chorus and audience at Covent Garden in *God Save the King*. After World War II she sang with the Chicago Opera, was professor of singing at Oklahoma University from 1950 to 1959, and after that taught in London, with Amy Shuard and Rita Hunter among her pupils.

tutti Italian for 'all' or 'everybody'. In music this calls for all the singers or instrumentalists to sing or play at once. It is also used to define the orchestral forces in a concerto as opposed to the soloist, especially when they are playing passages during which the soloist is silent.

twelve-tone (twelve-note) system Also known as *dodecaphony*. The organization of all twelve semi-tones in an octave to give equal value to each in the main theme of a composition. (*See also* **tone-row** and **serialism**.)

Tye, Christopher (*c.*1500–73) English composer. After serving as a choirboy and then a lay clerk at King's College in Cambridge, he was appointed choirmaster at Ely Cathedral in 1541 and remained there for twenty years. He is said to have been music tutor to the young King Edward VI, becoming also a Gentleman of the Chapel Royal. In 1561 he was ordained, and in due course held three livings in the Isle of Ely, though late in life he had to give them up because of financial irregularities. He wrote many anthems and motets, metrical versions of the *Acts of the Apostles* for four voices, and a number of instrumental *In nomines*.

tzigane *See* **zigeuner**.

U

uillean pipes The word *uillean* is Gaelic for 'elbow', referring here to bagpipes whose bellows are held under the player's arm.

ukulele Sometimes spelt *ukelele*, colloquially shortened to *uke*. A four-stringed instrument of Portugese origin which attained popularity in Hawaii early in the twentieth century. The name actually means 'jumping flea', and the instrument, a kind of small guitar, has never been seriously adopted other than in small dance bands, for use at parties, or as a strummed accompaniment to comic songs. Music for it is written in a form of tablature, a grid above the staffs of popular song sheets.

unison Two or more notes sounding together at the same pitch. In *unison singing*, successions of these are sung by everyone concerned in a monophonic tune with no harmonic separation.

upbeat The word has two common musical meanings: an unstressed note immediately preceding a barline and anticipating the accented first beat of the subsequent measure (common in the gavotte, rigaudon and bourrée); or the upward movement of a conductor's baton to signal his forthcoming downbeat on an accented note.

urtext German for 'original text', i.e. a composer's original scores (or 'autographs'), or editions adhering to the composer's supposed intentions without subsequent editing or arranging.

utility music *See* **gebrauchsmusik**.

V

valve A finger-key for a brass wind instrument. A number were added in the early nineteenth century to enable the tubing of a trumpet, horn, etc. to be effectively lengthened or shortened and so produce a complete chromatic scale instead of merely the natural harmonics. There are two types: for the trumpet family the *piston*, which goes down and up in its casing; and for the horn the *rotary*, which revolves to give four different stop-cock positions, controlled by a spring.

vamping A colloquial term for improvised accompaniment, usually by a pianist who can only play 'by ear' and not read music. On some popular music sheets there are frequently to be found two introductory measures marked by a repeat sign and also marked (or nowadays implicitly understood to mean) 'Vamp till ready', indicating that the player should repeat the short phrase until the singer or soloist is ready to enter with the theme.

Varèse, Edgard (1883–1965) French composer (American citizen 1926). He studied in Paris with d'Indy, Roussel and Widor, and between 1908 and 1913 worked in Berlin as a conductor and came under the influence of Busoni, being especially attracted by that composer-philosopher's *Sketch for a New Aesthetic of Music*. Returning to France, he served with the French army but was invalided out in 1915 and left for the USA, settling in New York and in 1921 becoming a founder of the International Composers' Guild to further the cause of new music. Early compositions which he had left in Berlin were destroyed in a fire.

He was vigorous in his denunciation of traditional musical forms, and began writing orchestral works which went beyond even the atonal disruptions of Schoenberg and Stravinsky. He favoured cumulative blocks of sound and explored convoluted melodic paths which had rarely been trodden before. Back in Paris between 1928 and 1933, he wrote *Ionisation* for thirty-five percussion instruments including gourds and rattles, and in *Ecuatorial* experimented with two *ondes Martenot*, completing the piece in the USA. For some years he produced little more, unable to get the help he pleaded for from film companies in the exploration of 'organized sound'. Early in the 1950s he was one of the first to work with tape, and in 1958 conceived his *Poème électronique* of natural and electronic sounds filtered and played through four hundred loudspeakers in the Philips pavilion designed by Le Corbusier for the 1958 Brussels Exposition. After this he relapsed again into virtual silence, but by this time had established himself as a major figure in the eyes of adventurous younger composers.

OTHER WORKS: Orchestral *Amériques*, including fire siren and cyclone whistle. *Déserts* for wind, percussion and tape.

variation A piece of music which takes an original theme or a theme by a favoured composer and varies or embroiders it melodically, harmonically or polyphonically. Many composers have used the title *Theme and Variations* for sets of these, including Brahms's piano *Variations on a theme by Handel*, and Britten's *Variations on a Theme of Frank Bridge*; others have used the form in a whole movement of a work, as in the finale of Mozart's clarinet quintet and that of Beethoven's *Eroica* symphony.

Vaughan Williams, Ralph (1872–1958) English composer. He was born in the village of Down Ampney, where his father was vicar. The composer was to commemorate his birthplace in a hymn tune of that name which he contributed to *The English Hymnal*. His father died less than three years after the boy's birth, and he was taken to live in his mother's family home at Leith Hill Place in Surrey. She installed a small organ for him to play, and his aunt gave him piano lessons as well as paying for a correspondence course in musical theory. He continued his musical interests at school, and after leaving Charterhouse went to hear Wagnerian performances in Germany. More formal studies began at the Royal College of Music and at Cambridge, and then with Bruch in Berlin. In 1908 he had a brief spell in Paris with Ravel.

The major compositions which followed were, from the start, influenced by his interest in English folksong, stimulated by his first hearing in 1903 of the song *Bushes and Briars* at the village of Ingrave in Essex, and feeling he had known it all his life. He wrote many songs of his own in an idiom almost indistinguishable from the rhythms and melodic lines of such pieces: *Linden Lea* has remained one of the most popular, and even the more ambitious cycle *On Wenlock Edge*, with its setting of A.E. Housman verses, breathes the same very English countryside atmosphere; as, indeed, do the instrumental *Six Studies in English Folk-Song* for cello or clarinet and piano.

He served in World War I, at the end of which he was appointed to the teaching staff of the Royal College of Music, where he showed the liveliest sympathy for younger composers and their differing talents, never forcing rigid rules

A pencil and chalk impression by Joyce Finzi, wife of the composer Gerald Finzi, of Ralph Vaughan Williams in 1947.

upon them. He also became conductor of the Bach Choir. At the same time he was composing more and more large-scale works, and was invited to the USA to conduct his *Pastoral Symphony*. His early symphonies frequently had titles expressing their mood, and he again used a title for his seventh, the *Sinfonia Antarctica*, based on incidental music he had composed for the film *Scott of the Antarctic* and incorporating a solo soprano and a women's choir. His symphonic style, with great broad gestures and harmonic structures as English as those of Brahms are German, owed a great deal — as did many of his choral pieces — to his instinctive rapport with the modal bases of both Tudor church music and folksong. This did not mean that he was a purely nationalist composer: his choral *Sea Symphony* made use of poems by Walt Whitman; his opera *Riders to the Sea* followed the Anglo-Irish rhythms of J.M. Synge's play with uncanny fidelity; and his palate appreciated many a tang of Ravel and Debussy.

Although an apparent agnostic, Vaughan Williams was always fascinated by sacred music, and found rewarding similarities between folksong and simple hymn tunes, many of them derived one from the other over the centuries. Commissioned to add new melodies to the outdated *Hymns Ancient and Modern*, he not only did so but after considerable research found himself with enough material for a quite separate volume which became *The English Hymnal*. The folksong tune *Monk's Gate* appears in this, named after the Sussex hamlet where the composer heard it; and he added some melodies of his own, following these up with similar contributions to *The Oxford Book of Carols*. One of his most glorious orchestral works sprang from this source: No.92 in *The English Hymnal* is a modal tune which he took from Thomas Tallis and later expanded into his *Fantasia on a Theme of Thomas Tallis* — a work of such power that the younger composers Herbert Howells and Ivor Gurney, when they first heard it in Gloucester Cathedral, roamed the streets all night unable to sleep.

For many years Vaughan Williams contributed generously to the annual Leith Hill Festival, and a great number of his works had their first performances at other major English festivals. He remained an enthusiast throughout his entire life: on the day he died, it had been arranged that he should attend a recording of his ninth symphony.

OTHER WORKS: Opera *Hugh the Drover*. Romance for violin and orchestra, *The Lark Ascending*. Overture *The Wasps*. Tuba concerto. *Serenade to Music* for sixteen solo voices and orchestra. Fantasia on *Greensleeves*.

Vauxhall Gardens In 1728 John Tyers acquired the lease of what had been the New Spring Gardens on the south bank of the river Thames in London and laid out lawns and vistas to charm the eye, restaurants and eating alcoves to satisfy the appetite, and entertainments of all kinds, including music to enchant the ear. In 1745 Dr Thomas Arne was appointed official composer, and his apprentice Charles Burney played in the orchestra. J.C. Bach wrote songs for performance there; the youthful Mozart made an appearance; and one first violinist, François Barthélemon, composed what must surely be the most beloved morning hymn tune ever written, *Awake my soul, and with the sun*. From 1774 to 1820 the resident organist and composer was James Hook, who wrote oratorios, cantatas, and over two thousand songs much heard in Vauxhall, among them *Sweet Lass of Richmond Hill*.

Saturday opening was abolished in 1806 because too many revellers stayed on into Sunday morning. The gardens prospered, however, for another half-century, with Sir Henry Bishop as official composer for much of the time, featuring some of his settings of Tom Moore's poems and one number which shows no sign of fading away: *Home, Sweet Home*. Unhappily, in 1859 Victorian puritanism led to increasing complaints about rowdyism and immorality, and after a final musical evening, billed 'The Last Night Forever', Vauxhall Gardens closed.

Végh, Sándor (1912–) Hungarian violinist. He studied in Budapest, where he later became professor of violin in the Hochschule. In 1931 he founded the Hungarian Trio; in 1935 the Hungarian Quartet. Leaving Hungary in 1946, he taught in Switzerland and Germany, and founded the Végh Quartet, paramount in their performances and recording of the Bartók string quartets.

Verdi, Guiseppe (1813–1901) Italian composer. The son of a village innkeeper near Parma, the boy had his first music lessons from the organist of the church across the road from the inn. At the age of ten he was sent to work for a merchant in Busseto, who encouraged his interest in music and, nine years later, arranged with a charitable trust for Verdi to go to Milan. Hopes of entering the Conservatorium were dashed when the examiners found his piano playing of poor standard, and also that he was four years older than the official admission age. Instead, Verdi studied privately with a conductor at La Scala, and returned to Busseto to apply for the post of church organist there. The townsfolk who had sponsored his studies were in favour of getting a return on their investment; but the ecclesiastical authorities had already chosen their own candidate. Verdi married the merchant's daughter and became director of the local Philharmonic Society, some members of which, enraged by the official snub to their protégé, invaded the church and carried off all their music which had hitherto been lodged and performed there.

In his spare time Verdi began to work on an opera, *Oberto*, which was eventually staged in Milan in 1839. It was well received, but the composer's happiness was clouded by the death of his two children; and shortly afterwards his wife died. He finished a second opera, which was a failure, and might have resigned himself to a humdrum life in Busseto if it had not been for the urging of an impresario for whom he wrote *Nabucco* (*Nebuchadnezzar*). In the humiliation of Hebrew slaves in ancient Babylon operagoers in Milan saw a parallel with their own subjection under Austrian rule, and joined in the choruses with revolutionary fervour.

Verdi's unconcealed nationalistic views won him no favour with the authorities, sacred or secular; but the public loved him, and he was soon embarked upon what he later referred to as his 'years in the galleys', writing operas at the rate of one or two a year. The most creative period was between 1851 and 1853, when he wrote *Rigoletto*, *Il trovatore* (*The Troubadour*), and *La traviata* (*The Woman Gone Astray*). By now he was establishing a new, more fluent and expressive style than had been possible in the formal operatic pattern of recitative, aria and ensemble, and was putting the *bel canto* tradition to his own use while at the same time infusing the characters with human, dramatic intensity.

The plot of *Rigoletto*, dealing with the cruelty inflicted on a hunchback jester by indolent noblemen, caused trouble with the censor, who banned the original libretto on the grounds that it displayed 'revolting immorality and obscene triviality'. Only after some toning down was permission given for the production to go ahead. Even worse, when commissioned in 1858 to write an opera for the royal theatre at Naples, Verdi chose a theme from a play by Eugène Scribe dealing with the assassination of King Gustav III of Sweden. With Italy already in rebellious mood against Austrian domination, the authorities were horrified at the idea of showing insurrection and a royal assassination on stage. *Un ballo in maschera* (*A Masked Ball*) was cleared for production only when the scene had been transferred to seventeenth-century Boston, Massachusetts, and the victim became an English governor. The absurdity of this was not redeemed until many decades later, when more modern productions were set in Italy or the original Sweden.

When the Austrian rule was finally shaken off and a free Italian parliament assembled, Verdi was invited to sit as a deputy. He carried out his duties for five years; and for thirty years did not write another opera for his own country. There were nevertheless commissions from elsewhere: *La forza del destino* (*The Force of Destiny*) for St Petersburg, *Don Carlos* for Paris. In 1869 he was asked by the Khedive of Egypt to write an opera to a text by a French Egyptologist to celebrate the opening of the Suez Canal. Time, however, was too short. The ceremony was marked instead by a production of *Rigoletto*. Two years passed before Cairo could welcome *Aida*, a sumptuous, spectacular work in which Verdi excelled himself with passionate melodies, choral edifices as massive as the pillars and pyramids of the scenery, and vivid orchestral splendour.

With the loss of his wife and children, Verdi's nature had become almost incurably melancholy, but after living for twelve years with a mistress, the soprano Giuseppina Strepponi, he married her and took her with him on most of his travels. In 1873, although an agnostic, he wrote a *Requiem* in honour of the dead Italian patriot, Manzoni, as dramatic in its construction and musical language as any of his operas. Subsequently, spending more and more time on a farm he had bought near Busseto, he showed little further interest in opera until tempted by a libretto by Arrigo Boito to begin work on a Shakespearean subject, Othello. The opera *Otello* which resulted was far beyond anything he had written before: he had moved on into more adventurous harmonies, a deeper feeling for tragic characters, and yet all of this without losing his gift for a continuous flow of melody.

The success of this late work brought demands from managements and the public for a successor. Verdi showed no interest for another five or six years, but then, remarkably, chose to conclude a creative career of largely tragic, dramatic works with a delicious comedy. Again choosing a Shakespearean subject, and again collaborating with Boito, he composed *Falstaff*, which had a triumphal première in Milan in his eightieth year, in spite of some quarrels during rehearsal with an arrogant baritone who wished to dominate all the other singers and ignore Verdi's specific instructions. 'I simply ask to be owner of my own belongings,' Verdi raged. 'If I were confronted with the alternatives – "Either accept these conditions or burn your score" – I would at once get the fire ready and myself throw on it Falstaff and his paunch.' Mercifully this catastrophe was

Giuseppe Verdi as seen by the painter Boldoni.

averted, and we have been left with a masterpiece: the chamber music quality of the scoring, the interplay of themes almost as if to show how in the hands of a master a *leitmotiv* need not be too earnestly assertive but can be combined skittishly with others, and above all the light yet loving characterization of Falstaff and his cronies, make it one of Verdi's most endearing and flawlessly polished achievements.

In 1897 his second wife died. Tired, Verdi composed no more, apart from four short pieces for chorus and orchestra, the *Quattro pezzi sacri* (*Four Sacred Songs*); but he devoted some of his time to setting up a rest home for aged musicians in Milan, which still bears his name and is supported by royalties from his works.

verismo Italian for 'realism'. It is used mainly in connection with operas whose stories are contemporary and down to earth – even what has been called, in twentieth-century drama, 'kitchen-sink'. Some critics frowned on realistic subjects such as those in Mascagni's *Cavalleria rusticana* and some of Puccini's works.

verse A solo passage in Anglican church music, as opposed to a passage for the full choir. A *verse anthem* is one consisting of alternating solo and choral sections. The word is also used for a Biblical verse in Gregorian chant.

vespers In Roman Catholic usage, the spoken or sung sixth of the canonical hours of the breviary, also known – especially in the Anglican rite – as evensong. The word is more loosely applied to any evening devotions. Monteverdi assembled a number of sacred pieces into his *Vespro della Beata Vergine* (*Vespers of the Holy Virgin* – sometimes referred to, because of their publication date, as *Vespers of 1610*). Verdi's opera *Les Vêpres siciliennes* (in Italian *I vespri siciliani*, in English *The Sicilian Vespers*) was based on the historical event of a late thirteenth-century Sicilian uprising against the French, signalled by the ringing of the vesper bells in Palermo.

Vestris, Lucia Elizabeth (1787–1856) English contralto. Granddaughter of the engraver Francesco Bartolozzi, she made her opera début in London in 1815, after which she became a star in Vauxhall Gardens and in Paris, and at the King's Theatre, London, where her husband Auguste Armand Vestris was ballet master. She became manager of Covent Garden and sang many male rôles including, according to reliable yet hardly credible records, the part of Don Giovanni. Also she created the rôle of Fatima in Weber's opera *Oberon*, composed to an English libretto expressly for production at Covent Garden and conducted at its first performance on 12 April 1826 by the composer himself.

Viardot-Garcia, Pauline (1821–1910) French mezzo-soprano. Of Spanish parentage, she was the sister of the flamboyant diva Maria Garcia (later Malibran), but seems to have had more self-control and a greater devotion to the music itself. Her friend George Sand once said to her: 'You are the priestess of the ideal in music, and your mission is to spread it, to make it understood, and to reveal to the recalcitrant and the ignorant the True and the Beautiful.' In danger of being featured as the inheritor of her sister's talent and coaxed into pushing her voice into higher registers, she resisted temptation and made a name for herself in dignified, moving interpretations such as that of Orpheus in Gluck's *Orfeo ed Eurydice*, which she sang more than a hundred and fifty times in the space of just over two years. After one such performance Charles Dickens admitted that his face was 'disfigured with crying'. In 1870 she was the first to sing Brahms's *Alto Rhapsody*.

Her private life was less austere. Alfred de Musset, Gounod and Berlioz all tried to entrap her, and she appears to have toyed very happily with their affections. The susceptible Berlioz had one of his tempestuous obsessions for a short time, but ultimately dismissed her as too cold for his tastes. Turgenev was in love with her for a large part of his later life, and there were rumours that he fathered one of her children. He wrote librettos for some lightweight operas which she composed; and Tchaikovsky wrote his song *None but the lonely heart* for her. After retirement she kept herself busy writing plays, painting, teaching at the Paris Conservatoire, and generously offering her time and encouragement to young composers.

vibraphone A percussion instrument invented by Hermann Winterhoff in 1916, similar to the xylophone but with tuned metal instead of wooden bars, played with padded hammers. Beneath are electro-mechanically controlled resonators which provide a wide vibrato. The instrument is more commonly used in jazz, where one of its greatest exponents was Lionel Hampton with the Benny Goodman Quartet and other ensembles, but it also appears in the score of Berg's *Lulu* and in works by Messiaen, Boulez and others. Milhaud wrote a concerto for marimba and vibraphone in 1947.

vibrato An Italian word describing undulation in the pitch of a note. Most singers other than choirboy trebles have a natural vibrato, sometimes too much so, making it a broad wobble rather than a pleasing tremor. Wind players produce a vibrato by breath control, string players by a slight rocking to and fro of the finger on the string. In unscrupulous hands this undulation between slightly higher and slightly lower pitches can be misused to disguise poor intonation and an inability to hit the actual note squarely.

Victoria, Tomás Luis de (*c.*1548–1611) Spanish composer. He studied at Segovia before going in 1565 to Rome to train for the priesthood. It is believed he also studied music with Palestrina, whose polyphonic style he certainly adopted in his choral works, all of them imbued with a mystical intensity. He became organist and choirmaster to a number of establishments in Rome, where he lived for so long that the Italians changed the spelling of his name to Vittoria. After some years in the service of the dowager empress Maria, sister of Philip II, he followed her on her return to Spain, and on her death in 1603 wrote an *Officium defunctorum* (Requiem Mass) for six voices. His Spanish nature added a rhythmic vigour and tonal colour to his works – all of them sacred music, and all worked out in the most superb counterpoint. Among these compositions were eighteen masses, forty-four motets, eighteen magnificats, and a great many hymn settings, published in a complete eight-volume edition during the first two decades of this century.

Vienna State Opera House Opera became the fashion in Vienna towards the middle of the seventeenth century, and a sequence of special theatres were built. The company was at first the Vienna Court

The Vienna State Opera House, opened as *Der Oper am Ring* in 1869, bombed in 1945, and rebuilt for reopening in 1955.

Opera, but changed its name in 1918 to Vienna State Opera (*Vienna Staatsoper*), with Richard Strauss and Franz Schalk as joint directors. Its tradition in presenting leading singers and conductors was as important in central and northern Europe as was that of La Scala, Milan in Italy. In March 1945 the theatre was severely damaged by bombing and was not rebuilt until 1955, when it reopened with a production of Beethoven's *Fidelio*. Herbert von Karajan was director from 1956 to 1964, and Leonard Bernstein and Zubin Mehta are among those who have conducted outstanding performances there.

Viennese School, the Second Following the dubious assumption that there was ever a First Viennese 'School', supposedly including Haydn, Mozart, Beethoven and Schubert, some musicologists have lumped together Schoenberg, Berg and Webern, along with some of Schoenberg's lesser pupils, into a second such group simply because they all worked in Vienna between 1910 and 1930. Looking back, their only common bond seems to have been a preoccupation for part of the time with twelve-tone methods.

Vierne, Louis (1870–1937) French organist and composer. Blind from birth, he studied in Paris with Franck and Widor, and became organist at the cathedral of Nôtre Dame and also professor of the organ in the Schola Cantorum. He toured Europe and the USA as a recitalist, and while in England in 1925 played at St Mary's church in Hinckley, Leicestershire, which led him to write a piece called *Les Cloches de Hinckley* (*Hinckley Bells*), as well as a London piece *Le Carillon de Westminster* (*Westminster Carillon*). Larger works were his five organ symphonies and fantasy pieces for the instrument. He died at the console in Nôtre Dame.

Vieuxtemps, Henri (1820–81) Belgian composer and violinist. At the age of six he performed a violin concerto in public, and was taken on tour by his father. After lessons in Paris he toured Germany, Austria, Russia and the USA. Between 1846 and 1852 he was Court violinist and professor of the violin in St Petersburg, and later professor at the Brussels Conservatoire until incapacitated by a stroke. Regarded as the leading virtuoso violinist of his day, he also wrote six concertos for the instrument, a sonata, and cadenzas for the Beethoven concerto.

Villa-Lobos, Heitor (1887–1959) Brazilian composer. He studied the cello and piano as a boy, but when his father died his mother sold the piano and insisted that he should study medicine and waste no more time on music. At sixteen he ran away from home and played the guitar with travelling musicians and in cafés with a *chôro*

The energetic Heitor Villa-Lobos, whose enthusiasm for European music and for his own Brazilian heritage kept him ceaselessly composing, experimenting, and using his own orchestra to introduce Bach and Beethoven to Brazil.

band – a Rio de Janeiro speciality, with flute, clarinet or cornet, ophicleide and baritone tuba, backed up by a couple of guitars to supply rhythm and harmonies. Many of the native melodies he heard in his travels through Brazil were transmuted into his suite *Chôros* for a number of different instrumental combinations.

An uncle helped Villa-Lobos with more formal studies, but he continued his wanderings. In 1923 he was able to travel to Paris, where he made a number of friends and found a publisher. His exotic instrumental compositions excited Satie, Milhaud and their circle almost as much as European influences excited Villa-Lobos. Having been introduced to the music of Bach, he attempted on his return to Brazil to combine baroque forms with his country's melodies and rhythms, resulting in a set of *Bachianas brasileiras* for different ensembles. One of the most popular with the public has been *The Little Train of the Caipira*.

In 1939 he composed an orchestral piece *New York Skyline* simply from a photograph of Manhattan, creating the melodic lines out of his own interpretation of that skyline. His most lasting work, however, may be the twelve solo *Etudes* for guitar, written for Segovia, which, as his admirer Julian Bream has pointed out, are much more French in style than the music one associates with the Spanish guitar, and dazzling with the composer's own flamboyant technique as an executant. Numbers seven to twelve are particularly expressive; and most tender of all are the fifteen *Preludes* of 1940, dedicated to his wife.

As well as composing, Villa-Lobos became superintendent of musical education in Rio de Janeiro, founded the Brazilian Academy of Music, and formed his own symphony orchestra in order to introduce European music which appealed to him to audiences in his homeland. In 1944 he visited the USA as conductor of his own music.

OTHER WORKS: Twelve symphonies. Harmonica concerto. Seventeen string quartets. Piano *Saudades das Selvas Brasileiras* and other suites.

villanella Italian for an unaccompanied rustic part-song, the literal meaning being simply 'country girl'. The French *villanelle* can mean roughly the same, or be applied to a musical setting of three-line verses in which the first and last lines of the first stanza are repeated alternately as the last line of succeeding stanzas.

viols, violins, etc. *See* **The Orchestra and its Instruments**.

Viotti, Giovanni Battista (1755–1824) Italian composer and violinist. His father, a blacksmith, was also a horn player and gave the boy his first music lessons. At the age of eleven he studied with a travelling lutenist and then was sent to Turin for lessons from Pugnani, a violin virtuoso of the day who took him on a tour of Germany and Russia. In 1782 he became accompanist and Court musician to Marie Antoinette, and although he had left her service when the Revolution broke out he soon decided it was wiser to flee to London. He played at Salomon concerts and shared in the management of Italian opera at the King's Theatre until he was unjustly accused of revolutionary activities and had to escape to Hamburg. Allowed to return in 1801, he set up as a wine merchant but found himself in financial difficulties. In spite of his problems he helped to found the Philharmonic Society and was invited to direct Italian opera in Paris. When this failed he returned to London, where he died in poverty.

Among his compositions were twenty-nine violin concertos and eighteen violin sonatas, twenty-one string quartets, and a number of serenades and divertimenti.

virtuoso A performer of outstanding technical and interpretative skill. Used as an adjective, the word is applied to a performance by such a masterly executant.

Vishnevskaya, Galina (1926–) Russian soprano. She studied in Leningrad and sang there in both operetta and then opera, joining the Bolshoi company in 1952. She took the leading rôle in Verdi's *Aida* at the New York Met in 1961 and at Covent Garden, London, in 1962. The soprano part in Britten's *War Requiem* was written for her: she did not appear in the first performance at Coventry Cathedral, but was on the 1962 recording conducted by the composer. In 1974 she and her husband, the cellist and conductor Rostropovich, left the USSR and four years later were deprived of their Soviet citizenship.

323

Vivaldi, Antonio Lucio (1678–1741) Italian composer. His father was a violinist in the orchestra of St Mark's in Venice, and is thought to have given the boy his first lessons, though little evidence remains of those early years. What is known is that at the age of fifteen Vivaldi began training for the priesthood and was ordained in 1703. He seems to have applied little time to his obligatory devotions, and gave up saying Mass on the grounds of a supposed chest ailment which somehow never afflicted him when he was writing, performing or conducting music. The combination of his red hair and clerical background led to his being dubbed by admiring or sceptical musicians and audiences 'The Red Priest'.

Although he was to teach and play most devotedly at the orphanage where he was employed, the *Ospedale della pietà*, there were gaps when his contract was not renewed, and others when he sought leave of absence to travel and present

A 1723 sketch by P.L. Ghezzi of 'The Red Priest', Antonio Vivaldi. At this time he was at the height of his fame. Throughout the 1730s a decline set in, church authorities banned production of his operas, his patron the Emperor Charles V died, and in 1741 Vivaldi himself died in penury.

less devout works than those composed for performance by the girls under his charge. Around 1705 he published a set of trio sonatas; in 1709 a set of twelve violin sonatas was dedicated to a royal visitor, King Frederik IV of Denmark; and in 1711 he dedicated to Ferdinando III of Tuscany *L'estro armonico* (*Harmonious Inspiration*), twelve concertos for different combinations of instruments which gradually became known across Europe for their ingenuity and fresh new style. Bach was one of many north of the Alps who recognized the power of the work and its melodic individuality: of the many Vivaldi pieces he was to adapt to his own uses, six came from this group of concertos.

In order to win public fame and fortune, operatic success was every Italian composer's goal. In due course Vivaldi was to write nearly a hundred, though less than half of these can now be traced. His first was *Ottone in villa*, for whose production in Vicenza in 1713 he was allowed one month's leave from the Venetian *Pietà*. After this he began to travel widely, not merely writing operas for Rome, Mantua and elsewhere but becoming for a time an impresario in Venice. In 1737 a production of one of his operas in Ferrara was forbidden by Cardinal Ruffio on the grounds that Vivaldi was a priest who did not say Mass and that he was living immorally with a singer. The woman, Anna Girò, was a gifted soprano for whom many of Vivaldi's leading rôles were written, and of whom he said 'a comparable prima donna is not to be found'. The truth of their relationship has never been firmly established, but it was no uncommon thing for composers to acquire a useful companion-cum-singer – though less tolerable for an ordained priest to do so.

While composing steadily for the stage, Vivaldi also continued writing his inventive instrumental music. Some of it was done so quickly (as indeed were operas such as *Tito Manlio*, on the score of which he boasted that it was 'written in five days') that envious rivals accused him of skimping much of the work by rattling off unison passages for all strings rather than working out full harmonies. There was some truth in this: accompaniments to some of the little chamber operas, for production by noble dilettantes, are sketchy in the extreme. But the instrumental lines themselves remain vigorous and exciting in their broad sweep, with exhilarating leaps between wide intervals which became almost the composer's trade-mark. At his most spacious, he foreshadowed the emergence of the eighteenth-century symphony in shape, harmonic progression, and rhythmic balance. Vivaldi himself was praised for his skill as a violinist, and he wrote as if every performer ought to be able to emulate his virtuoso technique. The most striking embodiment of his creative powers and imaginative use of strings is to be found in the four concertos making up *Le quattro stagioni* (*The Four Seasons*), where strikingly pictorial effects conjure up visions of the forest in spring, zephyrs in summer, huntsmen and drunkards in autumn, and the bleakness of winter.

His output of instrumental music included at least four hundred concertos, among them a number for bassoon, mandolin, cello and other soloists, and a cornucopia of sonatas for various combinations. Among his sacred music the most successful revivals in our own time have been three *Glorias*, two settings of *Dixit Dominus*, and three of *Laudate pueri*. By 1740 he was known and revered throughout Europe, and had notified the *Pietà* of his intention of finally severing his connection there; yet in the following year, visiting Vienna to sell a number of his concertos to Count Coltato and perhaps in hope of a Court appointment, he died of an 'internal inflammation' and was accorded the cheapest possible burial the very next day, having, it was recorded, 'through excessive prodigality died a pauper'.

vocal score Arrangement of the vocal parts of an opera or oratorio with piano accompaniment only in place of the full orchestral parts, useful for rehearsal or for amateur productions with limited resources.

vocalize A wordless vocal exercise (e.g. humming, or using a few meaningless syllables). A few songs have been written for performance in this way, including one so named by Rachmaninov; Medtner used the method in his *Sonata-V*; and experiments with wordless vocal effects, some of them employing electronic amplification, have been used by contemporary composers such as Berio (*Circles* and *Visage*) and Stockhausen (*Refrain* and *Stimmung*).

voice In its simplest meaning, the sound produced by the human vocal chords. In singing, there are four basic registers of voice: soprano, alto, tenor, and baritone. The word is also used for the separate strands or *parts* of a polyphonic composition, not just when sung but also when played instrumentally. *Voicing* is the adjustment of instrumental tone qualities by mechanical means, especially in the tuning of organ pipes. Certain such pipes have a distinctive tone known as a voice: *voix céleste* is French for an eight-foot stop with two pipes to each tone, producing a *vibrato* effect; *vox humana* is the Latin name for an eight-foot reed stop which supposedly produces a sound like the human voice, though in fact there is little resemblance.

volkslied German for 'folksong', often applied also to popular songs written in that vein by well-known composers, though strictly speaking these should be categorized as *volkstümliches lied*, which translates roughly as 'nationally popular'.

volta The Italian word means both 'time' and a 'turn' or 'jump', hence its use in *prima volta* — first time — and *volti subito*, meaning to turn the page over quickly. It was also the name of a quick dance, *La volta*, in 3/2 time involving a jumping step, similar to the *galliard*.

voluntary An organ solo played at the beginning or end of an Anglican church service, and occasionally at a break in the service itself. The word has also been applied to instrumental compositions for secular performance. One of the best-known is the *Trumpet Voluntary* arranged by Sir Henry Wood from a keyboard piece originally ascribed to Purcell but later found to be the work of Jeremiah Clarke.

vorhalt German for a suspension or syncopation.

Voříšek, Jan (1791–1825) Bohemian composer. By the age of eight he was proficient on the violin, organ and piano, and took up serious studies in Prague. In 1813 he went to Vienna, became friends with Beethoven and Hummel, and in 1822 was appointed Court organist. His style, particularly in his piano music, owed something to Beethoven, but there is a closer affinity with Schubert. He wrote little orchestral music, which is remarkable when one considers the swaggering confidence of his brilliant Symphony in D, which has all the gusto of Beethoven's Eighth without ever suggesting mere imitation.

vorspiel In German, literally a 'foreplay', it means a prelude or overture, and was thus preferred by Wagner in his operas.

W

Wagner, Richard (1813–83) German composer. After his widowed mother Johanna remarried, Richard, the ninth of her children, was given the surname of his stepfather, Ludwig Geyer. The fact that there was talk (apparently unfounded) of Geyer being partly Jewish, and of Richard being the result of a long-lasting liaison with Johanna before her widowhood (which the young man himself seems to have come to believe), has always raised psychological question-marks over the composer's later vicious anti-Semitism.

At the age of fourteen he resumed the name Wagner. At nineteen he composed a symphony and made an attempt at an opera *Die Hochzeit* (*The Wedding*) which his sister Rosalie, a successful singer in Prague, persuaded him to destroy.

A photograph of Richard Wagner taken about 1870 by F. Hanfstaegel.

Determined nevertheless to devote his life to music, he managed to obtain choral and theatrical conducting appointments in Würzburg and Magdeburg, had a couple of abortive love affairs, and in 1836 married one of the Magdeburg company's stars, Minna Planer. She could rely on well-paid engagements; her husband, a few years younger than herself, spent his time trying to persuade various theatres to put on some of his operatic ventures, including *Das Liebesverbot* (*The Ban on Love*), based on Shakespeare's *Measure for Measure*. At one stage Minna left him for another man, but he pleaded with her to come back, and during a cooling-down period in lodgings near Dresden he read Bulwer-Lytton's novel *Rienzi* and saw in it the basis of a grand opera.

Accepting a post as musical director in Riga, he persuaded his wife to join him there; but after two years was dismissed and had to flee from his creditors. In desperation he decided on a new career in Paris, reaching the city via a stormy journey which took in Norway and London. On a channel steamer he met the composer Meyerbeer, who offered useful introductions in Paris, helped with advice on the score of *Rienzi* ... and was later repaid by savage denunciation in Wagner's anonymous tract *Jewishness in Music*.

In Paris Wagner and his wife lived in poverty. At one stage Minna wrote to a well-to-do friend begging for money to save Wagner from the debtors' prison. Then plans were made in Dresden for the production of both *Rienzi* and another work, *Der fliegende Holländer* (*The Flying Dutchman*). While waiting for these the couple took a holiday in Bohemia during which Wagner began work on *Tannhäuser*. Although *The Flying Dutchman* was not the immediate success for which the composer had hoped, it aroused enough favourable attention to result in his being appointed *kapellmeister* to the Saxon Court. Able at last to rely on a steady salary, he completed *Tannhäuser*, but his personal extravagance was such that he was forever in debt. There was extravagance in his emotional and political views also: in 1848 he took noisy part in revolutionary demonstrations, and had to flee first to Weimar and then for a while to Switzerland.

It was in Zürich that he began work on the saga of *Der Ring des Nibelungen* (*The Nibelung's Ring*), for which he provided the whole text himself, as he was to do with all his works. Here also he wrote critical essays, including *Oper und Drama* (*Opera and Drama*), expounding his theories of the true function of art and above all of the 'music of the future' – which was in essence to be Wagnerian music-drama, in which would be unified poetry, narrative, drama and flawless music, subjugating the demands of histrionic singers and other performers to the overriding concepts of the presiding genius. While compounding such noble theories and continuing the libretti for the *Ring* tetralogy (in reverse order, beginning with *Götterdämmerung*), he found time to fall in love with Mathilde Wesendonck, the wife of his host and patron in Zürich. Characteristically he now abandoned other projects in order to pour his passions into the libretto and music of *Tristan und Isolde*, with its sensuous melodies and even more sensually suggestive harmonies below yearning, passionately interweaving duets. The advanced chromaticism of the work foreshadowed the atonality of the next century, and even the chromatic experimentation

of Schoenberg.

Wagner's justification for producing such a work at a time when his writings preached almost superhuman philosophical and aesthetic ideals was contained in notes for an unposted letter to Schopenhauer claiming to find in sexual love 'a path of salvation which itself leads to self-knowledge and self-denial of the will'. This self-denial was none too apparent when, after his admirer Hans von Bülow had conducted *Tristan* in Munich, Wagner fathered two children on von Bülow's wife Cosima (daughter of Franz Liszt), who eventually joined him in his villa Tribschen beside Lake Lucerne. When her husband had divorced her and Minna Wagner had died, they were married. She soon produced a son, inevitably named Siegfried after the hero of Wagner's still burgeoning tetralogy.

Rent of the idyllic villa was paid for by the young King Ludwig II of Bavaria, a homosexual who had fallen in love with Wagner's 'divinely inspired' concept of the *Ring* and was willing to provide financial support for whatever the composer might need. In spite of protests from the king's advisers, Wagner won from Ludwig the money to establish a theatre of his own in which his works could be presented exactly according to his overall vision, and a villa, Wahnfried, in which to live with his family. In 1876, after many disagreements, a *Festspielhaus* (*Festival-play House*) was opened at Bayreuth for the first complete performance of the cycle: *Das Rheingold* (*The Rhine Gold*); *Die Walküre* (*The Valkyrie*); *Siegfried*; and *Götterdämmerung* (*Twilight of the Gods*). In view of the time it had taken to complete the cycle, with so many interruptions and delays, and its construction out of chronological sequence, the cumulative power is amazing. Even the use of his favoured method of the *leitmotiv*, with motto themes summoning up memories in the huge, expressively handled orchestra and announcing the arrival or remote intervention of particular characters in the saga, does not explain the homogeneity and hypnotic assurance of the complete work. The composer's vision, so grandiose and easy to mock in the abstract, in performance imposed itself unfalteringly upon words, music, setting and the whole atmosphere.

All his ideas were conditioned by German romantic legend, and by a recurrent concern with the clash between sacred and profane love. *Tannhäuser* deals with a thirteenth-century minstrel tempted by the carnal pleasures of the Venusberg. *Lohengrin* blends myths of the Holy Grail with early German history. *Die Meistersinger von Nürnberg* (*The Mastersingers of Nuremberg*), his only comedy, uses tales of fifteenth-

A 1914 lithograph by Franz Stassen of a scene from *Das Rheingold*, one of the *Ring* cycle.

century guild singers to convey a resounding riposte to critics who had derided his music.

His last opera was *Parsifal*, a Christian music-drama on which he had worked for some years and which had its first performance at Bayreuth in 1882. After that he suffered recurrent heart attacks, the final one occurring when he and the family had gone to Venice for the early winter of 1883. The body was brought back for burial at Wahnfried in a tomb designed by Wagner himself. King Ludwig gave orders that all the pianos in his various palaces should henceforth be shrouded in black crêpe.

In spite of Wagner's outspoken detestation of Jews, the conductor of the first performance of *Parsifal* and of the music at the composer's funeral was Hermann Levi, son of a rabbi. After the 1883 festival, though mourning the loss of his idol, Levi wrote to his father: 'I do not think I have ever known such happiness ... my enchantment with this most glorious, most sublime of all works intensified from performance to performance, and so did my pride in being summoned to be its interpreter.'

waits Originally watchmen and keepers of town gates who patrolled at night with pipe, horn or drum, waits acquired in due course more advanced instruments and were expected also to serenade the townsfolk, provide fanfares and formal music for visiting dignitaries, give regular outdoor concerts, and sing and play for money and refreshment at Christmastime outside the homes of well-to-do citizens.

Walcha, Helmut (1907–) German organist. At the age of sixteen he went blind, but continued music studies at Leipzig and became assistant organist at the Thomaskirche and then organist in Frankfurt. He has been an influential teacher and has recorded Bach's organ works on instruments as close as possible to those of Bach's day, including that at Alkmaar in Holland, and in Germany the small organ of St Jakobi in Lübeck and the velvety-toned Schnitger baroque organ in Cappel.

Waller, Thomas ('Fats') (1904–43) American jazz pianist and composer. His father was a Baptist Church deacon, and the boy was encouraged to learn the organ. His interests turned to jazz, and after three years of playing a theatre organ in Harlem he became one of a group of pianists who broke away from ragtime and developed a style known as 'stride' piano playing. He made many recordings. A great number were of his own compositions, favourites among other jazz

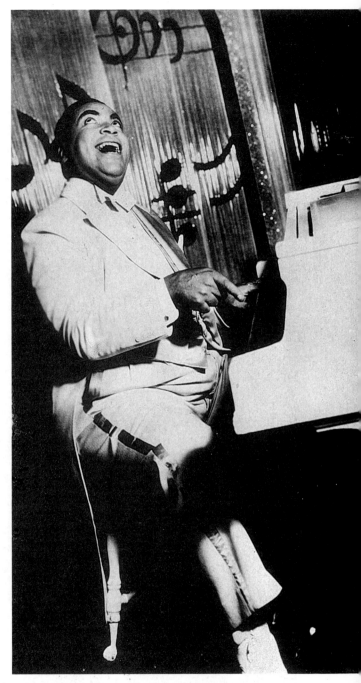

The ebullient pianist and vocalist 'Fats' Waller, who is reputed to have said, when asked to define rhythm, 'If you have to be told, you ain't got it.'

arrangers and improvisers. Among the better known are *Honeysuckle Rose* and *Ain't Misbehavin'*.

Walter, Bruno (1876–1962) German conductor (Austrian citizen 1911; French 1938; American 1946). He studied in Berlin, and in 1893 became coach and assistant conductor to Cologne Opera.

Later he conducted in Riga, Berlin, Vienna and Munich, presenting the first performances of Mahler's ninth symphony and of *Das Lied von der Erde* (which he was also to record later with Kathleen Ferrier). He made his American début in 1923 with the New York Symphony Orchestra, and his opera début at the New York Met in 1941 after fleeing from the Nazis to France and then

the USA. His conducting was broad and warm, drawing out the full tonal richness of orchestra and singers to irradiate the music of composers he particularly revered, most notably Beethoven, Schubert and Mahler.

Walton, (Sir) William (1902–83) English composer. As a choirboy at Christ Church, Oxford, he was helped by an observant tutor to enter the University proper as the youngest undergraduate since Henry VIII. He became a friend of the Sitwell family and was taken by them on holiday to Italy, with which he fell in love and to which he later returned to settle. While working on his oratorio *Belshazzar's Feast* in 1930-31, with its challenging amalgam of Handelian choruses and an orchestral palette owing much to Stravinsky, he was accommodated in the stables of a country house belonging to the Sitwells.

Walton's music was for a time on a par with the Sitwells' ironic, often prickly writing and sense of humour. His first work to attract attention, the suite *Façade*, a smart, febrile set of pastiche pieces designed as an accompaniment to the intoning of Edith Sitwell poems, caused him for a while to be regarded as an *enfant terrible*. By the time he came to his first symphony, however, he was becoming more serious, and produced a piece in the tradition of Elgar with big melodies and an orchestral architecture of noble proportions. His violin concerto, commissioned by Heifetz, had the same broad scope, but with a rhapsodic mellowness for the solo instrument which has assured it a regular place in the repertoire. He openly expressed a preference for classical conformity allied with lyricism; but romantic warmth was displayed in his opera *Troilus and Cressida*, perhaps as a result of his having found an ideal home in Italy.

The ability to write in pastiche, lightly and picturesquely, or with great feeling, made him one of the most accomplished composers of film scores: among his contributions to the cinema were the scores for *Escape me Never, Major Barbara, Henry V, Hamlet*, and the *Spitfire Prelude and Fugue* from *The First of the Few*.

OTHER WORKS: Opera *The Bear*. Ballet *The Wise Virgins*. Orchestral march *Crown Imperial* (for coronation of King George VI). Viola concerto. Overture *Portsmouth Point*. Five Bagatelles for guitar.

waltz A dance in 3/4 time, derived from the Austrian *ländler*, which found its way into fashionable ballrooms in the late eighteenth century and was taken up by the Strauss family in Vienna. Other

A photograph by Cecil Beaton of William Walton in 1926, the year when his provocative *Façade* suite had its first public performance in London, and the overture *Portsmouth Point* was first performed in Zürich and then in London.

composers who adapted it to their own instrumental and orchestral uses include Weber (*Invitation to the Dance*), Chopin, Tchaikovsky and Ravel (*La Valse*).

Warlock, Peter (1894–1930) English composer and critic. His real name was Philip Heseltine. At Eton he came across the music of Delius and, since there was no chance then of hearing full performances, transcribed some for piano solo or duet. At one stage he made an arrangement of Delius's *On Hearing the First Cuckoo in Spring* for brass band, known ever since as 'The Brass Cuckoo'. With his friend (and later biographer) Cecil Gray he founded a music magazine, *The Sackbut*, but adopted the pseudonym Peter Warlock when it came to composing music of his own. His main output was of songs, some in Elizabethan vein, others in rollicking half-folksong exuberance; but he also produced enchanting settings of old French dances in his *Capriol Suite* for string orchestra. Part roistering tippler, part contemplative musician, he fell into a depression just before Christmas 1930 after a quarrel with a woman he had been living with, put his kitten out with a dish of food, closed the doors and windows, and committed suicide by turning on the gas.

wassail An old English word for convivial songs and in particular songs addressed to fruit trees to make them bear. Christmas revellers would go *wassailing* from house to house, singing goodwill songs and especially carols.

Waterman, Fanny (1920–) English piano teacher. In 1963 she founded and became joint administrator of the Leeds International Piano Competition, which has become one of the most important regular contests for aspiring virtuoso players.

Webber, Andrew Lloyd (1948–) English composer. After a brief spell at Oxford, he went to the Guildhall School of Music and then the Royal College of Music in London to study orchestration so that he could pursue his determination to write 'musicals' for the stage in the vein of Americans such as Rodgers and Hammerstein. In 1965 he received a letter from twenty-year-old Tim Rice suggesting a collaboration, and in 1968 their *Joseph and the Amazing Technicolor Dreamcoat* was performed first by the Colet Court choir and later in St Paul's Cathedral. The following year they wrote the enormously successful *Jesus Christ Superstar*. In 1974 they began work on the story of the wife of the Argentine dictator General Perón: *Evita* opened in London in 1978 and on Broadway in 1979, and ran for several years. Their 1983 musical *Cats*, based on poems from T.S. Eliot's *Old Possum's Book of Practical Cats*, won seven 'Tony' awards in New York, including

A scene from 'the musical experience' *Starlight Express*, a roller-skating extravaganza by Andrew Lloyd Webber with lyrics by Richard Stilgoe.

one for the best score. In that same year Andrew Lloyd Webber bought the Palace Theatre in London as a showcase for his work.

Webber, Julian Lloyd (1951–) English cellist. He studied at the Royal College of Music and with Pierre Fournier, making his London début in 1971. In 1971 he gave the first London performance of Sir Arthur Bliss's cello concerto at the composer's own request, and soon became one of the country's leading soloists. In 1978 his older brother Andrew Lloyd Webber (*see* preceding entry) wrote for him *Variations* for cello and jazz ensemble.

Weber, Carl Maria von (1786–1826) German composer and conductor. His father was *kapellmeister* to the prince bishop of Lübeck, but shortly after his son's birth he became director of a travelling theatre company and took his family on protracted tours. He had hopes of turning Carl into an infant prodigy like Mozart, and ensured that by the time he was four the boy could sing and play the piano. In Salzburg, Carl took composition lessons from Michael Haydn, and had other lessons where he could get them on his travels. From the age of fifteen onwards he held positions as *kapellmeister* in Breslau, a musical secretary-ship in Stuttgart – from which he was dismissed because of disrespectful conduct and possibly a financial misdemeanour – and director of Prague Opera.

In 1817 Weber at last settled into a job he was to hold for the rest of his short life: that of director of the Dresden Court Opera. His brief was to build up a repertory of German opera worthy to compete with the prevailing Italian styles, a task which he gladly undertook in spite of continual clashes with the resident Italian director, Morlacchi. He worked at an exhausting pace preparing, staging and conducting operas with an overall concept which foreshadowed the theories and practices of his successor and ad-mirer Wagner. Yet in spite of his commitments he managed also to travel throughout Europe, presenting his own compositions and writing more of them as he went.

Weber's first great success was the opera *Der Freischütz* (*The Freeshooter*), produced to great acclaim in Berlin in 1821 with himself conducting. Its romanticism and use of German myth, with human beings pitted against supernatural forces, was very much in the national mood of the time; and the composer's orchestral tone colours and dramatic 'nature music', together with the vigour of solos and choruses, brought a new vividness to the operatic stage. The next opera, *Euryanthe*, had too confused a libretto to capture the public imagination, but the music itself is often played in concert suites and, like many of Weber's other orchestral works, has a dramatic expressiveness which the composer favoured above any rigidities of form: he was not a symphonist, and could not work happily within the confines of sonata form. His projected third piano concerto finished up as what he called a *Konzertstück* (*Concert piece*) and was even provided with a programme to explain its motivations. Debussy was to praise his unique ability to scrutinize 'the soul of each instrument'.

In 1826 Weber was commissioned by Covent Garden to write an English opera for London production. He chose *Oberon* as his subject, and spent some time in England conducting some of his other works while preparations were made for the staging of the opera. Suffering from a

Carl Maria von Weber as seen by the painter Caroline Bardua. When his corpse was returned from England to Germany, ships in Hamburg dipped their colours to the accompaniment of the Funeral March from Beethoven's *Eroica* Symphony.

throat disease, he found the English climate un-favourable, and was outraged by high prices, declaring that the only thing cheaper in England than in Germany was a haircut. He conducted several weeks of *Oberon* performances until, on the night of June 4th, he died. He was buried in Moorfields Chapel. Eighteen years later his suc-cessor as conductor of the Dresden Choral Society, Richard Wagner, put the Society's influence behind a campaign for the return of the body to Dresden, and delivered the graveside oration.

OTHER WORKS: Opera *Abu Hassan*. Two clarinet concertos. *Grand Duo Concertante* for clarinet and piano. *Aufforderung zum Tanz* (*Invitation to the Dance*) for piano (and in orchestral arrangement by Berlioz). Twenty piano duets. Many songs.

Webern, Anton von (1883–1945) Austrian composer. Son of a mining engineer who held posts in a succession of towns, the boy moved about during his childhood and, though taking private lessons in violin and cello playing, had little formal theor-etical instruction until his father agreed to let him study at the University of Vienna. Dissatisfied with the arid teaching methods there, he looked around for more stimulating company, and in

1904 became a pupil of Schoenberg, along with Alban Berg.

Webern's first compositions of any substance, a sonata movement for piano and a piano quintet in one movement, were still fairly traditional in style. For a time he had little opportunity of exploring new paths: attempting a career as a conductor, he held a number of posts but none of them for long, finding the work too irritating. Finally Schoenberg lit the necessary spark with his explorations of atonality and, ultimately, of serialism. The songs in Webern's Op.3 and Op.4 ventured into atonality, to be followed by small chamber and orchestral pieces with a brevity of material and style which became his hallmark. As the years went on he became more puritanical than his mentor, turning towards total serialism and working in even more concise forms. There are times when the notes and intervals, the economy of means and the calculated silences, have an almost oriental sparseness. In the first movement of his symphony of 1928 he allied serial methods with strict canonical devices, and in the second movement wrote symmetrical variations on a symmetrical theme. At the same time he attained an almost romantic beauty in some of his songs, and his love of medieval and baroque forms is shown in the pure lines of his three cantatas, his use of passacaglia and canon, and his stimulating orchestral arrangement of the *Ricercare* from Bach's *Musical Offering*.

Webern had married a cousin before World War I, who by the time the war was over had presented him with a son and three daughters. Dropping the aristocratic 'von' from his name now that Austria was a republic, he again sought work as a conductor. He was for a time conductor of the Workers' Symphony Orchestra in Vienna, and then in 1927 was appointed conductor and later musical adviser to Austrian Radio. Work with the orchestra ceased when political oppression loomed. The Nazis denounced Webern as a 'cultural Bolshevik' and banned his work in Germany and Austria. At the end of World War II, strolling in the evening outside his son-in-law's house near Salzburg, he was shot by an American soldier returning to barracks and misinterpreting a harmless gesture in the uncertain light. His influence lives on in the work of many younger composers who feel an even closer affinity with his radical style than with that of Schoenberg.

OTHER WORKS: Orchestral *Passacaglia*. Concerto for nine instruments. *Funf geistliche Lieder (Five Spiritual Songs)* for soprano and seven instruments. Six Bagatelles for string quartet. String trio.

Weelkes, Thomas (*c*.1575–1623) English composer and organist. He served in private households before becoming organist at Winchester College in 1600, taking a music degree at Oxford and spending the rest of his life as organist at Chichester Cathedral, apart from a few brief visits to London. He published volumes of daringly inventive madrigals for different consorts of voices, startling contemporaries with their calculated discords, chromatic explorations, and pictorial elements. *Thule, the period of cosmography*, is a remarkably dramatic work, virtually a guide to Iceland and other spectacular regions and sights of which travellers had brought back news to England. Weelkes married the daughter of a prosperous Chichester tradesman and built up a fine reputation among fellow musicians, but unfortunately took to the bottle so flagrantly that at one stage he was dismissed from his post as organist. Though soon reinstated, he is recorded as having continued to drink and 'curse and swear most dreadfully'. He died on a visit to London and was buried in St Bride's Church, Fleet Street.

Weill, Kurt (1900–50) German composer (American Citizen 1943). He studied with Humperdinck and Busoni, and after trying various styles found his métier in a brittle, tangy music influenced by jazz and Berlin cabaret life. Meeting Bertolt Brecht, he collaborated with the dramatist first on a radio cantata on the subject of Lindbergh's transatlantic flight and next on a short satirical sketch with music, *Mahagonny*, which they then amplified into a three-act opera *Aufstieg und Fall der Stadt Mahagonny (The Rise and Fall of the City of Mahagonny)*. Since they needed some source of income while working on this ambitious project, they hurriedly assembled a ballad opera for which the director of a popular theatre had asked. It proved to be their biggest success – *Der Dreigroschenoper (The Threepenny Opera)*, with its sardonic modern interpretation of John Gay's *The Beggar's Opera*, enlivened by the opportunities it offered Weill's wife, the singer Lotte Lenya. Weill declared that the piece had shown him the way to 'a new kind of popular (*volkstümlich*) melody' which in Germany might supersede 'the now exhausted American jazz'.

The next Brecht-Weill collaboration demanded by the theatre management took as its theme a conflict between dance-hall criminals and the Salvation Army in Chicago, a city which neither man had ever been near. In *Happy End* Weill used a skilfully manipulated jazz ensemble in the orchestra, and the crisp directness of the songs appealed immediately to the first-night audience during the early part of the work. The second half was less pleasing, with the aggressively left-wing propaganda of its final chorus,

A photograph by Suse Byk of Kurt Weill in Berlin, about 1930, when he and Bertolt Brecht were collaborating on small-scale operas for school performance, including *Der Jasager* (*The Yes-man*) based on a Japanese Noh play.

and the critics next day damned the whole thing. It was not revived until after World War II.

When Hitler showed signs of taking over Germany, Weill and his wife left for Paris where, in near poverty, he worked with Brecht on their last joint venture, *Die Sieben Todesünden* (*The Seven Deadly Sins*). He also tried to compose more serious orchestral work, but a symphony commissioned by Princess Edmond de Polignac was tepidly received when conducted by Bruno Walter in Amsterdam, and after further attempts to make money with musical comedies in Paris and London, husband and wife set off again, this time to New York.

In America, Weill wrote the music for an anti-war play, *Johnny Johnson*, and a Jewish epic *The Eternal Road*, but aroused greater popular interest with pieces such as *September Song* in the Broadway show *Knickerbocker Holiday* and scores for other musicals such as *Lady in the Dark* and *Love*

Life. At one stage he tried to create a more adventurous, truly American style of opera in an adaptation of Elmer Rice's *Street Scene* and, later, *Lost in the Stars*. While planning a collaboration with Maxwell Anderson on an opera based on Mark Twain's *Huckleberry Finn*, he died suddenly of a heart attack.

OTHER WORKS: Two symphonies. Concerto for violin and wind. Choral and orchestral *Das Berliner Requiem* (*The Berlin Requiem*).

Weinberger, Jaromir (1896–1967) Czech composer. He studied in Prague and Leipzig, and from 1922 to 1926 was professor of composition at the Ithaca Conservatory, New York, after which he returned to Europe to conduct and teach in various centres. He composed a number of operas, of which one was a profitable international success, *Švanda Dudák* (*Schwanda the Bagpiper*). His only other widely popular work was a scintillating set of orchestral variations and fugue on the song *Under the Spreading Chestnut Tree*. In 1939 he settled finally in the USA.

Weingartner, Felix (1863–1942) Austrian conductor, composer and writer. After studying at Leipzig and with Liszt at Weimar, he held various conducting posts before being appointed conductor of the Berlin Court Opera and of symphony concerts there. His American concert début was made in New York in 1905. In 1907 he succeeded Mahler in Vienna, but after 1910 travelled, made guest appearances with leading European orchestras, served for eight years as director of the Basle Conservatory, and conducted at Covent Garden, London. He composed seven symphonies, a number of operas, and choral works, but is better remembered as an inspiring teacher and the author of books on conducting and on Beethoven symphonies.

Wellesz, Egon (1885–1974) Austrian composer and teacher (British citizen). He studied in Vienna, at one period with Schoenberg, and became friends with Webern. Between 1913 and 1938 he taught at the University of Vienna, becoming professor of the history of music there. Although many of his own compositions were dodecaphonic, he maintained a lifelong interest in Byzantine music and Gregorian chant, which with a liking for baroque opera conditioned his work in a fruitful way. His opera *Alkestis* had a libretto by Hugo von Hofmannsthal; the *Persisches Ballett* (*Persian Ballet*) showed Eastern influences; but in the first of his nine symphonies one might almost be listening to a modern extension of his great idol, Mahler. In 1938 he settled in England and joined the music faculty of Oxford University, where from 1948 to 1956 he was reader in Byzantine music.

Wesley family Charles Wesley (1707–88) helped his older brother John, founder of the Methodist movement, to spread their beliefs by writing over six thousand hymns, including *Jesu, Lover of my Soul* and *Hark, the Herald Angels Sing*. One of his sons, also Charles (1757–1834), was a child prodigy who became a London church organist, gave public harpsichord recitals, and wrote a number of keyboard concertos and string quartets, but did not fulfil his early promise.

Another son, Samuel Wesley (1766–1837), was also a child prodigy and composed part of an oratorio at the age of eight. In 1784 he became a Roman Catholic. A few years later he injured his head in a fall, prompting strange moods and fits which necessitated his retiring into privacy for long periods. In his lucid spells he worked to revive interest in the music of Bach, conducted the Birmingham Festival in 1811, and lectured at the Royal Institution.

Samuel fathered an illegitimate son, Samuel Sebastian Wesley (1810–76), who became a chorister of the Chapel Royal and organist to a number of London churches. Later he held cathedral organ appointments at Hereford, Exeter, Leeds, Winchester and Gloucester, and composed many sturdy Anglican church pieces including anthems, hymns and services.

Wexford Festival An opera festival was founded in this Irish town in 1951 and has become an annual event, specializing in the revival of operas in the *bel canto* tradition and of neglected, once popular works.

Whiteman, Paul (1890–1967) American bandleader. He worked as violinist in the Denver Symphony Orchestra before forming the Paul Whiteman Orchestra to play what came to be called 'symphonic jazz', with unusually large forces including a string section, not a common feature in dance or jazz orchestras of the time. Famous jazz instrumentalists such as Bix Beiderbecke and Jack Teagarden played in the orchestra and recorded with it, but Whiteman tended to favour more symphonically flavoured pieces, and commissioned George Gershwin's *Rhapsody in Blue* for concert performance. He was dubbed 'The King of Jazz' – a misleading term in view of these predilections – and appeared in a film of that name. Many of his more ambitious orchestrations (including that of *Rhapsody in Blue*) were arranged by the composer Ferde Grofé.

whole-tone scale A scale which progresses in whole tones instead of including the usual semitone between the third and fourth and the seventh and eighth steps of the major scale, or the semitone intervals of the minor scale. There are in effect only two possible whole-tone scales, both starting from whichever note one chooses and embodying the academically deplored tritone, with no true sense of tonality and therefore no scope for modulation. Such a scale has only limited melodic uses but can be effective if employed sparingly, as Glinka discovered and as Ravel intuitively felt in certain ventures.

Whyte, Ian (1901–60) Scottish conductor and composer. He studied with Stanford and Vaughan Williams, and became music director of the Scottish service of the BBC in 1931, founding the BBC Scottish Orchestra and introducing much new music, including that of his fellow countrymen, in many years of adventurous programming. Two of his most characteristic compositions are the symphonic poems *Tam o'Shanter* and *Edinburgh*.

Whythorne, Thomas (1528–95) English composer. In 1925 the composer and critic Peter Warlock published a brochure containing twelve songs under the title *Thomas Whythorne, an Unknown Elizabethan Composer*. Warlock's friend E.J. Moeran took one of the melodies and built around it an orchestral rhapsody, *Whythorne's Shadow*. The name remained shadowy until in 1955 the manuscript of an autobiography turned up and was published by the Oxford University Press. The mysterious Mr Whythorne had, it was discovered, been a composer of some talent who worked as music teacher, instrumentalist, and writer of madrigals and duets, and according to his own story was forever dodging the amorous attentions of the lady of whatever house he happened to be working in. The book also contains a wealth of shrewd observations on organists, teachers, and wandering minstrels of his day.

Widor, Charles Marie (1844–1937) French composer and organist. He studied with his father, an organist at Lyons, and in Brussels. From 1870 until 1933 he was organist of St Sulpice in Paris, and in 1890 followed César Franck as organ professor in the Paris Conservatoire, later becoming professor of composition there also. He was as famous an improviser as his great predecessors Buxtehude and Bach had been, and with Albert Schweitzer edited the complete organ works of Bach. His own compositions included ten organ symphonies and many other works for the instrument, as well as three operas which have not survived, and six duets for piano and organ.

wiegenlied German for a cradle song or lullaby (in French, *berceuse*), used as a title for songs by Richard Strauss, Hugo Wolf and others, and by Brahms for one of his best-loved piano pieces.

Wieniawski family Polish composers and instrumentalists. Henryk Wieniawski (1835–80) entered the Paris Conservatoire at the age of eight, gave his first public concert as a violinist at the age of thirteen, and toured Poland and Russia, from 1850 onwards in the company of his brother Józef, a gifted pianist. In 1860 he was appointed solo violinist to the Tsar and taught at the St Petersburg Conservatory, leaving in 1872 to tour the USA with the pianist Anton Rubinstein. He composed two concertos and a number of fantasies and studies for the violin, and pieces reflecting his stay in Russia, *Souvenir de Moscou* and *Le Carnaval russe*. In 1874 he became professor of the violin at Brussels Conservatoire, but in spite of poor health continued to travel: he died suddenly during a return visit to Russia.

Józef Wienawski (1837–1912) studied, like his brother, in Paris, and then with Liszt in Weimar. Also like his brother, he became a professor in Russia – in his case, professor of piano at Moscow Conservatory. He wrote a concerto and various other studies for the piano, and a string quartet.

Henryk's nephew Adam (Tadeusz) Wienawski (1879–1950) studied composition in Warsaw and Berlin, and in Paris with d'Indy and Fauré. He served on the French front during World War I, then returned to Poland and in 1928 became director of the Chopin High School of Music. His works include two operas, *Megae* and *Escape*, a number of ballets, two string quartets, a concertino for piano and orchestra, and many songs and folksong arrangements.

Wilbye, John (1574–1638) English composer. He was the third son of a tanner who must have had some musical interests, since his will specified that John should have his lute. In his teens Wilbye was taken on as musician in the household of Sir Thomas Kytson of Hengrave Hall in the county of Suffolk, and remained with the family for more than thirty years. Sir Thomas also had a town residence, to which Wilbye accompanied the family on their visits to London and from which he issued his first volumes of madrigals. He was a master of varying styles, from the sprightliness of *Ye that do live in pleasures plenty* to the dark emotionalism of *Weep, Weep, mine Eyes*. His music was forgotten for centuries until revived with the republication of his madrigals in England and their performance by the Oriana Madrigal Society and, later, by such singers as the Deller Consort. On his death Wilbye left his best viol to the Prince of Wales, later King Charles II.

Willaert, Adriaan (1490–1562) Flemish composer. studying for the law, he went to Paris to pursue these studies but turned instead to music, travelled in Italy, spent some time in the service of King Ludvik of Hungary and Bohemia, and ultimately became *maestro di cappella* to St Mark's in Venice, where he also founded a singing school. Making use of the two choirs and two organs at St Mark's, he composed many antiphonal works, showing an innovative flair in his use of chromaticism, and was one of the pioneer madrigalists.

Williamson, Malcolm (1931–) Australian composer, pianist and conductor. He studied in Sydney with Eugene Goossens and in London with Mátyás Seiber and Elizabeth Lutyens, supporting himself in London by playing the piano in night clubs and the organ in church. He was commissioned to write an organ work for the opening of the restored Coventry Cathedral in 1962. Influenced both by jazz and by the works of Messiaen, Stravinsky and Britten – and, like Britten, enjoying writing for children – he combines a strong melodic gift with a freedom of harmonic styles and orchestration. His wittily scored opera *Our Man in Havana*, based on the Graham Greene novel, was produced in London in 1963. From 1970 to 1971 he was composer-in-residence at Westminster Choir College, Princeton. In 1975 he was appointed Master of the Queen's Music. One of the most delightful results of this official appointment has been the *Ode for Queen Elizabeth, The Queen Mother*, a suite sparkling with good humour and good tunes, some reminiscent of Scottish fiddle tunes with their frequent 'Scotch snaps'.

OTHER WORKS: Opera *The Violins of Saint-Jacques*. Miniature operas (for audience participation) *The Moonrakers, The Winter Star*. Five symphonies. Organ concerto. Three piano concertos. Two piano sonatas.

wire brush A drumstick with a head of wire strands fanned out in the shape of a brush, used to produce a swishing effect across a drumhead or cymbal, usually in a dance or jazz band.

Wirén, Dag (1905–) Swedish composer. He studied in Stockholm and Paris and became music critic of a leading Swedish newspaper. In his own compositions he has practised a 'metamorphosis' technique of building an entire work from a single cell or from a small group of notes. His works include five symphonies; concertos for violin, cello, and piano; and four string quartets. In 1940 he wrote a radio opera *Blått, gult, rött* (*Blood, Tears, Sweat*), inspired by the memorable phrase from one of Winston Churchill's World War II broadcasts.

Wittgenstein, Paul (1887–1961) Austrian pianist. He lost his right arm during World War I but, determined to continue playing, developed a powerful left-hand technique, and commissioned works for this hand from Ravel, Richard Strauss, Prokofiev, and Britten. In 1939 he settled in New York.

As a music critic Hugo Wolf made many enemies, but redeemed himself by writing over one hundred and seventy inspired songs in less than three years. Even after lapsing into insanity he continued trying to compose, but the flame had died.

Wolf, Hugo (1860–1903) Austrian composer. His mother was of mixed Slav and Italian ancestry, his father a German leather dealer with musical leanings. Hugo was taught piano and violin at an early age, but after a fire destroyed the family business he had little chance of formal training for some years. Expelled from a number of schools, he managed at last to gain entry to the Vienna Conservatory in 1875, only to quarrel with the director and be thrown out yet again. To make a living he gave piano lessons to the children of well-to-do parents, but was so impatient that they soon deserted him. A tolerant friend used his influence to have Wolf appointed as second conductor at Salzburg, where he quarrelled with the principal conductor and had to leave. Trying to compose a few songs and some chamber music, he realized he was making little headway, and resented those who did. For three years he held down a job as music critic in Vienna, but his attacks on successful composers, including Brahms, made him more enemies.

Early in 1887 Wolf produced a melodious little string quartet, the *Italian Serenade,* later arranged for string orchestra. In that same year a few of his songs were published and, plunging into the poetry of Eduard Mörike, he suddenly began pouring out a flood of new songs. Staying in a friend's house in the country, in three months he wrote over forty of the fifty-three *Mörike-Lieder.* Later in the year he completed fifty of his fifty-one Goethe settings in a similar space of time. An admirer of Wagner, he brought into the small-scale terrain of the *lied* the declamatory lines and harmonic unorthodoxies of his idol. Songs and accompaniments were often fashioned from tiny phrases taken up to almost symphonic dimensions. The union of literature and music was indestructible: even more than in the case of Schumann, it is impossible to separate the two elements, whether in the tiny, fragmentary pieces, the lyrical *An die Geliebte (To the Beloved),* or the grand declamations such as *Prometheus.* Friends who listened to his work spread their praise about, and he continued writing songs as if there could be no end to them, and embarked on an opera, *Der Corregidor (The Mayor),* which was poorly received and ran for only two performances.

In 1897 Wolf, in a fury against a supposed failure by Mahler to honour a promise regarding a new production of the opera, had a mental breakdown and was committed to a private asylum. He recovered for a while, tried to continue working but without success, and in October 1898 tried to drown himself. Taken again to an asylum, he slowly declined into general paralysis but survived until February 1903.

Wolf-Ferrari, Ermanno (1876–1948) Italian composer. Son of a German father and Italian mother, he was born in Venice, studied in Munich with Rheinberger, and returned to Venice to become, in 1902, director of the Liceo Benedetto Marcello. Five years later he went again to Munich, where he spent most of the rest of his life and where a number of his lighthearted operas in a pastiche of eighteenth-century style were successfully produced. The most frequently performed has been *Il segreto di Susanna (Susanna's Secret).*

Wolpe, Stefan (1901–72) German composer (American citizen 1944). He studied at the Berlin Hochschule and privately with Busoni, Scherchen and Webern. His left-wing leanings led to his providing incidental music for some of Brecht's theatrical productions, many of them with a jazz flavour; and also contributed to his having to flee first to Austria and then to Jerusalem when Hitler came on the scene. In 1938 he settled in the USA, teaching in various New York colleges and becoming head of the music department in Long Island University. The main influences on his compositional methods were Jewish music and an interpretation of serialism emanating from small tone cells rather than twelve-tone rows. Among his works were two operas, two cantatas, a ballet suite *The Man from Midian,* and a great deal of chamber music for different instrumental combinations.

Wood, (Sir) Henry (1869–1944) English conductor. His first music lessons came from his mother. At the age of ten he became assistant organist at the Church of St Mary's, Aldermanbury, in London, and later went on to other organ posts. While studying at the Royal Academy of Music he learned a great deal as accompanist to singers in the opera class. In 1889 he went as conductor with a touring opera company, and later conducted for the Carl Rosa company and a number of London and provincial concert organizations. In 1895 he was engaged to conduct Promenade Concerts at Queen's Hall in London, and became so identified with their programmes, the introduction of new music, and the improvement in orchestral standards that his name has been bestowed by the later sponsors, the BBC, on the annual Henry Wood Promenade Concerts at the Royal Albert Hall and their occasional supplementary concerts and recitals at other venues. He visited the USA several times, first in 1904 and later in the 1920s. As a tribute on his golden jubilee as a conductor in 1938, Vaughan Williams dedicated to him a *Serenade to Music,* with sixteen solo parts for the leading singers of the day.

Woodforde-Finden, Amy (1860–1919) English composer. She wrote a number of drawing-room ballads very popular in their day, especially the *Indian Love Lyrics,* which contained the much performed *Pale Hands I Loved beside the Shalimar.*

woodwind Instruments made of wood and blown directly (e.g. flute and recorder) or with the use of a reed (e.g. clarinet and oboe). (*See also* **The Orchestra and its Instruments**.)

Wordsworth, William (1908–) English composer. He studied with Tovey in Edinburgh and won the International Competition at the 1950 Edinburgh Festival with his second symphony. In all he has written six symphonies and a number of concertos, in a straightforward, traditional style with strong melodies and impeccable harmonic construction and orchestration. Although of London birth, he decided in the 1960s to make his home in Scotland, wrote a *Highland Overture,* and helped to form the Scottish branch of the Composers' Guild.

working-out Another name for the *development* section in *sonata form.*

Wunderlich, Fritz (1930–66) German tenor. He made his solo début in Freiburg with the Bach Choir in the early 1950s, and then on the opera stage as Tamino in Mozart's *Die Zauberflöte* in 1954. He soon established a reputation as a Mozartian tenor, sang at Covent Garden and for the Vienna and Berlin Operas, and appeared at Salzburg and Edinburgh festivals. He also shone in operetta. Just as his career seemed to be reaching its peak he died in a fall.

Wurlitzer An American firm of organ builders founded in 1856 whose name became associated between the 1920s and 1940s with theatre and cinema organs equipped with many special effects and a great deal of coloured lighting. After the decline of live music in such places, the firm concentrated on the manufacture of electronic organs and other keyboard instruments.

X

Xenakis, Iannis (1922–) Greek composer (French citizen 1965). He was born in Romania, but his parents returned to Greece when he was ten. He studied engineering at Athens Polytechnic, and during World War II worked with the Resistance, suffering severe facial injuries and having sentence of death pronounced on him. During the post-war turmoil in his country he finally fled to Paris, where he was helped by musicians, inclu-

The composer Iannis Xenakis admits that he was musically inspired by the fighting in Athens in 1944, when he was severely wounded, but stoutly denies that because his music often sounds violent he should be regarded as a violent man.

ding Honegger and Messiaen, and by the architect Le Corbusier, who gave him engineering work to do and whom he assisted with the design of the Philips pavilion at the Brussels Exposition of 1958.

As a composer Xenakis has applied mathematical and architectural principles to his works. His *Metastasis* for orchestra is built around geometrical concepts, with straight lines represented by glissandos within a dense orchestral pattern. Much of this he attributes to the precepts of his architect employer: 'I was very interested in his ideas of formal harmony, the massing of buildings, and the overall proportions of things, which was very close to the problems of musical form and rhythm,' he said in an interview. 'I found that I could *design* music which at first I couldn't write down on the stave.' As time went on, shunning strict serialism, he developed his own procedures of random composition deriving from the laws of probability, borrowing the term *stochastic* to describe his methods. In 1966 he founded a School of Mathematical and Automated Music in Paris, preached a similar gospel at Indiana University, and has used computer calculations in many subsequent works.

OTHER WORKS: Ballet *Kraanerg* (orchestra and tape). *Stratégie* for two orchestras and two conductors. *Hibiki-hana-ma* for tapes and loudspeakers. *Herma* for solo piano. *Nuits* for twelve voices.

xylophone *See* **The Orchestra and its Instruments**.

Y

yodel German spelling is *jodel*. It describes a form of singing in the Swiss mountains, usually sung in lively, leaping rhythm by men who alternate between normal voice and falsetto, echoing natural harmonics similar to those of the alphorn or Alpine horn.

Youmans, Vincent (1898–1946) American composer. He began in music publishing, but from 1921 onwards established himself as a leading writer of musical comedies, among them *No, No, Nanette*, with a song that has become a popular favourite and a jazz 'standard' for improvised choruses, *Tea for Two*.

Young, Victor (1900–56) American composer and violinist. He studied in Warsaw and played the violin in the Warsaw Philharmonic Orchestra, but returned to the USA at the outbreak of World War I. He worked in radio until 1935, when he began a successful career of composing film scores and popular songs such as *Sweet Sue* and *Indian Summer*.

Ysaÿe, Eugène (1858–1931) Belgian violinist, composer and conductor. As a child he studied the violin with his father, and appeared in public at the age of seven. After further studies at Liège Conservatory and with Henryk Wienawski and Vieuxtemps, he played in concert seasons in Cologne, Aachen, and Frankfurt, and from 1886 to 1898 was professor of violin at Brussels Conservatory. He founded and conducted the Ysaÿe concerts in Brussels, toured widely as an admired performer of the works of Bach and Franck, made his first American appearance in 1894, and from 1918 to 1922 was conductor of the Cincinnati Symphony Orchestra. Among his compositions were six violin concertos and a number of solo violin sonatas, *Variations on a Theme of Paganini*, and an opera in the Walloon dialect, *Piér li Houïeu* (*Peter the Coalminer*).

The Belgian violinist Eugène Ysaÿe, who introduced works by Franck and Elgar to European and American audiences.

Z

Zabaleta, Nicanor (1907–) Spanish harpist. He studied in Madrid and made his début in Paris in 1925. As well as appearing with orchestras and chamber groups as soloist in the main works in the instrument's repertoire, he has rediscovered and performed a great deal of early Spanish harp music, recorded the works of more modern composers such as Albéniz, Granados and Chavarri, and commissioned works from contemporaries including Milhaud and Křenek.

zapateado A Spanish dance for a solo performer, in 3/4 time, with the rhythm accentuated by stamping of the heels.

zarzuela A Spanish form of light opera in which the musical numbers are interspersed with spoken dialogue, often with an element of improvisation and sometimes allowing for interjections from the audience. The name comes from the royal palace of La Zarzuela near Madrid, where such pieces were popular in the time of Philip IV. They went through a period of neglect until the form was revived by nationalist composers in the nineteenth century, using strongly national music

and often devising librettos which were skits on existing, more solemn plays or on current political or social situations.

zeitoper A German term used during the 1920s and 1930s to describe the 'opera of the age', i.e. operatic works of social relevance to contemporary society (similar to *gebrauchsmusik*), favoured for a while by Hindemith, Weill and Křenek.

Zelenka, Jan Dismas (1679–1745) Bohemian composer. He studied in Prague and became double-bass player in the Dresden Court orchestra before continuing studies in Vienna. After travels in Italy he returned to Dresden and became director of church music there. Among his works were twenty-one masses, over a hundred psalms, and a *Melodrama de Sancto Wenceslao* (*Melodrama of Saint Wenceslas*) on the story of Bohemia's patron saint.

Zemlinsky, Alexander von (1871–1942) Austrian composer and conductor. The son of Polish parents, he studied at the Vienna Conservatory and made an impression on Brahms with some chamber music pieces. He became conductor at the Vienna Volksoper, then at the Court Opera, and later in Mannheim, Prague, and Berlin. In Prague he was responsible for the first perform-

Saint Wenceslas, prince-duke, martyr and patron saint of Bohemia, whose virtues are extolled in the Christmas Carol *Good King Wenceslas*, was the subject of one of his compatriot Zelenka's works.

ance of the atonal monodrama *Erwartung* by his pupil and son-in-law, Schoenberg, who in 1949 said of him: 'I owe almost everything I know about composing and its problems to Alexander Zemlinsky. I always thought he was a great composer, and I still think so. Perhaps his time will come sooner than one thinks.'

In fact, after Zemlinsky's death his music was neglected for some years, but a revival of interest was sparked off by a number of concerts at the time of his centenary, and later by BBC broadcasts. Although he had proved so helpful to Schoenberg, he did not follow his pupil's interest in serialism, but continued to write in the vein of Mahler and Richard Strauss. Among his operas were *Sarema*, with a libretto by Schoenberg, and two taken from Oscar Wilde, *Eine Florentinische Tragödie* (*A Florentine Tragedy*) and *Der Zwerg* (*The Dwarf*). He composed a 'lyrical symphony in seven songs' for voices and orchestra, and settings of psalms for chorus and orchestra. In 1927 he began working with Klemperer in Berlin, but fled from the Nazis, first to Vienna and then, in 1938, to the USA.

OTHER WORKS: Ballet *Der Triumph der Zeit* (*The Triumph of Time*). Two symphonies. Incidental music, *Cymbeline*. Four string quartets.

zigeuner A gipsy. The word is used for much Hungarian-based music, genuine or pastiche, as in titles such as *Der Zigeunerbaron* (*The Gipsy Baron*), an operetta by Johann Strauss II, and Brahms's *Zigeunerlieder* (*Gipsy Songs*), based on Hungarian folk poems. The word also appears as *tzigane*, *zingaro*, and *zingara*. The marking *alla zingaresca* means 'in gipsy style'.

Zimbalist, Efrem (1890–) Russian violinist and violist (American citizen). He studied in St Petersburg and made his début in Berlin in 1907 and his American début in Boston in 1911. In 1914 he settled in the USA, established himself as an outstanding soloist, and taught at the Curtis Institute, Philadelphia, becoming its director between 1941 and 1968. Among his own compositions are a violin concerto and an *American Rhapsody*.

Zimmermann, Bernd Alois (1918–70) German composer. He studied at Bonn, Berlin and Cologne, supporting himself as a labourer and by playing in a dance band. Called up into the army during World War II, he served in France and became interested in the music of Stravinsky and Milhaud. Later he was also influenced by Bartók and Schoenberg, and from his dance-band days retained an affection for jazz. His liking for symmetry produced *Perspektiven* for two pianos, which he also referred to, along with other of his works, as an 'imaginary ballet', quoting from other com-

posers in order to provide a kind of human characterization in the lines of the music. He also favoured an eclectic 'pluralism', using traditional resources along with electronic devices, as in his opera *Der Soldaten* (*The Soldier*), which is also pluralist in having scenes played out simultaneously on different stages. For two years he taught the history of music at Cologne University, and subsequently taught composition at the Musikhochskule there. His later music grew bleak and disorientated, and in 1970 he committed suicide.

OTHER WORKS: Symphony in one movement. *Antiphonen* for viola and orchestra. Cello sonata. *Tratto* and *Tratto II* for tape. *Requiem für einem jungen Dichter* (*Requiem for a Young Poet*), for soloists, choruses, orchestra, jazz group, and tape.

zither A stringed instrument of the dulcimer family, with a large number of strings (up to forty) stretched across a flat sound-box, played by the fingers and by a plectrum attached to the player's thumb. Common in folk-music ensembles, it has been used for creating atmosphere in Austro-Hungarian operettas, and a quite unforgettable atmosphere in the background music to the film *The Third Man*, which had its setting in Vienna immediately after World War II.

Zither.

Zukerman, Pinchas (1948–) Israeli violinist and conductor. He studied at the Israel Conservatory, The Tel-Aviv Academy of Music, and the Juilliard School in New York, making his début with the New York Philharmonic Orchestra in 1969. He has made an international reputation as a soloist, and also as a chamber player not only of the violin but also the viola. He has worked as one the conductors of the English Chamber Orchestra along with Daniel Barenboim, who has also been a regular companion in chamber music recitals.

Appendix I

MAJOR ORCHESTRAS OF THE WORLD

Orchestra	Founded	First conductor
Academy of St Martin-in-the-Fields	1956	Neville Marriner
Basle Chamber Orchestra	1926	Paul Sacher
BBC Symphony Orchestra	1930	Adrian Boult
Berlin Philharmonic Orchestra	1882	Franz Wüllner (1883)
Birmingham (City of) Symphony Orchestra	1920	Appleby Matthews
Boston Symphony Orchestra	1881	George Henschel
Bournemouth Symphony Orchestra	1893	Dan Godfrey
Chicago Symphony Orchestra (originally the Chicago Orchestra, then Theodore Thomas Orchestra until present name adopted 1912)	1891	Theodore Thomas
Cincinnati Symphony Orchestra	1895	Frank van der Stucken
Cleveland Orchestra	1918	Nikolai Sokolov
Concertgebouw Orchestra of Amsterdam	1883	Willem Kes
Czech Philharmonic Orchestra	1901	Ludvik Vitezslav Čelansky (*first full-time conductor, 1918*)
Detroit Symphony Orchestra	1914	Weston Gales
English Chamber Orchestra (originally Goldsbrough Orchestra until present name adopted 1960)	1948	Arnold Goldsbrough (*founder*)
Hallé Orchestra	1858	Charles Hallé
Israel Philharmonic Orchestra (originally the Palestine Symphony Orchestra)	1936	Bronislaw Hubermann

Orchestra	Founded	First conductor
Leningrad Philharmonic Orchestra (originally the Court orchestra, founded 1882)	1921	Emil Cooper
London Mozart Players (originally the London Wind Players, formed by Blech 1942)	1949	Harry Blech
London Philharmonic Orchestra	1932	Thomas Beecham
London Symphony Orchestra	1904	Hans Richter
Los Angeles Philharmonic Orchestra	1919	W.H. Rothwell
Minnesota Orchestra (originally the Minneapolis Symphony Orchestra until present name adopted 1968)	1903	Emil Oberhoffer
Moscow Philharmonic Orchestra (post-Revolution Moscow Philharmonic Society founded 1931)	1883	Pyotr Shostakovsky
NBC Symphony Orchestra *(disbanded 1954)*	1937	Arturo Toscanini
New York Philharmonic Orchestra	1842	Various
Paris, Orchestre de	1967	Charles Munch
Philadelphia Orchestra	1900	Fritz Scheel
Philharmonic Orchestra	1945	Walter Legge *(founder)* Various conductors
Pittsburgh Symphony Orchestra	1895	Frederic Asker
Royal Liverpool Philharmonic Orchestra (designation 'Royal' bestowed 1957)	1840	John Russell
Royal Philharmonic Orchestra	1946	Thomas Beecham
San Francisco Symphony Orchestra	1911	Henry Hadley
Stuttgart Chamber Orchestra	1945	Karl Münchinger
Vienna Philharmonic Orchestra	1842	Otto Nicolai

Appendix II

A BRIEF CHRONOLOGY OF MAJOR OPERAS

Date	Title of opera	Composer
1597	DAFNE	Peri
1607	ORFEO	Monteverdi
1673	CADMUS ET HERMIONE	Lully
1679	GLI EQUIVOCI NEL SEMBIANTE	Scarlatti (A.)
1689	DIDO AND AENEAS	Purcell
1724	GIULIO CESARE	Handel
1728	THE BEGGAR'S OPERA	Gay and Pepusch
1735	LES INDES GALANTES	Rameau
1737	CASTOR ET POLLUX	Rameau
1762	ORFEO	Gluck
1777	IL MONDO DELLA LUNA	Haydn
1782	DIE ENTFUHRUNG AUS DEM SERAIL	Mozart
1786	LE NOZZE DI FIGARO	Mozart
1787	DON GIOVANNI	Mozart
1790	COSI FAN TUTTE	Mozart
1791	DIE ZAUBERFLOTE	Mozart
1792	IL MATRIMONIO SEGRETO	Cimarosa
1805	FIDELIO	Beethoven
1816	IL BARBIERE DI SIVIGLIA	Rossini
1821	DER FREISCHUTZ	Weber
1826	OBERON	Weber
1829	GUILLAUME TELL	Rossini
1831	LA SONNAMBULA	Bellini
1831	NORMA	Bellini
1835	LUCIA DI LAMMERMOOR	Donizetti
1836	LES HUGUENOTS	Meyerbeer
1836	A LIFE FOR THE TSAR	Glinka
1838	BENVENUTO CELLINI	Berlioz
1841	NABUCCO	Verdi
1841	DER FLIEGENDE HOLLANDER	Wagner
1847	MARTHA	Flotow
1848-74	DER RING DES NIBELUNGEN	Wagner
1849	DIE LUSTIGEN WEIBER VON WINDSOR	Nicolai
1851	RIGOLETTO	Verdi
1853	LA TRAVIATA	Verdi
1856-9	LES TROYENS	Berlioz

Date	Title of opera	Composer
1858	ORPHEE AUX ENFERS	Offenbach
1859	FAUST	Gounod
1864	THE BARTERED BRIDE	Smetana
1867	DALIBOR	Smetana
1868	MEFISTOFELE	Boito
1874	CARMEN	Bizet
1874	BORIS GODUNOV	Mussorgsky
1877	SAMSON ET DALILA	Saint-Saëns
1879	EUGENE ONEGIN	Tchaikovsky
1882	PARSIFAL	Wagner
1883	LAKME	Delibes
1884	MANON	Massenet
1890	CAVALLERIA RUSTICANA	Mascagni
1892	I PAGLIACCI	Leoncavallo
1893	HANSEL UND GRETEL	Humperdinck
1893	MANON LESCAUT	Puccini
1893	FALSTAFF	Verdi
1896	LA BOHEME	Puccini
1898	MOZART AND SALIERI	Rimsky-Korsakov
1900	TOSCA	Puccini
1900	LOUISE	Charpentier
1901	RUSALKA	Dvořák
1902	PELLEAS ET MELISANDE	Debussy
1904	KOANGA	Delius
1904	MADAMA BUTTERFLY	Puccini
1905	SALOME	Strauss
1906	THE WRECKERS	Ethel Smyth
1906	MASKARADE	Nielsen
1907	ELEKTRA	Strauss
1907	A VILLAGE ROMEO AND JULIET	Delius
1909	THE GOLDEN COCKEREL	Rimsky-Korsakov
1911	DER ROSENKAVALIER	Strauss
1911	I GIOELLI DELLA MADONNA	Wolf-Ferrari
1914	THE IMMORTAL HOUR	Rutland Boughton
1914	HUGH THE DROVER	Vaughan Williams
1916	JEJI PASTORKYNA *(JENUFA)*	Janáček
1918	BLUEBEARD'S CASTLE	Bartók
1921	LOVE OF THREE ORANGES	Prokofiev
1921	KATYA KABANOVA	Janáček
1923	THE PERFECT FOOL	Holst
1924	TURANDOT	Puccini

A brief chronology of major operas

Date	Title of opera	Composer
1924	DIE GLUCKLICHE HAND	Schoenberg
1924	THE CUNNING LITTLE VIXEN	Janáček
1925	L'ENFANT ET LES SORTILEGES	Ravel
1926	WOZZECK	Berg
1927	OEDIPUS REX	Stravinsky
1927	SCHWANDA THE BAGPIPER	Weinberger
1927	HARY JANOS	Kodály
1928	DIE DREIGROSCHENOPER	Weill
1932	LADY MACBETH OF MTSENSK	Shostakovich
1933	ARABELLA	Strauss
1934	MATHIS DER MALER	Hindemith
1935	PORGY AND BESS	Gershwin
1937	JULIETTA	Martinů
1937	LULU (complete version not performed until 1979)	Berg
1945	PETER GRIMES	Britten
1946	THE RAPE OF LUCRETIA	Britten
1946	THE MEDIUM	Menotti
1946	WAR AND PEACE	Prokofiev
1949	IL PRIGIONIERO	Dallapiccola
1950	THE CONSUL	Menotti
1951	THE RAKE'S PROGRESS	Stravinsky
1954	THE TURN OF THE SCREW	Britten
1954	MOSES UND ARON	Schoenberg
1954	TROILUS AND CRESSIDA	Walton
1954	THE TENDER LAND	Copland
1955	THE MIDSUMMER MARRIAGE	Tippett
1956	ANTONY AND CLEOPATRA	Barber
1957	DIE HARMONIE DER WELT	Hindemith
1959	LA VOIX HUMAINE	Poulenc
1960	INTOLLERANZA	Nono
1960	DER PRINZ VON HOMBURG	Henze
1961	ELEGY FOR YOUNG LOVERS	Henze
1961	A MIDSUMMER NIGHT'S DREAM	Britten
1961	VANESSA	Barber
1962	KING PRIAM	Tippett
1968	PUNCH AND JUDY	Birtwistle
1972	TAVERNER	Maxwell Davies
1973	DEATH IN VENICE	Britten
1979	THE LIGHTHOUSE	Maxwell Davies
1983	WHERE THE WILD THINGS ARE	Knussen
1984	AKHNATEN	Glass

Appendix III

FUGUE

The opening page of Bach's *Die Kunst der Fuge (The Art of Fugue)* shows the basic principles of fugal and canonic writing before exploring further contrapuntal possibilities. The *Dux*, or 'leader', is the opening melodic subject which is to be imitated; the *Comes*, or 'companion', begins here 'at the fifth'; the original *Dux* is then taken up by the bass line, and the tenor follows with the same note sequence as the *Comes*, by which time the other voices are already striking out along new paths.

SLOW MOVEMENT FROM DVOŘÁK'S
'NEW WORLD' SYMPHONY

Appendix IV

A TYPICAL PAGE OF FULL SCORE

The page of full score on the left shows the generally accepted layout of orchestral parts, presented comprehensively so that the conductor can read each line in relation to all the others. Names of the instruments are generally given, as are the interpretative markings, in Italian.

Italian	Abbreviation	English
Flauti	Fl.	Flutes
Oboi	Ob.	Oboes
	(Corno inglese = cor anglais usually 'doubled' by oboist)	
Clarinetti	Cl.	Clarinets
	(pitch usually shown on score)	
Fagotti	Fg.	Bassoons
Corni	Cor.	French horns
	(pitch usually shown on score)	
Trombe	Tr.	Trumpets
	(pitch usually shown on score)	
Tromboni tenori	Trb. ten.	Tenor trombones
Trombone basso	Trb. basso	Bass trombone
Tuba	Tuba	Tuba
Timpani	Timp.	Timpani
Violoni I	Vl. I	First violins
Violoni II	Vl. II	Second violins
Viola	Vla.	Viola
Violoncello	Vcl.	Cello
Contrabasso	Cb.	Double bass

Acknowledgements

The Publishers would like to thank all the archives, agencies and individuals who have helped them to gather the illustrations for this book. Care has been taken to trace the ownership of the illustrations. Should any errors or omissions have occurred, notification should be sent to the publisher whereupon they will be corrected in subsequent editions.

Key *t* top, *b* bottom, *l* left, *r* right.

Front cover *clockwise* from *l* to *r* Dover Books/Beethoven-Hauses, Bonn/Archiv für Kunst und Geschichte/Royal College of Music/Archiv für Kunst und Geschichte.
Back cover *l* Archive für Kunst und Geschichte *r* The British Library.
Title page *l* to *r* Archiv für Kunst und Geschichte, National Portrait Galley, London. Archiv für Kunst und Geschichte, RCA, Erich Auerbach, J.L. Charmet.

l Erich Auerbach *r* National Portrait Gallery, London 10 Fotomas Index 11 Dover Books 12 Archiv für Kunst und Geschichte 13 Weidenfeld & Nicolson 14 Snape Crafts 16 *l* W. Neumeister/Deutsche Grammophon *r* Bart Mulder/Phonogram International BV 17 *l* & *r* Erich Auerbach 19 *l* Archiv für Kunst und Geschichte *r* National Portrait Gallery, London 20 *l* & *r* Erich Auerbach 21 Mary Evans Picture Library 23 *t* & *b* Archiv für Kunst und Geschichte 26 Archiv für Kunst und Geschichte 27 Mary Evans Picture Library 28 Toepffer/Deutsche Grammophon 29 Archiv für Kunst und Geschichte 30–31 Dover Books 33 Tate Gallery, London 34 *t* Zoë Dominic/Dominic Photography 6 J.L. Charmet 35 *t* Catherine Ashmore/Dominic Photography *b* London Contemporary Dance Theatre 38 Susesch Bayat/Deutsche Grammophon 39–41 Archiv für Kunst und Geschichte 42 *l* EMI Records *r* National Portrait Gallery, London 43 Beethoven-Hauses, Bonn 45 *t* Weidenfeld & Nicolson *b* Beethoven-Hauses, Bonn 46 *t* Dover Books *b* Archiv für Kunst und Geschichte 48 Deutsche Grammophon 50 Archiv für Kunst und Geschichte 52 Susesch Bayat/Deutsche Grammophon 54 J.L. Charmet 55 Archiv für Kunst und Geschichte 56 Mary Evans Picture Library 57 *l* Archiv für Kunst und Geschichte *r* Erich Auerbach 58–59 *all* Archiv für Kunst und Geschichte 62 Erich Auerbach 63 National Portrait Gallery 65–67 Archiv für Kunst und Geschichte 68 Erich Auerbach 69 Henmar Press Inc., New York, 1961, reproduced by permission of Peters Edition, London 70 Weidenfeld & Nicolson 72 *l* Royal Opera House, Covent Garden *r* Archiv für Kunst und Geschichte 73 Dover Books 74 Archiv für Kunst und Geschichte 75 Fotomas Index 77–79 *all* Archiv für Kunst und Geschichte 80 Erich Auerbach 83 Archiv für Kunst und Geschichte 84 Mary Evans Picture Library 85 Erich Auerbach 86 Dover Books 87 Royal Opera House, Covent Garden 89 Shiela Hodges 90 Network Photographers 91 The British Library 93 Weidenfeld & Nicolson 96 EMI Records 98 *t* Erich Auerbach *b* Archiv für Kunst und Geschichte 101 Mary Evans Picture Library 103 Archiv für Kunst und Geschichte 104 National Portrait Gallery, London 106 Melody Maker 108 Archiv für Kunst und Geschichte 110 *l* Royal College of Music *r* Archiv für Kunst und Geschichte 111 National Portrait Gallery, London 112 Susesch Bayat/Deutsche Grammophon 113 Royal College of Music 114 J.L. Charmet 115–116 Dover Books 119 Mary Evans Picture Library 120 National Portrait Gallery, Scotland 121 Archiv für Kunst und Geschichte 122 The British Library 123–126 *all* Archiv für Kunst und Geschichte 127 Guy Gravett/Picture Index 128 Erich Auerbach 129 Archiv für Kunst und Geschichte 130 J.L. Charmet 131 Archiv für Kunst und Geschichte 134 National Portrait Gallery, London 135 Bridgeman Art Library 138 Royal College of Music 141 Archiv für Kunst und Geschichte 142 Weidenfeld & Nicolson Archives 14? ?0 Donald Sheppard/BLA Publishing 151 National

Portrait Gallery, London 152–153 Archiv für Kunst und Geschichte 154 Melody Maker 155 Dover Books 156 Mary Evans Picture Library 158 Fotomas Index 159 *t* Archiv für Kunst und Geschichte *b* Sallie Alane Reason/BLA Publishing 161 Royal College of Music 164 *t* Royal College of Music/Weidenfeld & Nicolson Archives *b* Archiv für Kunst und Geschichte 165 Archiv für Kunst und Geschichte 167 Royal College of Music 168–172 Archiv für Kunst und Geschichte 173 Clive Barda/Deutsche Grammophon 176 Weidenfeld & Nicolson 177 Archiv für Kunst und Geschichte 178 Dover Books 181 Royal College of Music/Weidenfeld & Nicolson Archives 182 *l* & *r* Archiv für Kunst und Geschichte 183 The Mansell Collection 184 Weidenfeld & Nicolson 185 Erich Auerbach 186 Popperfoto 187 Mary Evans Picture Library 188 Erich Auerbach 190 Archiv für Kunst und Geschichte 192 BLA Publishing 193 Archiv für Kunst und Geschichte 195 Dover Books 196 Archiv für Kunst und Geschichte 197 by courtesy of the Trustees of the British Museum 199 Royal Danish Embassy 200 Erich Auerbach 201 Archiv für Kunst und Geschichte 202–204 Donald Sheppard/BLA Publishing 205 Archiv für Kunst und Geschichte 206 Van Walsum Management 208 *t* & *b* Archiv für Kunst und Geschichte 209 Guy Gravett/Picture Index *tr* Archiv für Kunst und Geschichte *br* Mary Evans Picture Library 210 Archiv für Kunst und Geschichte 211 Mary Evans Picture Library 212 Sallie Alane Reason/BLA Publishing 213 *l* & *r* Archiv für Kunst und Geschichte 214 Boosey & Hawkes 215–216 *all* Archiv für Kunst und Geschichte 217 Boosey & Hawkes 218–219 *all* Dover Books 220 *l* Boosey & Hawkes *r* Dover Books 221 Archiv für Kunst und Geschichte 222 Boosey & Hawkes 223 Donald Sheppard/BLA Publishing 224 Archiv für Kunst und Geschichte 226 Donald Sheppard/BLA Publishing 227 Dover Books 228 Royal College of Music 229 *t* & *b* Archiv für Kunst und Geschichte 230 Dover Books 232 National Portrait Gallery, London 234 Erich Auerbach 238 National Portrait Gallery, Smithsonian Institution/Weidenfeld & Nicolson Archives 239 Weidenfeld & Nicolson 241 Archiv für Kunst und Geschichte 242 *l* Archiv für Kunst und Geschichte *r* National Portrait Gallery, London 243–245 Mary Evans Picture Library 246 EMI Records 247 Archiv für Kunst und Geschichte 248 Weidenfeld & Nicolson 249 Dover Books 252 Archiv für Kunst und Geschichte 253 RCA Records 255 J.L. Charmet 256 Cantzler/Deutsche Grammophon 257 The Mansell Collection 258 Archiv für Kunst und Geschichte 259–260 Weidenfeld & Nicolson 262 Archiv für Kunst und Geschichte 263 Donald Sheppard/BLA Publishing 264 Weidenfeld & Nicolson 266–267 *all* Archiv für Kunst und Geschichte 270 Mary Evans Picture Library 272 Royal College of Music 273–274 Erich Auerbach 276 Dover Books 277–280 Archiv für Kunst und Geschichte 282 Mary Evans Picture Library 285–286 Archiv für Kunst und Geschichte 288 Steinway & Sons 289 Weidenfeld & Nicolson 290 Erich Auerbach 292–296 Archiv für Kunst und Geschichte 298–300 Erich Auerbach 301 Dover Books 303 Archiv für Kunst und Geschichte 305 Zoë Dominic/Dominic Photography 306 Archiv für Kunst und Geschichte 308 Popperfoto 310 Erich Auerbach 312 Weidenfeld & Nicolson 314 Dover Books 316 National Portrait Gallery, London 319 Archiv für Kunst und Geschichte 321 Zefa 323 Erich Auerbach 324 Archiv für Kunst und Geschichte 326–328 Archiv für Kunst und Geschichte 329 Melody Maker 330 National Portrait Gallery, London 332 Sue Hyman Associates 333–335 Archiv für Kunst und Geschichte 338 Royal College of Music 340 Erich Auerbach 341 Archiv für Kunst und Geschichte 342 Mary Evans Picture Library 343 Dover Books.